OXFORD HISTORY OF
THE CHRISTIAN CHURCH

Edited by
Henry and Owen Chadwick

OXFORD HISTORY OF THE CHRISTIAN CHURCH series is intended to provide a full survey of the Christian churches and their part in the religious heritage of humanity. Particular attention will be paid to the place of the churches in surrounding society, the institutions of church life, and the manifestations of popular religion, the link with the forms of national culture, and the intellectual tradition within and beyond Europe.

Titles in the series include:

Christianity in India
From Beginnings to the Present
Robert Eric Frykenberg (2008)

East and West: The Making of a Rift in the Church
From Apostolic Times until the Council of Florence
Henry Chadwick (2003)

Reformation in Britain and Ireland
Felicity Heal (2003)

A History of the Churches in Australasia
Ian Breward (2001)

The Church in Ancient Society
From Galilee to Gregory the Great
Henry Chadwick (2001)

The Early Reformation on the Continent
Owen Chadwick (2001)

England, Ireland, Scotland, Wales

The Christian Church 1900–2000

KEITH ROBBINS

OXFORD

UNIVERSITY PRESS

OXFORD
UNIVERSITY PRESS

Great Clarendon Street, Oxford OX2 6DP

Oxford University Press is a department of the University of Oxford.
It furthers the University's objective of excellence in research, scholarship,
and education by publishing worldwide in

Oxford New York

Auckland Cape Town Dar es Salaam Hong Kong Karachi
Kuala Lumpur Madrid Melbourne Mexico City Nairobi
New Delhi Shanghai Taipei Toronto

With offices in

Argentina Austria Brazil Chile Czech Republic France Greece
Guatemala Hungary Italy Japan Poland Portugal Singapore
South Korea Switzerland Thailand Turkey Ukraine Vietnam

Oxford is a registered trade mark of Oxford University Press
in the UK and in certain other countries

Published in the United States
by Oxford University Press Inc., New York

British Library Cataloguing in Publication Data

Data available

Library of Congress Cataloging in Publication Data

Robbins, Keith.
England, Ireland, Scotland, Wales: the Christian Church, 1900–2000 / Keith Robbins.
p.   cm. — (Oxford history of the Christian Church)
Includes bibliographical references and index.
ISBN 978–0–19–826371–5 (alk. paper)
1. Great Britain—Church history.—20th century I. Title.
BR759.R63 2008
274.1'082—dc22   2008015114

Typeset by SPI Publisher Services, Pondicherry, India
Printed in Great Britain
on acid-free paper by
CPI Antony Rowe, Chippenham, Wiltshire

ISBN 978–0–19–826371–5

1 3 5 7 9 10 8 6 4 2

PREFACE

A volume on 'the Christian Church' in England, Ireland, Scotland and Wales in the twentieth century is not a light endeavour. It has been long in contemplation, distillation and writing. The length of time is not solely because the author was for eleven years a vice-chancellor. It is a reflection of the complexity of the task and the coverage that is attempted. It could not have been done at all without a vast amount of secondary publication. That foundation is gratefully acknowledged. Even so, it is a distillation, not a totally comprehensive history of every ecclesiastical body in each of the territorial units under scrutiny. 'Ecclesiastical body' is a ponderous term. This is the appropriate place, however, to say that the word 'church' is used freely throughout the text. No 'privileging' of one 'ecclesiastical body' over another is implied. It is necessary, on occasion, to focus on their particular histories, but the main intention is not to write segmented Anglican, Free Church, Presbyterian or Roman Catholic 'histories' but to see all churches both in their individuality and their shared beliefs, behaviour and problems.

The same principle applies to the 'territories'. England, Ireland, Scotland, Wales, individuality and commonality live in uncertain balance. The term 'the British Isles' might alternatively have been used in the title, and it does slip into the narrative from time to time. However, awareness that its geographical utility is politically compromised has made it unpalatable in a title. In addition, of course, no significant church in this volume has been organized on an 'all-British Isles' basis. Nevertheless, this is a 'single story of two islands' and of churches inescapably caught up in their political, social and cultural evolution. Spatially, it aims to look north/south (or south/ north) and west/east (or east/west) in the complicated interaction of men (usually) and places. Yet the narrative can never be narrowly 'insulated'. America, Europe and a global empire have all had an impact, directly or indirectly, on British/Irish church life. Churches, being both national and international, have led a difficult double life, at least to some degree. When the century began, and perhaps for the first half-century or so, the church alignments of the British Isles referred back to, and perpetuated, the alignments of the centuries since the Reformation. They formed a commonly understood, if contested, framework of reference.

The transformations of the late twentieth century, however, have rendered that understanding of 'church history' precarious if not obsolete. Britain and Ireland—the latter to a lesser extent—have become 'global sites'. They are now 'home' to world religions, languages and peoples on a scale inconceivable in 1900. National narratives, in which 'church history' had played a significant role, have become problematic, though not dead. The context of the book is therefore inescapably political, in the widest sense of that term. No firm dividing line between 'religion' and 'politics' has been drawn, though individuals, on both sides of a supposed line, have sometimes thought that it should be. Inevitably, a book must concern itself, at least to some degree, with conferences, councils, assemblies, synods and other such places from which documents and declarations emerge and at which resolutions are passed. Church history can be a very wordy business. It can sometimes seem to consist of pronouncements from on high. How things appear to the churched millions may be very different. Necessarily, however, it is usually only 'leaders' who write autobiographies or have biographers. This book would not have been possible without such material. Such books disclose the assumptions, insights, vanities, visions and ambitions of great 'churchmen' in all churches. Nevertheless, occasionally at least, a glimpse from another perspective, and a little irony, is slipped in.

The distillation in this book does not simply draw upon published material. It draws, for the last half-century, on some observation of, and participation in, the life and work of all churches in all parts of the British Isles. The author has seen and heard, from one or more vantage points, many of the 'names' who feature in these pages. Over decades, too, he has also talked, at one level or another, to the 'unnamed' across the British Isles, though not explicitly 'interviewed' them. He does not propose to name them now. This book, however, could not have been written without an understanding, given by their 'anonymous' lives, of what it is to be 'church'. For extensive periods, he has lived and worked in England, Scotland and Wales during this half-century. He has not infrequently visited Northern Ireland and the Republic of Ireland for academic and other purposes. He has not escaped the agonies and awkwardnesses of the participant/observer. His purpose, however, is historical.

There are, however, some colleagues who must be named. He is grateful to Professor Owen Chadwick for the original invitation to write, his forbearance (and that of Oxford University Press) in the face of its slow delivery, and his commendation of its substance. It has been the inspiration of his example which kept the project alive. Professor Stewart J. Brown of the University of Edinburgh kindly read and commented on the entire text, to its great benefit. So did Professor Sir Brian Harrison. The fact that these two friends did not invariably direct the author along the same path in no way diminished the value of their observations! Professor Thomas O'Loughlin of the University of Wales, Lampeter, kindly read Irish material. Revd Dr Keith Clements advised from the substance of his ecumenical and historical knowledge. The responsibility for what is said naturally rests with the author. It has been a privilege, at different points, to use for this project the libraries of the University of Glasgow, the National University of Ireland, Maynooth, and the University of Wales, Aberystwyth. Above all, however, as vice-chancellor and now Honorary Professor and Honorary Fellow, it has been vital to draw, since 1992, on the excellent holdings in modern church history and theology of the University of Wales, Lampeter.

My mother knew of this project through most of its life but sadly did not live to see its completion. My father knows of its completion but sadly cannot see it. My wife has known about it for a very long time and may be surprised to see it completed: without her loving support and encouragement, it never would have been. All three have my gratitude, not least for the reminder their lives provide that there is more to church than writing books about church history.

K.G.R.

November 2007

CONTENTS

LIST OF ILLUSTRATIONS

LIST OF MAPS

Map 1. Catholic Dioceses in England

Map 2. Anglican Dioceses in England

Map 3. Catholic Dioceses in Ireland

Map 4. Anglican Dioceses in Ireland

Map 5. Catholic Dioceses in Scotland

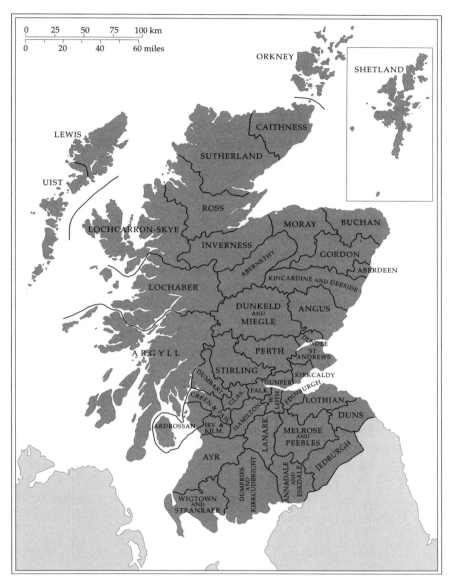

Map 6. Church of Scotland Presbyteries

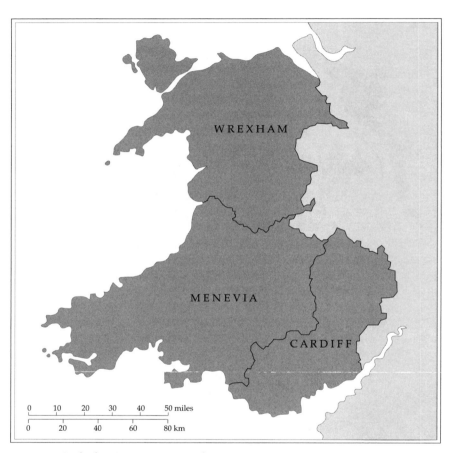

Map 7. Catholic Dioceses in Wales

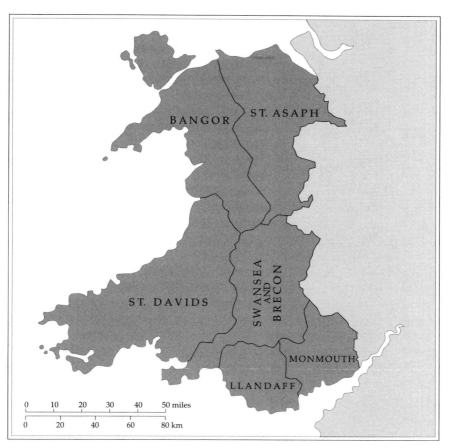

Map 8. Anglican Dioceses in Wales

I

NEW CENTURY, OLD FAITH

The Christian church, by its very nature, operates at the unstable point where time, place and public space come together. Studying its existence merely across one century, and in two islands and four complicated 'territories' (at least), constitutes only one glimpse of a phenomenon, whether perceived as 'institution' or 'movement', which is now universal and has had a long history. Yet environment, in its widest sense, is always crucial. In this instance, the church is bound up with the history of two islands which, in different but connected ways, have experienced profound change, both internally and externally. There is unity and conflict in their history. The church cannot stand outside time or pretend that 'Christianity' simply transmits certain timeless truths. It inherits and carries on, but also develops, a 'tradition'. It is enmeshed in particular societies and cultures. That tradition, almost invariably itself contentious, reached its second millennium at the close of the century with which this book is concerned. The church believes itself to have had its origins in a series of events, now distant, but still constantly re-presented. It is committed, on a regular basis, to performing certain acts 'in remembrance'. It cannot help looking back. The management of memory, therefore, is a central occupation. Church history, in turn, entails the study of a body which lives in the present but which is constantly engaged in 'incorporating' a particular past or pasts. A historian has to come to terms with a body of people who see themselves as living 'between the times' and therefore appropriates language which goes beyond the 'ordinary'. Its members, when they engage in remembering, experience the present as provisional. They reckon both with time— the exigencies of existence in a particular epoch—and with 'another world' which is perhaps 'beyond time'. What you get with a church, in short, is not only what you think you see. It would, of course, be more convenient for historians if this were not the case.

A history of the Christian church in England, Ireland, Scotland and Wales—'the [British] Isles'—in the twentieth century is therefore manifestly not concerned with its 'rise'. Insofar as it 'begins' in 1900, it does so with a past which, not unusually, was both its burden and inspiration. A narrative which ends in 2000, though it reaches a symbolic date, does not reach the 'end', even if some writers may think the end is near. It is not a revelation, however, to remark that *the* Christian Church does not exist. The historian has to contemplate, rather, a set of bodies which all laid claim to constitute *a* Christian church, some of which indeed, with certainty, though perhaps now less stridently, have supposed themselves to be *the* Christian church. The treasure, very obviously, comes in earthen vessels.

The word body is not casually used. The metaphor of 'the Body of Christ' has been central to reflection by twentieth-century theologians, in the British Isles as elsewhere, as they have sought to convey what 'being the church' entails.[1] Even here, however, interpretations have varied between those who have stressed the concept of the church's unity, the body, as that of a single physical entity and those who have emphasized the diversity inherent in the fact that the body has different parts. So, 'the Christian church', to some minds, might be bountifully broad and embrace bodies which might not entirely reject a Christian label (while at the same time absorbing other ideas and practices). That course has not been followed in a volume in a series avowedly devoted to the history of the 'Christian church' rather than a 'Christianity' of almost infinite breadth. Its focus is broad, but it could, even granted the inescapable limitations of space, have been broader. It is hesitant about giving attention to 'churches' which are themselves hesitant about, or indeed hostile to, the very term 'church'. Such a limitation, although naturally not beyond challenge, has inevitably meant that there has been limited attention to the Salvation Army, the Religious Society of Friends (Quakers) or Unitarians, to mention but three bodies who could, with looser criteria, have been more warmly embraced.

'Unity in diversity' constitutes a constant dialectic.[2] What it entails is a major concern of this volume. Its significance is given added weight in that it is written, distinctively, both 'transnationally' and 'transdenominationally' over four territories which have themselves been wrestling with 'unity in diversity'. All members of a Christian *koinonia* are equal in the sight of God but are they equal in the sight of each other? If there has to be hierarchy of some kind, how can the picture of a Christ the King with feet-washing skills be kept uppermost?

In the twentieth century the churches were to find themselves 'at the crossroads'. Many sought, as it wore on, to make a reality of 'unity in

---

[1] Colin E. Gunton and Daniel W. Hardy, eds., *On Being the Church: Essays on the Christian Community* (Edinburgh, 1989).

[2] Vaughan Roberts, 'The Church as Embodied Organization' in G. R. Evans and Martyn Percy, eds., *Managing the Church: Order and Organization in a Secular Age* (Sheffield, 2000), 164–7 summarizes the writing of Robinson, Macquarrie, Dunn, McFague and others on 'The Body'.

diversity'.[3] They entered the twenty-first century seemingly camped at this busy location, with signs still pointing in different directions. Even so, the history of *the* Christian church was something more than the aggregate history of particular churches. How much more, was a matter of opinion. The 'ecumenical century', however, did not 'create' *the* church. In turn, what is meant by 'ecumenicalism' or 'ecumenism' is not self-evident.[4] However, it is the fragile 'unity in diversity' or 'diversity in unity' in the British Isles which this history attempts to capture and convey.[5] It does so recognizing that these terms are themselves difficult. Is 'diversity' integral, or a threat, to 'unity'? It has reverberated throughout the history of the Christian church, arguably from the very outset.

It has also been an underlying political issue of the twentieth century.[6] The churches of the British Isles began the century within certain political 'unities', but those unities did not survive. After the first quarter of a century, the United Kingdom of Great Britain and Ireland was no more. In its last quarter, which 'unity' Northern Ireland should be part of was the subject of violent conflict. The dissolution of the worldwide 'unity' which the British Empire was claimed to be has been one of the major political changes of the twentieth century. The pursuit of 'European Union' has been enduringly problematic, perhaps particularly for the British people, in its attempted reconciliation of 'unity' and 'diversity'.[7] So has 'unity' and 'diversity' within the United Kingdom itself in the last quarter of the twentieth century. The 'unities' and 'diversities' of the churches have sometimes shared and sometimes resisted these wider realignments. Their own balance of 'unity' and 'diversity' could not be divorced from what was happening in the communities of which they were a part.

The fate of the churches has come most frequently to be perceived as part of a protracted process of 'secularization', which had begun in an earlier

    [3] J. H. Shakespeare, *The Churches at the Cross Roads* (London, 1918); Roger Hayden, 'Still at the Crossroads? Revd. J. H. Shakespeare and Ecumenism' in Keith Clements, ed., *Baptists in the Twentieth Century* (London, 1982), 31–54. Authors, at this time, were frequently standing at crossroads. J. N. Figgis, *Civilization at the Cross Roads* (London, 1912) deliberately referred to George Tyrrell, *Christianity at the Cross Roads* (London, 1910).

    [4] Ruth Rouse and Stephen C. Neill, eds., *A History of the Ecumenical Movement, 1517–1948* (London, 1954); Harold E. Fry, ed., *The Ecumenical Advance: A History of the Ecumenical Movement 1948–1968* (London, 1970); David Thompson, 'Theological and Sociological Approaches to the Motivation of the Ecumenical Movement' in Derek Baker, ed., *Religious Motivation: Biographical and Sociological Problems for the Church Historian*, Studies in Church History 15 (Oxford, 1978), 467–80.

    [5] Nicholas Orme, ed., *Unity and Variety: A History of the Church in Devon and Cornwall* (Exeter, 1991) happens to be a volume commended, in personal alphabetical order, by the Anglican, Free Church and Roman Catholic leaders in the south-west as an aid to Christian unity in the future. It concedes 'the enormous variety of Christian responses'.

    [6] James D. G. Dunn, *Unity and Diversity in the New Testament* (London, 1977).

    [7] Keith Robbins, *Britain and Europe, 1789–2005* (London, 2005).

century—for some simply the nineteenth, but, for others, much earlier. Industrialization and urbanization have also frequently been thought to provide the explanation. However, it has recently been argued that scholars failed to understand the robustness of 'popular religiosity' for two centuries after 1750. Before 1800, Christian piety had been located in masculinity. After 1800, it had become located in femininity. After about 1960, it is argued, 'women cancelled their mass subscription to the discursive domain of Christianity', with catastrophic consequences for the churches. There was 'no longer any femininity or moral identity for them to seek or affirm at the British Christian Church'. The 'Death of Christian Britain' has now arrived. It was the consequence of the 'Swinging Sixties'. New media, new gender roles and a 'moral revolution' shattered 'the culture which formerly conferred Christian identity upon the British people as a whole'. A route has been charted to a new understanding of 'the end of the Christian religion'. The churches are seen to be 'in seemingly terminal decay'. Despite their dramatic decline, it was concluded that churches would probably continue to exist in some skeletal form, with increasing commitment from decreasing numbers of adherents. From the 1960s, a suspicion of creeds arose which quickly rejected Christian tradition and all 'formulaic constructions of the individual'. Britain, on this analysis, was showing the world how 'religion as we have known it' could die.[8]

It would be a failing to ignore the 'death of Christian Britain'. Churches do not exist *in vacuo*. Their place in 'culture' and 'society' has always been enduringly problematic, both for themselves and for the cultures and societies in which they have existed.[9] That there was a continuous interaction

---

[8] Callum Brown, *The Death of Christian Britain* (London, 2001), 193–8. The author, of course, provides detailed arguments in favour of these assertions. His *Religion and Society in Britain: The Twentieth Century* (London, 2005) takes his case further in a contribution to a series, edited by this present author, looking at these issues over a *longue durée*. Earlier 'secularization' contributions by sociologists and historians include Martin E. Marty, *The Modern Schism: Three Paths to the Secular* (London, 1969); Owen Chadwick, *The Secularization of the European Mind in the Nineteenth Century* (Cambridge, 1975); David Martin, *A General Theory of Secularization* (Oxford, 1978); Steve Bruce, *Religion in the Modern World* (Oxford, 1996) and, ed., *Religion and Modernization: Sociologists and Historians Debate the Secularization Thesis* (Oxford, 1992); A. D. Gilbert, *The Making of Post-Christian Britain: A History of the Secularization of Modern Society* (London, 1980); Bryan Wilson, *Religion in a Secular Society* (London, 1966); E. Barker, J. A. Beckford and K. Dobbelaere, eds., *Secularization, Rationalism and Sectarianism: Essays in Honour of Bryan R. Wilson* (Oxford, 1993); A. D. Gilbert, 'Secularization and the Future' in Sheridan Gilley and W. J. Sheils, eds., *A History of Religion in Britain: Practice and Belief from Pre-Roman Times to the Present* (Oxford, 1994), 503–21; Jeffrey Cox, 'Secularization and Other Master Narratives of Religion in the Modern World', *Kirchliche Zeitgeschichte* 14 (2001), 24–35; Peter Berger, ed., *The Desecularization of the World: Resurgent Religion and Global Politics* (Grand Rapids, IL, 1999) brings another twist. See also the introductory discussion by Hugh McLeod in Hugh McLeod and Werner Ustorf, eds., *The Decline of Christendom in Western Europe, 1750–2000* (Cambridge, 2003), 1–28.

[9] H. R. Niebuhr, *Christ and Culture* (New York, 1951); J. H. Yoder, 'How H. Richard Niebuhr Reasoned: A Critique of *Christ and Culture*' in G. H. Stassen, D. M. Yeager and J. H. Yoder, eds., *Transformation: A New Vision of Christ and Culture* (Nashville, 1996).

between the churches and their environment is self-evident. This volume takes it as axiomatic that this awkward symbiosis can never be avoided. The issue is how this relationship should be characterized, at different points, and what 'accommodations' were sought and achieved, both within the churches themselves and between them and the wider society.

It also recognizes, however, what is not always recognized, namely that the history is not one simply of 'growth' or 'decline', 'success' or 'failure'. It accepts, too, that the 'identity' of any church is complex. It is, at one level, an institution 'like any other'. It has some organizational structure, some mechanism for policy-making, and some means of financing itself. It too has its own internal problems of power. It has, in varying ways and to different degrees, social power. It has 'aims and objectives', but not ones easily compressed into a 'mission statement'. It is a 'member organization', but there is no uniformity between churches in their understanding of what membership means and entails. It is this last point which makes numerical comparison hazardous. Some figures are scattered through the text but a detailed statistical presentation is not attempted. It recognizes that doctrinal differences, as expressed in denominational documents, do weigh heavily and 'explain' their separate existence. It also recognizes, however, that why people participate in the life of one church rather than another may depend as much on the 'accidentals' of family tradition or friendship, not to mention a good or bad heating system or the proximity of particular buildings on winter evenings.

i. Structures

The dialectic between past and present had long produced radically different and perhaps defining structures amongst churches in the British Isles. At one extreme stood those with a congregational polity. They were 'self-governing' through the instrument of a 'church meeting' which regulated its affairs and 'called' its own minister or pastor, who was in turn 'accountable' to it. Hierarchy was minimal. The ethos was 'democratic'. Such structures did not find their justification in political theory, though they did suit the emerging democratic age. A lord protector, even if one perhaps a little suspect as a democrat, had his latter-day admirers. 'I want living Cromwells,' proclaimed Dr Parker, the well-known minister of the City Temple (Congregationalist) in London at a Free Church celebration of the tercentenary of Cromwell's birth in 1899. Such a sentiment, however, did not stop him saying two years later that 'we all loved the Queen'. Nonconformists had lost a friend and a mother.[10] A local church was in a full sense *the* church gathered in a particular

---

[10] William Adamson, *The Life of the Rev. Joseph Parker* (London, 1902), 301–2, 327–8.

place. Baptists and Congregationalists started from a position in which there
was no central 'church' but rather a 'union' of freely associated 'independent'
bodies with executive 'general secretaries' operating from 'headquarters' in
central London, with annual gatherings presided over by annually serving
presidents or chairmen (respectively). The importance of regional areas and
associations reflected a polity that was 'bottom up' rather than 'top down'.
Approaching centenaries of such associations gave fresh impetus to the assertion of their importance in creating 'a deeper denominational consciousness'.[11]
Such churches had historically had no desire to be 'national' churches but such
extra-local structures as they possessed paradoxically related exclusively to the
British Isles. There was uncertainty, however, about what 'the British Isles'
meant. There was, for example, no Baptist Union of England but rather a
Baptist Union of Great Britain to which 'Ireland' was also added, though
somewhat uncertainly. English churches formed the preponderant membership and an English Baptist, J.H. Shakespeare, had just been appointed to
its influential general secretaryship in 1898.[12] There were also, however,
separate Baptist Unions in Ireland, Scotland and Wales.[13] The Congregational
Union was 'of England and Wales' alongside the Congregational Unions of
Scotland and of Ireland.

    Whether all this tangled inheritance was good enough for the new
century was another matter, at least as far as Baptists, Congregationalists,
Methodists and conceivably Presbyterians were concerned. Noting that
with a new century 'came new ideas into the minds of men' Parker's
biographer drew attention to his subject's frame of mind when he took up
office, for a second time, as Chairman of the Union on 1 January 1901. In
May Parker proclaimed that he no longer defended 'unorganised Congregationalism'. He wanted to create an institution to be known as the United
Congregational Church (which one day Baptists might join) and which
would embrace Congregationalists from England, Wales, Scotland and
Ireland. Presbyterians, noting the 'love of union' which he believed Congregationalists to be displaying might also come to appreciate the love of
liberty which was another characteristic. A dividing wall might then come

---

[11] *The Baptists of Yorkshire: Being the Centenary Memorial Volume of the Yorkshire Baptist Association*
(London, 1912), 317.

[12] Peter Shepherd, *The Making of a Modern Denomination: John Howard Shakespeare and the
English Baptists, 1898–1924* (Carlisle, 2001). Shakespeare was to serve until 1924, when he was
succeeded by a Welshman, M. E. Aubrey.

[13] E. A. Payne, *The Baptist Union: A Short History* (London, 1959); D. W. Bebbington, *The
Baptists in Scotland* (Glasgow, 1988); J. Thompson, *Century of Grace: The Baptist Union of Ireland:
A Short History, 1895–1993* (Belfast, 1996); T. M. Basset, *The Welsh Baptists* (Swansea, 1977); R. T.
Jones, *Congregationalism in England 1662–1962* (London, 1962); Harry Escott, *A History of Scottish
Congregationalism* (Glasgow, 1960); M. Coles, *I Will Build my Church: The Story of the Congregational
Union of Ireland 1829–1979* (Belfast, 1979).

down. He wanted to see the end of the word 'chapel', which he thought 'popish'. A year later, however, Parker was dead.

Methodism was more difficult to define. Surveying 'Methodism as it is' at the beginning of the twentieth century, one Methodist author could make the unusual claim that over the last half-century it had not been 'wholly absorbed in controversy'.[14] In so far as that was true, it represented a direct contrast with what had gone before.[15] It had not been issues of church order as such which had precipitated Methodism's eventual severance from the Church of England, though Wesley himself had refused to separate from the church of his birth. A new church and ministry had nevertheless been brought into being. How it should function had been a source of endemic subsequent controversy after Wesley's death and had resulted in successive splits and secessions—though that had not been their only cause.[16] The twentieth century began with no fewer than seven Methodist churches in England, though some eschewed the word church. It was claimed that they now constituted 'an unbroken fellowship' with an all-pervading spirit of mutual confidence, consultation and co-operation. Leaving aside the Wesleyan Reform Union and the Independent Methodists, there were in effect three groupings: the original (and still the largest) Wesleyan body, the Primitive Methodists (whose strength was in the Midlands and the north of England) and a third group consisting of the still separate United Methodist Free Church, the Methodist New Connexion and the Bible Christians (strong in the south-west of England). These latter three had agreed on an organic union which was to come into effect in 1907. In 1902 the Primitive Methodists decided to move beyond mere 'Connexionalism' and designate themselves a church. They recalled the great revivalist 'camp meeting' held on the Cheshire side of Mow Cop in 1807 which was their 'site of memory' and had led to the formation of the Connexion three years later. Centenary historians could not resist both recalling this event but also noting how their church had grown and developed in a century.[17] Its ethos, even so, was not that of the Wesleyans. There had been sporadic talk of achieving full Methodist union, but it remained to be seen whether this would be possible.

[14] William Redfern, *Modern Developments in Methodism* (London, 1906), 143.

[15] Rupert Davies, A. Raymond George and Gordon Rupp, eds., *A History of the Methodist Church in Great Britain*, vol. iii (London, 1983) is not a single narrative of nineteenth-century Methodism but a series of essays on various aspects of its life.

[16] A. B. Lawson, *John Wesley and the Christian Ministry* (London, 1963), 172–4.

[17] Authors were determined that 'our Church history' should not be lost amid the shadows of the past. See, for example, William Beckworth, *A Book of Remembrance: Being the Records of Leeds Primitive Methodism compiled during the Centenary Year, 1910* (Leeds, 1910) and W. M. Patterson, *Northern Primitive Methodism* (London, 1909). Patterson's focus was on the Old Sunderland District but he could not resist an opening chapter which expatiated on the significance of Mow Cop.

'Pastoral supremacy' as embodied in the ministerial conference which governed Wesleyan Methodism had been the major point of controversy. In 1878 it had finally been agreed that there should be lay representation, in equal numbers with ministerial.[18] That was indeed a significant change but the joint 'representative' session came after the 'pastoral' session attended by ministers only. It was the ministers who elected the president of the conference. So, in the eyes of the other Methodist bodies, the battle between the 'clerical ideal' and the 'brotherhood of the church' had not been finally won. They wanted to know, amongst other things, whether the laymen in the Wesleyan conference had been truly elected by the people and whether the functions of the pastoral conference had been really 'surrendered'. Detailed constitutional argument on such matters had long been found attractive. Whatever the variations which had emerged, the Methodist strands placed emphasis on the fact that they constituted 'Connexions' with elaborately articulated 'circuits' and 'districts'. The emphasis on 'relatedness' was reinforced by the regular and distinctive moving of ministers from place to place so that they did not become 'rooted' in one locality. Methodist ministers knew their railway timetables better than anyone else. Arriving in one destination, one of their number noted that he had preached there fourteen years earlier. In his intrepid old age, on another journey, getting out of a train, his leg slipped nastily down between the carriages.[19] This last experience was unusual but 'renewing acquaintance' with distant locations was common. Methodists, wherever they might be in the British Isles, were one 'people'. The intimate linkage between British and Irish Methodism had been stressed from the outset and was still in place in 1900.[20] The president of the British Wesleyan conference, an annual appointment, was also *ex officio* president of the Irish conference. For Charles Kelly, the peregrinating duties which occupied his year of office included a visit to Ireland: his grandfather had been an O'Kelly from Co. Galway.[21]

While there might appear to be an obsession with structure, Methodism was experiential. It sang hymns, particularly those of Charles Wesley. Its heart was to be found in its distinctive 'class meetings', its love-feasts and other 'refreshing ordinances'. It was the lay 'local preachers', who outnumbered the ministerial order by some ten to one, who conducted around three out of every four Methodist services. It had been their 'highest honour' to preach Sunday by Sunday—perhaps a million sermons a year

[18] H. W. Williams, *The Constitution and Polity of Wesleyan Methodism . . . down to the conference of 1880* (London, 1881).

[19] Eliza M. Champness, *The Life-Story of Thomas Champness* (London, 1907), 358–62.

[20] Alan Megahey, *The Irish Protestant Churches in the Twentieth Century* (Basingstoke, 2000), 16–17.

[21] Charles Kelly, *Memories* (London, 1910), 281–4.

were delivered. The true apostolic ministry, one such, a farmer, declared, was to be sought in a 'believing and preaching, not a priestly ministry'. There was to be 'no German obscurity about our theology'. The truth should shine forth in every sermon.[22]

Quite where Methodism 'fitted' on the church 'map' was a mystery, as much to Methodists as to others. It had been asserted in early nineteenth-century debates that Wesleyanism had no tradition of 'fierce, formal Dissent'.[23] Another author had then argued that 'In our form of government we are a Scripture presbytery, resembling, to a great degree, the Established Church of Scotland'.[24] In 1862, when Nonconformists had remembered the 2,000 ministers who had been ejected from their livings because they would not swear their unfeigned assent to everything prescribed in the new Prayer Book of 1662, the Methodist people had not seen fit 'to rouse themselves to any special effort' in connection with the bicentenary commemoration.[25] In 1891, one hundred years after the death of John Wesley, the then president of the Wesleyan conference sought an episcopal presence at a centenary gathering at which the Church of England alone would be represented. It would be a sign of a 'special relationship'—but no bishop was forthcoming.[26] Many Wesleyans would like still to have recognized their 'parentage' but it seemed to them that their parent was itself changing unacceptably. Oxford High Anglicanism, in the eyes of a leading Wesleyan minister and author, J.H. Rigg, had 'gone very far towards alienating the mass of English Methodists from the Established Church'.[27] It was sometimes acknowledged that the 'saintliness' of a Liddon or a Pusey was 'very beautiful' but their 'superiorness' would seem priggish to angels they subsequently encountered.[28] There might, therefore, be no alternative but to be identified as a 'Free Church', an outcome more acceptable in other Methodist bodies. Charles Kelly, however, made it clear that working with other Free Churches did not mean that denominationalism should be

---

[22] *Memoir of Joseph Smith . . . Wesleyan Local Preacher, with records from his diary, together with speeches and sermons from 1823 to 1898* (Malton, 1900), 284, 36.

[23] Asserted by Jabez Bunting: John Kent, *Jabez Bunting: The Last Wesleyan* (London, 1955), 59.

[24] Edmund Grindrod, *A Compendium of the Laws and Regulations of Wesleyan Methodism* (London, 1842), ix.

[25] Timothy Larsen, 'Victorian Nonconformity and the Ejected Ministers: The Impact of the Bicentennial Commemorations of 1862' in R. N. Swanson, ed., *The Church Retrospective,* Studies in Church History 33 (Woodbridge, 1997), 471.

[26] W. Fiddian Moulton, *William F. Moulton: A Memoir* (London, 1899), 250–2.

[27] J. H. Rigg, *Oxford High Anglicanism and Its Chief Leaders* (London, 1895), viii. For Rigg himself, see John Telford, *The Life of James Harrison Rigg D. D., 1821–1909* (London, 1909). Rigg wrote on these matters over half a century. His final view may be taken to be *A Comparative View of Church Organisation* (London, 1897); Martin Wellings, 'The Oxford Movement in Late-Nineteenth Century Retrospect: R. W. Church, J. H. Rigg, and Walter Walsh' in Swanson, *Church Retrospective,* 508–10.

[28] Champness, *Life-Story,* 355.

buried.[29] Hugh Price Hughes, however, promoter of the 'Forward Movement', editor of the *Methodist Times* and president of the Wesleyan conference in 1898, backed the 'Free Church' alignment more enthusiastically. Even so, he was coming to the conclusion, at the end of the century, that Christians in the English-speaking world must ultimately converge towards either Roman Catholicism or Methodism, properly interpreted. These churches, in their different ways, were 'most suited to the needs of humanity'. On an Italian visit, he looked back to what he thought was the purer Christianity of medieval Florence and Venice before the inventions and corruptions of the papacy took hold.[30] Hughes never lived to see this 'convergence'. Like Parker, he died in 1902.

His contention would have seemed absurd to the largest of all the churches in the British Isles, measured by any standard one cared to mention—parochial coverage, numbers of clergy, wealth and adherents in the British Isles. Yet, unlike any of the other 'structures' considered in this opening section, it was difficult to state categorically how the Church of England (embracing England and Wales) operated or, indeed, precisely what it was. It certainly had seen the arrival of new dioceses—St Albans, Truro, Liverpool, Wakefield, Southwell and Newcastle upon Tyne—over the preceding quarter of a century. Bristol had its first bishop after it was again separated from Gloucester in 1897.[31] The redrawing of ecclesiastical boundaries which this had entailed had been contentious. It had been a necessary recognition of the changed population pattern which the nineteenth century had produced. Great cities—Liverpool, Bristol, Newcastle—needed their own bishops. The names of at least some dioceses should not simply conjure up images of congenial country towns. Creating 'proper' cathedrals for these dioceses was of course a problem. Were they really necessary? If you had to have them, did you need deans? In Newcastle the largest financial contribution to the new bishopric came from a Quaker. 'Community' involvement in diocesan construction was also apparent in other ways. Who better than the duke of Northumberland to welcome the new bishop to Newcastle 'on behalf of the laity'?[32] Before returning to Alnwick Castle, His Grace reminded His Lordship that while the city had

---

[29] Kelly, *Memories*, 108. He became President of the National Council of Evangelical Free Churches in 1900.

[30] John Pemble, *The Mediterranean Passion: Victorians and Edwardians in the South* (Oxford, 1987), 219.

[31] Owen Chadwick, *The Victorian Church*, vol. ii (London, 1970), 346–7.

[32] Speaking to his diocesan conference in 1881, J. C. Ryle, bishop of Liverpool, thought a diocese should involve and 'command the affection of the middle classes'. Martin Wellings, 'J. C. Ryle "First words". An opening address delivered at the first Liverpool diocesan conference, 1881' in Mark Smith and Stephen Taylor, eds., *Evangelicalism in the Church of England c.1790–c.1890* (Woodbridge, 2004), 303.

risen to new levels of prosperity, the 'dark shadows of demoralisation and vice' followed in the train of wealth and luxury.[33] 'New' bishops (but no more than 'old'), on their extensive travels, did not join Methodist ministers in third-class carriages. No additional provision was made in the House of Lords for their increased number. The job specification for a bishop remained imprecise. Archbishop Benson, speaking in Birmingham on behalf of a project to create a bishopric for the city, had told its inhabitants in 1890 that they should place among themselves a citizen and ruler with the passion of the city at heart, a prophet who would speak plain things to both rich and poor. Only in 1905, however, was Birmingham to receive a bishop. A bishop should ideally be a 'local worthy', a consummate letter-writer, a passable preacher, a competent theologian and a shepherd capable of wielding an effective crook. It helped to have had a spell as a headmaster. Not all bishops passed all of these tests. Diocesan conferences, after some considerable controversy, had by now become prevalent, though it was thought necessary to state that their advisory proceedings paled before the rulings of a bishop. Bishops thought that the benefit of such conferences was that they would remind the laity that 'they are the Church as well as ourselves'. It did not apparently occur to bishops to remind the clergy not to treat the laity as superfluously peripheral.[34] Inevitably, some bishops were locally more 'popular' than others. The likelihood of a bishop's house—still frequently a 'palace'—being burnt by a mob, as had occurred in Bristol in 1831, was now remote. It was perhaps one more evidence of English calmness (or sublime indifference?) that the church, in the form of its clergy, was the object neither of the sustained invective nor the intense devotion evident contemporaneously in France.[35]

Calmness was not so evident in Wales, but there the situation was different. The Church of England had been experiencing decades of sustained assault from the Nonconformist denominations who used census and other evidence to demonstrate that it did not have the allegiance of a majority of people in Wales. Political, cultural and linguistic factors came together to make the church vulnerable.[36] That pressure had been successfully resisted, although bills had been introduced in the Commons in 1894 and 1895. Disestablishment had been the key issue in the ensuing general election in Wales. Liberals, who fared badly, would have to wait until a swing of the pendulum at Westminster would make it a reality. The animus against the church might, however, be

[33] Peter J. Jagger, 'The Formation of the Diocese of Newcastle' in W. S. F. Pickering, ed., *A Social History of the Diocese of Newcastle* (London, 1981), 48–51.

[34] Wellings, 'J. C. Ryle', 303.

[35] Hugh McLeod, 'Varieties of Anticlericalism in Later Victorian and Edwardian England' in Nigel Aston and Matthew Cragoe, eds., *Anticlericalism* (Stroud, 2000), 216.

[36] Kenneth O. Morgan, *Freedom or Sacrilege? A History of the Campaign for Welsh Disestablishment* (Penarth, 1966); P. M. H. Bell, *Disestablishment in Ireland and Wales* (London, 1969).

said to derive from feelings evoked in mid-century. There was some recognition that the church was renewing itself. While the situation varied in the four Welsh dioceses, the theological and liturgical changes were those which had also obtained in England, and indeed had their origin there. Archbishop Benson, preaching at the Church Congress at Cardiff, had wished to illustrate 'the undividedness of the Church of Wales and England in its history'.[37] It was still, therefore, in St Paul's Cathedral in London in 1897 that a young Welsh-speaking former Calvinistic Methodist, John Owen, was consecrated bishop of St Davids. He proved himself eager to maintain the establishment of one Church of England.[38] So did the archbishop of Canterbury, Temple. Sectional interests which disliked the church should not be allowed, in the latter's opinion, to sacrifice the 'religious welfare of the nation'.[39] Churchmen and Nonconformists in Wales asked themselves, with differing answers, what 'nation' it was to which the archbishop was referring.

A duke of Northumberland might not be taken to articulate the 'typical' sentiments of the church's laity in the north-east. But who were the laity? Supposing that they should be heard, how could that be best done? It could still be argued, but with reduced conviction, that the lay voice of the Church of England was properly and effectively expressed by the Crown in Parliament. It had seemed increasingly odd, however, that the manner in which the church conducted its worship should rest on the whim of MPs, at least some of whom might be irreverent. MPs, however, could make a rejoinder. They listened to the views of their constituents and those views might be ones which 'the church' might not want to hear. Whose church was it? Where was the 'true laity' to be found? 'Church Congresses' had for a time constituted, without statutory basis, a national sounding-board. Some of them had been so boisterous that they might almost be mistaken for the annual meetings of a Nonconformist body. By the 1890s, however, they had largely lost their appeal.

The clergy of Canterbury and York had their convocations. The two provinces—the former in 1885 and the latter in 1892 (an archiepiscopal death had had to supervene)—established Houses of Laity. The clergy had succeeded in retaining the discussion of faith and doctrine for themselves— though at least some bishops had thought the laity might have opinions on these matters. By what process 'laity' arrived in their House and what they should do on arrival was in process of clarification. It had not been officially decreed that the two bodies should meet together, so they did not. At the turn of the century, it was thought 'unofficially' that they might come into contact with each other. In the wings was a proposal for a 'Representative Church Council' which would combine all four bodies. Such rudimentary

[37] A. C. Benson, *Edward White Benson, Archbishop of Canterbury* (London, 1901), 366.
[38] Keith Robbins, 'Episcopacy in Wales', *Journal of Welsh Religious History* 4 (1996), 63–78.
[39] Peter Hinchliff, *Frederick Temple: Archbishop of Canterbury, A Life* (Oxford, 1998), 207–8.

'representativeness', however, still did not directly address how the Church of England should relate to the 'Representatives of the People' in Parliament.

It so happened that Lord Salisbury, the prime minister, a very wealthy man, was a devout though despondent High Anglican. He perceived that the relationship between church and state was in trouble.[40] The ideal of a church might be that it should be independent of the state, but he thought it could not escape from the entangling complexities and imperfections of the world. Anglicanism was gratifyingly 'sturdy, thickset and phlegmatic'.[41] His nephew, Arthur Balfour, shortly to succeed him, had ruminated on the subject of philosophic doubt. Balfour, in the Scottish part of his being, was a Presbyterian. To have 'Ritual' as additional burden on top of 'Free Trade' was more than any prime minister should have to deal with. So, for the moment, through the 'usual channels', accommodations could still be made. There was, however, a different climate. Perhaps the age in which bishops, and leaders of schools of thought within the church, were 'national' figures was passing or had passed.[42]

It was sometimes thought that this 'fudge' could not last indefinitely, which was one of the reasons why, both at diocesan and national level, the 'parties' of the church jostled so vigorously for position. They had been famously characterized in the mid-century as 'High', 'Low' and 'Broad'.[43] Yet, even though such terms became commonly used, they were widely recognized as generalizations riddled with exceptions. Those who deplored the 'party spirit' as embodied in the support organizations—the English Church Union for the 'very High' and the Church Association for the 'very Low'—as contrary to the essence of the church, perhaps formed the largest 'non-party' of all.[44] It was questionable, too, how far the 'party labels' of mid-century still applied in precisely the same way. All such caveats having been made, however, there had continued to be serious divisions on matters of theology, liturgy, politics and ecclesiology. 'Keeping the church together' had preoccupied all late-nineteenth-century archbishops. This condition of unresolved tension in the Church of England was one of the reasons which had led Hugh Price Hughes to believe that there could only be 'convergence' amongst the churches either towards Methodism or towards Roman Catholicism.[45]

---

[40] Frances Knight, 'From Diversity to Sectarianism: The Definition of Anglican Identity in Nineteenth-Century England' in R. N. Swanson, ed., *Unity and Diversity in the Church*, Studies in Church History 32 (Oxford, 1996), 377–86.

[41] Cited in Maurice Cowling, *Religion and Public Doctrine in Modern England* (Cambridge, 1980), 384 in the context of a more extended discussion of Salisbury's views.

[42] P. T. Marsh, *The Victorian Church in Decline* (London, 1969), 289.

[43] W. J. Conybeare: 'Church Parties' edited and introduced by Arthur Burns in Stephen Taylor, ed., *From Cranmer to Davidson*, Church of England Record Society 7 (Woodbridge, 1999), 213–385.

[44] R. Bayfield, *The History of the English Church Union, 1859–1894* (London, 1989).

[45] The most recent life is Christopher Oldstone-Moore, *Hugh Price Hughes: Founder of New Methodism, Conscience of a New Nonconformity* (Cardiff, 1999).

Certainly, the Roman Catholic Church now came into the picture in a way that it could not have done a century earlier.[46] Consideration of its structures and forms could not of course be considered simply on the basis of its presence in the British Isles—increasing numbers of British travellers had experienced it elsewhere. It was the *Catholic* church. Its insular self-understanding could not be different from its self-understanding in any other part of Europe, indeed of the world. It could not be said that it was 'unorganized'. It was felt important in some Anglican quarters, whose interpretation of 'catholicity' was different, to speak pointedly of the *Roman* Catholic church. The pope was in Rome, south of which city he happened to have been born. His only experience outside Italy had been as nuncio to Belgium in the middle-1840s. Whilst there, he had paid a short visit to London. Leo XIII, perceived to be fragile in health when elected in 1878, was still in office at the age of 90 in 1900. He had the novel experience, for a pope, of not having a state to govern. His predecessor had been (involuntarily) relieved of this task. Leo would like to have regained a state. He was, however, fortified by the conclusion of the Vatican Council in 1870 that in definitions of faith and morals a pope was infallible. Conciliarist interpretations of the role of the papacy had been rejected. It left him free to govern the church even more strenuously as a papal monarch. Bishops were firmly put in place and in their place. Congregations and orders were strictly supervised. Nuncios were elevated. Such liturgical or pastoral variation as existed was tightly restricted, if not eliminated—'Americanism' had received a very recent censure. If all roads had once led to Rome, railways now brought pilgrims more quickly. Nationally, it was with the newly united states of Germany and Italy and then, in different ways, with France, rather than with the United Kingdom, that the pope was chiefly engaged in dispute. His long reign had seen a series of pronouncements which, cumulatively, represented a grudging and qualified recognition of 'democracy' and 'liberty', together with the endorsement of workers' rights, though not of socialism. The pronouncements suggested that he was a kind of universal spiritual ruler. Put another way, he could be perceived as a dictator within a totalitarian system, underpinned by an anonymous bureaucracy.[47] It was, however, a church which thought it properly understood what 'democracy' meant. Its interpretation did not invariably coincide with that of democrats outside its ranks. 'Popery', declared the Wesleyan Charles H. Kelly in his presidential address to the National Council of Evangelical Free Churches in Sheffield in 1900, 'has not improved'. Notwithstanding all of the religious and civil liberty which it had been granted in the British Empire, it was 'still the foe of true liberty, of free speech, or private judgement'.[48] For the

---

[46] Dorothea Hughes, *The Life of Hugh Price Hughes* (London, 1904), 629.

[47] Klaus von Aretin, *The Papacy and the Modern World* (London, 1970), 125.

[48] Cited in Megahey, *Irish Protestant Churches*, 6.

papacy, however, none of its tentative 'accommodation', as it saw it, could put at risk the sense of the church as a spiritual fortress to be maintained against the fads of late-nineteenth-century Europe and its illusions of progress.[49] An index of forbidden books could still be made a reality.

Leo and his nineteenth-century predecessors well knew that in the British Isles it was only in Ireland that the fortress was well-manned. Westminster governments, too, had known that while Britain could have the image of a Protestant state, the Irish union had necessarily, if slowly, modified this picture as far as a 'United Kingdom' was concerned. It had been necessary to deal with the papacy, indeed to do deals with it. Now, for thirty years, with the disestablishment of the (Anglican) Church of Ireland, Ireland was the only part of the United Kingdom where the state no longer endorsed the status of any particular church though, even so, old habits died hard. For its part, a Catholic Church in Ireland which in periods of penal subordin-ation—although occasionally tinged with Gallicanism—had looked for support from the Vatican was not likely to wish to distance itself from an apparently strengthened papacy, even if its own insular circumstances had improved.[50] That improvement, however, could not detract from the fact that, in certain symbolic ways at least, the United Kingdom did remain constitutionally Protestant. The monarch could not be a Roman Catholic. The legislative removal of restrictions and disestablishment had sprung, of course, from the recognition that the subordination of the church to which the majority of the population adhered was no longer politically either feasible or desirable. A church which was indubitably the largest in the island of Ireland, whose development had been vigorously shaped by its clerical leadership, which had undergone a 'devotional revolution' in the aftermath of the disastrous national famine, and which had 'exported' itself to the British Empire and the United States, was therefore nevertheless locked within a United Kingdom in which it was a minority.[51] Further, as a

---

[49] Owen Chadwick, *A History of the Popes 1830–1914* (Oxford, 1998), 173–331 discusses Leo; L. P. Wallace, *Leo XIII* (Durham, NC, 1966).

[50] J. F. Broderick, *The Holy See and the Irish Movement for the Repeal of the Union with England 1829–1847* (Rome, 1951).

[51] Background to these general points can be found, for example, in O. MacDonagh, 'The Politicization of the Irish Catholic Bishops, 1800–1850', *Historical Journal* 18 (1975), 37–53; D. W. Miller, 'Irish Catholicism and the Great Famine', *Journal of Social History* 9 (1975), 81–98; E. R. Norman, *The Catholic Church and Ireland in the Age of Rebellion, 1859–1873* (London, 1965). See writings by Emmet Larkin, among them, for this purpose, being *The Roman Catholic Church and the Creation of the Modern Irish State* (Dublin, 1975) and 'Church and State in Ireland in the Nineteenth Century', *Church History* 33 (1964), 294–306. Additionally, see Desmond Bowen, *Paul Cullen and the Shaping of Modern Irish Catholicism* (Dublin, 1983); S. J. Connolly, *Religion and Society in Nineteenth-Century Ireland* (Dundalk, 1985); P. J. Corish, *The Irish Catholic Experience: A Historical Survey* (Dublin, 1985); Sheridan Gilley, 'Religion in Modern Ireland', *Journal of Ecclesiastical History* 47 (January 1992), 110–15 and 'Catholicism in Ireland' in McLeod and Ustorf, eds., *Decline of Christendom*, 99–112.

result of its traumatic experiences, Ireland, in mid-century substantially more populous than Scotland, was in 1901 narrowly less populous. At around four and a half million people, Ireland and Scotland together constituted 21 per cent of the United Kingdom population.

'Home Rule' for Ireland, whatever that precisely meant, could constitute one solution to the 'anomaly' of the church's position and allow it to assume what it would regard as its rightful guardianship of Irish life. Its stance had been greatly complicated by the personal conduct of Charles Stewart Parnell (a Protestant) and all that had stemmed from it. There was no way in which the church—by which one means the hierarchy—could detach itself from the 'Irish question' and little indication that it wished to do so. For *The Witness*, the Irish Presbyterian weekly (in 1886), however, the prospect had been found appalling. It reminded its readers that Ireland was merely one site in a global struggle in which Rome and the Reformation were still striving for mastery. The battle was by no means over. It was not being fought with sword and cannon, but it was no less real for that.[52] In the Ireland of the 1890s, it was far from clear how this situation would be resolved. Violence, or the threat of violence, was never far below the surface. While there were cities in Britain, perhaps Liverpool and Glasgow in particular, where sectarian tensions (or ethnic tensions using religious language?) might erupt, the possibility of some kind of civil war in Britain was not a context in which the British churches operated.[53]

In any case, while the strength of the Catholic Church in Ireland was unique in the British Isles, the island shared, though in markedly different proportions, the ecclesiastical pluralism of Britain—with the presence of Anglicans, Presbyterians, Methodists—the three largest—together with Baptists, Congregationalists, Quakers and Unitarians and other even smaller bodies. Collectively, they constituted 'the Protestant minority'. Although, according to the 1901 census—which in Ireland revealed denominational allegiance—their percentage had risen to 26 per cent from the 22 per cent half a century earlier, Protestants were more or less resigned to their minority condition. Ireland was not at long last on the brink of conversion to Protestantism.[54] Their very diversity, however, meant that they constituted a unity only in a loose manner—largely against the 'Other' of Rome. There was even a limited sense, until the Church of Ireland had been

[52] Cited by R. F. G. Holmes, 'United Irishmen and Unionists: Irish Presbyterians, 1791 and 1886' in W. J. Sheils and D. Wood, eds., *The Churches, Ireland and the Irish*, Studies in Church History 25 (Oxford, 1989), 187.

[53] F. Neal, *Sectarian Violence: The Liverpool Experience, 1819–1914* (Manchester, 1988); T. Gallagher, *Glasgow, The Uneasy Peace: Religious Tension in Modern Scotland* (Manchester, 1987).

[54] Desmond Bowen, *The Protestant Crusade in Ireland, 1800–70: A Study of Protestant–Catholic Relations between the Act of Disunion and Disestablishment* (Dublin, 1978) and *History and the Shaping of Irish Protestantism* (New York, 1995).

disestablished and disendowed, that other Protestants had been as much 'outsiders' as Roman Catholics had been. Even in 1902, the moderator of their General Assembly—an annual office—was not being given the precedence Presbyterians thought appropriate at state functions at the vice-regal lodge or at Dublin Castle. It was galling, they felt, that the head 'of a great Church like ours' had to accept a position behind a mere diocesan bishop.[55] This matter was in fact 'rectified' the following year. Such wounded sensibilities conveniently overlooked the extent to which, until disestablishment, the Presbyterians had for centuries been receiving a state subsidy, the *Regium Donum*.

Sensitivity about official recognition in Dublin also stemmed from regional dynamics within Ireland. While just over half of Irish Protestants were Anglicans and just under half were Presbyterians, the latter were emphatically concentrated in the north-east. However, although Armagh, in the north, was the primatial see, the administrative 'capital' of the Church of Ireland was in Dublin. Most of its largely graduate clergy had degrees from Trinity College and its *Gazette* and teacher training college were in the city. Belfast, on the other hand, was the 'capital' of the Presbyterian Church. The turn of the century saw the construction of a splendid set of buildings there—naturally in Scottish baronial style—in which to hold its Assembly and for other purposes. Here was an example of 'city culture' with a vengeance.

The Church of Ireland, on disestablishment and disendowment, had had to begin again: a constitution, a hierarchy of governing bodies (which of course included the question of how bishops should be chosen henceforth) and a new Prayer Book.[56] Urgent financial issues had to be addressed. Inevitably, reconstruction and revision had been the initial preoccupations. By the end of the century, however, a self-governing body in which the two archbishops of Armagh and Dublin, and the other bishops, shared authority with a mixed annual synod of clergy and laity, was held to demonstrate that, despite 'worldly or financial injustice' allegedly done to it, 'spiritual advantage' had accrued.[57] The scattered nature of many congregations was an additional reason why, so long as church regulations were not being infringed, individual congregations were not subject to much

---

[55] Cited in Megahey, *Irish Protestant Churches*, 15; T. Hamilton, *History of Presbyterianism in Ireland* (Belfast, 1992); R. F. G. Holmes and R. B. Knox, eds., *The General Assembly of the Presbyterian Church in Ireland 1840–1990* (Belfast, 1990).

[56] Richard Clarke, 'Imperfect with Peace . . . Lord Plunket and the Disestablishment Revision of the Irish Prayer Book' in John R. Guy and W. G. Neely, eds., *Contrasts and Comparisons: Studies in Irish and Welsh Church History* (Welshpool/Armagh, 1999), 115–34.

[57] The judgement of a layman, Anthony Traill, Provost of Trinity College, Dublin cited in R. B. McDowell, *The Church of Ireland, 1869–1969* (London, 1975), 70; A. Acheson, *A History of the Church of Ireland 1691–1996* (Dublin, 1997); M. Hurley, ed., *Irish Anglicanism* (Dublin, 1970).

supervision. In Co. Cork in 1881, for example, Protestants constituted 8.3 per cent of the total population, of which 29 per cent resided in various county towns. In parish terms, the range of Protestant presence could vary between 19.4 per cent and 0.04 per cent. The life of a Protestant family in a 'Big House' could be virtually self-contained. Such a pattern of distribution makes generalization about the Church of Ireland, even on a county level, virtually impossible. In Cork city, for example, the Protestant population was such that it could sustain a life of its own and indeed most social, cultural and charitable organizations were arranged on a denominational basis.[58]

Further, the two largest Protestant churches in Ireland, the Anglican and the Presbyterian, had different 'kinships' across the Irish Sea, though the depth of that 'kinship' should not be exaggerated. Leaving aside issues of ethnicity for the moment, the connections of the Church of Ireland were with the Church of England (and English theological scholarship) whilst those of the Presbyterian Church were with Scottish Presbyterianism and theological scholarship. Some Irish ministers traditionally studied in Scotland. What both minority churches felt closest to, therefore, had been, and still was, largely determined by geography and history. The same factors also combined to make both Catholics and Protestants in Ireland look across the Atlantic, though the connections and interactions which developed had the effect of strengthening rather than dissipating the differences between them. Its circumstances had, however, broadly given the Church of Ireland a more pronounced Protestant tone than the Church of England on the whole now felt proper. Whatever their own disagreements, and against a long history, however, all Protestants felt alarm, perhaps fear, in the face of the Vatican as they saw it evolving.[59] The restrictions and exclusions still experienced by Protestants in certain 'Catholic' countries of Europe, with the blessing of the Vatican, seemed ominous. It was not accidental that the Church of Ireland developed a special affection for the scanty number of Iberian Protestants. Lord Plunket, Anglican archbishop of Dublin, with two other bishops, was to be found in Madrid in 1894 conferring episcopal orders on one such Spaniard.

In 1895 Leo had addressed a letter *Ad Anglos* which recalled the ancient union of the noble English nation with the mother church and indicated a special concern for the conversion of England. It made no mention of 'the Church of England'. He was the first pope to use the expression 'separated

---

[58] Ian d'Alton, *Protestant Society and Politics in Cork, 1812–1844* (Cork, 1980) and 'Southern Irish Unionism: A Study of Cork Unionists,1884–1914', *Transactions of the Royal Historical Society*, 5th series, 23 (1972), 75–6.

[59] Jacqueline Hill, 'Popery and Protestantism, Civil and Religious Liberty: The Disputed Lessons of Irish History 1690–1812', *Past and Present* 118 (1988), 96–129.

brethren' to refer to Protestants and Orthodox, but Anglicans had just been left in no doubt that their orders were invalid (*Apostolicae curae*, September 1896). It was a pronouncement which had followed a series of conversations between Anglicans and Roman Catholics in Rome. The archbishop of Canterbury, Edward Benson, happened to be in Dublin, celebrating the restoration of the cathedral of Kildare, when the news came through. He told his audience that the result was a lesson to those who had been led in quiet years to believe that the Church of Rome had become other than what it was.[60] The Anglican rebuttal—though not by Benson, for he died shortly afterwards—made no impression in Rome.[61] Lord Halifax, president of the English Church Union (the Anglo-Catholic organization), who had been personally involved in cultivating conversation, was most disappointed.[62] Benson had told him that while secret diplomacy might be part of the machinery of the Church of Rome it was contrary to the genius and sense of the English church. Halifax, for his part, hearing of Irish Anglican goings-on in Madrid, took it upon himself, speaking on behalf of 'members of the catholic church', to write to the archbishop of Toledo deploring Lord Plunket's initiative.

There was perhaps something to be said for entering the new century with clarity. Evangelicals had in any case been apprehensive that an aristocratic Anglican coterie was trying to persuade Rome that the Church of England was something it was not.[63] The Church of England and the Roman Catholic Church in England now knew, apparently, how they stood in relation to each other. The former could not expect that a 'federation' would be on offer. Presbyterians and Nonconformists, confident that their ancestors had recovered the primitive constitution of the church, saw a sort of piquancy in the situation. Rome pronounced Anglican orders to be null and void: Canterbury pronounced Nonconformist orders null and void.

Herbert Vaughan, archbishop of Westminster since 1892, was gratified that reunion was 'not even on the most distant horizon'. The only possible course for Anglicans was 'a gradual submission'. It could only come when the 'fact of unity' had been recognized.[64] He wrote to the archbishop of Toledo to explain that Lord Halifax was not a Catholic, merely the head of 'one of the sects of the Anglican church'. When that description of him

[60] A. C. Benson, *The Life of Edward White Benson, Archbishop of Canterbury* (London, 1901), 522.
[61] The documents are reproduced in R. P. Flindall, ed., *The Church of England, 1815–1948: A Documentary History* (London, 1972), 167–81.
[62] J. J. Hughes, *Absolutely Null and Utterly Void* (London, 1968).
[63] Nigel Scotland, *Evangelical Anglicans in a Revolutionary Age, 1789–1901* (Carlisle, 2004) provides an assessment of their importance, though he does not specifically comment on their attitude to Leo's initiative.
[64] Cited in E. Norman, *The English Catholic Church in the Nineteenth Century* (Oxford, 1984), 370–1.

appeared in the press, Vaughan wrote to Halifax to say that the phrase must have been caused by faulty translation (Vaughan had written in Latin). It was, nevertheless, what he believed. He thought it obvious that, as things were, Anglicans were widely separated from one another in doctrine, more widely separated indeed within than they were from the Nonconformists without. Such bluntness might have been expected from a former Anglican—such as Manning, his predecessor. Vaughan, however, came from a landowning 'old' Catholic family in Herefordshire. He brought with him to Westminster knowledge not only of the slums of Salford but also of Catholic life in Europe and South America. Just as a 'strong Papal adherence' had been growing up in England, he had written thirty years earlier, so it was important that it would also be weaved into 'pagan lands' and British colonies. If it had been possible, at this juncture, to be more Roman than the Romans, Vaughan would have been a candidate. It was not only in England that 'papal adherence' was growing. The restoration of a Catholic hierarchy in 1851 had only been to England (and Wales as part of England). It had not been until 1878 that the hierarchy had been restored in Scotland. It was not conceivable that there could have been a 'British' hierarchy since it was in the aspect of its church life that the distinctiveness of Scotland remained most evident. Apart from the small Scottish Episcopal Church, which hesitated to call itself Protestant, there was in Scotland no *via media* such as the Church of England, or at least parts of it, considered itself to be in England. No Presbyterian peer was to be found seeking 'recognition' from Rome on behalf of his church.

By the close of the century, however, it did appear that incessant fissiparousness, deemed characteristic of Scottish Protestant church life, had almost exhausted itself. The wounds of the 'Great Disruption' of 1843, which had seen the departure of a large body of ministers and people from the Church of Scotland on the issues revolving around lay patronage, had not been healed.[65] Since many of those who left its ranks were from its most energetic membership, the Church of Scotland was gravely weakened and had lost its clear pre-eminence. The resulting Free Church was not opposed in principle to establishment but to 'Erastian' establishment. The consequence of the disruption, though not in equal proportions in all areas, was that Scotland witnessed a competing parallelism between the Church of Scotland and the Free Church of Scotland—Free Church against the old parish

[65] A. L. Drummond and J. Bulloch, *The Church in Late Victorian Scotland 1874–1900* (Edinburgh, 1978); John F. McCaffrey, 'Scottish Church History in the Nineteenth Century: A Select Critical Bibliography', *Records of the Scottish Church History Society* 23/3 (1989), 417–36; S. J. Brown, *The National Churches of England, Ireland and Scotland, 1801–46* (Oxford, 2001); Callum Brown, *Religion and Society in Scotland since 1707* (Edinburgh, 1997), 48–9 gives maps which illustrate the comparative regional strength in 1891 of the three main Presbyterian churches.

church, manse against manse, school against school, divinity college against university divinity faculty. Earlier eighteenth-century 'secessions' had come together in 1847 to form the United Presbyterian Church, a body committed to the voluntary principle. Throughout the latter decades of the nineteenth century, committees from the Free and United Presbyterian Churches engaged in discussions—which sometimes had to be broken off because they appeared to be deadlocked—with a view to achieving a union. The strong commitment of the latter to disestablishment was one obstacle. It had seemed, on the Free Church side, that to advocate a purely secular state was a form of unbelief. Its power of intervention suitably circumscribed, the state should nevertheless support a national church. After 1874, only a minority, based primarily in the Highlands, continued to hold this position. The schismatic spirit had spread to Scottish Australia, but there, union was achieved. Eventually, in October 1900, though not without a secession on the Free Church side, chiefly in the Highlands, the United Free Church of Scotland came into being. It claimed to be larger than the Church of Scotland. Could they come together?

The union that was eventually achieved might suggest an inexorable process. Such was not the case. There were important differences of social and intellectual ethos between the two churches, reflecting in part their regional distribution, and, within that, between urban and rural Scotland. The strength of the Free Church in Gaelic-speaking areas of the Highlands and Islands was not matched by the United Presbyterians and it was there that the seceders of 1900 found their residual strength. The controversial issues which had so much engaged the committees touched raw nerves over a long Scottish past. In their minutiae, they were only dimly perceived or understood in England. Even though *de facto* the Free Church had been driven in a 'voluntary' direction it had not been a 'free church' as the classical English Nonconformists understood the term. Baptists and Congregationalists, as has been mentioned, were only small and marginal to the main streams of Scottish church life. However, Parker's 1901 hope that the Presbyterians might come into his envisaged new church was in part based on his knowledge of the creation of the United Free Church of Scotland. A United Free Church of Britain would indeed be a novelty because it would mean an ecclesiastical incorporation never previously achieved. Presbyterians, however, notwithstanding their nineteenth-century and earlier splits, and the variations in government that accompanied them, still retained their understanding of church order which might make a Scottish 'national' Presbyterianism a more likely outcome. Although fraternal greetings were exchanged across the border between annual assemblies, and there were occasional 'pulpit exchanges', there was no in-depth familiarity. Ministerial 'traffic' tended to be in one direction. It might not be an exaggeration to suggest that English Congregationalism, at this time, was being dominated, intellectually at least, by Scotsmen.[66]

ii. Particular Places

Grappling with the passage of time is a problem which inescapably confronts a church in any country or continent. It is its occupation of particular 'places' which gives its existence a specific character. In turn, the 'feel' of particular places has a profound impact on religious life.[67] Even when particular churches have felt uncomfortable with the concept of 'holy ground', all have had 'sites of memory'. Thanks to Mr Thomas Cook, late Victorians who visited the 'Holy Land' did so more as 'pilgrims' than as simple 'tourists'. Special meetings for prayer and meditation were arranged for them.[68]

It is arguable, therefore, that it is at the 'local' level that 'church history' really comes to life. It is in the pattern of Christian behaviour displayed by 'ordinary people', whose conduct and priorities can often relate only obscurely to the formal pronouncements and statements which are frequently taken by historians to constitute 'what the church thinks', that church history 'comes alive'.[69] Yet, 'congregational studies', whether 'extrinsic' or 'intrinsic', and however sophisticated, can be equally partial if there is no 'big picture'.[70] Attempts to consider the Christianity of 'the North', or of any other region of England or the British Isles, encounters the difficulty that 'regions' are manufactured and have different resonances at different times.[71] Populations and boundaries shift. In short, a 'typical' church is elusive, but this author attempts to integrate 'church history', perceived both from 'above' and 'below', from its centres and its peripheries, from 'inside' and from 'outside', though well aware that to contrive such an integration is no more easy in a book than it is in life.

---

[66] The names of A. M. Fairbairn, P. T. Forsyth, A. E. Garvie, and J. Hunter stand out in this regard.

[67] Geoffrey Lilburne, *A Sense of Place: A Christian Theology of the Land* (Nashville, TN, 1989).

[68] Timothy Larsen, 'Thomas Cook, Holy Land Pilgrims, and the Dawn of the Modern Tourist Industry' in R. N. Swanson, ed., *The Holy Land, Holy Lands, and Christian History*, Studies in Church History 36 (Woodbridge, 2000), 341.

[69] The contours of this relationship, for an earlier period, are specifically addressed in Jeremy Gregory and Jeffrey S. Chamberlain, *The National Church in Local Perspective: The Church of England and the Regions, 1660–1800* (Woodbridge, 2003).

[70] Matthew Guest, Karin Tusting and Linda Woodhead, *Congregational Studies in the UK: Christianity in a Post-Christian Context* (Aldershot, 2004). See Haddon Willmer, 'Writing Local Church History' in Anthony R. Cross, ed., *Ecumenism and History: Essays in Honour of John H. Y. Briggs* (Carlisle, 2002), 208–24.

[71] A. R. H. Baker and Mark Billinge, eds., *Geographies of England, Imagined and Material* (Cambridge, 2004); Keith Robbins, *Nineteenth-Century Britain: Integration and Diversity* (Oxford, 1988), 63–96.

However it situates itself in time, a church can function only in a given social, physical and cultural environment. The universal has to be confined. Not every church architect had followed the example of R.G. Thomas of Charles Street chapel, Cardiff, in incorporating in its façade a stone 'from every nation' as a symbol of universality incorporated within a particular place. What a church presents itself as may seem obscure or obnoxious to the community in which it is set. It may be treated with approval, indifference or hostility. Churches may not only be transmitters of their own traditions, however, but those traditions may be accepted, perhaps passively and unconsciously, as part, a significant part, of local, regional or national identities.[72] Churches, in such a situation, may be so entwined with the rhythms and rifts of a community that their purchase on universality fades. An institutional ability to transcend 'place' is no more common than is the ability to transcend time. The assumptions and conduct of churches may, therefore, in reality, be lightly anchored in 'the Christian past' and be, predominantly, those of the wider society in the present. That wider society, however, may have been unwillingly coerced, by legislative enactment or political pressure, into the acceptance and enforcement of 'norms' which stemmed from Christian 'norms', or what churches in previous generations had judged to be Christian 'norms'. Churches and their members would not be able to escape these issues in the new century. Corporately and individually they occupied substantial social space. The further complication was that they did so, however uncomfortably, in a political system which, for men, now verged on being democratic.

A century earlier, in 1802, William Cobbett, a man much given to rural rides, noted that whenever one looked around the country and saw 'the multitude of regularly distributed spires' the wonder was that any such thing as disaffection or irreligion should prevail.[73] The 'feel' of the British Isles at the beginning of the twentieth century would have been quite different without places where Christians assembled (though their buildings did not all have spires). Churches as 'markers' occupied prominent physical space throughout the British Isles. They were the visible indications of 'a Christian country'. 'Our old parish churches', many but lately restored and 'improved', could be 'owned' by the people at large, whether or not they attended. Attachment by 'locals' to a particular place and its associations, and the 'occasional' attendance which accompanied it, indicated a certain kind

[72] The use of the word 'our' in a nineteenth-century dictionary of Preston's places of worship by 'Atticus' (A. Hewitson), *Our Churches and Chapels: Their Parsons, Priests, & Congregations* (Preston, 1869) indicates local 'ownership'. Timothy Jenkins, *Religion in English Everyday Life* (Oxford, 1999) concerns itself with 'Congregational Cultures' and 'the Boundaries of Identity' in Kingswood outside Bristol.

[73] William Cobbett to William Windham, 27 May 1802, in L. Melville, ed., *The Life and Letters of William Cobbett in England and America*, vol. i (London, 1913), 156–7.

of belonging, even if the accompanying doctrinal foundations were slender. The observer would be aware, however, that the Christian landscape did not consist exclusively of aesthetically satisfying constructions. Some were made of red brick. William Cobbett would not have seen squat and perhaps unappealing structures without spires when standing on his high hill, but now there were many more of them. It was possible to gain a sense of the ecclesiastical 'feel' of any village or town by the character and spatial distribution of its religious buildings. Size, 'impressiveness' and density all constituted indicators of local 'strength' and 'weakness'. The pattern would probably reveal where power and influence lay within a community. Foundation stones testified to the involvement of families locally prominent in business and commerce. The Wills 'tobacco' family in Bristol, for example, active in Redland Park Congregational Church (a building equipped with tower and spire) gave generously to its enlargement. No one dreamt that a building on which the congregation was lavishing such care would be shattered in 1940 by a German incendiary bomb.[74] It is significant, however, that Redland was one of the middle-class citadels of the city's westwards expansion on high ground. The Wills factories were on low ground in Bedminster and out of sight. Any generalizations about the religious complexion of a city had in turn to take account of its suburban segmentation and fluid character in a scene of constant 'development'.[75]

The distribution of buildings for worship was not in itself 'historic'. The previous half-century had seen an energetic programme of construction and renovation. The dowry bequeathed to the twentieth century was substantially Victorian.[76] The observer in 1900 could expect to see 'church' and 'chapel' (or 'chapels') in most English villages.[77] It would not have been difficult by their external appearance to distinguish 'church' (Anglican) from 'chapel' (Protestant Nonconformist).[78] A 'church' would be dedicated to a saint. A 'chapel' would normally only be known by its location (though occasionally incorporating the name of a local, though uncanonized, 'saint') or by an Old Testament reference—such as Zion or Ebenezer. A church noticeboard might be reticent about the name of the vicar. A chapel noticeboard would give the name of the minister and, where available,

---

[74] William Edwards, *Redland Park Congregational Church, Bristol* (Bristol, 1941); J. C. G. Binfield, 'The Wills Family of Bristol', *Congregational History Circle Magazine* 2/6 (1990), 3–14. The connection between men of business and church/chapel life can also be seen also in many other places. See, in particular, essays in David J. Jeremy, ed., *Business and Religion in Britain* (Aldershot, 1988).

[75] J. H. S. Kent, 'The Role of Religion in the Cultural Structure of the later Victorian City', *Transactions of the Royal Historical Society*, 5th series, 23 (1972), 166.

[76] C. Brooks and A. Saint, eds., *The Victorian Church: Architecture and Society* (Manchester, 1993).

[77] Frances Knight, *The Nineteenth-Century Church and English Society* (Cambridge, 1995).

[78] Royal Commission on the Historical Monuments of England, *An Inventory of Nonconformist Chapels and Meeting-Houses in Central England* (London, 1986) is one such guide.

the degree or degrees he possessed. Roman Catholics, though not invariably, tended to speak of their buildings as 'chapels'.

'Tabernacles', rectangular buildings with Greek temple fronts, bore scarcely any resemblance to the biblical sanctuary tents from which the name was drawn. They had spread through south-east London on the inspiration of the Metropolitan Tabernacle erected for C.H. Spurgeon at the Elephant and Castle in 1860. 'One of the sights of London', it provided seats for 5,000 together with standing room for a further 1,000. Some aspiring Nonconformists, however, had now succumbed to spires. In 1900 Lavender Hill Congregationalists in London added a tower and spire to a church built in 1883. Wesleyan Methodists in New Inn Hall Street felt a need to supplement the quota of Oxford's dreaming spires. In Wales, Welsh-language congregations preferred Classical styles, rather than the Gothic which they associated with Anglican churches, but English-language congregations in Wales tended to be less worried by such similarity. However, 'The cathedral of Welsh Nonconformity', Tabernacle, Morriston, Swansea had received a spire from its deacon and architect in 1872.[79] All this building had come at a price, sometimes an exorbitant and debilitating price. The greatest single Nonconformist expenditure had arisen from the building in 1894 of a Baptist church in Paisley. Its stone-built Gothic magnificence, drawing on 'the best traditions of mediaeval church architecture' but with adaptations to meet the requirements of Protestant worship, was made possible by the generosity of the Coats family. It was a memorial to Thomas Coats, founder of the world-wide cotton-thread firm.[80] The defining stance of Baptists was that infants were not baptized. Baptism, by total immersion, was for believers on profession of faith. Where there was provision for a baptistery in the chapel, however, it was normally totally obscured by a platform or other covering when not in use—so the emblem of denominational distinctiveness was hidden from sight.

The process of competitive church building between denominations expressed a desire to control space, whatever else it did. It entailed an expenditure on the part of Wesleyans, Baptists and Primitive Methodists which has been calculated at over £8 million in the 1890s (in contemporary values). Spending by Congregationalists, for which statistics are not available, would boost that figure further. We may be looking at a total of some £350 million in present values. Maintaining a balance between 'supply' and 'demand', however, proved problematic.[81] Much of the building could also

---

[79] Anthony Jones, *Welsh Chapels* (Stroud, 1996 edn.).

[80] J. C. G. Binfield, 'The Coats Family and Paisley Baptists' I and II, *Baptist Quarterly* 36/1 and 36/2 (January and March 1995), 29–42, 80–95.

[81] Robin Gill, *The 'Empty' Church Revisited* (Aldershot, 2003) discusses provision in the context of his overall evaluation of nineteenth-century attendance.

latterly be classified as 'upgrading'. When even Primitive Methodists claimed that some of their buildings were 'sumptuous in their appointments' the days of the sneers at 'ugly conventicles' might be numbered.[82] Failing a major increase in attendances, however, it had already become apparent that there was significant 'over-provision'. It was probably better, as Roman Catholics were finding, to use limited provision intensively rather than to find more generous provision of space 'empty'.

The informed observer would realize that behind the varied styles and sizes lay questions of money, but also more than money. It would be ambitious to suppose that ecclesiastical tourists would know, in each instance, whether the building should be categorized primarily as a *domus dei* or a *domus ecclesiae*, but form certainly immediately conveyed a diversity of understanding of purpose. 'Temple' and 'Meeting-house' expressed different theologies and expectations of congregational participation.[83] Some buildings clearly more consciously encapsulated 'sacred space' than others. The churches in the landscape in any part of the British Isles disclosed a pervasive but differentiated presence of Christianity. The visitor could sense, at a glance, notwithstanding the frequent proximity, even juxtaposition, of different styles in many parts of the islands, which denomination was in *de facto* local domination of space by virtue of size, 'impressiveness' or sheer density. It might disclose, for example, 'Methodist Cornwall', but it might also reveal significant variations in denominational strength between adjacent towns and villages.[84] The distribution, style and size of Roman Catholic, Church of Ireland, Presbyterian and Methodist buildings in the north of Ireland told one a great deal about land ownership, 'territory' and community in the local population. The 'ground' of Ulster was narrow.

External differences could of course deceive. Cathedrals, in particular, were sometimes perceived by Roman Catholics to be 'in the wrong hands' and should, in due season, be returned to their 'original' and rightful owners.[85] An expectation, or at least hope, that the Church of Ireland, on disestablishment, would hand over to Roman Catholics, as surplus to

---

[82] James Munson, *The Nonconformists: In Search of a Lost Culture* (London, 1991), 140–1.

[83] H. W. Turner, *From Temple to Meeting House: The Phenomenology and Theology of Places of Worship* (The Hague, 1979).

[84] T. Shaw, *A History of Cornish Methodism* (Truro, 1967); N. Yates, 'Urban Church Attendance 1850–1900' in Derek Baker, ed., *The Church in Town and Countryside*, Studies in Church History 16 (Oxford, 1979), 390.

[85] Stanford Lehmberg, *English Cathedrals: A History* (London, 2005) is a general survey. Many individual cathedrals are now equipped with good recent histories, normally by teams of writers who examine different facets and periods of their life, e.g. G. E. Aylmer and Reginald Cant, eds., *A History of York Minster* (Oxford, 1977) or Ian Atherton, Eric Fernie, Christopher Harper-Bill and Hassell Smith, eds., *Norwich Cathedral: Church, City and Diocese, 1096–1996* (London, 1996). For Canterbury see Keith Robbins, 'The Twentieth Century, 1898–1994' in Patrick Collinson, Nigel Ramsay and Margaret Sparks, eds., *A History of Canterbury Cathedral* (Oxford, 1995), 297–340.

its small requirements, at least some of the more than two dozen pre-Reformation cathedrals it maintained, was not realized.[86] The space cathedrals occupied sent significant messages, perhaps most notably in Dublin where the city's two ancient cathedrals remained in the possession of the Church of Ireland. Two cathedrals, Roman Catholic and Church of Ireland, in Armagh jostled for physical supremacy. Castle Square Calvinistic Methodist Chapel, Caernarfon competed for attention not with a cathedral but with a substantial castle. The 'cathedral' of St Giles in Edinburgh had long since become a High Kirk and indeed, to rub home the point, the space had housed several 'ordinary' kirks. Visiting it in mid-century, the Anglican Henry Parry Liddon came away with 'a deep and unutterable aversion to a system whose outward manifestations are so hatefully repulsive'.[87] There could be no more graphic testimony to the importance of particular places.

Whether 'rightful owners' of cathedrals should simply wait for the demise of their temporary occupiers and then resume their own use, or whether they should seek to build their own, on a substantial if not commensurate scale, was a moot point. It was indeed possible, as was evident in Londonderry, to construct in such a way that an 'occupied' cathedral could be 'cut down to size'. Londonderry was the only Anglican cathedral proudly to have a cannon ball on display, perhaps as a reminder of a past that had not disappeared. In 1899, recognizing what a noted and populous city Belfast had become, with a growing Episcopalian population, both absolutely and proportionately, the Church of Ireland synod decided that it was time to build a cathedral, St Anne's, on the site of an eighteenth-century parish church.

iii. Sight and Sound

External difference was replicated internally. It would be difficult to say precisely what configuration of internal space one would expect in an Anglican church. Colour, smell and ornaments, however, or their absence, would give a clear clue to the 'tendency' which prevailed in specific cases. It would be possible for the discerning eye to see how far spatial arrangements emphasized the division between clergy and laity.[88] The pattern and frequency of services, together with the words used to describe them, would give further clue. So, if one attended a service, would the attire favoured by the incumbent, even if one might not be able to attach the appropriate words in describing it. A vicar in an Anglo-Catholic parish in London might wear a biretta and green chasuble and be accompanied by acolytes wearing

---

[86] P. Galloway, *The Cathedrals of Ireland* (Belfast, 1992).

[87] J. O. Johnson, *Life and Letters of H. P. Liddon* (London, 1904), 15.

[88] Nigel Yates, *Buildings, Faith and Worship: The Liturgical Arrangements of Anglican Churches 1600–1900* (Oxford, 2000 edn.) provides a full background.

scarlet cassocks and cottas.[89] The altar might be a blaze of candlelight.[90] It
was at one such in 1898 that John Kensit, Protestant denouncer of ritualism,
obtained great publicity when he seized the crucifix as the congregation on
Good Friday went up to kiss it, denouncing idolatry in the name of God—
an action which brought him a fine of £3 for brawling but which no doubt
helped him to secure 4,693 votes when he stood as the 'Protestant' candidate for Brighton in the 1900 general election.[91] Such actions seemed likely,
so one evangelical bishop thought, to cause the good name of Protestantism
to stink in the land, but there was a 'Protestant underworld' which would
not be ignored. Controversy had swirled for decades, and was to continue
to swirl, on the question of 'ritualism'. Liturgical correctness, for certain
clergy, was everything. There had not infrequently been a struggle between
incumbents and parishioners in relation to the management of church
buildings. It was a topic which had occasioned much episcopal agony.
Bishops, besieged by zealous pressure groups, wrestled with what should
and should not be permitted in churches.[92] Ceremonial might be one thing,
Romanist doctrines another.

'Ritualism' proved to be sufficiently contentious and disruptive for the
prime minister, A.J. Balfour, in 1904 to appoint a Royal Commission on
Ecclesiastical Discipline which began to identify in which churches lighted
candles were on the altar and where incense was used. Two years later,
it recommended that all but the most extreme demands of ritualists be
accommodated and urged a period of reflection on the contending parties.[93]
A 'temple', enthusiasts urged, was a place where sight and sound, movement
and music fused mysteriously on hallowed ground in an act of worship. It
was a conception in which the role of the priest as president was crucial. Yet
it was far from the case that 'ritualism' had entirely captured the churches of
the Anglican Communion in the British Isles. It has been calculated that in
1900 as a percentage of the total number of Anglican churches in England
and Wales the number of ritualist ones was never very great. Their geographical spread was pretty even, probably weakest in Wales and East
Anglia. As a general rule, 'ritualism' was weaker the further one travelled

---

[89] J. Mayo, *A History of Ecclesiastical Dress* (London, 1984).

[90] From a description of the scene at St Cuthbert's, Philbeach Gardens, in P. F. Anson,
'Confusion and Lawlessness', *Church Quarterly Review* 169 (1968), 182. See also Anson's *Fashions
in Church Furnishings, 1840–1940* (London, 1960).

[91] Martin Wellings, *Evangelicals Embattled: Responses of Evangelicals in the Church of England to
Ritualism, Darwinism and Theological Liberalism 1890–1930* (Milton Keynes, 2003) and 'The First
Protestant Martyr of the Twentieth Century: The Life and Significance of John Kensit (1853–1902)'
in Diana Wood, ed., *Martyrs and Martyrologies*, Studies in Church History 30 (Oxford, 1993), 347–58.

[92] James Bentley, *Ritualism and Politics in Victorian Britain: The Attempt to Legislate for Belief*
(Oxford, 1978).

[93] Nigel Yates, *Anglican Ritualism in Victorian Britain 1830–1910* (Oxford, 1999), 326–31. The
conclusions can be found in Flindall, ed., *Church of England 1815–1948*, 293–7.

from London. As to clergy, it has been estimated that at the end of the century only 15.1 per cent were members of one or other of the Church of England ritualist societies.[94] It would be a mistake, therefore, to consider 'ritualism' dominant across the country. Indeed, the observer might conclude, moving from parish church to parish church, that there were 'three Churches of England, not one'.[95] The Church of England congregation now did sing, though not from the same hymn book, again reflecting the preferences of 'parties'.[96] At the turn of the century, however, *Hymns Ancient & Modern*, though a scheme to make it the 'official' book had failed, clearly led the field. A revision was in prospect. Hymns on the subject of heaven were causing the revisers most difficulty.[97] Yet the very fecundity of Victorian hymn-writing and its quality, or lack of it, judged from some literary or aesthetic standpoints, appeared likely to bring it under the cloud which would hang over all things 'Victorian'.[98]

Herbert Vaughan had come to London from Salford as Roman Catholic archbishop of Westminster in 1892.[99] What his church needed, he thought, was a cathedral in the metropolitan city (and the selection of the title for the see, as yet the only archiepiscopal one, signified that the church was not going to allow itself to be consigned to the suburbs of national life). The site of the old Middlesex County Prison offered the opportunity to escape from ecclesiastical confinement. It was to be in the style of a Roman basilica and could not therefore be accused of seeking to rival Westminster Abbey. It would also be cheaper than a Gothic building. Even so, there could be no doubting that its construction signified Catholic resurgence in English space. Begun in 1895, Westminster Cathedral was completed in eight years. 'Churches', Vaughan had declared, 'are not merely buildings *in* which, but *with* which, we worship God'.[100] The language of the Mass was Latin but some observers felt that it was only marginally more incomprehensible, for worshippers, than the English of the 'King James' Bible or the Book of Common Prayer. The clustering (even cluttering) and conjunction of particular visual images would identify Catholic space. What 'Catholic devotion' meant in Victorian England had undergone considerable change.[101]

[94] Yates, *Anglican Ritualism*, 322 and Yates, *Buildings, Faith and Worship*, 143.

[95] Horton Davies, *Worship and Theology in England: The Ecumenical Century 1900 to the Present*, vol. v (Princeton, 1965), 284.

[96] Nicholas Temperley, *The Music of the English Parish Church* (Cambridge, 1979).

[97] W. K. Lowther Clarke, *A Hundred Years of Hymns Ancient & Modern* (London, 1960), 70.

[98] Ian Bradley, *Abide With Me: The World of the Victorian Hymn* (London, 1997).

[99] R. O'Neil, *Cardinal Herbert Vaughan* (London, 1995).

[100] Cited in Norman, *English Catholic Church*, 368–70.

[101] Susan O'Brien, 'Making Catholic Spaces: Women, Décor, and Devotion in the English Catholic Church, 1840–1900' in Diana Wood, ed., *The Church and the Arts*, Studies in Church History 28 (Oxford, 1992), 449–64; M. Heimann, *Catholic Devotion in Victorian England* (Oxford, 1995).

A visitor to a Nonconformist building would find a different internal ordering of space. A central pulpit would normally be found. Nothing would cause the presiding minister to turn his back on the congregation. The wearing of a white tie showed his status but some declined to wear one. Such colour as was to be found was brown or black. It was likely that an organ would be prominently sited, costing anything from 5 to 1,000 guineas. The size of the instrument was a clear indication of what a congregation could afford. It had been necessary to overcome the view, held by Spurgeon, that the placing of an organ was an act of profanation—a view also strongly held in Scotland. The controversy over the propriety of a 'kist o'whistles' had rent many a kirk session asunder before the instrument had generally triumphed. A choir might be identifiable—'well-trained voices' were admitted to be an asset—but it would probably not be robed. Whether a choir 'performed' separately, with an anthem or introit, or whether it was there simply to 'give a lead' to the congregation was still contentious. It would be likely to be a mixed choir, though not invariably. The view that singing (and praying) could not be done 'by proxy' was not dead. 'First-class' artists were brought in as soloists at Baptist services in Barnoldswick on the Lancashire/Yorkshire border, though it had first been ascertained that they were all Christians. The orchestra playing at services in the Woolwich Tabernacle was very unusual.

The hymns which the members of the congregation sang came from the book on the ledge of the pew in front of them. Whether one stood or sat to sing (or stood or sat to pray) could not be forecast with complete accuracy. 'Free-lance' collections of hymns had been steadily replaced by 'official' publications. Over a million copies of the *Congregational Church Hymnal*, for example, had been sold in the decade before 1900. The *Church Hymnary* of the Church of Scotland appeared in 1898.[102] The use of hymns rather than metrical psalms and paraphrases had been gaining ground in the last third of the century. A new *Baptist Church Hymnal* was produced in 1900. The 'turnover' from earlier books could be considerable. In this last case, for example, a thousand out of sixteen hundred hymns found in the two preceding books were dropped.[103] The respective merits of 'words' and 'music' could sometimes be much disputed. It was noted that Welsh hymn tunes were being employed in England. They had a certain melancholy and for 'some strange reason', as one commentator put it, appeared to appeal very strongly to English congregations.[104] Alongside such denominational enterprises, there were 'gospel hymns', legacies of the visit of Dwight

---

[102] Douglas Murray, 'From Disruption to Union' in Duncan Forrester and Douglas Murray, eds., *Studies in the History of Worship in Scotland* (Edinburgh, 1984), 89–90.
[103] W. T. Whitley, *Congregational Hymn-Singing* (London, 1933), 203.
[104] Eric H. Thiman in Whitley, *Congregational Hymn-Singing*, 214.

L. Moody and of Ira D. Sankey to Britain in 1873–5. Sankey's *Sacred Songs and Solos* (1874) in its subsequent editions, still told 'the Old, Old Story' of 'unseen things above' in 'easily remembered verses, with plenty of repetition and obvious rhyming'. They mingled threats and promises. Repetition allowed many of these hymns to become incantatory.[105] They could be brought out, instead of the *Methodist Hymnbook*, on special 'Mission' Sundays.[106] Reared in Anglican evangelical piety, the Catholic convert Ronald Knox had been much influenced as a boy by hymns, but refused his 'homage' to Moody and Sankey, with the solitary exception of 'There were Ninety and Nine'.[107]

The seating arrangements in a chapel were made with preaching in mind. The pews in the City Temple, built a quarter of a century earlier on Holborn Viaduct, were slightly curved so that the occupant of its famous 'Great White Pulpit' could be seen from every part of the building. Preaching was at the heart of a chapel service. There was no liturgy (and no microphone) to carry a stumbling expositor forward. His prayers would be ex tempore. 'Princes of the Pulpit' were celebrities, though not all preachers were princes. Postcard photographs of the most famous could be purchased and sent to friends in the country. The absence of 'star' preachers from their own pulpits was considered ruefully by chapel treasurers. When Dr Parker was away from the City Temple it was estimated in the 1890s to cause a loss to the Sunday collection of between ten and fifteen pounds and the 'supply' had also to be paid.[108] He vigorously defended congregational applause when it occurred during a sermon. While no one stood up when the president—the 'minister' or 'pastor'—arrived at his place to commence the service, often supported by a phalanx of office-bearers, his pre-eminence was unchallenged. Sermon preparation and delivery was a craft. Preaching could be physically exhausting. It would not be sufficient to deliver a ten-minute homily. A man could not infrequently descend from the pulpit wreathed in sweat. The unrivalled claim of C.H. Spurgeon, the Baptist preacher, to the hearts of so large a body of his fellow-countrymen was explained by one of his biographers as 'a triumph of character'. His listeners had known that he was absolutely sincere, simple, unpretending and straightforward.[109] Preachers were as one in defence of their task. Hugh Price Hughes, the Welsh, but London-based Wesleyan Methodist, held that 'when Ritualism was rampant' the preacher should hold fast to Protestant teaching and preaching. Anyone, apparently,

[105] J. R. Watson, *The English Hymn: A Critical and Historical Study* (Oxford, 1999), 494.
[106] Basil Willey, *Spots of Time: A Retrospect of the Years 1897–1920* (London, 1965), 47.
[107] Ronald Knox, *A Spiritual Aeneid* (London, 1919), 7.
[108] William Adamson, *The Life of the Rev. Joseph Parker, D.D.* (Glasgow and London, 1902), 259.
[109] W. Y. Fullerton, *C. H. Spurgeon* (London, 1934 edn.), 324.

could tell you what Romanism, Anglicanism or Nonconformity was, but what was 'Christianity?'[110]

iv. Time Past and Time Present

Study of the past of the church has not infrequently been undertaken within the confines of particular churches with the purpose, implicitly or explicitly, of confirming their 'legitimacy' or 'authenticity' and in order to impugn the claims of others. At the beginning of the twentieth century, 'ecclesiastical history' had therefore frequently been undertaken by 'church professionals' within the confines of, and to suit the purposes of, one or other church. Further, 'amateurs' had joined with them in forming historical societies, with their own journals, meetings and networks, whose primary purpose was to study their 'tradition', their own form of what it was to be a Christian church. Amongst Nonconformists, this happened formally in the two decades before 1914. Wesleyan Methodists were first in the field, with their society being formed in 1894, and *Proceedings* followed four years later. The Congregational Historical Society was established in 1901, the Baptist in 1908 and the Presbyterians in 1913. The Scottish Church History Society was formed in 1922, initially among adherents of the Presbyterian churches.[111] Whether it was possible to study ecclesiastical history, as Mandell Creighton, first holder of the Dixie Chair of Ecclesiastical History at the University of Cambridge in 1884, had urged, by dismissing 'all preconceived opinions', was perhaps optimistic. 'There was' he thought 'no branch of study more important', a view about their own discipline common to holders of university chairs. He himself, for example, thought he would begin by trying to find out what the Reformation *really* was. He was to do so in a university which had declined to admit as an undergraduate, on the grounds of his being a Roman Catholic, a man who, at the turn of the century, was its Regius Professor of Modern History.

The events in the ancient world, which had seen the emergence of a Christian church, remained central to the self-understanding of any ecclesiastical body. The structures, forms, dogmas and practices which had then crystallized in 'the early church', often after intense controversy and dispute, constituted the shared past which in some way shaped the present. A church conducted itself in a constant dialogue between past and present. The Apostolic Age constituted the 'charter' of the church. When R.W. Dale (1829–95), the celebrated nineteenth-century Birmingham Congregationalist minister, had attempted to write the history of English

---

[110] J. Morgan Gibbon, *Evangelical Heterodoxy* (London, 1909), 170.
[111] Dale A. Johnson, *The Changing Shape of English Nonconformity, 1815–1925* (New York, 1999), 170–3.

Congregationalism, a body which might be said to have 'begun' in Elizabethan England, he had no doubt that he ought to 'begin' with 'church
polity in the apostolic age' and attempts thereafter, as he saw it, 'to recover
the lost ideal of the Communion of Saints'.[112] His use of 'recovery' was
central to his thinking. What had once been 'the church' could be recreated.
The passage of time had seen decay, decline, even degeneration, but there
was an original template which could be put to fresh use. The Reader in
Ecclesiastical History at Oxford, Edwin Hatch, had published controversial
Bampton Lectures on the subject in 1881.[113] Other scholars with different
allegiances, however, when they pored over the same material and the same
sources, saw a very different Apostolic Age and a different church emerging
from its ancient chrysalis from the one Dale had identified.[114] There was,
such historians suggested, not only an Apostolic Age but also an Apostolic
Succession. A church that could demonstrate, at least to its own satisfaction,
that it shared in this succession, had a means of linking time past and
time present and ensuring its enduring 'authenticity'. For others, however,
'continuity' might only preserve the continuity of an early corruption.

The 'quest for the historical church' had engaged nineteenth-century
minds with fresh vigour. Even if it were to have proved possible to reach a
scholarly consensus, and the topic had of course been debated over many
centuries, it now presented itself in a somewhat different guise. The notion
of 'evolution' had seeped into late-Victorian consciousness. 'I have been
struck again and again at the new aspect that the old questions take when
looked at from the standpoint of Evolution'—a comment made in a letter
by a Cambridge fellow in 1903.[115] His comments could stand for a whole
generation of men. Much of the long debate had revolved around 'origins',
on the assumption that a pure and binding Christian church had once
existed. If necessary, and 'the Reformation' had deemed that it was necessary, pristine understandings could be 'recovered' or 'restored'. In practice,
of course, there had been much disagreement about what that would entail.
Some questioned whether it was in fact possible ever to 're-form' in any
comprehensive sense. To believe that the church could be 'brought back'
would be to adopt the position, at least a difficult one, that the society in

---

[112] R. W. Dale, *History of English Congregationalism* (London, 1907). The title of 'Book I' of this
work.

[113] Edwin Hatch, *The Organization of the Early Christian Churches* (Oxford, 1881).

[114] A Professorship of Ecclesiastical History had been established in Edinburgh in 1702. A. C.
Cheyne, 'Church History in Edinburgh' in his *Studies in Scottish Church History* (Edinburgh, 1999)
indicates the ways in which church history in that university came to be seen in the twentieth
century as being related as much to history in general as to theology. He notes, nevertheless,
the continuing 'churchly' character of Edinburgh's church historians. Holders of chairs were
church ministers.

[115] Forbes Robinson, *Letters to his Friends* (London, 1909), 181.

which it had come into being could also be brought back. It seemed more plausible, therefore, to recognize both continuity and discontinuity. The church 'developed' and one might even say that it was inescapably 'evolving'. Churches might all claim to express authentic and 'original' Christianity, but in fact it could never be 'recaptured'. They all adapted, adjusted and modified as they passed on the deposit of the past. To speak in this way might be a way to understand what the church itself referred to as the Holy Spirit. If so, that Spirit could seem to blow in wayward directions. How was one to distinguish between 'true' and 'false' development? John Henry Newman was not the only wrestler with this question. If churches were always evolving, as seemed likely, could their direction be controlled or directed, and if so, by whom? Were they simply caught in the 'flux of time'? The 'Christian past' often seen as clear and authoritative might only have been made to cohere by the suppression of 'alternative voices'. 'Christian history' might be better seen as always polyphonic, and all the better for it.[116]

The tension between continuity and difference confronts all churches everywhere. Their preoccupation with what had once been, but also with that which is 'to come', is a universal Christian one. How that preoccupation is regarded, however, is related to the 'spirit' which, broadly, characterizes any age. The 'Victorian Age' in the British Isles, shortly to come to an end with the death of Victoria herself, had been a time of extraordinary change in many spheres, though perhaps for that reason some pasts, particularly 'the Middle Ages', had held particular attraction.[117] However, noting the extraordinary scale of change in so many spheres, public expectation looked forward, though not without some apprehension. It was not the kind of public mood which encouraged attention to institutions which appeared to be, in the widest sense, conservative. The thrust of the new century, it was frequently suggested, should surely not be on the imprint of the long past, as exemplified by 'the church' but rather on the new context offered by the present. It was inevitable, too, that this new century, coupled as it fortuitously was with the 'overdue' advent of a new monarch, should give fresh impetus to the pursuit of 'the new'. Speaking back in 1885, the then bishop of Peterborough had spoken of his belief that there was still 'in the heart of the nation some reverence for the past, some love of old ways and old institutions'.[118] The antiquity of an institution, he thought, was

---

[116] In *Why Study the Past? The Quest for the Historical Jesus* (London, 2005) Rowan Williams argues for a 'conversation with the past which avoids both fundamentalism and progressivism'. In *Interpreting Christian History: The Challenge of the Churches' Past* (Oxford, 2005) Euan Cameron argues that the 'Christian essence' will always strike people differently. He suggests that the time when any single tradition or body of heritage documents could be thought all-sufficient and timeless is 'long past'.

[117] Veronica Ortenberg, *In Search of the Holy Grail: The Quest for the Middle Ages* (London, 2005).

[118] C. S. Magee, ed., *Speeches and Addresses by the late W. C. Magee D.D.* (London, 1893), 56.

testimony to its intrinsic worth. That perspective began to sound rather dated at the turn of the century. Indeed, a reaction against 'Victorianism' was already taking place. Eminent Victorians were within a few years to be put under scrutiny by the next generation—and were soon found wanting. Cardinal Manning's ambition was 'exposed' by Lytton Strachey. The young historian G.M. Trevelyan thought that Strachey had hit the right note.

A Christian church, in such circumstances, quite apart from any other consideration, could be left behind simply because it was 'old'. It was always in danger of being a prisoner of the past. The Dixie Professor who had immersed himself in the history of the papacy, but who was now Anglican bishop of London, told an audience in the Albert Hall in October 1899, however, that the great work of the church of Christ was 'to mould the future'. Its eyes, Mandell Creighton added, were turned to the past for instruction and warning, not for imitation. That was easier said than done. It might be necessary, in the process, to jettison parts of the received past if such moulding of the future was to be achieved.

v. Public Space

That same question had direct relevance to the public space the churches occupied, or sought to occupy. There was a long past. Pondering on whether it would be sufficient to anoint King Edward on the forehead at his coronation in 1902, Frederick Temple, archbishop of Canterbury, concluded that this was the model to be drawn from the Bible, and what was biblical was 'best for Englishmen'. He had usefully been occupying himself in conducting a thorough investigation of what headgear, if any, bishops had worn at each coronation from the Reformation onward. He wanted to be certain in the matter of precedents. In this he testified to the long intimacy of church and state in England. The coronation of the king of the United Kingdom of Great Britain and Ireland, notwithstanding that kingdom's now manifest ecclesiastical plurality, would still be a matter for the Church of England.

While the peoples of the far-flung British Empire owed allegiance to the British monarch, it had become clear at the end of the century that the 'Anglican' churches world-wide were not disposed to owe allegiance to the archbishop of Canterbury in parallel. The first 'Lambeth Conference' had been held in 1867 and over the subsequent decades it had become clear that the 'Anglican Communion' would consist of autonomous provinces in communion with each other—another 'unity in diversity'. At the last conference, held in 1897, the American Episcopalians in particular had made it clear that they did not remotely wish to return, even spiritually, to the British Empire. The establishment in the same year of a province of

Japan confirmed that the Anglican Church was not merely an 'English' phenomenon.[119] Even so, as the communion felt its way forward, it remained an awkward fusion of 'missionary' work carried out in the non-Christian world and the shepherding of transplanted English. A compendium on 'Bishops of the Day', designed to give 'members of the Church of England at home and abroad' a wealth of detailed episcopal information, and incidentally 'confirm the practical sagacity with which she is governed' revealed their substantial English provenance. Eton, Winchester, Rugby, Harrow, Merchant Taylors' and St Paul's comfortably headed the list of the schools at which bishops had been educated. Only one, unsurprisingly, had been born in Poland and educated there in Rabbinic schools. Episcopal university educations had overwhelmingly been at Oxford or Cambridge, with the General Theological Seminary, New York and Trinity College, Dublin next. Only American bishops were revealed to have formerly been engineers. The archbishop of York had held an army commission, as had the bishop of St Helena (perhaps in prudent anticipation of guarding a successor to Napoleon) but they were out-gunned by the vast combatant experience of American bishops which they had acquired during the American civil war. The vehement outbursts of the bishop of Lahore, whose diocese contained a larger number of British troops than that of any other diocese of the English church, whether at home or abroad, were thought to be 'only the more impressive from their comparative rarity'.[120]

It was perhaps oddly appropriate that one of the most comprehensive contemporary accounts of 'The Church in Greater Britain' should have been given in a course of lectures delivered before the University of Dublin in 1900–1. The archdeacon of Achedon spoke warmly there of the growth of the colonial church among 'our countrymen' abroad and among 'the various heathen tribes' with which they had come into contact.[121] It had been suggested that, since 1897 would mark the 1300th year since the arrival of St Augustine of Canterbury [to convert the 'English'], the bishops attending Lambeth should make special pilgrimage to a site with a close connection to the early Christianity of 'the British race'. American and colonial bishops availed themselves of the special train obligingly organized by the bishop of Bath and Wells so that they could process in the ruins of Glastonbury Abbey. The bishop of Gloucester was the only one not to need a ticket, being the possessor of a free pass from a grateful railway company in return for services rendered—a privilege which was perhaps

---

[119] W. M. Jacob, *The Making of the Anglican Church Worldwide* (London, 1997), 244–5.

[120] F. S. Lowndes, *Bishops of the Day: A Biographical Dictionary of the Archbishops and Bishops of the Church of England, and of all churches in communion therewith throughout the world* (London, 1897), 5, 145, 303–4.

[121] G. Robert Wynne, *The Church in Greater Britain* (London, 1901), v.

some consolation for his disappointment at not becoming archbishop of Canterbury. It is not recorded whether the world-wide communion felt that such a visit to a quintessential English (or was it perhaps Arthurian?) site of memory was really appropriate.[122]

Whether churches should anywhere be 'established' within the United Kingdom, and what establishment meant, remained a live issue. Unlike the crisis which was shortly to come to a head in France, however—watched with some concern from across the Channel—the pressure for the formal separation of 'church' and 'state' came not from a secularist lobby but from opposed views in and between the churches themselves.[123] The very idea of a 'national church', in the eyes of P.T. Forsyth, the Congregationalist theologian and minister—'one of the most brilliant minds in Europe' according to the agnostic John Morley—was one of the greatest impediments to missionary success. An 'Established Church' was 'in standing contradiction to the first principle of the religion for which it was established'. He had no wish to submit to the Vatican but 'The Church of Rome rests upon a more truly spiritual foundation than the Church of England.'[124] Established religion sanctioned 'the passion for power of unredeemed man'.[125]

Mandell Creighton, now a bishop, had formed an ideal of the Church of England. He saw it as a church 'not existing in indefinite space, and founding claims to universality on the ground that it has no particular home' but rather it was a church 'rooted in the hearts and minds of the English people'. It was an unashamed acknowledgement on his part that the form, structure, ethos and doctrine of that church had been fashioned in the circumstances of English history. The Church of England was both an expression of and a support to Englishness. Looking round the world, he could find 'no other home so well suited for a divine institution'. It was a church 'fitted for free men'. Such a statement may have been unusually explicit, but the underlying sentiment was widespread. It had found expression in many places in the nineteenth century. 'I think it deplorable', a young Anglo-Catholic priest, Arthur Stanton, had written in 1874, 'when any young Englishman becomes a papist and associates himself with a system which can never be English or liberal. It blights his whole life and the

---

[122] Alan M. G. Stephenson, *Anglicanism and the Lambeth Conferences* (London, 1978), 109.

[123] That is not to say that there was no 'secularism' or 'progressive humanism' but it lacked the strength which it possessed in France. Ian D. MacKillop, *The British Ethical Societies* (Cambridge, 1979); Edward Royle, *Victorian Infidels* (Manchester, 1974) and *Radicals, Secularists and Republicans: Popular Free Thought in Britain, 1866–1915* (Manchester, 1980).

[124] P. T. Forsyth, *The Charter of the Church* (London, 1896), vi, 80.

[125] Cited and discussed in Keith W. Clements, 'P. T. Forsyth: A Political Theologian?' in Trevor Hart, ed., *Justice the True and Only Mercy: Essays on the Life and Theology of P. T. Forsyth* (Edinburgh, 1995), 156.

freshness of his character goes'. The possibility that the Host might be carried in procession at the conclusion of the nineteenth international eucharistic congress, to be held in London in September 1908, caused a furore. Protestant petitioners were outraged at the dishonour to 'the religion which has made England great' which such a procession would represent. It did not occur.[126]

The Church of England, in such a perspective, occupied a very definite space. It was a 'national' space.[127] It neither could nor should detach itself from the English people whose 'religious organ' it was. Creighton deplored those who talked of 'freeing the Church from the bondage of the State'. To speak thus was to represent the state as something inherently unholy and stifling to spiritual aspirations. 'Religion' was not a space only to be occupied by 'the church'. The state should not divest itself of its 'religious character'. The 'general trend' of the church had to be regulated by the wishes of the English people. It was their church. Moreover, as Edward King, bishop of Lincoln, put it at the turn of the century, 'the truth as we have it in the Church of England is the secret of England's highest happiness and of England's power'. What was to be encouraged was 'godly patriotism'. The nation had a divine calling and could look back on its history with pride.

Creighton died in 1900. That he had written so much history may have contributed to his early demise. He felt for the England of small towns. He could not resist writing a history of his native Carlisle. His *Story of some English Shires* was coming out in a second edition as he lay dying. Perhaps this was *fin-de-siècle* nostalgia for a dying world. He did not live to see the young man he had taught (and also advised that a good speech should last for fifteen minutes) become foreign secretary in December 1905. He did have some sense, however, that this England, *his* England, whose international destiny Sir Edward Grey would direct, was under threat. In conversation, he had expressed the view that England was the most artificial of states. Coal could not last for ever. A single defeat at sea might suffice to bring catastrophe. The war in South Africa was not going to be swiftly concluded.

It was therefore important that the church should stand 'in an organic relation to the national life of the country'. It should be national without ceasing to be 'the maintainer of catholic truth'. That did not mean that it should succumb to small national prejudices. It should, however, understand

---

[126] G. I. T. Machin, 'The Liberal Government and the Eucharistic Procession of 1908', *Journal of Ecclesiastical History* 34 (1983), 562.

[127] Keith Robbins, 'England, Englishmen and the Church of England in the Nineteenth-Century United Kingdom of Great Britain and Ireland: Nation, Church and State' in Nigel Yates, ed., *Bishop Burgess and his World: Culture, Religion and Society in Britain, Europe and North America in the Eighteenth and Nineteenth Centuries* (Cardiff, 2007), 198–232.

national aspirations and seek to direct them 'in accordance with the eternal principles of truth and righteousness'. It would be wrong, indeed antagonistic to all development of human activity, for the state to stand absolutely under the tutelage of the church. It was also undesirable for the state to stand outside the church, as in the United States. Although he had never been there, he thought it meant that 'religious organizations', in competition with one another, lost real hold on their principles and ceased to be 'operative in directing the conscience of the community'. The intricate interweaving of church and state achieved in England—the spirit of which could not be captured merely by reference to its legal and constitutional formulation—was an insular treasure. Not that Creighton stayed at home. He had listened to Wagner in Dresden. He had married the daughter of a Baltic German from Russian Estonia who had married a Scottish wife and become a naturalized British subject.[128] He had witnessed the 'extraordinary' sight of Russian peasants doing their devotions in the streets in front of icons. He received the (Russian) archbishop of Finland at Fulham Palace. He bothered himself with the problems of the French Reformed Church in London. Common sense, which he supposed constituted the foundation of Italian character, seemed to him to harmonize with the English disposition. He ascended the Montenegrin mountain. He even holidayed in Wales. The German Emperor was represented at his funeral. Yet, even so, he had to admit that 'we English' were 'hopelessly insular'. He was not to know that a third of the books on Forsyth's shelves were in German, but Forsyth, though resident in Cambridge, was a Scot.[129] Creighton felt that it was no good attempting a *rapprochement* with any continental people in the belief that the English were animated by a strong cosmopolitan spirit. They were not. The great object of history, he had told one of his first audiences in the diocese of London, was to trace 'the continuity of national life' and to discover and estimate the ideas on which it was founded. Churchmen and churchwomen had of course taken part in the vast explosion of continental travel over the previous half-century. They had seen (and smelt) services across the European continent. When travelling in Catholic areas they had felt themselves to be Protestant but in Protestant areas not only was Protestantism not quite like any of their forms but also, travelling as 'British', they became more aware of particular brands of Protestantism across the British Isles. Orthodoxy, at least as encountered on Mount Athos by Dean Stanley, was something else.[130]

---

[128] James Covert, *A Victorian Marriage: Mandell and Louise Creighton* (London, 2001).

[129] Keith Robbins, *Protestant Germany through British Eyes: A Complex Victorian Encounter* (London, 1992); John Davis, *The Victorians and Germany* (Bern, 2007).

[130] Marjorie Morgan, *National Identities and Travel in Victorian Britain* (Basingstoke, 2001), 83–118.

Creighton's 'national life' was English. It was obvious, however, that there were other 'national lives' in the United Kingdom. On disestablishment, the Church of Ireland had retained that style and had resisted the notion that it was some mere 'Episcopalian' sectarian apparition in Ireland. Ireland was its proper territory. Its purported inheritance of insights from the early Celtic church was one aspect of the armour of its Irish authenticity. Likewise, Presbyterians, despite their regional concentration, rejected any notion that they were a 'Church of Ulster'. Both assertions were important in a context in which Irishness and Catholicism were being presented as synonymous. The churches of Scotland were equally adamant that they were *of* Scotland. The High Kirk of St Giles had been 'dignified' in the 1880s to offer suitable provision for national occasions, both 'Scottish' and 'British in Scotland'.[131] A service had been held in the cathedral on the day of Gladstone's funeral attended by the town council in their robes, although the kirk had stipulated that the occasion should be as simple and non-official as possible, Mild changes in the forms of service might even have mildly mollified Dean Liddon. These were years in which one prominent but 'High Church' Presbyterian, James Cooper, Professor of Ecclesiastical History at Glasgow University since 1898, chose to advocate a United Church for the British Empire, but the tide was not with him.[132] In Wales, too, while the line against disestablishment was held by the bishops, some other voices in the church wished to see its 'Welshness' more firmly asserted. In 1895 Leo XIII had proclaimed a Catholic vicariate in Wales. The formation of a separate Anglican province, if indeed that was to be the eventual outcome, would give the opportunity to make a real Welsh church.[133] Such discussion took place in a context in which the church had long been characterized by Nonconformists as 'alien'. Nonconformity saw itself as embodying the 'real' Wales. The piety of its people marked them out from the oppressiveness and rapacity of the English.[134] Wales might be

[131] John Wolffe, 'Civic Religious Identities and Responses to Prominent Deaths in Cardiff and Edinburgh, 1847–1910' in Robert Pope, ed., *Religion and National Identity: Wales and Scotland c.1700–2000* (Cardiff, 2001), 178.

[132] James Cooper, *A United Church for the British Empire* (Edinburgh, 1902). Two years earlier, he had written *The Church Catholic and National* (Glasgow, 1898). Cooper had run into trouble as a parish minister in Broughty Ferry and Aberdeen when he had introduced Christmas and Holy Week services. Yates, *Anglican Ritualism*, 309–10.

[133] Frances Knight, 'Welsh Nationalism and Anglo-Catholicism: The Politics and Religion of J. Arthur Price (1861–1942)' in Pope, ed., *Religion and National Identity*, 103–122.

[134] Keith Robbins, 'Religion and Identity in Modern British History' reprinted in *History, Religion and Identity in Modern Britain* (London, 1993), 85–104 and 'Religion and Community in Scotland and Wales since 1800' in Gilley and Sheils, eds., *Religion in Britain*, 363–80; D. W. Bebbington, 'Religion and National Feeling in Nineteenth-Century Wales and Scotland' in Stuart Mews, ed., *Religion and National Identity*, Studies in Church History 18 (Oxford, 1982), 489–503.

difficult to define in political or constitutional terms but it was presented as being distinctively and intensively 'religious'. It was in 'the sacred' that the 'language of heaven'—spoken at the turn of the century by more people in Wales than ever before, but a diminishing percentage of the population (50 per cent in 1901)—found its haven. Religion, language and culture appeared to form a seamless whole, existing in mutual interdependence.[135] Yet, at the turn of the century, at least in border counties, the church had the peculiar challenge of trying to minister to people in two very different languages within the same parish.[136]

A problem with these emphases on the 'rootedness' of religion and the stress upon the inextricable intertwining of 'church' and 'nation' to be found across the British Isles, though neither uniformly nor completely, derived from the fact that the 'ethnic' homogeneity of these 'nations' had become somewhat problematic. That was most evident in the Irish presence in nineteenth-century Britain.[137] Although by no means entirely Roman Catholic, Ireland was almost invariably presented as so being. Irish immigration had been a major element in the growth of the Roman Catholic Church in the three territories of Britain. In that very fact, however, had lain a dilemma for a church seeking to assert itself as properly 'national' within England, Scotland and Wales.[138] Within the context of trying to limit 'seepage' to Protestantism, or out of religious practice altogether, in British cities which were very different from the Irish countryside, would that task be less or more likely to be successful if the 'Irish Catholic' communal symbiosis was maintained, or dissolved in the British 'melting pot'? While it would be over-simple to paint a complete contrast between 'poor' incomers and 'comfortable' natives within the Catholic community, that

---

[135] Dorian Llywelyn, *Sacred Place, Chosen People: Land and National Identity in Welsh Spirituality* (Cardiff, 1999); Paul Ballard and D. H. Jones eds., *This Land and People: A Symposium on Christian and Welsh National Identity* (Cardiff, 1979); Keith Robbins, 'Locating Wales: Culture, Place and Identity' in N. Garnham and K. Jeffery, eds., *Culture, Place and Identity* (Dublin, 2005), 23–38.

[136] Frances Knight, 'Anglican Worship in Late Nineteenth-Century Wales: A Montgomeryshire Case Study' in R. N. Swanson, ed., *Continuity and Change in Christian Worship*, Studies in Church History 35 (Woodbridge, 1999), 418.

[137] The literature is large and includes the following: Graham Davis, *The Irish in Britain, 1815–1914* (Dublin, 1991); T. M. Devine, ed., *Irish Immigrants and Scottish Society in the Nineteenth and Twentieth Centuries* (Edinburgh, 1991); Brenda Collins, 'The Irish in Britain, 1780–1921' in B. J. Graham and L. J. Proudfoot, eds., *An Historical Geography of Ireland* (London, 1993), 366–98; David Fitzpatrick, 'The Irish in Britain, 1871–1921' in W. E. Vaughan, ed., *A New History of Ireland, vol. vi: Ireland under the Union, pt. II (1871–1921)* (Oxford, 1996), 653–98; Paul O'Leary, *Immigration and Integration: The Irish in Wales, 1798–1922* (Cardiff, 2002).

[138] Bishop Goss of Liverpool, more strongly than most, asserted that he was English, a real John Bull and a Lancashire man. P. Doyle, 'Bishop Goss of Liverpool (1856–1872) and the Importance of being English' in S. Mews, ed., *Religion and National Identity*, Studies in Church History 18 (Oxford, 1982), 442.

aspect too affected relationships across Catholic Britain.[139] If the 'Irish question' returned to the centre of British politics there would be awkward times ahead for all the churches. And, while it was in its Irish aspect that the question arose most conspicuously, the relationship between ethnicity and denominational allegiance was also an issue, for example, for Welsh Nonconformists on Merseyside or Scottish Presbyterians in Newcastle—and, of course, for all comers, in London. If both 'church' and 'nation' were providentially provided, the relationship between the two was under considerable strain. Was it the case that the Christian state was the Christian church 'in another character' as Archbishop Benson had claimed in 1891 in an address in Wales?[140]

In any case, the British Isles had to find their place in an apparently globalizing Christianity. Leading figures, particularly from churches which considered themselves to be in spiritual kinship with the Pilgrim Fathers, had made regular visits across the Atlantic.[141] They preached and gave lectures on preaching. They had not infrequently returned with a useful honorary doctorate.[142] The Free Church evangelist Rodney 'Gipsy' Smith (he was born in a Gipsy tent) had paid his fifth visit to the United States in 1896, where he was placarded as 'the greatest evangelist in the world'. The opening weeks of the twentieth century saw this man, who had been presented to two Presidents of the United States, conducting a 'Simultaneous Mission' under the aegis of the Evangelical Free Churches of England and Wales.[143] Randall Davidson, on his first visit to the United States in 1904, and the first ever by an archbishop of Canterbury, seems to have been identified by American Episcopalians as 'a democrat' with whom one could do business.[144] George Adam Smith, then Professor at the Free Church College in Glasgow and shortly to be Principal of Aberdeen University, undertook lecture tours in America in 1896, 1899 and 1903. He was not the only Scot on circuit, though he was perhaps

---

[139] Steven Fielding, *Class and Ethnicity: Irish Catholics in England, 1880–1939* (Buckingham, 1993); Sheridan Gilley, 'Irish Catholicism in Britain' in Donal A. Kerr, ed., *Religion, State and Ethnic Groups: Comparative Studies on Government and Non-dominant Ethnic Groups in Europe, 1850–1940*, vol. ii (Aldershot, 1992), 229–60 and 'The Roman Catholic Church and the Nineteenth-Century Irish Diaspora', *Journal of Ecclesiastical History* 35 (1984), 188–207.

[140] Cited and discussed in E. R. Norman, *Church and Society in England, 1770–1970: A Historical Study* (Oxford, 1976), 202.

[141] Keith Robbins, *Foreign Encounters: English Congregationalism, Germany and the United States c.1850–c.1914* (London, 2006).

[142] Timothy Larsen, 'Honorary Doctorates and the Nonconformist Ministry in England' in D. Bebbington and T. Larsen, eds., *Modern Christianity and Cultural Aspirations* (London, 2003), 139–56; Roger L. Brown, 'The Tale of the DD', *Journal of Welsh Religious History*, new series, 3 (2003), 69–77.

[143] Gipsy Smith, *His Life and Work by Himself* (London, 1903), 305.

[144] G. K. A. Bell, *Randall Davidson: Archbishop of Canterbury* (London, 1952 edn.), 452.

unique in being asked to sum up the significance of Melchizedek in two sentences.[145] American divinity filtered into Welsh Nonconformity as significant figures went to and fro across the Atlantic.[146] By 1900, 62 per cent of Roman Catholic bishops in the United States were Irish, and half of them Irish-born and half of US Catholics were Irish.[147] An 'Irish Catholicism' which spanned the Atlantic constituted a new reality.

There was in fact something of a 'cosmopolitan spirit' abroad. A World Presbyterian Alliance had been formed in 1878, an International Congregational Council in 1891. Methodists too were world-wide, with a World Council, though in the early 1880s, Hugh Price Hughes, then ministering in Oxford, had had difficulty in persuading Mark Pattison, rector of Lincoln College (where Wesley had been a fellow) that they numbered twenty-five million rather than twenty-five thousand.[148] There was also the paradox that 'American Methodism' was now growing in Germany. The initiative for a 'world alliance of Baptists' came from Kentucky in 1903 but it was in London two years later that what was inaccurately claimed to be 'the greatest Protestant evangelical community on earth' held its first world congress.[149] Even if blessed, the ties that bound such burgeoning global pan-denominationalism were necessarily loose and unproven. They existed in a world of states, and even 'Christian' states could be at war with each other. Indeed, the United Kingdom itself was at war with a South African Republic whose farmers might not quite be like the Presbyterians of Princeton but who were, nevertheless, part of the Reformed family. There was a sense, therefore, that the history of the churches of the British Isles could not be confined to what happened in the Isles but neither could they be, or did they wish to be, detached from whatever was taken to be 'national life'.

Sentiments in these matters frequently derived from personal experiences and associations. Creighton's own 'national life', for example, was that of England, not that of the United Kingdom. His perspective came naturally to a boy educated in the shadow of Durham Cathedral and at Merton College, Oxford. The vision of symbiosis seemed natural too in his other transient locations—Worcester, Peterborough, Cambridge, even London. Fulham Palace was its domestic expression. Here was the continuity of the 'English

---

[145] Lilian Adam Smith, *George Adam Smith: A Personal Memoir and Family Chronicle* (London, 1943), 122; Bernard Aspinwall, 'The Scottish Religious Identity in the Atlantic World 1880–1914' in Mews, ed., *Religion and National Identity*, 505–18.

[146] D. Densil Morgan, 'Wales, the Princeton Theology and a Nineteenth Century Battle for the Bible', *Journal of Welsh Religious History*, new series, 2 (2002), 51–81.

[147] Owen Dudley Edwards, 'The Irish Priest in North America' in W. J. Sheils and Diana Wood, eds., *The Churches, Ireland and the Irish*, Studies in Church History 25 (Oxford, 1989), 333.

[148] D. P. Hughes, *The Life of Hugh Price Hughes* (London, 1904), 161.

[149] F. Townley Lord, *Baptist World Fellowship* (London, 1955); Ian Randall, *English Baptists of the 20th Century* (London, 2005), 49–50.

church', with judicious weight placed upon both words. It was an interlocking world in which a bishop of London spoke in the House of Lords,
staggering on blindly, as Creighton put it, not knowing whether he was
making an ass of himself. No one ever cheered, looked at the speaker, or
even seemed to listen, but perhaps, he thought, he did good. There had
been, too, a 'rather nice' garden party at Buckingham Palace. The queen
summoned him to Windsor oftener every year and he was always glad to
see her. This was establishment at its peak. Throne and altar buttressed
each other.

During her childhood years, however, Victoria had developed 'a great
horror of *Bishops* on account of their wigs and aprons'. A reception for
black-gaitered and aproned bishops during her Diamond Jubilee celebrations in 1897 had led to a private expostulation that she did not care for
them.[150] Thirty Nonconformists, for the first time in English history, had
been allocated places at St Paul's for the short act of worship that took place.
It is not clear whether the queen liked them, or indeed registered their
presence. Her companion mentioned two bishops who might be an exception to her dislike, only to be told that it was that she liked them as *men*, not
as *bishops*. She liked Randall Davidson, who was to become archbishop of
Canterbury after her death, on both counts. The previous decade had seen
him bishop of Rochester and then of Winchester. It had been no handicap,
at least in royal eyes, that the man who was rising to the summit of the
English church was a Scottish boy born in Edinburgh, though educated at
Harrow and Oxford. The Scottish path to Lambeth Palace had already been
established by his father-in-law, Archibald Tait, the first Scot to be archbishop of Canterbury.

Queen Victoria's last English archbishop, Frederick Temple, had been
brought up in an exotic location. He was born and lived his first nine years
in the Ionian Islands, off the coast of Greece, where his impecunious soldier
father played a modest part in the 'protection' Great Britain afforded this
'independent' republic. Deprived locally of the English church, his Cornish
mother had successfully inoculated him against modes of thought and
superstitions evidently entertained in the islands by nurses and servants.
Certainly, when Temple, previously bishop of Exeter and of London,
became archbishop of Canterbury at the age of 76 in 1897, no influences
from the Ionian Islands appeared to seep into the English church with him.
Although he preached in St Paul's on the Sunday after Queen Victoria's
death, he does not seem to have been present at her funeral. He had never
enjoyed the confidence of the queen or been granted access to the inner

---

[150] W. L. Arnstein, 'Queen Victoria and Religion' in Gail Malmgreen, ed., *Religion in the Lives of English Women, 1760–1930* (London, 1986), 109.

circles of the Palace.[151] Whatever the pattern of individual likes and dislikes, however, in the nation at large a set of arrangements and relationships remained intact. Church bells tolled across the country as news spread of Victoria's death. Loyalty to her, a preacher in Chicago cared to observe, had been 'almost a religion'. And, according to the *Morning Post*, the distinctive feature of the queen's life had been religion. Moreover, to the chagrin of the church of which she was Supreme Governor, she had taken the sacrament in Crathie parish church according to the uses of the Church of Scotland.[152] In the year of her Diamond Jubilee, the aristocratic bishop of Aberdeen and Orkney in the Scottish Episcopal Church had caused a storm by declining to permit the dean of Norwich to preach in the chapel of Aberdeen University on the grounds that it was a Presbyterian place of worship. It was a ban which led the principal of the university to speak in strong terms, as principals sometimes do.

The complex rituals following Victoria's death contrived, after careful planning, a delicate balance. Massed bands and numerous military and naval detachments paraded in public places while an impressive choral service was held at St George's Chapel, Windsor. There was a universal wearing of black: great ladies in carriages and flower girls with rags of crape were demonstrations, as Beatrice Webb conceded, of a true national 'wake' by the whole people in favour of the monarchical principle. In the fortnight following, it was widely reported that churches were packed. At this level, there could apparently be no more convincing demonstration of a 'national church' and a common public space.[153]

The Coronation Ode written by a son of an archbishop of Canterbury for the new king-emperor—who had wisely chosen for himself the 'good old English name of Edward'—declared that God had made the land of hope and glory mighty. Might He make her mightier yet! The territory of this magnificent realm, however, had long ceased to be coextensive with that of the Church of England. The one-to-one relationship, endorsed in such public ceremonial, was in this sense a fiction. True, England was at the heart of this state. Queen Victoria had sensibly died not at Balmoral but on the Isle of Wight. Her obsequies had occurred in English places. It was not conceivable that they could have occurred anywhere else. The United Kingdom no doubt reflected the predominance of England and one might, indeed, speak of its domination. If so, however, it was a domination which had not required uniformity within the realm. The Church of

---

[151] Hinchliff, *Frederick Temple*, 281–96.

[152] Owen Chadwick, 'Sacrament at Crathie 1873' in S. J. Brown and G. Newlands, eds., *Scottish Christianity in the Modern World* (Edinburgh, 2000), 177–98.

[153] John Wolffe, *Great Deaths: Grieving, Religion, and Nationhood in Victorian and Edwardian Britain* (Oxford, 2000), 221–31.

England was not the 'religious organ' of the British people, even less of the British Empire. No church was. While it could still be argued, therefore, that the Church of England continued to occupy English public space in a significant manner, it could not in a religious sense comprehensively undergird the United Kingdom. Indeed, in its existence in the British Isles outside England, it could be presented, inaccurately but not implausibly, as an unwelcome intrusion of Englishness. The increasing adoption of the word 'Anglican' identified the church not by any doctrinal or ecclesiological benchmark but by its English origins. It left adherents of the Church of Ireland in Ireland or of the Church of England in Wales vulnerable to the charge, thought to be wounding, that they were, even if inadvertently, agents of Anglicization. The enthusiasm displayed by clerical cricketers in Ireland might count as a prime example of such subversion. It had become increasingly uncomfortable to be 'Anglo-Irish' or 'Anglo-Welsh'.[154] An ecclesiastical allegiance which was compatible with, indeed presented as being integral to, Englishness, was bound to cause tension outside England.

In summary, in 1900 the Christian churches in the British Isles, in their myriad identities, still functioned in territory that was Christian in its general ethos, although that ethos was under pressure. That reality could be publicly stressed by pointing to Christianity's long history in these islands, a history that could not be understood without reference to it. Apart from a Jewish minority, which was being augmented by immigration from Eastern Europe, and a very small number of Hindus and Muslims, it was still possible to speak of 'a Christian country'. In so far as 'religion' was expressed in both the public and private spheres in the British Isles, it could reasonably be assumed to be 'Christian'. Against the background of the structures, locations and assumptions at the turn of the century that have been outlined in this opening chapter, it is now appropriate to consider what that reality entailed.

---

[154] L. P. Curtis, 'The Anglo-Irish Predicament', *Twentieth-Century Studies* 4 (1970), 46–62; Basil Jones, bishop of St Davids, had famously declared in 1886 that Wales was no more than a 'geographical expression'. He wanted to be a bishop *in* Wales not a *Welsh bishop*. When he died in 1897, however, his remark seemed to express an Anglo-Welsh sentiment that was becoming 'incorrect'.

2

A CRISIS OF CHRISTENDOM, 1900–1914

In autumn 1915, leading Anglican theologians and historians addressed what the bishop of London called 'our place in Christendom' in a series of lectures in St Martin-in-the-Fields. They moved magisterially from reflecting on unity and authority in the primitive church to considering the vocation of the Church of England in the present. What they did not do, however, was to give any sustained attention to what they thought 'Christendom' still was, had been or might yet become. The bishop of London clearly thought of it as a present reality.[1] A few years earlier the Congregationalist R.F. Horton had argued that while the churches seemed to be dying, Christianity was very much alive. Indeed, 'Christendom is more clearly defined than ever as the progressive part of humanity'.[2] The 'progressive part of humanity' had not always been its definition in the past. It might be argued that the First Amendment to the United States Constitution, with its prohibition of 'establishment' and protection for the 'free exercise' of religion, albeit with a Christian motivation, constitutes 'the end of Christendom'—if whether the State should offer deliberate assistance to the Church's mission is the test. One might take the French Revolution as another indication of the 'end of Christendom'. But perhaps it was the war that was raging in 1915 that was *the* 'turning point'? The rulers of the Earth, it might appear, had ceased to believe that they owed service to the rule of Christ. Contemporaries did not expect them to.[3]

So, was Christianity now simply a 'mystery for initiates'? If so (and these matters will be returned to), the years from 1900 to 1914 were ones in which the strains of 'modernity' had already appeared. The 'challenges' present in the perceived 'questions of the day'—class, gender, culture, war, nation, empire most prominently—could not be side-stepped. 'We were, like you, going about naked . . . with our war paint on,' Sir Harry Johnston, explorer

---

[1] *Our Place in Christendom* (London, 1916). Amongst the contributors were Neville Figgis, Henry Scott Holland and Charles Gore. The title was provided by Winnington-Ingram, the bishop of London.

[2] R.F. Horton, *Great Issues* (London, 1912), 58–9.

[3] Oliver O'Donovan, *The Desire of the Nations: Rediscovering the Roots of Political Theology* (Cambridge, 1996), 244–5.

and colonial administrator, had informed the Basoga people of East Africa in the 1890s, 'but when we had learned Christianity from the Romans we changed and became great. We want you to learn Christianity and follow our steps and you too will be great.'[4] Sir Harry's parents had been members of the Catholic Apostolic Church but he himself was a Social Darwinist who thought Africans were 'savages'. A decade or so later, neither 'learning Christianity' nor British 'greatness' seemed so straightforward.

The British people were indeed not going about naked, but there were more than a few traces of war paint to be seen. 'Small colonial wars' had always featured in late Victorian life. The war in South Africa which had just begun as the century opened loomed larger, lasted longer and proved more difficult than had been anticipated. It was not one which the Church of England opposed. Aged Archbishop Temple was, however, very concerned that there should be enough money to support victims of the war and their families. Bishop Winnington-Ingram perhaps put it a little more forcefully than others when he declared that the young volunteers departing for South Africa were experiencing 'the joy of sacrifice'. It was perhaps only to be expected, given that it was a Conservative government which had gone to war, that such opposition as there was came from Nonconformists, though this was a matter of action taken by individuals rather than by their churches as such. W.T. Stead, erstwhile supporter of the earlier Jameson Raid, now brought out a weekly paper with a masthead beseeching 'Deliver us from Bloodguiltiness, O Lord'. The *Daily News* orchestrated the opposition from a significant number (but still a minority) of ministers, particularly Congregationalists and Baptists. Silas K. Hocking, former United Methodist minister, novelist and aspiring Liberal politician, launched a 'Stop the War' Committee. The Baptist minister John Clifford became its president. The Peace Committee of the Society of Friends, however, hesitated to make any public statement—a stance which infuriated Quaker radicals. The reality was that the Free Churches, as one minister, J.D. Jones, observed at the time, were 'as hopelessly divided as the politicians themselves'.[5] Hugh Price Hughes was not an aberrant Wesleyan in arguing that the cause of the British Empire was just. R.J. Campbell, coming to the fore as a Congregationalist preacher, believed that God had granted to the British people

    [4] Roland Oliver, *Sir Harry Johnston and the Scramble for Africa* (London, 1957), 297.
    [5] S.C. Carpenter, *Winnington-Ingram, The Biography of Arthur Foley Winnington-Ingram, Bishop of London, 1901–1939* (London, 1949), 279; D.W. Bebbington, *The Nonconformist Conscience: Chapel and Politics, 1870–1914* (London, 1982), 121–4; John Kent, 'Hugh Price Hughes and the Nonconformist Conscience', in G.V. Bennett and J.D. Walsh, eds., *Studies in Modern English Church History in Memory of Norman Sykes* (London, 1966), 196–200; A.H. Wilkinson, *Rev. R. J. Campbell: The Man and his Message* (London, 1907), 26–8; Martin Ceadel, *Semi-Detached Idealists: The British Peace Movement and International Relations, 1854–1945* (Oxford, 2000), 156–64; Thomas C. Kennedy, *British Quakerism 1860–1920: The Transformation of a Religious Community* (Oxford, 2001), 253–64.

certain powers which other races did not possess. Britain could not recede from her responsibilities in the world, even if she wanted to.

Sabine Baring-Gould, son of an army officer, had knocked off 'Onward Christian Soldiers' in ten minutes, as a hymn for a children's parade in Horbury, West Yorkshire, but it had been taken up and sung round the English-speaking world. Its original lines spoke of the 'soldiers' being 'one in faith and doctrine' and claimed that 'we are not divided'. In the early twentieth century, however, he was persuaded to substitute 'one in hope and purpose' and 'though divisions harass' for his original lines. It was a more sober assessment of the position. The church was not a mighty army, only *like* one. Whether even that was an accurate picture would shortly become clear.

The South African War ended in 1902. It had been a 'crisis of empire'. Victory, of a kind, had been won, but it left in its wake lingering anxieties about the future of the providential enterprise, anxieties shared very substantially in the churches. It was an anxiety mingled with some sense of shame at the ease with which a 'jingoism' had taken hold. Baring-Gould's Christian soldiers had only been marching as to war. Over the next decade, the thought that they might be marching in a real war, perhaps of unimaginable horror, sometimes came to the surface. Who would be inside and who outside the national tent then?

i. People: Inclusions and Exclusions

It had been a commonplace, for decades, at least in Britain, that 'church' was not something that the working class 'did', a commonplace which did not prevent it being frequently presented as a new discovery.[6] Bishops had addressed diocesan conferences on the subject.[7] Hugh Price Hughes, according to his daughter, had always been 'haunted' by the knowledge

---

[6] K.S. Inglis, *Churches and the Working Classes in Victorian England* (London, 1963); H. McLeod, *Class and Religion in the Late Victorian City* (London, 1974); *Religion and the Working Class in Nineteenth-Century Britain* (London, 1984); *Piety and Poverty: Working Class Religion in Berlin, London and New York* (New York, 1996) and, ed., *European Religion in the Age of Great Cities 1830–1930* (London, 1995). Much of the early discussion of religion and 'the working class' betrays a greater confidence in the existence of the latter than is perhaps now felt by social and cultural historians. Trevor Griffiths, for example, is sceptical of the notion of a peculiar homogeneity of class culture between the later nineteenth and the mid-twentieth centuries in his *The Lancashire Working Classes c.1880–1930* (Oxford, 2001), 332. One contemporary discussion is G. Haw, ed., *Christianity and the Working Classes* (London, 1906); R.Q. Gray, 'Religion, Culture and Social Class in Late Nineteenth and Early Twentieth Century Edinburgh' in G. Crossick, ed., *The Lower Middle Class in Britain* (London, 1977), 134–58; Donald J. Withrington, 'Non-church-going, Church Organisation and "Crisis in the Church" c.1880–c.1920', *Records of the Scottish Church History Society* 24 (1991), 199–236; Michael Watts, *Why Did the English Stop Going to Church?* (London, 1995).

[7] J.C. Ryle, *Can They Be Brought In? Thoughts on the Absence from the Church of the Working Classes* (London, 1883).

that the great majority of European and British manhood lay outside the churches and was more or less hostile to their ministry.[8] According to the Congregationalist Silvester Horne, in the early twentieth century, many churches in London were fighting desperately for their bare existence. They were too much exercised with the problem of keeping their head above water to be able to do anything substantial to help their struggling semi-submerged neighbours.[9] The 'multitudes' or the 'masses' lay outside the life of the church, or at least outside its day-to-day activity as an institution. 'Church', on this reading, was something 'the middle class' did.

Two contemporary, but rather different, surveys in the capital filled out this picture of working-class absence. Charles Booth, of Liverpool Unitarian background, published *Life and Labour of the People of London* in seventeen volumes in 1902/3. He devoted seven volumes to 'religious influences' in great detail. Science, he had personally concluded, in the wake of the publication of Darwin's *Origin of Species*, had as clearly disposed of the existence of God as Galileo had demonstrated the correct solar system.[10] In Booth's investigations, however, consideration of 'abstract truth' fell below the horizon, as he put it. He produced a mass of information on the extraordinary variety of religious practice to be found in the capital—detail which precludes easy generalization—but the 'working class' was not substantially present. It was a story told in the first person. He came to decide that he wished to evaluate rather than enumerate. Bald statistics of church attendance said relatively little. He was searching for the effect of religion on the lives of the people. The Roman Catholic archbishop of Westminster and the Anglican bishops of London, Rochester and Southwark had urged their clergy to facilitate Booth's work, but they could not have been greatly encouraged by his findings.[11]

The *Daily News* carried out a survey of the religious life of London in 1903. Its superintendent, Richard Mudie-Smith, himself a deacon at Westbourne Park Baptist Church, concluded that the total number of worshippers in London amounted to 832,051 and, deducting various categories, he estimated that 2,355,152 people could have gone to a place of worship if they had chosen to do so. The Free Church worshippers narrowly outnumbered the Church of England (545,317 to 538,477), the Baptists being the largest Free Church denomination. There were 96,218 Roman Catholic

    [8] D.P. Hughes, *The Life of Hugh Price Hughes* (London, 1904), 161.
    [9] C. Silvester Horne, *Pulpit, Platform, Parliament* (London, 1913), 21.
    [10] B. Norman-Butler, *Victorian Aspirations: The Life and Labour of Charles and Mary Booth* (London, 1972), 36.
    [11] Some historians have been dismissive of the importance, from a historian's point of view, of Booth's 'religious' work but see the valuable discussion in Rosemary O'Day and David Englander, *Mr Charles Booth's Inquiry: 'Life and Labour of the People in London' Reconsidered* (London, 1993), 161–98.

attendances. The results for London and Greater London revealed combined attendances of 1,514,025, which gave a ratio of 1 in 4.11 of the population. Individual authors then commented in detail on the religious life of particular areas of London.[12] In East London, those who failed to attend were identified as 'the working classes, and not the shopkeepers, except the very small shopkeepers of the lowest type'. The non-attenders were classified as being either 'estranged and antagonistic' or 'apathetic and careless'. It was suggested, however, that there was now far less 'undisguised hatred' of the church than there had been a decade earlier.[13]

It is not easy to interpret this information. That some contemporaries painted the picture in the terms that have been described cannot be dismissed. On the other hand, more recent research, with a focus on boroughs in London, has brought out a more complicated pattern of 'belonging' and blurred boundaries of involvement, alienation and indifference.[14] The more both categories and concepts are refined, the more it becomes difficult to think in terms of a deep gulf separating 'middle-class culture' and 'working-class culture' in relation to religion. Any generalization would have to be modified by reference to gender, region and type of community. It was sometimes supposed that London was exceptional, but information on Liverpool and other cities in this period makes that unlikely. Perhaps it was city life itself which cut off people from 'nature' and thus damaged one source of 'religion'. Charles Masterman, after a temporary incarceration in Camberwell, concluded that 'The tide is ebbing within and without the Churches. The drift is towards a non-dogmatic affirmation of general kindliness and good fellowship . . .'.[15] Seebohm Rowntree's investigation of the archiepiscopal city of York also painted a grim picture. Broadly speaking, it was being suggested that 'only a section of the middle class ever attends church at all; the workers, as a body, absent themselves; the professional and upper classes do the same'.[16] 'Non-church-going', it was felt, was the normative assumption which had to be made, at least about England, but commentators could not quite make up their minds when the British people had ceased to be 'in the main a church-going people'.[17] It might have followed a shift in 'convention'. Church-going, like the wearing of a black coat or a tall hat, may have been a piece of conventional respectability.

[12] R. Mudie-Smith, ed., *The Religious Life of London* (London, 1904), 15–18.

[13] Percy Alden in Mudie-Smith, ed., *Religious Life*, 28–9.

[14] Jeffrey Cox, *The English Churches in a Secular Society, Lambeth, 1870–1930* (New York, 1982) and S.C. Williams, *Religious Belief and Popular Culture in Southwark c.1880–1939* (Oxford, 1999) examine two London boroughs.

[15] C.F.G. Masterman, *The Condition of England* (London, 1909), 268.

[16] R.J. Campbell, *Christianity and the Social Order* (London, 1907), 1–2.

[17] Prebendary Carlile (founder of the Church Army) in W. Forbes Gray, ed., *Non-Church-Going: Its Reasons and Remedies* (Edinburgh and London, 1911), 45.

'Public opinion' had required it, but now it no longer did. Empty churches, some said, formed the outward and visible sign of separation from God.

It has sometimes been thought, in these circumstances, that 'the working class' in particular may only 'ever' have been tangential to the Christianity of the churches. The church, on this reading basically a 'service provider', had offered 'its limited range of social services in return for nominal loyalty' but 'provided little further sustenance to the majority'.[18] Church attendance, where it occurred, had been very largely a matter of 'rites of passage'. Working-class people turned up for a New Year watch night service but not for more specifically Christian festivals. In the country, harvest thanks-giving brought attendance from many who were not otherwise seen. Knowledge of the Bible was weak. The creeds were perceived to constitute 'dogma' and to get in the way of a Christianity largely construed as a matter of 'decent behaviour'.[19] Workers, it was thought, found the whole atmos-phere of the Church uncongenial. They were not prepared to face the humiliation of being asked to 'move on' by a well-dressed person who had paid a pew-rent (though pew-rents were being phased out). Frothy effu-siveness in church about the principles of the Sermon on the Mount seemed compatible with sublime indifference to their fulfilment in the affairs of everyday life.[20] Christianity was a class act, in every sense of that term.

Clergymen or ministers might be quite poor, if considered as 'professionals' alongside other professionals, but, particularly the former, were certainly not 'working men'. They found themselves in ambiguous social circumstances where the expectation that the clergyman would be a 'gentleman' collided with financial constraints and recruitment needs. By 1914, it is argued, the clergy were well on their way to their position as 'rather awkward and shabby professionals'.[21] At the top, however, 10 per cent of bishops in office between 1900 and 1919 had received their early education from private tutors.[22] Some

---

[18] Standish Meacham, *A Life Apart: The English Working-Class 1890–1914* (London, 1977), 200. Such a perspective accords with the author's view that, as religion lost whatever slim hold it may have had upon it, the urban working class felt free to visit vengeance upon its middle-class tormentors.

[19] H. McLeod, *Religion and the People of Western Europe, 1789–1970* (Oxford, 1981), 124–5; S.J.D. Green, *Religion in the Age of Decline: Organisation and Experience in Industrial Yorkshire 1870–1920* (Cambridge, 1996), 338–42.

[20] Forbes Gray, *Non-Church-Going*, 23–6.

[21] A. Haig, *The Victorian Clergy* (London, 1984), 358–61; Anthony Russell, *The Clerical Profession* (London, 1980) ranges more generally; K.D. Brown, *A Social History of the Nonconformist Ministry in England and Wales, 1800–1930* (Oxford, 1988).

[22] This figure—an indication of aristocratic connection—is cited in Kenneth Medhurst and George Moyser, eds., *Church and Politics in a Secular Age* (Oxford, 1988), 86. It is derived from a Hull MA thesis by D.J. Morgan. See also D.J. Morgan, 'The Social and Educational Background of Anglican Bishops: Continuities and Changes', *British Journal of Sociology* 20 (1969), 295–310; Kenneth A. Thompson, 'Church of England Bishops as an Elite' in Philip Stanworth and Anthony Giddens, eds., *Elites and Power in British Society* (London, 1974); James Bentley, 'The Bishops 1860–1960: An Elite in Decline' in M. Hill, ed., *A Sociological Yearbook of Religion in Britain*, vol. v (1972).

bishops did not like their social classification. Charles Gore, consecrated bishop of Worcester in 1902, declined to live in the episcopal residence, Hartlebury Castle. When he moved to the new see of Birmingham three years later, he rejoiced in a villa in Edgbaston which he freely described as the ugliest in western Europe. Frederick Temple, on becoming archbishop, rid himself of Addington Palace, Croydon and made a new home for himself in Canterbury.[23] He was able to lease a substantial part of his extensive grounds at Lambeth Palace to the London County Council.[24] The thought of 'the beautiful house' which was the bishop's palace at Wells had not earlier been enough to persuade Randall Davidson to come to a diocese which was in a big county a great distance from London and with a bad slow train service.[25] Others, however, evidently could be persuaded. The suffragan bishop of Stepney lived in a medium-sized house at Clapton and said his Office on the omnibus.[26] By no means all bishops, however, particularly those who, unlike Gore, did not have earls as grandfathers, followed his example in declining to be referred to as 'My Lord'. Episcopal insistence that candidates for ordination should have a university degree substantially weakened the efforts of the Revd Herbert Kelly, who had tried to deal with 'the unbridged gap' by training—at Kelham in Nottinghamshire—priests with elementary school backgrounds. Masterman, whose brother became a bishop, dismissed the idea that if the church abandoned 'the stiff and formal ways of its class traditions' all would be well. It was impossible to assume that a transformation of organized Christianity would bring the people back to what he called 'the spiritual affirmation of their fathers'.[27]

Ecclesiastical life was shot through with the distinctions of speech, dress and manners built into the structure of the time. Viewed nationally, social diversity existed to some degree within all denominations and it was not difficult to gauge the predominant social composition of particular congregations. Social identities, cultural expectations and financial conditions all played their part in uniting or dividing congregations. In some cases, diversity was 'managed' by the provision of separate services for 'the poor' or 'the working class'. Yet there were also conscious efforts to 'integrate'. To what degree, however, could depend on a multiplicity of factors. 'Middle-class' consciousness and 'working-class' consciousness was not

---

[23] A large bequest had enabled Temple to take a more energetic interest in church extension in Croydon. J.N. Morris, *Religion and Urban Change: Croydon, 1840–1914* (Woodbridge, 1992), 46.

[24] Tim Tatton-Brown, *Lambeth Palace: A History of the Archbishops of Canterbury and their Houses* (London, 2000), 94–6.

[25] Melanie Barber, ed., 'Randall Davidson: A Partial Retrospective' in Stephen Taylor, ed., *From Cranmer to Davidson: A Miscellany*, Church of England Record Society 7 (Woodbridge, 1999), 395.

[26] Emma K. Paget, *Henry Luke Paget* (London, 1939), 172–3.

[27] Masterman, *Condition of England*, 272.

uniform across the British Isles and varied, in both categories, from region to region. Prevailing patterns of occupation and employment (mono- or multi-industrial) shaped the structures of communities and the place churches and chapels occupied within them. Even to speak, as is sometimes done, of church/chapel participation as being, amongst the 'working class', the preserve of 'the aristocracy of labour' oversimplifies. In such circumstances, generalizations about 'inclusion' or 'exclusion' across all the territories of the British Isles remain hazardous.[28]

What was perhaps new was the degree of unease which awareness of 'class difference' produced. Public-school and university men sought spells in sponsored 'Missions' or 'Settlements' in inner-city locations—by 1914 over forty such settlements existed. The very term conveyed a sense of moving into an unknown land, as indeed the East End frequently was—despite its problems having been under discussion for decades. Settlement instruction was not confined to pugilism, though that featured. Those being instructed, however, often proved unreasonably resistant to changing their ways. If the mores and manners of the 'residents' were those which should characterize Christian men, unrespectable workers, it seemed, did not wish to qualify. Christianity, for them, could appear as esoteric as the funny game of Fives which the university men played in their spare time at 'Oxford House' in Bethnal Green. William Temple's use of his spare time, spent reading Bosanquet's *Logic* on a rickety three-legged chair, when he had a spell at the Oxford Medical Mission in Bermondsey, was equally esoteric. A certain Stanley Baldwin did time at the Trinity (Cambridge) Mission in Camberwell, though his leisure was not spent engrossed in logic. Nor was this only an Anglican activity. The Leysian Mission, founded by the Wesleyan public school in Cambridge, had its new premises in the City Road opened by the Prince and Princess of Wales in 1904. At Bishopthorpe Palace in 1911 the archbishop of York plotted how young men of wealth, position and leisure could be induced to pledge themselves to a life of service. It was felt that a new London club, of the old-fashioned kind, but with a chapel, might assist. A convalescent Dick Sheppard coaxed the Cavendish Club into existence with the support of the duke of Devonshire.[29] A spell in one of these 'Missions' might

---

[28] Chris Williams paints a picture of the Rhondda valleys before the First World War as being 'physically and ideologically marked by religion' in *Democratic Rhondda: Politics and Society 1885–1951* (Cardiff, 1996), 19–20. See also Robert Moore, *Pitmen, Preachers and Politics: The Effects of Methodism in a Durham Mining Community* (Cambridge, 1974). Men and women of the same social category might be 'respectable' or 'reckless'—with very different consequences. Paul Johnson, 'Conspicuous Consumption and Working-Class Culture in Late-Victorian and Edwardian Britain', *Transactions of the Royal Historical Society*, 5th series, 38 (1988), 41–2.

[29] R. Ellis Roberts, *H.R.L. Sheppard: Life and Letters* (London, 1942), 66–7. Carolyn Scott, *Dick Sheppard: A Biography* (London, 1977).

constitute 'experience of the poor' for undergraduates in their vacations. It sometimes changed their political outlook, but it did not lessen the social gap. Nor did the Cavendish Club.[30]

An alternative 'remedy' for this 'alienation', often seized upon by the Free Churches, was to be found in the 'institutional church'. The church of the people had to become the home of the people. Many existing buildings, particularly Nonconformist buildings, reminded an East End observer of 'nothing so much as a second-rate mortuary'. They were not fit for purpose. He wanted to see them all swept away and replaced by bright halls. Chairs should replace pews. The church itself would be nothing but a central auditorium, round which would be small halls and rooms set aside for lectures, classes, games, gymnasia and many other purposes and designed to cater 'in the round' for all age groups.[31] Silvester Horne left Kensington to inspire such an institute at Whitefield's church in Tottenham Court Road. Though there was a well-used billiard table, young men were to be taught more than how 'to go in off the red'.[32] In the event it was not an institute for the 'outcast' but one for 'assistants', clerks, young people 'in business' or 'in service'.[33]

The 'institutional church', as a notion, with variants, was widely taken up. The result was a formidable array of activities and organizations conducted under church auspices. Here was a lively 'open' but cohesive society which might satisfy from cradle to grave. It looked to one United Free Church minister in Scotland in 1901 as though 'a Christian would not need to go outside the Church for culture or amusement'. The ancient 'fear of God', he thought, seemed to have departed completely.[34] The young people of Redland Park Congregational Church, Bristol, for example, were spoilt for choice: Young Men's Mutual Improvement Society; Book Society; Recreation Club for Young Men; Penny Readings Society; Redland Field Club; Young Men's and Young Women's Christian Association: Sunday School Teacher's Preparation Class: Evening Classes Association; Concerts and Lectures in the Redland British School; Young Men's Missionary Society; Youth's Bible Class; Young Men's Literary Society; Young Men's Liberal Association. If these failed to satisfy, there was always the Society for giving Prizes for Clean and Tidy Homes. The minister, who

---

[30] Edward Norman, *Church and Society in England, 1790–1970: A Historical Study* (Oxford, 1976), 163–6; Standish Meacham, *Toynbee Hall and Social Reform, 1880–1914: The Search for Community* (New Haven, 1987); David McIlhiney, *A Gentleman in every Slum: Church of England Missions in East London, 1837–1914* (Allison Park, PA, 1988).

[31] Alden in Mudie-Smith, *Religious Life*, 32.

[32] Horne, *Pulpit, Platform, Parliament*, 38.

[33] For this assessment and commentary see Clyde Binfield, *So Down to Prayers: Studies in English Nonconformity 1780–1920* (London, 1977), 204–13.

[34] Cited in Callum Brown, *Religion and Society in Scotland since 1707* (Edinburgh, 1997), 129.

asserted that he had a strong 'working-class' element in his congregation, had thrown himself into voluntary organizations in the city. His impact was such that his three-mile journey to his grave was lined all the way with Bristol admirers.[35] The building of Central Halls seemed to Methodists to be the way forward in cities.[36] Laymen could be vastly enthusiastic. As well as planning (in London) the biggest flour-mill in England, Joseph Rank threw himself into planning the Tooting Central Hall. After its opening in November 1910 it was reputedly crowded on Sunday evenings with working men and their families, as many as 1,700 people. The fact that they came in their caps, and were not sure whether or not to take them off, proved to Rank that he was reaching the right audience. Fortunately, apart from an occasional game of golf or billiards, Rank had no other interest besides making money and advancing Methodism. He gave generously.[37] Suburban churches in Scotland were being built with multiple church halls to cater for the panoply of church activities, described by one minister as 'links in the chain of full Church membership'. Yet, despite some signs of 'success', it became evident that 'the institutional church' was a difficult operation to run. The more complex it became, the more it demanded managerial skills—which were by no means invariably present. Further, the commitment required in order to sustain this organizational pattern was held to 'partly account' for the small attendances which were reported at prayer and devotional meetings.[38] Mission halls established in working-class districts by 'middle class' congregations might attract locals, but they were likely to be run from outside.

ii. Leisure's Temptations

Such an apparent order of priority in organized church life provoked some reflection on the place of 'leisure', 'recreation' and 'pleasure' in a Christian existence.[39] It had been noted that too many Saturday afternoon cycle-rides—even though a cycle had been identified as a 'thoroughly Christian machine'—could sap enthusiasm for the following morning's Bible class. The bicycle, according to Randall Davidson, as bishop of Winchester in his 1899 charge to his diocese, was undermining Sunday attendances—though clergy, like the young Hensley Henson, could testify to its utility in

---

[35] David Morgan Thomas, *Urijah Rees Thomas: His Life and Work* (London, 1902), 125.

[36] For Manchester, see George Jackson, *Collier of Manchester* (London, 1923) and for Edinburgh, see Annie Jackson, *George Jackson* (London, 1949). For Birmingham, see Rita Armitage, *Mission in the Second City: The History of the Birmingham Methodist Central Mission 1887–1987* (Birmingham, 1987).

[37] R.G. Burnett, *Through the Mill: The Life of Joseph Rank* (London, 1945), 119, 149–51.

[38] W. Edwards, *Redland Park Congregational Church, Bristol* (Bristol, 1941), 17.

[39] Helen Meller, *Leisure and the Changing City, 1870–1914* (London, 1976).

extending their own pastoral range.[40] However, Christianity should concern itself with 'the whole person', not just 'the spiritual life'. Davidson
himself was a keen fisherman and shot, not to mention being addicted to
cricket. Commentators have sometimes interpreted this 'comprehensiveness' as an attempt to compete, ultimately unsuccessfully, with the burgeoning entertainment industries of the wider society.[41] It was that, but there was
also a serious attempt to give 'recreation' a full meaning.[42]

It appeared obvious, however, that more insidious examples of the
pleasure principle were available than were offered by cycling. It seemed
that Edwardian society as a whole was seeking to shed Victorian constraints.[43] The luncheon parties at Marlborough House thrown by King
Edward when Prince of Wales, not to mention his presence at Lord
Rosebery's tennis parties at Epsom, both activities on Sundays, had violated
sabbatarian principles. The accusation that the new monarch was licentious,
made on at least one occasion in a pulpit, could certainly not have been
levelled at his mother. The 'Victorian Sunday' still survived, but came under
pressure.[44] The Lord's Day Observance Society struggled manfully to keep
it intact. Attempts were made at resorts to draw a line in the sand, that is to
say to restrict activity to sea bathing and deny access to a golf course, but
lines on beaches are in their nature impermanent. In a 1906 Golf Yearbook,
virtually no English club advertised Sunday play but by 1913 nearly half did
(only 18 of 83 Welsh clubs). A.J. Balfour, the prime minister, played golf on
Sundays.[45] To depart from 'God's Law'—in so far as 'the Sabbath' was
protected in British legislation—seemed to its supporters to threaten grave
consequences. It was appalling to contemplate Sunday becoming a kind of
Bank Holiday recurring every week, as one speaker at the Congregational
Union in 1910 put it.

At one level, here was an apparent conflict between 'religion' and 'sport'
in which the latter was winning, game and set, though not yet match. At
another, however, what was happening was a transition from the rhythms
and requirements of a particular kind of industrial society to another, as yet
uncertain, one. It could also be the case, as one contemporary claimed, that
there was reason to dislike Sunday golfers as a breed: they did not pay their

[40] Peter Hammond, *The Parson and the Victorian Church* (London, 1974), 104.
[41] A.D. Gilbert, *Religion and Society in Industrial England: Church, Chapel and Social Change
1740–1914* (London, 1976), 182.
[42] Hugh McLeod, ' "Thews and Sinews": Nonconformity and Sport' in David Bebbington
and Timothy Larsen, eds., *Modern Christianity and Cultural Aspirations* (London, 2003), 28–46.
[43] Samuel Hynes, *The Edwardian Turn of Mind* (Princeton, 1968); D. Read, ed., *Edwardian
England* (London, 1982).
[44] John Wigley, *The Rise and Fall of the Victorian Sunday* (Manchester, 1980).
[45] Nevertheless, Balfour continued to assert that not only was he a Theist but he was a Christian.
Keith Robbins, 'The Churches in Edwardian Society' in Read, ed., *Edwardian England*, 115.

debts. Also at stake, however, was a certain conception of 'Britishness'. To 'go continental'—Prince Albert had indeed played chess on Sundays, but unobtrusively—would be a 'national' as much as a 'Christian' catastrophe. From the perspective of Sussex, 'southern Ireland' was part of the continent.[46] It was indeed in Ireland that the 'Sunday' question most sharply divided the Christian camps. Some Presbyterian households used their Sundays in ways which allegedly would have given Calvin some hints in austerity (such households did not dwell on Calvin's willingness to play bowls on Sunday afternoons). The Church of Ireland conference in 1910 debated 'The Secularization of Sunday' at length. The earl of Donoughmore was not alone in lamenting that modern transport facilities had engendered a spirit of restlessness amongst the people. Dublin Presbyterians, believing that the use of Sunday was 'the Greatest Question for the Church today', emphatically did not feel that Catholic habits provided the answer.[47]

In his presidential address to the National Council of Evangelical Free Churches in 1906, the Wesleyan Scott Lidgett saw evidence of vulgar materialism all around him.[48] He daily witnessed intemperance, impurity, gambling and speculation.[49] The integrity of home and society was at risk. A contributor to the *Daily News* survey suggested that West London was 'rapidly becoming the pleasure-ground not merely of England but of Europe'. It created an atmosphere 'unfavourable to religious work'. The presence there of 25,000 foreigners, 'largely and avowedly irreligious', was disturbing.[50]

The churches, between them, had a plethora of societies designed to counteract all the evils Scott Lidgett observed. The National Gambling League, founded in 1890, continued to enjoy interdenominational support from clergy and ministers. The National Vigilance Association, whose director, James Marchant, had originally been a Presbyterian minister, sponsored the National Purity Crusade against prostitution.[51] The Band of Hope had battled for half a century against drink.[52] A membership of around

---

[46] Material in these sentences is drawn from John Lowerson, 'Sport and the Victorian Sunday: The Beginnings of Middle-Class Apostasy', *British Journal of Sports History* 1/2 (Sept. 1984), 202–18.

[47] Alan Megahey, *The Irish Protestant Churches in the Twentieth Century* (Basingstoke, 2000), 69.

[48] J. Scott Lidgett, *Apostolic Ministry* (London, 1910), 236.

[49] G. Thompson Brake, *Drink: Ups and Downs of Methodist Attitudes to Temperance* (London, 1974); R. McKibbin, 'Working Class Gambling in Britain, 1880–1939' in R. McKibbin, ed., *The Ideologies of Class: Social Relations in Britain, 1880–1950* (Oxford, 1991), 101–38.

[50] Arthur Shadwell in Mudie-Smith, *Religious Life*, 94.

[51] For further details see G.I.T. Machin, *Churches and Social Issues in Twentieth-Century Britain* (Oxford, 1998).

[52] Brian Harrison, *Drink and the Victorians: The Temperance Question in England 1815–1872* (Keele, 2nd edn. 1994), 192–4. A final chapter considers these matters in Edwardian England. Gerald W. Olsen, 'From Parish to Palace: Working Class Influences on Anglican Temperance Movements, 1835–1914', *Journal of Ecclesiastical History* 40 (1989), 239–52.

three millions was claimed at the turn of the century.[53] The choice between 'rough' and 'respectable' styles of life, campaigners argued, faced every individual. The outcome of that choice, in turn, could be observed in every individual face. Zeal in these matters had come to be particularly associated with Nonconformity—'the Nonconformist Conscience' seemed to be particularly sensitive.[54] Concern, however, was not limited to Protestant Nonconformists. Cardinal Manning had been a temperance reformer.[55] Even earlier, Father Mathew had campaigned in Ireland and had obtained pledges (in Irish) in England.[56] The Scottish temperance movement was vigorous, as it needed to be.[57]

Beneath the rhetoric of 'crusade', however, awkward questions were posed both by the plight of the poor and the pursuit of pleasure. Was what might now be identified as 'conspicuous consumption' or 'incipient consumerism'—albeit on the part of the Edwardian 'rich' elite—an engine of economic 'progress' or an example of hedonistic frivolity? Further, was the solution to 'poverty' only obtainable by redistribution (which might also be seen as retribution)? Could only so much be done by individuals? Evangelical emphasis had been and still was heavily placed upon individual behaviour and personal responsibility. A converted man was a new being. The evils of society would be eradicated inexorably, if not immediately, by the elevation of 'character'. The 'terrible consequences of unpardoned sin' as expounded in a Primitive Methodist Chapel in Louth, as elsewhere, had led a hearer to a consciousness of personal guilt and then to liberation and newness of life.[58] It was an example of 'conversion' which could still be replicated in many other contemporary instances and seemed particularly to happen to young men at the age of 26. Evangelicals had supposed that the moral regeneration of the country depended on the multiplication of such life-transforming experiences. If so, it was still some way off.

It is not likely, however, that the preacher in Lincolnshire on this occasion had taken stock of the late-Victorian elite's rejection of Hell— Samuel Butler's satire on the use of the threat of Hell in *The Way of All Flesh*

[53] L.L. Shiman, *Crusade against Drink in Victorian England* (London, 1988), 154.

[54] D.W. Bebbington, *The Nonconformist Conscience: Chapel and Politics, 1870–1914* (London, 1982).

[55] Brian Harrison, 'Religion and Recreation in Nineteenth-Century England', *Past and Present* 38 (1967), 124–5. Harrison, citing Newman, suggests that Manning's zeal was in fact tending 'to the destruction of religion altogether'. For further on Manning as a temperance reformer see A.E. Dingle and B.H. Harrison, 'Cardinal Manning as Temperance Reformer', *Historical Journal* 12 (1969), 485–510.

[56] Elizabeth Malcolm, 'The Catholic Church and the Irish Temperance Movement, 1838–1901', *Irish Historical Studies* 5/23 (1982), 1–16.

[57] Elspeth King, *Scotland Sober and Free: The Temperance Movement 1829–1979* (Glasgow, 1979); Norma Denny, 'Temperance and the Scottish Churches, 1870–1914', *Records of the Scottish Church History Society* 23 (1988), 217–39.

[58] George Shaw, *The Life of Parkinson Milson* (London, 1893).

was published posthumously in 1903. A recognition of the exceeding sinfulness of sin did not commend itself to the intellectual *Zeitgeist*. Even so, there was a little anxiety, which Mr Gladstone had felt at the end of his life, that the relegation of hell to 'the far-off corners of the Christian mind' would adversely affect moral behaviour.[59] There might, even so, still be something to say about sin but the identification of particular sins divided opinion. The drink question was a case in point. Some thought temperance sufficient, others thought teetotalism imperative. Some wanted legislative restriction, others wanted prohibition.

These specific issues were all aspects of the underlying question which the churches faced, namely how they should position themselves as society evolved in what was described as a 'liberal' direction. The earl of Chichester, vicar of Yarmouth, in a campaign against Sunday golf apparently believed that the church could still properly insist on preventing citizens from engaging in harmless activities, or so those citizens supposed them to be. Attenders at the 'holiness' conventions held at Keswick in Lakeland worried about the propriety of playing croquet on Sundays. Such narcissistic moralism, critics said, should not be inflicted on society as a whole. Theatre censorship, another burgeoning issue, was another instance where 'Christian standards', as upheld in legislation, came under challenge. Could or should the state be 'neutral' in such matters and leave them to the individual? Much depended on what 'the state' was supposed to be. The coming generation of leading Anglicans meditated on the writings of T.H. Green and Bernard Bosanquet. It was through membership of the state, Henry Scott Holland declared, that 'we are knit into a single fabric. We are welded together into an organic structure. We live one life.' A man's 'whole being', according to William Temple, was comprised in the fact that he was a member of a state.[60] If this was so, *how* it was 'welded' was no small matter. 'Neutrality' could not be left in the hands of a set of arcane guardians, even judicial ones. Decisions, one way or another, involved the political arbitration of competing conceptions of public good. To treat Sunday like a perpetual Bank Holiday, if that were ever to happen, would not be a 'neutral' act.[61]

Fuzziness in such matters was not congenial to those who were alarmed by the inroads of Vanity Fair. The churches should warn their members and denounce the advance of Mammon. Prophetic utterance is in its nature

---

[59] Michael Wheeler, *Heaven, Hell and the Victorians* (Cambridge, 1994), 185.

[60] Holland (1911) and Temple (1904) are both cited in Matthew Grimley, *Citizenship, Community and the Church of England: Liberal Anglican Theories of the State between the Wars* (Oxford, 2004), 54.

[61] David Fergusson, *Church, State and Civil Society* (Cambridge, 2004), 58–9. Fergusson's discussion is contemporary, but has pertinence to the evolving Edwardian situation. See also Susan Mendus, *Toleration and the Limits of Liberalism* (London, 1989).

non-negotiable. 'It is a discernment', it has been argued, 'that comes either from God or from the devil, and has to be taken or left as such.'[62] The prophet addresses the church and, through the church, the world. Charles Gore and Neville Figgis were amongst those who assumed this role.[63] Personally content with a tin bath, iron bedstead and no carpet, Gore manifestly disliked Edwardian excess. He was of the view that Jesus had a profound contempt for majorities. However, a political system existed in the United Kingdom which depended on them, even if, as yet, the electorate did not consist of the majority of the adult population. The 'condition of England' was a political question. Any 'social gospel' would have to make its way in the arena of compromise which was politics.

iii. Collectivism and Individualism

It was time, one contemporary wrote, for the state to 'render existence easier by clearing away the thick undergrowth of thorns which make the road of virtue painful to tread'. The verdict of the future, he thought, would rest with Augustine, identified with 'collectivism', rather than with Pelagius, identified with 'individualism'. The policy of inaction was the policy of suicide. The desired haven of prosperity would never be reached 'in a bark of prohibitions floating jauntily on a sea of negations'.[64] Fearing that the bark of Christ had allowed itself to be a bark of prohibitions, there was a mood abroad to consider 'poverty' primarily as an economic question. While not going so far as to suppose that the road of virtue should be painless, there was widespread, though not universal, Christian endorsement of a shift in emphasis. Writers displayed no lack of self-confidence in their attempt to construct a social Christianity which would meet the needs of the hour.[65] The distinctly marked peculiarity of 'our age', in the eyes of many observers, was that social problems were approached by means of legislation and administration.[66] It was common ground that Western civilization was 'passing through a social revolution unparalleled in history for scope and power' as the American Walter Rauschenbusch put it in a book widely applauded on both sides of the Atlantic. The men, like himself,

[62] O'Donovan, *Desire of Nations*, 188; Keith Robbins, 'On Prophecy and Politics: Some Pragmatic Reflexions' reprinted in Robbins, *History, Religion and Identity in Modern Britain* (London, 1993), 105–18.

[63] D. Newsome, 'The Assault on Mammon: Charles Gore and John Neville Figgis', *Journal of Ecclesiastical History* 17 (1976), 227–41.

[64] Reginald A. Bray, *The Town Child* (London, 1907), 70.

[65] W.R. Ward, 'The Way of the World: The Rise and Decline of Protestant Social Christianity in Britain' in his *Faith and Faction* (London, 1993), 301–8 emphasizes that this shift was not simply a British phenomenon but, unlike in Germany or France, a closely interlinked doctrinal system or *intégrisme* did not emerge. As he puts it, no one in Britain was trying to make a 'system' work.

[66] Scott Lidgett, 'The Church and Social Problems' in *Apostolic Ministry*, 169.

who had worked out 'the new social Christianity' constituted 'a new type of Christian'.[67] The 'social' emphasis is evident in most denominations.[68] Life could not be compartmentalized. The Catholic Social Guild, formed in 1909, drew a direct line between the 'economic and social tyrannies of modern England' and leakage from the faith.[69] The social order of the Middle Ages was held to protect the individual. The extremes of wealth and poverty which now prevailed had supposedly not existed in the past. It was time to return to an organic society underpinned by religion.[70] There was an attempt to revive the notion of 'the just price' in the ordering of commerce. R.J. Campbell, minister of the City Temple in London, could not see why 'the whole problem of the poverty of Great Britain could not be solved in twelve months'. The state ought to become as a church—a family, if you like. The social gospel, he conceded, was not the whole gospel, but it was a large part of it.[71] That the state was an organic unity was claimed as much by the Baptist John Clifford as by the Anglican Scott Holland.[72]

There were, however, many meanings to be attached to 'socialism' and little certainty about how this 'social Christianity' translated into the competitive world of party politics. What the term meant had been much bandied about ever since Sir William Harcourt had had his revelation that 'we' were all socialists now. The view of socialism which seemed to emerge from the Christian Social Union (formed in 1889) was too anodyne for more radical spirits. A clerical group, encouraged by the increased Labour representation after the general election, formed the Church Socialist League in 1906 to give a harder edge to socialism. The land and capital were to be run collectively for the good of all. Laymen who became involved included Maurice Reckitt, R.H. Tawney and, from a very

[67] Walter Rauschenbusch, *Christianity and the Social Crisis* (New York, 1907), xi, 352; R.T. Handy, ed., *The Social Gospel in America, 1870–1920* (New York, 1966). It is difficult to be certain about the direct influence of Rauschenbusch. It has been pointed out that in Wales (as elsewhere in Britain) his basic tenets were echoed by those who had been influenced by the Germans, Harnack and Ritschl. Robert Pope, *Seeking God's Kingdom: The Nonconformist Social Gospel in Wales 1906–1939* (Cardiff, 1999), 104–5.

[68] P.d'A. Jones, *The Christian Socialist Revival, 1877–1914: Religion, Class and Social Conscience in Late Victorian England* (Princeton, 1968).

[69] J.M. Cleary, *Catholic Social Action in Britain, 1909–1959* (Oxford, 1961); C.C. Martindale, *Charles Dominic Plater, S.J.* (London, 1922).

[70] Barbara Wraith, 'A Pre-Modern Interpretation of the Modern: The English Catholic Church and the "Social Question" in the Early Twentieth Century' in R.N. Swanson, ed., *Church Retrospective*, Studies in Church History 33 (Woodbridge, 1997), 529–45.

[71] R.J. Campbell in C. Ensor Walters, ed., *The Social Mission of the Church* (London, 1906), 199–202.

[72] David M. Thompson, 'The Emergence of the Nonconformist Social Gospel in England' in Keith Robbins, ed., *Protestant Evangelicalism: Britain, Ireland, Germany and America c.1750–c.1950* (Oxford, 1990), 255–80, fills out the background in the 1890s; William King, 'Hugh Price Hughes and the British "Social Gospel" ', *Journal of Religious History* 13 (1984), 66–82.

different background, George Lansbury. Membership was small—around a thousand—but the character of some of its leading figures perhaps compensated for its lack of numbers. Conrad Noel, born in a royal cottage at Kew, where his father was a gentleman-in-waiting to Queen Victoria, had early moved beyond a loathing of cricket to a more comprehensive rejection of his early surroundings. In due course, thanks to the patronage of the Countess of Warwick, it led him to the vicarage at Thaxted in Essex in 1910. His father, a poet, had written *The Red Flag*. Noel had a belief that his stately ceremonial and reasoned doctrine could put Romish practices into the shade. His wife, except for beautifying the church and making the garden, devoted her time entirely to taking morris-dancing classes. He supplied whisky to visiting inspectors of boy scouts and was able to persuade Gustav Holst to train the 'throaty voices' of Essex people. Noel concluded that some of his curates were eccentric.[73]

Whatever colourful synthesis was emerging in rural Essex, it seemed undeniable that socialism on the continent was frequently linked with anti-clericalism and revolution. The papacy had condemned it. Was socialism in the United Kingdom something quite different?[74] There was certainly no major political party which could be compared with the Socialist parties of France or Germany, but that might only be a matter of time. A new Catholic Federation (1906), seems at least partly to have been founded in order to disabuse those gullible Christians who were being told that socialism merely meant the redress of economic wrongs. 'Don't swallow socialism' a Blackburn priest warned working men. The Jesuit George Tyrrell had expressed bitter opposition to socialism, as did his fellow Jesuit Joseph Rickaby.[75] It might be that in England Socialists flew the Union Jack, but this was mere tactics. James Larkin, leader of the great Dublin strike—not himself a great flyer of the Union Jack—visited Manchester in search of support and roundly declared that whoever said that it was impossible to be a Socialist and a Catholic was a liar.[76] If that was so, there were clerical liars on Clydeside.[77] By 1908, however, the Roman Catholic archbishop of Glasgow took a more conciliatory line and John Wheatley of the Catholic Socialist Society emerged as a significant political figure.

[73] Conrad Noel, *Autobiography* (London, 1945); Reg Groves, *Conrad Noel and the Thaxted Movement* (London, 1967).

[74] S. Yeo, 'A New Life: The Religion of Socialism in Britain, 1883–1896', *History Workshop* 4 (1977), 5–56.

[75] Writing, respectively, in *The Month* 87 (1897), 280–8 and *The Month* 118 (1911), 160–76. I am indebted for these references to Mr Bernard Aspinwall.

[76] Peter Doyle, 'The Catholic Federation, 1906–1929' in W.J. Sheils and Diana Wood, eds., *Voluntary Religion*, Studies in Church History 23 (Oxford, 1986), 470–1.

[77] S. Gilley, 'Catholics and Socialists in Glasgow 1906–1912' in K. Lunn, ed., *Hosts, Immigrants and Minorities* (Folkestone, 1980).

Fabian Tracts, published in the 1890s, and still being reprinted, had included *Socialism and the Teaching of Christ* by John Clifford (also published in a Welsh translation) and *Christian Socialism* by Stewart Headlam. Some leading figures in the Fabian Society, it was true, could not be accused of Christian sympathies. However, while George Bernard Shaw, another Dubliner, could be accused of many things, most strikingly by G.K. Chesterton, even he did not appear to be a likely assassin or incendiarist.[78] In any case, perhaps more 'representative' of the course British socialism was to take was Arthur Henderson, Methodist local preacher, teetotaller and trade union official who was elected, somewhat fortuitously, to the Commons in 1903.[79] And it was the Wesleyan minister of the Kingsway Hall in London who was preaching on 'The Socialism of Jesus' to a packed congregation in 1907. Was there any irony in the fact that two prominent Wesleyan businessmen and MPs, Robert Perks and Thomas Ferens, had given £1,000 each to build the Hall?[80]

Whether there was compatibility or not, came back, time and again, amongst both Catholics and Protestants, to what socialism really entailed. It might be, according to R.F. Horton, that socialism could be defined as 'Christianity applied to our industrial organisation and to our State life'.[81] Robert Flint, Professor of Divinity at Edinburgh, had written a weighty treatise which endeavoured to sift what was true from what was false in the idea of socialism. His book had been so well-received in Britain and Europe that a second edition appeared in 1908.[82] Was socialism one thing and state socialism another? R.J. Campbell, however, who appeared on Independent Labour Party platforms, had made up his mind. The rise of socialism was best interpreted as simply the revival of Christianity in the form best suited to the modern mind. Primitive Christianity was not identical with contemporary socialism but it was far nearer to the socialism of the present than it

---

[78] G.K. Chesterton, *George Bernard Shaw* (London, 1909).

[79] F.M. Leventhal, *Arthur Henderson* (Manchester, 1989), 10–11.

[80] David Jeremy, *Capitalists and Christians: Business Leaders and the Churches in Britain 1900–1960* (Oxford, 1990), 307. Jeremy's book demonstrates both the substantial extent of 'Christian influences' amongst the British business elite in this period but also how difficult it is to trace a coherent Christian 'business morality'. 'Christian socialism', as espoused by clergy, could lead to irritation, to put it no more strongly, on the part of 'practical' Christian men of business. Some even doubted whether R.J. Campbell was correct in his assertion that poverty could be ended in twelve months. Keith Robbins, 'British Culture versus British Industry' in Bruce Collins and Keith Robbins, eds., *British Culture and Economic Decline* (London, 1990), 1–24.

[81] R.F. Horton, 'Socialism' in *Great Issues*, 163.

[82] Robert Flint, *Socialism* (Edinburgh, 1894); Donald Macmillan, *The Life of Robert Flint* (London, 1914), 432–7. Flint, a founding Fellow of the British Academy, was an influential thinker in Scotland with a European reputation. D.S. Smith, *Passive Obedience and Prophetic Protest: Social Criticism in the Scottish Church 1830–1945* (New York, 1987) and D.J. Withrington, 'The Churches in Scotland c.1870–c.1900: Towards a New Social Conscience?', *Records of the Scottish Church History Society* 19 (1977), 155–68.

was to the Christianity of the present.[83] The view that socialism needed to be 'Christianized' and Christianity needed to be 'socialized' was an alternative formulation suggested in Scotland. Thomas Chalmers's 'godly commonwealth' could still be appealed to in the laboratory of municipal reform that was the city of Glasgow. There, and elsewhere in Scotland, Christian socialist ministers, trade unionists and professional social workers formed a united front.[84] In Wales, socialist assertions were a matter of vigorous debate. While some ministers claimed to have been converted to socialism by reading Robert Blatchford's *Merrie England*, others criticized Blatchford's atheism. The issue could sometimes sharply divide churches and pit ministers against leading figures in their congregations. A political struggle could not be kept out of the vestry. For some, 'socialism' was 'a virus', for others, it was the hope of the present and the aim of the future.[85] Whether 'the basis of the Christian faith' really did consist in ensuring decent living conditions of life and labour was being argued over in community after community, chapel after chapel.

iv. Education Battles

Socialism might be 'the next stage' in human development, but it still looked as though the party struggle in Britain lay between Conservatives and Liberals. In Ireland, of course, the issue of Home Rule meant that the party contest was different. The broad alignment of Nonconformity in Scotland and England/Wales with the Liberal Party and the Church of England with the Conservative Party remained. Redland Congregational Church, it will have been noted, had not offered rooms for Young Conservatives. The bitter struggle which had ensued around the 1902 Conservative Education Bill appeared to demonstrate just how deep was the divide between church and Dissent—and that this divide still had a substantial social element.[86] Whatever the merits of the government's attempt to create a unified structure of elementary schools and to secure full public control, it was the provision of rate aid for voluntary schools which proved most contentious. Robertson Nicoll, editor of the Nonconformist *British Weekly*—a Scotsman much given to gossip in the Reform Club—declared that Dissenters would be paying to enable church schools to pervert their children—'we should have to pay for the destruction of

---

[83] Campbell, *Christianity and the Social Order*, 17–20.

[84] Brown, *Religion and Society in Scotland*, 134–9.

[85] Robert Pope, *Building Jerusalem: Nonconformity, Labour and the Social Question in Wales, 1906–1939* (Cardiff, 1998), 67–70.

[86] See the chapter 'Passive Resistance and Nonconformist Power, 1902–1914' in James Munson, *The Nonconformists: In Search of a Lost Culture* (London, 1991), 244–89.

Nonconformity'.[87] Clifford, who became the best-known opponent of the Bill, saw it as an attempt by the intolerant and grasping holders of privilege (the Anglican clergy), to strengthen the tyranny of the state church.[88] Church schools, in single-school areas, would suborn Nonconformist children. A Passive Resistance League was founded in 1902 and organized the non-payment of rates. Clifford's parents had been charged double fees because they had refused to send him from the village school to the Anglican Sunday School. He declared that 'the function of government was exclusively secular' and he was as much opposed to 'undenominational' teaching as he was to 'Romanism'. He led a formidable campaign in the country, though 'passive resistance' was a contentious tactic, particularly for Wesleyans. Rate refusals began early in 1903 and, by March 1906, 176 persons had been sent to prison, rather a disappointing figure. In the interval, up and down England and Wales, energetic steps had been taken to strengthen the ties between the Free Churches and the Liberal Party. Nonconformists knew that they could only expect a different measure with a change of government. Liberal tacticians, for their part, hoped that Nonconformist Liberal Unionists could be made to respond to ancestral voices and return to the fold. While Nonconformist militancy was only one of the factors which produced the dramatic 1906 Liberal victory, it gave a particular flavour to that campaign.[89] It suited the prime minister, Campbell-Bannerman, to say that his party had been put in office by the Nonconformists. His Cabinet was the most non-English and non-Anglican that there had yet been. He and the Irish Secretary, James Bryce, were Presbyterians. A little Congregationalism might still linger around Asquith. Lloyd George was a Baptist, of a kind. Augustine Birrell, 'lapsed' son of a Baptist minister, became president of the Board of Education. His parliamentary secretary, Lough, was a Wesleyan. The Liberal backbenches were inhabited by men who could be claimed in large numbers, perhaps a maximum of 180, to be Nonconformists. For a time, there was a heady atmosphere of expectation.

It did not last. Two years of protracted discussion and negotiation on a new Education Bill failed to produce an acceptable outcome.[90] This time, Anglicans and Roman Catholics had grave anxieties (not precisely the same

[87] Norman Sykes, 'Church, State and Education since 1815' in his *Man as Churchman* (Cambridge, 1959), 117–67 gives a general overview; M. Cruickshank, *Church and State in English Education, 1870 to the Present Day* (London, 1963); D.W. Bebbington, *The Nonconformist Conscience: Chapel and Politics 1870–1914* (London, 1982), 142; G.I.T. Machin, *Politics and the Churches in Great Britain, 1869 to 1921* (Oxford, 1987).

[88] John Clifford, *The Fight against the Education Bill: What is at Stake* (London, 1902).

[89] Stephen Koss, *Nonconformity in Modern British Politics* (London, 1975), 70–1.

[90] N.J. Richards, 'The Education Bill of 1906 and the Decline of Political Nonconformity', *Journal of Ecclesiastical History* 23 (1972), 49–63.

ones) and could look to the House of Lords to sustain their objections. The fact that the 1902 Act remained on the statute book revealed that Nonconformist stridency could be ineffective in the thickets of parliamentary manoeuvre. Such benefit as there might have been in the 1906 proposals, viewed from a structural standpoint, had been lost.[91] There could be no disguising the fundamental cleavage which emerged during the course of the deliberations. Roman Catholics wanted to keep total control of their schools. A Christian community had the right to provide an education within a context which passed on its understanding of the meaning and purpose of life. Anglican schools could be similarly conceived as private enterprises, though serving public purposes. Yet, while the Roman Catholic community seemed demonstrably to be self-contained, the Anglican community was almost indefinable and Nonconformists resented the fact that in particular localities they had little option but to attend 'church schools'. Nonconformists had come to accept the 'Bible teaching' which had been in place in board schools for thirty years. With the partial exceptions of the Wesleyans, and in some other instances, they no longer, and in some cases never had, aspired to their own school teaching.[92] The exclusion in board schools of any 'catechism or religious formulary distinctive of any particular denomination' might suggest, however, that there was a 'Christianity' floating free of any particular denomination. Many Nonconformists did seem prepared to accept that this school 'Bible Teaching' did actually convey 'essential Christianity', a supposition which to Anglican and Catholic eyes revealed their defective understanding of Christianity.

The control of the educational system and controversy over the place Christianity should or should not occupy within it had been contentious, though different in particulars, throughout the United Kingdom. In Scotland, after the 1872 Act, burgh and parish schools had been transferred to local boards consisting entirely of ratepayers. Any school which stood outside this system had to survive without rate aid. Those that did so were Roman Catholic and Episcopalian but by 1914 only 10 per cent of schools were outside the state system. That system, however, did not mean the exclusion of church influence. Ministers and laity frequently maintained a major role through their participation in the management of school boards. Elections to these boards were contested but the outcomes normally ensured that 'Religious Instruction', which was now timetabled, reflected Presbyterian understandings. It is argued, however, that there was a discernible shift away from the 'evangelical design' of Scottish education. The

[91] John Wigley, 'Educational Aspirations versus Social Hierarchies: The 1906 Education Bill', in Bebbington and Larsen, eds., *Modern Christianity and Cultural Aspirations*, 246–65.

[92] F.C. Pritchard, 'Education' in Rupert Davies, A. Raymond George and Gordon Rupp, eds., *A History of the Methodist Church in Great Britain*, vol. iii (London, 1983), 279–308.

role of the Scotch Education Department ensured that Scotland was coming to have one of the most centrally organized educational systems in the world.[93]

In Ireland, there had been no strong lobby for a purely secular system of education but the question of control within the 'national' system set up in 1831 had been bitterly contested.[94] That system had provided for religious instruction to be given in separate classes. The Congregation of Propaganda in Rome, on enquiry, had given an opaque ruling on its acceptability. It was not unknown for Catholic bishops to complain that English Nonconformists and Irish and Scottish Presbyterians had forced 'a system of godless education' on Ireland. They knew that such a system would be 'pernicious to Catholic interests'.[95] Their answer was that educational institutions should be under the direct control of the Catholic Church, that is to say of the clergy—something which substantially did happen in the denominationally based secondary system set up in 1878. Anglicans might have liked to instruct the nation but had come to realize that they did not have the resources to do so. Presbyterians, without such aspirations, were broadly content with 'non-denominational' Bible teaching in schools. It was at the level of higher education, however, that the first decade of the twentieth century saw the most protracted struggle to find an acceptable structure. Successive Chief Secretaries wrestled with 'the Irish University Question'. The eventual solution was to enlarge the National University, which would be open to all. In it, Trinity in Dublin remained an Anglican institution. The Catholic College in Dublin was subsidized but did not become a fully-fledged university. Cork remained as Queen's College and its sister, Belfast, became the Queen's University of Belfast. The complex arrangements that were put in place tried to accommodate Roman Catholic, Anglican and Presbyterian positions (this was far from being a straight Catholic/Protestant polarity) and, from the perspective of government, to give a measured but not full support to denominationally aligned institutions. An expanded 'National' University came into being just at the point when the meaning of 'nation' within the British Isles was again coming to the fore.[96]

These arrangements indicate a situation of considerable cultural confusion across the British Isles in the period up to 1914. The United Kingdom could not be said to have *a* policy with regard to the implanting of

[93] Brown, *Religion and Society in Scotland*, 143–4; T.M. Devine, *The Scottish Nation 1700–2000* (London, 1999), 396–8; R.D. Anderson, *Education and the Scottish People 1750–1918* (Oxford, 1995); W.M. Hume and H.M. Paterson, eds., *Scottish Culture and Scottish Education* (Edinburgh, 1983).

[94] D.H. Akenson, *The Irish Education Experiment: The National System of Education in the Nineteenth Century* (London, 1970). His *Small Differences: Irish Catholics and Irish Protestants, 1815–1922: An International Perspective* (Kingston and Montreal, 1988) looks at wider issues.

[95] Bishop Conroy, cited in Megahey, *Irish Protestant Churches*, 31–2.

[96] D.W. Miller, *Church, State and Nation in Ireland 1891–1921* (Dublin, 1973).

'Christianity' in the coming generation. It was accepted that there should be 'Religious Instruction', an instruction, however, which could not be a catechistical exposition of 'what the state believed'. At the same time, its provision also suggested that the state did believe something. Parents could withdraw their children from such instruction should they wish to do so—a right not exercised on a substantial scale. The relationship between 'knowledge' and 'belief' stood uncertain and was probably best left in this condition. With the exception of R.B. Haldane, no front-rank United Kingdom politician relished, or indeed was capable of, venturing into deep reflection of a philosophical character on what the relationship between education, religion and morality might be. It seemed likely that he was an agnostic, a fact, if fact it was, which did not prevent a fellow-Scot, the archbishop of Canterbury, regularly staying with the Haldanes at Cloan during summer holidays in Scotland. Scots like Bryce and Balfour of Burleigh (a 'convinced Presbyterian' but happily one apparently 'in the fullest harmony with the Church of England') were Davidson's 'very old friends'. His intimacy with 'leading men on both sides of politics' was indeed something to which he attached great importance. Dining with them at Grillions Club, and exchanging confidences there, in Davidson's estimation, placed 'not the Archbishop only, but the Church, in quite a different relation to public life in its religious and secular aspects'.[97] It was indeed the suspicion of this 'establishment' intimacy which had angered Nonconformists throughout the 'Education' controversy.[98] Echoing his Baptist minister father, the 'lapsed' Augustine Birrell, at a 'complimentary' dinner which, ironically, followed the failure of his Education Bill in 1907, declared that he could hardly think of a word which 'the bishops' had ever said 'in the cause of humanity'. Davidson thought his history faulty: Birrell should stick to literary essays.

v. Gender Rules

Even if beautifying Thaxted church, supplemented by morris-dancing, satisfied Miriam Noel, it was becoming evident that the role allocated to women in the arrangements of institutional Christianity no longer satisfied some, perhaps many, women. What that role should be had deep ramifications.[99] Women in the Church of England, and in most other churches, were

---

[97] Barber, 'Randall Davidson' in Taylor, ed., *From Cranmer to Davidson*, 423–5.

[98] Davidson's position in particular years of the dispute can be followed in G.K.A. Bell, *Randall Davidson, Archbishop of Canterbury* (Oxford, 1952 edn.), (1902) 372–81, (1906) 510–30, (1908) 532–40.

[99] D.A. Johnson, *Women in English Religion 1700–1925* (New York and London, 1983); Frances Knight, ' "Male and Female He Created Them": Men, Women and the Question of Gender' in John Wolffe, ed., *Religion in Victorian Britain*, vol. v: *Culture and Empire* (Manchester, 1997), 24–57.

excluded 'both from spiritual leadership and from secular management'.[100] The sphere of women continued to be determined by men. Yet the surveys which have been alluded to made it clear that women, in all classes, formed the 'backbone' or the 'mainstay' of churches of all kinds. The Mudie-Smith survey demonstrated that nearly twice as many women attended Church of England services as men. Nor should this be seen as a new phenomenon or one peculiar to the British Isles.[101] Why this should be so admitted a variety of explanations. It might be that 'religion' was something which was particularly a facet of a woman's 'nature'. The language of Sigmund Freud in which maleness was identified with the 'super-ego' and femaleness with 'id' reached ecclesiastical recesses only gradually but, when it was explained, it seemed gratifyingly to be able to confirm that only men understood order. Women had a special 'feeling'. It was all tied up with the primacy of their familial role. The home was the place where women transmitted Christianity to their children, though within a framework in which a highly patriarchal model of domestic life was prevalent. And was not patriarchy 'biblical'? Separate spheres were providential. There was an 'order of nature' which Christianity upheld rather than destroyed. The public realm in church and community was one for men.

The fear that Christianity might be thought to be 'essentially' effeminate had been one of the reasons behind 'muscular Christianity'.[102] The 'further masculinising of women and the feminising of the Church' was publicly deplored by one Scottish Presbyterian, but he spoke for many.[103] There was, however, no lack of debate about gender.[104] Were 'women' (and 'men') born or made? Was the new century witnessing the birth of a 'new woman'? The subordination of women had to some extent been eroded by legislation after 1850 but if equality of the sexes is taken to mean that men and women should have the same rights, that condition had not been reached.[105] How far subordination entailed oppression, and what degree of subordination

[100] Brian Heeney, 'The Beginnings of Church Feminism: Women and the Councils of the Church of England 1897–1919', *Journal of Ecclesiastical History* 33 (1982), 90.

[101] See contributions in W.J. Sheils and D. Wood, eds., *Women in the Church*, Studies in Church History 27 (Oxford, 1990) and R.N. Swanson, ed., *Gender and Christian Religion*, Studies in Church History 34 (Woodbridge, 1998).

[102] Norman Vance, *The Sinews of the Spirit: The Ideal of Christian Manliness in Victorian Literature and Religious Thought* (Cambridge, 1985).

[103] Cited in Lesley A. Orr Macdonald, *A Unique and Glorious Mission: Women and Presbyterianism in Scotland 1830–1930* (Edinburgh, 2000), 173.

[104] Barbara Caine, *English Feminism, 1780–1980* (Oxford, 1997), 131–72; R.J. Evans, *The Feminists: Women's Emancipation Movements in Europe, America and Australia, 1840–1920* (London, 1977); Jane Rendall, *The Origins of Modern Feminism: Women in Britain, France and the United States 1780–1860* (Basingstoke, 1985); Myrtle Hill and V. Pollock, *Women of Ireland, Image and Experience, c.1880–1920* (Belfast, 1999); E. Breitenbach and E. Gordon, eds., *Out of Bounds: Women in Scottish Society 1800–1945* (Edinburgh, 1992): Deirdre Beddoe, *Out of the Shadows: A History of Women in Twentieth Century Wales* (Cardiff, 2000).

[105] Jane Rendall, ed., *Equal or Different?: Women's Politics 1800–1914* (Oxford, 1987).

entailed what degree of oppression, was a matter, however, on which, unsurprisingly, neither all men nor all women were in agreement. In any case, perhaps the reality of the relationships between the sexes could not be encapsulated in legislation. It was not only in fiction that the subordinated wives of bishops exercised power, even if they did not have authority. Personal patronage had provided many aristocratic women with a significant role in the religious affairs of their parishes. It has indeed been argued that it is not feasible to think of them operating in 'separate spheres' defined by any rigid definition of femininity.[106] 'Gender' no more than 'class' or 'nation' determined how all women felt and acted.

'Votes for Women', whether sought sedately by the National Union of Women's Suffrage Societies (1897) or stridently by the Women's Social and Political Union (1903) became a central issue of the moment. For some women it was an end, for others a means to an end. It divided families, political parties—and churches. No one could tell what a greatly expanded electorate would mean for the political system, particularly if one assumed, as some did, that the political behaviour of women would contrast with men and be 'irrational'. Did not men, in any case, vote not merely on their own behalf but as heads of their households? It did not escape attention that men fought wars. Since no one surely supposed that women should fight, it was wrong that decisions to go to war might in future be made by an electorate in which women might be a majority. Politicians might be 'progressive' in public but 'conservative' in private. While it was in general 'progressive' to support enfranchisement, it might be that a progressive measure would produce conservative voters. The issue became entangled, too, with the question of a further extension of the male franchise. Despite dramatic gestures and sustained campaigning by supporters of women's suffrage, the Liberal governments did not change the 'representation of the people'.[107]

A Church League for Women's Suffrage had been founded in 1909. The bishop of Lincoln, Edward Hicks, was its president.[108] Its 'chairman' was Maude Royden, in private a woman deeply involved in a complex three-fold love relationship, who threw herself into a public campaign.[109] The

---

[106] K.D. Reynolds, *Aristocratic Women and Political Society in Victorian Britain* (Oxford, 1998), 84–5, 220–1.

[107] Brian Harrison, *Separate Spheres: The Opposition to Women's Suffrage in Britain* (London, 1978), 55 discounts a simple equation between anti-suffragism and anti-feminism and between suffragism and feminism.

[108] Hicks was always willing to support 'progressive' causes. G. Neville, *Radical Churchman: Edward Lee Hicks and the New Liberalism* (Oxford, 1998).

[109] Her personal affairs are considered in her autobiography, *A Threefold Cord* (London, 1947). Royden had read history at the new and tiny Lady Margaret Hall, Oxford, a women's college with an Anglican ethos. Gillian Sutherland, 'The Movement for the Higher Education of Women: Its Social and Intellectual Context in England, *c.*1840–80' in P.J. Waller, ed., *Politics and Social Change in Modern Britain* (Brighton, 1987), 91–116.

League did not doubt that most Anglicans opposed votes for women. The notion, advanced at the Church Congress at Southampton by Ruth Rouse, that the aims of the women's movement approximated to 'the ideals of the Kingdom of God' received short shrift in the dean of Durham's diary. He had listened, he wrote, to a succession of young women 'bleating the *suffragist-nonsense* with variant degrees of absurdity'.[110] Henson had a well-developed sense of the absurd—in others. Some thought that his own action, at the age of 38, and having made a vow of celibacy, in proposing marriage (successfully) to a young woman four days after meeting her at a dinner party, was absurd. He was not moved, however, by Maude Royden's contention that the women's movement 'was the most profoundly moral movement . . . since the foundation of the Christian Church'. She began to move out of 'a little suffrage circle' onto a wider stage.[111] The archbishop of Canterbury, in the eyes of suffrage enthusiasts (such as his connexion by marriage, Ethel Smyth, the composer), seemed alarmed by what demonstrators might do inside a church building rather than show awareness of what she termed 'the greatest moral revolution the world has ever seen'.[112] Even 'men of goodwill', witnessing the way in which suffragettes courted punishment, and forced the authorities into appearing brutal, were not impressed.[113] The title of Ethel Smyth's opera—*The Wreckers*—seemed very fitting to wags in London's male clubland.

To some bishops, that moral revolution had unnervingly become apparent in the disconcerting revelation by their colleagues of Salisbury and Chichester that there were some—perhaps dubiously legal—women churchwardens in their dioceses. A line was held, however, by the all-male, all-clerical Lower House of Convocation, in excluding women from election to voluntary parochial councils (though they could vote in the elections). Such a step seemed to the wife of the bishop of London to be one which would alienate thinking women from parish work. It would separate 'the more advanced woman' from the church. After her husband's death, Louise Creighton continued to be an impressive advocate of the women's cause and, in her own manifold activities, particularly as president of the National Union of Women Workers, demonstrated their capacity. It was men, she had written, who had been responsible for the degradation of numberless women. The granting of suffrage, by recognizing the full

---

[110] Cited and discussed in Sean Gill, *Women and the Church of England: From the Eighteenth Century to the Present* (London, 1994), 207–8.

[111] Sheila Fletcher, *Maude Royden: A Life* (Oxford, 1989), 78–107.

[112] Bell, *Davidson*, 664–6.

[113] Brian Harrison, 'Women's Suffrage at Westminster, 1866–1928' in Michael Bentley and John Stevenson, eds., *High and Low Politics in Modern Britain* (Oxford, 1983), 115; L. Leneman, *A Guid Cause: The Women's Suffrage Movement in Scotland* (Edinburgh, 1985) and 'The Scottish Churches and "Votes for Women" ', *Records of the Scottish Church History Society* 24 (1991), 237–52.

citizenship of women, would banish the idea that women existed simply to please men.[114]

Yet a certain ambiguity remained. The Mothers' Union, started in 1876 by a woman, albeit daughter of a bishop and niece of an archbishop of Canterbury, with its commitment to prayer, purity in family life and, latterly, to the upholding of the sanctity of marriage, was certainly a 'women's voice', even if some women found it insufficiently militant. The Church of Scotland Woman's Guild was a comparable body.[115] There were women's organiza-tions, under a variety of names, in all churches, all performing 'services', locally and nationally, which women were particularly equipped to carry out. Maude Royden, daughter of a Liverpool shipowning and shipbuilding millionaire, with her own handsome Hampstead house, might well want moral revolution and desire to upset the world ruled by men, but other women, less well-placed, were less ambitious.

There were other ways. Some women in England, Ireland, Scotland and Wales in a sense bypassed the power structures of their churches at home by going out boldly to the 'mission field'. The unstructured circumstances which they necessarily experienced there gave them scope which might well have eluded them at home. Jeanette Owen, daughter of a Merioneth-shire shepherd, having mastered the English language, after a fashion, wanted a wider role than working on a hill-farm. She felt that the mis-sion-field was such a work 'that the heavenly Angels would be glad to leave there [*sic*] golden crowns and share in it'. However, she invented being shipwrecked *en route* from North Wales to the Mission College in Glasgow and, when found out, her missionary career did not even begin.[116] Women might still be confined within existing notions of femininity but those who did get overseas found opportunities normally reserved for men. In Ireland, a professional female missionary body emerged which enabled women to support themselves and become regarded as authorities in mission affairs.[117] No doubt, in many instances, they carried with them, either implicitly or explicitly, not only their Christian message but also assumptions about cultural superiority. To put it crudely, women might be still 'inferior' at home but they were 'superior' to those to whom they sought to bring

---

[114] Susan Kingsley Kent, *Sex and Suffrage in Britain, 1860–1914* (Princeton, 1987), 21, 171; Elizabeth Crawford, *The Women's Suffrage Movement in Britain and Ireland: A Regional Survey* (London, 2006).

[115] M. Magnusson, *Out of Silence: The Woman's Guild 1887–1987* (Edinburgh, 1987).

[116] Rosemary Seton, 'Welsh Women Missionaries of the London Missionary Society in the Nineteenth and Twentieth Centuries', *Journal of Welsh Religious History: Wales, Women and Religion in Historical Perspective* 7 (1999), 115–18.

[117] Myrtle Hill, 'Women in the Irish Protestant Foreign Missions c.1873–1914' in Peter N. Holtrop and Hugh McLeod, *Missions and Missionaries*, Studies in Church History, Subsidia 13 (Woodbridge, 2000), 185.

health and enlightenment abroad. It was permissible for their supporters to give such distant women heroic and perhaps exaggerated stature. They were, however, emphatically achievements of women, and their missionary 'auxiliary' bodies frequently sought to preserve an autonomy or independence from missionary societies controlled by men.[118]

The church, it was repeatedly said, supported 'the family'. There were words of warning which made it clear that 'service' which led to a neglect of a woman's primary responsibility was reprehensible. Yet the church also saw itself as a family, a 'family of love' and within a family there were surely different roles. On this analogy, it was not wrong still to see a place for gender-based organizations both for adults and young people. Boys had their organizations—Boys' Brigade, the Boy Scouts (founded in 1907 and with a membership of 150,000 by 1914) and the Church Lads' Brigade, all loosely or closely linked to particular congregations (circumstances varied quite considerably) while girls had their Friendly Society or Girl Guides. It was not, however, a situation of 'equal but separate development'. The Church Congress at Southampton in 1913 which had so upset Hensley Henson had indeed discussed 'The Kingdom of God and the Sexes', but wide differences were apparent. Some speakers thought that if men only treated 'the weaker sex' with Christian chivalry then the suffrage issue would go away. Awkward questions concerning sexuality lurked below the surface, sometimes not very far below, in all the churches.[119] Did 'dressing up' and ceremonial 'acting', for example, have a particular appeal for homosexuals? Did Anglo-Catholicism 'create' homosexuality or, tacitly at least, gave homosexuality a home?[120] Male church leaders knew these issues were there, but did not know how to handle them.

The Roman Catholic hierarchy, untroubled by the burgeoning appearance of 'representative' bodies in other churches, and certain that the ordering of the church should remain a matter for men, could conclude that the evidently 'disturbed' state of Protestant women stemmed from the failure of Protestant culture to provide adequate space for the feminine.[121]

---

[118] See the chapters 'Women in the Mission Field' in Gill, *Women and the Church of England*, 173–205 and 'Women and the Foreign Missionary Movement' in Orr Macdonald, *Unique and Glorious Mission*, 104–66; A.S. Swan, *Seedtime and Harvest: The Story of the Hundred Years Work of the Women's Foreign Mission of the Church of Scotland* (London, 1937).

[119] K.M. Boyd, *Scottish Church Attitudes to Sex, Marriage and the Family* (Edinburgh, 1980) is a fuller study than exists for church attitudes in England, Ireland or Wales.

[120] D. Hilliard, 'Un-English and Unmanly: Anglo-Catholicism and Homosexuality', *Victorian Studies* 25 (1982), 181–210. W.S.F. Pickering, *Anglo-Catholicism: A Study in Religious Ambiguity* (London, 1989), 200–5. See also the essays in J.A. Mangan and J. Walvin, eds., *Manliness and Morality: Middle-Class Masculinity in Britain and America 1800–1940* (Manchester, 1987) and M. Roper and J. Tosh, eds., *Manful Assertions: Masculinities in Britain since 1800* (London, 1991).

[121] F. Mason, 'The Newer Eve: The Catholic Women's Suffrage Society in England, 1911–1923', *Catholic Historical Review* 72 (1986), 620–38 reveals that some Catholic women were concerned.

The number of women in convents had dramatically increased in the Victorian period. In 1900 there were probably 10,000 Roman Catholic sisters in around 600 houses. Their situation (and that of their Anglo-Catholic counterparts) has been described as combining 'institutional subordination and self-determination'.[122] They had to do a lot of domestic drudgery (i.e. be female) but also found themselves with considerable responsibility for acquiring and managing property (i.e. be male). The foundress of the Society of the Holy Child Jesus had urged her sisters to become 'strong women' who would not lose their 'sweetness and gentleness' but would have a masculine force of character and will.[123]

The Virgin Mary had been interpreted as appearing in place after place in continental Europe. Marian devotion had given Catholic women a 'role model' which was more satisfying and obviated any need to 'ape' men. The Virgin had a message of warning to give—though it seemed to be increasingly by words of consolation—and imparted it particularly to women or children of low social status or marginal within their communities.[124] The Marian apparitions at Knock in County Mayo in 1877 have their place alongside Lourdes and Marpingen, both sites where women outnumbered men as pilgrims and vastly outnumbered them as 'cures'.[125] In 1907, Pope Pius X approved, for the whole Catholic world, the Festival of the Appearances of the Virgin Mary. British Protestants might be prepared to admit that their attention to Mary had been too limited, but rampant Marianism did not appeal.

vi. Church Unity: Looking

The educational controversy had brought to light much unedifying inter-ecclesiastical rancour. Its outcome, as has been noted, meant that in different parts of the British Isles, the churches interpreted the requirements of Christian formation very differently. Some required a self-contained and, in practice, clerically dominated if not clerically controlled 'church' educational system. Others accepted a system which excluded a 'church' presence, though not 'Christianity', altogether. There were various gradations in between. The United Kingdom had reached a series of accommodations on these matters, but they were fragile and 'unsystematic'. Whether the state should, or could, seek greater coherence was problematic and, in the new

---

[122] M. Vicinus, *Independent Women: Work and Community for Single Women 1850–1920* (London, 1985).

[123] Cited in Susan O'Brien, '*Terra incognita*: The Nun in Nineteenth-Century England', *Past and Present* 121 (1988), 136–8.

[124] D. Blackbourn, *Marpingen: Apparitions of the Virgin Mary in Bismarckian Germany* (Oxford, 1993) and R. Harris, *Lourdes: Body and Spirit in the Secular Age* (London, 1999).

[125] J. Devlin and R. Fanning, eds., *Religion and Rebellion* (Dublin, 1997).

political situation after 1906, bound up with the question of its own constitutional unity. Since the Liberal governments accepted, at least in general terms, that there were distinct nations and that they all exhibited ecclesiastical peculiarities, acceptance of plurality in educational provision was inescapable. The continued universal, though minimal presence of 'Religious Knowledge' did not satisfy critics who supposed, in the matter of religion, that there was nothing to be knowledgeable about.

This messy state of affairs left the churches in a quandary. Their leaders were well aware of the currents, both social and intellectual, which seemed to imperil or at least challenge their position in society. What was appearance and what was reality in 'late-Christendom'? Winston Churchill, brightest, youngest and most belligerent of Cabinet members, had been converted to 'rationalism' by Winwood Reade's *Martyrdom of Man* but cheerfully married Clementine Hozier in St Margaret's, Westminster. David Lloyd George signed the marriage register. He no doubt listened to the injunction upon Winston to forsake all others with a certain detachment. Lord Hugh Cecil, Churchill's best man, took it very seriously.

If, notwithstanding the ambiguous continuing Christian absence/presence in public life, symbolized at this wedding, 'Christianity' was under strain, might not the fact that there was no single Christian church have some bearing on the matter? The fissiparousness of the nineteenth century should surely not be a defining characteristic. It has already been noted that the new century was beginning with some 'reunions' within Scottish Presbyterianism and English Methodism. Even though, in these instances, the 'family likenesses' were clear and the divisions had only been of relatively recent origin, the reunions had been difficult to achieve. A reunion which brought together churches whose polities were episcopal, presbyterian, connexional or congregational had to reckon with much longer histories and much deeper divisions. And that would only be to consider questions of structure. It was inconceivable, so the evidence had but recently suggested, that there could be a 'reunion' between the Roman Catholic Church and the Anglican churches of the British Isles on any basis other than the submission of the latter to the former. There was no mind to take any such step. In so far as all other churches in the British Isles might be generically labelled as 'Protestant', it seemed, at least on paper, that some coming together might be feasible. However, the extent to which a substantial section of the Church of England jibbed at the notion that it was 'Protestant' needs little additional emphasis here. A relationship with the Church of Sweden was more attractive than one with the non-episcopal churches of the British Isles. A report on this possibility was published in 1911. It contained a long section on 'Presbyterian and other Non-Episcopal Churches' which noted that any reunion with them would require general agreement in doctrine and practice. The Historic Episcopate would be essential. It was noted that there was no strong desire on the part of any of the Presbyterian churches for a closer union with the Anglican churches.[126] 'Reunion' seemed a very hazy prospect. Indeed, the stresses and strains within the Church of England were such that it would break apart. It did not offer a very inspiring example of unity since its contending parties seemed more bent on expanding their own strength than in celebrating its diversity and 'catholicity'.

The talk about Free Church unity continued. Councils and Federations had been set up across England and Wales. It became common for ministers from different Free Church denominations to share the same platform. Even so, while it was frequently argued that only in unity would the Free Churches constitute the force in national life which their collective numbers appeared to make possible, the nature of that unity remained problematic. Moreover, there was an uncomfortable awareness, at least in some quarters, that the 'Nonconformist moment' might be passing and even unity might not bring it back. A.M. Fairbairn, principal of the new Mansfield College in Oxford—itself a significant presence—had noted in 1897 that it was perhaps harder to be a Nonconformist than at any previous date in English history. Previous generations had laboured under disabilities but their very substantial, though not complete, removal made dissent harder than it had been for previous generations.[127] The Nonconformist Union at Cambridge University celebrated its thirtieth anniversary in 1913 but, in retrospect at least, it came to be seen as its swan-song. Bernard Manning, its secretary in 1914, concluded a decade later that 'Nonconformity cannot live as a protest against injustices removed and errors that are dying'.[128] The vehement language of the educational campaign could not altogether disguise a 'loss of zest'. The 'dissolution of dissent' might be particularly sensed in a university in which, by definition, ideas and assumptions were challenged, but it was not confined to young men who were being seduced by their academic environment.[129] It was time to look again at 'traditions'. The form of worship came under fresh scrutiny in all the Free Churches, though the liturgical enthusiasms of some authors were not invariably shared by congregations. Amongst Congregationalists, the *Devotional Services*

[126] Alan M.G. Stephenson, *Anglicanism and the Lambeth Conferences* (London, 1978), 123–4.

[127] Cited in E.K.H. Jordan, *Free Church Unity: History of the Free Church Council Movement 1896–1941* (London, 1956), 47–8.

[128] Cited in David M. Thompson, 'Nonconformists at Cambridge before the First World War' in Bebbington and Larsen, eds., *Modern Christianity and Cultural Aspirations*, 199–200.

[129] Dale A. Johnson, *The Changing Shape of English Nonconformity, 1815–1925* (New York, 1999) and his earlier article 'The Oxford Movement and English Nonconformity', *Anglican and Episcopal History* 59 (1990), 76–98; Mark D. Johnson, *The Dissolution of Dissent, 1850–1918* (New York and London, 1987).

compiled by John Hunter, already in existence for two decades by 1901, had grown to 300 pages and was to be regularly reprinted. Amongst Baptists, G.P. Gould and J.H. Shakespeare produced a *Manual for Free Church Ministers* in 1905. A Wesleyan Guild of Divine Service was formed by ministers and laymen in 1905 with the aspiration to promote greater reverence and intelligent participation in worship. Amongst other things, it advocated kneeling for prayer, a fuller observance of the church's year, and more frequent communion. The scale of the change which was taking place should not be exaggerated, but the trend was clear.[130] It might suggest, as J.H. Shakespeare contended in 1910, that denominationalism was 'a tree which was rapidly becoming hollow'.[131] Even so, if 'Free Church unity' meant entire theological or ecclesiological agreement, it was not present. The Baptist authors of the manual could not refrain from referring, with regard to baptism, to 'the strange deviation from primitive practice' in other Free Churches.

The 'interdenominational principle' was being promoted by the Student Christian Movement which began in 1893 at a conference of students interested in mission work.[132] Interdenominationalism was not to be 'weak and colourless' but in 1908 saw itself as working to 'prepare the way for ultimate unity in the Christian Church'.[133] At its conferences, 'the delight of discovering what jolly good fellows High Churchmen and Baptists can be' had often 'obliterated' all thought of the differences which separated them.[134] This was a very different level of interdenominational contact from the meeting of great men from the British churches which Sir Henry Lunn, now, unusually, an English adherent of the American Methodist Episcopal Church, had entrepreneurially orchestrated in Switzerland in the early 1890s—'off piste' as it were. This contact had led, briefly, to the publication of the *Review of the Churches*. Individuals tried their own forays across ecclesiastical boundaries. Never able to resist an independent line, Hensley Henson in 1909 accepted an invitation to preach at the first anniversary of the Digbeth Institute (which had been set up under the auspices of Carr's Lane Congregational Church in Birmingham).[135] The

---

[130] For further information see Norman Wallwork, 'Developments in Liturgy and Worship in Twentieth-Century Protestant Nonconformity' in Alan P.F. Sell, and A.R. Cross, eds., *Protestant Nonconformity in the Twentieth Century* (Carlisle, 2003), 102–31.

[131] Cited in Ian Randall, *English Baptists of the Twentieth Century* (London, 2005), 63.

[132] The participation was some 40 per cent Anglican, 30 per cent Presbyterian and 30 per cent Free Church—a distribution broadly maintained in the evolving movement. Tissington Tatlow, *The Story of the Student Christian Movement* (London, 1933).

[133] Cited in Tatlow, *Student Christian Movement*, 332.

[134] Martyn Trafford, cited in Johnson, *Dissolution of Dissent*, 285.

[135] In 1901, reflecting on 'our unhappy divisions', he had pleaded for recognition of non-episcopal churches. Herbert Hensley Henson, *Cross-Bench Views of Current Church Questions* (London, 1902), 341–55.

vicar of the parish in which it was situated spied a clerical stranger entering it without his consent and complained to Gore, his diocesan. Henson defied the inhibition which was then placed upon him.[136] J.H. Jowett, minister of Carr's Lane, wrote to the *Birmingham Daily Post* to say that the older he became the less he was concerned about formal etiquette. It strangled and suffocated the liberty of Christian communion. Preoccupation with it could only result in deeper alienations and divisions and provide further material for scornful outsiders.[137] In 1911, still languishing in 'Tory Hereford', Bishop Percival invited Nonconformists to receive communion in the cathedral at the time of the coronation of George V. Many accepted. However, its clergy thought 'mad' the suggestion that they might accept a reciprocal invitation from the Congregational minister.

It was evident, therefore, that there remained many matters which 'jolly good fellows' would have to address. Central was the nature of 'unity' itself. At one level, the analogy was with commercial rationalization. Viewed from the top, it was a matter of the eradication of duplication and the efficient deployment of 'plant' and resources, both human and financial. It was a point of view particularly attractive to laymen who had to think in such terms in their working lives. The multiplicity of 'challenges' faced by all the churches could be more effectively met by a degree of 'rationalization'. Yet engagement with the language of 'optimum size' was not congenial. It could be argued—or at least privately admitted—that this apparent duplication (competition?) might actually be to the continuing benefit of 'Christianity' in the round. It was perhaps no accident that the British Isles were not witnessing, or not yet, that polarization between 'church' and 'anti-church' evident in those other European countries without the United Kingdom's range of churches. Variety had made 'space' for segments of the population to remain within a Christian orbit who might otherwise have left it altogether.[138] In countries where only one church significantly existed the temptations of power had been too strong and had prompted anti-clerical hostility. Nevertheless, whatever view was or is taken of such an analysis, contemporaries began to take seriously the notion that the manifest 'disunity' of the church constituted a standing reproach. Did its divided condition not make a mockery of its own message?

Missionary heroes continued to penetrate the most diverse locations. Twenty-six-year-old Archibald Fleming, for example, was spending the

---

[136] 'Bishop Gore and Canon Henson, 1909' in R.P. Flindall, ed., *The Church of England, 1815–1948: A Documentary History* (London, 1972), 298–9.

[137] Arthur Porritt, *John Henry Jowett* (London, 1924), 118–20.

[138] Hugh McLeod suggests that Nonconformity had this religious safety-valve effect in England in his ''Dissent and the Peculiarities of the English, *c*.1870–1914' in Jane Shaw and Alan Kreider, eds., *Culture and the Nonconformist Tradition* (Cardiff, 1999), 124–36.

winter of 1909–10 living in an igloo with two Eskimo (Inuit) families. He did not exactly find the acrid smoke from the blubber lamps an aromatic disinfectant but, as they battled for survival, he found that there was a remarkable at-one-ness in the settlement. Missionary stories from across the globe, relayed through the multiplicity of denominational and non-denominational missionary societies, formed part and parcel of church life. It has been argued that the missionary project was one of the primary ways in which 'community' was imagined at home.[139] A World Missionary Conference assembled in Edinburgh in 1910 in a mood of some optimism.

Looking back on the British Isles from their distant vantage point in Africa or Asia, however, missionaries from the various churches frequently understood the extent to which the divisions they were accustomed at home had social and cultural dimensions which made little sense in a different environment.[140] Converts should not be expected to embrace the full baggage of British history. A conviction that a united Indian church would appeal to non-Christians in a way that divided churches could not was widespread—though unproven. India, it was said, already had divisions enough without Christians multiplying them. On the other hand, some-times the very plurality of India was held to give scope for non-English missionaries from Britain. The Tamil language, some supposed, was 'similar to the Welsh' and its poetry unlike any other save Welsh in apparently sharing an enthusiasm for elaborate alliteration.[141] Even so, there was a limit to possible 'identifications'. A Scottish Presbyterian missionary in Rajputana felt that insistence upon Presbyterianism without the 'Scotch character' would not work.[142] His remark has parallels in many other contexts. The missionary enterprise put the internal discords of British Christianity in

[139] The further assertion, that the 'seemingly irrational' act of giving away 'precious pennies' by the working class 'forged a spiritual terrain that enabled poor and working-class Congregationalists to affirm their moral dignity against the manifold humiliations that characterize daily existence in a class society' is more questionable. Susan Thorne, *Congregational Missions and the Making of an Imperial Culture in 19th-Century England* (Stanford, 1999), 158–9.

[140] More detailed consideration of matters sketched in the following paragraphs can be found in histories of individual missionary societies, as N. Goodall, *A History of the London Missionary Society, 1895–1945* (London, 1954) and B. Stanley, *History of the Baptist Missionary Society, 1792–1992* (Edinburgh, 1992); R. Gray, *Black Christians and White Missionaries* (New Haven, 1990); A.N. Porter, 'Cultural Imperialism and Protestant Missionary Enterprise 1780–1914', *Journal of Imperial and Commonwealth History* 25/3 (1997), 367–91; 'Religion, Missionary Enthusiasm, and Empire' in Andrew Porter, ed., *The Oxford History of the British Empire: The Nineteenth Century* (Oxford, 1999), 222–46; and *Religion versus Empire: British Protestant Missionary Overseas Expansion, 1700–1914* (Manchester, 2004).

[141] John P. Jones of Madura (South India) cited in Aled Jones, 'Gardens of Eden: Welsh Missionaries in British India' in R.R. Davies and Geraint H. Jenkins, eds., *From Medieval to Modern Wales* (Cardiff, 2004), 278.

[142] Bengt Sundkler, *Church of South India: The Movement towards Union, 1900–1947* (London, 1954), 354.

perspective. The points on which the churches were agreed were all-important, and those on which they differed were comparatively trifling.[143] Moves towards unity in India, largely though not exclusively on the part of churches which were 'British-created', would show an example to the 'mother' churches: *Ex oriente lux*. 'Has not the reunion of Scottish Presbyterianism begun in India?' wrote one author in 1901. The imperative, it was widely agreed, was to put non-Europeans and Europeans on an equal footing. V.S. Azariah became the first Indian Anglican bishop in 1912. According to the English Congregationalist R.F. Horton, who happened to be in India at the time, the presence of the American J.R. Mott at the first Indian National Missionary Conference in Calcutta was causing denominational rivalries or differences to melt away. It would, of course, be too simple to suppose that all Indians wanted unity. Those that did could be mystified by how 'the British' perceived themselves. An English Congregationalist, for example, writing home in 1905 suspected that the chief trouble in unity discussion would centre on subscription to creeds and confessions. His 'Scotch brethren', he thought, were inordinately fond of such things.[144]

It was goings-on in East Africa, however, that provided the most dramatic example of how the home boat could be awkwardly rocked. In 1913 the 'Kikuyu Conference' was held at a Church of Scotland mission station in Kenya to consider closer union between Anglican, Presbyterian and Methodist missionary bodies in British East Africa. The Anglican bishops of Uganda and Mombasa, who were evangelicals, invited a visiting Church of Scotland minister to preach at the concluding Communion Service and invited the non-Anglicans present to receive Holy Communion. Norman Maclean, the preacher, reported in *The Scotsman* on his return that the missions had 'solved the problem of how to coalesce Episcopacy and Presbyterianism'. Linkage was made, in this respect, to the 1910 world missionary conference, though that was controversial.[145] Frank Weston, the Anglican bishop of Zanzibar, an Anglo-Catholic, denounced his episcopal colleagues for heresy and demanded that they be brought to trial. The archbishop of Canterbury did not rush to judgement. Advised by the Consultative Body of the Lambeth Conference, he sagely concluded that a growing 'native church', in East Africa or elsewhere, should not be held back because of 'accidental happenings of English or Scottish life', political,

---

[143] A view expressed back in 1874 by Sir Bartle Frere in his *Indian Missions*.

[144] Sundkler, *Church of South India*, 355 n. 26.

[145] S.P. Mews, 'Kikuyu and Edinburgh: The Interaction of Attitudes to Two Conferences' in G.J. Cuming and D. Baker, eds., *Councils and Assemblies*, Studies in Church History 7 (Cambridge, 1971), 345–59 argues that 'Kikuyu' had nothing to do with 'Edinburgh', though its repercussions subsequently did.

social and ecclesiastical over the previous two centuries. He also concluded that joint communion services gave rise to misunderstandings and should not be repeated. A summation of these conclusions, attributed to a mischievous Ronald Knox, was that the Communion Service had been eminently pleasing to God but was on no account to be repeated.[146] The controversy in England, particularly on the question of inter-communion, which involved Gore, Talbot and Henson, amongst others, was somewhat stilled, but not settled. Pursuit of unity outside England might yet cause schism at home.[147] The Kikuyu mission station might be at 'an out-of-the-way place' in East Africa but the reality was that British and Irish denominational relationships had ceased to be self-contained. At the 1908 Lambeth conference, puzzled English bishops had to get used to their Canadian brethren occupying their lunch breaks shooting tin bears down a tube at a nearby rifle range. The challenge of diversity was everywhere.

vii. Faith: The Spirit and the Letter

What an 'Episco-Presby-gational-Bapto-Methodist Church' might look like—to use an imaginatively succinct term coined in India at this time—could indeed only be a matter for prayer and speculation. Discussion of issues of 'order' might well become bogged down in detail. But what of faith? Here again, 'abroad' and 'at home' interpenetrated, though in rather restricted circles. Missionaries in India inevitably asked themselves about the relationship of Christianity to the other religions of the sub-continent (and to the emerging national aspirations of Indians). In what sense, if indeed in any, could Christianity be presented as fulfilling elements in Hinduism or Sikhism? Could it oust Islam? Not surprisingly, there was no single answer. Those who addressed it, however, knew that living as a Christian in India raised questions about 'religion' which had no parallel social context at home except in very restricted circles.[148] There were very small immigrant Hindu and Muslim communities, although late Victorian 'native' adherents of Islam or of varieties of Hinduism provided some growth. It was in 1912 that the Woking mosque was revived.[149] Only Jewish communities

---

[146] 'Kikuyu, 1913' in Flindall, ed., *Church of England*, 299–307.

[147] David M. Thompson, 'The Unity of the Church in Twentieth-Century England: Pleasing Dream or Common Calling' in R.N. Swanson, ed., *Unity and Diversity in the Church*, Studies in Church History 32 (Oxford, 1996), 507–31.

[148] D. Forrester, *Caste and Christianity: Missions and Caste in India* (London, 1984); E. Sharpe, *Not to Destroy but to Fulfil: The Contribution of J.N. Farquhar to Protestant Mission Thought in India before 1914* (Lund, 1965) and *The Theology of A.G. Hogg* (Madras, 1971); Gerald Studdert-Kennedy, *British Christians, Indian Nationalists and the Raj* (Delhi, 1991).

[149] G. Beckerlegge, 'Followers of "Mohammed, Kalee and Dada Nanuk": The Presence of Islam and South Asian Religions in Victorian Britain' in John Wolffe, ed., *Religion in Victorian Britain*, vol. v: *Culture and Empire* (Manchester, 1997), 221–70.

constituted a socially significant non-Christian presence. The nature of that population had changed dramatically with the influx of Jews from Russia.[150] The Aliens Immigration Act (1905), as was intended, did curb the inflow, but in 1914 there were 180,000 Jews in London—and considerable communities in other British cities.[151] The bishop of Stepney moved amongst Jews in Whitechapel and Spitalfields. He and church workers thought they ought to be 'won', but they were not confident in their 'line of approach'. He had many Jewish friends and, on one occasion, gave the stately Blessing of the Old Covenant in Hebrew when he happened upon a Jewish man on the point of death.[152] The new arrivals disturbed the accommodation which long-settled Jews had made with British society over many generations. In South Wales in August 1911, in an area where there were many 'incomers', not least English, there were riots and looting directed against Jews. The Monmouthshire Welsh Baptist Association dropped a motion supporting the local Jewish population.[153] In Glasgow in 1909, in a notorious murder case, a Jewish immigrant was found guilty. Twenty years later, appeal judges found that the presiding judge in the original case had misdirected the jury. The judge was Lord Guthrie, son of the Revd Thomas Guthrie, and himself a temperance reformer and president of the Boys' Brigade.[154] Since the larger Jewish population was so new and was itself so diverse, both religiously and linguistically, formal Jewish–Christian dialogue had little or no place. In the matter of 'religion' the United Kingdom was a Christian country.[155] The extent to which 'passive anti-Semitism' was the 'prerogative of English gentlemen', at this time, of *Christian* English gentlemen, is not easily answered.[156]

It was not necessary to be in contact with other faiths, whether at home or abroad, to seek to probe the heart of Christian faith. Where did it lie? It had, of course, been hammered out historically in creeds at once both succinct and complex. Most Christians publicly repeated 'I believe...'.

[150] Geoffrey Alderman, *Modern British Jewry* (Oxford, 1992); K. Collins, *Second City Jewry: The Jews of Glasgow in the Age of Expansion 1790–1919* (Glasgow, 1990); U. Henriques, 'The Jewish Community of Cardiff, 1815–1914', *Welsh History Review* 14 (1988), 269–300.

[151] B. Gainer, *The Alien Invasion: The Origins of the Aliens Act of 1905* (London, 1972).

[152] Paget, *Henry Luke Paget*, 187–90. Bell's life of Davidson contains no reference to Jews.

[153] C. Holmes, 'The Tredegar Riots of 1911: Anti-Jewish Disturbances in South Wales', *Welsh History Review* 11 (1982), 214–25.

[154] Ben Braber, 'The Trial of Oscar Slater (1909) and Anti-Jewish Prejudices in Edwardian Scotland', *History* 88/2 (2003), 267–8.

[155] D. Feldman, *Englishmen and Jews: Social Relations and Political Culture 1840–1914* (London, 1994); L.P. Gartner, *The Jewish Immigrant in England, 1870–1914* (London, 1973 edn.).

[156] T.G. Otte, '"Alien Diplomatist": Antisemitism and Anti-Germanism in the Diplomatic Career of Sir Francis Oppenheimer', *History* 89/2 (2004), 233–55 uses this term coined by Gertrude Himmelfarb. He notes a number of British diplomats who put their dislike of Jews on paper.

But were there not different ways of 'believing'? In relation to the Thirty-Nine Articles of the Church of England, clergymen had been able since 1865 to give their 'general' assent, which did not commit them to every proposition. Such issues naturally most affected men seeking ordination. The bishop of Oxford had refused to ordain William Temple because at that point Temple could not affirm the two miracles of the Apostles' Creed—the Virgin Birth or the bodily resurrection of Jesus. The archbishop had to step in to make ordination possible. Lectures Temple published in 1910, just after becoming headmaster of Repton, may have helped persuade Davidson that his predecessor's son was, after all, theologically sound.[157] Episcopal attitudes varied, but it was clear now that if the question was 'What must I believe to be saved?' different answers could be accepted. Certainly, the seven Oxford contributors to *Foundations: A Statement of Christian Belief in Terms of Modern Thought* (London, 1912) put forward rather different propositions.[158] 'Being saved', in any case, might be a matter of 'doing' rather than 'believing'. The combined impact of biblical scholarship and new scientific thinking had dissolved many certainties, even if, in relation to both, there was no consensus about their import.[159] It was far more urgent, wrote Flint in Edinburgh, to keep the leaders of thought in Germany, France and Britain Christian than to make those of Turkey, India or China Christian. The churches seemed to be more rapidly losing the former than gaining the latter.[160]

The precise implications of this state of affairs were uncertain. The dispute between 'the spirit' and 'the letter' as P.T. Forsyth put it, had now burned itself out in favour of the former. When it had been the letter which had been held in honour there had appeared to be something fixed but, with its defeat, it was unsatisfactory that the plea of 'spirituality' was being made to cover 'anything from inspiration to eccentricity'.[161] R.J. Campbell of the City Temple shot to fame as he proposed a 'New Theology' (1907) in which, he thought, the gospel of the Kingdom of God and the religion of science were combined. Religion was necessary to mankind but churches were not. Campbell's ethereal personality made a big impression on his congregations and, for a time, a 'New Theology' movement

---

[157] William Temple, *The Faith and Modern Thought* (London, 1910).

[158] See the discussion in Peter Hinchliff, *God and History: Aspects of British Theology 1875–1914* (Oxford, 1992), 233–41.

[159] W.B. Glover, *Evangelical Nonconformists and Higher Criticism in the Nineteenth Century* (London, 1954); D.N. Livingstone, *Darwin's Forgotten Defenders: The Encounter between Evangelical Theology and Evolutionary Thought* (Edinburgh, 1987); J.R. Moore, *The Post-Darwinian Controversies* (Cambridge, 1979); Martin Wellings, *Evangelicals Embattled: Responses of Evangelicals in the Church of England to Ritualism, Darwinism and Theological Liberalism 1890–1930* (Milton Keynes, 2003).

[160] Macmillan, *Robert Flint*, 492.

[161] P.T. Forsyth, *Faith, Freedom and the Future* (London, 1912).

swept the country.[162] The looseness of Campbell's terminology particularly upset theologians trained in Scotland. Bishop Gore published a firm rebuttal.[163] An analogy from photography sprang to the minds of critics. Campbell was 'over-exposed and under-developed'. That may indeed have been the case, but it was equally true that Campbell's language seemed to resonate with 'the public' where more orthodox formulations failed.

The search for something new, or at least the reformulation of something old, was not merely the final floundering of a Protestantism whose anchor had ceased to hold. The Jesuit George Tyrrell, born in Dublin the son of a Protestant journalist, who converted to Rome when he arrived in London at the age of eighteen, found himself, over time, increasingly impatient with his new church, as his writings revealed—though the impatience was mutual.[164] He was dismissed from the Jesuits in 1906 and forbidden to say Mass. Pius X, from the moment of his accession in 1903, was determined to stamp on 'modernism'. The movement in the church under that label, which originated in various European countries in 1890, was formally condemned in 1907 and may be said to have been snuffed out by 1910. When Tyrrell died in 1909, he was refused a Roman Catholic burial.[165] The language in which Pius X told priests that they should obey him (and the Vatican bureaucracy which acted in his name) without apparently setting any limits seemed 'monstrous' to Baron von Hügel.[166] Other Catholics, however, welcomed this papal display of intransigence. It might be the case that von Hügel, a Hampstead resident Austro-Scot, and his friends in London were devout and admirable people but 'modernism' would destroy the church.

Catholic Modernism, in its brief efflorescence, was not the same as Liberal Protestantism, yet Campbell, for one, recognized a fellow spirit in Tyrrell.[167] The City Temple minister thought that extreme anti-Romanist Protestants, who were amongst his critics, were in reality 'in the same boat with Rome'. Both of these camps wanted an external standard of belief—in either Bible or

---

[162] R.J. Campbell, *The New Theology* (London, 1907). Campbell was subsequently to become an Anglo-Catholic. *A Spiritual Pilgrimage* (London, 1916) is his autobiography. Keith Robbins, 'The Spiritual Pilgrimage of the Rev. R.J. Campbell' reprinted in Robbins, *History, Religion and Identity*, 133–47; Keith Clements, *Lovers of Discord: Twentieth Century Theological Controversies in England* (London, 1988) has a chapter on Campbell, as does Hinchliff, *God and History*, 198–222.

[163] Charles Gore, *The New Theology and the Old Religion* (London, 1907); J. Warschauer, *Problems of Immanence* (London, 1909).

[164] Nicholas Sagovsky, *On God's Side: A Life of George Tyrrell* (Oxford, 1990).

[165] A.R. Vidler, *The Modernist Movement in the Roman Church* (Cambridge, 1934) and *A Variety of Catholic Modernists* (Cambridge, 1970) and commentary in Hinchliff, *God and History*, 150–78.

[166] L.F. Barmann, *Baron Friedrich von Hügel and the Modernist Crisis in England* (Cambridge, 1972), 248.

[167] B.M.G. Reardon, ed., *Liberal Protestantism* (London, 1968), introduces and publishes selections of the writings of Ritschl, Herrmann, Sabatier, Réville and others who were much read at this time. Campbell, *New Theology*, 13.

church—but that was no longer available. So, how could 'religions of authority' and 'religion of the spirit' be reconciled?[168] Could one, somehow, be a 'Free Catholic'? A Welshman in Birmingham wanted 'the atmosphere and some of the human symbolism of Catholic piety' but Catholicism needed that piety corrected and purged 'in an austerer ethic of veracity'.[169] A combination of the two would be ideal. In the King's Weigh House (Congregational) in London, W.E. Orchard sought to combine evangelical and catholic practice in a way which he described as 'a revelation to many', but it could already be suspected, correctly, that he would eventually 'cross over' to Rome.[170]

The difficulties in relation to creeds were most acute in Scotland. The United Free Church, in the act of its creation, had taken the view that the church had absolute power over her creed. The continuing Free Church, however, held that loyalty to the creed defined what the church was. It was an issue which had led Christian men on the Isle of Arran to break into a United Free Church through a skylight and threaten the church officer with a revolver.[171] In 1904, though not held at gunpoint, the House of Lords ruled that the name and property of the Free Church belonged to the small minority which declined to enter the union. The consequences rumbled on. Trust Deeds, and the difficulties that accompanied them, made the United Free Church theologian James Denney in 1904 wish sometimes that he was 'a Quaker or a Congregationalist, and had only to believe in the gospel, and not in a creed at all'.[172] 'Declaratory Acts' passed by the United Presbyterian Church in 1879 and the Free Church in 1892 had allowed ministers, at their ordination, to affirm that the Westminster Confession expressed the 'essentials' of the faith. It was left to conscience to determine what the 'essentials' were. With its 1910 New Ordination Formula, the Church of Scotland also relaxed its terms of subscription to the Westminster Confession. It was perhaps salutary, amidst these controversies, to be reminded that God had revealed himself not to the theologian or philosopher but to fishermen

---

[168] Auguste Sabatier's *The Religions of Authority and the Religion of the Spirit* appeared in London in English translation in 1904.

[169] J.M. Lloyd Thomas, *A Free Catholic Church* (London, 1907), 6. Thomas was minister of the Old Meeting in the city. Elaine Kaye, 'Heirs of Richard Baxter? The Society of Free Catholics, 1914–1928', *Journal of Ecclesiastical History* 58/2 (2007), 232–55.

[170] W.E. Orchard, *From Faith to Faith* (London, 1933), 149.

[171] Kenneth R. Ross, *Church and Creed in Scotland: The Free Church Case 1900–1904 and its Origins* (Edinburgh, 1988); David M. Thompson, ' "Unrestricted Conference?" Myth and Reality in Scottish Ecumenism' in Stewart J. Brown and George Newlands, eds., *Scottish Christianity in the Modern World* (Edinburgh, 2000), 210–14.

[172] James Moffatt, ed., *Letters of Principal James Denney to his Family and Friends* (London, n.d.), 119: Denney, who had himself taken a First in Classics and Philosophy was certain that the words 'Christ died for our sins' constituted the central truth in the Christian religion. James Denney, *The Atonement and the Modern Mind* (London, 1903); Alan P.F. Sell, *Defending and Declaring the Faith: Some Scottish Examples 1860–1920* (Exeter, 1987), 212–13.

and peasants, as Tyrrell put it in 1891. However he was 'met', Jesus was the author and finisher of the faith.[173] An Orkney man, then ministering in Northumberland but later an academic eminence in Cambridge, pondering on the confused ecclesiastical scene, concluded that true unity in the church would never be found by attempting to go back. Contrasting the unity of a building with the uniformity of a quarry, it seemed wise to conclude that 'hasty endeavours after uniformity' would not succeed.[174]

viii. Kingdom in Trouble: Churches and Nations

The United Kingdom was also a building, but its structure was in difficulty. The return of Liberal governments after 1906, with their strong electoral support outside England and a galaxy of non-English Cabinet members, inevitably opened the way for the attempted resolution of 'Celtic' issues. Even Englishmen like Asquith and Churchill represented Scottish constituencies. The state, too, had to wrestle with unity.[175] If the task for the churches was at least to seek to build 'unity' from a condition of separation, the task for the state was perhaps to preserve its 'unity' by recognizing at least some element of separation. 'Home-Rule-All-Round', for example, might be a way of recognizing 'diversity-within-unity'.[176] The reality, too, was that these two processes were themselves by no means entirely distinct. Many of the issues already discussed in this chapter, it will have been noted, have been common across the British Isles. In this decade, however, additional attention has to be given to Ireland, Scotland and Wales because it was in these territories that 'religious' and 'national' issues intersected most closely and, potentially at least, most explosively.[177]

Ireland presented the most obvious example. Initially, just as the previous government had dallied with a scheme which was 'less than maintaining the Union pure and simple' so the Liberals, with James Bryce, the veteran Scoto-Ulster Presbyterian Chief Secretary, tried an Irish Councils scheme which could be represented as either a substitute for Home Rule or a step

---

[173] The introduction by F.C. Burkitt of Cambridge to the English translation of Albert Schweitzer's *The Quest for the Historical Jesus* (London, 1910) told readers to accept that the eschatology of the Christian gospel was historically the eschatology of Jesus. The *Hibbert Journal* had published a special supplement in 1909 in which fourteen writers of different persuasions addressed the question *Jesus or Christ?* See James Peter, *Finding the Historical Jesus* (London, 1965).

[174] John Oman, 'The True Unity' in his *Vision and Authority* (London, 1902).

[175] Keith Robbins 'Core and Periphery in Modern British History' reprinted in *History, Religion and Identity*, 239–58.

[176] J.E. Kendle, 'The Round Table Movement and Home-Rule-All-Round 1909–14', *Historical Journal* 11/2 (1968), 332–53 and *Ireland and the Federal Solution* (Kingston and Montreal, 1989) and *Federal Britain* (London, 1997).

[177] David Hempton, *Religion and Public Culture in Britain and Ireland: From the Glorious Revolution to the Decline of Empire* (Cambridge, 1996).

towards it.[178] It failed. After 1907, his successor embarked on a full measure of Home Rule (one which gave no special place to 'Ulster'). Detailed consideration of the complex politics of 'the Irish question', both at Westminster and in Ireland, in the years leading up to 1914 cannot be undertaken here.[179] What is material, however, is the extent to which it was a 'Church question'—on both sides of the Irish Sea. Enough has been said earlier about the turn-of-the-century ecclesiastical composition of the island of Ireland. Did Christian divisions cause, stiffen, sharpen, modify, underpin, or merely reflect a conflict which appeared likely to engulf Ireland, and possibly the British Isles, in what might be 'civil war'. For individuals and their 'communities', 'Catholic' and 'Protestant' labels covered a multiplicity of personal sentiments and alignments. The content of 'nationalism' is always protean. Was Catholicism inextricably bound up with a nationalism which could only be satisfied with 'Home Rule' or 'Independence'? Was Protestantism likewise inextricably bound up with another nationalism which wanted neither?[180] Behind the debate lay contested issues of power and status, of conquest and settlement, of the 'right to belong', of 'racial equality'. What place expressed the 'essential Ireland'?[181] Was 'Ulster' no place at all, but only a 'delusion of the mind'?[182] A view of 'Ulster' could be projected in which Catholics were not visible.[183] A view of 'Ireland' could also be projected in Irish nationalist writing in which Protestants were not visible.[184] Some could portray Catholicism as 'natural' and 'permanent' whereas Protestantism was seen as 'unnatural' and 'temporary'. Stereotypes abounded on all sides. Popular demagogues in the north were able to fulminate against Catholicism before an expanded

[178] D.G. Boyce, *The Irish Question and British Politics 1868–1986* (London, 1988), 38. Not that there had ever been anything 'pure and simple' about the government of Ireland under the Union. Alan J. Ward, 'A Constitutional Background to the Northern Ireland Crisis' in Dermot Keogh and Michael H. Haltzel, eds., *Northern Ireland and the Politics of Reconciliation* (Cambridge, 1993), 35–6.

[179] Patricia Jalland, *The Liberals and Ireland: The Ulster Question in British Politics to 1914* (Brighton, 1980); A.T.Q. Stewart, *The Ulster Crisis* (London, 1967); Stephen Howe, *Ireland and Empire: Colonial Legacies in Irish History and Culture* (Oxford, 2000).

[180] Whether the unionism of Ulster constitutes 'nationalism' is much debated in the relevant literature.

[181] Brian Graham, ed., *In Search of Ireland: A Cultural Geography* (London, 1997).

[182] Brian Graham, 'Ulster: A Representation of Place Yet to be Imagined', in P. Shirlow and M. McGovern, eds., *Who are 'The People'? Unionism, Protestantism and Loyalism in Northern Ireland* (London, 1997), 34–54.

[183] J.J. Lee, *Ireland, 1912–1985: Politics and Society* (Cambridge, 1989), 1–6, presents a picture of a Protestant *Herrenvolk* dedicated to sustaining a sense of racial superiority. It has been pointed out, however, that he makes no allowance for the obverse side of supremacy, namely fear and insecurity—'a precarious belonging'. Patrick Mitchel, *Evangelicalism and National Identity in Ulster 1921–1998* (Oxford, 2003), 40. The turn of the century had seen Catholics outnumbering Protestants in talismanic Derry/Londonderry. One source of the fear was the Catholic sectarian secret society, the Ancient Order of Hibernians.

[184] Marianne Elliott, *The Catholics of Ulster* (London, 2000), 367.

electorate.[185] Henry Montgomery, the Presbyterian moderator, in 1912 pointed to the threats to religious liberty from Home Rule: nationalist assurances were 'not worth the breath used in speaking of them or the ink required to write them'.[186] C.F. D'Arcy, the new Anglican bishop of Down, a philosopher not given to using words lightly, stressed that behind Ulster's opposition to Home Rule there was an immensely strong conviction which was 'essentially religious'.[187] He had apparently taken this view without consulting his fellow bishops. This was just the man to represent the Church of Ireland bishops at the coronation of George V.[188] The Anglican bishop of Cork, however, took the view that the Anglican laity in the South objected 'to being identified in any way with the Ulster movement'.[189] Exclusive noise in Ulster might possibly scupper Home Rule, but it might also, eventually, result in an Ulster 'exclusion' which would leave Southern Irish Protestants as a small minority under a Dublin Parliament. After the Liberals introduced the Home Rule Bill in April 1912—the Parliament Act made passage through the Lords ultimately inevitable—most adult Ulster Protestant males, nearly half a million men, pledged themselves to a 'Solemn League and Covenant' which would resist the authority of Westminster. Use of the term 'covenant' in this context was deliberate, because of its both Scottish and biblical resonances.[190] According to a former Presbyterian moderator, Christ had bestowed a priceless gift of spiritual liberty which 'Rome rule' would jeopardize. There would be no surrender. The Ulster Volunteer Force would soon be armed with guns brought in from Germany. That was evidently one way of bolstering that humble reliance on the God of their fathers expressed in the Covenant. Belfast, though not all of Belfast, sang 'O God our help in ages past'.

[185] J.W. Boyle, 'The Belfast Protestant Association and the Independent Orange Order', *Irish Historical Studies* 13 (1962), 117–52.

[186] Cited in R.F.G. Holmes, ' "Ulster Will Fight and Ulster Will be Right": The Protestant Churches and Ulster's Resistance to Home Rule, 1912–1914', in W.J. Sheils, ed., *The Church and War*, Studies in Church History 20 (Oxford, 1983), 321–36. See also his 'Ulster Presbyterianism and Irish Nationalism' in S. Mews, ed., *Religion and National Identity*, Studies in Church History 18 (Oxford, 1982), 535–48. The most conspicuous Presbyterian ministerial Home Ruler was the Revd J.B. Armour of Ballymoney, but he was exceptional. R.B. McMinn, *Against the Tide: J.B. Armour, Irish Presbyterian Minister and Home Ruler* (Belfast, 1985).

[187] Cited in Megahey, *Irish Protestant Churches*, 30.

[188] C.F. D'Arcy, *Adventures of a Bishop* (London, 1934). It was when he became bishop of Clogher in 1903 that he records himself as having first come into contact with the intellectual and spiritual life of the Church of England. He moved from there to Ossory, Ferns and Leighlin 'one of the most beautiful parts of our country' before briefly becoming archbishop of Dublin and then moving to Armagh in 1920.

[189] Cited in R.B. McDowell, *The Church of Ireland, 1869–1969* (London, 1975), 104.

[190] Christopher Harvie, however, sees the reinvoking of the Covenant as 'a publicity stunt, thought up in a London club, rather than any radical outburst against the abuse of parliamentary sovereignty'. 'The Covenanting Tradition' in Graham Walker and Tom Gallagher, eds., *Sermons and Battle Hymns: Protestant Popular Culture in Modern Scotland* (Edinburgh, 1990), 17. See also Steve Bruce, 'The Ulster Connection', 231–55 in the same collection.

So, perhaps religion was indeed the heart of the matter.[191] It was rather extraordinary that at this juncture the Leader of the Opposition was Andrew Bonar Law, born in Canada but brought up in Glasgow—with Ulster forebears. He attended the massive parade and service at Balmoral (outside Belfast) on Easter Tuesday 1912. He was not an Englishman. However, even so, on his return to London, he wrote that the demonstration had been a big surprise. It might seem 'strange to you and me, but it is a religious question'. The people were in serious earnest and were prepared to die for their convictions. It rather seemed as though London-based ministers had lost an ability to reckon with religion as an independent variable. Three months later, at a gathering at Blenheim Palace in Oxfordshire, however, Bonar Law made a ringing declaration that he could not imagine any length of resistance to which Ulster could go which he would not support. He believed that in doing so he would be supported 'by the overwhelming majority of the British people'. In the event, that contention was never put to the test.

If the strangeness of Ulster to a Bonar Law lay in its being 'a religious question' one might think *a fortiori* that this was the case for Englishmen who lacked his peripheral antennae. The 'Britishness' of Ulster was as problematic in Britain as it was in Ulster itself.[192] The rituals of Orangeism, although still more Anglican than Presbyterian, even when they made an appearance in Glasgow or Liverpool, seemed exotic from 'middle' England.[193] When the (English) President of the Wesleyan Conference reached Belfast to preside over the Irish conference he found Methodist opinion sharply divided, largely on generational lines. He feared that the church was going to be set ablaze 'with unholy fire'. Differences at the gathering were not extinguished but it was held by Irish Methodists that it was the moderating influence of an Englishman which changed the atmosphere.[194] The 'Glorious Twelfth' had little resonance in Great Britain as a whole.[195] Certainly, Irish Protestants, by correspondence and publications, sought to enlist that support from quarters across the water likely to be sympathetic. The virtues of Protestantism were still not without some appeal in Britain. An Edinburgh publisher brought out a work which looked at the *Los von Rom-Bewegung* ('Away from Rome movement') occurring in some

---

[191] It is a question, of course, on which different views have continued to be offered ever since. Some writers cannot believe that 'antediluvian religious discourse' is really significant. 'Religion' must just be a cover for ethnic or economic conflict. Other writers who do not believe that all religious discourse is antediluvian believe, nevertheless, that in this instance 'religion' has long since been corrupted by its ethnic entanglement and its essence strangled.

[192] J. Loughlin, *Ulster Unionism and British National Identity since 1885* (London, 1995).

[193] Ruth Dudley Edwards, *The Faithful Tribe: An Intimate Portrait of the Loyal Institutions* (London, 1999). When Sir Edward Carson, the Dubliner who led Ulster Unionism, came to speak in Glasgow, only 8,000 people turned up, whereas 150,000 did when he spoke in Liverpool.

[194] Jackson, *Collier of Manchester*, 178–80. He had noted, of course, that 'these Irishmen are feeling very deeply on this Home Rule question'.

[195] S.S. Larsen, 'The Glorious Twelfth: A Ritual Expression of Collective Identity', in A.P. Cohen, ed., *Belonging: Identity and Social Organization in British Rural Cultures* (Manchester, 1982).

parts of Europe. Even in Ireland, the more intelligent Roman Catholics, it was claimed, were waking to a knowledge of the evil influences of Rome. They could see that to put their country under the feet of the Roman priest-hood would be 'a disaster of appalling magnitude'.[196] Yet an emblematic Protestantism as 'British national' might not be sufficient to move most Eng-lishmen to go to 'any length' to support 'Protestant Ulster'.[197] Besides, under such a description, a conflict might exacerbate and inflame Protestant–Catholic relationships throughout Britain itself. It is no surprise, therefore, that the archbishop of Canterbury was busily meeting and corresponding with both Asquith and Bonar Law in the spring of 1914.[198] Exclusion of Ulster from Irish Home Rule, at least temporarily, might be the answer—if such an 'Ulster' could be acceptably defined. The issue was no less problematic for the arch-bishop of Westminster, given the size of his Irish-descended flock (though the two archbishops were not on such terms as would enable them to share their anxieties with each other).

The possibility of conflict spreading was perhaps most acute in Scotland. Perhaps 10 per cent of the Scottish population at the turn of the century was Roman Catholic—heavily concentrated in the dioceses of Glasgow, Mother-well and Paisley. Although Italians, Poles and Lithuanians had added to the mix, the community's collective identity remained Irish.[199] But not all the Scottish Irish were Catholic. At the Convention in Belfast in 1912 an Edin-burgh minister expressed solidarity with Irish Protestants in their quest to avert 'a great calamity to their beloved Emerald Isle'. The Glasgow *Herald* thought that if 'Glasgow and Clydeside' ever found itself in the same position as 'our kinsfolk' across the Irish Channel it would react as they were doing. Yet despite the resolutions and the rhetoric, the 'common agenda' should not be exag-gerated. Scottish Presbyterians, it was noted, would sympathize with their Irish brethren but that might not be sufficient to divert them from liberalism. It was also a little awkward to talk about Home Rule as weakening the Empire when some of those who favoured Home Rule for Scotland said it would do no such thing. There was also, for some, the galling spectacle of a Scottish Presbyterian winning Derry City at a parliamentary by-election in January 1913 on a Home Rule platform.[200] Things were never quite as straightforward as they seemed.

[196] John A. Bain, *The New Reformation: Recent Evangelical Movements in the Roman Catholic Church* (Edinburgh, 1906), 4.

[197] John Wolffe, 'Change and Continuity in British Anti-Catholicism, 1829–92' in Frank Tallett and Nicholas Atkin, eds., *Catholicism in Britain and France since 1789* (London, 1996).

[198] Bell, *Davidson*, 720–30.

[199] Irene Maver, 'The Catholic Community' in T.M. Devine and R.J. Finlay, eds., *Scotland in the Twentieth Century* (Edinburgh, 1996), 269–84.

[200] These matters are discussed further in Graham Walker, *Intimate Strangers: Political and Cultural Relations between Scotland and Ulster in Modern Times* (Edinburgh, 1995), 36–46. The interpreter of Presbyterian opinion was William Whitelaw, Chairman of the Highland Railway. He would never have envisaged that his son, whom he sent to be educated at Winchester, would one day become a Secretary of State for Northern Ireland.

The 'religious issue' in Ireland, in its political dimension, was primarily played out between England, Ireland and Scotland. In Wales, as the campaign for disestablishment of the Church of England in Wales moved to its climax and when success at last seemed politically achievable—the Bill had just been introduced by the Home Secretary, McKenna (who sat in the Commons for Monmouthshire). This was hardly a moment at which to seek to mobilize pan-Protestant expressions of solidarity with Irish Protestantism. The monster demonstration in Swansea, itself the climax of two massive processions, addressed by Lloyd George in May 1912 was focused on Wales, not Ireland. Banners proclaimed 'A Wronged Nation Demands Redress' and, perhaps more optimistically, 'Religious Equality'. Students at St David's College, Lampeter, in a daring raid, had denuded the 'sandwich van' of its stock of leaflets advertising the demonstration, as a counter-protest.[201] The Royal Commission on the Church (1906–10) was testimony to the centrality which the question was still supposed to hold in Wales. Its report produced the customary argument over numbers, but now, 'by a supreme effort', campaigners thought success was going to be achieved. Speeches by the archbishop of Canterbury, whether delivered in Caernarfon—following up, at a decent interval, a visit to Wales made by a predecessor in 1282—or in the Albert Hall, in London, were not going to stop it. Neither, in the end, because of the Parliament Act, could the House of Lords. Four Welsh dioceses, as they saw it, were unhappily prised away from the bosom of Canterbury into an uncertain future, though still one which was to be delayed by the outbreak of war. A Wales basking, apparently, in a glorious unity of nation, Nonconformity and the Liberal Party—no Tory MP had been elected in Wales in 1906—was not going to start marching under Bonar Law's Tory banner, even for Ulster's Protestants.[202]

Such self-absorption should not lead to the supposition of Welsh indifference to the deficiencies of Roman Catholicism, even if militant Protestant organizations had not recruited substantially in Wales in the previous century.[203] Firm adherence to 'Protestant values' was proclaimed,

---

[201] Neil Evans, ' "A Nation in a Nutshell": The Swansea Disestablishment Demonstration of 1912 and the Political Culture of Edwardian Wales' in R.R. Davies and Geraint H. Jenkins, eds., *From Medieval to Modern Wales* (Cardiff, 2004), 214–29.

[202] The bishop of St Asaph stated that he was half English and half Welsh and that he had been 'labouring' between the two all his life. His 'identity problem' has been held to constitute the basis for the 'out-and-out war against popular Nonconformity and the voluntary, democratic and proletarian Welsh-speaking culture from which it had grown'. Densil Morgan, ' "The Essence of Welshness"? Some Aspects of Christian Faith and National Identity in Wales, *c.*1900–2000' in Robert Pope, ed., *Religion and National Identity: Wales and Scotland c. 1700–2000* (Cardiff, 2001), 144.

[203] The exact nature of anti-Catholicism in Wales in the twentieth century and its relationship to the previous century is the subject of a vigorous exchange. Tristan Owain Hughes, 'Anti-Catholicism in Wales, 1900–1960', *Journal of Ecclesiastical History* 53/2 (2002), 312–25 is challenged by Paul O'Leary, 'When was Anti-Catholicism? The Case of Nineteenth- and Twentieth-Century Wales', *Journal of Ecclesiastical History* 56/2 (2005), 308–33.

[Territorial Army], whose chaplain he had been since his installation in 1901. Urged by the commanding officer to 'put a little ginger' into his sermon on the subsequent Sunday, the bishop obliged: 'We would all rather die, wouldn't we, than have England a German province?' Men let out a low growl of assent and immediately volunteered to fight overseas. His message over the new few months was clear and uncomplicated: national freedom, national honour and national faith formed an inseparable trinity. His flock recognized and responded to their bishop's unquenchable adolescence as he developed his themes in a series of public addresses.[2]

It could not be said that the possibility of war had altogether eluded the episcopate. Cosmo Gordon Lang, made archbishop of York in 1909 at the age of 44, had had a dream, earlier on in 1914, in which war had broken out with Germany. In the dream, he had been summoned to Lambeth Palace. Davidson told him that five thousand German women had landed on the Essex coast. Clergy, with the archbishops at their head, had then processed out of London to urge the invaders 'by moral suasion' to turn back. The women, it seems, were disinclined to do so. At which, when one of his clergy cried, 'Let's get at 'em!', the archbishop awoke from his dream. Interpreting dreams, perhaps particularly archiepiscopal ones, is never easy. Few commentators in the press, even those most apprehensive about German aims, had been predicting an Amazonian advance-guard. The archbishop's dream, however, is at least evidence of the subliminal extent to which it was not only *National Review* which had Germany 'on the brain'.[3]

Decades earlier, visiting Germany after coming down from Oxford, the Glaswegian Lang, son of a moderator of the General Assembly of the Church of Scotland, had found many Germans amiable and hospitable. He had enjoyed talking a sort of German. But that had been a quarter of a century ago. The world had apparently changed, as had his own life. He had succeeded Winnington-Ingram as bishop of Stepney in 1901 on the latter's translation to London. It was a remarkable progress for a young man who had professed himself as an undergraduate at Oxford 'wholly ignorant of English ecclesiastical affairs', a condition which apparently made it possible for him, though unconfirmed, to receive Holy Communion in the Church of England.

Now, at this hour of crisis, with his fellow Scot, and fellow ex-Presbyterian, the archbishop of Canterbury, he would have to say what 'England expected'. His house guests at Bishopthorpe Palace spent the weekend before the British declaration of war in deep discussion. Lang was 'harried with anxiety' about what he should say and do and took himself off to Cuddesdon—the theological college outside Oxford—to consider his

[2] S.C. Carpenter, *Winnington-Ingram: The Biography of Arthur Foley Winnington-Ingram, Bishop of London 1901–1939* (London, 1949), 282–3, 292–301.

[3] J.G. Lockhart, *Cosmo Gordon Lang* (London, 1949), 245.

stance. Concluding that the church could not rightly oppose the war, he threw himself into the recruiting campaign, addressing meetings in most of the cities and larger towns of his diocese.

Davidson at Lambeth Palace was now 65, seasoned in diplomacy and at ease in office after eleven years, although in gloomier moments he felt that 'nobody cared a rap about anything I said about anything in heaven and earth'. The 'battlefield', to use his word, which chiefly engaged his attention in the last week of July 1914, had little connection with the enveloping European crisis. The Lambeth Conference Consultative Body had been meeting to ponder the vexed issue of 'intercommunion' arising out of the 'Kikuyu' affair in 1913. At breakfast on 31 July, however, Davidson took an unexpected telephone call. A young man felt war was certain and wanted to be married immediately before he went off to fight. The wedding took place two days later. Something was happening which might even make the 'Kikuyu' question seem of secondary importance. And indeed, even Frank Weston, bishop of Zanzibar, who had raised that storm, was shortly to turn his attention to enrolling puzzled African recruits to fight in East Africa for British civilization against German civilization.

i. Imminent (Religious?) War: Ireland

The intensification of the European crisis to the imminent point of war did indeed come as a shock, but Davidson had been well aware that the political scene was uncertain. All sorts of things appeared to be coming to a head. Whatever happened in continental Europe, the United Kingdom itself—or at least Ireland—might be on the brink of civil war. It was indeed the bitter polarization of opinion in Ireland, replicated in the conflict between the Liberal government under Asquith and the Unionists led by Bonar Law, which was uppermost in the archbishop's mind. The country was at 'a crisis hour', he had written to *The Times* in March 1914, and he had come privately to the conclusion that 'with respect to the political deadlock' he ought actively to attempt to break it. He had a series of meetings with Asquith and Bonar Law and acted as something of a go-between. Defining the area of Ireland which might be 'excluded', with whatever time-limit, from a 'Home Rule Ireland' would obviously be difficult, yet it seemed to be the only solution. Speaking in the House of Lords on 8 July, Davidson urged that exclusion should be on the basis of geography and not by distinguishing Protestant- from Catholic-inhabited areas. King George V summoned a conference of all sides at Buckingham Palace to try to find a way forward, but it collapsed on 24 July.[4]

---

[4] G.K.A. Bell, *Randall Davidson: Archbishop of Canterbury* (London, 1952 edn.), 720–30.

The Home Rule Bill was indeed enacted in September 1914—with its exclusion of 'Ulster'—but was suspended for the duration of the war. (The act disestablishing the Church of England in Wales was similarly suspended.) In seeking a territorial exclusion of Ulster on the basis of geography, the archbishop had been seeking to avoid its resulting character being perceived as 'Protestant'. He did not succeed. In these circumstances, to apply the terminology of 'Protestant' and 'Catholic', in apparent confrontation, could not be avoided. Davidson was well aware of the extent to which the supposed coherence of 'Ulster' as 'Protestant' would marginalize Protestants in the rest of Ireland—an anxiety most naturally felt by Southern Protestants.

It remained difficult for visitors from England to grasp the meanings attached to the words Protestant and Catholic. The 15th of June had found the dean of Durham, Hensley Henson, visiting the great shipbuilding works of Messrs Clarke & Co. in Belfast. He had come to preach in the new Church of Ireland cathedral which was being built in the city. He realized that the situation in the North had reached 'a critical stage' and found his feelings to be 'mixed'. He combined, or so he thought, a long-standing sympathy for Irish patriotic aspirations with a belief that the Unionist case against the Home Rule Bills was 'irresistible'. He understood, and largely shared, the distrust of the Roman Catholic Church which he found in his conversations. On his return to England, he wrote a letter to *The Times* on 23 June stating that Home Rule was an impracticable policy. Rhetorically, it might sound appealing, but it could be implemented only at a cost ruinously great alike to Ireland itself and to the British Empire. He had returned home in no doubt that the men he had met in Belfast were serious. He concluded that the question was mainly 'religious'. Nothing would induce them to accept 'a supremacy of the Papists'.[5]

That Henson placed inverted commas around 'religious' is significant. It reflected a continuing uncertainty, at the height of the crisis, as to its fundamental nature. Was it 'religious' or 'political'? Where did 'ecclesiastical' and 'national' sentiments begin and end? It might be theoretically possible to distinguish one from the other but perhaps only in theory. The dean of Canterbury, the evangelical Dr Wace, had lent his name to a 'national appeal' launched in London in March in which the signatories had demanded a dissolution of Parliament. They further declared that if the Home Rule Bill were passed without being put to the electorate they would support any action which might prevent its implementation. Davidson had enough personal history in his veins to know how far unity/disunity in the Christian church marched in tandem with unity/disunity in the United

[5] H. Hensley Henson, *Retrospect of an Unimportant Life*, vol. i (Oxford, 1942), 170–3.

Kingdom. There did not exist a sufficient consensus within Ireland, as events were demonstrating, for the Irish people to make a Home Rule Ireland viable and successful. It would not, of course, be an independent state, though it might irreversibly lead to one.

The mood in Ireland was shifting in the opposite direction. Ireland could not see itself as a 'partner' in a common project which was 'the United Kingdom'. Foreigners always knew where the weak spot of the United Kingdom was. When Winnington-Ingram, on a visit to Moscow in 1908, ventured a few critical remarks in conversation with the Tsar about Russian conditions, he found himself, in turn, having to defend British policy in Ireland. 'Time', some suggested, would not heal British–Irish relations. It was the differing approaches to 'time' which made it so difficult for the two peoples to get on. For 'the Irish', time past was always more potent, in the present, than it was for 'the English'.[6] The former saw history as a kind of perpetual oscillation between coercion and conciliation, between negotiation and the threat of violence. The latter saw it as a steady path of improvement, whether identified with the march of reason or moral benevolence. Both Irish Protestants and Irish Catholics shared this view of the past (though canonizing and celebrating different events and dates for the purpose). A gulf separated the two islands.

The archbishop, nevertheless, continued to offer himself as 'non-partisan' but he could be of little help in grappling with the deeper connotations of the crisis. 'The Christian church' could not offer a way out since the chasm which evidently separated 'Catholic' and 'Protestant' was a central feature of the political struggle. It was not a 'purely' religious conflict—if such conflicts ever exist—but neither was religion an insignificant element in the cluster of values, beliefs and attitudes which were held to define the ethnicities and nations of the British Isles. How these elements were reconciled naturally varied in individual instances but the burden of the past seemed to be imposing a 'package' which was communal. The prime minister had authority in, and operated over, the whole United Kingdom in a 'British' party system, although the Home Rule party had come to be a majority in Ireland. The archbishop of Canterbury had no such United Kingdom ecclesiastical authority or operational base. Indeed, having lost the battle in Wales, he would soon 'lose' Wales. After the war, there would be an archbishop of Wales and a new province of the Anglican Communion. Nor could he speak for Scottish Episcopalians—though they were, admittedly, the least weighty Anglican presence in the four territories of the United Kingdom. Only in England was Canterbury's authority

---

[6] Oliver MacDonagh, *States of Mind* (London, 1983), 6–7; Stephen Howe, *Ireland and Empire: Colonial Legacies in Irish History and Culture* (Oxford, 2000), 94–5.

direct, notwithstanding his status within the world-wide Anglican Communion. That it should fall to a Scot to preside over this final contraction of the Church of England to England was a piquant accident. It was also an accident that at the height of the political conflict 'Glasgow' (Bonar Law) and 'Edinburgh' (Davidson) were in conversation, a circumstance not always productive of healing outcomes. It was impossible to say what an 'Anglican' pan-insular view on the United Kingdom crisis might be. No mechanism existed whereby it could be formulated.

This was even more true when all the churches of Britain and Ireland are considered: the notion of an ecclesiastical 'Buckingham Palace Conference' was inconceivable. There was no standing forum which brought together the leaders of its ecclesiastical groupings on a regular pan-insular basis. The perceptions each held of the other, with only rare exceptions, were not explored in dialogue but were reinforced within the respective denominational and national structures. On all sides, they continued to draw heavily on persecuted pasts and derive satisfaction from maintaining a sacred and untarnished deposit of faith—be it Catholic or Protestant: the scene, after all, was a competitive one. Their networks were quite different and it was only occasionally that churchmen found themselves in the same room. Use of 'Christian names' between them was strictly rationed. Yet, something was happening. In September 1913, Davidson privately noted that contemporary religion in Britain found natural expression 'in a more dramatic, aesthetic, symbolic form than was habitual a generation ago'. This was not simply the outcome of the Oxford Movement in the Church of England. Scottish Presbyterians or English Baptists, he thought, were quite as Protestant as they used to be but in their worship and demeanour they were drawing on 'the general aestheticism of the time'.[7] Doctrinal convergence might be still far away but the spirit of the age was at work. He felt himself to have 'contributed steadily and with considerable effect to the maintenance of a reasonably comprehensive spirit in our Church's polity'. From across the water, however, England could present 'a sorry spectacle' to a Catholic priest in Ulster. It was a battleground for sects. The English people, robbed of their priceless inheritance of Catholic Faith, were running after every form of human error. Catholic Ireland would hold the fort against their disturbing influences and dissolving, not to say dissolute, tendencies.

The litany of the past, therefore, remained powerfully present. The terms on which a 'union' of Christians might be contemplated or dismissed, or on which a United Kingdom might be maintained or broken up, were not dissimilar. 'No surrender' could be heard in many quarters. The struggle for

[7] Melanie Barber, ed., 'Randall Davidson: A Partial Retrospective' in Stephen Taylor, ed., *From Cranmer to Davidson: A Miscellany*, Church of England Record Society 7 (Woodbridge, 1999), 437 n.

hegemony, whether conceived as 'religious', 'national' or 'cultural/linguistic' or, in many instances, a bewildering fusion of all these elements, was clearly in evidence. The struggle, however, did not in the end turn into an internal pan-insular battle in summer 1914. The advent of the European war subdued but, as events were to show, did not eliminate the areas of internal tension. Indeed, though now in a European and even global context, all these elements were again in play. The stakes, it seemed, could not be higher.

ii. War, 1914: Church and State 'Shoulder to Shoulder'

As the European crisis unfolded in parallel with the Irish crisis (the latter for a time seemingly being more grave than the former) the British Cabinet wrestled with its own course of action. If the country was to go to war it should do so, as far as possible, unitedly. In so far as 'public opinion' mattered, it would have been significant if, collectively, all the churches had publicly opposed intervention. There is no record, however, to suggest that individual members of the Cabinet, in considering their positions, thought such a stance likely. Politicians were left to ponder whether, without a formal alliance, the United Kingdom had 'obligations of honour' to France. Church leaders were not privy to the details of diplomacy or the calculations of the military. Statecraft, in any case, was a matter for statesmen. The archbishop of Canterbury nevertheless saw the prime minister privately on 31 July. Davidson had been asked to endorse a memorial being drawn up by some Liberal MPs in favour of non-intervention but he wanted to know first whether the government would find it 'helpful and not harmful'. The prime minister said that it would be harmful. Asquith further commented generally on the position. The scene, he said, were it not so tragic, was almost ludicrous. Europe was in crisis because of the vagaries of a wild little state like Serbia, a country for which nobody had a good word. France, Russia and still more Germany, he supposed, were averse to going to war. It was vital, however, Asquith stated, not to enable the military party in Germany to say that England would not intervene. If that came to be believed, it might precipitate an attack on France through Belgium. For this reason, the prime minister urged the archbishop to do all he could to prevent demonstrations or memorials opposing intervention. Davidson agreed to preach in Westminster Abbey as a means, hopefully, of preventing a general sense of confusion and even panic.[8]

Opinion in the Cabinet shifted and swayed. There might be significant resignations. The Liberal government might not be able to carry on. And if

---

[8] Bell, *Davidson*, 733–5.

the government split, so might the country at large. A country divided would not be an effective belligerent. In the event, however, few resigned and the government carried on. In the Commons, on 3 August, the foreign secretary, Sir Edward Grey, made it clear that peace could no longer be preserved. He urged the House to approach the crisis 'from the point of view of British interests, British honour, and British obligations'. Matters had gone far beyond the original quarrel between Austria and Serbia. He suggested that the United Kingdom would suffer terribly even if it stood aside (from the collapse of trade). In placing that suffering more or less on a par with the suffering which joining the war would bring, Grey revealed that he had little conception of what lay ahead. He was, of course, not alone. With the exception of the mid-century battles in the distant Crimea, it had been a century since British troops had fought on the European continent. How long would the war last? How great would be the number of casualties? Where would it be fought and by what means? Nobody knew the answers.

A foreign secretary, at such a juncture, naturally based his argument on what he conceived to be British interests, British honour and British obligations. There could be, and indeed were, arguments in the House of Commons that he had misinterpreted them, but policy could not have any other basis. The archbishop heard Grey speak in the Commons and came away convinced that no other course was possible. Two days later he spoke in the House of Lords. The country should try together to face the inevitable difficulties 'standing shoulder to shoulder'. He was recognizing that he lived in a world of sovereign states. The purpose of diplomacy was to reconcile their respective interests, honour and obligations, but it could not invariably succeed. If it did not, despite allusions to the 'Concert of Europe', there was no detached and independent arbiter available to resolve conflicts. States went to war, as they had always done, from a mixture of fear and ambition. That was the way of the world.

It was the world in which the churches had to exist. They were part of the fabric of the state, as the United Kingdom crisis was itself demonstrating. Yet, however firmly embedded in constitutional or cultural structures they were, they professed not to be confined by them. Although in 1914, in two of the United Kingdom's territories, there were 'state churches', the churches did not profess a 'state religion'. Their 'Christianity' was 'universal'. No doubt, through time, they had 'compromised' and one might speak loosely of 'English religion' but it was not a national ideology existing in insular isolation. Davidson knew that Charles Gore was unhappy when he spoke of 'the National character of the Church of England', but the expression, he thought, was simply a harmless fact. The Christianity of the peoples of the United Kingdom, it was difficult not to believe, had been an element in their global 'success'—a position which in 1914 might be explained by referring to 'manifest destiny' or 'the design of Providence'.[9]

British interests, honour and obligations, at this juncture, therefore sprang from such an ambience. Sir Edward Grey, a Wykehamist and Balliol man, may have been Wordsworthian in outlook, but his grandfather, born in Gibraltar, had been a member of the committee of the Church Missionary Society and of the British and Foreign Bible Society. The foreign secretary, bird lover and fly fisherman was the very epitome of an English gentleman.[10] A young soldier with the Argyll and Sutherland Highlanders, who came from a long line of eminent Church of Scotland ministers, but also educated at Winchester and Oxford, could not have put it better when he wrote home from the trenches in France in 1915: 'The more one sees of other countries, of other interests, and the ideals of other people, the more one realizes what a splendid type the *Britisher* is . . . no superficiality, just *genuine* and there's nothing finer in the world than "the real thing".'[11] Young George MacLeod, subsequently awarded the Military Cross, was a little sad, however, that there weren't quite enough Britishers to go round. Such a sense of cultural solidarity to be found in the 'establishment', both political and ecclesiastical, rendered implausible any notion that collectively 'the churches' might take a stance which self-consciously and deliberately placed them in opposition to the course on which the government embarked.

Moreover, the likelihood of 'Church' and 'Chapel' reacting differently was reduced because it was a Liberal government which was going to war. It was as close to being 'their own' as Nonconformists were likely to have. The European war was not a further piece of British imperial expansion. Significant figures in its ranks, even the prime minister himself, had a purchase on Nonconformity. Lloyd George, chancellor of the exchequer, but latterly given to making pronouncements on international issues, knew the language which a Nonconformist audience would need to hear. He soon found an opportunity to speak in the City Temple. A man who had once opposed the Boer War was surely to be believed.

However doubtfully a Baptist, Lloyd George was indubitably Welsh. London Welshmen had been present in his audience to hear that Belgium, like Wales, was a small nation. The 'hulking bully' that was Germany would have to be fought. Nonconformist ministers back home in Gwynedd opined that to take up arms was 'a sacred calling'. The princes of the pulpit had no qualms about becoming recruiting officers. In due time,

[9] Stewart J. Brown, *Providence and Empire* (London, 2007).

[10] Keith Robbins, *Sir Edward Grey: A Biography of Lord Grey of Fallodon* (London, 1971), 2–17.

[11] Ronald Ferguson, *George MacLeod: Founder of the Iona Community* (London, 1990), 36.

Lloyd George was able to create the 38th (Welsh) Division commanded by an Anglesey Congregationalist, the only senior Welsh-speaking officer in the regular army.[12] There was little sign of dissent in the Church of Scotland either. The minister of St Giles, Edinburgh claimed on 9 August that the church stood 'as we have always stood, for the great apostolic principles of humanity, patriotism, loyalty, and religion'.[13] Speaking as the moderator at the 1915 General Assembly, he reiterated that the nation had entered the war conscious that if it had not done so it would stand as a criminal before God.[14] By the same year, it was calculated that around 90 per cent of 'sons of the manse' had volunteered and their fathers were already mourning losses. The prominence of non-English figures in the government, together with such recent Dundonians as Winston Churchill, gave the decision to go to war a 'United Kingdom' character, though it is evident that little prompting was really needed. Even John Redmond, the leader of the Irish Home Rule Party, declared that Britain was fighting 'in defence of right, of freedom and of religion'. He, like many others, supposed that the war would not last long. In the context of the Irish situation Redmond's stance was a gamble.[15] He was buttressed, if that is the word, by firm support from the Church of Ireland hierarchy. In appealing for recruits, J.H. Bernard, the newly appointed archbishop of Dublin, took the view that the war would make the great realities of life stand out in bold relief. Religion, he said, would again become a great factor in human life: a little later, he lost his own son at Gallipoli.[16] Presbyterian ministers were no less committed. The Ulster Volunteer Force, which formed the new 36th (Ulster) Division, found itself fighting in Flanders, not in Ulster. It was even possible to have a 'selfish and petty' sense of relief that the 'lurid cloud hanging over Europe' had burst and, apparently, taken Irish minds away from Irish issues.[17]

---

[12] D. Densil Morgan, *The Span of the Cross: Christian Religion and Society in Wales, 1914–2000* (Cardiff, 1999), 41–4.

[13] Cited in S.J. Brown, ' "A Solemn Purification by Fire": Responses to the Great War in the Scottish Presbyterian Churches, 1914–19', *Journal of Ecclesiastical History* 45/1 (1994), 90. Similar sentiments, also cited in this article, emerged from the other Presbyterian churches. See also P. Matheson, 'Scottish War Sermons', *Records of the Scottish Church History Society* 17 (1972), 203–13; S.D. Hendry, 'Scottish Baptists and the First World War', *Baptist Quarterly* 31 (1985), 52–65.

[14] Dr Wallace Williamson cited in A.C. Cheyne, *The Transforming of the Kirk* (Edinburgh, 1983), 181.

[15] J.J. Lee, *Ireland 1912–1985: Politics and Society* (Cambridge, 1989), 22.

[16] R.B. McDowell, *Church of Ireland, 1869–1969* (London, 1975), 105–6. If Bernard had been an English prelate, his biographer observed, he might have left a name which would have put him in the same class as Tait or Davidson.

[17] This reaction from a leading Irish Quaker, James Richardson of Bessbrook, is cited in Alan Megahey, *The Irish Protestant Churches in the Twentieth Century* (Basingstoke, 2000), 58.

iii. Finding the Path to Peace

The ease with which the princes of the pulpit apparently prostituted the message of the Prince of Peace has made them a target. Historians, a little self-righteously, have criticized 'jingoistic and self-righteous' remarks, spoken of the 'pollution of the pulpit' or, in the specific case of Wales, disapproved of Nonconformity's 'compromise with the political establishment of the time'.[18] Contemporaries, however, less comfortably in armchairs, could not know what the next four years would bring. If they had known, to go to war might have seemed the greater rather than the lesser of two evils. 'Compromising with the political establishment of the time' was not at all what Christian leaders thought they were doing. Their reactions stemmed from the shared assumptions with 'the political establishment' about the kind of polity the United Kingdom, even more the British Empire, represented or was becoming. The 'Public Right' of Europe had been shattered by German conduct. The strength of the rhetoric being deployed reflects the fact that the United Kingdom, unique amongst the major belligerents, had no military conscription. Its relatively small regular army needed urgent supplementation. Men would come forward whether they believed their country to be right or wrong, but to believe it to be right would help.

The British Empire no doubt had its flaws and imperfections. Even so, it remained common, both in church circles and beyond, to regard it as a kind of Christian engagement. At least to some eyes, the British Empire and the Anglican Communion continued to reinforce each other. When the king and queen came to dine with the archbishop of Canterbury at Lambeth Palace in February 1914 it was not a matter of surprise that fellow subjects present included the archbishop of Brisbane and the bishop of Yukon. J.P. Whitney, an ecclesiastical historian in Cambridge, serenely working, in the early years of the war, on a volume on the episcopate and the Reformation, unexpectedly inserted a reference in it to the strong love of the more distant churches for the mother see of Canterbury. It was, he thought, 'a sentiment of extraordinary power, and may yet do for our Empire what the see of Augustine did in the olden days for our own island'. To abandon the 'national mission', or to portray it as corrupt, or nothing more than exploitative self-interest, would be to compromise with Christian duty. Even the Quaker J.W. Graham, though critical of empire in many respects, thought natives in the tropics were too indolent to do the needful work. Continued European control was necessary.[19]

---

[18] J.A. Moses, 'The British and German Churches and the Perception of War, 1908–1914', *War and Society* 5 (1987), 24 speaks of church leaders as succumbing to the intoxication of vulgar nationalism.

[19] Cited in Michael Bentley, *Modernizing England's Past: English Historiography in the Age of Modernism 1870–1970* (Cambridge, 2005), 72: J.W. Graham, *Evolution and Empire* (London, 1912), 115–16.

Of course, whether Christians should ever support war had controversially resonated throughout the history of the church.[20] By the early twentieth century, the possibility of a 'just war' had been debated for centuries. Theologians and casuists revisited the stock of theory in 1914 but, even as they did so, had to acknowledge that the march of events had passed them by. Besides, in seeking to judge whether British intervention was 'proportionate', it was difficult to say what had 'caused' Britain to enter the war. When had the fuse been lit? Asquith had spoken privately to the archbishop that he would not have been sorry if Serbia had been given a 'thrashing', but could not permit Belgium to be similarly treated. The violation of Belgian neutrality, for most church leaders, made the war 'just' and took it beyond more abstract and perhaps dubious 'balance of power' arguments. Yet, the more 'just' the war the more impossible it might be to stop. 'Unjust' wars, fought blatantly for scraps of territory or commercial advantage, could perhaps more readily be concluded by compromise.[21] War in the twentieth century, some suggested, might well be an altogether different phenomenon from what it had been when discussed by St Thomas Aquinas. The horrible toll in the civil war which had ravaged 'Christian America' was a warning of what a new European war might be like.

A variety of peace societies had arisen in the nineteenth century. It was hoped that war, like other evils, could be 'abolished'. 'Pacifism', much in the air, was a new word in the early twentieth century.[22] 'Peace Congresses', with international participation, blossomed. The people would speak peace unto the people. Even governments, under the unlikely inspiration of the Tsar of Russia, agreed to talk at The Hague in 1907, though unsuccessfully, about possible disarmament measures. The nineteenth-century 'Peace Movement' had had a strong Nonconformist aura—successive secretaries of the Peace Society had been Nonconformist ministers (preferably Welsh).[23] In 1910, with the formation of a Church of England Peace League, the established church too began to dabble with the issue. The bishop of Lincoln became its president.[24] These were straws in the wind,

---

[20] R.H. Bainton, *Christian Attitudes to War and Peace* (London, 1968).

[21] David Martin, *Does Christianity Cause War?* (Oxford, 1997). For a recent discussion, see Oliver O'Donovan, *The Justification of War* (Cambridge, 2003).

[22] Martin Ceadel has written fruitfully on both the terminology and history of pacifism in *Thinking about Peace and War* (Oxford, 1987) and *Pacifism in Britain 1914–1945: The Defining of a Faith* (Oxford, 1980).

[23] Martin Ceadel, *The Origins of War Prevention: The British Peace Movement and International Relations, 1730–1854* (Oxford, 1996): Keith Robbins, 'A Welshman and the Pursuit of Peace: Henry Richard and the Path to the 1850 Frankfurt Peace Congress' in W. Elz and S. Neitzel, eds., *Internationale Beziehungen im 19. und 20. Jahrhundert: Festschrift für Winfried Baumgart* (Paderborn, 2003), 19–36.

[24] G. Neville, *Radical Churchman: Edward Lee Hicks and the New Liberalism* (Oxford, 1998). In 1914, however, Hicks supported the war.

however, rather than mass movements. A year on, only just over 100 members of the Church of England committed themselves to 'promoting universal and permanent peace by encouraging arbitration, conciliation and international friendship'.[25]

It was not difficult to speak favourably about peace, although whether it was something more than the absence of war was more problematic.[26] Europe seemed to be in a condition which was 'neither war nor peace'. Rather than speak about 'peace' in the abstract, therefore, the churches should speak across frontiers and seek to calm specific tensions. J. Allen Baker, a Liberal MP, had met German church leaders when he had presented a memorial on the subject of disarmament to the 1907 The Hague conference.[27] A Quaker himself, he was able to arrange funding from Quaker sources for a high profile visit the following year of German pastors and a visit of British religious leaders to Germany in 1909 (meeting the Kaiser and other prominent German figures). These exchanges resulted in the formation, in the two countries, of the Associated Councils of Churches for Fostering Friendly Relations between the British and German Peoples. The archbishop of Canterbury became President of the British Council. A quarterly magazine, *The Peacemaker,* had achieved a circulation of 94,000 by 1913. Signs of advancing cordiality between the two peoples were identified. Boyd Carpenter, the bishop of Ripon, rather optimistically, recognized in the Kaiser someone who was 'a lover of peace' and devoted to the welfare of mankind. His imperial majesty had a simple trust in divine guidance.[28]

So 'successful' did the Associated Councils appear to be, that those involved wanted to form a 'World Alliance' for promoting global friendship through the churches. Andrew Carnegie in the United States made funding available. A conference was scheduled for Lake Constance on 1–3 August 1914. In the event, all that those assembled could do was to pray and pass a

---

[25] Paul Laity, *The British Peace Movement 1870–1914* (Oxford, 2001), 185.

[26] Keith Robbins, 'L'ambiguité du mot "Paix" au royaume-uni avant 1914' in *1914: Les Psychoses de Guerre* (Rouen, 1984), 59–73.

[27] E.B. and P.J. Noel-Baker, *Allen Baker, M.P.: A Memoir* (London, 1927). The other Liberal MP heavily involved was W.H. Dickinson. H.C. White, *Willoughby Hyett Dickinson* (Gloucester, 1956).

[28] Keith Robbins, *The Abolition of War: The 'Peace Movement' in Britain, 1914–1919* (Cardiff, 1976), 17–18. The Kaiser had regained popularity in Britain by this juncture. It is argued that in placing great hopes on Wilhelm in July 1914 the British press seriously overestimated his influence. Lothar Reinermann, *Der Kaiser in England: Wilhelm II. und sein Bild in der britischen Öffentlichkeit* (Paderborn, 2001). The archbishop of York was shortly to run into a press storm when he referred publicly to a 'sacred memory' of the Kaiser—referring to seeing him kneeling with King Edward VII at the bier of Queen Victoria—which made him feel that the German emperor could not lightly have embarked on war. How terribly hard it was, Lang thought, 'to get even a hearing for some faint voices of the Christian spirit'. Lockhart, *Lang*, 248–9.

resolution—and struggle to get home somehow. Dr Clifford was jostled when he went to get his luggage. Until he got to Cologne, he had to make do with a solitary German sausage for nourishment. He eventually proceeded safely to London.[29] J.H. Rushbrooke, a fellow Baptist minister and editor of *The Peacemaker*, whose German wife was visiting her relatives on the Baltic coast, plunged into Germany to find her. He was arrested *en route* and only with difficulty was the family reunited and returned to England.[30] His story was only more dramatic than that of many other clergy and ministers holidaying in Switzerland, Italy or France. Principal Lindsay of the Free Church College in Glasgow was convinced that his abominable journey back from the south of France had strained his heart and called the doctor. By the end of the year, he was dead.[31]

It was not only in a physical sense that hearts were being strained. Small numbers of Christians concluded that an explicit and fundamental 'pacifism' was now needed. Friends, colleagues and families argued whether 'justice' came before 'peace' or 'peace' before 'justice'. There were some swift and unexpected shifts of opinion. Was pacifism the same as 'non-resistance'? Was it not now time to contemplate 'solitary acts of divine madness'? The secretary of the National Peace Council concluded that 'the kind of internationalism that alone could result in a world at peace was of the order which Quakerism offered—a deep spiritual life expressed in a very vital and realistic practice'. He joined the Society of Friends.[32] Not that Quakers were all of a mind. The place of the 'historic testimony' had been a topic of lively debate for some time as leading figures sought a renaissance in Quaker life. 'Our Testimony for Peace' had but recently been given fresh emphasis. It was not some artificial appendage but rather the organic outcome of Christian faith. Even so, when it came to the point, 200 young Quakers enlisted promptly (and by the end of the war one-third of all male Friends of military age served). This was more than just the defection of 'birthright' Quakers whose participation in the Society had been minimal.[33] The corollary, of course, was that the Society thus 'purged' presented a pretty united front thereafter.

A further development was the formation, in December 1914, of the Fellowship of Reconciliation. Its first national secretary was a Welsh

---

[29] James Marchant, *Dr John Clifford* (London, 1922), 186–8. It was not long before Clifford decided that the issue in the war was plain. It was Kaiser or Christ. J. Clifford, *The War and the Churches* (London, 1914).

[30] E.A. Payne, *John Henry Rushbrooke 1870–1947: A Baptist Greatheart* (London, 1954), 29–31.

[31] *Letters of Principal T. M. Lindsay to Janet Ross* (London, 1923), 259–61. For Lindsay, see the assessment by Donald K. McKim in Michael Bauman and Martin I. Klauber, eds., *Historians of the Christian Tradition* (Nashville, TN, 1995), 351–75.

[32] Laity, *British Peace Movement*, 228.

[33] Thomas C. Kennedy, *British Quakerism, 1860–1920: The Transformation of a Religious Community* (Oxford, 2001), 313.

minister serving in London—a remarkable continuity with the past of the Peace Society. By the following July, with branches across the country, it had 2,000 members. Christians, the largely middle-class and Nonconformist Fellowship declared, were forbidden to wage war. Their loyalty to country, to humanity, to the Church Universal and to Jesus Christ called them to enthrone love in personal, social, commercial and national life.[34]

Christian pacifists, it is clear, had by no means captured the churches for their stance. Nevertheless, their position had to be seriously addressed and, so far as possible, effectively rebutted. J.M. Lloyd Thomas, minister of the Old Meeting House, Birmingham, came to the conclusion that, in its unconditional form, non-resistance was 'not merely illegal and criminal but irrational, immoral and unchristian'.[35] Yet, while disagreeing with them, other preachers were not slow to praise Quakers. Their testimony, declared Hensley Henson in Norwich Cathedral in September 1914, had 'a priceless value as a protest against Christian acquiescence in a lower level of practice than the Christian conscience'.[36] D.S. Cairns, a Scottish theologian, wrote to Henry Hodgkin, the Fellowship's Quaker guiding figure, in November 1914 indicating his disagreement but also expressing gratitude for the fact that Friends stood for 'an ideal in a mad and wicked world'.[37] P.T. Forsyth, however, was more dismissive. The founders of the Fellowship of Reconciliation, he wrote, were no doubt pleasant people, but they were offering 'sugar-coated pills for an earthquake'.[38] In Scotland, James Barr, a United Free Church Minister in Govan, was a rather lonely voice in denouncing the war.[39]

In pledging their 'loyalty' to country, humanity, the Church Universal and to Jesus Christ, members of the Fellowship of Reconciliation seemed to assume that their pledge contained no internal contradiction. Loyalty to country, however, was a specific pledge and, at this particular juncture, the Fellowship's loyalty to 'King and Country' did not seem evident to its critics. Loyalty to humanity was a pledge which could not be readily cashed—in the condition in which humanity found itself. Loyalty to 'the Church Universal' was scarcely less difficult, as all Christians, not only pacifists, found.

On 17 July Dr Ernst Dryander, the senior court chaplain to the Kaiser, had written privately to the archbishop of Canterbury to enquire whether the Anglican Church 'with its world-wide influence' would take part in the

[34] Jill Wallis, *Valiant for Peace: A History of the Fellowship of Reconciliation 1914 to 1989* (London, 1991), 6–7.

[35] J.M. Lloyd Thomas, *The Immorality of Non-Resistance* (Birmingham, 1915), vi.

[36] H. Hensley Henson, *War-Time Sermons* (London, 1915), 21.

[37] Cited in Kennedy, *British Quakerism*, 317.

[38] P.T. Forsyth, *The Christian Ethic of War* (London, 1916), 44.

[39] James Barr, *Lang Syne* (Glasgow, 1948). After the war, Barr became an MP.

jubilee of the four-hundredth year of the Reformation. Courteously, Davidson replied that while important figures in the Church of England would be sympathetic, corporate and official co-operation would not be possible. The Church of England could not align itself with a coherent and solidly united Protestantism against a coherent and solidly united Catholicism: it had a double relationship to European Christianity.[40] The extent to which it 'faced both ways', however, left the church rather isolated in the European ecclesiastical landscape. In the future its complicated character might enable it to be a bridge. In the present it had no European 'partner'.

In his reply, on 1 August, Davidson added that war 'between two great nations of kindred race and sympathies is, or ought to be, unthinkable in the twentieth century of the Gospel of the Prince of Peace'. A 'special relationship' had been commonly referred to, but it had latterly become brittle. The outbreak of the war swiftly brought to the surface mutual resentments and recriminations, on both sides of the North Sea/German Ocean.[41] Ferocity was by no means absent in the ecclesiastical exchanges. Leading scholars and churchmen in Britain and Germany, in open letters, explained to the outside world why the cause of their countries was the cause of Christian civilization.[42] A personal element entered and complicated the picture. The dean of Canterbury, declaring that war, as a last resort, had been shown for a thousand years to be the only effectual means of punishing and preventing unjust violence, had married as his second wife the daughter of a German scholar who had taught in Edinburgh. Less so for Anglicans, but for Nonconformists and the Scottish Presbyterian churches, Germany had been the favoured place for study for its intellectually able ministers.[43] John Baillie, for example, a notable church figure in subsequent decades in Scotland and beyond, wrote of his experiences studying in pre-war Germany that he was 'fond of Germany beyond all other continental countries which I have seen'.[44] Now, individuals turned in revulsion from

---

[40] Bell, *Davidson*, 732–3.

[41] Roland N. Stromberg, *Redemption by War: The Intellectuals and 1914* (Lawrence, KS, 1982); Stuart Wallace, *War and the Image of Germany: British Academics 1914–1918* (Edinburgh, 1988) does not have a specific chapter on British academic theologians or biblical scholars. See also A.J. Hoover, *The Gospel of Nationalism: German Patriotic Preaching from Napoleon to Versailles* (Stuttgart, 1986) and *God, Germany, and Britain in the Great War: A Study in Clerical Nationalism* (New York, 1989).

[42] These, and other exchanges, are collected in Gerhard Besier, *Die protestantischen Kirchen Europas im Ersten Weltkrieg: Ein Quellen- und Arbeitsbuch* (Göttingen, 1984); J.C. O'Neil, 'Adolf von Harnack and the Entry of the German State into War, July–August 1914', *Scottish Journal of Theology* 55/1 (2002), 1–18.

[43] C.E. Bailey, 'The British Protestant Theologians in the First World War: Germanophobia Unleashed', *Harvard Theological Review* 77 (1984), 115–21.

[44] George Newlands, 'John Baillie and Friends, in Germany and at War' in Stewart J. Brown and George Newlands, eds., *Scottish Christianity in the Modern World* (Edinburgh, 2000), 138.

ideas, and persons, they had once admired.[45] Perhaps a little rashly, a young
Baptist minister set out for Germany, where he had earlier enjoyably studied
in Berlin and Marburg, for a holiday at the end of July. After being detained,
he did not reach England until December. He had tried to attend public
worship but had then abandoned it. Anyone really alive to the universalism
of the gospel could not listen to purely German notes.[46] The scholars of
Glasgow felt that German scholarship had taken a wrong turning. There had
been, T.M. Lindsay felt, a fatal severing in Germany of the connection
between the professor's chair and the active work of the ministry. James
Cooper wrote that he had long feared 'that the critical and philosophical
extravagances of Germany were sapping the authority, alike of Scripture, of
the Church, and of Christ'.[47] The result was now palpable and he hoped that
all British churches would take the lesson. Young Geoffrey Fisher, preaching his first sermon as headmaster in Repton School chapel, identified
arrogance as the cause of the war. The Germans thought themselves
intellectually superior and thereby felt justified in using force to increase
their dominion. Britain, he told the boys, was fighting for God's cause
against the devil's. Others, although not blessed like Fisher with first class
degrees from Oxford, came to the same conclusion.[48] Individuals, in this
atmosphere, sometimes made symbolic gestures towards 'the fellowship of
Christians in their common faith'. The Polish-born Scottish principal of
New College (Congregationalist), London, read his daily portion in the
New Testament in German, and the German New Testament scholar Adolf
Deissmann read his in English. It was not clear how 'loyalty to the Universal
Church' could be otherwise expressed in wartime.[49]

iv. *Roman Catholics and the Patriotic Drum*

Roman Catholics were in a different but scarcely less problematic position.
Baron von Hügel no doubt spoke for many when in September 1914 he felt
himself face to face 'with an upheaval, a testing of values, such as occurs only
once in, say, three or four centuries'. He had a particular pain in seeing
Austria (his father's country) and Britain (his mother's) at war with each
other and being forced to choose between them. Having lived for over forty

---

[45] Adolf von Harnack was a case in point. Harnack published a selection of his own relevant
writings in *Aus der Friedens- und Kriegsarbeit* (Giessen, 1916).

[46] L.H. Marshall, *Experiences in German Gaols* (London, 1915) cited in J.C.G. Binfield, *Pastors
and People: The Biography of a Baptist Church, Queen's Road, Coventry* (Coventry, 1984), 161.

[47] A.D. Lindsay, ed., *T.M. Lindsay: College Addresses, and Sermons Preached on Various Occasions*
(Glasgow, 1915), 85–6: H.J. Wotherspoon, *James Cooper* (London, 1926), 275–6.

[48] Edward Carpenter, *Archbishop Fisher—His Life and Times* (Norwich, 1991), 18.

[49] A.E. Garvie, *Memories and Meanings of My Life* (London, 1938), 166; H. Strachan, *The First
World War*, vol. i: *To Arms* (Oxford, 2001), 1115–16.

years in England, as against two and a half in Austria, he had no doubt about his allegiance. The only consolation he could draw was that it was 'coarse Prussianism' which for the moment had captured the German soul.[50] Anglicans, in all probability, would not find themselves fighting Anglicans, but Catholics would certainly find themselves fighting Catholics (just as Reformed Protestants would find themselves fighting Reformed Protestants). It was this certainty which faced the aristocratically raised, newly elected and diplomatically trained pope, Benedict XV, in August 1914. The issue of the 'Temporal Power'—the 'Roman Question'—still lingered on unresolved (and Italy was not at war). His pontificate, von Hügel thought, would consist in little more than helping to settle Europe again into 'happier conditions' (as early as September von Hügel thought that the war had gone on too long). But could, or should, Benedict seek to reconcile the warring states and bring peace? Two days after his enthronement, he indicated 'so far as it is in our power' his determination to leave nothing undone to this end. His first encyclical, *Ad Beatissimi*, published on 1 November, spoke of his anguish at what European men were doing to each other. Who could conclude from their behaviour that they were sons of a single Father in Heaven? This diminutive man, however, soon discovered, if he did not know from the outset, that his power was also slight. He had to be 'neutral', whatever that precisely meant, aware that he would be denounced respectively as the 'Boche pope' or the *Franzosenpapst*.[51] Neither in the United Kingdom, nor throughout Europe as a whole, were all Christians suddenly disposed to regard him as 'their' pope, although R.J. Campbell, from the pulpit of the City Temple, hoped that he would convene a Christian peace conference—after the war.

The map of belligerent European 'Christendom' was complicated.[52] It might be thought that 'secularization' had already rendered out of date the historic descriptions of countries as 'Catholic' or 'Protestant'. Yet the cultural inheritance and prevailing ethos remained potent. Participating countries could still be slotted into one category or the other. Even leaving aside Orthodox Russia (a not inconsiderable thing to do), neither alliance grouping in the war was homogeneously 'Catholic' or 'Protestant'. It was a point seized on in Co. Down. The war was not being fought 'between different branches of the Church of God' but between those who believed in 'justice, liberty and truth' and those who did not.[53] Britain might still be

---

[50] Bernard Holland, ed., *Baron von Hügel: Selected Letters 1896–1924* (London, 1927), 211–13.

[51] J. Derek Holmes, *The Papacy in the Modern World* (London, 1981), 2–3: J.F. Pollard, *The Unknown Pope: Benedict XV (1914–1922) and the Pursuit of Peace* (London, 1999).

[52] See the useful discussion by Michael Snape, 'The Great War' in Hugh McLeod, ed., *The Cambridge History of Christianity: World Christianities c.1914–c.2000* (Cambridge, 2006), 131–50.

[53] Dean Grierson cited in Megahey, *Irish Protestant Churches*, 39.

labelled 'Protestant' in such a context, but the United Kingdom of Great
Britain and Ireland could not be. For Catholics in Britain, the war came at
an awkward juncture. They now constituted a significant element in the
religious life of the country. Yet, despite their now episcopally sanctioned
presence in Oxford and Cambridge—at least one kind of yardstick of
Catholic participation in the life of England—they were still not fully
'mainstream' and some, though not all, itched to be so.

To demonstrate a supercharged commitment to the war would show that
Catholics did not wish to live perpetually on the margins, whether in
England, Scotland or Wales. They could be and wished to be as patriotic
as any Protestant.[54] Born in Clapham, the archbishop of Westminster
appeared indisputably English and had no doubt about the justice of the
cause.[55] Before the war, he had written a pamphlet *The Paramount Need of
Training in Youth* which in retrospect appears anticipatory. Part of his
education had been in Leuven/Louvain, a fact which strengthened his
ready identification with the plight of Belgium. He made no suggestion
that English and Welsh Catholics should be 'neutral'. The Roman Catholic
archbishops of Glasgow and Edinburgh also gave their full public support to
the war, as did the editor of the Catholic *Glasgow Observer*. There was a
favourable initial response from the Irish in Scotland to the recruiting
drive.[56] It seemed that for them, too, there was an opportunity to achieve
acceptance, this time in Scottish society.[57] The 'Scottish soldier' would
perhaps cease to be as strongly Presbyterian as both image and (substantially)
reality made him out to be.[58] Even so, the future fate of Ireland did not
disappear as an issue, particularly in the life of the west of Scotland. Contacts
remained strong, illustrated, for example, by the Irish-born wine and spirit
merchant who became, in 1903, the first Catholic bailie on Glasgow City
Council since the Reformation, who was elected a few years later, though
only briefly, as the Irish Nationalist MP for Co. Monaghan.

Yet a beating of the patriotic drum risked compromising the catholicity
of Catholicism. It would be a mistake, in the pursuit of 'acceptance', to

---

[54] M. Snape, 'British Catholicism and the British Army in the First World War', *Recusant
History* 26 (2002), 314–58.

[55] Francis, Cardinal Bourne, *The Nation's Crisis* (London, 1918).

[56] J. Cooney, *Scotland and the Papacy* (Edinburgh, 1982), 17; T. Gallagher, *Glasgow. The Uneasy
Peace: Religious Tension in Modern Scotland* (Manchester, 1987), 84.

[57] Wartime could produce departures from peacetime practice. The Roman Catholic commander of the 2nd Battalion Royal Scots regularly attended the Presbyterian services of his unit, an
overwhelmingly Protestant one. Edward Spiers, 'The Scottish Soldier at War' in Hugh Cecil and
Peter H. Liddle, eds., *Facing Armageddon: The First World War Experienced* (Barnsley, 1996), 320.

[58] Ian Wood, 'Protestantism and Scottish Military Tradition' in Graham Walker and Tom
Gallagher, eds., *Sermons and Battle Hymns: Protestant Popular Culture in Modern Scotland* (Edinburgh,
1990), 112–36 is concerned with a later period but makes some observations on long-standing
regimental traditions.

suppose that the church was other than 'international'. Indeed, the writer and Liberal MP Hilaire Belloc, of Anglo-French parentage, perhaps the most prominent Catholic publicist at this time, brought together 'the Faith' and 'Europe' in prolific publications. In *An Open Letter on the Decay of Faith*, he asked his British readers to remember 'that we are Europe: we are a great people'. It had been Europe which had enlarged the faith and given it visible form. It was, as he chose to put it, 'the service we Europeans have done to God. In return He has made us Christians'.[59] Belloc was soon writing well-paid articles on the war, collected and published in 1915 and 1916 as *A General Sketch of the European War*. England's future should be as part of a 'Catholic Europe': the path, in other words, led to Rome. When Maurice Baring, author, diplomat, soldier, linguist, traveller, decided to take Christianity seriously, this 'citizen of Europe' opted for Rome: Anglicanism was simply a 'lopped off branch' of Catholicism.[60] Many of the church's native-born priests had been trained abroad. Former students at the English or Scots colleges in Rome were already, or were to become, bishops. Their cultural formation as well as their theological outlook was therefore different.[61] In addition, priests and nuns from the continent were working permanently in England. Amongst the laity, Lithuanians and Poles in the Lanarkshire coalfield and Italian ice-cream vendors in South Wales inhabited a rather different world from Baron von Hügel's Hampstead, but illustrated the diversity of the British Catholic population.[62] And England could be said to be present at the highest levels in the Vatican—if, stretching matters, Cardinal Merry del Val, Secretary of State in Rome, is admitted to be English, as he apparently claimed to be.[63] The fact that the Roman Catholic Church included more non-native-born in its ranks than any other church did not, however, hinder its commitment to the war effort, indeed, it may even have enhanced it.

v. Home Front

The 'war experience' as it affected the inhabitants of the British Isles immediately bifurcates between home and overseas. At home, German warships bombarded Whitby and Scarborough, and as a consequence two

[59] Cited in Joseph Pearce, *Old Thunderer: A Life of Hilaire Belloc* (London, 2003), 115.

[60] Emma Letley, *Maurice Baring: A Citizen of Europe* (London, 1991), 143.

[61] Michael E. Williams, *The Venerable English College Rome* (London, 1979), 146–7.

[62] Kenneth Lunn, 'Reactions and Responses: Lithuanian and Polish Immigrants in the Lanarkshire Coalfield, 1880–1914', *Journal of the Scottish Labour History Society* (1978), 23–38; T. Colpi, *The Italian Factor: The Italian Community in Great Britain* (Edinburgh, 1991).

[63] For a further discussion of the composition of Roman Catholicism see Adrian Hastings, *A History of English Christianity 1920–1990* (London, 1991), 137–9. Born in London, del Val's father was a Spaniard.

shells unexpectedly crashed through the roof of a parish church during the celebration of the Eucharist. The archbishop of York watched Zeppelins passing over his palace at Bishopthorpe on their way to bombing the nearby city. It was, he thought, clearly time to remove priceless glass from the city's minster. The dean of York, now aged 86, confessed himself, when this idea was put to him, too old to oversee such an unexpected task. And, indeed, he died at Christmas 1916, having caught a fatal chill while surveying the windows.[64] Dean Beeching at Norwich, as did his counterparts in other cathedrals, had to take steps to insure cathedral property against the hitherto unknown contingency of an air attack.[65] All told, airship raids killed 654 people, and the raids by Gotha and Giant aircraft killed 835—not to mention destruction of property. There were, of course, deprivations and restrictions imposed on the civilian population. Innumerable church social occasions, normally blessed with tea or coffee and cake, had to do without 'owing to food shortage'. All sorts of emergencies had to be coped with somehow, such as the departure of the organist on military service.

Yet, for the insular populations, and particularly those living outside eastern and southern England and eastern Scotland, war did not have the grim immediacy to be found overseas on both the eastern and western fronts. It was reported on formally in the press and informally through correspondence, albeit with some degree of censorship, but for the bulk of the population, it remained a conflict which had to be envisaged. It could not be seen. So, most of those who kept the home fires burning in clerical grates found it hard to imagine 'what the war was really like'. The prime minister painted a vivid picture of German troops being devoured by wolves as they fell in snow-covered Poland—not that Asquith had seen them—when he and his family came to lunch with the archbishop on New Year's Day 1915. Asquith went on to immerse himself in the heraldry to be found in Canterbury Cathedral. For less exalted clergy and their congregations, however, it was simply a case of the old things having to be done, but 'the things that mattered did not happen here'.[66] Little things, however, could connect. Here, an organ recital for the relief of distress in Serbia, there, a concert in aid of Belgian refugees. A Belgian sculptor, stranded in Edinburgh, was found work. The congregation at Free St George's sent special gifts to the Indian sappers and miners in France, having been told by a former Lieutenant Governor of Bengal of the hardships being suffered by

[64] G.E. Aylmer and Reginald Cant, eds., *A History of York Minster* (Oxford, 1977), 312.

[65] Ian Atherton, Eric Fernie, Christopher Harper-Bill and Hassell Smith, eds., *Norwich Cathedral: Church, City and Diocese, 1096–1996* (London, 1996), 629. The Canterbury Chapter, however, decided not to place any special insurance. Keith Robbins in Patrick Collinson, Nigel Ramsay and Margaret Sparks, eds., *A History of Canterbury Cathedral* (Oxford, 1995), 365.

[66] Wotherspoon, *Cooper*, 274–5.

Indians in the imperial cause.[67] The examples of such activity could be multiplied. Being humdrum and ordinary, it has rarely been chronicled, but it represented significant social support.

Services and church life carried on 'as usual' but always against a background of anxiety and uncertainty. Only rarely, and in the Free Churches, did opposing views on the war disrupt the relationship between minister and congregation.[68] Clergy and ministers found themselves writing more letters, abroad and at home, than had been customary. They became conduits of information as well as being purveyors of consolation. Even so, and the further away a congregation was from the south coast of England where the firing of guns could sometimes be heard across the Channel, the war continued to be 'distant'. A city like Durham had naturally been affected in many ways but there was still a sense, as Hensley Henson noted when preaching in his cathedral, of 'battles far away'. The greetings sent 'o-er the foam' to their absent men by Free Churches reflected the high degree of congregational solidarity of a 'gathered church'.[69] In fact, nothing could quite be 'as usual'. Here was an opportunity, thought Charles Gore, 'to get rid of some of the stiffness and formalism which has beset our church'. Dick Sheppard, however, new vicar of St Martin-in-the-Fields, might be taking his injunction a little far. Sheppard's introduction of a daily Eucharist would have been welcome, but the special Sunday afternoons for servicemen, and later, women, at which the Guards' bands played—only one of his many innovations—was perhaps more suspect.[70] It was not seemly to produce what were thought to be 'stunts'.

The pastoral task for clergy extended from the highest to the lowest in the land. It fell to the archbishop of Canterbury to write to the prime minister on hearing of the death of his son, Raymond. He knew he could cite a passage from the New Testament *in Greek*. The death of another young Raymond had prompted another father to write a memoir which contained 'supernormal communications' from his dead son. Sir Oliver Lodge, principal of Birmingham University, neither a historian nor a philosopher, had published a book which offered his thoughts on England and Germany. Lodge looked to a future in which politics would not be treated 'as an

---

[67] G.F. Barbour, *Life of Alexander Whyte, D.D.* (London, 1923), 568–9.

[68] Clyde Binfield describes the interplay of tensions and responses between the Revd Leyton Richards and the members of Bowdon Downs Congregational Church in *So Down to Prayers: Studies in English Nonconformity 1780–1920* (London, 1977), 238–44; Nathaniel Micklem, *The Box and the Puppets* (London, 1957), 59–60.

[69] Binfield, *Pastors and People*, 158–81, gives an account of 'A Church at War'. He describes a particular greeting sent to troops as 'a simple mixture of sentiment, mateyness, bad poetry, and music-hall comedy, pitched just about right'. Its minister, Arthur Dakin, had studied in Halle and Heidelberg and had a doctorate from the latter university.

[70] R. Ellis Roberts, *H.R.L. Sheppard: Life and Letters* (London, 1942), 100.

opportunity for a career and personal advancement'. Since Lodge, the pioneer of radio, was a scientist of repute, the 'supernatural communications' caused something of a sensation.[71] The bishop of Winchester, who had himself lost a son in the war, engaged him in critical private correspondence.[72] Lord Halifax published a rebuke—an address which he had given in St Martin-in-the-Fields—but it did not seem to stem the 'spiritualist' tendency.[73] The fact that it was increasing 'by leaps and bounds' seemed to Neville Figgis to be a nemesis on the church for neglect. Instead of getting angry about spiritualism, the corrective was the doctrine of angels.[74] The black-edged announcements of death became all too familiar but recipients could only speculate on what had actually happened to their loved ones. R.J. Campbell, in the process of becoming an Anglican, meditating in France on All Souls' Day 1915, felt ever more strongly that death was only a bend in the road of life. Hensley Henson, preaching in Durham Cathedral on Easter Day 1915 referred to death as 'but an episode of existence, the Gate of Life'.[75] Later in the war he came to deplore what he called spiritualism, occultism, faith-healing and a debased sacramentalism. For Campbell, the body as the medium of communication was struck away, but that was all.[76] It was with some difficulty that priests, in comforting mourners and in holding out the hope of glory, retained a proper agnosticism about the nature of the life to come.

The gap between Protestant and Catholic views on the subject of prayers for the dead narrowed. In the Church of England, public prayers for the dead had been rare indeed, but in the summer authority was given for their use—with the bishops of Liverpool and Manchester dissenting. Death in battle raised other questions too. The possibility that there might be a second chance of salvation after death was implicitly or explicitly contemplated in evangelical circles where it had not previously been entertained.[77] Some preachers, not least the bishop of London, seemed to be suggesting that the self-sacrifice of the soldier in itself conveyed immortality.[78] Christ

---

[71] Sir Oliver Lodge, *The War and After* (London, 1915); *Raymond* (London, 1916); J. Oppenheim, *The Other World: Spiritualism and Psychic Research in England, 1850–1914* (Cambridge, 1985).

[72] Edward S. Talbot, *Aspects of the Church's Duty* (London, 1915).

[73] Viscount Halifax, *'Raymond' Some Criticisms* (London, 1917).

[74] J.N. Figgis, *Hopes for English Religion* (London, 1919). The sermon was preached in September 1917. J. Winter, 'Spiritualism and the First World War' in R.W. Davis and R.J. Helmstadter, eds., *Religion and Irreligion in Victorian Society* (London, 1992).

[75] H. Hensley Henson, *War-Time Sermons* (London, 1915), 186.

[76] R.J. Campbell, *The War and the Soul* (London, 1916).

[77] D.W. Bebbington, *Evangelicalism in Modern Britain: A History from the 1730s to the 1980s* (London, 1989), 200.

[78] This aspect is considered more fully in A. Wilkinson, *Church of England and the First World War* (London, 1978), 180 ff.

might greet as a comrade-in-arms the hero who had died in a righteous cause. The soldier who shed his blood on the field of battle in a just cause was only doing what Christ did, declared *Y Llan* the Welsh Anglican periodical.[79]

The churches would surely pray in time of war. The bishop of Stepney was only one of many who sought to interpret the Lord's Prayer 'in the day of battle'. He noted, as some sign of hope, that 'Our Father' was being said, daily, in their own languages, by soldiers across the battlefields of Europe.[80] Charles Gore reminded his clergy of the duty to pray for the Germans and supplied 'A Prayer for Germany'. They should pray for a people who had now become enemies 'though they are our brethren in Christ'.[81] But should one pray for victory? The seaside and university town of Aberystwyth was the scene of a bitter dispute. Whether a German national on the university's staff should retain his post became a *cause célèbre* involving town and gown. On hearing the minister pray for British victory, a man dramatically walked out of the Calvinistic Methodist chapel in the town during a Sunday evening service in September 1915. Such a prayer, he thought, was 'no better than a barbarian's appeal to the god of his tribe'.[82] He would never darken the doors of the chapel again. It is, of course, impossible, at this juncture, to be certain about what precisely was being said—in any language—in extempore prayers across the British Isles. The question excited public discussion. J.R. MacDonald, a guarded opponent of the war, not yet identifiable as a future prime minister, delivered a scathing attack on what he judged to be the hypocritical absurdity of both sides invoking the same God. God, as Sir John Squire was later famously to put it, evidently had his work cut out in dealing with the conflicting imprecations addressed to Him. Scott Holland, Regius Professor of Divinity at Oxford, took comfort in the fact that both sides did acknowledge one supreme God and Father of all. No one who knew what Christian prayer was could possibly be praying that God would hear England simply because it was England, or Germany because it was Germany. What mattered was righteousness.[83] Soon after the war began, the archbishop of Canterbury had prepared special prayers for use up and down England. To the dismay of some, they contained no direct prayer for victory. Hensley Henson cautioned against the simplicities he heard from some of his brethren. Victory would not prove British

---

[79] Morgan, *Span of the Cross*, 58; Gavin White, 'The Martyr Cult of the First World War' in D. Wood, ed., *Martyrs and Martyrologies*, Studies in Church History 30 (Oxford, 1993), 383–8.

[80] H.L. Paget, *In the Day of Battle* (London, 1915).

[81] Charles Gore, *The War and the Church* (London, 1914), 38–9.

[82] The man was T. Gwynn Jones, a journalist who had recently been appointed to the university staff. Morgan, *Span of the Cross*, 56–7.

[83] Henry Scott Holland, 'Praying for Victory' in *So As By Fire* (London, 1916), 108–9.

goodness nor defeat be the punishment of British sins. Bishops who said that victory would surely come because justice was on the British side were simply wrong. He wondered at 'the archaic thinking' which suggested that 'the proper consequences of events' could be arrested by repeated petitions.[84]

Events, as the war proceeded, did indeed provide a context for the innumerable sermons, addresses and articles produced throughout the British Isles. Sermons given by best-known preachers or holders of high office often appeared in print, though they represent only a fraction of what was said (and is now irrecoverable). Those delivered by Winnington-Ingram, described by Asquith in private conversation with Davidson in February 1918 as 'utterly deplorable', were not unique in their 'shallowest jingoism' but neither should they be taken as 'representative'. Hensley Henson, perhaps the most celebrated Anglican preacher, was clear that preachers should aim to be able to recall their words retrospectively without shame.[85] Not every sermon passed that test. For the greater part of the conflict, notwithstanding the scale of loss caused by its unanticipated duration, the issues at stake, as originally identified, still seemed worth fighting for. Even so, there was no option but to address the questions which naturally surfaced. What was to be understood by Providence? Why did not God stop the war? What did the Sermon on the Mount really imply? It would be rare to find a preacher who did not understand their urgency and seek to provide answers, though they were not necessarily the same answers. Scott Holland thought that he and his contemporaries had better material with which to read the soul of history than Gibbon or Grote: others were not so sure that they could.[86]

Himself a *quondam* historian, Hensley Henson felt that the Christianity of the future could not be the Christianity of the past. It was necessary to accept 'the privation of doctrinal certitude, the burden of reverent agnosticism with respect to many solemn and infinitely pressing questions'.[87] A general belief in angels did not require one to accept, as his bishop apparently did, that there had been a specially beneficial angelic visitation during the retreat from Mons. It seems that that episode began life as a fictional short story but became translated into fact, with eyewitnesses to hand. Having read a book on the subject by 'A Churchwoman', which had reviewed all the evidence, the Congregationalist Dr Horton concluded 'If

[84] H. Hensley Henson, *Christian Liberty* (London, 1917), 134–6.

[85] Keith Robbins, 'The War Sermons of Hensley Henson' in G. Teuillé, ed., *War Sermons* (forthcoming).

[86] The contributors to J. Estlin Carpenter, ed., *Ethical and Religious Problems of the War* (London, 1916), largely Unitarians, were all convinced that the war could only be understood as springing out of 'a long historical development'.

[87] Henson, *War-Time Sermons*, 224–5.

we are victorious in the war it will be because God saved us at Mons and on the Marne.'[88] Preachers across the country found themselves requested by their congregations for a sermon on the 'Angels at Mons'. In Glasgow, however, in a letter to his sister, James Denney said, 'they are not exactly a burning question with me'. He was more interested in the 'good angels' who were making it possible to pay the same ministerial stipend as the previous year.[89]

Henson's critics felt that his dismissal of angelic assistance was typical of the man. He found himself, in 1917, in an ecclesiastical rumpus on a par, as far as some clergy were concerned, with the war itself, when he was appointed bishop of Hereford. The bishop of Oxford thought Henson unorthodox and it required much skill on the part of the archbishop (and Henson) to find appropriate words to avoid a doctrinal schism.[90] It was to this disturbed world that Dr J.H. Jowett returned from New York to take up the pulpit of Westminster Chapel in March 1918—gaining in his congregation, in the process, the occasional presence of a British prime minister instead of an American president. He found that the spirit and morale of the people had sagged. It perhaps took a man charged up by the New World to revive in the old country the belief in a final victory of good over evil.

vi. Foreign Service

Whatever church leaders and congregations said about it at home, the war was going on 'over there'. Wallace Williamson, the minister of St Giles, Edinburgh and eloquent supporter of the war, visited the trenches in May 1915. He came back shaken. A close friend recalled that he was thereafter burdened with the grim horror of war. Having heard from a former student, now soldier, the Professor of Divinity at Edinburgh University thought that it was not war as formerly understood. All the romance and honour had gone out of it. The horror was unimaginable.[91] Clergy and ministers of all denominations went out to see for themselves.[92] It was not until May 1916, however, that the archbishop of Canterbury paid a call at the front.

---

[88] R.F. Horton, *An Autobiography* (London, 1917), 341.

[89] James Moffat, ed., *Letters of Principal James Denney to his Family and Friends* (London, n.d.), 193.

[90] The creedal controversy can be followed in R.P. Flindall, ed., *The Church of England, 1815–1948: A Documentary History* (London, 1972), 324–33.

[91] Cited in Brown. 'A Solemn Purification by Fire', 93.

[92] An invitation to one clergyman to minister to wounded and convalescent soldiers in northern Italy was declined because the region was too cold, too expensive and it was only young men's teeth that could cope with bully beef. Cited in Robert Lee, *Rural Society and the Anglican Clergy 1815–1914: Encountering and Managing the Poor* (Woodbridge, 2006), 192.

Fortunately provided with a 'strong rapid car', he covered a good deal of ground in eight days. Travelling around, he had never seen so many dead partridges. He observed the trenches through field-glasses. Forty assembled generals told him that the army chaplains were first-rate chaps. Finding sleep difficult, Davidson felt 'more and more the fearsomeness of all this going on between Christian peoples, and the helplessness of religious leadership to intervene'.[93] The archbishop of York, who had already hopped from ship to ship visiting the Grand Fleet for a month in 1915, came out to the Western Front two years later, staying with each army commander in turn. The army took pains to provide the 62nd (2nd West Riding) Division for a large parade service. The war had taken its toll on Lang. What little hair he had left was white. His words to the troops, however, were not without some effect. Having heard his remarks, a brigadier who had been telling his men that live Germans were a curse, and that therefore no prisoners should be taken, amended his instructions and stated that a few could be allowed to survive.[94] The archbishop of Armagh, Crozier, came to see Irish soldiers. The bishops of London and Birmingham, with supporting clerical entourages, eagerly arrived. The archbishop of Westminster followed, as did the successive moderators of the Church of Scotland and the Chief Rabbi. R.J. Campbell became so familiar a figure that on his third visit he was allowed to bring his own car.[95]

The ecclesiastical top-brass expected and received proper appointments at GHQ. Generals and bishops, sensing parity of rank, sized each other up. Haig apparently thought the archbishop of Westminster 'neither eminent in appearance nor in conversation'. Davidson, supposing Haig to be a semi-Presbyterian, found him initially rather shy, but later considered the frankness of his conversation delightful. The archbishop did not know that, after January 1916, hardly a Sunday passed without Haig reflecting on the sermon preached by 'the earnest young Scotch man', the minister, George Duncan, in the Scotch church which Haig attended. 'Our Douglas', his brother had written, was the instrument God would use to crush the German invaders. Haig himself wrote to his wife later that '*I feel* that every step in my plan has been taken with the Divine help.'[96] Those historians who have been less impressed by Haig's plans have been inclined to credit him with possessing

---

[93] Bell, *Davidson*, 778–84.
[94] Lockhart, *Lang*, 258.
[95] R.J. Campbell, *With our Troops in France* (London, 1916), 17–20.
[96] Gerard DeGroot, *Douglas Haig, 1861–1928* (London, 1988), 217–19, 251. The same author has written more fully on this relationship in ' "We are safe whatever happens"—Douglas Haig, the Reverend George Duncan and the Conduct of War, 1916–1918' in N. McDougall, ed., *Scotland and War AD 79–1918* (Edinburgh, 1991). Duncan's own account is *Douglas Haig as I Knew Him* (London, 1966). When Haig appeared before the General Assembly of the Church of Scotland in May 1919, he was received as the Christian hero who had won the war.

an unhelpful delusion of infallibility.[97] Nor was Haig alone amongst senior generals in his convictions. It has been pointed out that generals Horne (First Army), Plumer (Second Army), Byng (Third Army), Rawlinson (Fourth Army) and Gough (Fifth Army) were all Christian gentlemen.

Haig's inner conviction, however, did not prevent him from developing, according to Duncan, an 'instinctive dislike' to visitors from British civilian life, not least to churchmen, unless they came on 'a highly responsible mission' (whatever that might be). Episcopal 'joy rides', and subsequent books about their visits, were deprecated.[98] He thought of the army as a self-contained entity. In relation to a particular service at GHQ in 1918, Haig wanted it not to be taken 'by a visitor from outside'—the bishop of Kensington was on hand—but by an official army chaplain. Davidson, for his part, was rather surprised to find how little the soldiers knew about what was going on in England. It was difficult to keep alive a sense of one church 'at home and abroad'.

The chaplains were the men in the middle. Conflicting comments on their work and role reveal them caught in the cross-fire of different expect-ations. Wyn Griffith, in his memoir of his experiences, has a Welsh soldier speak in such admiring terms of a Welsh padre that if he got through 'this bloody business' he would like to attend the padre's church.[99] On the other hand, 'most chaplains out here' wrote one Scottish lieutenant 'are only a nuisance, occupying good billets and drinking our drinks and doing nothing noticeable toward the spiritual welfare of the troops. As a class they are cordially disliked with very few exceptions.'[100] Caricatures of useless chap-lains, particularly Anglican ones, became subsequent standard literary issue. Then again, there were those in the churches who thought chaplains were inherently compromised figures. They wanted all ties with the military to be broken. It would scarcely be surprising if some individuals left poor impressions, but the generalizations seem loaded.[101] The context of their

[97] Haig's religion is explored further in Snape, *God and the British Soldier*, 61–7.

[98] A shaft apparently directed at the bishop of Birmingham rather than the bishop of London. It was Winnington-Ingram's chaplain, Guy Vernon Smith, who provided *The Bishop of London's Visit to the Front* (London, 1915).

[99] Morgan, *Span of the Cross*, 53. Discussion of Welsh chaplains is to be found on the surrounding pages.

[100] Cited by Edward Spiers, 'The Scottish Soldier at war' in Hugh Cecil and Peter H. Liddle, eds., *Facing Armageddon: The First World War Experienced* (Barnsley, 1996), 325. There has been no published recent study of Presbyterian chaplains and their interaction with troops to enable one to evaluate such a comment. Official sources give a figure of 97 chaplains being killed in action or having died from wounds received.

[101] The general issues can be followed in works which come at them from different perspectives as John Smyth, *In This Sign Conquer: The Story of the Army Chaplains* (London, 1968); M. Moynihan, ed., *God on Our Side: The British Padres in World War One* (London, 1983); S. Louden, *Chaplains in Conflict: The Role of Army Chaplains since 1914* (London, 1996).

activity was inescapably complicated and denominational jockeying for position was not absent. The creation of the United Navy and Army Board in January 1915 had allowed Free Church chaplains to serve in the forces, but such a step could be portrayed alternatively as 'proper parity' or 'subordination to the military'.[102] Chaplains came across regional dialects. There was 'bad language' in all of them. They were forced to witness a closer intermingling, in practice, between 'superstition', 'luck', 'fatalism' and 'faith' than their theology considered appropriate. Catholics and Protestants, too, differed about what was and what was not a miracle.[103] Inevitably, too, the simple fact of its major expansion, from an Army Chaplaincy Department consisting of 117 in August 1914 to 3,416 in August 1918, brought in men who, initially at least, had received little specific training for what lay ahead of them.[104] The war did not stop for Sundays.

The maintenance of morale might be a fundamental objective but it had to subsist alongside philosophical issues of a predictable kind, even if not many philosophers were fighting. It would be as misleading to suggest a wholesale abandonment of a Christian framework by the British at war as it would be to argue that a Christian army sailed sublimely through the conflict. Beliefs and lives were changed but not in a simple pattern. 'Christianity' John Henry Newman had written 'is dogmatical, devotional, practical all at once.'[105] War saw the interplay 'all at once' between those elements in an intense fashion leaving the balance between them precariously poised and their continuing integration uncertain.

vii. Women Waiting

One foundation which might be shaken in the future was a world in which only men spoke from positions of power. When the eager Geoffrey

---

[102] The then chairman of the Congregational Union, in his May 1916 address, drew enormous satisfaction from the establishment of this Board. Alan Ruston, 'Protestant Nonconformist Attitudes towards the First World War' in Alan P.F. Sell and Anthony R. Cross, *Protestant Nonconformity in the Twentieth Century* (Carlisle 2003), 260; Neil E. Allison, 'Shakespeare's Man at the Front: The Ministry of the Revd William Cramb Charteris OBE MC during the Great War (1914–1918)', *Baptist Quarterly* 41 (2005), 224–35 is a rare picture of the work of a Free Church chaplain.

[103] Katherine Finlay, 'Angels in the Trenches: British Soldiers and Miracles in the First World War', in Kate Cooper and Jeremy Gregory, eds., *Signs, Wonders, Miracles: Representations of Divine Power in the Life of the Church*, Studies in Church History 41 (Woodbridge, 2005), 443–52.

[104] There were 89/1941 Anglican chaplains, 17/298 Roman Catholic, 11/298 Presbyterian, 0/256 Wesleyan Methodists and 0/248 United Board (Baptists, Congregationalists, United Methodists and Primitive Methodists), over this same period. Snape, *God and the British Soldier*, 89. Snape's discussion of the role of chaplains in this section of his book takes the discussion on to a new level.

[105] Cited and discussed in S.W. Sykes, *The Identity of Christianity: Theologians and the Essence of Christianity from Schleiermacher to Barth* (London, 1984), 27.

Studdert-Kennedy was at last able to get permission to go out to the Front as a chaplain he wrote his wife a poem which remarked on how the summons of the Lord had cut their little pleasant world in two:

> One sad world where women wait
> One fierce world of strife and hate
> And we wander far apart, dear, I and you.[106]

The encapsulation of these two worlds in these lines did indeed appear to reflect reality. Men controlled the political and military worlds. Men offered ecclesiastical commentary. Men fought. Could women, Christian women, make them see sense? Alternatively should women join them?[107]

Maude Royden wrote to the liberal *Church Weekly* claiming that war could never be ended, except by refusing to have anything to do with it. She became travelling secretary for the Fellowship of Reconciliation, having signed an appeal in January 1915 from British women pacifists to the women of Germany and Austria.[108] Women should not be fooled by the claim of the bishop of London, who had explained to her that this was 'the last Armageddon of the world' after which 'the great sun of Love' would shine out in its permanent strength.[109] But neither in church nor state did women have power. Yet perhaps to seek some kind of parity with men was to risk being corrupted by power. In their powerlessness, women, Christian women, understood the gospel better than Christian men who had for so long succumbed to its charms. Just as the cause of peace might demand 'a martyr nation', so women might be martyrs for a new order and allow Christianity to escape from its early corruption. Royden admitted that women throughout Europe had accepted war as an inevitable evil and that, when they had the power, they might be no more likely to 'vote against war' than men. However, she believed that the Women's Movement and 'militarism' were in eternal opposition. The victory of one would be the defeat of the other. The Women's Movement would move to its inevitable triumph when moral force came to be recognized as the

---

[106] 'By his Friends', *G.A. Studdert Kennedy* (London, 1929), 101; William Purcell, *Woodbine Willie* (London, 1962).

[107] For general considerations of this issue see P.P. Pierson, *Women and Peace: Theoretical, Historical and Practical Perspectives* (Beckenham, 1987); Jill Liddington, *The Long Road to Greenham: Feminism and Anti-Militarism in Britain since 1820* (London, 1989); R.J. Evans, *Comrades and Sisters: Feminism, Socialism and Pacifism in Europe 1870–1914* (Brighton, 1987).

[108] She also wrote a pamphlet at this time *The Great Adventure: The Way to Peace* (London, 1915).

[109] Winnington-Ingram to Royden, 13 August 1914, cited in Sheila Fletcher, *Maude Royden: A Life* (Oxford, 1989), 112.

supreme governing agency in the world.[110] Such arguments were contentious in the circumstances, even amongst her women friends.

Quite apart from the specific issue of war, the majority of church leaders
remained apprehensive about any manifestation of female aspirations. The
Church Times was not alone in fearing the monstrous regiment not only as
politicians but as priestesses. The latter, it thought, would be a thousandfold
worse than the former. The council of the National Mission had initially
proposed that during its course women should be allowed to speak in
church, but withdrew this proposition when some clergy said they would
not take part if this were to be the case. A leading Anglo-Catholic layman
detected a conspiracy, though one happily nipped in the bud, which aimed
at opening the priesthood to women. Also lurking, though not often
articulated, was the thought that some women might wish to go further,
feminize God and shatter male-dominated hierarchical structures. The next
chapter notes one attempt to create a female-dominated church. It was not
an example widely copied but there appeared to be a very small minority
which wanted more than 'parity'.

In Scotland, noble pronouncements by Presbyterian men about the place
of women in the scheme of things had been frequent. Some feared that
women were increasingly disillusioned and disappointed. The United Free
Church set up a committee of fifteen men to consider the matter. Modification not revolution was to be the order of the day. It is difficult to
judge how far such moves were conscious efforts to respond to 'pressure
from without' whilst not losing control. It is notable, however, that the
moderator in 1915, a church historian, left his chair to denounce John
Knox as 'utterly wrong' in his thinking about women. On the other hand,
those clear that women were not fitted for public life detected 'the thin
edge of the wedge' in the changes that were being mooted. There was
also a realistic recognition that, unless something was done, 'because of
the demands elsewhere for competent and well-paid workers' many of the
finest women with special aptitude would be lost to church service.[111]
The theologian James Denney considered that in his church there was
'no reason why women should not be ordained'—such a step would

    [110] A. Maude Royden, 'War and the Woman's Movement' in Charles Roden Buxton, ed.,
Towards a Lasting Settlement (London, 1915), 145–6. Although Quaker women, such as Theodora
Wilson Wilson and Isabella Ford, were heavily involved in peace activities under various auspices,
Ceadel argues that a fully articulated feminist perspective did not emerge until the 1970s. Martin
Ceadel, *Semi-Detached Idealists: The British Peace Movement and International Relations, 1730–1854*
(Oxford, 2000), 209. See also G. Bussey and M. Tims, *The Women's International League for Peace
and Freedom, 1915–65* (London, 1965).
    [111] Lesley A. Orr Macdonald, *A Unique and Glorious Mission: Women and Presbyterianism in
Scotland 1830–1930* (Edinburgh, 2000), 192–202.

happily also help to 'eradicate every fibre of the sacramental conception of ordination'.[112]

In Wales, women seem to have accepted that the ministry and eldership should be confined to men without much public sign of discontent. However, in 1920 one headmistress, observing the multitude of outstanding opportunities for social service and leadership, asked whether Welsh women could continue to regard their sphere as that of sewing garments, preparing meals and decorating church buildings and to see Sunday School and Band of Hope work as their highest achievements.[113]

In England, it was again Maude Royden who raised the stakes. She accepted an invitation to be an assistant at the City Temple (Congregationalist).[114] Further controversy could be anticipated when a report on the ministry of women, commissioned by Davidson in 1917, reported after the war.[115] Women, Charles Gore thought, should have the vote in ecclesiastical as well as political matters. Nevertheless, there was 'an essential headship of man over woman which neither physiology nor Scripture will allow us to ignore' and some day, he stated, he would find himself in collision with the 'Women's Movement'.[116] It looks, therefore, as though the hierarchy was aware of an impending storm but wanted to push the issues into the future rather than confront them during the war. Gore's endorsement of 'votes for women' can be seen as part of a wider attempt in the middle of the war to defuse suffragette militancy.

Charitable activity, in which women had a major role, was being allied to national purpose to a degree unknown since the Napoleonic wars. Many women were being called upon to take over jobs from the men who were fighting. Some of them had less time for 'women's work', including church activity. It was being reported as early as 1915 that the number of volunteers turning up for work at charitable agencies was falling.[117] Even if that holds good as a generalization, however, the wartime circumstances did mean that women had more scope within church life than hitherto. In Baptist

---

[112] Moffat, ed., *Letters of James Denney*, 192.

[113] Cited in Morgan, *Span of the Cross*, 165. Morgan detects virtually no feeling of unfairness on the part of the men who allocated pastoral tasks to women, or complaint by women.

[114] R.M.B. Gouldbourne, *Reinventing the Wheel: Women and Ministry in English Baptist Life* (Oxford, 1997) explains developments amongst Baptists.

[115] Sean Gill, *Women and the Church of England: From the Eighteenth Century to the Present* (London, 1994), 235–6. Constance Coltman, the first ordained Congregational woman minister, was assistant at the King's Weigh House, London.

[116] Charles Gore, *The War and the Church* (London, 1914), 89.

[117] Frank Prochaska, *Christianity and Social Service in Modern Britain: The Disinherited Spirit* (Oxford, 2006), 85–6. Even so, to take but one example, the Baptist Women's League, which had been founded in 1908, spread through Baptist communities and Baptist women became more prominent in their denomination's social work. Arthur Marwick reflects generally on the impact of the war in *Women at War 1914–1918* (London, 1977).

churches, for example, vacancies caused by male absences led to gentle consideration, though normally nothing more, of the possibility of electing women to the diaconate (chapel office-holders). It seems, in the Free Churches at least, that women took advantage of such vacancies where they occurred rather than mounting a concerted effort. Nor should it be thought that it was only the war which gave women their opportunity. Hettie Rowntree Clifford was preaching to 900 people at the West Ham Central Mission before the war began and, although her minister husband was also well-known, she was spoken of as the 'life and soul' of the Mission. In short, while many women 'also served' by sewing and waiting, the war gave others a welcome opportunity to extend their role in church life.

viii. Peace Notes

The special pain of seeing Catholics fighting on both sides had never ceased to sadden the new pope. The Vatican had spent huge sums in relief work to alleviate the suffering of soldiers and civilians, but Benedict sought a diplomatic role. He tried, but despite lack of enthusiasm for the war amongst Catholic peasants, failed, to prevent Italian entry in 1915. He also failed to persuade the United States not to intervene. The big question, however, was whether he could bring the belligerents to seek peace by negotiation. Mgr Eugenio Pacelli (later Pope Pius XII) was sent to Bavaria in May 1917 to take soundings. In August the pope issued a 'Peace Note' setting out proposals which might provide the basis for such negotiation, but they fell on deaf ears. The fact was that the particular papal solicitude for Austria-Hungary seemed palpable in western capitals. Nor was it the case that Catholics themselves, in belligerent countries, rejoiced at the prospect of negotiation. In France it appeared that church and state had rediscovered a common purpose, at least for the moment; Cardinal Mercier, archbishop of Mechelen/Malines and Belgian primate was the very embodiment of patriotic resistance (after the king of the Belgians), a fact which could be used in Catholic Ireland to buttress its participation in the war. The pope, in short, could not come forward with a basis for talking on which all belligerent governments could agree. The fact that he had tried, however, had at least established the principle that a pope ought to cast himself as an intermediary. Even so, perhaps inescapably, the Vatican had its own interests (in this instance anxiety about Russia).

The reception of the Note in Roman Catholic circles in Britain and Ireland was cautious. English Catholics were anxious not to forfeit the improved public standing which the war had brought, though some complained that the press had not given it sufficient attention. The Irish Catholic hierarchy, having been anxious not to be too overtly enthusiastic about Irish participation in the war was equally discreet about promoting peace. The official magazine of the Church of Scotland concluded in June 1918 that the Roman Catholic Church was not only 'the enemy of Great Britain and the friend, more or less avowed, of Germany', but had itself been responsible for various outrages against international right and human liberty since the war began.[118]

The 'neutrality' of the papacy irritated Protestant opinion, therefore, when and where it took notice of it.[119] Early in the war the Roman Catholic bishop of Northampton had endeavoured to explain papal neutrality but the pope's failure to condemn those 'German atrocities' which so exercised public opinion still rankled.[120] The veteran Lord Bryce (a Presbyterian) had accepted an invitation from the prime minister at the beginning of the war to investigate allegations of German brutality and violation of the laws and established usages of war. The Swabian peasants whom Bryce had known in 1863 had been 'simple kindly folk', but now he found German conduct 'sheer murder'. His report, published in May 1915, had been widely used thereafter in British propaganda.[121] A papal pursuit of peace still smacked somewhat of a papal pursuit of power, and in particular of a solicitude for the Central Powers. For P.T. Forsyth, the Roman form of internationalism, as he put it, was 'not only useless to humanity', which the attitude of the pope to the war was demonstrating, but 'mischievous to it'. He conceded that the difficulties in the way of a real internationalism were indeed great, but they could not be got over by ignoring the nations. The divisions of the churches were 'incurable on the line of absorption in one imperial Church'.[122] The degree to which so much in the Roman Catholic Church was being centralized in the Vatican had not escaped Protestant attention.

The archbishop of Uppsala was more likely to receive a sympathetic response. Not only was Sweden itself neutral, but Dr Söderblom himself had a career which sent neutral messages—a student in Leipzig, a chaplain to

[118] Cited in Brown, 'A Solemn Purification by Fire', 101.

[119] James Cooper, now moderator of the General Assembly of the Church of Scotland, was one who was irritated by appeals for peace, appeals which in his opinion lacked any suggestion of righteousness being a needful way to it. Wotherspoon, *Cooper*, 275. The papal initiative was not thought worth mentioning by George Bell in his biography of Randall Davidson.

[120] Bishop of Northampton, *The Neutrality of the Holy See* (London, 1915). As Strachan points out, the German army was heir to two traditions, the *Kulturkampf* and the identification of Catholic priests as orchestrators of local resistance (the Peninsular war).

[121] Keith Robbins, 'Lord Bryce and the First World War' reprinted in his *Politics, Diplomacy and War in Modern British History* (London, 1994), 192–4. Trevor Wilson, 'Lord Bryce's Investigation into Alleged German Atrocities, 1914–15', *Journal of Contemporary History* 14 (1979), 369–83 questioned the evidence which had been used to substantiate the conclusions reached by the Bryce Committee, but see also John Horne and Alan Kramer, *German Atrocities, 1914: A History of Denial* (London, 2001).

[122] Forsyth, *Christian Ethic of War*, 3.

the Swedish ambassador in Paris, an exchange with the bishop of Salisbury, and an honorary DD from the University of St Andrews.[123] Together with the primates of Norway and Denmark, he issued an invitation in February 1918 to Davidson to send representatives to an ecumenical conference which he proposed to hold in Uppsala. It would not have quite the same direct peacemaking aspiration as the Papal Note, being a 'sign and signal' that henceforth the churches would want to see Christian principles applied in international relations. As a matter of timing, however, the invitation was awkward, given the situation on the Western Front. Put thus, the agenda seemed to Davidson platitudinous, but if it got down to talking about actual terms of peace it would be dangerous 'without having the Government and country behind it'. It made no sense to him to suppose that the Church of England might send representatives. His reply indicated that Anglican delegates could be sent only if the other great 'organized' Churches, the Roman and Eastern, were doing likewise—a contingency he knew to be unlikely. It was not a matter on which 'the mind of the church'—supposing one can use such a term—had been elicited.

Instead, Davidson talked the matter over with four senior politicians: Lansdowne, Asquith, Balfour and Lord Robert Cecil. Meeting the latter pair together, the conversation had an explicitly Christian framework. Balfour, however, thought it was a blunder when Christian spokesmen, feeling that they had not adequately asserted the Christian position in the world's life, tried to make amends. They deceived themselves by thinking that they were following Christ. They were not. They were trying to be politicians rather than Christians. They should concentrate on making people everywhere Christian and then the 'political lines' would be automatically sound. Cecil disagreed. Christians, like himself, were right to want to affect politics by making Christianity permeate the whole body. The archbishop was left to ponder this advice from the man who was Minister for Blockade.

Lord Lansdowne, former Foreign Secretary, turning his mind from seeking to prevent Irish Home Rule, published a 'Peace Letter' in the *Daily Telegraph* (*The Times* having declined it) on 29 November 1917. It urged a restatement of Allied war aims, hinted that they might not all be attainable and suggested the ending of the war because on both sides the people felt that it had already lasted too long. He feared a world-wide catastrophe if it continued. A political storm ensued and the noble marquess found himself being hailed as a fount of sagacity by some 'negotiate peace' Liberals and by Labour, an accolade never previously awarded him. A curious Lansdowne/Labour campaign got under way.[124] The archbishop

[123] Bengt Sundkler, *Nathan Söderblom* (London, 1965).
[124] Robbins, *Abolition of War*, 149–53.

read the letter carefully—it seemed to him 'as anti-pacifist as it could be'—and evidently Lansdowne counted Davidson as a supporter. However, the archbishop made no public statement. He was increasingly convinced in the early months of 1918 that 'sheer victory' was unobtainable and there would have to be some sort of negotiation, but did not know how that could be achieved.

As these references indicate, the archbishop continued to enjoy access to the highest political levels and sought to influence policy where he thought it appropriate. The churches indicated their willingness to be 'understanding'. Together with the archbishop of Westminster, Davidson agreed in the spring of 1917 that the soil could be tilled for food on Sundays—so long as agricultural workers did not neglect their essential religious duties. It would be a temporary concession, with adequate safeguards for conscience. He realized the limits of his influence. It had been wrong, he thought, to respond in kind to German use of poison gas—only one of a number of instances where the war seemed inexorably to be propelling politicians towards retaliation and reprisals beyond what he thought appropriate, but he could not stop them. He did not object to the introduction of conscription, though he did not welcome it with the enthusiasm displayed, for example, by Hensley Henson, for whom it was a belated expression of fairness. He made it plain that he disagreed with the convictions of conscientious objectors, but wished them to be respected and welcomed the provisions for them. He took up individual cases, though found it difficult to extend his sympathy to 'absolutists' who refused the 'alternative service' open to them.[125]

ix. *Repentance and Hope: Reviving England*

If the issues inherent in the war were what most church leaders thought them to be, part of their duty was to stiffen the sinews. However tired and weary the people might on occasion feel, they should be exhorted to keep right on until the end of the road. Christianity was itself a 'Way' even if Harry Lauder's popular song had no explicit theological intent. There was now, churchmen proclaimed, added justification for the standards in personal conduct which Christians had sought to uphold, and indeed, where possible, enforce. Morale, morals and mission were all linked, though what might be ideal, from a Christian standpoint, might not be feasible.

---

[125] Robbins, *Abolition of War*, 70–82: John Rae, *Conscience and Politics: The British Government and the Conscientious Objector to Military Service 1916–1919* (London, 1970); R.J.Q. Adams and P.H. Poirier, *The Conscription Controversy in Great Britain, 1900–1918* (Columbus, OH, 1987); Keith Robbins 'The British Experience of Conscientious Objection' in Cecil and Liddle, eds., *Facing Armageddon*, 691–708.

This was a world in which perceptions of 'class' were strongly present and in which suppositions about how 'ordinary working men' or how 'public school men' should and did behave were freely bandied about. 'If England fails,' S.P.B. Mais disarmingly wrote, 'it is our [the public schools] fault; if England leads the world, the praise is due in no small measure to us.' A chapel in a public school was where it could be shown that 'Christianity is an optimistic, buoyant, cheerful, absolutely happy religion where human feelings and failings, successes and misadventures, loves and hatreds are taken into account'.[126] 'If we are to win this War' wrote one soldier in November 1916, 'it will only be through gigantic efforts and great sacrifices. It is the chief virtue of the public-school system that it teaches one to make sacrifices willingly for the sake of *esprit de corps*.' If public school men held back, 'the others' would not follow. The author Paul Jones had won a history scholarship to Balliol College, Oxford from Dulwich College in 1914, but never lived to take it up. For his christening, a vessel containing water drawn from the Pool of Bethesda had been used. According to his father, however, as a soldier his son cared nothing for 'religious dogmas'. He did, however, bow 'in reverent homage before the Christ'. Reading Froude's essay on Newman's *Grammar of Assent*, the young lieutenant thought that what mattered was following 'the example of great teachers like Christ, who had nothing to do with creeds or ritual'. 'Hear, hear', he said, to the necessity for a campaign against 'administrative incapacity, against swindling and cheating, against drunkenness and uncleanliness, against hunger, squalor and misery'. The Master of Balliol recalled how well the young man had written in the scholarship examination on the subject of the character of Oliver Cromwell.[127] The expressed disregard for 'creeds or ritual' would not have satisfied church leaders, at least outside the Free Churches, but the general message conveyed by these remarks was one the churches endorsed. Whether 'the others' would follow, was another matter. Morale, morals and mission were being mixed together in a heady brew.

The brew, however, should not be alcoholic. One of the archbishop of Canterbury's earliest actions was to beg the Home Secretary to secure means for the early closing of public houses. Urged on by Kitchener, the secretary of state for war, he wrote a letter to *The Times* in which he deplored the public's apparent habit of treating men in uniform to strong drink. The country needed fit men. He urged as many citizens as possible to abstain for the duration of the war. Leads were needed. King George obliged in March 1915 by issuing an order against consumption of alcohol

---

[126] S.P.B. Mais, *A Public School in War-Time* (London, 1916), xii, 49.

[127] Paul Jones, *War Letters of a Public-School Boy* (London, 1918), 112, 266.

in the royal household. It was a matter, the following month, which produced a rare, if not unprecedented, letter under the names of the archbishops of Canterbury and York, the cardinal archbishop of Westminster and the president of the Free Church Federal Council (in that order). At the front, the commander of the 33rd Division, a devout and non-smoking teetotaller, abolished the rum issue for his men in favour of a cup of hot tea and one small biscuit. He was thereby thought by one of his regular soldiers to be more fitted to command a church mission hut at the base than a division of troops. In 1916, Hensley Henson, dissenting from the view that the absence of total abstinence was all that stood between the British nation and divine blessing, thought the whole campaign in favour of it was misguided and demonstrably futile. Inevitably, he said so publicly.

Drunkenness was not the only evil. Gambling, prostitution and the pursuit of blatant luxury were all thought to be on the increase. These evils might perhaps only be comprehensively addressed by a National Mission of Repentance and Hope. Launched in the autumn of 1916, following much discussion on how the church might best respond to the 'needs of the hour', it took as its starting point that there was 'something radically wrong among ourselves'. Evangelicals, in particular, wished to make sure that any focus on national sins should not lead anyone to think lightly of individual ones.[128] Under the aegis of a central council, bishops in diocese after diocese also stressed 'the opportunity of the hour'. 'Repentance' was required because of the sins which had stained British civilization but 'Hope' was to be found in Christ for the rebuilding of a new world. Winnington-Ingram toured every diocese. Individual bishops took their own initiatives. Some emphasized the need for individual amendment of life while others stressed corporate regeneration. The objective was to meet the man in the street and, quite possibly, the woman too. The newly appointed bishop of Peterborough, whose aggressive chin, we read, was mitigated by the moulding of his mouth, addressed large gatherings, including one of 15,000 people in Northampton. The message was simple: 'We must get back to God.' Though he found individual Nonconformists 'very agreeable' and supportive, there was no formal co-operation. This was still a *national* mission being undertaken by the *national* church. Once it came to an end, individual bishops sustained the effort in their own dioceses in whatever way they thought effective. Peterborough earned attention in the press by becoming known as the 'walking bishop'. Beginning in 1917, he walked from village to village in his diocese in the summer months wearing a purple cassock, holding a shepherd's crook as his pastoral staff, and shaking people

[128] Kenneth Hylson-Smith, *Evangelicals in the Church of England, 1734–1984* (Edinburgh, 1989), 280.

by the hand. He apparently radiated hope and kindliness wherever he went. Reporters scoured the countryside seeking news on his whereabouts in order to tell their readers about this massive effort.[129] On the Western Front, the National Mission received public support from three army commanders, Horne, Gough and Allenby, the latter pronouncing that, having made an act of repentance, and having purged every base motive, 'we may go forward in high hope to the sure triumph awaiting us'.[130] The bishop for Northern Europe, on an extraordinary visit to the Ruhleben internment camp in Germany, had the difficult task of explaining the National Mission to its inmates. He came away conscious of what he described as the true and strong Christian life and witness to be found amongst the men, thanks largely to the YMCA. A Canadian inmate, however, whilst acknowledging the 'tremendous emotional response' to the bishop's visit, thought its effect was short-lived. The rigidities of ecclesiastical institutions, with their absurd divisions, could have no purpose, he claimed, for the social body that was Ruhleben. It was not a comment which the bishop would have wanted or perhaps expected.[131]

Since the National Mission and its diocesan successors did not have 'targets' that were measurable, opinion differed on whether it had been a success. Hensley Henson was predictably scathing. He saw little point in missioners running about the country exhorting little companies of puzzled women. Such 'dervish-like fervour', he thought, could not be maintained and was neither illuminating nor morally helpful. The 'slump in religion', which the National Mission had been designed to arrest, had continued. Others who, unlike him, had taken an active part, drew encouragement from these signs of life. Lang had little sympathy with what he called the war-weary and disgruntled spirits who criticized it. He had devised a very elaborate organization to send out the best available clergy, two by two, into all the towns and villages of the diocese of York. He was sure it had been worthwhile.

The National Mission was an English/Welsh and Anglican affair but it was noted in Scotland. The General Assemblies both of the Church of Scotland and of the United Free Church appointed special commissions at their annual meetings in May 1916 whose purpose, as one speaker put it, would be to find answers for those who were saying that Christianity was a failure and the church worthless. The thrust of both reports was that the church should focus on ensuring that Scotland should not return to what was

---

[129] Edward S. Woods and Frederick B. MacNutt, *Theodore, Bishop of Winchester: Pastor, Prophet, Pilgrim* (London, 1933), 72–86.

[130] Cited in Snape, *God and the British Soldier*, 70.

[131] Herbert Bury, *My Visit to Ruhleben* (London, 1917), 53–63; J. Davidson Ketchum, *Ruhleben: A Prison Camp Society* (Toronto, 1965), 246–9.

described as 'the chaos of pre-war conditions'. The churches should stand 'shoulder to shoulder' in the 'coming Great War against Poverty'. Repentance and reform were again placed together. But, at a time when paper was scarce, there were some who had little patience with all this 'windy talk'. They disliked seeing Scots ecclesiastics 'imitate' what was referred to as the 'whining tone of the Anglican "Mission"'. That was not a good thing. It would take a good deal to prove that 'our baptised and confirmed people, fighting and dying, are to be roughly called to a confession of national sins'.[132]

A call to repentance, however, never particularly welcome, was likely to be resisted by a nation convinced that the enemy stood in greater need of it. The National Mission concluded on the eve of the political crisis which brought David Lloyd George, 'the man to win the war', to 10 Downing Street. There was the man on whom more immediate hope rested.

x. Sacrifice and Hope: Resurrecting Ireland

On 24 April 1916, the day after Shakespeare's birthday, an anniversary which the *Irish Times* had particularly wanted its readers to note, an insurrection occurred in Dublin. An army of less than 2,000 rebels, proclaiming an Irish republic, occupied much of central Dublin for the best part of a week. The Church of Ireland archbishop, from his residence overlooking St Stephen's Green, predictably proclaimed the duty of obedience to the existing order. His letter to *The Times*, the following month, declared that this was not the time for amnesties and pardons in Ireland but for punishment swift and stern. In a letter to Lloyd George in June, he was able to report that 'the one class in Ireland which has *not* had resort to arms in support of its political options in 1913–16 is the Unionist class in the South and West'. At a time when new organizations were mushrooming, Protestants in Connaught, Leinster and Munster formed neither party nor army and, with only tiny exceptions, kept outside anyone else's.[133] The Easter Rising took place on the first anniversary of the death of the archbishop's son when leading his men in the Dublin Fusiliers in a bayonet charge. The Church of Ireland bishop of Tuam, unexpectedly finding his car commandeered for barricade purposes, presented his card to the rebels and was gratified by the return of his vehicle. It was evidently encouraging, if perhaps a little surprising, that all Church of Ireland bishops were thought worthy of such respect.

---

[132] Material in this paragraph, and the citations, are derived from Brown, 'A Solemn Purification by Fire', 97–9. Brown takes the view that Scottish Presbyterianism had become individualistic in its piety and largely voluntary in its organization and could not understand what corporate repentance was supposed to entail.

[133] Quoted and commented on in Peter Hart, *The I.R.A. at War 1916–1923* (Oxford, 2003), 228.

The Presbyterians in Lower Abbey Street were appalled at the complete destruction of their church hall in the violence. It was, they thought, the supineness of those responsible for the government of Ireland which had led to the rebellion.

A few further sentences here cannot do justice to the complexity of the reactions to what was taking place. Stupefaction at stupidity, admiration of heroism, and condemnation of treason, all were felt in the quarters where one would expect to find them. It is difficult to judge the balance of opinion in Dublin (and even more in Ireland as a whole) on a day-to-day basis. Most contemporaries, and historians, seem to agree, however, that the stern punishment sought by the archbishop—which did see the execution of Patrick Pearse, James Connolly and other leaders after their trial by court-martial—had the consequence, which he did not desire, of steadily increasing sympathy for them and their cause. Blood sacrifice had not been in vain—or so it could seem.

On 1 July 1916, the date on which the Battle of the Boyne had been fought, and henceforward remembered, the British army began its ill-fated offensive on the Somme. In the first three days, the 36th (Ulster) Division—almost exclusively Protestant—suffered around 5,500 casualties, some 3,000 being fatalities, a substantial proportion of its total strength. Ulster soldiers were the only ones to reach the German second line anywhere, but they were not adequately supported. At a crowded watch night service at New Year 1915 a young officer had told his men that before the year was out 'we may all be killed' but added, 'to a Christian, death is only beginning to live'.[134] The scale of this disaster had a profound impact in the local communities from which particular battalions of the division had been drawn. There was scarcely a home, it was said with pardonable exaggeration, where there was not a death in the family. Immediately, though capable of being given other meanings with the passage of time, the loss of life was taken to be an indication of Ulster's commitment to the British Crown and to the imperial cause. A debt, in turn, had been incurred. Blood sacrifice had not been in vain—or so it could seem.[135]

The churches did not, or could not, stand outside these developments. Even in the act of declaring itself 'a strictly non-political body', the Irish Guild of the Church, recently founded to promote 'Irish ideals' within the Church of Ireland, affirmed its loyalty to the Crown and deplored the recent rising. It wished to make it plain that it had 'no connection whatever with

[134] Cited in Snape, *God and the British Soldier*, 157.

[135] B. Graham and P. Shirlow, 'The Battle of the Somme in Ulster Memory and Identity', *Political Geography* 21 (2002), 881–904 and 'The Place of Ulster: Alternative Loyalist Identities' in Helen Brocklehurst and Robert Phillips, eds., *History, Nationhood and the Question of Britain* (Basingstoke, 2004), 99–111. Keith Jeffery, *Ireland and the Great War* (Cambridge, 2000).

it'. Dublin Methodists seem to have thought it was 'business as usual'. They opened the 'Soldiers' Rendezvous' in Abbey Street in May 1916 and provided 1,000 meals a day, together with a variety of recreational facilities. It was reported that 600 voluntary ladies from the Dublin churches made the work 'the success which it proved to be'.[136] The Co. Kerry-born Lord Kitchener expressed his appreciation of their efforts. But clearly it was not business as usual. The 'Tommies' being given tea in the Abbey Street Lecture Hall—'our lads'—were, in other circles, perceived as no less an army of occupation than German forces in Belgium.

The air was thick with assertions of loyalty and accusations of treachery— but to what?[137] Protestants in the South, if they had reluctantly reconciled themselves to Home Rule of the 1914 variety, nevertheless still saw Ireland's place as within the United Kingdom and the British Empire. Protestants in the North now looked to the permanent exclusion from Home Rule of a six-county Ulster. Indeed, after the Easter Rising, Lloyd George and Carson cobbled together such a plan, but it collapsed. The former brought the latter into his coalition government, where he occupied several posts until January 1918. Carson's presence was a symbol of that devotion to the British cause which had been so recently sealed in blood on the Somme. 'Protestant unity', however, was precarious, reflecting the uneven distribution of the Protestant population. That was most evident in the case of the two Church of Ireland archbishops. Dublin rejected partition but was prepared to contemplate self-government for all Ireland. The granddaughter of one of his predecessors, he would have been shocked to discover, had thrown herself passionately into the cause of an Irish Ireland and had associated herself with the Rising even as her horrified brother fought at the Front as a British soldier.[138] Armagh said he regarded the prospect of partition 'with horror', but rejected Irish self-government. Less exalted churchmen changed their minds as it became clear which way the wind was blowing. The Annual General Meeting of the Irish Guild of the Church in May 1918 overturned the condemnation of the Rising which its Executive Committee had passed in June 1916, whereupon its president, the bishop of Killaloe, resigned and walked out, together with many others. In the aftermath, two competing organizations existed, one claiming to be traditional and the other claiming that the tradition was reactionary.[139]

---

[136] Alexander McCrea, ed., *Irish Methodism in the Twentieth Century* (Belfast, 1933), 78–9.

[137] O.D. Edwards, 'Divided Treasons and Divided Loyalties: Roger Casement and Others', *Transactions of the Royal Historical Society* 32 (1982), 153–74; Jane Leonard, 'The Reactions of Irish Officers in the British Army to the Easter Rising of 1916', in Cecil and Liddle, *Facing Armageddon*, 156–68.

[138] Cesca Chenevix Trench.

[139] Megahey, *Irish Protestant Churches*, 42.

The Convention chaired by Sir Horace Plunkett (in which Sinn Féin did not participate) passed month after month from July 1917 exploring options. Every member was supposed to use his best efforts to submit to the British government a constitution 'for the future government of Ireland, within the Empire'. The new factor—as Plunkett, from direct personal experience, was well aware—was the United States. The sympathy and perhaps direct intervention of Washington might make all the difference in the war. A deal between Southern unionists and nationalists, as from time to time seemed possible, might be such that no British government, with an eye to the United States, could refuse to agree to it. Writing to Bonar Law in January 1918, Lloyd George suggested that the Irish were 'paralysing the war activities of America'.[140] Ulster talked about the empire; now was the time for it to demonstrate that it placed the empire above everything. If the 'little Protestant communities of the south' who were 'isolated in a turbulent sea of sinn féinism and popery' could agree to the scheme associated with their leader, the Earl of Midleton, surely the powerful Protestant communities of the north would take the risk. If America went 'wrong', he concluded, 'we are lost'.[141] Indeed, with the Allies facing possible defeat in France in the late spring of 1918, it did look momentarily as though Ulster might wobble. On the other hand, Midleton had difficulty in keeping Southern unionism together. In the event, however, the Convention came to an end in April 1918 without an agreed solution. Its discussions having spun out time, it looked as though Lloyd George was going to implement partition. The pursuit of some kind of pan-Ireland accommodation was over. The Northern mystic, poet, painter and philosopher George W. Russell (AE), tendering his resignation from the Convention to Plunkett in February 1918, felt that the only thing which could now be done was to let the 'new forces of nationalism manifest themselves in their full strength'. A man had to either be an Irishman or an Englishman. Russell was Irish.[142]

John Redmond died in London in March 1918. His funeral service at the Brompton Oratory apparently resembled that of a royal personage. Midleton later contrasted that tribute with the perfunctory honour shown Redmond in Dublin. 'The Catholic authorities' had shown their hand by ignoring the arrival of Redmond's remains there prior to interment at Wexford. In his view, the Catholic bishops who had taken part in the Convention sabotaged its chances and, in so doing, apparently fulfilled the

[140] F.M. Carroll, *American Opinion and the Irish Question 1910–1923* (Dublin and New York, 1978) explores this aspect of the situation.

[141] Cited in Trevor West, *Horace Plunkett, Co-operation and Politics: An Irish Biography* (Gerrards Cross, 1986), 169–70.

[142] West, *Plunkett*, 173.

prediction of a Catholic farmer that 'a mist, emanating from the Church, would come over the Convention'.[143] He had singled out the bishop of Raphoe who was boasting an expert, though possibly exaggerated, knowledge of the impact which the English rate of tax on articles like tea and sugar would have on his flock in Donegal. A certain mist had also come over Midleton, because his daughter, Albinia, had turned republican, although there was perhaps consolation for him in that, unlike Dorothy Stopford, her fellow Protestant republican, she had not also taken to smoking a pipe.[144]

This need to think in terms of 'either/or' was frequently felt most compulsively at this juncture by those who, whether by cultural ambience, double domiciles or personal ancestry, were in reality, to one degree or another, and in different social milieux 'both/and'. Patrick Pearse had blotted out his English father and James Connolly had been born and early brought up in Edinburgh. Some, but few, prominent individuals had bolted, in whole or in part, from the ecclesiastical enclosures or sense of identity in which they had been raised, but the equation of Protestantism with u/Unionism and British/Irishness (even if both of these identities might be thought suspect by their 'real owners') was pervasive, though not the complete picture. Those Protestants who, from conviction or prudence, now wanted a complete severance of the British connection or, as it might alternatively be put, freedom from the British yoke, if so minded, could invoke Wolfe Tone or Robert Emmet, to mention only two talismanic names. Douglas Hyde, president of the Gaelic League, and Standish O'Grady, narrator of heroic Ireland, were both sons of Church of Ireland rectors. Remaining Protestants, like W.B. Yeats, not that there were many Protestants who were quite like Yeats, were indeed not Catholics but they could hardly be said to share the mental or cultural 'Ulster-Scots' world inhabited by Presbyterians in the north-east, socially stratified though that in turn was.[145] The political strategies of Protestants, North and South, Presbyterian, Anglican or Methodist, were defensive whatever precise version of the medley of federal, confederal or unitary possibilities for the future of Ireland being dangled in front of them (and not all Protestants were specialists in constitutional theory). The men on the Somme had made the blood sacrifice in a Division whose motto was 'For God and Ulster'. The blood sacrifice in Dublin had been 'For God and Ireland'.[146]

[143] Earl of Midleton, *Records and Reactions 1856–1939* (London, 1939), 244.

[144] Léon Ó'Broin, *Protestant Nationalists in Revolutionary Ireland: The Stopford Connection* (Dublin, 1985) traces the realignments of another important family.

[145] R. Munck, 'Class and Religion in Belfast: A Historical Perspective', *Journal of Contemporary History* 20 (1985), 241–59; H. Patterson, *Class Conflict and Sectarianism: The Protestant Working Class and the Belfast Labour Movement 1868–1920* (Belfast, 1980).

[146] Guillemont, on the Somme battlefield, had been taken by the 16th Division, the self-styled 'Irish Brigade'.

A Rising that takes place over Easter cannot escape symbolic associations, nor did most of the participants wish it to do so. The resurrection of Ireland lay before them. A proclamation 'In the name of God and of the dead generations' made explicit connections. Nationalism, for Sinn Féin, in theory transcended confessional allegiance, but reality was rather different. Rebel garrisons during the Rising regularly recited the rosary together. Piety was conspicuous. Of the 1916 leaders, only Tom Clarke, an old Fénian, died without the last rites of the Catholic Church. Even Roger Casement was received into its ranks before his execution. Not surprisingly, Casement was the only one of those about to die who was known personally to the archbishop of Canterbury, who had admired his agitation about the Congo. Davidson attempted to intervene with the home secretary and the lord chancellor. He did not attempt to deny that Casement deserved hanging, but policy 'in the largest sense of the word' could not be ignored and another course should be found. He was not successful. James Connolly, having made his confession, perhaps a firm indication of his return to the faith, was anointed by a Capuchin friar. On the eve of his execution, he asked his Protestant wife, Lily, to convert to Catholicism. The capitalist, William Martin Murphy, who had been his bitter enemy during the 1913 Dublin lock-out, nevertheless apparently felt 'every drop of Catholic blood' surge up in his veins following Connolly's execution.

Such facts might suggest the complete unity of Catholicism and revolutionary nationalism. Yet the position was not that simple. Individual priests in particular situations might think differently, but the hierarchy had broadly identified itself with constitutional nationalism and the parliamentary path to a new Ireland. The Easter Rising, the work of a tiny conspiracy, could only with difficulty satisfy the conditions for a just rebellion.[147] Cardinal Logue condemned it, as did seven other members of the hierarchy unqualifiedly and one qualifiedly. One, in effect, condoned it. A total of twenty-two bishops judged that it was best to say nothing. The seven unreservedly condemned the rebels on theological grounds, though, pragmatically, one thought it simply madness when the 'English army' amounted to five million men (though he had presumably noted that there was a European war on).[148] Logue had a soft spot for the Empire and kept on stating that he could not see why patriotism should stand between the duty of Irishmen to the 'higher powers' and their attachment

---

[147] J. Newsinger, 'Revolution and Catholicism in Ireland', *European Studies Review* 9 (1979), 457–80.

[148] John Whyte, '1916: Revolution and Religion' in F.X. Martin, ed., *Leaders and Men of the Easter Rising: Dublin 1916* (London, 1967), 221–3 and discussion in Michael Laffan, 'The Sacred Memory: Religion, Revisionists and the Easter Rising' in Judith Devlin and Ronan Fanning, eds., *Religion and Rebellion*, Historical Studies 20 (Dublin, 1995), 174–91.

to their country and their religion. The cardinal denied that the young clergy were in favour of Sinn Féin. Down in Limerick, however, Bishop O'Dwyer was striking a rather different tone and, unlikely though it appeared at the time, two years later it was to be the right one.

A republic established in the circumstances of April 1916 seemed to most bishops a dubious proposition. Even so, there was no doubt that the subsequent executions had to be condemned. And, to say the least, Connolly's Catholicism was suspect. When directly asked by a friend in 1908 whether he was still in the bosom of the church, he had replied that though he usually posed as a Catholic he had not the slightest tincture of faith left. His pose would help strengthen the appeal of the socialist message to the Catholic working class.[149] He was a Marxist. Bit by bit, however, the church had to adapt itself to the evolution of public opinion. By 1918 the hierarchy's general support for the war had melted away. In the crisis of 1918 the clergy could not have forced Irishmen to have accepted conscription. Bishops had to look to what appeared to be the future. Eventually, de Valera was to be the man to back.[150]

Pearse's 'Catholic vision' also drew on, and to some extent hallowed, a semi-pagan past. The picture he painted of a future in which the Gael, who was not like other men, would instruct the nations of the world, linked into a popular piety. He had translated into English a seventeenth-century Irish poem which had forecast victory to the host of the Gael over the clans of Calvin and Luther. A welding together of the Gael for this purpose in the early twentieth century might recreate a Gaelic Catholic Ireland but hardly constituted a welcoming scenario of an Irish future when viewed from the north-east.[151]

The notion that the corollary of love of Ireland was hatred of England was certainly not a particular recipe for harmony in the British Army at this juncture. It was not as though it was only the Ulster Division which was fighting in France.[152] Listowel-born though he might be, Kitchener had set

---

[149] Cited in W.K. Anderson, *James Connolly and the Irish Left* (Blackrock and Melbourne, 1994), 26–7. Subsequent pages discuss Connolly and religion. O.D. Edwards, *The Mind of an Activist: James Connolly* (Dublin, 1971); R.D. Edwards, *James Connolly* (Dublin, 1981). A general discussion is E. Larkin, 'Socialism and Catholicism in Ireland', *Church History* 33 (1964), 462–93.

[150] See the chapters on 1916 and 1918 in J. aan de Wiel, *The Catholic Church in Ireland 1914–1918: War and Politics* (Dublin, 2003), 78–126 and 203–54.

[151] This exposition draws on Sheridan Gilley, 'Pearse's Sacrifice: Christ and Cuchulain Crucified and Risen in the Easter Rising, 1916' in Jim Obelkevich, Lyndal Roper and Raphael Samuel, eds., *Disciplines of Faith: Studies in Religion, Politics and Patriarchy* (London, 1987), 479–97. Ruth Dudley Edwards, *Patrick Pearse: The Triumph of Failure* (London, 1977) and Brian P. Murphy, *Patrick Pearse and the Lost IRB Idea* (Dublin,1991). For more general discussion see M. Goldring, *Faith of our Fathers: The Formation of Irish Nationalist Ideology, 1890–1920* (Dublin, 1982).

[152] In general see Terence Denman, 'The Catholic Irish Soldier in the First World War: The Racial Environment', *Irish Historical Studies* 27 (1991), 352–65 and *Ireland's Unknown Soldiers* (Dublin, 1992); see also specific pieces in David Fitzpatrick, ed., *Ireland and the Great War* (Gigginstown, Mullingar, 1988).

himself against Redmond's suggestion that predominantly Catholic and nationalist regiments be grouped into an Irish Brigade. It had been only reluctantly that he had agreed to the Ulster Division, but agree to it he had. The contrast was obvious. Augustine Birrell, the Chief Secretary for Ireland until April 1916, commented that Kitchener was not a real Irishman, only an accidental one. Even so, there were two other Irish Divisions, the 10th and 16th. Redmond provided a list of Roman Catholic officers and the GOC of the 16th was replaced specifically in order to appoint a Roman Catholic. Redmond's son joined up, and his brother, Willie, died at the Front. He had been carried off the battlefield in an Ulster ambulance.[153] This touching episode, a soldier wrote home, 'should go far to reconcile the mutually antagonistic Irish parties'.[154] Willie, and Charles Craig (brother of the man who was later Northern Ireland's first prime minister), had been gazetted on the same day in the French Legion of Honour. There was symbolism here, but only for those who wished to see it.[155] Although denounced by his opponents, Redmond's supporters appealed for recruits at public meetings. In Galway, three cheers were given for the Connaught Rangers and the large crowd sang 'God Save the King'. The volunteers from Dublin, though only initially around a third of those volunteering in Belfast, were Catholic and Protestant in roughly equal numbers (the Protestant population, of course being much smaller). In the South as a whole Protestants did not volunteer in proportionately higher numbers. All told, 145,000 Irishmen were to volunteer, of whom 65,000 were Catholics. The 'allegiance' of the Divisions was closely watched. The *Weekly Northern Whig* claimed that there were more Ulster Unionists than nationalists in the 10th and it should not therefore be viewed as 'Redmond's'. Protestants were apprehensive that their greater recruitment rate—and hence likely casualties—would adversely affect their relative strength in Ireland when the war ended. Redmond visited the Front in the autumn of 1915 and, on his return, at a recruiting meeting for the Royal Irish Rifles in London, spoke emotionally about the Ulsters and the Dubliners side by side 'like comrades and brothers'. He prayed that whenever an Irish battalion went into action there would be an Ulster division alongside them. Basil Brooke, later prime minister of Northern Ireland, promised, in this elevated and fraternal atmosphere, that he would never again resort to anti-Catholic rhetoric.[156]

The rising of April 1916, whatever else it did, shattered this expressed spirit (and apparently absolved Brooke from his promise). It naturally

[153] Terence Denman, *A Lonely Grave: The Life and Death of William Redmond* (Blackrock, 1995).
[154] Jones, *War Letters* (18 June 1917), 248.
[155] Paul Bew, *Ideology and the Irish Question* (Oxford, 1990) discusses the project of 'Redmondism', 118–52.
[156] Bew, *Ideology*, 140, cites Redmond and Brooke.

created a new situation in France, though one observer the following month noted that a football match being played between the 6th Battalion, Connaught Rangers, and an Ulster battalion, was played 'in a spirit of friendliness which, so far as I am aware, seems unattainable on Ireland's native soil'.[157] Redmond felt the horror of knowing that on the same day as men of the Dublin fusiliers had been killed by Irishmen on the streets of Dublin the Irishmen of the 16th Division had shown unconquerable bravery in recapturing certain German trenches. Over a year later, preaching to the men of that same division at St Omer, the Roman Catholic chaplain, William Doyle, linked their impending exploits to those of the Irish 'Wild Geese' in Flanders two centuries earlier. It was no mean diplomatic achievement on his part to establish a continuity between men who had fought against England with men who were now fighting with, if not for, England.[158] Ironically, however, the bloodletting diluted the Protestant and Catholic character of the respective Irish divisions even as Protestant and Catholic divisions became ever stronger in Ireland itself. The archbishop of Canterbury was being told in September 1916 that Roman Catholics only constituted 45 per cent of the 16th division. Irish recruits were not coming forward in sufficient numbers. The vacancies in the Irish divisions were increasingly filled by English conscripts. By the end of the war, it had only one Irish battalion. The Ulster division's composition was such that, on St Patrick's Day in 1918, Mass was being celebrated and shamrock distributed.[159] A final unexpected twist was that the 10th Division latterly found itself in Palestine, but with so many Indian battalions that it lost its 'Irish' designation. The British government in April 1918 had attempted to extend conscription to Ireland as a way of making good this dilution, but all over Ireland thousands declared their opposition to what was described as a 'blood tax'. Such opposition, however, had led to Tom Johnson, the Irish Labour leader, receiving a bloody head in front of City Hall Belfast from a missile despatched by pro-conscription Unionist workers. It was Cardinal Logue of Armagh who organized a strongly-worded anti-conscription pledge. In the circumstances, the measure could not be implemented. Irishmen were not going to make one last push for the British Empire.

The armistice of November 1918 brought one war to a conclusion. The future of Ireland (and its relations with Great Britain) might be decided only by another war, or wars. They would be more limited in scale but possibly even more intense because of their fratricidal intimacy and indeterminate

---

[157] Cited in J.G. Fuller, *Troop Morale and Popular Culture in the British and Dominion Armies, 1914–1918* (Oxford, 1990), 89.

[158] A. O'Rahilly, ed., *Father William Doyle, S.J.: A Spiritual Study* (London, 1932), 522.

[159] Snape, *God and the British Soldier*, 145–6.

boundaries. Our analysis of Ireland in the Great War has necessarily only skimmed the surface of a complex and rapidly shifting political scene. The politics have been examined from contrasting and often conflicting perspectives as historians have explored the roads taken and not taken. Our summary narrative has naturally drawn particular attention to the pervasive presence of the labels 'Catholic' and 'Protestant' as markers and identifiers. Yet what is striking, historiographically, is the absence, largely, of attempts by historians to write about the churches in this crisis.[160] What were the thoughts and the actions of leaders and people, at a time of cultural conflict, contested ethnicity and, apparently in all likelihood, further bloodshed? The reticence in this regard, however, may suggest that such an unpicking is impossible, or has been too painful. 'The church', or rather its non-existence, encapsulated the crisis. Nor was this, though British churchmen tended to suppose it was, a peculiarly Irish question. 'The experience of Christianising countries', wrote Father Benson, the founder of the Society of St John the Evangelist, the Cowley Fathers, 'leads one to believe that the country is Christianised at the expense of souls, and when all are Christians none are.'[161] Was this true everywhere?

xi. *Patriotism, Peace and Progress*

'I realize', a 50-year-old nurse told the chaplain attending her on the eve of her death, 'that patriotism is not enough. I must have no hatred or bitterness towards anyone.' Edith Cavell, daughter of a Norfolk rector, working in a Red Cross hospital in Brussels in August 1915, had been arrested by the Germans for having assisted Allied servicemen to escape to the non-belligerent Netherlands. She was tried by court-martial and shot. Perhaps ironically, she became a 'national martyr' and, in due time, had a commemorative statue off Trafalgar Square. Nine months earlier, also in Belgium, Cardinal Mercier's message to his flock was that 'the religion of Christ makes patriotism a law: there is no perfect Christian who is not a perfect patriot'.[162]

---

[160] It is perhaps significant that aan de Wiel's substantial recent study was written as a French doctorate. Peter Hart, in arguing from Newfoundland that the Irish revolution needs to be 'reconceptualized', lists 'religion and ethnicity' together with many other categories—gender, class, community, elites and masses, the nature of violence and power, periodization and geography—which need to be explored 'without compartmentalization' but nevertheless in the process has already compartmentalized 'religion and ethnicity' as 'one category' rather than two. Hart, *I.R.A. at War*, 28.

[161] R.M.C. Jeffery, ' "When All are Christians None Are": Church and Mission in the Teaching of Father Benson' in M.L. Smith, ed., *Benson of Cowley* (Oxford, 1980), 119.

[162] Cited in Strachan, *First World War*, i. 1118; Cardinal Mercier, *An Appeal to Truth* (London, 1915).

Patriotism was a word with a contested British history, being 'claimed' by both Left and Right in different periods.[163] As these two quotations indicate, war had served to heighten its significance. Patriotism had been proclaimed *ad nauseam*, but was it enough? Mercier had become something of a hero in Britain but might it be rather better to be an imperfect patriot, at least for imperfect Christians? Patriots, zealous for their country's freedom or 'rights', had been noisy in all belligerent countries and had needed little governmental stimulus. It had not proved difficult to find causes which had engaged the zeal of Christians. Therein lay the difficulty. It was tempting to suppose, with Nurse Cavell, that patriotism had had its day. The Enlightenment had tried to present a 'love of humanity' ruled by rationalism, dissolving nationalism and flouting historical tradition or obligation. Ironically, cosmopolitanism, however, according to P.T. Forsyth, had worked itself out in the 'fine tenderness to life' which marked the French Revolution. What he called a 'cosmopolitan humanitarianism' was morally sterile. It could not be realized. The only hope of nations (as of churches) was by way of a federation based on common rights and reciprocal respect. Such a federation, however, would also have to include 'the past'. The future could not be jumped into except by violence, and then it was insecure. Humanity was a chaotic sum of individuals who cohered, if at all, in a unity that was vast, remote and feeble. A nation, perhaps a federation of free nations, small enough for the members to love each other yet not large enough to lord the world, was the form in which the supranational unity of man had a real home.[164]

Forsyth, though too often tempted by paradox, had a shrewd grasp of where the war might leave Europe. There could be no jump into a cosmopolitan fantasy. There was, however, a widespread feeling in the British churches that 'something had to be done' (though not in conscious imitation of Lenin's injunction). Was the United Kingdom of Great Britain and Ireland (and its empire) both 'small enough' and yet 'not too large'? In these circumstances, exegetical attention turned to the Tower of Babel— and to Pentecost. The Book of Revelation, in eschatological terms, talked of healing rather than eradicating nations. And at Pentecost, as it has been put, when the Spirit comes, all understand each other 'not because one language is restored or a new all-encompassing meta-language is designed, but because each hears his or her own language spoken'. Pentecost, on this reading, did not overcome 'confusion' by 'reverting to the unity of cultural uniformity, but by advancing towards the harmony of cultural diversity'.[165]

[163] Hugh Cunningham, 'The Language of Patriotism, 1750–1914', *History Workshop Journal*, 12 (1981), 8–33.
[164] Forsyth, *Christian Ethic of War*, 1–5.
[165] The argument of Miroslav Volf, *Exclusion and Embrace: A Theological Exploration of Identity, Otherness and Reconciliation* (Nashville, TN, 1996), 228.

What unit, in such a context, was small enough for its members to love one another, or at least to feel that they constituted a 'community'? Enough has already been said to indicate that, for most inhabitants of Ireland, the United Kingdom was not small enough, though also that, in turn, for others, Ireland itself might be too big. For the moment, also, no disposition 'to love one another' was particularly manifest. Great Britain, however, still seemed small enough for most of its inhabitants, but it also contained 'nations' of uncertain import for whom it might seem too big. Emrys ap Iwan (d. 1906) was a Welshman who had left a legacy to the next generation in preaching Christian nationalism, or perhaps it was nationalist Christianity. He had asked his fellow Welshmen, not all of whom were responsive, to remember that God had made people as nations. They were therefore not to be ashamed of things, language in particular, which distinguished themselves from other nations. It was especially important not to imitate the nation next door [England] 'in her pride, her arrogance, her boastfulness, her love of war, her frivolity, her narrowness of thought and her lack of sympathy with other nations'.[166] Confronted by such a list of his nation's attributes, an Englishman might blink a little, but according to the bishop of Stepney (who was not averse to giving blessings in Hebrew) variety of speech was significant. A nation's language was a wonderful thing. It was 'the very express image of all that goes to make it a nation; its past, its present, its future . . . National endowment and character and aspiration have shaped and toned it. The nation's language is the nation's soul.' He did not want to merge 'the divers tongues into some eccentricity of a universal language'.[167] It was a sentiment, though not about the English language, which drove Patrick Pearse and indeed enthusiasts for language revival and national regeneration throughout Europe amidst the collapse of the three great empires—Romanov, Hohen-zollern and Habsburg—which had existed in 1914. Evidence of an intensity of belonging was everywhere. Boundaries between peoples were not dissolving, they were simply being redrawn. Religious and national discourse had been drawing so deeply on the same terminology—faith, hope, liberation in par-ticular—that separation might prove impossible, except in a sense that was academic. The acknowledgement of both 'Christian belonging' and 'Christian distance' in the British Isles, in particular in those areas where history had bequeathed a complex and fragile ethno–linguistic–cultural–religious in-heritance, might be more easily proclaimed than put into practice.[168]

---

[166] Cited and discussed in Dorian Llywelyn, *Sacred Place, Chosen People: Land and National Identity in Welsh Spirituality* (Cardiff, 1999), 54–5.

[167] Paget, *In the Day of Battle*, 3.

[168] The terminology of 'distance and belonging' has been derived from Volf. It is discussed with particular relevance to Ireland/Ulster in Patrick Mitchel, *Evangelicalism and National Identity in Ulster 1921–1998* (Oxford, 2003), 61–8 but has application here throughout the British Isles.

The hope for the future, therefore, might be that nations would 'league' together rather than struggle against each other. The last years of the war, particularly in the 'Anglo-Saxon world', had seen the development of the idea that another inter-state war, like that of 1914, could be avoided by forming a 'League of Nations'. Not surprisingly, the various discussion documents that had been drawn up differed in considerable detail, but they seemed to offer a 'new world order'. Lord Bryce, who had been chairing one such group, enlisted the support of the archbishop of Canterbury. Lord Robert Cecil saw the proposal, in whatever form it might eventually take, as giving 'a special opportunity for the church'. Davidson wanted to give more than lip-service to a great ideal. The issues involved were world-wide, the archbishop wrote to *The Times* in late September 1918, and 'our vision and our purpose must be world-wide too'.

The British Empire was world-wide, but was it merely a form of domination or was it (which a League, it was claimed, was not) a 'going concern' no doubt flawed in detail but capable of being an example to the world at large? It was the empire as a whole, rather than just the United Kingdom, which had won the war. It was obvious, at its conclusion, that some new statement would have to be made which recognized the status of 'the Dominions'. 'In plain words', wrote Lionel Curtis, who had been working on these matters with 'Round Table' groups throughout the empire, 'the issue . . . is whether the Dominions are to become independent republics, or whether this world-wide Commonwealth is destined to stand more closely united as the noblest of all political achievements'.[169] A strain of Christian idealism expressed by Curtis and, with variation, by Sir Alfred Zimmern, came close to believing that the British Empire was the nearest realization on earth of the Kingdom of God. It was a unique agency for the moral improvement of the world's inhabitants.[170] It was not an English, nor an Anglo-Saxon, but a 'world experiment'. The fact was that the British had a special genius for governing. It was perhaps not advisable to say so too publicly, but they really ought to be 'lords of the whole earth'. In places such as Nigeria, Egypt or India there was 'no practicable alternative' to empire.[171] British administration throughout the world, Lord Milner had told a missionary meeting presided over by the archbishop of Canterbury in

---

[169] Lionel Curtis, *The Problem of the Commonwealth* (London, 1916); Deborah Lavin, *From Empire to International Commonwealth: A Biography of Lionel Curtis* (Oxford, 1995); G. Studdert-Kennedy, 'Political Science and Political Theology', *Journal of Imperial and Commonwealth History* 24 (1996), 197–217.

[170] If God meant Germany 'to do for Asia Minor what we have done for India and Egypt' why had Germany allowed the Armenians to be massacred, one writer asked. H.L. Goudge in G.K.A. Bell, ed., *The War and the Kingdom of God* (London, 1916), 177.

[171] G.K. Pleatling, 'Globalism, Hegemonism and British Power: J.A. Hobson and Alfred Zimmern Reconsidered', *History* 89/3 (2004), 381–98.

1909, ought 'always to be based upon Christian principles, and to be animated by Christian ideals, but that is only in the broadest sense. As between different religious communities the British administrator is pledged to perfect tolerance and impartiality.' No other attitude was practicable.[172] Such even-handedness, supposing it to be the reality, was admirable, but it seemed to presuppose that the conquered peoples of the empire would be content to be subjected to government on this basis.

The empire might be becoming wider still and wider. There was no lack of symbolism in the fact that it was a British general, Sir Edmund Allenby, whose support of the National Mission of Repentance and Hope has been noted, who entered Jerusalem on foot on 9 December 1917. The devout study of George Adam Smith's *Historical Geography of the Holy Land*, it was claimed, had given him tactical help.[173] Notwithstanding that this was a Protestant presence, the bells of Rome apparently rang in celebration of a Christian triumph—if that was what it was. There was, however, another reality. The British Empire contained more Muslims than any other state in the world. John Buchan's *Greenmantle*, described by a contemporary reader on the Western Front as 'a thoroughly live story', has his hero Richard Hannay crushing a German plot which would aim to provoke an Islamic Holy War against the British.[174] Setbacks for the Ottoman forces, together with the 'Balfour Declaration' of the previous month, in which the British government had stated its support for a 'national home' for Jews in Palestine, led to the formation of the Advent Testimony Movement whose members, under the presidency of Dr F.B. Meyer, felt called to prepare the way for the coming again of the Lord Jesus Christ.[175] Miss Christabel Pankhurst, to the surprise of those who knew her only as a militant in the suffrage cause, had become of that persuasion, having been aroused by a notable volume on *The Approaching End of the Age*. The return of the Jews to Palestine was interpreted in such circles as a sure sign of the Second Coming. Even if that were not to happen, the mandate over Palestine under the League of Nations, which Britain was shortly to assume, placed it at the very heart of Christian–Jewish–Muslim relations—with consequences which, at the time, could scarcely have been imagined. In such a context, Britain itself was perceived as a Christian state. There had been some indigenous converts to Islam,

[172] Lord Milner, *The Nation and the Empire* (London, 1913), 414.

[173] Iain D. Campbell, *Fixing the Indemnity: The Life and Work of Sir George Adam Smith (1856–1942)* (Carlisle, 2004), 91. I owe this reference to Professor S.J. Brown.

[174] Jones, *War Letters*, 228.

[175] W.Y. Fullerton, *F.B. Meyer: A Biography* (London, n.d.), 158–9; Bebbington, *Evangelicalism in Modern Britain*, 223 notes that two bishops were in membership and eighteen military and naval officers. Residence in Greater London and on the south coast was particularly favoured by the members.

but the largely immigrant Muslim population in wartime Britain has been estimated to be around 10,000.[176]

The assumptions that have been sketched naturally do not present a full picture. They were, however, widespread, if not universal, and invited (and received) the criticism that they constituted an implausible moral justification for having painted red one-fifth of the habitable globe. These assumptions constituted a mind-set largely shared by church leaders, since they had been formed and articulated in the educational and social circles in which they moved. There was, however, a recognition, in some quarters, that British governments might be trying to have things both ways. If immediate national independence was in itself desirable for every people in the world then it should not only apply to Belgians, Czechs and Croats but for Poles, Irish and Egyptians. If, on the other hand, it was maintained that independence from the British Empire might be a curse rather than a blessing, might that not also apply to the multi-national empires of Europe?[177]

It is arguable that 'at long last' those who saw themselves as sensitive Christians became ever more aware during the war of the dangerous as well as the contradictory character of their dividedness, yet their problems paralleled those which have been just considered: the particular and the universal.[178] The war brought some unanticipated conjunctures. Without it, the archbishop of Canterbury would never have received the sash and broach of the first-class grade of the Serbian Order of St Sava from the prime minister of Serbia at Claridge's Hotel in October 1918. It was in recognition of the help which the Anglican Church had been giving to the Serbian Church. Early in the war, Davidson had also had a most courteous correspondence with the Roman Catholic archbishop of Rouen—who had signified his assent to the Church of England using certain Roman Catholic chapels for services. Greetings were sent to the Russian Orthodox Church both before and after the Bolshevik revolution in 1917. It was obviously not possible for such Anglicans as might wish to do so to join in the Luther celebrations in Germany in 1917, but Luther was not to be traduced simply because he was a German. Hensley Henson was one of those who felt that denominations had lost their religious *raison d'être*. The Protestant agitator of pre-1914 England, he thought, would not in future gain a hearing from men who had received the tender ministries of French priests and nuns in hours of desperate need. R.J. Campbell of the City Temple, feeling that he needed 'the corporate unity of the Catholic Church' rather than 'Protestant

---

[176] John Wolffe, 'Fragmented Universality: Islam and Muslims' in Gerald Parsons, ed., *The Growth of Religious Diversity: Britain from 1945* (London, 1993), 144.

[177] Goudge, in Bell, *War and the Kingdom of God*, 182.

[178] D.J. Hall, ' "The Great War" and the Theologians' in G. Baum, ed., *The Twentieth Century: A Theological Overview* (London, 1999), 12.

individualism', resigned his ministry. There was for him, however, a liberty and comprehensiveness in the Church of England which was foreign to the genius of the Church of Rome. The Protestant unity which he desired, however, was only a step along the path to a greater unity still. No unity which excluded Rome or which Rome excluded could be regarded as ultimately satisfactory.[179] Such sentiments only constituted straws in the wind of uncertain import. Denominations, as became evident, were fully as capable as nations of demanding absolute 'loyalty'.

It was possible, as Ronald Knox argued in explaining in 1919 his leaving the Church of England for the Roman Catholic Church, that the disintegration of the world, and of Europe in particular, was going to be far greater than anyone realized. If that was so, 'men will look for guidance to the two institutions which override the boundaries of country—International Socialism and the Catholic Church'.[180] One of the great attractions for him of the Roman Catholic Church was that it was 'everywhere spoken against'. In April 1917, of course speaking about the 'February' rather than the 'October' revolution, the archbishop of Canterbury had written to a friend saying that he did not feel quite as hopeful as she did about 'the doings in Russia'. He was not certain that Russia would be able to escape the bloodthirstiness which was apt to enthuse revolutionaries. He was, however, glad to see an emancipation from archaic ways and from *misrulers*. Five years later, together with other church leaders, Davidson was engaged in vigorous protest to the Soviet government concerning its treatment of Patriarch Tikhon. Speculating on 'The Church and the Future' in 1915 he stressed, 'we have real enemies; and they hate Christ'. Perhaps they were now at the gates.[181] It might be that the competing 'guidance' offered by International Socialism and the Catholic Church (or conceivably all churches in some kind of alliance with it) would come to dominate the future of Britain, Ireland and of Europe. One or other would win.

The British royal family did not immediately seem likely to share the fate of the Russian. Throne and altar remained intact. On the Sunday after Christmas 1918/19, the bishop of Peterborough, at royal command—from what was now the House of Windsor—preached at Sandringham and then spent time with the royal family. After dinner, he was asked to accompany the singing of hymns which each member chose in turn. One of the princes chose the American 'Battle-Hymn of the Republic'.[182] Their royal eyes had seen the glory of the coming land in the west. It was a prudent choice. Even if the United States appeared to be withdrawing from Europe, it had saved

---

[179] R.J. Campbell, *A Spiritual Pilgrimage* (London, 1916), 273–4, 331–2.
[180] R.A. Knox, *A Spiritual Aeneid* (London, 1919), 254.
[181] Figgis, *Hopes for English Religion*, 113.
[182] Woods and MacNutt, *Theodore, Bishop of Winchester*, 128.

the intimate social order which the bishop at the piano with his royal singers represented. Would it last?

Whether the word selected in public addresses was 'earthquake', 'thunder-clap' or merely 'upheaval', spokesmen in all the churches had a sense that the European world was being shaken to its foundations. The explanations they offered for the war, dwelling not on faulty structures or systems but on deep-seated aspects of the human condition—greed, materialism, pride—were not of the kind favoured by diplomatic historians. 'War', John Baillie proclaimed in June 1915, 'is God's judgement on our sins—the sins of militarism, the lust for power, the desire for material and military supremacy, international jealousy—there are lessons for us all'.[183] The bloody collapse of European civilization, some thought, might even be seen as a judgement on its arrogant pretensions. Christians, according to Charles Gore, had been 'acquiescing in belonging to a civilization which rested on a fundamentally anti-Christian basis'.[184] It was not 'Christian civilization'. The hour of *kairos* had come. Who could tell what might be the implications for Europe's global imperialism? Yet there seemed so much to admire in what Europe had achieved. The tragedy, indeed, lay in the cutting short of what had appeared, for all its limitations, to be 'progress'. So perhaps, when the war did end, the forward march would be resumed. Equally, however, the lights might be going out in 'bourgeois' Europe forever. The continent of com-pliant 'Christian monarchies' might be doomed. But what might replace them? The mantra of 'freedom and justice', which so readily passed so many lips, left little clue as to its practical meaning. Clearly, some European proponents of progress equated it with the elimination of the church from the public sphere.[185] The intellectual discarding of Christianity, evident in so many quarters, might find its corollary in the notion that political systems needed no reference beyond themselves.

When they reflected on these things, both publicly and privately, church leaders could not quite decide whether to be optimistic or pessimistic. The events in Dublin in 1916 and those in St Petersburg in 1917, to take but two examples, illustrated how war spawned unanticipated revolutionary devel-opments. The one, in reopening the 'Irish question' with violence, again raised issues which directly concerned the churches of the British Isles. The other, however, though more distant, raised an even more alarming pro-spect for 'Christian civilization'. Foundations had been shaken, but the buildings might yet be kept standing.

[183] Cited by Newlands, 'John Baillie' in Brown and Newlands, eds., *Scottish Christianity*, 146.
[184] Gore, *War and the Church*, 16–17.
[185] Christopher M. Clark and Wolfram Kaiser, eds., *Culture Wars: Secular–Catholic Conflict in Nineteenth Century Europe* (Cambridge, 2003); Michael Burleigh, *Earthly Powers: Religion and Politics in Europe from the French Revolution to the Great War* (London, 2005).

4

POST-WAR DISLOCATIONS, 1919–1932: 'MODERNITY' AND 'MODERNISM'

After 1919 it was never possible fully to 'make sense' of the Great War or to 'come to terms' with it, though that was not for want of trying. The flood of interpretation has not abated, since the passage of time naturally produces fresh perspectives. Its 'aftermaths' lingered on in the lives of individuals and their societies. There has been no universal 'closure'. For some contemporaries, as for some subsequent historians, the war, in all its manifold aspects, constituted an absolute caesura, not merely in the history of the British Isles, but in the history of Europe and indeed the world.[1] The situation of humanity 'before' and 'after' the Great War, some thought, differed absolutely. A disposition to think in cataclysmic terms was particularly rampant amongst continental writers living amidst collapsed empires. Franz Kafka believed that the gates of chaos had been opened and the outer bulwarks of human existence broken apart. This, however, was not merely an exaggeration born of a disintegrating central Europe. Englishmen of very different dispositions too could feel the sense that the world might have changed utterly. H.G. Wells suggested that no intelligent brain that passed through the experience of the Great War could emerge without being profoundly altered.[2] The 30-year-old Arnold Toynbee, a very different figure, walking along Buckingham Palace Road in London in 1919 suddenly found himself 'in communion, not just with this or that episode in History, but with all that had been, and was, and was to come'. The moment passed, but it left behind the desire to write a great work of history. Was the individual perhaps merely like a wave in the flow of history's vast tide?[3] It was a desire

[1] Jay Winter, *Sites of Memory, Sites of Mourning: The Great War in European Cultural History* (Cambridge, 1995) and *Remembering War: The Great War between Memory and History in the Twentieth Century* (London, 2006); Paul Fussell, *The Great War and Modern Memory* (Oxford, 1975); Modris Eksteins, *Rites of Spring: The Great War and the Birth of the Modern Age* (New York, 1989); Keith Robbins, *The First World War* (Oxford, 1984); George Robb, *British Culture and the First World War* (Basingstoke, 2002).

[2] Roland N. Stromberg, *Redemption by War: The Intellectuals and 1914* (Lawrence, KS, 1982), 193.

[3] W.H. McNeill, *Arnold Toynbee: A Life* (Oxford, 1989), 90.

which, in the end, was to entail twelve volumes. The place in 'the Great Society' of the future to be occupied by Christianity (and what kind of Christianity) was enigmatic. There would certainly be no place for any churches that remained on the establishment of local sovereign states.[4] Edward Elgar completed an elegiac Cello Concerto (1919) but 'Gerontius', although retreating to the security of Worcester, became less confident whether, at the end, he would go forth as a Christian soul.

i. *Managing Memory*

The pain of wartime memory therefore mingled with this sense of nostalgia for the passing of an era (though there were millions, of course, in whose experience the Edwardian age had been less than golden). There was also a fear of cultural disintegration. In Lausanne, in Switzerland, a young American poet, recuperating from a nervous breakdown and the catastrophe of his marriage, was completing *The Waste Land* (1922). It was widely taken to encapsulate the fragmentation of Europe, together with the shattering of its institutions and its illusions about 'progress'.[5] When war began again in 1939, another poet and critic, Herbert Read, lamented that, contrary to much of the public rhetoric two decades earlier about 'peacemaking', 'the world was not renewed'. He wrote that in 1919 there had been hope in the homestead and anger in the streets, but the old world had been restored and his generation—though perhaps not he himself—had returned to 'the dreary field and workshop' and what he termed the immemorial feud of rich and poor. 'Our victory', he concluded 'was our defeat' and power had been retained where power had been misused.[6] Such poetic summaries, of course, while testifying to a mood, do not do justice to the complex social and political changes that did take place 'between the wars'. Nevertheless, the years after 1919, for many, and not only for poets, came to be given the character of an 'interlude' before the resumption of conflict which had not been truly settled in 1914–18. The 'dark continent'—even though it had not been without flashes of light—was apparently bent on self-destruction yet again.

Churches, from one perspective 'naturally' and 'traditionally', functioned as 'sites of mourning'. Their buildings offered a location, alongside the memorials being erected in public places, to commemorate the fallen, either by plaques listing names, memorial windows, or some other means.

---

[4] M. Cowling, *Religion and Public Doctrine in Modern England* (Cambridge, 1980), 32.

[5] T.S. Eliot's arrival in England to study philosophy at Oxford more or less coincided with the outbreak of the war in 1914.

[6] The poem 'To a Conscript in 1940' is cited and discussed in Trevor Wilson, *The Myriad Faces of War* (Cambridge, 1986), 820–7.

In addition, churches and chapels not infrequently provided premises for the holding of public meetings to discuss a proposed public memorial (where precisely a monument should be sited was an intensely local affair). There was almost invariably a place for clergy in the unveiling of these monuments, with the established church, in England, taking the lead. In post-disestablishment Wales, however, such events often provided the first public opportunity to demonstrate the parity of clergy and ministers, though there was no 'all-Wales' uniformity in the participatory clerical 'batting order'. What happened in Bedwellty Park in South Wales in 1924, for example, gives a flavour of the new plural ecclesiastical world in Wales. The local Baptist minister opened the proceedings with a scripture reading, the Calvinistic minister led those assembled in prayers, the Congregational minister and the Anglican vicar shared the consecration and dedication prayers and the Wesleyan minister gave the concluding benediction.[7] There was also a strong inter-church presence at the opening of memorial halls. Clergy were likewise called upon for addresses, short or long, in connection with Armistice Day services. In his in 1923 the archbishop of Canterbury spoke of looking back in 'proud bereavement' at those who had gone forth 'at their country's call just because it was their country's call'. Two years earlier, on the same day in Bradford, its bishop had spoken of pride in those who had gone out 'to serve humanity and save the world from tyranny and domination of material force'.[8] Death and loss, it seemed, could very frequently be 'accommodated' within cultures that locally perceived themselves to be Christian, at least in some sense.

Yet, whatever might be happening 'locally', there was a different message to be derived from two of the most important British war memorials: the Cenotaph in Whitehall and the memorial to 'the Missing' at Thiepval on the Somme, both the work of Sir Edwin Lutyens. A pantheist with theosophist connections, Lutyens created abstract forms which eschewed Christian (or indeed patriotic or romantic) symbolism. It is not surprising that there were complaints from the churches. Lloyd George had apparently proposed that the unveiling should not be accompanied by prayers but the archbishop of Canterbury successfully protested. 'O God our help in ages past' was sung by surpliced choristers and the Lord's Prayer was said. However, steps were taken to include the Chief Rabbi and Muslim and Sikh representatives. Several Indian princes ensured a Hindu presence. The interment of the Unknown Warrior at Westminster Abbey on Armistice Day 1920 also

---

[7] Angela Gaffney, *Aftermath: Remembering the Great War in Wales* (Cardiff, 1998), 125.
[8] Cited in Adrian Gregory, *The Silence of Memory: Armistice Day 1919–1946* (Oxford and Providence, 1994), 35–6.

raised questions of 'ownership'. The choice of hymns endeavoured to combine a Christian with a patriotic but not jingoistic tone. The congregation sang Cecil Spring-Rice's 'I Vow to Thee, My Country'—which became a 'remembrance favourite'. The tombstone was inscribed both with biblical texts and elevating phrases which commemorated those who had given life for God, king and country. Over future years, the Cenotaph became the site of public commemoration and the Tomb the place for private devotion. The dean of Westminster, well aware that some had wanted a more 'secular' occasion, was confident that nine-tenths of those who visited the grave were Christian people. The brethren who had fallen in France, he asserted, were by great majority Christians either by conviction or profession. On one level, the centrality of Christianity in national mourning, as John Wolffe notes, had been successfully reasserted.[9] Yet it is also arguable, despite the fact that remembrance was 'rooted in the language of the Eucharist and the Passion of Christ', that it was also 'strangely irreligious'. The common equation of the soldier's sacrifice in the war with the sacrifice of Christ, although it could be heard from clerical lips, hardly constituted theological orthodoxy. It is probably going too far, however, to suggest that despite hymnody and liturgical elements these occasions were 'religious occasions in form only'.[10]

Every British cemetery in France and Belgium (there were more than 1,800 of them) had at its centre both a 'Stone of Remembrance' designed by Lutyens and a 'Cross of Sacrifice' designed by Reginald Blomfield.[11] Such a joint presence symbolized the uneasy coexistence of comprehensive inclusiveness with Christian expression. Above all, when the king, the prime minister, the heir to the throne, and former prime ministers and the archbishop of Canterbury came together at the Cenotaph, they were pledging the nation to remember the past.

It is more difficult to determine whether Christianity remained central in life as well as in death. Was the war *the* turning point? 'Loss of religious faith' has indeed often been taken to be one of the major legacies of the war. The churches, it is sometimes asserted, never 'recovered' from this massive exposure of the impotence or indifference of the God in whom men and women had placed their trust. 'God is a devil who rejoices in human suffering. He may be. There's no evidence to show He isn't.'

[9] John Wolffe, *Great Deaths: Grieving, Religion and Nationhood in Victorian and Edwardian Britain* (Oxford, 2000), 261–4.

[10] Bob Bushaway, 'The Great War and Remembrance' in Roy Porter, ed., *Myths of the English* (Cambridge, 1993), 159.

[11] Catherine Moriarty, 'Christian Iconography and First World War Memorials', *Imperial War Museum Review* 6 (1991), 63–74; Alan Borg, *War Memorials from Antiquity to the Present* (London, 1991).

C.F.G. Masterman had written in his diary in February 1918.[12] A London army private, surveying the earth-covered ossuary that was Passchendaele in 1917, had a moment of truth. Where was God? From that day onwards, his belief in a church which condoned killing 'faded away'. He would not again voluntarily attend or take part in a church service. That was that. It is not difficult to find other such 'moments of truth'. The scale of suffering was indeed massive but it did not need the war to raise the question of why God 'allowed' (or indeed 'rejoiced in') suffering of any kind. Chaplains, perhaps particularly Catholic chaplains, emphasized that the war was a consequence of human sin. It was a very nice world, another London private concluded, and 'if we choose to muck it up that's our fault'.[13] God was not to be blamed.

Two such differing reactions from the same military background point up the difficulty of making generalizations which apply to British society across the board. It would, of course, be quite misleading to suppose that circumstances were conducive to the presentation of seminar papers on the subject of theodicy. It was evident, however, that many had looked for evidence of a benevolent God who 'intervened' in the face of pain and suffering, and had not found it. At the very least, the collapse or at least decline of popularly held assumptions, perhaps not necessarily Christian, forced theologians to revisit how God 'acts' in the world. Even a 'spectrum model' cannot do full justice to the complexity of shifting emotions and convictions which such issues posed, in the immediate aftermath of war and enduringly thereafter. Nor, however, should any overall assessment overlook the existence of a sense of gratitude and pride on the part of some survivors—they had played their part, under God, in delivering their country and Europe from a barbarous militarism.[14]

Any generalization about 'loss of religious faith', however, reopens the issue of what counts as 'religion' and how far, if at all, it can be distinguished from 'religiosity'. Clergy did not quite know how to interpret what they had encountered in the army. A number disdainfully supposed that what was being characterized in the forces as 'religion' was in fact 'superstition' (though they did not often feel called upon to explain the difference). Some

---

[12] Lucy Masterman, *C.F.G. Masterman* (London, 1939), 290. In citing this diary entry in *The Deluge: British Society and the First World War* (Harmondsworth, 1967), Arthur Marwick gives it as an example of the 'direct effect' of the war on religious belief but also acknowledged 'other long-term forces' at work in the decline of organized religion.

[13] In citing these two quotations, Michael Snape, *God and the British Soldier: Religion and the British Army in the First and Second World Wars* (London, 2005), 194 has concluded that 'the experience of the First World War does not seem to have had an immediate and negative impact on public religious observance in Britain'.

[14] R. Schweitzer, 'The Cross and the Trenches: Religious Faith and Doubt among some British Soldiers on the Western Front', *War and Society* 16 (1998), 33–57.

discovered an ignorance of 'the fundamental ideas of our religion' which they found 'amazing'.[15] The frequent verdict was that the war had brought neither a general revival of religion nor a mass alienation from it. The churches might have to decide whether the 'folk religion' which evidently did exist was the 'spiritual stratum' on which 'the church' should seek to build or whether it might even constitute an obstacle to 'real' Christianity as 'the church' understood it. The churches, thought the editor of the report on the army and religion, needed to have 'the real state of matters brought before them', namely that they had lost or were in danger of losing 'the faith of the nation'. He appears to have taken it as axiomatic both that they had indeed possessed 'the faith of the nation' and that its 'retrieval' was both a laudable and achievable objective for the churches to have.

So, for the churches, 'beginning again' in 1919 meant confronting awkward and, for many, unpalatable questions: about their institutional structures and identity; about their relationship to 'the faith of the nation' (and 'what nation?' in a context in which, in the British Isles, the Irish struggle came to its bitter and bloody climax); about 'peace and justice' (and, living in a nervous imperial power awkwardly engaged with a European 'mainland', the possible tension between them); about class and gender (a matter for self-analysis as much as for social commentary); about power, leadership and democracy; about money, health and welfare. Churches in the British Isles inescapably set in the particular culture(s) of (now) two states had long wrestled with such matters in different circumstances. The 'modern age' brought them into sharper focus.

ii. *Broadcasting Truth*

Meeting 'the modern' in the post-war world was a disconcerting experience. Churches had to react to it—whatever it was deemed to be. They did not control or drive modernity. Preachers who had grown accustomed, in earlier decades, to receptive congregations sometimes felt stranded in the new age of challenge and change. At the age of 73, R.F. Horton, minister of Lyndhurst Road Congregational Church, Hampstead, became a father in 1928 for the first time. His belated paternity, however, offered no certainty that he would feel 'at home' with young people. Those he met seemed to him 'typically modern, so good, so Christless'. They seemed to give all their time to enjoyment untrammelled by duty and care. This godless and unworshipping generation, as he called it, made his heart break. He was

---

[15] Cited in D.S. Cairns, ed. *The Army and Religion* (London, 1919), 121. The conclusions, drawn by Cairns, a Church of Scotland minister, are discussed by Snape, *God and the British Soldier*, 2 and Callum Brown, *Religion and Society in Twentieth-Century Britain* (London, 2006), 93–4.

not on their 'wave length'. He had indeed been persuaded by this new British Broadcasting Company (set up earlier in the year) to broadcast from Savoy Hill in 1923 but in the following year he complained of 'the vile "listening-in" which breaks up worship and home, conversation, and the Word of God'. The note of resentment at the inrush of 'the modern world' is readily apparent.

'Listening-in', however, proved to be here to stay. The managing director of the British Broadcasting Company, John Reith, was a son of a Free Church of Scotland manse, a man who had 'earned his spurs' in the war. Mankind could be best served, he thought in 1920, by 'an unqualified deliberate manly aggressive doctrine of the principles expounded by Christ'. The best political guidance could be found in some of the 'volcanic utterances' of the Old Testament Jehovah. The inwardly troubled but outwardly dominant Reith certainly wanted 'a definite and considerable place' for the Christian religion. Much concerned with manliness, he wanted to bring Christ's kingdom to men in whatever capacity God called him. The churches, however, were a bit of a problem, since there was 'mighty little in many churches to attract'.[16] Fortunately for Reith, however, Dick Sheppard, maligned by some as an ecclesiastical stunt man at St Martin-in-the-Fields, thought that 'a lack of interest in churches and church affairs may be perfectly compatible with a genuine and sincere enthusiasm for Christianity'.[17] He was the man Reith needed, but first the managing director had to go to the top ecclesiastical manager.

In March 1923, he invited the archbishop of Canterbury and his wife to his home. He then startled his guests by switching on something called a 'wireless' which had, until this juncture, the innocent appearance of a sideboard. They were staggered. Davidson soon recognized that something had to be done to cope with this phenomenon. Swift steps were then taken to set up a 'Sunday Committee', chaired by the bishop of Southwark, but with representatives from different churches, to advise on appropriate 'names' (to be paid expenses but not fees) of possible broadcasters. But what about church services? The chapter of Westminster would not permit the wedding of the duke of York and Lady Elizabeth Bowes-Lyon to be broadcast. A canon of St Paul's, on another occasion, did not want to see 'sensational methods' introduced into worship. A canon of Westminster offered the opinion that there were not in the country fifty men in all the

---

[16] Kenneth M. Wolffe, *The Churches and the British Broadcasting Corporation 1922–1956* (London, 1984), 3–15; Asa Briggs, *The History of Broadcasting in the United Kingdom, vol. i: The Birth of Broadcasting* (Oxford, 1961); J.C.W. Reith, *Broadcast over Britain* (London, 1924) and his autobiography *Into the Wind* (London, 1949), 96; C.H. Stuart, ed., *The Reith Diaries* (London, 1975); Andrew Boyle, *Only the Wind will Listen* (London, 1972).

[17] R. Ellis Roberts, *H.R.L. Sheppard: Life and Letters* (London, 1942), 112–13.

denominations put together who were qualified to speak to such an audience as radio provided. However, attitudes were to change quite rapidly. Cathedral deans, in relation to broadcasts, quickly asked each other over the next few years for advice on how to deal with the fees for organists, lay clerks and choristers, and for that other novelty, 'records'. Precentors had to learn that if they coughed during carol services they ruined the transmission to the listening multitudes. Bell, the archbishop's chaplain, who had facilitated Davidson's initiation into the mysteries of the 'sideboard', was, five years later, as dean of Canterbury, arranging for the enthronement in Canterbury of Davidson's successor to be broadcast. The BBC told him that it would be 'their biggest effort so far'.[18]

Questions of parity and access, therefore, came in thick and fast in the years after the first broadcast from a place of worship, St Martin's, which took place on 6 January 1924. Dick Sheppard was very conscious that the gospel could be brought into the homes of millions who would not otherwise hear it. That was true, but alongside it, within the churches themselves, there was a growing realization—and in some quarters growing alarm—at the extent to which 'BBC religion', unless itself 'controlled' (but who by and how?) could prove a solvent undermining particular denominational ownerships of Christianity. The Catholic archbishop of Liverpool called in 1931 for a 'less emasculated' Christianity over the airwaves. As Dean Inge recognized with dismay, no method of taking a collection at a broadcast service had yet been discovered.[19] As the BBC became a chartered corporation, should it in religious broadcasting, as in other areas, provide an opening for all kinds of Christians or only 'approved' ones? The national consensus might still be Christian but what about 'religious space' for the largest non-Christian minority, the Jews? And what about space for critics of all religion? Clergy, too, had to face the uncomfortable prospect that their congregations might come to regard 'radio preachers' and broadcast services as 'better' than 'the real thing'. Also, more generally, the marvellous manifestation of modernity that was radio might also, in due course, by providing both 'serious' enlightenment and 'light' entertainment, insidiously undermine what the 'institutional church' sought to provide. The significance of space and place and the associational habits of centuries were threatened, though so were newspaper barons and political parties by the same developments.[20] Broadcasting House, in due course erected in Portland Place, had somewhat the appearance of a ship (now sailing in chartered but uncharted waters).

[18] Keith Robbins, 'The Twentieth Century, 1898–1994' in Patrick Collinson, Nigel Ramsay and Margaret Sparks, eds., *A History of Canterbury Cathedral* (Oxford, 1995), 312–15.

[19] W.R. Inge, *Assessments and Anticipations* (London, 1929), 221.

[20] Ken Ward, *Mass Communications and the Modern World* (London, 1989).

Perhaps, however, for the moment at least, when Horton, under domestic pressure, agreed to have a 'wireless' in his home, 'broadcasting', was not quite the disaster he feared. A place for 'religious broadcasting' had been secured and, by its exclusions, confirmed the prevalence of a Christian culture. The two Houses of Canterbury Convocation passed resolutions in 1931 expressing grateful appreciation of the service rendered to the cause of religion by the BBC. Religious provision, however, might come to imply that all other broadcasting could and should not be constrained or informed by Christian perspectives. It did seem, however, that there was no way in which the 'modern world' could be 'switched off'. When he preached his last sermons at Lyndhurst Road in 1930—the scene of his life's work over a half-century and which church seemed to him to embody *The True Theory of a Christian Church* about which his own father had written—the church was half-empty.

Horton was of course not the only elderly man in the 1920s to confess that he belonged to the nineteenth century and had got 'out of sympathy with the trend of things to-day'. The supersession of the generations in the post-war world was even more painful to live through than it normally is, as other erstwhile great clergy were also finding. 'The modern', however, was apparently something more than that set of changed circumstances which makes every generation uncomfortable with its successors. Here was not only 'the modern' but 'modernism'.[21] Whether in literature, architecture, music or painting here was a concerted presentation of a New Style and a New Vision as the New Man (and Woman) could be presented with new social realities made possible by technological revolution. What 'modernism' amounted to in these fields cannot be pursued in detail here. Such unity as it possessed as a 'movement' can perhaps ultimately only be found in the self-conscious reiteration of novelty. Some of this enthusiasm could be dismissed as 'continental' and it did indeed take longer to 'take off' in the British Isles than elsewhere in Europe. It was of course also the case that 'modernity' in all these artistic spheres was by definition controversial. 'Middlebrow' culture could seek a different accommodation with the past and, unlike Yeats, Joyce, Lawrence, Huxley and Eliot, who had not in fact participated in the war, the most popular literary figures in the inter-war period—such names as Priestley, Sherriff, Hutchinson and Deeping—had all been officers. They had been 'there'.[22] It would be a mistake, accordingly, to suppose that 'modernism' engulfed the culture of the British Isles at all social levels. Adolf Hitler, in opening the House of German Art,

[21] A. Hastings, 'Modernity' in A. Hastings, A. Mason and H. Pyper, eds., *The Oxford Companion to Christian Thought* (Oxford, 2000), 443–4.

[22] Rosa Maria Bracco, *Merchants of Hope: British Middlebrow Writers and the First World War, 1919–1939* (Providence and Oxford, 1993), 200.

proclaimed that Cubism, Dadaism, Futurism 'and the rest' had nothing in common 'with our German people'. There were those who felt that they also had nothing to do with 'our British people'.

That might be true in relation to the new forms of elite culture but, even so, there was no mistaking a pervasive unsettlement of convention and a widespread corrosion of certainty at all social levels. It had so often been assumed that 'respectability' had required 'religion' and 'religion' had entailed 'respectability'. Now the bond began to dissolve as the social meanings to be attached to 'respectability' mutated once more. Insofar as 'religion' had been used as a means of social control—a case frequently alleged—it appeared that the controllers were losing interest in its efficacy for this purpose. 'Sunday Best' religion began to dissolve. It was becoming sufficient, it seemed, for 'pillars of society', if so minded, to become 'flying buttresses'—still in many cases supporting 'the church' but from outside. There was, however, no need to go inside with any regularity. High-minded and comfortably-provided-for dons, flitting between Cambridge, Bloomsbury and France, took pride in not knowing at what time church services were held. Lowes Dickinson, fastidious don, liked the *sound* of what went on in his college chapel (King's), but it made no *sense* to him.

This shifting pattern left the churches in a quandary. If 'respectability' was another way of describing a life of responsible and virtuous conduct in both private and public life, supposing agreement was possible on what that entailed, it should surely not be scorned. Such a respectable life, of course, need not be totally without happiness. 'Duty' and 'care', therefore, should not be mocked, as was seemingly increasingly the case, by hedonistic 'moderns'. Yet, the ease with which respectability could slide into self-righteousness had not escaped the attention of Christian moralists over centuries. Some of the ingredients of 'respectability', it had to be admitted, were always time- and culture-specific. There was no call to uphold everything that now appeared to be under assault, but it would be equally wrong to acquiesce in the assumption, evident in some quarters, that 'anything goes'. What might count as 'responsible and virtuous conduct' might be possible without religion—no one knew—but it would be foolish to underestimate the social value of that buttress of 'respectability' which the churches provided, or at least sought to provide. They did not see themselves as mere suppliers of social cement but, to a degree at least, they did still provide it. The communities they tried to be were flawed, but they were communities. The question for the churches was how the course between these conflicting pressures should be steered, and who should steer it.

'The church', some churchmen thought, could not cope with 'the modern' unless it too became thoroughly modern and that might mean a reformulation of what Christianity should be taken to be. But how and where should such engagement take place? Universities, primarily Oxford and Cambridge, were places where modern thought might be managed. Modernity, amongst other things, meant 'Science'. It was no less a person than Arthur Balfour, former prime minister and foreign secretary and now chancellor of Cambridge university who was prevailed upon by a Cambridge biochemist, Joseph Needham, a man disinclined to be restricted by his specialism, to contribute an introduction to a volume of essays on *Science, Religion and Reality*. Balfour advocated what he called a provisional acquiescence in the unresolved dualism presented by the 'material' and the 'spiritual'. Both 'science' and 'religion' seemed very different but they were both in their way 'real'. Somewhere, somehow, they had to be in contact along a common frontier.[23] He, and other contributors—anthropologists, psychologists, philosophers, scientists, theologians—made suggestions where the frontier might be drawn. Clement Webb, from Oxford, had no doubt that a mental revolution was happening but did not believe that it had 'the appearance of heralding the disappearance of Christianity'. His religion had shown, over the centuries, 'a wonderful capacity of retaining an unmistakable identity through changes of a far-reaching kind'.[24] But just what was that 'identity'?

'Catholic Modernism' and 'Liberal Protestantism', as has earlier been noted, had both had their pre-war moment. It was clear that post-war modernity would not lead the papacy to reconsider 'modernism'. A kind of 'liberalism' or 'modernism', however, manifested itself across the non-Roman churches, though what it precisely implied admitted, almost by definition, of no simple statement.[25] Its leading advocates drew not only of the heritage of the Victorian Broad Church but also of German and French Liberal Protestantism, Roman Catholic Modernism, American Liberalism and Liberal Judaism.[26] Since one of the aims of the Churchmen's Union (which added the word Modern in 1928) as set out in 1919, was to defend the freedom of responsible students, clerical and lay, in their work of

---

[23] Earl Balfour, 'Introduction' in Joseph Needham, ed., *Science, Religion and Reality* (London, 1926), 16–17. Michael Oakeshott, the political philosopher, had been associated with Needham in the preparation of this volume and at this date was reviewing theological books as he reflected on religion and the moral life. Cowling, *Religion and Public Doctrine in Modern England*, 263–7. Peter Bowler, *Reconciling Science and Religion: The Debate in Early-Twentieth-Century Britain* (Chicago and London, 2005).

[24] Clement C.J. Webb, 'Science, Christianity and Modern Civilisation' in Needham, ed., *Science, Religion and Reality*, 342.

[25] See the introduction by Bernard Reardon to his collection *Liberal Protestantism* (London, 1968), 9–65.

[26] Alan M.G. Stephenson, *The Rise and Decline of English Modernism* (London, 1984) 86–7 identifies the interaction of these elements in his assessment of H.D.A. Major, widely seen as English modernism's most forceful, if not most subtle, exponent. Paul R. Smythe, *A Bibliography of Anglican Modernism* (Cambridge, 1947).

criticism and research, it is not surprising that opinions on the 'restatement of the doctrines of the Church of England' differed. The 'continuous and progressive character of the revelation given by the Holy Spirit' was affirmed. The vehicle for debate was *The Modern Churchman*, started by H.D.A. Major in 1911, together with annual conferences which were normally held in Oxford or Cambridge colleges. That held at Girton College, Cambridge in 1921 on the subject of 'Christ and the Creeds', with papers, amongst others, from M.G. Glazebrook, F.J. Foakes Jackson and E.W. Barnes, proved particularly controversial. The detailed positions adopted by individual speakers on such matters as miracles, the incarnation and the divinity of Christ, at this and other conferences, cannot be charted here but all sought substantial 'restatement'. The focus of discussion can be judged by the annual themes—for example 'Christianity as the World Religion', 'The Scientific Approach to Religion' and 'Christianity and History'. The church and the 'modern world', and the Bible and 'modern man' were themes identified in the early 1930s. Ripon Hall in Oxford from 1919, with Major as its principal, became the liberal citadel.[27]

The modernity of these conference-minded modern men who talked to each other (only a tiny number of women ever spoke) had a somewhat restricted basis. MCU presidents in the 1920s, for example, all had their glimpses of 'modern England' from an Oxbridge window. One of them (1915–22), Percy Gardner, Professor of Classical Archaeology at Oxford, was a numismatist who was once so enthusiastic about Auguste Comte that he had read every word the French master had written, but now argued that modern man needed the evolutionary Christianity of which he, Gardner, was an exponent. What modern man did not need, in Gardner's estimation, was democracy, feminism or the spread of American culture.[28] Gardner was followed, though in what was to be the last year of his life, by Hastings Rashdall, Oxford historian of medieval universities, philosopher on the subject of good and evil, and theologian of the Atonement. He was succeeded in 1924 by W.R. Inge, dean of St Paul's since 1911, who held office for a decade until his retirement from St Paul's.

Inge, an Etonian, had been a Cambridge undergraduate prizewinner in Classics and unsuccessful Eton master before becoming a fellow of Hertford College, Oxford (his father was provost of Worcester College). After a brief spell as a vicar in the fashionable West End of London, he had returned to Cambridge as Lady Margaret Professor of Divinity in 1907. In offering him

[27] Clive Pearson, Allan Davidson and Peter Lineham, *Scholarship and Fierce Sincerity: Henry D.A. Major. The Face of Anglican Modernism* (Auckland, 2006).

[28] Gardner (1846–1937), amongst other works, wrote *Modernism in the English Church* (London, 1926) and an autobiography, *Autobiographica* (Oxford, 1933). His sister Alice, however, was capable of assessing *Our Outlook as Changed by the War* (Cambridge, 1914), a paper read at Newnham College.

the deanery, the prime minister had suggested that he might restore the traditions of scholarship and culture which had been associated with it in the past, but he should also maintain the sober beauty of its services. It was the former rather than the latter which appealed to Inge—he was on occasion to be observed reading a book during moments of sober beauty. His deafness and dislike of music could be accounted impediments to sharing fully in the cathedral's life. In 1911 he addressed the Women's Diocesan Association in London on 'The Co-operation of the Church with the Spirit of the Age'. It turned out, as the subsequent publication made clear, that he was not enamoured of the spirit of the age.[29] His remarks earned him the title of 'the gloomy dean' from the *Daily Mail*, a description which stuck, though he professed to think it not entirely accurate. In fact, over the next forty years, in a journalistic career which took him to the *Evening Standard* and many other journals, Inge's well-honed lugubriousness brought him not only public reputation but also substantial income. No other Fellow of the British Academy at this time was in the same earnings league. He did, however, decline a substantial offer to write his own autobiography, a refusal, he relates, which was followed by an invitation to write the life of Christ for a rather smaller sum.

Just as he was self-taught in theology, there was scarcely any topic on which Inge was not prepared to offer an opinion. He could express himself equally on what made a successful man and on cosmology.[30] Eugenics was an enduring if not endearing speciality.[31] Deep Sea Fisheries was the only topic on which he admitted to have spoken without any knowledge whatsoever, but there may have been others. At London dinners, he picked up tit-bits of useful information. In 1930, for example, Lord Lothian told him that large houses were now almost worthless. One had been lately sold for 12s 6d. In retirement a few years later, Inge was able to pick up an Oxfordshire manor.

It was not altogether certain, therefore, for a variety of reasons, that Inge's 'modernity' was quite what was to be expected in an MCU president. Indeed, in various addresses, he made it relatively clear that his 'modernism' was particularly personal. Indeed, his *magnum opus* had been the Gifford Lectures at St Andrews in 1917/18 on the philosophy of Plotinus, the mystical pagan.[32] He formed a friendship with Lord Haldane. It was gratifying to join Balfour and Asquith in apparently being the only people able

---

[29] W.R. Inge, *The Church and the Age* (London, 1912).

[30] W.R. Inge, *God and the Astronomers* (London, 1933). It apparently sold out within a few days of publication.

[31] W.R. Inge, *Outspoken Essays (Second Series)* (London, 1922), 254–75. Inge was a prolific author and lecturer. Adam Fox, *Dean Inge* (London, 1960) provides in his Appendix C a full list. Information on Inge referred to in this paragraph is derived from this biography.

[32] W.R. Inge, *The Philosophy of Plotinus* (London, 1918).

to understand everything Haldane said. Inge, however, was particularly at home in the intellectual world of the second and third centuries. He believed that he was revivifying a 'third type' of Christianity, alongside what passed for Catholicism and Protestantism. It could be more fruitful for its future. As he put it in Cambridge lectures in 1925/6, he wanted Christian Platonism to be recognized as a legitimate and independent type of Christian theology and practice.[33] It fell to him to attempt a 'conclusion' to Needham's 1926 collection of essays. He warned against any facile statements, particularly from the pulpit, which suggested that theology and science were reconciled, but he had no doubt that they could be reconciled—if God was thought of less anthropomorphically and heaven was considered a state rather than a place.[34]

Subsequent theological assessments of 'modernism' in this period have tended to be negative.[35] However, its 'moment' can be seen to have been substantially in the 1920s.[36] It receded as a 'movement' since its stress on the virtues of free enquiry ceased, very largely, to be contentious throughout the Church of England.[37] Perhaps a distinction between 'liberality' and 'liberalism' in this regard can be sustained.[38] Certainly, with the foundation of the journal *Theology* in 1920, edited from a vicarage until 1933 by E.G. Selwyn (at which date he became dean of Winchester) and the publication, in 1926, of *Essays Catholic and Critical*, it was being vigorously asserted by other writers that one could be modern without being modernist. And, personal issues apart, under Inge's successor, W.R. Matthews (both as dean of St Paul's and as MCU president), the extent to which the modernist movement, as Matthews himself put it, was 'derived from two different and partly incompatible sources' led to an internal crisis and to his own resignation in 1937.[39] In his own much later autobiography Matthews came

---

[33] W.R. Inge, *The Platonic Tradition in English Religious Thought* (London, 1926), v–vii.

[34] W.R. Inge, 'Conclusion' in Needham, ed., *Science, Religion and Reality*, 360.

[35] Adrian Hastings, *A History of English Christianity 1920–1990* (London, 1991), 232 recognizes that the negative criticisms of the modernists were often to the point but suggests that 'their positive constructions suffered from a vagueness and a dull lack of any great sense of mystery feebly inadequate to bear the weight of Christian spiritual experience'.

[36] Stephenson, *Rise and Decline of English Modernism*, 3 thinks that the 1920s were its 'golden age'. Major's own account is *English Modernism; Its Origin, Methods, Aims* (London, 1927). See also H.P.V. Nunn, *What is Modernism?* (London, 1932).

[37] A.M. Ramsey, *From Gore to Temple: The Development of Anglican Theology between* Lux Mundi *and the Second World War 1889–1939* (London, 1960), 74.

[38] A.R. Vidler, *Essays in Liberality* (London, 1957), 21 urges 'liberal' to mean not a creed or set of philosophical assumptions, or any 'ism, but a frame of mind and a quality of character.

[39] Cited in Stephenson, *Rise and Decline of English Modernism*, 153. Matthews had professed the philosophy of religion at King's College, London, from 1918 to 1934, at which point he became dean of Exeter. He had written *Studies in Christian Philosophy* (London, 1921) and was to publish *God in Christian Thought and Experience* (London, 1939). His autobiography is *Memories and Meanings* (London, 1969).

to the conclusion that while he had thought of himself as a Liberal Protestant he was probably more of a Liberal Catholic—an illustration of the uncertainty surrounding categories.

He was followed in the presidency by Sir Cyril Norwood, newly installed as president of St John's College, Oxford where, as an undergraduate, he had distinguished himself in Classical Moderations and 'Greats'. His headmasterships at Bristol Grammar School, Marlborough and Harrow were sufficient to make him the authority on English education. Before him lay his Report of 1943 which provided the basis of the 1944 Education Act. Norwood was prepared to speak on 'The Christian Teacher and the Modern World'. It took a layman who was not a theologian—albeit with a clerical father—to keep some semblance of order.

Matthews noted that one wing of the MCU did hold that 'the Church was an essential element in the complex which is called Christianity' but not all did. The relationship between 'dogma' or 'creed' and the 'life of the church' remained subtle. The 'complex called Christianity', it seemed to be generally agreed, had three elements—the institutional, the prophetic and the individual/internal (be that spiritual, mystical or intellectual), but was one element 'fundamental'? Were all three so mutually interconnected that to neglect or even dismiss one would in fact undermine the totality of the complex? How did they relate to each other? Matthews subsequently confessed that his own preaching and lecturing too often took the form of discussions about problems in religion 'as if the Church of Christ was a fellowship of students of Comparative Religion'.[40] Evelyn Waugh, after an 'idle, dissolute, and extravagant' life at Dean Inge's former Oxford college, wrote his first novel, *Decline and Fall* in 1928 which had wicked fun at the expense of a 'Modern Churchman'.

The 70-year-old Inge reflected at the end of 1930 on what he called his 'extraordinary and incomprehensible vogue as a preacher and lecturer'.[41] He had been told again and again that 'hundreds were turned away'. He rushed around the country, 'meeting a need', but his audiences were largely those assembled for special occasions in special places—university sermons and the like. Vice-chancellors were particularly worth visiting. He had a cousin who was one in Bristol. William Henry Hadow, adviser on the education of adolescents, like Inge son of an Anglican clergyman and an enthusiast for cricket—but unlike him in being an enthusiast for music—was frequently visited when Hadow was in post at Durham and Sheffield. Hadow had been a fellow of Inge's father's college. So the dean too was not to be found frequently 'in the parishes'. He had a dislike of what he termed

---

[40] Matthews, *Memories and Meanings*, 119.
[41] W.R. Inge, *Diary of a Dean: St. Paul's 1911–1934* (London, 1949), 153.

'ecclesiasticism'. Finding organized religion to be 'lamentably weak', he felt little urge to do anything to inject fresh life into it. The task of the church of Christ was to rescue a little flock, here and there, from materialism, selfishness and hatred. There was no likelihood that it would ever be otherwise. Although claiming that he would not quite go so far himself, the religion of Christ might be a greater power in the world if its professional custodians were removed.[42] It was more important to be a *thinker* than to be a 'yes-man' among the bishops—who had given such wretched guidance from the days of *Essays and Reviews* onwards.[43]

William Temple, enthroned as bishop of Manchester in 1921 at the age of 39, still hoped to remain a thinker (once he had polished off the life of his old headmaster, the subsequent bishop of Hereford, John Percival). Unfortunately, his official residence was some miles away from the university where intelligent laymen were to be found, though the subsequent provision of a car afforded some access to them. He soon found that Manchester did not expect just a thinker. Helped by a notoriously hearty laugh and a developing rotundity, though hindered by gout, Temple was well-received, even on the sands at Blackpool. In his study, however, he was working away at providing a 'mainly theological' counterpart to the 'mainly philosophical' volume *Mens Creatrix*, frantically completed on the night before his wedding and published in 1917. Published as *Christus Veritas* in 1924, the new volume aimed to be a 'Christo-centric metaphysic' and to address modern men, or at least those who used a quasi-Hegelian vocabulary. He was himself a modern man—too modern for some—and in the 1920s he was optimistic and seemed to be in tune with the times.[44]

Temple did not think that the one thing needful in a bishop was to stay in his study. Episcopal impact had to stretch broad and far, both in Manchester and in England (as a start). He was good at being busy, a man of 'a very rare mental and moral type' as the *Bolton Evening News* sagely observed on hearing news in 1928 that he was to become archbishop of York. He was a man, as the editor of the *Manchester Guardian* told him, of 'uncomfortably wide and various sympathies, and affiliations'.[45] 'Yes-man' he was certainly

---

[42] W.R. Inge, 'Conclusion', in Needham, ed., *Science, Religion and Reality*, 387–8.

[43] Inge reached this conclusion in 1951 in reflecting on the autobiography of his friend and frequent, though not invariable ally, Herbert Hensley Henson, who had, Inge thought, ceased to be a thinker. Fox, *Inge*, 263,

[44] Extensive commentary on Temple's writing is to be found in Hastings, *History of English Christianity*, 232–3 and Cowling, *Religion and Public Doctrine in Modern England*, iii. 289–91. Hastings has another assessment of Temple in *The Shaping of Prophecy: Passion, Perception and Practicality* (London, 1995), 53–68.

[45] The pattern of his activity in his Manchester years is portrayed in F.A. Iremonger, *William Temple* (London, 1948), 282–362. The adulatory tone in Iremonger's biography is not repeated in J.H.S. Kent, *William Temple: Church, State and Society in Britain, 1880–1950* (Cambridge, 1992).

not, but, perhaps unfortunately, he was not very good at saying 'No' to invitations. 'The Church', he was certain, was not just a place in which to hold philosophical seminars. It was an institution, even if, as Temple himself put it, it existed, at its best, for others rather than for itself. What that meant, in this period, will be explored more thoroughly in a subsequent section. Its 'professional custodians' had to 'run the shop'—and Temple, in the name of efficiency, had to carry through the long-mooted division of the diocese of Manchester, resisted by his predecessor, leading to the creation of the new diocese of Blackburn. The custodians did not believe they could prosper without seeking a degree of acceptable doctrinal clarity. Whether what would be acceptable would be clear, and whether what was clear would be acceptable, constituted the challenge.

The 'modernism' controversy at the Girton Conference in 1921, which also reached the non-ecclesiastical press, was one of the factors leading to the establishment of the Archbishops' Commission on Christian Doctrine on which sat representatives of various 'parties'. It would not proceed rapidly. Some of its members were relatively young and might hope to survive the end of the deliberations, even if only to be excommunicated.[46] Some hoped to see a drastic revision of the Thirty-Nine Articles. One of the theologians most adept at seeking accommodation was Oliver Quick, who became Professor of Divinity at Durham in 1934. Quick's *The Doctrine of the Creeds* was published in 1938 (he was appointed to the Regius Chair at Oxford in the following year). He had been urging 'wholeness' for decades and sought to resist finding in liberalism, modernism or traditionalism 'the sole representatives of the essence of the Christian faith'. Origin, tradition, and the latest discoveries of the contemporary mind, had to make 'their full contribution'.[47] It took a long time for the commission to make its full contribution. As different viewpoints were elaborated by the members, any idea that it would swiftly produce an 'agreed statement' was unrealistic. The irony was that by 1938, when *Doctrine in the Church of England* was published, the theological landscape of the early 1920s was already 'history'. As William Temple noted in his introduction to the report, if the Commission's members had been starting again, their perspectives would have been different. It was a recognition that 'doing theology' was inextricably 'contextual'.

Thus far, the 'modern age', and adjusting to it, has been seen in this section from an angle that has been Anglican, English and university-orientated (almost without exception men from Oxford or Cambridge,

---

[46] Matthews, *Memories and Meanings*, 145 put matters thus.

[47] O.C. Quick, *Liberalism, Modernism and Tradition* (London, 1922), 149. A.R. Vidler, *20th Century Defenders of the Faith* (London, 1965), 69 expressed admiration for the acuteness of Quick's mind, though that showed itself more in criticism than construction.

or both, with an admixture of King's, London) as articulate men reacted to each other intellectually and socially in a privileged environment.[48] In Oxford and Cambridge, the 'lead' that was given reflected a context in which the Church of England (as expressed in college chapels and 'university churches') still retained a prominent place. And if the variety these offered did not suffice, town churches catered for every shade of opinion, custom and practice. The divinity faculties were staffed by men, normally Englishmen in Anglican holy orders, and the study of theology could be presumed to be Christian theology (after a struggle, post-war Oxford had agreed that non-Anglicans could be admitted to divinity degrees).[49] Individuals, however, might differ in the extent to which they perceived their function as being the intellectual preparation of intending ordinands or the detached search for Truth (supposing that these pursuits were different). In either event, whereas it was frequently suggested that theology in German universities had very little to do with 'the church' on the ground, that was not the case in Oxford. Colleges, particularly in Oxford, still had substantial patronage and to this extent, willy-nilly, there were connections with parsons and parishes. It is only to be expected, therefore, that dialogue on church/Christianity reflects these circumstances.

Even so, Oxford and Cambridge were, of course, no longer Anglican universities and the Anglican dominance in the consideration of 'modern Christianity', though still constitutionally entrenched in certain aspects—in Oxford several of the major chairs remained tied to canonries at Christ Church—was to an extent being modified by non-Anglican presence (a presence which happened also to be often less English—either by intellectual formation or personal descent). The Baptists had it in hand, in stages, to transfer their London Regent's Park College, under the same name, to Oxford from the late 1920s and thus to be alongside the Congregationalist Mansfield College.[50] Manchester College contributed a Unitarian presence, though its principal, L.P. Jacks, editor of the *Hibbert Journal*, withdrew his name in 1928 from the official list of Unitarian ministers in protest against the decision of the Unitarians, for the first time in their history, to become an organized denomination.[51] In Cambridge, the Methodists built Wesley

[48] The 'Modern England' which was supposedly the subject of Mr Cowling's combative volumes, appears virtually to be found in the antagonisms, intellectual and otherwise, present in the University of Cambridge. In terms of individuals, the detail of his engagement with them cannot be repeated on the same scale in this volume but his assessments endlessly stimulate (or perhaps infuriate).

[49] A.R. Vidler has some remarks on this matter in his essay 'The Future of Theology' in *Essays on Liberality* (London, 1957), 29–30.

[50] R.E. Cooper, *From Stepney to St. Giles: The Story of Regent's Park College, 1810–1960* (London, 1960); Elaine Kaye, *Mansfield College, Oxford: Its Origin, History and Significance* (Oxford, 1996).

[51] L.P. Jacks, *The Confession of an Octogenarian* (London, 1942), 202.

House in 1926 (the first principal being a Welshman), the Congregationalists had moved Cheshunt College there in 1905 and the Presbyterians had
built their Westminster College in 1899. While all these institutions might
in a certain sense be 'peripheral' and not yet colleges as Oxbridge understood colleges, the scholarly calibre of some of their staff was at least the
equal of Anglicans in established university posts.[52] Indeed, if still perceived
to be culturally peripheral, the Nonconformist colleges, with their many
links to Scotland, Germany and the United States, were more outward-
looking and international than their Anglican counterparts.[53] The first
Oxford-based principal of Regent's Park College, H. Wheeler Robinson,
was an eminent Old Testament scholar—some said the most outstanding
of his generation in Britain—a field in which other Baptists in this period,
as later, were excelling.[54] C.H. Dodd, to become perhaps the most distinguished British New Testament scholar of his generation, taught at Mansfield before succeeding the Methodist layman, A.S. Peake, in the Chair of
Biblical Criticism and Exegesis at the University of Manchester in 1930 (still
at the time the only theological chair in an English university open to a
Nonconformist). He moved to Cambridge as Norris-Hulse Professor in
1935. His formation as a Welsh Congregationalist from Wrexham never left
him.[55] Robinson had an Edinburgh degree (besides an Oxford one) and, in
paying German study visits, he had followed in a well-established Nonconformist pattern. While some Oxbridge Anglican theologians of the 1920s
(E.C. Hoskyns in Berlin and N.P. Williams in Strasbourg) had also done
this pre-war, the German Protestant 'bloodline' ran more directly into
Nonconformist intellectual life. In London, there were increasingly close
connections between the Free Church colleges then still in the capital and
King's College in the University of London's Faculty of Theology, a
partnership symbolized by the books in the *Library of Constructive Theology*
jointly edited by Matthews and Wheeler Robinson.[56] As the English provincial university colleges in the major cities obtained full university status
so, where there was provision for theology, Nonconformist colleges moved
closer to them with students taking their degrees and their staff becoming

[52] John Tudno Williams, 'The Contribution of Protestant Nonconformists in Biblical Scholarship in the Twentieth Century' in Alan P.F. Sell and Anthony R. Cross, eds., *Protestant
Nonconformity in the Twentieth Century* (Carlisle, 2003), 1–32.

[53] F.M. Turner, 'Religion' in Brian Harrison, ed., *The History of the University of Oxford*,
vol. viii: *The Twentieth Century* (Oxford, 1994), 298.

[54] Henry Wheeler Robinson, *The Christian Experience of the Holy Spirit* (London, 1928) and
'Hebrew Psychology' in A.S. Peake, ed., *The People and the Book: Essays on the Old Testament*
(Oxford, 1925); E.A. Payne, *Henry Wheeler Robinson* (London, 1946); Rex Mason, 'Henry
Wheeler Robinson Revisited', *Baptist Quarterly* 37/5 (1998), 213–26.

[55] F.W. Dillistone, *C.H. Dodd: Interpreter of the New Testament* (London, 1977).

[56] Matthews, *Memories and Meanings*, 123–6.

'recognized' teachers.[57] The calibre of such emerging men—Vincent Taylor (New Testament) and Norman Snaith (Old Testament)—at Wesley College, Headingley (Leeds) could be seen in their early published work.[58]

That there was some academic flowing together of these 'streams' can be inferred from the fact that they did refer to each other's books (often but not invariably), but the channels in which the streams flowed were still distinct. A broad, though by no means complete, distinction can be drawn between Nonconformist concentration upon (and distinction in) biblical studies and Anglican absorption in the relationship between philosophy and theology. Nonconformist scholarship, with rare exceptions, did not come from scholars who had been moulded, as their Anglican contemporaries had been, in the culture of English public schools. The Bible as 'authority' was a common concern, but not quite for the same reasons or in the same way.

There was virtually no formal place for Roman Catholic theology in this academic scene, though an individual like von Hügel was a familiar figure in the London study of religion. In Oxford, for example, in 1926 Ronald Knox, as an Anglican a chaplain of Trinity College, returned to the Roman Catholic chaplaincy at its location 'The Old Palace' but he apparently neither sought nor was offered admission to the Faculty of Theology.[59] His impact in Oxford, and the Catholic advocacy which came from the Jesuit Martin D'Arcy installed at Campion Hall, together with the intellectual work of the Dominicans at Blackfriars, remained at a distance from and substantially in opposition to the 'theology of the university'.[60]

The Jesus of History (1917) by T.R. Glover is an example of the way in which the distinct strands were to some degree coming together.[61] A Scot

---

[57] For example, in Bristol, the college moved to a site close to the university in 1919: N.S. Moon, *Education for Ministry: Bristol Baptist College, 1679–1979* (Bristol, 1979), 67–70.

[58] William Strawson, 'Methodist Theology 1850–1950' in Rupert Davies, A. Raymond George and Gordon Rupp, eds., *The History of the Methodist Church in Great Britain*, vol. iii (London, 1983), 182–231 gives an overview of Methodist scholarship in this period but finds no occasion to use the word 'modernism'. There were exceptions, but Strawson commented, 'Methodism had not in fact produced many outstanding scholars, and has depended upon other Churches for leadership in theological matters'. Methodists, he suggested, were never professional theologians and even those set aside to teach theology in colleges remained biased towards circuit ministry—a situation which he welcomed.

[59] E. Waugh, *Monsignor Ronald Knox* (London, 1959).

[60] Turner, 'Religion' in Harrison, ed., *History of the University of Oxford*, viii. 299–300. H.J.A. Sire, *Father Martin D'Arcy: Philosopher of Christian Love* (Leominster, 1997). Waugh was received into the Roman Catholic Church by D'Arcy (himself a convert). Waugh wrote a life of Edmund Campion. Perhaps a little oddly, Lutyens was selected as the architect for Campion Hall. Waugh was later to write the life of Knox. E. Waugh, *A Little Learning: The First Volume of Autobiography* (London, 1964). The Dominican house was opened in Oxford in 1921 and in Cambridge in 1938. The journal *Blackfriars*, started in 1924, sought both to develop a Catholic and to some extent 'European' perspective on contemporary culture, but also to be open to that culture in a manner that was mildly 'progressive'. A. Nichols, *Dominican Gallery: Portrait of a Culture* (Leominster, 1997).

[61] T.R. Glover, *The Jesus of History* (London, 1917).

by pedigree, but schooled in Bristol where his father had become a leading
Baptist minister, he had a distinguished record as a classical scholar and tutor
at St John's, Cambridge. He remained a layman and a Baptist (though not
without certain wobbles), becoming president of the Baptist Union for
the year 1924. The archbishop of Canterbury was persuaded to write a
commendatory foreword to the book. It was published by the Student
Christian Movement Press, a notable addition, Davidson thought, to its
publication programme. He called it a book of great value to the student or
exponent of dogmatic theology. It was a vast publishing success, selling
50,000 copies within three years and running into nineteen impressions over
the next couple of decades (and incidentally making possible the expansion
of the SCM Press). First delivered as lectures in India, Glover's Jesus can
be taken to be *the* 'middle of the road' picture of Jesus as presented by non-
Catholic Christians throughout the English-speaking world—Glover had
taught in Canada and retained connection with it.[62] He was apparently
'never much at home on the Continent'. This was an Englishman's Jesus for
the British Empire and the United States. The date of publication coincided
with the entry of the United States into the war. Glover was a popular
lecturer in America in the early 1920s. He saw no need to say anything in
his book about Jesus's miracles.

There were those in his denomination who thought Glover was a
'modernist' and were irked by the pungent line he took in the column
which he wrote for *The Daily News*. Indeed, a small number of churches left
the Baptist Union, on doctrinal grounds, at the time of his period in office as
president. However, while being quite acerbic about his conservative
critics, he continued to assert his evangelicalism.[63] There were Baptist
modernists of various shades but the core of denominational leadership
wanted to avoid the denomination being labelled either as modernist or
fundamentalist. 'Fundamentalism', of course, saw itself as the antithesis of
'modernism'. The choir of the Metropolitan Tabernacle in 1922 was singing
'Bible battle-songs' as part of an All-Day Bible Demonstration. In the same
year, *The Bible Call*, a journal of the Baptist Bible Union, thundered against
'the Modernist movement' which was identified as the religious wing of
anarchy, revolution and Bolshevism. Lawlessness and the rebellion against
authority were judged to be characteristic of 'the last days'. The controversy
rumbled on, amongst Baptists in particular, and also amongst Anglican

[62] T.H. Robinson, *Terrot Reaveley Glover, M.A., D.D., LL.D: Scholar and Christian* (London,
1943); H.G. Wood, *Terrot Reaveley Glover: A Biography* (Cambridge, 1953); B. Stanley, '"The
Old Religion amd the New": India and the Making of T.R. Glover's *The Jesus of History*' in
D.W. Bebbington, ed., *The Gospel in the World* (Carlisle, 2002), 295–312.
[63] Ian Randall, *English Baptists of the Twentieth Century* (London, 2005), 134–5.

evangelicals, though there was no mass support for 'fundamentalism'.[64] There was, however, something of a paradox. The United States was at one and the same time the stronghold of that 'fundamentalism' with which *The Bible Call* hoped to work in close co-operation but the country was also perceived, at least in refined circles, as the very paradigm of a distasteful modernity. The methods, if not the messages, of the Americans were 'modern'.

Free Church 'modernism' was more likely to be found in Congregationalism. Dr Horton had noted the existence of Anglican Modern Churchmen. In April 1926, in an article in the *Congregational Quarterly*, he proposed a 'Modern Free Churchmen's Conference' whose members could present a Christianity 'equally removed from Romanism and Fundamentalism'.[65] Since Free Churchmen were not in any case so hung up on the subject of creeds (not being in the habit of reciting one or other of them during divine service) their outlook was not so constrained by them. Creeds were all human productions and could not be regarded as necessarily and absolutely infallible. They should not be used as a ground for excluding from the church of Christ anyone who could not entirely accept them.[66] The 'Modern Free Churchmen's Conference' first met in Oxford in 1927, with Horton in the chair, as he continued to be over the next few years. He was accorded great respect, but some of the younger members found him too 'orthodox'. Frank Lenwood's *Jesus—Lord or Leader?*, published in 1930, was more to 'radical' taste. At Mansfield, C.J. Cadoux was working on his own version of modernism in some friction with his new principal, Nathaniel Micklem, once thought to be 'one of us' but, on his return from Canada, found not to be.[67] It was a Congregational layman and Cambridge college bursar, preacher and historian who put the matter starkly. There was much talk, Bernard Law Manning wrote in 1927 in an essay on 'Christian Experience through the Centuries', about the cultivation of a religious attitude which was Christian but did not require a church. He was quite

---

[64] D.W. Bebbington, 'Baptists and Fundamentalism' in Keith Robbins, ed., *Protestant Evangelicalism: Britain, Ireland, Germany and America c. 1750–c. 1950: Essays in Honour of W.R. Word* (Oxford, 1990), 298; Bebbington, *Evangelicalism in Modern Britain: A History from the 1730s to the 1980s* (London, 1989), 217–20.

[65] A. Peel and J. Marriott, *Robert Forman Horton* (London, 1937), 282–3.

[66] So argued C.J. Cadoux in *Catholicism and Christianity* (London, 1929), 242–8.

[67] The book appeared as *The Case for Evangelical Modernism: A Study of the Relation between Christian Faith and Traditional Theology* (London, 1938). Nathaniel Micklem, *The Box and the Puppets* (London, 1957), 81 ff. comments on his relationship with Cadoux but is rather coy on his own early 'liberalism'. Elaine Kaye, *C.J. Cadoux: Theologian, Scholar and Pacifist* (Edinburgh, 1988); Norman Goodall, 'Nathaniel Micklem', *Journal of the United Reformed Church History Society* 1/10 (1977), 286–95.

clear, however, that the article 'I believe in one Catholick and Apostolick Church' could not be separated from the rest of the faith.[68]

It was possible, in other words, that trying to 'meet' modernity, in the ways that have been so far discussed, was simply misdirected. 'The Church', one eloquent author declared, 'cannot move with the times; simply because the times are not moving...We do not want, as the newspapers say, a Church that will move with the world. We want a Church that will move the world.' It was a voice which came not from the world of academic theology, but from 'men of letters' who knew what they thought had to be said and knew how to say it. Brimming with versatility and vitality, G.K. Chesterton had dealt with *Heretics* (1905) and *Orthodoxy* (1908) pre-war. After the war, thinking that England had 'got into so wrong a state, with its plutocracy and neglected populace and materialistic and servile morality', he suggested that it needed to take a sharp and sensational turn. Leaving the Church of England, he made his own march on Rome in 1922. He would be showing that Christianity was a religion of repentance which stood 'against modern fatalism and pessimistic futurism'.[69] Inge, somewhat under the impression that Chesterton had become a Roman Catholic in order to show his contempt for all Inge stood for, was dismissive. It was impossible to take such a fat Falstaffian man seriously. Nevertheless, the Christ Chesterton presented to the public a couple of years later in *The Everlasting Man* (1925) had a challenging directness which by-passed the Christ of academic debate. It seemed, after all, that there was no need to be in the thrall of modernity.[70]

Virginia Woolf, at the cutting edge of modernity, was shocked in 1927 when T.S. Eliot was baptized and confirmed in the Church of England. He had been editing the literary magazine the *Criterion* since 1922 and writing poetry. Eliot did not have Chestertonian girth and might therefore be a serious figure. Woolf's interview with him on Christianity she found both shameful and distressing. He would be 'dead to us all from this day forward'. A corpse would be more credible than a living person sitting by the fire and believing in God. 'Us all' did not mean just her friends but the 'all' of the modern age since they embodied that age's essential character. Adding, for good measure, as he did, that he was an Anglo-Catholic and a royalist, there was obviously an element of deliberate reaction in the stance that Eliot took at this juncture, yet his complicated path to Christianity was not

[68] Published in *Essays in Orthodox Dissent* (London, 1939), 25. For an assessment of Manning see J.M. Turner, 'Bernard Law Manning (1892–1941)—as Church Historian', *Journal of the United Reformed Church History Society* 1/5 (1975), 126–38. See also Cowling, *Religion and Public Doctrine in Modern England*, i. 200–4.

[69] Maisie Ward, *Gilbert Keith Chesterton* (London, 1944), 398, 390; G.K. Chesterton, *Autobiography* (London, 1936); A.S. Dale, *The Outline of Sanity: A Life of G.K. Chesterton* (London, 1982).

[70] Jay P. Corrin, *G.K. Chesterton and Hilaire Belloc: The Battle against Modernity* (London, 1981).

mere provocation. Its impact was all the greater for its 'lay' character and the evident working of a mind which ruminated on the quality of culture. It was also shockingly disturbing in that conversion to 'Christianity' was evidently not some generalized cultural profession but actually entailed active involvement in the treadmill life of the clumsy hippopotamus that was the church: in time, indeed, it was to see poet as churchwarden.

In Oxford a young don who had been wounded on the Western Front in March 1918 read *The Everlasting Man*. One of his pupils, Mr Betjeman, was proving particularly irksome, in equal measure, for both his frivolity and his attendance at Pusey House. The don, C.S. Lewis, was a colleague at Magdalen of its erstwhile chaplain, J.M. Thompson, whose views on miracles had upset when they were aired before the war. Reinstated in his fellowship by supportive colleagues, he was now turning his attention to the bloody inauguration of the modern world, the French Revolution. In the late 1920s, mingling with J.R.R. Tolkien and other literary men in Oxford, men with creative as well as critical instincts, Lewis moved to Christian belief. It was an obscure event and did not seem of much consequence. Dons immersed in medieval English literature, even if they had unusual inklings, were not necessarily in the front line of modernity.[71]

The espousal of Christianity by these three men, following different intellectual trajectories as they did, expressed, to different extents, a dissatisfaction with a 'modernist' agenda which eliminated God, or at least the 'ordinary one'. It also manifested some element of grumpiness about modern life as a whole. How their writing might fare in this 'modern world' was beyond even their imaginations (though Chesterton did take to broadcasting). They were of course not unique in their professions of new faith. Others did not find it necessary to clash, rather self-consciously, with 'the modern' in order to be sensible Christians. In the cases of Eliot and Lewis, however, there was a further element in their journeys. They were both— leaving aside their 'domestic' lives—struggling with what it was to be English. Eliot's transformation into an Englishman—naturalization as a British subject seemed to be part and parcel of his conversion—was the more obvious 're-location'. He had 'Catholic tendencies' but to become both English/British and Roman Catholic simultaneously seemed incongruous. The Church of England was the national church of an Englishman and it was conveniently possible to be rather Catholic within it. Lewis, born in Belfast in 1898, needed no naturalization. The Britishness of a Church of Ireland family in an Ulster in crisis had surrounded him in childhood and

[71] Lewis himself wrote an account of his religious experiences until he reached the age of 31 in *Surprised by Joy* (London, 1955); A.N. Wilson, *C.S. Lewis: A Biography* (London, 1990); Humphrey Carpenter, *The Inklings: C.S. Lewis, J.R.R. Tolkien, Charles Williams and their Friends* (London, 1979).

early schooling before he was shunted off, unhappily as it turned out, to Malvern College and then, more happily, to Oxford. He fought as a British soldier. He had the appearance of being an Englishman, but there was, of course, more to Englishness than the smoking of a pipe.

iii. *Global Politics: Self-Determination and a 'Christian' Empire*

What it was to be a Christian, and what it was to be a church in the post-war decade, could not be separated from the overall political environment in which 'modern' rethinking had been taking place. The more optimistic had supposed in 1919 that a 'new order' had been created in Europe. The three pre-war empires—Habsburg, Hohenzollern and Romanov—were no more. 'National self-determination' was the order of the day though, as the peacemakers had discovered, the application of this 'principle' in ethnically mixed territories defied easy solutions. There was scarcely a new state in central Europe without a simmering internal 'minority' grievance which hindered the consolidation of state-building. 'Minority' treaties supposedly protected rights but monitoring them was difficult. It was apparent, also, in many instances, that ethnicity was virtually inseparable from religious allegiance, whether Catholic, Protestant or Orthodox, to put it simply.

The 'self', in 'self-determination', could not easily be identified. Europe was 'in convalescence' but some observers did not believe that the 'so-called Christian Churches' would be able to play the part which they should in the process of reconstruction. Religion, it was sometimes stated, had been imprisoned by its professional keepers and needed to be released.[72] It could also be hoped, however, that after the upheaval, Europe would experience a new harmony. British enthusiasts for the reordering of Europe, on supposedly 'national' lines, from the Baltic to the Balkans, were unhappy at some particular outcomes of the settlement but remained optimistic. *Nations*, it could be supposed, would speak peace unto nations in a continent where, in the past, *states* had failed to do so. With the exception of the kingdom of Serbs, Croats and Slovenes (as Yugoslavia was initially called) all the new states (including Germany) were republican democracies (though Hungary had a regent). British 'realists', however, were deeply sceptical about these developments. Pig-headed idealists, General Sir Philip Chetwoode told the wife of the dean of St Paul's, had created 'silly little nations ready to drop like a ripe cherry into anyone's mouth'.[73]

---

[72] A.E. Zimmern, *Europe in Convalescence* (London, 1922), 73–5.

[73] Inge, *Diary of a Dean*, 82. Chetwoode, later field-marshal and commander-in-chief of the Indian Army, had a daughter, Penelope, who was a playmate of the dean's daughter. She later married, for better or worse, C.S. Lewis's recalcitrant and reluctant pupil, John Betjeman.

It could be thought that the United Kingdom had escaped this upheaval. After all, the monarch still sat on his throne. The British Empire still existed, indeed by virtue of new 'mandates' under the new League of Nations in Iraq, Palestine and elsewhere, its territorial extent was greater than ever before. Yet there were clear signs both that the constitutional relationships between the 'mother country' and the 'dominions' required redefinition and that there was increasing opposition to British rule in India. Both of these issues, in different ways, occupied politicians through the 1920s. The 1931 Statute of Westminster gave formal character to the parity of status (though not of power) which the 'old dominions' now possessed. 'Round Tables' on the future of India continued.

The implications of these changes, even if only partially perceived in the churches, were profound. The end of the Ottoman Empire, followed by the 'secularization' of Turkey, had removed the largest Muslim power (although it had caused Muslim unrest in British India) and thus gave the impression of the triumph of a Britain conceived as a 'Christian power'. The establishment of a 'National Home' for Jews in the Palestine for which Britain bore direct responsibility further complicated the picture. The British assumption of the Palestinian mandate was a political act, but it was encouraged by those British Christians who supposed that the gathering back of Jewish people to the Holy Land would herald the Second Coming of Christ.[74] This new development did not mean, however, that Christian missionary work amongst Jews was inappropriate. The Anglican 'Church Missions to the Jews' was supporting some 200 missionaries seeking to convert Jews both in Britain and in continental Europe. It was not the only such society. In practice, however, in comparison with Germany, relatively few Jews in Britain became Christians. One British Jewish writer calculated that converts cost an average of £1,000 apiece.[75] The extent to which the long inheritance of Christian polemic against the Jews, which may be labelled 'anti-Judaism', fed into or can be distinguished from racial anti-Semitism remains contentious and cannot be resolved here.[76] In the charged atmosphere of 1916 Ireland, the Roman Catholic bishop of Limerick had thought it appropriate to refer disparagingly to the then Chief Secretary, Sir Matthew Nathan, as a 'Jew from Shoreditch'. It would be reasonable to suppose, however, that 'conversionist' modes of thinking predominated in the churches. The view that it was the church which had turned 'normal xenophobia' into 'the unique evil of anti-Semitism' which a young Anglican clergyman, James Parkes, began to formulate in

[74] Barbara Tuchman, *Bible and Sword: How the British Came to Palestine* (London, 1984).
[75] Israel Zangwill, *The Voice of Jerusalem* (London, 1921), 333.
[76] See the discussion in Richard Harries, *After the Evil: Christianity and Judaism in the Shadow of the Holocaust* (Oxford, 2003).

the late 1920s while working in Geneva, would not have been one which church leaders accepted.[77] Continental developments in the next decade were to bring these questions to the fore, exposing the degree of ambiguity that existed.

The relationship (or lack of it) between Jews and Christians in Britain (and, in a rather different context, in Palestine) was in certain respects a 'special case'. More generally, in the 1920s, the churches could not ignore 'inter-faith relationships'. They played a part in the foundation in 1921 of the International Missionary Council. In different parts of the world there was an emerging clash between 'independence' movements and 'imperialism' which found churches 'on the frontier' where national aims and universal beliefs were in tension.[78] A second World Missionary Conference, held at Jerusalem in 1928, issued a report *Rethinking Mission* which acknowledged that there was a new climate, but asserted Christianity's distinctiveness.[79] For the moment, however, while these issues were to some extent addressed at such international gatherings, they seemed somewhat remote in islands where 'religion' and 'Christianity' still seemed virtually coterminous. It was difficult, however, to decide whether what was happening, in global terms, represented the further advance of that complex intertwined politico-religious entity called 'the Christian West', with Britain still in the van, or whether it indicated its precariousness and perhaps imminent collapse. Dean Inge was not the only leading churchman to feel in his bones that the 'old country' was finished. He fell to speculating on 'the White Man and His Rivals'. Europeans, he wrote, had recently enjoyed an unfair advantage over their rivals. They would not have it in the future.[80] Prognosticating on the condition of the world in 2000, he felt it to be 'inevitable that we shall cease to be one of the Great Powers of the World', though that need not be a great loss.[81]

---

[77] Parkes wrote his own account (under the pen name 'John Hadham') in *Voyages of Discovery* (London, 1969); Colin Richmond, *Campaigner against Antisemitism: The Reverend James Parkes 1896–1981* (London, 2005); Tony Kushner, 'The Impact of British Antisemitism, 1918–1945' in David Cesarani, ed., *The Making of Modern Anglo-Jewry* (Oxford, 1990), 191–208; more generally, see Gisela Lebzelter, *Political Anti-Semitism in England, 1918–1939* (London, 1978) and William and Hilary Rubinstein, *Philosemitism: Admiration and Support in the English-Speaking World for Jews, 1840–1939* (London, 1999).

[78] Keith Clements, *Faith on the Frontier: A life of J.H. Oldham* (Edinburgh, 1999). Oldham, in practice a Scottish Presbyterian layman, had a prominent role in formulating responses to these challenges.

[79] The contributors to Norman Etherington, ed., *Missions and Empire* (Oxford, 2005) caution against any simple notion that Christian missions in this (as in other periods) were merely adjuncts of imperialism and colonial conquest.

[80] W.R. Inge, 'The White Man and His Rivals' in *Outspoken Essays* (*Second Series*), 230.

[81] W.R. Inge, *Assessments and Anticipations*, 183.

The Great War, as has earlier been noted, had changed the terms of a possible Irish 'solution'. Certainly, the kind of state which the United Kingdom of Great Britain and Ireland had purported to be in 1914 could not continue. It was apparently not only in 'new Europe' that people wanted 'silly little nations'. This unstable condition pulled the churches of the British Isles in different directions. It has already been made abundantly clear in this book that ecclesiastical had not followed political union in the United Kingdom. In one sense, therefore, whatever political change took place, over whatever span of time, the churches, almost without exception, were already territorially structured. They would have to adjust to constitutional change but had already 'anticipated' it—indeed they could be said to have been carriers of cultural identity in the absence of its political expression (or potent demand for it). Yet the interplay of these considerations made it unlikely that there would be any uniform outcome throughout the British Isles. In particular, the word 'nation' remained problematic and left the churches in a quandary, not to say a quagmire.

The quandary was this. The 'national principle' was being elevated at one and the same time as its ferocious undertow was apparent. Preachers perhaps exaggerated how far they had succumbed to xenophobic utterance in the late war but they sought now to 'make amends'. 'Whatever else the religious history of the last three centuries has shown' an English theologian, Oliver Quick, declared in lectures in 1922 in New York, 'it has at least demonstrated the abject futility of merely national Churches, and we may add that the Papal State of the Ultramontanes has done no better. The Church stands for a higher principle of association than the group or race, and when it fails to be true to that principle it is a mere encumbrance to progress.'[82] He spoke, of course, as a member of a national church. It was an observation which can be found in many other contemporary places. But was this empty rhetoric in the wake of a war which had disclosed the impotent paralysis and cultural captivity of Europe's churches? The contributors to the wartime volume edited by George Bell, the archbishop's chaplain, had agreed that the cause of the Kingdom of God was greater than the cause of the patriot.[83] Yet they did not cease to regard themselves as patriots. Patriotism was a sound virtue.

How, if at all, could this dichotomy be resolved? Subsequent sections of this chapter will separately explore some of these implications, though in reality they could not be kept separate. It might be right that some things should fall apart but what 'centre' should be held? If the church did indeed stand for 'a higher principle of association' how could that association be

---

[82] Quick, *Liberalism, Modernism and Tradition*, 125.
[83] G.K.A. Bell, ed., *The War and the Kingdom of God* (London, 1915).

practically, as opposed to theoretically, manifested? 'The church' might be 'higher' than the 'group or race', or a class, but 'the church' was itself only code for a multiplicity of associations, by no means all in harmony with each other. Did 'Christendom' still have any transcendent utility in that 'new Europe' from which 'Throne and Altar' had all but disappeared? Might not what constituted the 'height' represented by the church be itself differently determined by groups and races? And did the pursuit of the 'higher' require at least scepticism about 'group' or 'race' and the solidarities each might properly expect and evoke? A 'unity', whether of nations or churches, achieved by eliminating or disparaging diversity, in order to produce 'uniformity', might not be desirable, and would certainly not be achievable. Yet the maintenance of a perceived identity, whether 'invented' or not, seemed to be a fraught matter, trembling on the brink of violence. The sections that follow illustrate how, in different ways, these issues came to the fore.

iv. Domestic Politics: Defining Christian Citizenship

Forebodings about the implications of a global shift in power were not confined to the dean of St Paul's. Even so, writing as one who loved his own country dearly, Inge felt in 1926 that its greatest danger came 'not so much from the aggressions of foreign nations . . . as from anti-social and unpatriotic sectionalism which is the curse of industrial civilisation'.[84] Unsettlement clearly began at home. It was fortuitous, but his book *England* appeared a few months after the May General Strike. During that crisis, he had felt, the bishops had come out of it very badly, 'bleating for a compromise while the nation was fighting for its life'.[85] Bishop Woods (together with Garbett of Southwark) published a letter in *The Times* on the day it began advocating a subsidy for the mining industry. 'Bleating', however, was not how Archbishop Davidson saw his document, *The Crisis: Appeal from the Churches*, which had called for the cancellation of the strike but also for the continuance of government financial support to the coal industry and withdrawal of the wage rates being offered by the mineowners. The director-general of the BBC had refused to allow him to broadcast it—a fact which had the incidental benefit of giving it a prominence it might not otherwise have commanded. Temple, with some other bishops and Free Church leaders, attempted subsequently to mediate between owners and miners but only gained a response from the latter. One conclusion has been that 'faced with hard, practical, highly divisive issues involving the bread

---

[84] Preface to *England* quoted in Fox, *Inge,* 190.
[85] Inge, *Diary of a Dean* (May 1926), 111.

and cheese of poor heavily burdened men' the well-intentioned generalities of churchmen were of little use.[86]

Of course there were many conservative Anglicans who thought, as W.C. Bridgeman put it, that the robust condemnation of the strike—portrayed as a direct challenge to lawfully constituted authority and a sin against the obedience owed to God—delivered at High Mass in Westminster Cathedral by the archbishop, was preferable to the 'miserable paper' from the archbishop of Canterbury. In Scotland, the moderator of the United Free Church of Scotland declared that the outcome constituted 'a victory for God'. The principal of New College, Edinburgh, criticizing the archbishop of Canterbury, had been adamant that the General Strike, an attempt at *force majeure*, had to be broken at whatever cost.[87] Others, in Scotland and elsewhere, wanted to make clear that they nevertheless had sympathy for the plight of miners and hoped, in an unspecific way, that once the strike had indeed failed, 'something could be done'. In Liverpool, however, the Catholic archbishop stated firmly that if private enterprise could not provide the worker with a living it had to 'clear out' for another system which could. One might surmise, with Canon Peter Green, that in the upshot, clergy and laity, even in all churches, believed both that the archbishop of Canterbury had been right to make his appeal and that Baldwin had been right to ignore it: the best, or worst, of both worlds.[88] The Scottish middle classes, it has been concluded, who formed the backbone of the Scottish churches, were no longer prepared to condone the preaching of Christian Socialism.[89]

Criticism of 'generalities' extended too to the work which had been undertaken in the early 1920s, culminating in the Conference on Christian Politics, Economics and Citizenship (COPEC) which had been held in Birmingham under Temple's chairmanship for a week in April 1924. It was claimed by the organizers that the social ethics of Christianity had been greatly neglected by Christians 'with disastrous consequences to the individual and to society'. The king sent a message of encouragement—as did the leaders of the political parties—stating that such discussions 'must surely be welcomed by the citizens of a Christian country'. Temple stressed three features of the assembly—its scope, its representative character and its spiritual basis. The scope did indeed leave room for the expression of opinions on a wide range of matters. Lord Aberdeen (Church of Scotland),

---

[86] Hastings, *History of English Christianity*, 191. Hastings has an entire chapter on the strike.

[87] S.J. Brown, ' "A Victory for God": The Scottish Presbyterian Churches and the General Strike of 1926', *Journal of Ecclesiastical History* 42 (1991), 596–617.

[88] Cited in S. Mews, 'The Churches' in Margaret Morris, *The General Strike* (Harmondsworth, 1976), 337.

[89] Brown, 'A Victory for God', 616.

for example, emphasized the importance of folk-dancing as a way forward. Resolutions were passed, amongst others, on education, the home, the relation of the sexes, leisure, the treatment of crime, international relations, industry, and property. The final exhortation was that Christians should do battle against the evils of the press.[90] It was with sadness that Temple reported that the Roman Catholic Church, 'that great Church' had felt unable to be officially represented. Two Jesuit priests, Leslie Walker and Leo O'Hara, had originally served on the preparatory commission. Catholics had also served on the commissions which prepared the reports on which the resolutions were passed. The Balliol fellow Francis Urquhart had been active on one of these, no doubt on the basis that 'we must try to give Protestants the principles of Christianity which they ought to have'.[91] In the event, however, Cardinal Bourne wrote to O'Hara that Catholics should not co-operate formally with COPEC or in future participate in any of its activities. The bishop of Salford wrote to congratulate the archbishop of Birmingham (McIntyre) for the broadside he had delivered *ad clerum* against all that COPEC seemed to stand for. 'Our Common Christianity', he wrote, was so much eye-wash. The neglect of 'social ethics' was not something for which Catholics should accept any responsibility. The social chaos was all the product of Protestantism.[92]

There was little doubt at the conference that the existing industrial system was 'radically unChristian'. What should be done about it was another matter. A great many questionnaires were issued. Reports and conferences tried to establish a way forward. Temple, enthusiastic about 'middle axioms', tried to steer a middle course, but critics of different persuasions, on the one hand dismissed COPEC as unrealistic waffle, and, on the other hand, condemned its stance as insufficiently radical. A.D. Lindsay took a rather different view. In modern industrial society, the fundamental antagonism was not between those who owned capital and those who did not, but between managers and the managed.[93] The General Strike exposed a power struggle in which the churches were powerless. The secretary of the Congregational Union, S.M. Berry asked, 'What part have we to play in the controversies and struggles which have shifted from the political to the economic plane?' It was a rhetorical question.[94]

---

[90] *The Proceedings of C.O.P.E.C* (London, 1924).

[91] A general stance which he had adopted for some years. K. Aspden, *Fortress Church: The English Roman Catholic Bishops and Politics, 1903–1963* (Leominster, 2002), 130.

[92] The issues are discussed in Aspden, *Fortress Church*, 146–53 and in his article 'The English Roman Catholic Bishops and the Social Order, 1918–26', *Recusant History* 25 (2001), 543–64.

[93] A.D. Lindsay, *Christianity and Economics* (London, 1933). The lectures were given in 1930.

[94] Cited in Peter Catterall, 'The Party and Religion' in Anthony Seldon and Stuart Ball, eds., *Conservative Century: The Conservative Party since 1900* (Oxford, 1994), 646.

A 'just' social order remained elusive. The degree of inequality evident in many spheres was unacceptable, but what was meant by 'equality'? R.H. Tawney, who had first met Temple on the platform of Rugby station as the boys made their way for their first day at Rugby School, was keen on equality. He thought he knew what it implied. He did not like the acquisitive society. Christian Socialists, of whatever variety, and whether lay or ecclesiastic, constantly reiterated that the existing system had to change to a more collectivist order, but did not know how to get there. Schemes for the creation of industrial harmony were many and various. A school of 'Christian Sociologists' sought the revival of 'Christendom'.[95] Men were tugged to or from 'politics' as the means of getting to the right destination. 'After many years of strenuous political activity,' wrote the Revd P.E.T. Widdrington, an eager prophet, in 1925, 'I have come to question its usefulness.' It was partly that there was no political party with which he was in wholehearted sympathy, but he was also coming to believe that 'no secular civilization can be stable, and this applies to socialist civilizations just as much as capitalist or Fordian schemes'.[96] The Industrial Christian Fellowship, with G.A. Studdert-Kennedy as its 'messenger', did manage, within limits, to bring together 'captains of industry', Labour politicians and trade unionists. Baldwin threatened privately to proscribe from promotion any bishop who had appeared with the ICF during the Coal Strike.[97]

Some individual Christian 'captains', implicitly or explicitly, sought to apply their convictions to the management issues before them. Some Quakers thought co-ownership the solution. Sometimes, however, unhappiness was expressed with the clerical view that the quest for private profit was incompatible with Christianity. Josiah Stamp, Wesleyan chairman of the London, Midland & Scottish Railway, addressed the question of social ethics in various publications. In 1926, he emphasized that 'the ethical' could make many systems work and did not prescribe either capitalism or state socialism.[98] Others questioned whether 'nationalization'—described by some churchmen as 'a flowing tide'—was really the answer to everything. There was still something to be said for 'competition'. These varying

---

[95] These ideas are considered, not without criticism, in E.R. Norman, *Church and Society in England, 1770–1970: A Historical Study* (Oxford, 1976), 279 ff.: John Oliver, *The Church and Social Order: Social Thought in the Church of England, 1918–1939* (London, 1968). See also G.I.T. Machin, *Churches and Social Issues in Twentieth-Century Britain* (Oxford, 1988), 29–41 and Kent, *Temple*.

[96] Maurice B. Reckitt, *P.E.T. Widdrington: A Study in Vocation and Versatility* (London, 1961), 75.

[97] Gerald Studdert-Kennedy, *Dog-Collar Democracy: The Industrial Christian Fellowship, 1919–1929* (London, 1982).

[98] David J. Jeremy, *Capitalists and Christians: Business Leaders and the Churches in Britain 1900–1960* (Oxford, 1990), 181–2.

reactions point to something deeper. The expression of broad social principles derived from Christian insights ran up increasingly against the complexity of industrial (and other) organization and 'specialized knowledge'. It might be that there were 'middle axioms' which could bridge the gulf but they were increasingly difficult to 'translate'.

Ideas apart, individual reactions to these problems were shaped by personal explorations in the maze of the class structure and in the experience of life.[99] Temple, in Manchester, deplored the 'escapism' of those businessmen who relished Sunday because going to church was so different from what they did on the other six days of the week. That was a dangerous dichotomy. It was wrong to exercise emotions in one field and 'practical activities' in another.[100] Laymen, for their part, wondered how ecclesiastics with limited experience of 'practical activities' could write with such assurance on 'the industrial system'. Some bishops, it is true, did move into unknown territory—'determined to get first-hand experience'—as Theodore Woods, bishop of Peterborough, did when the Trades Union Congress met at Glasgow. There was clearly 'religion' in the labour movement. It was 'implicit', the first Labour lord mayor of Bristol declared. It was George Lansbury who urged his fellow socialists to 'Come back to the Galilean!' Jesus had been the greatest revolutionary force of his times. He now lived on to give men and women the revolutionary spirit.[101] The TUC's chairman allowed Woods onto the platform in Glasgow, though Clydesiders were puzzled by such an episcopal presence, and an English one to boot. In every ounce of demeanour, he was not 'one of us'. What was he up to? Woods himself, believing that the TUC was the most powerful organization in the country, knew that its thinking could not be ignored.[102] That it was apparently so powerful, however, alarmed some of his fellow bishops. The idea of bowing before 'King Demos' did not appeal to them. They preferred the prime minister, Baldwin, surely a man to be trusted. He was undoubtedly a Christian. Indeed, the *Church Times* discovered in him 'not a little of the spirit of St George'.[103] When Baldwin, unprecedentedly, visited general assemblies of both the Church of Scotland and the Free Church of

---

[99] Ross McKibbin, *Classes and Cultures: England 1918–1951* (Oxford, 1998).

[100] Iremonger, *Temple*, 327.

[101] Both men were speaking at the conference held in September 1919, a record of which is published as *The Religion in the Labour Movement* (1919?), 46–55. J. Shepherd, *George Lansbury: At the Heart of Old Labour* (Oxford, 2004); more generally, see S. Mayor, *The Churches and the Labour Movement* (London, 1967).

[102] Edward S. Woods and Frederick B. MacNutt, *Theodore, Bishop of Winchester: Pastor, Prophet, Pilgrim* (London, 1933), 118–19.

[103] Cited in Matthew Grimley, *Citizenship, Community and the Church of England: Liberal Anglican Theories of the State between the Wars* (Oxford, 2004), 122. The illuminating discussion of 'Temple, Baldwin, and the Strike' is on 116–28.

Scotland in June, he was given a hero's welcome.[104] In private, he expressed his exasperation with 'the bishops' who could not see that what they were doing was 'to keep in power the latent atheist bolshevists, like Cook'.[105] The 'England' of which Baldwin spoke with such rapture was not going to become a Soviet state, though it would appear that the beacon of Bolshevism did beckon some in the 'working classes'. The strike had unexpectedly passed without comment from Hewlett Johnson, newly appointed dean of Manchester. Although he later developed more comprehensive plans for the human future, for the moment, as a former engineer, he was more impressed by the liberations made possible by the spread of the T-model Ford. Petrol and electricity, he thought, offered bright prospects for humankind.[106]

v. England: Establishing Democracy and Disestablishing Church?

The underlying question was 'democracy'. When democracy had come to the United Kingdom, if it indeed had fully come, would depend on what meaning was attached to the word. The adult male suffrage under the Representation of the People Act (1918), together with the enfranchisement of most women over 30, gave it a new and unpredictable dimension. 'Democracy' did not come to the churches with the same degree of disconcerting unsettlement which had occurred, for example, in Germany in 1919. Indeed, its post-war 'forward march' was broadly seen and welcomed as a further step in that seamless process of evolution which was the story of the British constitution. Even so, and the political instability of governments in the early 1920s seemed to suggest this, assumptions about 'freedom', 'party', 'citizenship', 'community', 'class' and 'leadership' were all in disarray.[107] The rise of Labour, even if it was a faltering one, brought a new situation. There was a loss of direction, support and morale in the Liberal Party. There was a loss of direction, support and morale in the Free Churches. Was it the same crisis? 'Democracy', learned Christian writers argued from eminent academic citadels, would need to be 'educated'. What might be less palatable was the extent to which the churches might be constrained by democracy, if democracy entailed letting majorities have

---

[104] Philip Williamson, 'The Doctrinal Politics of Stanley Baldwin' in M. Bentley, ed., *Public and Private Doctrine: Essays in British History presented to Maurice Cowling* (Cambridge, 1993), 181–208; Philip Williamson and Edward Baldwin, *Baldwin Papers: A Conservative Statesman 1908–1947* (Cambridge, 2004).

[105] T. Jones, *Whitehall Diary*, vol. ii, ed. K. Middlemas (Oxford, 1969), 63.

[106] Robert Hughes, *The Red Dean* (Worthing, 1987), 50. Temple (and his wife) drove an Austin 12 in Manchester and Johnson was able to forsake his Ford for a magnificent 14hp Crossley which he had been given by his parishioners in Altrincham as a parting gift on his new appointment.

[107] Grimley, *Citizenship, Community and the Church of England* gives a full account.

their way 'in principle' even if, in the process, they trampled on Christian conviction and hallowed structures. In short, the respective boundaries of church, nation and state were again under pressure.

Hensley Henson, in letters to *The Times* in 1919, had declared that the proposals for church self-government then coming before Parliament would mean that 'the Church of the English nation' in which every Englishman had rights, and for which he had responsibilities, would come to an end. The new Church Assembly could be dominated by Anglo-Catholics. The passage of the legislation to 'enable' its creation was by no means a foregone conclusion. Ecclesiastical lawyers, 'Life and Liberty' enthusiasts (who were not all themselves of one mind) liked to see themselves as prophetic. It was unlikely that administrators would be prophetic.[108] There was some irony in the fact that it was a non-Anglican, non-Englishman, Lord Haldane, who considered that the outcome was that the Church of England had ceased to be 'the assembly of the nation at large' and had become but a 'fragment'. He believed that 'in the long run, a current had been set moving which would lead to the Disestablishment of the Church'.

A new National Assembly of the Church of England was created. The inclusion of the word 'national' was important. Any measure which it wished to see enacted was to be placed, in the first instance, before a new ecclesiastical committee consisting of 15 members from each of the two Houses of Parliament. If approved there, the measure would have to be passed by a single division in each House before gaining royal assent. In the event that this ecclesiastical committee would not consent, a measure could still be submitted for royal assent if both Houses so resolved. The National Assembly could make ordinances in relation to its own government but, unless passed through this procedure, they did not become the law of the land. In the aftermath, there was much talk about whether the Church of England had become a 'denomination' or even a 'sect' but these words meant different things to different people.

Whether the National Assembly was itself 'democratic', or ought to seek to be, was not clear. One critic in the Commons had even supposed that the archbishop of Canterbury was at one with Lenin in wanting 'to combine a democratic form with autocratic effects'.[109] A parliamentary democracy

---

[108] Kenneth Thompson, *Bureaucracy and Church Reform: The Organizational Response of the Church of England to Social Change* (Oxford, 1970), 156–78 describes the forces at work. David M. Thompson, 'The Politics of the Enabling Act (1919)', in Derek Baker, ed., *Church, Society and Politics*, Studies in Church History 12 (Oxford, 1975), 383–92 looks closely at the political manoeuvres; R.P. Flindall, ed., *The Church of England, 1815–1948: A Documentary History* (London, 1972), 342–5.

[109] Major Baines cited in Thompson, *Bureaucracy and Church Reform*, 155.

needed contending parties to make the system work. There were very obviously 'parties' in the church, but they were not supposed to behave like 'real' ones, though often did. Did the new representatives—not thought likely to be significantly drawn from the 'working classes'—have 'constituents'? No one was sure. But perhaps, as the bishop of Norwich sagely observed, in relation to the Assembly, logic and academic coherence were 'foreign to the English mind'.[110] Nonconformists, with whom there had been some consultation, thought that, despite the liberty that had been obtained, the Church of England still wanted an 'established' status and had largely succeeded in retaining it. Taken in the round, however, it looked a reasonable deal, that is to say it fudged certain issues in a way which satisfied the players, both in church and state. The importance of one of these issues was soon to be made clear. The National Assembly was 'representative' of the baptized, but not necessarily confirmed, Anglican English, but Parliament was representative of the diversity, political and ecclesiastical, which was the United Kingdom.

A vital question, in some minds, was whether the church could make changes to its Prayer Book without parliamentary approval.[111] Davidson said it could not. The long process of trying to effect them in such a way as to keep the church 'abreast of modern needs' (not least from the point of view of satisfying its own strands of opinion) yet remain loyal to 'ancient order', was coming to a head. In the early 1920s, the three Houses of the Assembly—clergy, laity and bishops—debated at length the proposals for amendment which were brought forward. Reservation of the sacrament aroused much controversy, as did the possibility that a shortening of the services of Morning and Evening Prayer might lead to the omission of prayers for the king and the royal family. In June 1927, all three Houses adopted the new Prayer Book by substantial majorities. The aforementioned ecclesiastical committee of Parliament, in turn advised by a sub-committee, gave its approval. It considered that the doctrine of the Church of England was not being changed and that the king's promise at his coronation to maintain the Protestant Reformed Religion was not being compromised.

Although the Lords approved by an overwhelming majority in December, the Prayer Book was defeated in the Commons by 238 votes to 205. In party terms, the Conservatives split almost evenly—Baldwin, the prime minister, had spoken in favour. Twice as many Labour MPs voted against as voted in favour. Nearly all the Liberals who voted were against. Post-war parliaments, in the absence of MPs from Southern Ireland, were of course

---

[110] Bertram Pollock, *Twentieth-Century Bishop: Recollections and Reflections* (London, n.d.), 130.

[111] Robert Currie, 'Power and Principle: The Anglican Prayer Book Controversy, 1927–30', *Church History* 33 (1964), 192–202; G.I.T. Machin, 'Parliament, the Church and the Prayer Book Crisis, 1927–8', *Parliamentary History* (2000).

more Protestant in composition than they had been for a century, though the small number of Catholic MPs chose to abstain. However, some English and Welsh MPs who were Nonconformists, and Scottish MPs who were Church of Scotland or United Free Church members, did participate—not all of whom voted against (though Lloyd George did). William Temple thought that the best speech in favour of the measure had been made by a Labour MP who was also a Baptist minister—Herbert Dunnico. In a rare, if not unprecedented, display of oratory, it was the home secretary, Joynson-Hicks, an evangelical Anglican, who effectively rallied the opponents, one of whom was the Communist MP for Battersea North, who happened to be a Parsee. It was left to the dean of Lincoln to point out in a letter to *The Times* that if voting had been restricted to MPs from English constituencies—on a measure which would have applied in England only—it would have been carried by a majority of 21 votes. When a revised version of the Revised Prayer Book came before the Commons again, in June 1928, it was defeated by an even larger majority. It was observed, however, that 53 MPs from Scotland and Wales voted against.

No one in the Church of England wanted to try again. The archbishop of Canterbury reaffirmed his view that the church had 'an inalienable right' to order its own worship. The Revised Book had no standing in civil law, but it was used. A legal challenge to such use might indeed have precipitated a crisis in the relations between church and state. but it was never made. By a rather unexpected route, the Church of England came to experience some liturgical diversity, but its general position seemed unsatisfactory to those no doubt few English minds—*pace* the bishop of Norwich—who worried about logic. They were to find in Hensley Henson a champion who was as articulate as he was unpredictable. It was time, he now thought, to disestablish the Church of England.

Even though 'the English' accepted this parliamentary rebuff to 'their church' with their customary humility, it was an odd outcome. It illustrated the continuing ambiguity of 'the English Church'. Its standing could be said to have been enhanced 'nationally' by the war. The Nonconformity which, before 1914, had appeared to be so vocal and to constitute a 'challenge' to its position, no longer seemed to do so, or to want to do so, in any serious manner. There was no doubt that the Church of England was still comprehensively 'bundled up' with the life of England but these very entanglements irritated those who thought that they impeded the ability of the church to be the church. Its Englishness, however, was somewhat muted by the extent to which it was at the established heart of the British state. If, as the sections which follow suggest, the churches outside England were, to one degree or another, bound up in the assertion of distinctive identities, the Church of England was wedded, for better or worse, to a United Kingdom whose Parliament had just settled its Prayer Book for it.

vi. Wales: Disestablished and Distressed

The war had been 'won' under a Welsh-speaking and publicly Nonconformist prime minister. Few would have predicted that in 1914—when there had been some supposition that David Lloyd George was going to oppose British intervention in the war. He was prime minister, but in a Conservative-dominated coalition government. It was, therefore, for the first time ever, a Welshman who played his part in 'settling' Europe. It also, ironically, fell to a 'Celt' to partition Ireland (or, one might alternatively say, divide Great Britain/Ireland). Wales had never had such a figure at the helm of Britain and the British Empire. Not all Englishmen were happy with this state of affairs. Dean Inge, for one, was tired of hearing Lloyd George described as 'the man who won the war'. That was silly. Lloyd George 'was never a true friend to England; he can only understand the smaller patriotism of Wales. He disliked us; all his friends were Welsh.' And, in relation to his post-war conduct, it seemed to Inge in 1924 that Lloyd George had 'brought down the whole of political life'.[112] He would, and should, never return to power. That there was an uncongenial Celtic darkness about Lloyd George had also occurred to John Maynard Keynes. It was true, however, that Lloyd George did understand 'the smaller patriotism' of Wales, if in a Machiavellian way. His own period of power, brief though it turned out to be, coincided with the disestablishment of the Church of England in Wales. A 'new' and 'Nonconformist' Wales seemed to be being born. The reality was more complicated and, for Nonconformists, dispiriting. Coal and Christianity were evidently and perhaps unexpectedly in crisis together.

At least in the eyes of English ecclesiastics, disestablishment served to highlight how different 'Wales' and 'the Welsh' were. Of course, in its detail, how this new 'province' of the 'Anglican Communion' provided for its governance did not greatly trouble the English public, even the English Anglican public. Its implementation in Wales was also, and perhaps unexpectedly, a curiously muted affair. The war and the social issues of the inter-war period combined to relegate the 'disestablishment' issue to a different era. It produced an outcome which, arguably, neither side in the controversy had envisaged. The 'church' had undoubtedly suffered a loss of status and deference. It struggled to decide whether it could function simply as one denomination among many, 'the largest sect', or whether

---

[112] Inge, *Diary of a Dean*, 92.

it still had about it an element of being the 'official' form of Christianity in Wales. Its cathedrals still seemed 'natural' places in which to hold public events. The Church itself still felt that the disendowment provisions—with some of its property being distributed to Welsh local authorities and to the University of Wales—had been vindictive.

Anguished messages from the Welsh front line were delivered over the border by the new archbishop of Wales, though at no great personal risk, to the effect that disestablishment had all been a great mistake. The Nonconformists, he wrote, as it still seemed right to call them, were being only slightly less tiresome than formerly. Such messages were received in England but could have no consequence. The Welsh bishops were on their own.[113] Even so, some Welsh clergy still wrote to the archbishop of Canterbury to tell him of acute local poverty and suffering. Never had South Wales been as depressed as it was in 1930. In Pontypridd, the vicar said, the only colliery which provided employment had just closed and had only been on part-time working for several years.[114] A disestablished Wales, in short, was a depressed Wales.

What should the disestablished church call itself? After some debate, it was decided to use the form 'The Church *in* Wales' rather than 'The Church *of* Wales'. The first archbishop, A.G. Edwards, was enthroned in St Asaph Cathedral in June 1920 and, at the age of 73, settled down to a further fourteen years in office. Both he and his successor, as it happened, held the archiepiscopal position from their sees in North Wales, there being no designated archiepiscopal see. Since Wales had no capital, there was no need for such a see to be fixed at Llandaff on the edge of Cardiff, the city that was aspiring to be the capital. Prime Minister Lloyd George, who was present at Edwards' enthronement, received communion—an act, from his point of view, which had the advantage of shocking Anglican and Nonconformist alike. Much effort had to be put into planning the new province and to coping with 'the catastrophe of impoverishment' as the archbishop of Canterbury described disendowment. A diocese of Monmouth was created in 1921 and, two years later, 'Swansea and Brecon' was created by dividing the huge diocese of St Davids. The new bishop of the former, C.H.G. Green, was unusual in combining, in equal measure, a real enthusiasm for liturgy, ecclesiastical law and administration. After moving to Bangor, he succeeded Edwards as archbishop in 1934. The constitution of the church was allegedly the result of consultation between the bishops and 'their' clergy and laity. It bore, however, the strong imprint of Green's predilections. He took pains to point out that the church was not a

[113] Keith Robbins, 'Episcopacy in Wales', *Journal of Welsh Religious History* 4 (1996), 63–78 and 'Establishing Disestablishment: Some Reflections on Wales and Scotland' in Stewart J. Brown and George Newlands, *Scottish Christianity in the Modern World* (Edinburgh, 2000), 231–54.

[114] Revd Illtyd Jones to Cosmo Gordon Lang cited in Machin, *Churches and Social Issues*, 41.

democracy. He published a work on the constitution at his own expense, a volume ambiguously greeted by the Cardiff-based *Western Mail* as having said all that could possibly be worth saying about the Church in Wales. It was a document which testified to its claim that it was 'a Catholic and National Church'. 'The supreme question for the Church in Wales' a contemporary writer observed 'is the combination of its religion with the modern progress of Wales.'[115]

The 'modern progress of Wales' was a fine phrase, but what did it mean? Was 'modernity' something which had no respect for frontiers? Did it mean that the churches in Wales would find themselves buffeted by the intellectual and cultural forces evident in England? Might the 'modern progress of Wales' be found, on the contrary, in self-consciously reacting against modernity as encountered in all that was happening in England. 'Modernity' added another element to an already existing multi-layered ambivalence. The writer of these words, Merionethshire-born Dr Maurice Jones, was himself returning to Wales in 1923 to become principal of St David's College, Lampeter—then nursery of so many clergy for the Welsh church, at least in its southern dioceses—after serving outside Wales, as army chaplain and in the pastoral ministry, for thirty years.

The situation, however, was not clear-cut. Archbishop Green (Charterhouse and Oxford) stated at the Church Congress held at Bournemouth in 1935 that there was still free communication between England and Wales, something which perhaps came as no great surprise to his audience.[116] He was speaking, after all, at a seaside town where the Welsh Congregationalist, the Revd J.D. Jones, had been exercising a celebrated ministry at Richmond Hill—and a concomitant role in English Congregationalism—since 1898.[117] The archbishop may have been overstating matters when he told his audience that all was well in Wales. He was right, however, to indicate that the border was porous. Visitors from England were not unknown and Welshmen as unlike as Ingli James, Ponthir, Monmouthshire-born minister, 1931–43, of Queen's Road Baptist Church, Coventry and Arthur Duncan-Jones, Oldham-born but Welsh-descended dean of Chichester, were by no means unique 'expatriates'. Dean Inge, despite his dislike of Lloyd George, travelled to Aberystwyth to lecture on 'A New Twilight of the Gods?' and returned unscathed. T.R. Glover, in so far as he represented 'modernizing tendencies' amongst English Baptists, had 'difficulties' with Wales. One of his biographers, admittedly Cardiff-based, thought that this Scottish-descended, Cambridge-based Bristolian 'never appreciated

---

[115] More detail on the 'restructuring' is available in D.T.W. Price, *A History of the Church in Wales in the Twentieth Century* (Penarth, 1990) and the chapter by David Walker in the volume *A History of the Church in Wales* (Penarth, 1976), 164–74.

[116] A.J. Edwards, *Archbishop Green: His Life and Opinions* (Llandysul, 1986), 87–8.

[117] J. Trevor Davies, *Richmond Hill Story* (London, 1956).

Wales'.[118] There was an irony in the fact that his induction to the presidency of the Baptist Union of Great Britain and Ireland in 1924 took place in Cardiff. Certain Welsh Baptist ministers made their dissatisfaction with him apparent, though there were no formal protests (and a coterie of Welsh Baptists in England also made their voices heard in the Baptist Missionary Society).[119] In South Wales, in particular, 'fundamentalism' had a considerable appeal, again with strong links to the United States. Rhys Bevan Jones, originally a Baptist minister in the Rhondda, inspired an evangelical network in South Wales outside the existing denominations—though he did not restrict his activities to Wales. The Bible College of Wales set up in Swansea by Rees Howells in 1924 took as its model the Moody Institute in Chicago.[120]

One of the objectives in establishing this college was to counter the 'liberalism' believed with some reason to be prevalent in the colleges for ministerial training established by the various denominations in Wales. Certainly, by the 1920s, seminary professors in Bala-Bangor, Carmarthen and Brecon put forward views which differed in detail but which were as impeccably 'modernist' in tone and temper as anything being written in England. Miall Edwards at Brecon wrote a substantial systematic theology in Welsh designed to meet 'the mind of the present age' by, in effect, accepting its axioms, abandoning dogmatic formulae and relying on the individual's experience of the spiritual. Calvinistic Methodism, whose standard of faith had legal status, witnessed a number of controversies at this time involving ministers whose views were comparable to those of Edwards.[121] It was particularly important to Edwards that he should write in Welsh. England should not be 'modern' and Wales 'conservative'. A biblical dictionary, *Y Geiriadur Beibleidd*, appeared in Welsh between 1924 and 1926 under the auspices of the Guild of Graduates of the University of Wales. Edwards now envisaged three volumes on the gospel in its relation to thought and life— in Welsh. 'Up-to-dateness' would be confirmed if C.H. Dodd would write in Welsh. It transpired, however, both that Dodd could not really write Welsh—he proposed to restrict his use of Welsh to the title of his

---

[118] Robinson, *Glover*, 5.

[119] Bebbington, 'Baptists and Fundamentalism', in Robbins, ed., *Protestant Evangelicalism*, 306, 316–19.

[120] D. Densil Morgan, *The Span of the Cross: Christian Religion and Society in Wales, 1914–2000* (Cardiff, 1999), 137–41. Welsh emigration to the United States and resulting Presbyterian–Calvinistic Methodist links had earlier brought 'Princeton Theology', admittedly of a rather different ilk, into Wales. Not all good things, Nonconformists were aware, needed to come through England. D. Densil Morgan, 'Wales, the Princeton Theology and a Nineteenth Century Battle for the Bible', *The Journal of Welsh Religious History*, new series, 2 (2002), 51–81.

[121] Morgan, *Span of the Cross*, 131–3 outlines Edwards's position and in surrounding pages gives a picture of the general theological scene.

contribution—and that he was so tardy in delivery that the project—in which his role was to be central—had to be abandoned.[122]

Collectively, in their different individual ways, the colleges had been responsible for 'doing theology' in Wales, in the absence, until the late nineteenth century, Anglican Lampeter apart, of institutions which could award degrees. Sound statesmen in the federal University of Wales, from 1893, in a context of ecclesiastical conflict over disestablishment, had shown reluctance to allow further academic theological study. After the war, however, the situation gradually changed. Even so, the emphasis, both in Bangor and in Cardiff, was heavily linguistic and, perhaps reflecting linkages with associated 'Nonconformist' theological colleges, produced Old Testament scholarship of great distinction in the persons of T.H. Robinson, Aubrey Johnston and H.H. Rowley. In 1916 Robinson told Lord Haldane, who was considering the structure of the University of Wales, that 'a good many of us, in the theological colleges in Wales' were 'under suspicion of heterodoxy'. Haldane apparently replied that people were prone to look for aberrations and added 'you are very fond of aberrating in Wales'. Bangor in 1926 was boasting that the number of students studying Hebrew there was larger than in any other university college in the United Kingdom. Such vitality might not be enough to counter the allegation, made rather surprisingly, though by a Welshman, from the pulpit of the City Temple in London, that teachers and professors at the Welsh colleges were showing 'definite pagan tendencies'.[123]

Wales was different, in other words, though not invariably that different. There was a border with England but its precise delineation was elusive. The Welsh Church Acts (1914 and 1919) contained provisions to determine which way parishes which straddled the England/Wales border would go—Church in Wales or Church of England? Wales itself remained a country of subtle though unmarked frontiers—north, south, east and west. There was even an important part of its religious and cultural life to be found in Liverpool (not to mention London). Mothers, in particular, reading their 'Welsh Bibles' constantly on Merseyside, felt that there was only one way to keep going the Welsh life they had known in their childhood in rural Caernarfonshire. They put 'all their eggs in one basket; the chapel' perhaps fearing that at no distant point in the future the struggle might be lost, though believing that miracles might happen.[124]

---

[122] R. Pope, 'The Gospel according to C.H. Dodd', *Journal of Welsh Religious History*, new series, 1 (2001), 90–1.

[123] J. Gwynn Williams, *The University of Wales, 1893–1939*, vol. ii (Cardiff, 1997), 368 and *The University College of North Wales: Foundations 1884–1927* (Cardiff, 1985), 395.

[124] D. Ben Rees, ed., *The Liverpool Welsh and their Religion: Two Centuries of Welsh Calvinistic Methodism* (Liverpool, 1984) and his 'Welsh Calvinistic Methodists and Independents in Toxteth Park, Liverpool', *Journal of Welsh Religious History*, new series, 3 (2003), 86.

But surely, in Wales itself, the 'new Wales' was Nonconformist Wales—
the 'real Wales'? After decades of campaigning, it had triumphed and would
be able to place an indelible stamp on the Wales that was to be. Why this did
not happen, or at least not to the extent that might have been anticipated,
remains the question which is perennially asked, but not easily answered.
Some ministers, grown used to a public role during the disestablishment
campaign, found other avenues of service. The scale of post-war industrial
crisis experienced in Wales, it is sometimes argued, pushed 'religion' aside in
a hard-edged class struggle which led to a mass exodus from 'chapel',
though to place exclusive emphasis upon this aspect underplays the extent
of continuing 'chapel' involvement in social issues, even if ministers were
nevertheless not offering sufficient leadership to the working class in its
struggle.[125] The division amongst Nonconformists as between Liberalism
and Socialism (and indeed Conservatism) was a common feature in rural and
industrial England and Wales in this period.

What made Wales different was its cultural/linguistic context, as experienced in both predominantly English and predominantly Welsh language
milieux. Men could hold seemingly opposed views at once, or shifted
uneasily between them. Idris Davies, an English-language poet in South
Wales, combined some spasmodic attendance at his local Baptist chapel with
the belief that Wales would benefit from the eradication of Christianity.
One Welsh miner reportedly joined the Communist party, giving as reason
the news that Baptists in the Soviet Union were being persecuted, but other
Communists did not entirely sever their chapel links.[126] David James
Jones—'Gwenallt'—nurtured a Welsh-speaking Calvinistic Methodist in
the Swansea Valley, wartime conscientious objector in Princetown and
Wormwood Scrubs, now impending poet in Welsh studying at Aberystwyth, for a time wanted proper paganism. Welsh poetry needed to get rid of
every single image that was Christian. By the mid-1930s, however, but in
stages, he had been drawn back to Christianity, though the discontented
snarl with which he had departed from it did not altogether disappear on
his return. The Communist revolution, he concluded, seemed a mere flea-
bite beside the Christian. He found a home in the Church in Wales, only
to think that it was not really Welsh after all, and eventually returned to
the Calvinistic Methodism in which he had begun.[127]

---

[125] Robert Pope, *Building Jerusalem: Nonconformity, Labour and the Social Question in Wales,
1906–1939* (Cardiff, 1998), 173.

[126] H. Francis, *Miners against Fascism* (London, 1984), 60.

[127] A.M. Allchin, D. Densil Morgan and Patrick Thomas, *Sensuous Glory: The Poetic Vision of
D. Gwenallt Jones* (Norwich, 2000) consists of two assessments together with the annotated
translations of certain poems.

The insights of poets may always be heightened beyond the general. Public people slid away with less drama. Thomas Jones, CH, had a career which had taken him from Rhymney, via Glasgow and Belfast, to the very heart of Whitehall. It also took him from initial candidature for the Calvinistic Methodist ministry to an agnosticism which made education into a religion.[128] Megan Lloyd George, who became the first Welsh woman MP in 1929, slipped lightly away into the religion of humanity from whatever slender Nonconformist mooring to which her father was tethered.[129] Even so, Nonconformity and her politics still seemed somehow to mix for her—just as she could comfortably combine, as a young girl, being a cottager under Snowdon and conversing at Claridge's with Margot Asquith.[130]

A substantial segment of the Welsh population was haemorrhaging into England in search of employment from the late 1920s. As hundreds of thousands left, it looked as though Wales was 'dying'. The mood was black. Nonconformity too was barren and bible-black. Safely in London, a Welsh writer prised open what he considered to be the poisonous and pernicious, not to say hypocritical, piety of his native Ceredigion. The Welsh language was in crisis. Its decline and possible fall was so intimately linked with 'chapel' in communal life that it seemed inevitable that language and Nonconformity, if not Christianity, would decline and fall together. So, Nonconformity might need to shed its cultural clothing to survive, but if it did so it would only be contributing, perhaps fatally, to the downfall of that 'Wales' which members cherished.[131] The dilemma was not yet apparent everywhere but, in those places where it was acute, it was also too painful to be tackled. 'Welsh religion', so often perceived outside Wales to be characterizing, even defining, the existence of Wales as a nation, had not been 'settled' by disestablishment. Its 'modern' locus looked elusive and uncertain.

From the outset, some members of the Church in Wales, clerical and lay, wanted to make an effective appeal to 'the principle and sentiment of nationality'. The church would be coming to the Welsh people in its 'corporate national capacity'. There was some evidence that the 'national

[128] E.I. Ellis, *T.J: A Life of Dr Thomas Jones CH* (Cardiff, 1992).

[129] Lloyd George, in 1932, took on the job of chairing the Welsh Religious Advisory Council of the BBC. John Reith declared that the Welsh language constituted 'a bond of enormous value and importance'. Aled Jones, *Press, Politics and Society: A History of Journalism in Wales* (Cardiff, 1993), 234.

[130] This happy conjuncture struck Emlyn Williams, whose own dramatic seed had been sown in Wales but whose full corn had flourished in England. The cultural fate of Lloyd George's progeny is discussed in Paul Ward, *Unionism in the United Kingdom 1918–1974* (Basingstoke, 2005) though the religious fall-out is not specifically addressed.

[131] See the chapter 'Spiritual Skeletons: Religion, Superstition and Popular Culture' in Russell Davies, *Secret Sins: Sex, Violence and Society in Carmarthenshire 1870–1920* (Cardiff, 1996), 186–213.

inheritance' might simply fall into its lap. It was noted that there was a steady
trickle, which might become a stream, of Nonconformist ministers who
sought Anglican ordination. Such men could help to eradicate the debilitating stain of being described as 'the English Church', although this
devastating charge had always been overstated for propaganda purposes.
John Owen, bishop of St Davids, a prominent figure, had a Nonconformist
and 'humble' background himself. That pedigree was to be frequently
repeated in the Welsh episcopate in the future.[132] The Church in Wales,
on this analysis, could simply get on with its own life and wait for Nonconformity to 'come home'. The reality, however, was that 'Nonconformity' was a fiction, only given a degree of reality in a common opposition to
'establishment'. Its organizational life existed only in the distinct structures
of Baptists, Independents, Methodists (both Calvinistic and Wesleyan),
bodies of varying strength in different parts of Wales. The term 'Nonconformity' to describe these denominations continued perforce to be used—
though it made no sense—because to speak of 'non-episcopal' churches had
no resonance. Such an anachronism in itself suggested that their place was
in a past which no longer existed.

There was, however, another church to which Wales might 'come
home'. The first pastoral letter of the Roman Catholic archbishop of Cardiff
in 1921 reflected his long-held belief that the Welsh people would eventually 'return' to the faith. *The Tablet* in 1924 had not the smallest doubt that
'Cambria' would soon rival 'Hibernia' in her Catholic faith and zeal—
though the prognosis, as time passed, seemed a little ambitious. Protestantism, a meeting of the Catholic Mission Society was told in 1936, 'is on its
death-bed'. Pope Pius XII announced a plenary indulgence for those
visiting the new Catholic church at Porthmadog on condition that they
prayed for the return of Wales to the Faith.[133]

Saunders Lewis, scion of Merseyside Welsh Nonconformist pulpit
princes and, though more distantly, of peasants in Wales, wounded soldier,
English graduate of the University of Liverpool and emerging great literary
figure in Welsh in Wales, announced his conversion (prudently after the
death of his father) to Catholicism in 1932. Eleven years earlier, as a librarian
in Cardiff, and no doubt mischievously, he had expressed a wish to have
lived in the fourteenth century, adding, 'Welshmen had never dreamed of

---

[132] The Lampeter–Llandovery axis was seen by some to be excessively dominant, from the rural
west, in the affairs of the church. (Owen had been Professor of Welsh at Lampeter and Edwards,
Warden of nearby Llandovery, an Anglican public school.) See the *Life of Bishop Owen* (Llandysul,
1958 and 1961) written by his daughter, Eluned.

[133] Trystan Owain Hughes, *Winds of Change: The Roman Catholic Church and Society in Wales,
1916–1962* (Cardiff, 1999) and 'The Roman Catholic Church and Evangelism in Twentieth-
Century Wales', *Journal of Welsh Religious History*, new series, 1 (2001), 74–89.

Nonconformity then.' The 'black barbarism' of Nonconformity, as even then he put it, contrasted, at least at the time, with the beauty of Catholicism.[134] In his spirit, fortified by his reading of French Catholic writers, he felt himself to be a man of European Catholic civilization. Such a sensibility also had the advantage of making the Wales of the future distinct from the supposed latitudinarianism of England. The conviction that Wales should have its own Christian future led Lewis to be one of the founders of *Plaid Genedlaethol Cymru* (later *Plaid Cymru)* the Welsh Nationalist Party in 1925, though others of his associates, while sharing the political objective, remained Nonconformists.[135] One of the latter, J.E. Daniel, differing somewhat from Lewis, at least in the source of his ideas, was a little later to develop a strong Christian nationalism. A central part of his argument was that whole societies as well as individuals were divine creations. It was wrong to infer, from the fact that it was a sin to make the nation an idol, that its very existence was a sin.[136] Lewis issued a rallying call the following year at Machynlleth where the rebellious Owain Glyndŵr had held a 'Welsh Parliament' in 1404. A decade later, Lewis had become perhaps the most controversial figure in Wales. He and others took part in burning an RAF bombing school on the Llŷn peninsula. Uproar ensued when he was tried at the Old Bailey, and then imprisoned for nine months, after refusing to give evidence in English. The University College of Swansea, where Lewis was employed as a lecturer in Welsh, sacked him, to further uproar, before his sentence was actually pronounced. A certain admiration for him, however, by no means entailed agreement with the vision of 'Christian Wales' offered in his plays and poetry (he stepped down as party president in 1939 on the grounds that his Catholicism was impeding its progress).

In any event, to be talking of 'Christian Wales' appeared to be whistling in the black. Churches and chapels were still present everywhere but there was a consciousness of an apparently inexorable decline. Far from there being any sign of a mass movement towards religion, the evidence, as presented by clergy and ministers, was that there was a steady drift away from it, or at least away from what it had been traditionally thought to entail in the way of commitment and participation.[137] The situation appeared to

[134] Letters from Lewis to his wife cited in Branwen Jarvis, 'Saunders Lewis: A Welsh Catholic View of Women', *Journal of Welsh Religious History* 7 (1999), 122–4. John Harvey observes, however, in *The Art of Piety: The Visual Culture of Welsh Nonconformity* (Cardiff, 1995), 1 that indifference to beauty was being overstated since 'while Nonconformity opposed the use of art as a means of worship, it did not repudiate it as a handmaid to religion'.

[135] D. Hywel Davies, *The Welsh Nationalist Party 1925–1945: A Call to Nationhood* (Cardiff, 1983).

[136] Dorlan Llywelyn, *Sacred Place, Chosen People: Land and National Identity in Welsh Spirituality* (Cardiff, 1999), 56, and surrounding discussion.

[137] Morgan, *Span of the Cross*, 172–4.

present a striking contrast with Ireland. The Christendom of another 'Celtic land' aroused interest in those who hoped that it might yet be transplanted. From Fishguard, where D.J. Williams, one of the arsonists of 1936, was a schoolmaster, ships left for the new state on the other side of the Irish Sea. 'New Ireland' might be more congenial for Wales than the 'Old England' to which it was yoked. The wife of Saunders Lewis, who became a Catholic some years before him, was from an Irish Methodist family in Co. Wicklow. She had set to learning Irish in Liverpool where they met. It was on a visit to Connemara in the 1920s that 'Gwenallt' saw the significance of national tradition and began his return to a politically imbued Calvinistic Methodism. Here was a world away from the crippling (and crippled) industrialism of South Wales ('Gwenallt's' father, a steelworker, had been killed in an industrial accident). Conversely, Kilkenny-born Michael McGrath arrived as a priest in Flintshire in 1919. After several other posts and after learning Welsh, he was appointed bishop of Menevia in 1935 (the first graduate of the National University of Ireland to become a member of the hierarchy of England and Wales) and five years later became archbishop of Cardiff. He had been publicly proclaiming that North Wales was moving fast, and with it all Wales, back to the faith. In Brittany in 1932 Dom Louis Gougaud published his *Christianity in Celtic Lands* covering the period from its earliest years to the twelfth century. It became a classic scholarly study with a resonance beyond the academic world. New Ireland would again be characterized by saintly sanity—in the same year the most fulsome biography of Pearse to date was published in Rennes. The 'Celtic world' was alive.

vii. Ireland: Divided Unities

In June 1932, the year of Saunders Lewis's conversion, G.K. Chesterton arrived in Dublin, staying at the erstwhile vice-regal lodge, to witness the Eucharistic Congress held to celebrate the 1500th anniversary of St Patrick's mission to convert Ireland to Christianity.[138] It was an event on a massive scale. The papal legate sailed into Dun Laoghaire to be greeted by an air force display making the sign of the cross in the sky. Cardinal Bourne, by comparison, slipped in unobtrusively to pay only his second visit to the city of his mother's birth. His ship was named the *SS Cambria* but this may have been accidental rather than a specific tribute to the 'Welsh' St Patrick or an indication or an encouragement of Catholicism in Wales. The Congress climaxed with a Solemn Pontifical High Mass in Phoenix Park followed by

---

[138] David G. Holmes, 'The Eucharistic Congress of 1932 and Irish Identity', *New Hibernia Review* 4 (Spring 2000), 55–78. *Thirty-First International Eucharistic Congress, Dublin 1932: Pictorial Record* (Dublin, 1932).

2. The cardinal legate blesses the military guard of honour, Dublin, 1932

a procession, reputedly five miles long, towards O'Connell Bridge and a final benediction from the legate. It seemed that everybody was there—an estimate was that the final Mass had been attended by one million people, more than one-third of the total population of the Irish Free State. Although this was the largest assembly, about half that number had been present in 1929 for an outdoor Mass in celebration of the 100th anniversary of Catholic Emancipation. Corpus Christi processions in these years attracted very large numbers in other Irish cities. Chesterton was delighted with what he saw. *Christendom in Dublin* was the book about it all which he speedily produced. His awe and reverence for priests was enormous. The bad statues and fripperies were a trial, but it all showed the wisdom of the church. The whole thing was so 'terrific' that if people did not have these let-downs, he thought, they would go mad. His biographer, who was also present, thought that Dublin 'had become for the time Rome or the Christian Centre'. After all that had been said, from Cardinal Manning onwards—and much had been said—about the great mission and destiny of the Irish nation to spread the faith on earth, here was a living demonstration of its vitality. Irish bishops came from far afield—from Boston and Los Angeles, from Wagga-Wagga and Manila, and elsewhere. Here was what it was like to be living in a Catholic state. Chesterton could not have written *Christendom in London* and there was quiet satisfaction that it was an English writer who came to tell the story to the world. Members of the Dáil and the Senate and civic dignitaries had all eagerly taken part in the procession, naturally behind cardinals, archbishops and bishops. After Edward Byrne, the new archbishop of Dublin, had received the papal legate on Irish soil the visitor had been greeted, in Irish and Latin, by de Valera, the new President of the Executive Council, followed by other government ministers.

The event had symbolic attractions all round. A massive display of national solidarity might help to heal the wounds—though they went deep—still raw from the civil war, lasting some eleven months, which had only come to an end in 1923. It might also be compensation for disappointment.[139] The 'Free State' had survived, but there was no economic miracle. Between 1924 and 1930 Irish migration to Britain averaged about 9,700 persons per annum.[140] It was clear that the new election victor, taking advantage of the global need to redefine constitutional relationships within the British Empire/Commonwealth, would seek to release the state from the constraints on its full freedom, constraints which had made its creation possible in the first place but to which he had then been opposed. He would do so, however, 'from within' and, in all probability, would be able to carry with him those opponents who had successfully fought to enforce the 'Free State' solution in 1922–3.

How this situation had come about needs to be briefly sketched. The UK general election of December 1918 was a triumph for Sinn Féin, which immediately set about establishing Dáil Éireann as a republican constituent assembly. Its manifesto claimed that it stood less for a political party than for the nation. The 'first shots' in a military campaign designed to rid Ireland of its centuries-old oppressor were fired in January 1919. It began to become clear that it would be the military campaign which would count. In 1920, 232 police and soldiers were killed. In the following spring, 24 Volunteers were shot or hanged for murder. An Ireland of two 'Home Rule' entities, as provided for under the Government of Ireland Act (1920), was not going to work in the South. Elections there in May 1921 were an uncontested walkover for Sinn Féin, which proceeded to constitute itself as the second Dáil. 'Terrorism' and 'counter-terrorism' (in the form of the 'Black and Tans', non-Irishmen recruited into the Royal Irish Constabulary to replace Irishmen who were resigning) worsened. A truce was agreed in July 1921. Eventually a 'treaty' was signed after negotiations between Lloyd George as prime minister (of a coalition government) and an Irish delegation led by Arthur Griffith and Michael Collins. The 26 counties of 'Southern' Ireland

---

[139] Dermot Keogh, *Twentieth-Century Ireland: Nation and State* (Dublin, 1994), 70; Ronan Fanning, *Independent Ireland* (Dublin, 1983), 59.

[140] Enda Delaney, *Demography, State and Society: Irish Migration to Britain, 1921–1971* (Liverpool, 2000), 45.

were to have full dominion status—though 'dominion status' was itself in flux—rather than the restricted 'Home Rule' of the 1920 Act. It was to be styled the Irish Free State. The members of its parliament were to swear allegiance not only to its constitution but also to King George V by virtue of the 'common citizenship' of Ireland with Great Britain and her adherence to the British Commonwealth. It was this framework which de Valera set out to dismantle. Whether the negotiators should ever have accepted these terms became a matter of acute division in the South and the terms were only accepted in the Dáil by a majority of 64 to 57. Opponents of the treaty claimed that the republic which had been established could not be 'abolished' in this way. The oath of allegiance was a sticking point. The political struggle turned into a military one between the state forces and their opponents. Both sides claimed legitimacy and democracy in support of their struggle. The state won, though at a price. The 1932 congress had great symbolical and functional significance in that it brought both 'treaty' and 'anti-treaty' sides together.

The massive events in Dublin in June 1932, however, could not altogether obscure an irony. If one was persuaded by the seventh-century legend-makers, St Patrick had begun his mission in 432 in Co. Down—a county not within the territory of the Irish Free State. It was in 1932, too, though not in the presence of Mr Chesterton, that a massive event of another kind took place at Stormont outside Belfast—the opening of the Parliament Building. In the 'North' the original proposals under the 1920 Government of Ireland Act had gone ahead. There had been elections for a House of Commons in which Unionists held 40 of the 52 seats. Northern Ireland consisted of six of the nine counties of the province of Ulster. The area was the largest possible extent which could still ensure an overall Protestant majority. Sir James Craig became the first 'Prime Minister of Northern Ireland'. D'Arcy, now Anglican archbishop of Armagh, read prayers at the first session of the parliament. Unionists stated that they accepted the constitutional outcome reluctantly—and of course the 'province' remained within the United Kingdom and continued to send MPs to Westminster.

In their different ways, the events of 1932 showed that the administrations in both Dublin and Belfast had 'come of age'. Ministries had been established and bureaucracies were functioning. The process of state-building was being consolidated in both jurisdictions, though whether the devolved government of Northern Ireland was really building a 'state' was another matter. Westminster and Whitehall had no experience of dealing with a devolved administration. The best way of dealing with it was probably to leave it to its own devices, however suspect some of these devices might be.

At a party meeting in October 1931, some months before his election victory, de Valera had declared that he was a Catholic first and an Irishman or politician second. The applause which greeted him suggested that he had struck the right note. Nor was such an ordering of priorities confined at this time to his Fianna Fáil party (whose devotion to Irishness could scarcely be doubted). A few years later, the Labour Party thought it appropriate to send a draft of its new constitution to the Catholic hierarchy for vetting.[141] De Valera's assertion could be taken to mean that there was no aspect of the life of the Free State which should not be subordinate to the church, and what 'the church' was could only mean the Roman Catholic Church. The intertwining of church and state, on public display in 1932, seemed to suggest a relationship which made the Free State look very like those other overwhelmingly Catholic European states—Italy, Poland, Spain and Portugal, to be followed shortly by Austria—which, to one degree or other, had authoritarian regimes, either backed by the church or where there was direct clerical participation. There was no need, either, to suspect that de Valera's assertion was merely a cynical piece of politics, though it was a piece of politics.

The Roman Catholic Church had an extraordinary opportunity to stamp its mark on a new state with very considerable confidence that it could do so with the willing compliance of a Christian people.[142] The context, however, was more complicated than at first sight might seem likely. Its leaders, in the *ancien régime*, had been accustomed to steering its fortunes in relation to three arenas—the 'Irish people', the UK government through its administration in Dublin Castle, and the papacy. There had been occasions, clearly, either tactically or strategically, when they had bent before whichever wind was blowing most strongly. Now, the Westminster government was removed as a direct factor in the equation, but the papacy naturally remained. It so happened that the new pope, who followed Benedict XV in 1922, had been in Warsaw as nuncio during the 1919–20 Soviet–Polish war. A distinguished palaeographer, he saw writing on the wall and proved himself no mean epigrapher. Bolshevism would destroy the church. He looked benevolently on the regimes that appeared between 1922 and 1926 in Italy, Spain, Poland and Portugal, whether described as fascist or authoritarian, which would give to the church the status which 'Catholic peoples' would expect. Certainly, the new pope had no commitment to 'liberal democracy' or 'freedom of religion'. Concordats could be concluded and, in Italy itself, it might be possible to conclude one with the Fascist regime

---

[141] R.V. Comerford, *Inventing the Nation: Ireland* (London, 2003), 135.

[142] Patrick Murray, *The Oracles of God: The Roman Catholic Church and Irish Politics 1922–1937* (Dublin, 2000); John Cooney, *The Crozier and the Dáil: Church and State in Ireland 1922–1986* (Dublin, 1986).

which at long last would settle 'the Roman question'. Such, briefly, was the European world into which the Free State was born. It could appear that the shape of its politics would fall into this pattern. What was the 'freedom' of the Free State? How 'modern' was it? How 'modern' did it wish to present itself as being?[143]

The reality was that, though significantly poorer than Britain (still its 'Other'), it was probably more prosperous than those overwhelmingly Catholic European states which became 'authoritarian' in the 1920s. The Free State developed a political system in which two major parties—both avoiding the demeaning word 'party'—confronted each other (though with the normal internal tensions). A third party struggled to make an impact. The whole formed a system of government and administration in which 'British' assumptions and practices blended over time with innovations (and improvements). Firm and efficient government, it has been argued 'became the hallmark of the Free State'.[144]

The church, through the hierarchy, had no doubt that it should suffuse every aspect of the life of the state with its teaching and influence.[145] That hierarchy in turn, it is suggested, became from 1925 onwards 'a self-selecting oligarchy', one, if necessary, willing to cold-shoulder any papal delegate who appeared to think that the Vatican knew best in matters of nationalist politics.[146] The 1922 Free State constitution repeated the prohibitions of the 1920 Government of Ireland Act on the endowment of religion, or the enactment of any law discriminating on the basis of religious belief.[147] That did not prevent the archbishop of Dublin from making it clear that the church would look to legislative underpinning of Catholic teaching.[148] 'The modern' had been so feared before 1914. Now there was an opportunity to cage it.[149] Film censorship was introduced in 1923 followed, six years later, by a Censorship of Publications Act which did

---

[143] For further reflection on the management of 'the Irish inheritance' see Stephen Howe, *Ireland and Empire: Colonial Legacies in Irish History and Culture* (Oxford, 2000).

[144] The term used by F.S.L. Lyons, *Ireland since the Famine* (London and Glasgow, 1973 edn.), 479; Ronan Fanning 'Britain's Legacy: Government and Administration' in P.J. Drudy, ed., *Ireland and Britain since 1922* (Cambridge, 1986), 45–64.

[145] D.H. Akenson, *A Mirror to Kathleen's Face: Education in Independent Ireland 1922–1960* (Montreal, 1975); B.M. Coldrey, *Faith and Fatherland: The Christian Brothers and the Development of Irish Nationalism 1838–1921* (Dublin, 1988).

[146] K. Theodore Hoppen, *Ireland since 1800: Conflict and Conformity* (London, 1989), 232 [drawing on D. Keogh, *The Vatican, the Bishops and Irish Politics, 1919–1935* (Cambridge, 1986)].

[147] Charles Townshend, 'The Meaning of Irish Freedom: Constitutionalism in the Irish Free State', *Transactions of the Royal Historical Society*, sixth series, 8 (1998), 45–70.

[148] Byrne wrote to Cosgrave in 1923 on the specific matter of Catholic teaching on marriage. Cosgrave himself had suggested 'a theological senate to evaluate the Catholic orthodoxy of all mooted legislation'.

[149] Tom Garvin, 'Priests and Patriots: Irish Separatism and Fear of the Modern, 1890–1914', *Irish Historical Studies* 25/97 (1986), 67–81.

not limit itself to dealing with pornography.[150] Divorce was made practically impossible and, in the 1937 revision of the constitution, formally prohibited. A Dance Halls Act endeavoured to regulate behaviour therein. The sale of contraceptive devices was made a criminal offence in 1935. It was possible, in advocating many of these measures, to make Britain the source of social evil (as well as the normal amount of political or economic evil). It was galling that the London *News of the World* had a circulation in the Free State of around 190,000 in the late 1920s. Bishop McKenna of Clogher thought it a sound idea in 1924 that the newsagents involved should be imprisoned or submitted to the lash. A diocese like his, which straddled the border, was of course particularly susceptible to the insidious infiltration of alien print. Its clergy thought the partition a catastrophe but were divided amongst themselves as to the stance they should take in relation to it.[151] Why should the people be subjected to the worst English influence? Of course, it was assumed that the vigorous promotion of the Irish language throughout the education system would further assist in saving the soul of the nation. 'Modern forces', the *Irish Monthly* had declared in 1925, 'are not for but against the Church's mission. Today the enemy is invisible and omnipresent.'

It did look, however, as though 'modern forces' were being kept at bay. It was also possible to harness technical modernity for traditional devotional purposes. In 1932 during the Congress, prayers in Latin appeared in the sky in coloured lights. The Catholic Truth Society was extremely active in propaganda, publishing over a million pamphlets in 1925/6. The 'success' was an endorsement of the view that a church speaking on behalf of 'the great majority' should properly devise a state which would safeguard the values for which it stood. Its postage stamps should link the new state with pre-conquest Ireland by drawing heavily on Irish early Christian visual sources. The material culture of popular Catholic devotion, so evident in home, school and church, did not predispose towards modernism in religious art. Neither did the Academy of Christian Art, founded in 1929, open only to Catholics, which aimed to stimulate the imaginative qualities of the Irish mind and release the soul from bondage to material aims.[152]

In drawing attention to the prohibitive legislation, it should not be assumed that it was imposed against the will of the people or with physical

---

[150] M. Adams, *Censorship: The Irish Experience* (Dublin, 1968).

[151] Eamon Phoenix, 'Patriotism, the Catholic Church and the Diocese of Clogher *c*.1912–1928' in Henry A. Jefferes, ed., *History of the Diocese of Clogher* (Dublin, 2005), 221–2; Malcolm Anderson and Eberhard Bort, *The Irish Border: History, Politics, Culture* (Liverpool, 1999) look at the area's significance from multi-disciplinary perspectives.

[152] John Turpin, 'Visual Culture and the Irish Free State', *Journal of Ecclesiastical History* 57/1 (2006), 59.

violence (even bishops could not imprison or employ the lash at whim).[153] Writers who fell foul of censorship on occasion were generally muted in their protests, or simply left the country. The church's stance also reflected the view that the state should not aim to take over functions which should remain with voluntary bodies—the church itself being pre-eminent among them. No legislation on matters referred to above, it was argued, could ever be 'neutral'. It was simply a fact that a Christian society was superior either to the valueless individualism into which a 'liberal' state across the water appeared, from this angle, to be 'degenerating', or to the form of society which went under the name of Communism. Neither church nor state was 'totalitarian'—whatever this new word quite meant—but neither was it 'liberal'. The church's position buttressed that ambiguous 'conservatism within revolution' which characterized the Free State. Its position at the heart of society was unlikely to be challenged by a de Valera government.

Its dominance reflected the conviction that there was only one church. The first Free State census of 1926 revealed that its Church of Ireland population had dropped by 34 per cent since 1911. It stood at 164,215 (against a Catholic population of 2,751,269—only marginally down). The Presbyterian fall was from 45,486 to 32,429. Such a decline had various causes. The departure of the British army and the 'Castle bureaucracy' was one factor. In Munster and Connacht in particular, with the destruction of the 'Big Houses' and the social order which they represented, the communities to which the Church of Ireland ministered and which supported it, departed. The aspirations embodied in the nineteenth-century 'Protestant Crusade' now seemed far-fetched. Some Catholic commentators took exception to the 'Church of Ireland' so describing itself. An indication of the 'staggering' displacement that was taking place can be found in the decision of Bernard, the Anglican archbishop of Dublin, to resign and become, instead, provost of Trinity College, Dublin. He seemed to be saying that the church as such could not in practice hope to be 'of' the Irish Free State. What it needed to do was to try to ensure that it stayed 'in'. That meant preserving, so far as possible, its educational and other institutions. If Trinity's financial basis could be sustained, it would certainly continue to be a Protestant institution since the Catholic hierarchy forbade Catholic attendance. Bernard flew the Union Jack from the college roof on the king's birthday and on Armistice Day. He regularly contributed unsigned articles in London periodicals from 1919 to 1925 on the state of things, as he saw it, in Ireland. The archbishop of Canterbury wrote to his

---

[153] Lyons, *Ireland since the Famine*, 687 suggests that this 'puritanism' on the part of government 'reflected rather than distorted the idealism of the people'. He sees it as 'an important element in the Irish character'.

widow that no Irishman had ever had more friends on the English side of the water.[154]

The Church of Ireland and other Protestants could take some comfort from the constitution's endorsement of freedom of worship. It was also well aware, however, of the social pressures experienced by its members. Some also could not forget the nightmare which had been their experience during the civil war. Thousands of Protestant families had suffered burnings, thefts, vandalism and boycotts and unarmed assaults—though rarely murder. Yet, whatever the motivation behind intimidation and violence, it neither reached 'eliminationist' levels nor could it be said to have been undertaken with the connivance or support of the Free State government, or indeed of the political parties.[155]

In these circumstances of dislocation the Church of Ireland community's political discourse has been described as 'conservative and defensive, though by no means cowed'.[156] Few deliberately 'went over' to Rome, though the consequences of inter-marriage remained as contentious and draining as ever. Its Dublin members, still strongly present in its southern suburbs, had to come to terms with a loss of status. It was, however, inexorably driven in on itself, seeking to preserve and support 'its own'. Its 'identity crisis' was not easily resolved. Thousands of Freemasons, after attending a service at St Patrick's cathedral, held a banquet which toasted the king at its conclusion. Since the Irish Free State and the United Kingdom allegedly shared a 'common citizenship' such an act was not illegal, but it was not being widely done. His Majesty thanked the General Synod in 1929 for its message of good wishes which had been sent during an illness. The entire assembly rose to its feet and applauded the king over the water. The new Free State national anthem, 'The Soldier's Song', did not appeal, for reasons which it was not difficult to discern. It had been composed in 1907 (in English) and adopted by Sinn Féiners. It spoke of a land in which 'despots' had ruled over 'slaves'. Doubt was cast on the utility of the Irish language, but a minority took a positive view.[157] Irish-speaking Protestant teachers

---

[154] Robert H. Murray, *Archbishop Bernard: Professor, Prelate and Provost* (London, 1931), 369.

[155] These matters are discussed in Peter Hart, *The I.R.A. at War, 1916–1923* (Oxford, 2003) in the chapters on 'The Protestant Experience of Revolution in Southern Ireland' and 'Ethnic Conflict and Minority Responses'. However, whether this kind of language is appropriate remains deeply contentious, it being argued that 'opposition to actions carried out in pursuit of a sectarian pro-British objective does not in itself imbue the Republican position with sectarianism'. Meda Ryan, 'The Kilmichael Ambush, 1920: Exploring the "Provocative Chapters" ', *History* 92/2 (2007), 248.

[156] Martin Maguire, 'The Church of Ireland in Dublin since Disestablishment' in Raymond Gillespie and W.G. Neely, eds., *The Laity and the Church of Ireland, 1000–2000: All Sorts and Conditions* (Dublin, 2002), 286.

[157] Designation of the language as 'Irish' rather than 'Gaelic' or 'Erse' could carry the implication that those who did not speak it—the great majority of Protestants—were not fully Irish.

were available to assist in the teaching at the Church of Ireland Training College in Dublin.

The reality, too, was that in their social values Anglicans, Presbyterians and Methodists in the Free State were in general not out of sympathy with the legislation which has been referred to—indeed, in relation both to drink and gambling might have wished to go further. Most members of the minority might be judged to be closer to contemporary Catholic attitudes than they were to Yeats and other literary figures of Protestant tradition who had become theologically heterodox.[158] All lingering pan-British associations of sentiment were tempered by gradual adjustment to political reality and a grudging acknowledgement of the extent to which (in membership of the Senate, for example, where in 1922 there were 24 non-Roman Catholics in a total membership of 60) Protestants were a small minority with a kind of privileged position. Not that the Senate proved to be very important.[159] The Church of Ireland did not, however, give up on its claim to St Patrick, even if its organized celebrations in 1932 could scarcely be compared with the Eucharistic Congress. It was also revealing that an invitation to preach on this occasion had gone to an Englishman, the bishop of Durham, though, in the event, illness prevented Hensley Henson from obliging.

The Irish Free State, paradoxically, could only have taken on its character between 1922 and 1932 because of partition. Its Protestant community, even if broadly interpreted, constituted only a small and largely impotent minority. Its rate of decline might have suggested that decline would be followed by a fall. If partition had not occurred, an Irish state would have had a much more significant, if internally divided, Protestant percentage. Its presence would have made 'Catholic Ireland' much more difficult and perhaps impossible. Their condemnation of partition did not mean that bishops in the South had overlooked this fact.[160]

'Northern Ireland' also took on something of the character of a 'confessional state'. Its Unionist political leadership in the new parliament did not hesitate to claim that the new regime epitomized Protestant freedom. That freedom, however, in its early years, was enjoyed in a context of violence. 'Northern Catholics' a recent analysis has concluded 'were far worse off than their Southern Catholic counterparts'. In Belfast, the Catholic 25 per cent of the population suffered two-thirds of the casualties and 80 per cent of the damage in the city—though Catholics were at least as violent as their

---

[158] See essays by Augustine Morris and J.H. Whyte in M. Hurley, ed., *Irish Anglicanism* (Dublin, 1970) and the discussion by Kenneth Milne, 'Disestablishment and the Lay Response' in Gillespie and Neely, *Laity and the Church of Ireland*, 242–5.

[159] Kurt Bowen, *Protestants in a Catholic State: Ireland's Privileged Minority* (Dublin, 1983).

[160] Mary Harris, *The Catholic Church and the Foundation of the Northern Irish State* (Cork, 1993).

Protestant neighbours. There were more than 300 civilian deaths and hundreds more wounded.[161] In the North, as in the South, in so far as 'justification' was attempted, it was claimed that violence was in retaliation for what was happening in the other: reciprocity ruled OK. The 'religious territory' of Belfast, always more pronounced than Dublin, became even more segmented. Each side saw its actions as defensive. Although the Protestant churches and the Northern Ireland government did not discourage popular sectarianism, there was no grand plan of ethnic cleansing. The 'battle for Belfast' of 1922, at bottom, was a struggle for supremacy in which the forces of Unionism proved successful. The IRA in the North collapsed. Some refugees, perhaps 1,500, went south in 1922 but many probably returned home later. There was, therefore, no massive transfer of population (both ways) analogous to the contemporaneous transfers between Turkey and Greece. The result was a Protestant Northern Ireland but one in which the minority, unlike the minority in the South, was substantial.

As its first election approached, Catholics decided to campaign but to abstain if elected. Bishop MacRory of Down and Connor had a letter read at Sunday Masses urging voters to deal a 'death blow' to the insulting measure which he thought partition to be. Dealing with the Northern Ireland government amounted to collaboration with the enemy. If there had to be some contact, MacRory normally deputed particular clergy to make it for him. Thereafter Catholics were at best only sullenly acquiescent in the new regime and unwilling, by active participation in its organs, to give it a spurious legitimacy.[162] Proportional representation in local elections was withdrawn, a step which reinforced Unionist ability to dominate. There was, in the event, no revision of the boundaries between North and South. 'Abstention' on the one hand and 'Discrimination' on the other became the perpetual cries of the two sides. What had become clear by 1932, itself a year in which more than half of Belfast's shipbuilding workforce was unemployed, however, was both that the Northern Ireland government was not going to fade away and that its Catholic minority (33.5 per cent in 1926) was not going to accept its legitimacy.[163] There was little inclination on the part of the British government, or little ability on the part of the Free State government, to intervene in the consequential struggles.

---

[161] Hart, *I.R.A. at War*, 243 and surrounding pages. See also the discussion in H. Patterson, *Class Conflict and Sectarianism: The Protestant Working Class and the Belfast Labour Movement 1868–1920* (Belfast, 1980).

[162] Harris, *Catholic Church and Foundation of the Northern Irish State*, 259–62. The author considers the church to be 'in no small way' responsible for the delay on the part of Northern Nationalists in recognizing the state.

[163] Marianne Elliott, *The Catholics of Ulster* (London, 2000), 373–83.

Numbers apart, however, there was another difference between the situation in the North and in the South. The 'Protestant' majority in 1926 continued to be made up of Presbyterians (31.3 per cent) and Church of Ireland (27.0 per cent) and Methodist (3.9 per cent). Their leaderships were no less anxious than the hierarchy in the South to have a powerful input on social issues. Yet they did not always speak with one voice. This was only to be expected in churches with different leadership structures. Educational provision continued to be contentious, for Catholics and Orangemen alike.[164] The Northern Catholic bishops described the treatment of Catholics by the 'Six-County Parliament' in this regard as 'a grave menace to the peace of the whole community'.[165] It was sometimes stated that the government had it in mind to forbid the Mass. The United Education Committee of the Protestant churches did largely manage to achieve an outcome which they regarded as satisfactory. Their unity, however, was not complete on other matters. In 1927 some Presbyterians attacked the Church of Ireland for its 'moderatism' and 'flunkeyism' in social life, reacting adversely to the Down diocesan synod's refusal to support 'local option' as a way of countering the drink evil. They added, for good measure, that Anglicans in Down had always been 'lukewarm in the furtherance of any Christly cause'. There was a determination that Protestant Ulster would keep Sunday special. Sunday concerts were banned at holiday resorts. It would be wrong to suggest, even so, that there was complete unanimity on these matters but, where differences did exist, there was anxiety that they should not destabilize the Unionist government to which they were committed. A Methodist author in 1931 spoke glowingly of how 'with their fellow-citizens of all denominations, Methodists in Northern Ireland have greatly benefited through the progressive and enlightened policy which Lord Craigavon's government has pursued in matters of education and the improvement of the social conditions of the people'.[166]

In short, all the churches of the island seemed firmly locked into their cultural heritages. They expressed the fears of their members that their particular social and economic aspirations could only be safeguarded, or advanced, within particular political arrangements, North and South, which were responsive, in large measure, to their wishes. That could only mean

[164] Alan Megahey, *The Irish Protestant Churches in the Twentieth Century* (Basingstoke, 2000), 92–7.

[165] Cited in Mary Harris, 'The Catholic Church, Minority Rights, and the Founding of the Northern Irish State' in Dermot Keogh and Michael H. Haltzel, eds., *Northern Ireland and the Politics of Reconciliation* (Cambridge, 1993), 74. The author discusses the educational issue in detail on surrounding pages. The fullest treatment is D.H. Akenson, *Education and Enmity: The Control of Schooling in Northern Ireland 1920–50* (Newton Abbot, 1973).

[166] Revd James Alley, 'Irish Methodism and Political Changes' in A. McCrea, ed., *Irish Methodism in the Twentieth Century: A Symposium* (Belfast, 1931), 21.

the perpetuation of self-sustaining stereotypes of the 'Other'. The churches did not, however, take the further step of matching, in their own internal structures, the political division of the island. There was, in this sense, a commitment to 'Ireland' above and beyond the reality of two jurisdictions. 'The unity of our Church', Presbyterians declared, 'will not be impaired by being under separate legislatures'—and comparable statements can be found elsewhere.[167] Inevitably, however, the churches in both jurisdictions had to react to increasingly different cultural and legislative environments. The awkwardness this produced was most striking in the case of the Church of Ireland. Its representative body and other institutions continued to be in Dublin, whereas the great majority of its members lived in Northern Ireland. Catholic bishops in Northern Ireland, for their part, had to balance their opposition to the North's very existence with the need to have some day-to-day dealings with government. And the new two jurisdictions, 'North/South' of Ireland, related not just to the 'England' of Irish rhetoric but to the complexity of 'Britain'—England, Scotland and Wales.

viii. Scotland: Healing Disruption, Strengthening Borders

The tensions of Ireland did not pass Scotland by. Indeed, there had been a sense in which a 'Home Rule' solution for Ireland would be matched by one for Scotland. A Speaker's Conference on Scottish Home Rule was called in 1920 but its proposals seemed obsolete once Irish events had taken their different course. The great majority of Scots had no wish to emulate the Free State. But partition in Ireland raised issues which touched on the raw nerve of Scottish identity. If the Scots were a Protestant, indeed a Presbyterian people, their sympathy was with what the 'Protestant people' of Northern Ireland had done. There was much post-war talk of 'covenanting together' to achieve a 'Protestant commonwealth' but, despite the historical resonance of such language, its translation into reality proved elusive. Scotland had ceased to be homogeneously 'Presbyterian' even if both its friends and its enemies supposed that it, or at least 'Calvinism', still had a purchase on 'the Scottish soul'. The Episcopalians continued to be only a small element in the religious picture, though socially significant. They only approached 'popularity' in particular parts of the country. Their prevalent 'High Church' outlook, however, contrasted with the predominantly 'Low Church' Anglicanism of Ireland (both being ways of distinguishing themselves from the majority ethos in which they existed).

---

[167] John M. Barkley, 'The Presbyterian Church in Ireland and the Government of Ireland Act (1920)' in Derek Baker, ed., *Church Society and Politics*, Studies in Church History 12 (Oxford, 1975), 398.

In Scotland, Roman Catholicism now stood in 'second place'. Where Scotland itself 'stood'—in relation to Ireland, within Britain and within the British Empire—could not be detached from ecclesiastical perceptions and positions. No more than in Ireland could 'the church' speak with 'one voice' in seeking to shape the future. Its divisions replicated, if they did not fuel, the debate about Scotland's self-understanding. Once again, what had 'the church' to do with 'the nation', and vice versa?

As the war drew to a close, the Church of Scotland set up a special commission which reported to the General Assembly in 1919 on *The Life and Efficiency of the Church*. One of its recommendations was that the church should set up a permanent committee to deal with such matters affecting the church and 'national life' as from time to time might arise. It was anticipated that 'emergencies' would be more frequent in the future. There were many domestic matters in which moral and spiritual considerations were vital to a 'right settlement'. Abroad, it was stated, imperial relations to the backward races in the British Empire could only be rightly adjusted by a steadfast regard for Christian principles. The 'Church and Nation Committee' was duly established, being at the same time both the voice of the General Assembly and the source of advice to it: a happy conjuncture. Scotland had no parliament of its own and the committee's bid was to 'speak for Scotland' and to be taken as doing so in Westminster. That view could be made more plausible if, at length, a reunited Church of Scotland, about which both the Church of Scotland and the United Free Church had agreed before the war that there should be 'unrestricted conference', could be achieved.

The joint conference between the two Churches considered the issues of establishment and doctrine under the headings of 'national recognition of religion' and 'spiritual independence (or freedom)'.[168] When post-war discussion resumed, division within and between the churches still centred on the precise meanings to be attached to these terms. Progress was made, however, in drafting articles of a constitution which would embody the spiritual powers claimed to be inherent in the church. These were approved by the General Assembly of the Church of Scotland in 1919 by an overwhelming majority and became a Schedule to the Church of Scotland Act (1921). This measure, though still subject to judicial interpretation, gave recognition to the church's freedom. Such interpretation would have to be consistent with the articles. The churches had left the question of 'temporalities' to be finalized once the preliminary question of spiritual freedom had been settled, but were agreed that the new church would hold its property as freely as the United Free Church held its. In the event,

---

[168] David M. Thompson, 'Unrestricted Conference', in Brown and Newlands, *Scottish Christianity in the Modern World*, 207. Thompson's article is a valuable assessment of the issues involved.

the Act had been passed without a division, though not before a number of Scottish MPs had expressed great anxiety and forecast that on entering into union with 'the State Church' there would be another Disruption. Thomas Johnston, an elder of the United Free Church, suspected that the leaders of the Church of Scotland had in view the possibility of union with episcopacy. The people of Scotland should not be humbugged. So, was the result to be a 'State Church'? Was it to be 'established' or 'disestablished'? Some MPs felt they could get no clear answer. It was unfortunate, one of them felt, that a measure to promote church union depended upon an exhibition of casuistry which would apparently have been a credit to the Middle Ages.[169] The new church would apparently still be 'the national church' but now she would be free, with the jurisdiction of her ecclesiastical courts confirmed by the state. The complex property questions then took time to resolve, but an accommodation, though still not a final settlement, was reached in an Act of 1925. The way was now open for the final stage of this protracted process. The two churches drew up a document which indicated their substantial agreement in matters of doctrine, worship, government and discipline and also set out the steps which would have to be taken to turn two structures into one. It was approved in assemblies and presbyteries in May 1929 and in October the Church of Scotland was formally reunited in the presence of the lord high commissioner, the duke of York, who was in Edinburgh with his Scottish wife. Only a minority of the United Free Church—around 25,000—continued a separate existence.

There could be no doubt that there had been a significant healing of the great division which had occurred in Scottish national and ecclesiastical life in 1843. It had needed ecclesiastical 'statesmen', with John White of the Barony Church in Glasgow pre-eminent among them (and almost inevitably the first moderator). It had required a formidable grasp of legal technicalities to negotiate a way through. It was hardly surprising, and perhaps necessary, that some ambiguity remained. There were liberal references to 'heritages' being 'intact' but also 'new paths' being stepped into. It was, however, perhaps the former rather than the latter which were most evident. The union, although the outcome of a protracted and complicated process, had been made possible because there was no deep cleavage between the two churches once a way had been found to deal with 'establishment' and 'spiritual freedom'. It was not a moment for the reconsideration of old doctrinal standards or to re-evaluate hallowed assumptions about government. 'Old Scotland' had been apparently restored. The ideal of a national church, both representing and fostering the Christian faith of the whole people, was 'in a manner realized' as the Professor of Ecclesiastical

---

[169] Augustus Muir, *John White* (London, 1958), 203–13.

History at Edinburgh put it in 1960. The great majority of Presbyterians, forming some four-fifths of the church-going Protestant population of Scotland, had now been incorporated in one body. The middle-aged men of the two Union committees, assembled for 'a historic photograph' in New College, Edinburgh, had certainly—after due process—accomplished something. Quite what, was another matter.

The process of achieving 'union' had been time- and energy-consuming, at least for those most heavily involved, but to what end? The vast 'duplication' which had run through Scottish church life since 1843 was no longer sustainable and was considered simply as a matter of finance. There would be 'savings' and a better allocation of resources in a merged institution. The reality was that although this could be obtained 'at the centre', how 'union' was to be made a reality in towns and villages across Scotland where there was deep attachment to particular 'uneconomic' arrangements could not be speedily settled. In theory, the church was 'uniting for action' but uniting was such an absorbing activity that the 'action', whatever it was, had to wait. The fused objectives can be seen in the aphorisms attributed at this time to John White as he carried the gospel of goodwill among the Scottish people, being received, it was claimed, 'with thanksgiving' in every town and hamlet. Churchmen, it seemed, had rendered obsolete the reply 'Physician, heal thyself' thrown back at them by both sides of industry. There was, however, another concern. Democracy was in danger of 'septic dissolution' but church union would prevent that. Further, western civilization had to 'cross a dangerous river' and the new Church of Scotland would provide a national bridge.[170]

These were fine, if delphic, expressions. The reality was more complicated. The 'unity' that was being proclaimed was neither fully catholic nor comprehensive, whether ecclesiastically or nationally. Some of its impetus and appeal had stemmed from the desire to 'safeguard' Scotland from an 'Other' which challenged what was taken to be its self-understanding. That 'Other' was identified as simultaneously 'Irish' and 'Catholic'. The 'gospel of goodwill' as delivered by John White might be being received in every town and hamlet with thanksgiving but in the city of Glasgow, and more generally in the West of Scotland, it was not perceived nor received as such by its non-Presbyterian population. It had been an initiative from Glasgow which had led the General Assembly to appoint a special committee of ministers and elders to consider 'Irish Immigration'.[171] Having received a report, it instructed the Church and Nation committee to organize a

---

[170] Muir, *White*, 257.

[171] It was, of course, the Catholic element in that immigration on which attention focused. It was some three or four times the size of the Protestant Irish in Scotland. For the latter, however, the Orange Order had strong working-class roots in Glasgow and the West of Scotland. G. Walker, 'The Orange Order in Scotland between the Wars', *International Review of Social History* 37/2 (1992), 177–206.

campaign (into which all the Presbyterian churches were drawn) against the 'menace' which the Irish constituted. John White, in correspondence with the Scottish secretary in late 1925 claimed that a 'superior race', to which he himself presumably belonged, was being supplanted by an 'inferior race'.[172] It was stated that 'Irish Catholics', some 25 per cent of the population of Glasgow, consumed over 70 per cent of public and private relief funds. The issue, he claimed, was being pressed 'entirely as a racial and not as a religious issue'. True Scots, another minister opined, were being faced by a menace more formidable than that of the German emperor and his multitudinous legions. White himself did not hesitate to speak of the 'corruption' which came with the 'horde' of Irish immigrants. The Scottish Office, however, made it clear that its statistics, considering the matter in merely numerical terms, did not support Presbyterian claims. No specific legislation would be introduced.[173] The sense that Scotland was being left to the Irish whose desire, according to the Glasgow Unionist Association in 1927, was 'to gain this country for Roman Catholicism' was accentuated by the massive haemorrhage of population out of Scotland—some 392,000 in the decade after 1921—which aroused presentiments of doom. Scotland was dying. It is not surprising, in such a context, that in 1929 and immediately thereafter, writers emphasized that the reformed religion 'had done more for the unity of the Scottish race' than the victory at Bannockburn or the defeat at Flodden. It had 'made' lowland Scotland.[174] The implication seems to be that only lowland Scotland mattered.

The 'ethno-religious' issue was of central importance in the shaping of Scottish political identities (with Liberalism in crisis) amongst both Unionists and Labour. Both in Glasgow and Edinburgh, at local government level, 'Protestant' parties had an impact, though not an enduring one, particularly in the decade after 1930.[175] It is not difficult to highlight these examples of

---

[172] In 1930, according to his account, Margaret Bondfield, the minister of labour in 1930, talked to Dean Inge about 'the Irish invasion of Lancashire and Scotland' which she described as 'a remarkable instance of a lower civilisation pushing out a higher'. Inge said that it was up to her to keep them out, to which she replied that she had no power to keep out British subjects, though she could and did keep out aliens. Inge, *Diary of a Dean*, 152.

[173] S.J. Brown, 'Presbyterians and Catholics in Twentieth-Century Scotland' in Brown and Newlands, *Scottish Christianity in the Modern World*, 262–9 and his ' "Outside the Covenant": The Scottish Presbyterian Churches and Irish Immigration, 1922–1938', *Innes Review* 42 (1991), 19–45; R.J. Finlay, 'Nationalism, Race, Religion and the Irish Question in Inter-War Scotland', *Innes Review* 42 (1991), 46–67. Sir John Gilmour, Secretary of State for Scotland at different points in the 1920s and 1930s, was himself an Orangeman, albeit an 'honorary' one.

[174] Professor Archibald Main cited in G. Walker, 'Varieties of Scottish Protestant Identity' in T.M. Devine and R.J. Finlay, eds., *Scotland in the Twentieth Century* (Edinburgh, 1996), 256.

[175] T. Gallagher, *Glasgow: The Uneasy Peace: Religious Tension in Modern Scotland* (Manchester, 1987) and *Edinburgh Divided: John Cormack and No Popery in the 1930s* (Edinburgh, 1987) and 'Protestant Extremism in Urban Scotland, 1930–1939: Its Growth and Contraction', *Scottish Historical Review* 64 (1985), 143–67.

sectarian fervour. Yet two pieces of legislation specifically applying in Scotland indicate that the Westminster parliament showed a considerable degree of sensitivity to Catholic aspiration and grievance. The Education Act (1918) brought Catholic schools into the state system with the proviso that their religious character should be preserved. Over time, a path to improved Catholic educational progress (and social mobility) was opened up. The Catholic Relief Act (1926) made it clear that Catholic priests could parade in public wearing formal vestments (a matter of some controversy). Presbyterian voices considered both measures to be concessions which jeopardized their vision of what Scotland should be. Seeing 'Scotland in Eclipse', the Professor of Private Law in the University of Glasgow in 1930 feared for the future of his intelligent but dwindling race. It was being threatened by an expanding but inferior one who were being guided by 'obscurantist magic-men'. Andrew Dewar Gibb spoke as a founder-member of the new National Party of Scotland (1928) and others prominent in its limited ranks shared his opinion. They were balanced, however, by Catholics. One of them, the English-accented novelist Compton Mackenzie, steadily turning himself into a Catholic Scot, stormed to victory in 1931 in the contest for the rectorship of Glasgow university with a very different vision. It was not, however, a post which enabled him to determine the future course of Scottish history.

The burden of being an 'inferior race' was hard to carry, The air was thick with perceptions of discrimination in the job market which only rarely diverged from reality. There were, however, important senses in which Catholicism in Scotland was not simply 'Irish'. That its strength was derived from Irish immigration could not be denied, but there were also 'real' Scots, Lithuanians and Italians, not to mention even English accents, though not so many English persons. The 'mother country' just across the water still held a sentimental attraction but it was Scotland which would be 'home' (one firmly British, not a Scottish—but Protestant—Free-State-in-embryo). No one could tell when the superior race would cease to feel so superior, but it would one day happen. Even a Presbyterian church historian in 1933 had reluctantly come to the conclusion that the Irish were here to stay. No agitation for their repatriation would be successful.[176] There was, therefore, no future, for the Catholic Church, in the self-conscious promotion of 'Irishness' in perpetuity. To do so could hinder the attractiveness, actual or potential, of Catholicism for all the people of Scotland. But, similarly, from the church's standpoint, the path to social acceptance and cultural assimilation also brought danger. Rampant 'anti-Catholicism' had the benefit of cementing a 'Catholic community' which might 'leak' even

---

[176] J.R. Fleming, *History of the Church of Scotland, 1875–1929* (Edinburgh, 1933), 150.

more alarmingly than it already did. As a short-hand term, therefore, 'community' did duty, but the reality was more complex.[177] There was even the possibility that a softened Presbyterianism or an ever-accommodating Episcopalianism might prove attractive as Catholics began their ascent of the educational, and hence social, ladder. It was necessary, from time to time, for the hierarchy to make it clear that there was only one church and seek to protect the flock from the entanglements, amatory and otherwise, which assimilation might bring with it. Cardinal MacRory, across the water, had stated with great clarity in 1931 that the Presbyterian Church in Ireland, and the Protestant Church anywhere else, was not only not the rightful representative of the early Irish church, 'it was not even a part of the Church of Christ'.[178] In its Declaratory Articles, however, the Church of Scotland insisted itself to be part of the 'Holy Catholic or Universal Church'.

Such bold, but contradictory assertions made it clear why 'the church' could not bring 'unity' to Scotland. What is not so clear, amidst the obvious manifestations of hostility and separateness which have been cited, is the extent to which hostility was omnipresent at all social levels and in all types of community. A Catholic Corpus Christi procession, for example, caused no trouble in an upland miners' village in 1923. The *Motherwell Times* reported that the village had a majority of Catholics—of Scottish, Lithuanian and Irish descent—who were on the best of terms with the Presbyterian minority. A decade later, as Harry Whitley, later minister of St Giles in Edinburgh, recalled, he had ventured out jointly with the local Irish-born priest in Port Glasgow, with whom he was on excellent terms, on a joint and successful expedition to break up a brawl between local 'Protestant' and 'Catholic' mobs. He left it to the priest to carry a stick. Mobs, it seems, would be mobs and any pretext of religious group identity would do. The stance of their pastors might be nearer to the mind of Christ.

ix. Church Unity: Starting

In the decorous mob which assembled to process to St Giles in Edinburgh in October 1929, the civic robes of the cities of Scotland mingled with the crimson and white of the Lords of Session. 'Union' was a great Scottish occasion. Also present was another Scotsman, the archbishop of Canterbury, in purple cassock and scarlet-and-black gown and hood, together with the archbishop of Wales and the primus of the Scottish Episcopal Church. The Roman Catholic Church was not represented. The Anglican presence,

---

[177] Bernard Aspinwall, 'Faith of our Fathers Living Still . . . The Time Warp or Woof! Woof!' in T.M. Devine, ed., *Scotland's Shame: Bigotry and Sectarianism in Modern Scotland* (Edinburgh, 2000), 105–14.

[178] Cited in Megahey, *Irish Protestant Churches*, 98.

and of course that of the duke of York, gave it the appearance of being a British occasion, but that was only superficial. It is true that 'reunion' with the Anglicans had been in the minds of some 'High Church' Presbyterians but the suspicion that this was the case reinforced the determination of others to leave that door firmly shut.

In 1926, beset by bishops and Free Church leaders who thought they might be able to reconcile the coal-owners with the leaders of the miners, Stanley Baldwin aimed a dart in their direction. He commented that if he saw it announced that the Federation of British Industries was trying to bring about a reunion of the Particular Baptists with the Anglo-Catholics he would not be optimistic. Another of his jibes was to suggest that the Iron and Steel Federation might be asked to undertake the revision of the Athanasian Creed.[179]

Church leaders did not need a prime minister to tell them how unpersuasive were their observations on social and international reconciliation—given their inability to resolve the matters on which they were themselves divided. It was obvious, wrote Arthur Cayley Headlam in 1930, previously principal of King's College, London and Regius Professor of Divinity at Oxford, but now lord bishop of Gloucester, that 'the Christian divisions which separate us from one another, which prevent us from exercising in any real or effective way our brotherly relations, which destroy our fellowship in Christ, are fundamentally inconsistent with the Christian ideal'.[180] It was already apparent that 'reunion' would be difficult and, in Headlam's words, would demand 'courage and faith'. There would need to be much reflection and it might only be a new generation which would be able to move forward. The progress, or lack of it, made since an 'Appeal' had gone out from the Lambeth Conference in 1920 seemed to justify this view. The 'Appeal', besides making some specific suggestions, took the view that in inter-church conversation the 'truly equitable' approach would be by way of mutual deference to each other's consciences. A new age demanded a new outlook and would require a willingness to make sacrifices for the sake of a common fellowship, a common ministry, and a common service to the world.[181] Sometimes a little ambitiously characterized as the most

---

[179] Grimley, *Citizenship, Community and the Church of England*, 120.

[180] R.C.D. Jasper, *Arthur Cayley Headlam* (London, 1960); A.C. Headlam, *Christian Unity* (London, 1930). He had set out his basic position a decade earlier in his Bampton Lectures, *The Doctrine of the Church and Christian Union* (1920); David Carter, 'The Ecumenical Movement in its Early Years', *Journal of Ecclesiastical History* 49/3 (1998), 465–85.

[181] Printed in Flindall, ed., *Church of England*, 359–64. That the 'collected religious dignitaries of the English-speaking world', as he called them, should have supposed that the Nicene Creed constituted a sufficient statement of the Christian faith for this new age seemed to A.E. Zimmern to be a piece of absurdity. The churches could not help a Europe materially and spiritually in chaos by reiterating a set of formulae, antiquated in expression if not in meaning, drawn up in Asia Minor sixteen centuries earlier. Zimmern, *Europe in Convalescence*, 74–5. Sir James Marchant, ed., *The Reunion of Christendom: A Survey of the Present Position* (London, 1925) collected together various denominational comments.

important initiative since the Reformation—the era, allegedly, when 'the church' divided—it was not so much an 'initiative' as a response to work that was already being done in England and elsewhere in preparation for a world conference on 'Faith and Order'.[182]

Such an anticipated 'world conference' was in itself an indication that 'church unity' could not be contemplated in insular isolation. By this juncture, all the British churches who might be involved formed part of 'global' communities, though they were loosely structured and without a central authority such as the papacy provided. The Church of England developed further its relations with the Church of Sweden, which had maintained the historic episcopal succession. An Eastern Churches Committee sought to develop relationships with the various Eastern Orthodox churches and steadily succeeded in gaining recognition from them of the validity of Anglican Orders. The 1600th anniversary of the Council of Nicaea was celebrated in Westminster Abbey in 1925 in the presence of the Patriarchs of Alexandria and Jerusalem, two Russian Metropolitans and representatives of the Greek and Romanian churches. The Nicene Creed, with and without the *filioque*, was recited. The aspiration to manifest 'mutual deference' in these approaches was not a pious window-dressing hiding 'imperialist' ambitions, but it would take time for mutual trust to emerge. Politics could never be excluded. It would be idle to suppose that the desire to enhance the global stature of Anglicanism was not present in these approaches, but it would be misleading to suggest that it was the only motive. Inter-church personal networks took time to be established. It was going to prove possible to spend a lot of time talking about episcopacy. Perhaps, however, it was not so much whether it should be seen as emerging 'from above' or 'from below' that mattered as how individual bishops looked and behaved when, in exploring 'unity', they strayed across denominational boundaries. Headlam, for example, had no small talk and his tenacious enthusiasm for his top hat, wearing it even in a car, was not invariably taken to identify him as the kind of bishop who was carrying himself in the 'representative and constitutional manner' (with King George V as model?) recommended in the Lambeth Appeal.

The 'Call to Unity' issued from the unprecedentedly representative and carefully prepared 'Faith and Order' conference at Lausanne in August 1927, presided over by the Episcopalian Bishop Brent of New York, had entailed British churches—not all, for the Baptists declined to send anyone—meeting foreigners from a wide variety of confessions. Even so, it

---

[182] David M. Thompson, 'The Unity of the Church in Twentieth-Century England: Pleasing Dream or Common Calling?' in R.N. Swanson ed., *Unity and Diversity in the Church*, Studies in Church History 32 (Oxford, 1996), 514 and *passim*.

looked as though 'Anglo-America' (and even Anglican/Episcopalian Anglo-America) was taking the lead. Before the opening service, it was the organist of the English church who played the overture to *The Messiah* in Lausanne Cathedral. It was also decided that it was the English text of the 'conclusions' which should be authoritative. The notion that they should also appear in the Greek language used by the apostles and evangelists was not taken up. The reports on some important areas did not disguise the differences but endorsed an ongoing commitment to seek unity. William Temple supposed that 'all tendencies are towards unity'. Collectivism, in one form or another, was sweeping everything before it. Yet the pendulum might swing back and divisive tendencies come to the fore. It was therefore vital that the form of unity should be such as would curb and check them if they should once more become prevalent. Unity should not be expressed in uniformity. It had to be elastic and welcome a rich variety.[183] The task, wrote one of the participants, was now to broadcast 'the reunion movement' throughout the whole Christian church. He alleged that one of the greatest obstacles was the apathy of churchmen and churchwomen.[184]

The remarks of Temple, some supposed, were in fact painting a picture of the Church of England and offering it as an example to the world. If so, however, he well knew that its own 'divisive tendencies' threatened its own coherence. 'Anglo-Catholics' were in no mood to encourage a catholicity which would be gained without Catholicism. The post-war decade appeared to demonstrate a mood of jubilant flamboyance among them. 'Congresses' rather than mere 'conferences' were held, packing the Albert Hall in 1923, for example, and requiring overflow meetings in Kensington Town Hall. Between 15,000 and 20,000 people were said to be present at the High Mass held in the White City Stadium during the 1930 congress. In 1933, the centenary year of the Oxford Movement, even more were present. Yet there remained a profound ambiguity about 'Anglo-Catholicism'. Was it merely a stage on the road to Rome, as evangelicals or 'Modern Churchmen' frequently supposed?

Indeed, from 1921, a series of 'unofficial' but acknowledged meetings took place between a group of Anglicans and Roman Catholics reviving the earlier 'Malines' conversations. The stock of Cardinal Mercier of Malines, the 'voice of Belgium', was high in the 'Anglo-Saxon world'. Visiting the United States in 1919, he had addressed the Episcopalian House of Bishops. Now he presided over what has sometimes been seen as the first sustained dialogue between the Roman Catholic Church and (elements of) the

---

[183] H.N. Bate, ed., *Faith and Order: Proceedings of the World Conference, Lausanne, August 3–21, 1927* (London, 1927), 135.

[184] E.S. Woods, *Lausanne, 1927* (London, 1927). For Woods see Oliver Tomkins, *The Life of Edward Woods* (London, 1957).

Church of England since the Reformation. The participants discussed, amongst other matters, how the Church of England might be regulated within the Roman Communion. The fact that there were such conversations, though they did not continue beyond 1926, when Mercier died, alarmed Anglican evangelicals.[185]

The bishops of the Church of England, in general, conspicuously kept their distance from the Anglo-Catholic congresses. Bishop Furse of St Albans was a lonely, though not insignificant episcopal presence at the 1930 White City High Mass. He was 6'6" and, in some minds, the embodiment of the church militant. The 'Roman' canopy which sheltered him had indeed to be capacious. Perhaps the most significant battles at this time occurred in the diocese of Birmingham. Bishop Barnes, newly equipped with the regulation episcopal Austin 12, had pledged himself to banish and drive away false sacramental teaching.[186] St Aidan's, Small Heath, for a time moved to the centre of the ecclesiastical stage. Religious zeal, the bishop believed, unless purified by 'quiet thought', was extravagant. In Exeter, Lord William Cecil, who certainly had no intellectual aspirations and stuck to a yellow (rather than purple) bicycle for his peregrination in the city, was no friend to Anglo-Catholicism during his twenty years in the see. His maladroitness in his dealings in the diocese, with an effort, could be regarded as agreeably eccentric, though perhaps not by the clerical widower of long standing who, when asked a second time within the hour how his dear wife was, replied tartly, 'still dead, my lord'.

The less than quiet thoughts of the only Fellow of the Royal Society on the episcopal bench were, however, no more congenial to evangelicals than to Anglo-Catholics. Evangelicals remained vigilant against any attempt to turn the Church of England into 'an annexe of Rome'. The parliamentary defeat of the Revised Prayer Book had been greeted as a triumph in which evangelical laymen had played a notable part. Even so, it was far from clear that Parliament would always be the effective defender of the Church of England which most evangelicals supposed it ought to be. Evangelicals girded up their loins to try to stop some local centenary 'celebrations' of the Oxford Movement. Their unity, however, was more easily expressed in denouncing 'Romeward' tendencies than in addressing the issues raised by biblical criticism. 'Liberal' and 'conservative' evangelicals tried to maintain a common stance, but divisions of opinion could not really be disguised. The lack of a 'weighty' (though not necessarily tall) evangelical on the bench meant that they were curiously like their polar opposites in being a vociferous but 'powerless' minority.

---

[185] B. Barlow, '*A Brother Knocking at the Door*' (Norwich, 1996).
[186] John Barnes, *Ahead of his Age: Bishop Barnes of Birmingham* (London, 1979).

In short, the 'party' allegiances within the church remained conspicuous—though it was also still the case that many other 'ordinary Church of England people' resisted exclusive labelling. The existence of such divisions, however, meant that they acted as a brake on any rapid movement in 'interchurch' discussion. The questions of faith and order raised in such discussion exposed the variety of positions which could be found within the Church of England itself. To 'tilt' too decisively in one direction or another risked its own delicate internal balance. There were those, however, the bishop of Durham among them, who thought that it was time to 'call the bluff' of those Anglo-Catholics who threatened schism, but they did not prevail.

It would be wrong, however, to suppose that this was a problem for the Church of England alone. A pursuit of 'unity' exposed divisions in every denomination. J.H. Shakespeare, general secretary of the Baptist Union, wrote powerfully on the need for the Free Churches to come together, perhaps initially in a federation as a step to organic union—a United Free Church.[187] Denominationalism made no sense in the post-war world. He further expressed the hope that the Free Churches and the Church of England might ultimately be brought together. However, while there were some voices within his own denomination which were sympathetic, the general reaction was critical (and, naturally, baptism was distinctively significant for Baptists).[188] Shakespeare appeared ready to accept some modified form of episcopacy and even some form of re-ordination. Such a willingness suggested to some, perhaps most, in his denomination that Shakespeare would 'sell the pass'. He had clearly moved ahead of the 'rank and file' (whoever they quite were).

A Federal Council of the Evangelical Free Churches did come into existence in October 1919 and over the course of the next four years some twenty meetings were held between Anglicans (the two archbishops and nine diocesan bishops) and Free Churchmen (twenty-five 'representative figures'). The latter, however, although they met among themselves and prepared a formal statement, were not plenipotentiary negotiators mandated by their particular denominations. These 'Lambeth conversations' came to an end by mutual agreement, foundering on the question

---

[187] J.H. Shakespeare, *Churches at the Cross-Roads: A Study in Church Unity* (London, 1918); A.J. Carlyle, S. Clarke, J.S. Lidgett and J.H. Shakespeare, eds., *Towards Reunion* (London, 1919); Michael Townsend, 'John Howard Shakespeare: Prophet of Ecumenism', *Baptist Quarterly* 37/6 (1998), 298–312; R. Hayden, 'Still at the Crossroads?: Revd. J.H. Shakespeare and Ecumenism' in K.W. Clements, ed., *Baptists in the Twentieth Century* (London, 1982); Peter Shepherd, *The Making of a Modern Denomination: John Howard Shakespeare and the English Baptists, 1898–1924* (Carlisle, 2001).

[188] Between them, A.R. Cross, *Baptism and the Baptists: Theology and Practice in Twentieth-Century Britain* (Carlisle, 2000) and David M. Thompson, *Baptism, Church and Society in Modern Britain* (Carlisle, 2006) offer a comprehensive analysis of thinking about baptism.

of episcopal ordination.[189] There was certainly an improved 'atmosphere', as compared with twenty years earlier, but misunderstanding and suspicion had not disappeared. The Wesleyan Methodists had been uncertain about the 'Federal Council'—a continuing reflection of some doubts about 'Free Churchism', but they did participate in the conversations. Dr Scott Lidgett emerged as one of the leading figures.[190] The Methodist position was complicated by the fact that, at long last, it looked as though the three strands into which they had come to be consolidated—Wesleyan, United and Primitive—would succeed in coming together. Union was indeed achieved in 1932, though the consequential 'consolidation' was to take many years. Since the adherents of these strands were not equally spread across the country, north–south tensions continued to exist.[191] No one involved in these discussions could be unaware of how difficult circuit consolidation would be. It was the local church which had association and meaning. The process had necessarily taken time and energy internally and reduced, for the time being, the capacity of Methodism to be a 'bridge' between Congregationalists and Baptists on the one hand and the Church of England on the other—a role which some, but not all, thought consonant with its history. The fact that Methodist union and Presbyterian union (in Scotland) had been achieved did, however, show that 'unity' could be realized—but there was also a recognition that these were as yet 'family reunions' and did not engage with wider ecclesiastical issues. It was also clear, even at this juncture, that 'rationalization' by no means necessarily made the participating bodies more effective.[192]

In short, a way of putting all 'the church' together again was not readily discernible. Even to speak of 'compromises', for some, was to speak the language of the world. Truth was at stake. There were others, T.R. Glover among them, who thought that the 'unity' being considered was not the kind of 'oneness' which Jesus had meant. If reunion required an artificial fog to bring it about he would have none of it. Straight thinking and straight

---

[189] G.K.A. Bell and W.L. Robertson, *The Church of England and the Free Churches* (London, 1925) gives details of the discussions.

[190] J.S. Lidgett, *Christ and the Church* (London, 1927); Alan Turberfield, *John Scott Lidgett, Archbishop of British Methodism* (London, 2006).

[191] Rupert Davies, 'Methodism' in Rupert Davies, ed., *The Testing of the Churches 1932–1982: A Symposium* (London, 1982), 37–8; J.H.S. Kent, 'The Methodist Union in England, 1932' in N. Ehrenstrom and W. Moelder, eds., *Institutionalism and Church Unity* (Geneva, 1963), 195–220. Robert Currie, *Methodism Divided: A Study in the Sociology of Ecumenicalism* (London, 1968); Clive Field, 'A Sociological Profile of English Methodism, 1900–1932', *Oral History* 4 (1976), 73–95.

[192] Currie's remains the most extensive published treatment. See also A.J. Bolton, *The Other Side: Opposition to Methodist Union 1913–32* (Peterborough, 1994). David Peter Easton, ' "Gather into One": The Reunion of British Methodism, 1860–1960, with particular reference to Cornwall' (University of Wales, Lampeter, Ph.D., 1997) takes a longer perspective, and notes that the nineteenth-century progenitors of 'union' were not motivated by concern for falling membership.

talking was what was required. Archbishop Lang, pleased by the reception he received when addressing the Baptist and Presbyterian assemblies in 1921, seems nevertheless to have concluded that the 'good people' he met there, did not have any real care about a visible church at all. They would be content, he supposed, if they were invited to preach at St Paul's Cathedral and 'communicate at our altars'.[193] The 1930 Lambeth Conference did make some complex modifications in this latter regard, though not in terms which satisfied Free Churchmen. The conference as a whole devoted little attention to the discussions with the Free Churches and left some of those who had been involved in them feeling somewhat slighted. The English Presbyterian minister, Carnegie Simpson, who had taken a leading part in the conversations, thought that during their course Anglicans had shed some of their superiority and Free Churchmen some of their inferiority, but a degree of social tension remained. It was agreed formally in 1931 that conversations would resume, but rapid progress was not to be anticipated.

Most accounts of these exchanges have indeed written about them in terms of 'the leaders' being 'far in advance of the rank of their followers'.[194] David Thompson, however, has reasonably suggested that this picture—with its corollary that clergy and ministers wanted unity and the laity did not—is too simple. The obvious fact is that the 'leaders' who failed to 'find a formula' were themselves clergy and ministers who knew that what they were talking about deeply involved their own status and self-perception. What the 'followers' thought about the issues being argued over was not clear since they were not participants. That does not mean, of course, that 'the laity' straightforwardly wanted unity and were deprived of it by the special concerns of the clergy. Rather, it pointed to a situation in which questions of structure, power and authority were in confusion in all the churches. 'Churches', 'Denominations' or 'Sects' had to be 'run' by somebody, but where could the balance be found between 'bureaucratic centralization' and 'local initiative'? There was so much inherited and confusing terminology in relation to titles for particular offices that it obscured 'rational' consideration of how any church should function. It might be, under different labels—be they bishops, general superintendents, chairmen of districts or whatever—that each wrestled with the same problems. In 1924 the bishop of Exeter wondered whether the latest developments—he was referring to the way the Church Assembly was evolving—were not 'robbing the locality of some of their interest and

---

[193] J.G. Lockhart, *Cosmo Gordon Lang* (London, 1949), 274.
[194] E.K.H. Jordan, *Free Church Unity: A History of the Free Church Council Movement, 1896–1941* (London, 1946), 174.

rightful powers, and endangering the new life of the Church by creating a bureaucratic government'. The secretary of the Central Board of Finance replied that he thought that 'the Church of England has avoided alike the Roman autocracy in organism and the Protestant isolation of unit'.[195] Amongst Baptists, by means of various funding appeals, there was a conscious effort to develop 'interdependence' but even as a policy was developed 'at the centre'—Baptist Church House in London—so local churches apparently developed something of a 'them and us' culture.[196] There were some, but not many, who suspected that the only way forward for all the churches was to be 'prepared to think everything *de novo* . . . even to the creation of a totally new organization with marks that are not found in any existing church'. Perusal of statements being made did not suggest that this would be very likely.[197]

At the 1930 Lambeth Conference, Carnegie Simpson made a joke, though if indeed it was one, the Anglican bishops were not very happy with it. He said that if Free Churchmen had to take episcopacy into their system, perhaps it would be safer to take the Roman rather than the Anglican form, mindful as he was that the former still regarded the latter as null and utterly void. All the non-Roman churches were well aware in their conversations that they were not considering simply 'Home Reunion'. A.S. Peake, the Methodist lay biblical scholar, recognized this in his presidential address to the Free Church Council in 1928. Anglican insistence on principles which he found distasteful did not stem from any spirit of arrogance but because for Anglicans to 'surrender' on them would cause insuperable difficulties as regards reunion with the Eastern Orthodox churches and with Rome.[198]

It appeared, however, that those two churches could contemplate unity only on the basis that others accepted their own claims. The Vatican reiterated the traditional 'ecclesiology of return'. In the encyclical *Mortalium Animos* (1928) Pius XI called for submission to the see of Rome as the way to reunion. Occasionally, individual clergy or ministers were persuaded and submitted, but there was no tide. One of them, W.E. Orchard, erstwhile minister of the Congregational King's Weigh House, in retrospect suggested that his dreams of a Catholic order within Nonconformity had not been 'anything but stages towards further reunion and as a preparation for

[195] Cited in Thompson, *Bureaucracy and Church Reform*, 198–9.

[196] W.M.S. West, 'J.H. Shakespeare: The Secretariat of the Baptist Union and Effective Denominational Action' in *Baptists Together* (London, 2000), 47.

[197] H.H. Rowley, *Aspects of Reunion* (London, 1923) cited in John F.V. Nicholson, 'H.H. Rowley on "Aspects of Reunion"', *Baptist Quarterly* 38/4 (1999), 196.

[198] J.M. Turner, *Conflict and Reconciliation: Studies in Methodism and Ecumenism, 1740–1982* (London, 1985), 187–9.

the final reconciliation with Rome'.[199] The 'peripheral' discussions at 'Malines' notwithstanding, emphasis on 'return' meant that there was no dialogue and very little contact, although it has been claimed that Bishop Barnes was on 'quite amicable' terms with the Catholic archbishop of Birmingham despite the fact that Catholics in the city had staged a Mass of Reparation for Barnes's 'attacks on the Real Presence'. It would appear, however, that it was only in relation to such matters as the after-care of schoolchildren that the two men would share the same platform.

The Anglican cultivation of Eastern Orthodox connections was sustained and seemed to be being received more sympathetically (although there was no single 'Eastern Orthodox' voice) but statements made at Lausanne more than hinted at difficulties in the path of full mutual acceptance. While this relationship was important in terms of global ecclesiastical politics, it had little significance 'on the ground'. In the British Isles the small Orthodox churches, almost exclusively formed by immigrant communities, did not feature significantly in the ecclesiastical landscape (contrasting, of course, with the Roman Catholic presence). In another aspect of diversity, however, the presence in Lausanne of an Armenian bishop from Manchester no doubt came as something of a surprise to the other British church representatives.

The reiteration that unity did not mean uniformity was a commonplace of speeches and sermons but rarely was there illumination on what that might in practice mean. Such reticence was not surprising. The position of the churches of the British Isles mirrored the general condition of the British Isles. There was only a degree of uniformity in the unity of the United Kingdom of Great Britain and Northern Ireland. The unity of Great Britain and Ireland, whether conceived to be a unity that was 'colonial' or not, was at an end. Differences, which might be conceived as 'small', showed every aspiration to become 'great'. 'Ireland' evoked contrasting and competing notions of the relationship between uniformity and unity. In beginning a search for a 'unity' that was not 'uniformity' the churches of the British Isles remained circumscribed by the circumstances in which they existed. Lloyd George, shackled with his coalition partners, firmly told his Free Church supporters that 'the Irish Question is one of those in regard to which the churches are unfitted to pass an opinion'.[200] But nor was it only a matter of circumscription. Inter-church conversation, where it existed, took place frequently in a British Isles context in which confessional consolidation

---

[199] W.E. Orchard, *From Faith to Faith* (London, 1933), 195. In *The New Catholicism* (London, 1917), 160, he had looked for 'one really Catholic Church' which would transcend the intransigence of Rome and the equal intransigence of Nonconformity. The 'Society of Free Catholics' entertained similar aspirations. W.G. Peck, *The Coming Free Catholicism* (London, 1918).

[200] Cited in Stephen Koss, *Nonconformity in Modern British Politics* (London, 1975), 159.

seemed to be reinforcing and indeed even to an extent being made possible by 'national' considerations. When J.D. Jones, the Welshman who ministered in England, ventured to suggest at a meeting of the International Congregational Council in Edinburgh in 1929 that a 'union between Scottish and English and Welsh Congregationalism' should be contemplated, he was met with responses which argued that it would be 'unwise of us to throw over our honoured national heritage for the sake of the comfort which union with England would bring us'.[201] 'Honoured national heritages' were not negotiable in many places.

The various divides of the British Isles were complicated and could be problematic. Clergy and laity who strayed across them found their identities in contention. Archbishop Lang, when in Scotland, occasionally let slip that the ways of the English were strange, and he may even have been serious. If only Scottish professors could all become bishops, he thought, they would raise the level of episcopal discussion. The 'average parish priest' in England was frequently supposed to be well below the level of intellectual attainment achieved by the 'average parish minister' in Scotland. Scottish theologians and English theologians did not have frequent personal or intellectual intercourse, the Scots situating themselves frequently in an 'American' or 'continental' context rather than in a pan-British one. Indeed, from 1919 until his return to the Chair of Divinity at Edinburgh in 1934, John Baillie held posts in North America. In a different context, Sir John Reith, from the height of the BBC, found it difficult to understand how the Church of England worked. Dean Inge travelled to address the assembled bishops of the Church in Wales. In 1927, he preached in a packed Belfast cathedral, met the prime minister, held various anti-Roman conversations and, flanked by Lord Londonderry, delivered a university address on the causes of the fall of the Roman Empire, a topic which might be seen by his audience to have analogies. T.R. Glover travelled to Trinity College Dublin to receive an honorary degree and lecture. William Temple came to talk about St John's Gospel and to conduct a mission. It was a Scottish Presbyterian layman, John Anderson, as under-secretary, who had administered in Dublin Castle the last rites of British government in Ireland, before becoming an English Congregationalist, then a nonconforming Anglican and, ultimately, viscount Waverley.

It was, however, the 'Irish question' which proved most difficult for Catholics in England to handle. It split families and revealed a gulf between sections, at least, of the lay elite (as embodied in the Catholic Union of Great Britain) and some of the bishops, three of whom were Irish-born. One of them, Cotter of Portsmouth, in a letter to Amigo of Southwark,

---

[201] Cited in Harry Escott, *A History of Scottish Congregationalism* (Glasgow, 1960), 223.

compared the rough heroism of Irish Catholicism with what he called the polished and expedient profession characteristic of English Catholicism. It was an analysis he could safely make to a man who was not English and who loved the holy and learned bishops in Ireland, as he called them, with whom he was pleased to correspond. Archbishop Bourne, however, was determined to be an Englishman, and saw no call to tie the hierarchy to the Irish cause. People had to expect a slightly different view on the Irish question 'from one whose duty it is to be English as well as a Catholic and an Archbishop'. Amigo, whose relations with Bourne had never been harmonious ever since he feared that Bourne planned to extinguish his diocese, was appalled at what he regarded as the failure of the cardinal of England to denounce the scarlet regime of the Black-and-Tans. It was especially galling, reading the criticisms of them being made by Davidson in the Lords on 2 November 1920, to find a *Protestant* archbishop protesting against reprisals upon a *Catholic* country. A Requiem Mass was held in Westminster Cathedral for the three Catholics who, with other British soldiers, had been shot in their beds in Dublin on the morning of 21 November 1920. Bourne made no reference in the service to the shootings at Croke Park by troops in search of IRA men. Some interpreted his action as his own reprisal for what had taken place in the diocese of Southwark a few weeks earlier. On that occasion, the emaciated body of Terence MacSwiney, lord mayor of Cork, who had died in Brixton prison after a protracted hunger strike, was carried into Southwark Cathedral for a Requiem Mass in the presence of two bishops and Archbishop Mannix of Melbourne. His coffin was opened overnight and an Irish Republican uniform placed on the body. An inscription in Irish stated that he had been murdered by the foreigner. A correspondent complained to Bourne that murders and suicides seemed to be being all mixed up with Masses and rosaries. The cardinal was well aware that such mixtures compromised his own efforts to give his church a proper 'English face'. Yet he was also worried that Irish working-class Catholics in England might be alienated if he had condemned MacSwiney. One way of resolving the moral issue of what should, or should not be said, was to contemplate the financial consequences if 'Irish' or 'English' faithful 'voted' at the collection plate. Such examples of tangled allegiances and behaviour across the churches could be multiplied.[202]

---

[202] These matters are discussed further in Aspden, *Fortress Church*, 76–109 and M. Clifton, *Amigo: Friend of the Poor* (Leominster, 1987), 71–86. Although positions can be presented as polarized in this way, attitudes both amongst clergy and laity were not straightforward. George Boyce, *Englishmen and Irish Troubles: British Public Opinion and the Making of Irish Policy, 1918–22* (London, 1979) and Stuart Mews, 'The Hunger Strike of the Lord Mayor of Cork, 1920: Irish, English and Vatican Attitudes' in W.J. Sheils and D. Wood, eds., *The Churches, Ireland and the Irish*, Studies in Church History 25 (Oxford, 1989), 385–99. G.K.A. Bell, *Randall Davidson: Archbishop of Canterbury* (London, 1952 edn.) 1055–66; T. Greene, 'English Roman Catholics and the Irish Free State', *Eire-Ireland* 19 (1984), 48–73.

It is not surprising, therefore, that Ernest Barker, then principal of King's College, London, chose to reflect in his college in 1927 on 'Christianity and Nationality'. The gist was that the two were not enemies. Their interpenetration might be 'conceived as a natural stage of the historical process of human life'. Writing as an Englishman, and one who himself straddled both social and ecclesiastical divides, he argued that a nation was 'no ignoble thing'. It lifted men out of their selfish and partial concerns. The churches, however, could help to ensure that nations could escape 'from the broader and corporate selfishness which is the defect of nationalism'. A common Christian effort should play its part in 'ensuring that common understanding among the nations which is at once the root and the fruit of any abiding friendship'.[203] Such sentiments might be unexceptionable when delivered before an academic audience, but neither what had happened in the British Isles over the previous decade, nor what was to happen thereafter, suggested that any simple and sustainable balancing of the virtues and vices of nationalism would be possible.

x. Women: Voting

There was further unsettlement in the relations between men and women in the public sphere. The restriction of the franchise to 'mature' women would not be likely to endure for long (it went within the decade). The 'feminization' of politics might take a long time but it would be idle to suppose that it would not, in turn, influence the life of the churches. That unsettlement of an ecclesiastical world, controlled, as much as was the political, by men, might be longer delayed but, whether greeted with relief or apprehension, it could already be discerned.

In England, in September 1917, Constance Mary Todd (to become Coltman on her marriage the following day) was ordained in the King's Weigh House Church in London as a Congregational minister.[204] She had studied in Oxford at Somerville and Mansfield. The preacher on this occasion spoke of a new age 'travailing at the birth'. It would be one in which men and women 'would be in partnership'. The Congregational Assembly had decided eight years earlier that a woman who had undergone

---

[203] Ernest Barker, *Christianity and Nationality* (Oxford, 1927), 31–2. He was delivering the first lecture given in memory of Hubert Murray Burge, latterly bishop of Oxford, who had played a leading part in the English section of the World Alliance for Promoting International Friendship through the Churches.

[204] Elaine Kaye, 'A Turning Point in the Ministry of Women: The Ordination of the first Woman to the Christian Ministry in England in September 1917' in W.J. Sheils and Diana Wood, eds., *Women in the Church*, Studies in Church History 27 (Oxford, 1990), 509. Further biographical information can be found in Elaine Kaye, 'Constance Coltman: A Forgotten Pioneer', *Journal of the United Reformed Church History Society* 4/2 (1988), 134–45.

the full ministerial training could become a fully ordained and accredited minister. Constance herself believed that her very existence as the first minister was a valuable symbol of the equality of all human beings. In the short term, however, only a trickle of women followed. College principals, apprehensive that women ministers might not find employment, looked with special favour on applicants who had private sources of income. The council of the Baptist Union stated in 1926 that it saw no bar to women becoming 'pastors' though the reality was that churches remained reluctant to invite women to serve in this capacity. It took a further three decades before they could be called 'ministers' and they were still listed separately in the *Baptist Union Handbook*. Violet Ledger, who settled at Littleover, Derby in 1926, became the best-known pastor in the denomination, but she experienced much loneliness, anxiety and disappointment, not to mention hostility, in relation to work opportunities.[205] God, she was certain, was not a man. The church needed to think again about the masculine and the feminine. That meant that St Paul had to be put in his context, if not in his place. The idea of a 'Woman's Church' made a radical if fleeting appearance. Not the removal, but the reversal, of gendered boundaries of space was proposed. Women would do everything—preach, pray, make music and take the collection. After all, it was pointed out, there was nothing novel in the church being governed by *one* sex only. It was just that, in a new scheme of things, the sex which had usually been governed was itself to govern.[206]

Baptists and Congregationalists in England moved cautiously, but their example was not likely to move the Church of England or the Roman Catholic Church (or, indeed, Methodists). Nevertheless, the possibility of ordination rumbled on in the Church of England. Maude Royden remained the gadfly. In *The Church and Woman* (1924), in her preaching at the special Guildhouse, and in her tussles with bishops, her activities were deemed at the very least unladylike. Men in the English Church Union were confident that women 'were against other women haranguing them in church', it being confidently assumed, apparently, either that men never harangued or, if they did, that they harangued agreeably. Those few bishops willing to countenance conferences in their dioceses on the role of women

---

[205] Randall, *English Baptists*, 142; J. Briggs, 'She-preachers, Widows and Other Women', *Baptist Quarterly* 31 (1985–6), 337–52. Clive Field, 'Adam and Eve: Gender in the English Free Church Constituency', *Journal of Ecclesiastical History* 44/1 (1993), 63–79, ranging more widely, presents interesting data on the higher proportion of women at worship than in the population as a whole.

[206] Krista Cowman, ' "We Intend to Show what Our Lord has Done for Women": The Liverpool Church League for Women's Suffrage' in R.N. Swanson, ed., *Gender and Christian Religion*, Studies in Church History 34 (Woodbridge, 1998), 485.

found women somewhat reluctant to take part. Royden believed that the 'last worst enemy'—the idea of uncleanness in woman and in sex—had to be defeated if the relations between men and women were to be what God surely meant them to be.[207] Whether there was indeed a 'non-rational sex-taboo' at the heart of the matter was strongly contested in both formal and informal discussion at this time. So, inevitably, was whether what had obtained in 'the sacred past' should be true for all time.[208] Church arguments advanced before 1914 that women were not equipped with the capacity for legislative duties, or for deliberative and administrative roles, were certainly not dead, but it was difficult to sustain them in the affairs of the church when the state, no doubt mistakenly, had in theory at least now admitted women to precisely such roles, in principle if not yet substantially in practice. Even Oxford university had moved to admit women to degrees. Women could, therefore, have a voice (Royden's among them) in the 'business' of the church, though it proved unsurprisingly to be a minority one in the House of Laity. Hensley Henson had tried to stop the admission of women there but had failed. To admit women to councils, he had argued, there being no security against their obtaining a majority in due course, was to open the door to a demand which could not and would not stop short of entire admission to the ministry itself, even to the episcopate. Churchmen worried that if women 'got control' it might make your average man consider church to be 'women's work' even more than the imbalance of men and women in the pews already made it seem, 'on the ground', that this was the case.[209]

The negotiations which had produced the reunited Church of Scotland in 1929 had been the work of men. It is after this date, however, in the Fellowship of Equal Service, that some women began campaigning to change the institutional church. Put positively, men had to ask themselves not how they could silence the calls of women but rather how women could be put to efficacious use. It was for the Christian church to provide encouragement and example to society. 'Spiritual equality' it was argued, meant little when for men it meant determining women's contribution and for women it meant conformity or repression.[210] The Marchioness of Aberdeen was the fellowship's president. It seems likely that the equality

---

[207] Sheila Fletcher, *Mande Royden: A Life* (Oxford, 1989), 199–200.

[208] Sean Gill, *Women and the Church of England: From the Eighteenth Century to the Present* (London, 1994), 236–40.

[209] For further general comments on gender roles and relations in this period see Susan Kingsley Kent, *Making Peace: The Reconstruction of Gender in Interwar Britain* (Princeton, 1993) and Brown, *Religion and Society in Twentieth-Century Britain*, 120–3.

[210] Lesley A. Orr Macdonald, *Unique and Glorious Mission: Women and Presbyterianism in Scotland 1830–1930* (Edinburgh, 2000), 352.

members craved was in turn dependent upon a network of domestic support provided by 'servant women'.

G.K. Chesterton weighed in with the view that women should be womanly and men manly. He hated women who 'gate-crashed' what he thought was 'the male side of life'. There was no getting away from the fact that St Paul had taught as a matter of principle that the female sex was subordinate in certain respects to the male. Subordination, it was often helpfully explained, should not be taken to imply inferiority. The Lambeth Conferences of 1920 and 1930 held the line. The status of the Order of Deaconess had been much discussed. It was concluded that it should be 'for women the one and only order of the ministry'. But the argument would not go away. Charles Raven came out with *Women and Holy Orders* in 1928, advocating their admission. Women meant a great deal to him. Henson feared such advocacy. In an article, 'Most Menacing Evil of our Time', he thought that what the world wanted most desperately was not female priests and bishops but Christian wives and mothers. At any rate, those bishops without Christian wives did try to acquire them as a contribution to this goal. The bachelor bishop of Norwich, formerly master of Wellington College, despite the attendance of his maids and servants 'below stairs', found living in his palace lonely. Fortunately, one wet day, a Christian lady was ushered into his presence by his tall and elegant footman. She was surprised to find his lordship greeting her with his feet up on a sofa—only later learning that this was a characteristic deployment. She was disarmed and put at her ease by the generous offer of egg sandwiches. It proved a good opening move. They later married and had a family. This little episode is a reminder that most Christian women still found happiness and service within the domestic context of their family. There was plenty for the wives or widows of bishops to do in the life of the church locally and beyond without yearning for roles which men still believed they should occupy. No one had a more energetic life than Louise Creighton but she could not quite bring herself to believe that women could be ordained. There seems little reason to doubt that many, perhaps most, women of less prominent status felt similarly.

Church leaders, in the wake of the Great War, had shared the general hope that the world could be made a better place. There had been a serious attempt to grapple with social issues and define what it meant to be a Christian citizen. They sought accommodation of a kind with 'modernity' but could not ignore that sizeable section of their memberships for whom 'church life' constituted a conservative and reassuring bulwark in the face of social, political and economic upheaval. The mixed feelings of women themselves, which has just been alluded to, illustrates this dichotomy. The

Christian Conservative politics of Stanley Baldwin had great appeal for 'ordinary' Christians. There had been no lack of social and economic tension but a kind of accommodation had been reached. In 1931, after political and economic turmoil, he returned to office heading a 'National' government. The omens then in Europe were not good. The word 'crisis' was increasingly used. The churches might have solutions to offer, or they might simply be engulfed.

5

'CHRISTIAN CIVILIZATION'
IN JEOPARDY, 1933–1953

'I can't take Hitler seriously', wrote that impatient parson, Dick Sheppard, in March 1933, a few months after the Führer had come to power. He was 'too like Charlie Chaplin with that moustache—but Heaven knows we may have to'.[1] The Fascisms and Communism of Europe after 1933 had to be 'taken seriously' by all the churches. The ideologies inexorably advancing on the continent seemed, in their different ways, to imperil the very survival of 'organized Christianity'. 'Western civilization' was at stake, although precisely what was happening in Germany, Italy, the Soviet Union and Spain—to name only four countries—was controversial. It could sometimes all seem very far away from insular 'ordinary church life'. The Second World War, so much feared in anticipation, was then fought and won. In 1953, as a young Christian queen was crowned in London and a vicious dictator and wartime ally died in Moscow, it could look as though the world might have been 'restored'. The reality, of course, was more complex. The war might have been just but the 'peace' that ensued was fragile. Allies had become enemies. The Cold War still had a long time to run. Christianity and communism, it appeared, remained in contention. However, although the uplands were proving less sunlit than some had hoped, and mushroom clouds hung over the international scene, the churches could be forgiven for supposing that, after all, some kind of 'Christian civilization' had survived. Yet they had generally been mindful of too simple an identification of Christian faith with the objectives of any state. The centenary of the Oxford Movement in 1933 provided a reminder, some said, that the spheres of church and state always had to be renegotiated in every generation. How these issues were 'negotiated' in different circumstances and at different levels is the concern of this chapter.

---

[1] L. Housman, ed., *What Can We Believe? Letters Exchanged between Dick Sheppard and L.H.* (London, 1939), 210.

i. Pledging Peace, Being Reasonable, Taking Sides

War was not what the churches wanted. Something had to be done. Sheppard had resigned as dean of Canterbury in 1931 and, wandering around France in search of health and happiness, he continued to hit out at the institutional church. The Church Assembly, he wrote to the *Church Times* in May, was not only ridiculous. It was 'a positive menace to the presentation of the Christianity which its Founder revealed and these days so urgently require'. Gazing over the Mediterranean in the early morning, he asked, 'Dear Lord, can anything be done or must You raise up another civilization to do Your Will?' How could Sheppard help? He had become clear that he could not 'work through the Churches until they are refilled with different and more passionate people'—but he accepted a canonry at St Paul's Cathedral.[2]

In October 1934, he had a letter published in certain newspapers which claimed that the 'average man' had become convinced that war, for any cause, was not only a denial of Christianity but a crime against humanity. It should no longer be permitted by civilized people.[3] The 'Sheppard Peace Movement' was launched, attracting to its ranks men who indicated that they renounced war and would never again, directly or indirectly, support or sanction another. A meeting in the Albert Hall in July 1935 attracted 7,000. The movement was relaunched as the Peace Pledge Union in May 1936 with 'sponsors' who included such quintessentially 'average men' as Aldous Huxley and Bertrand Russell.[4] Merely to mention these latter names is to indicate that the asthmatic Sheppard's charisma brought together different strands of pacifism, at least for a time. The pledge gained 100,000 signatures and in the heady summer of 1936 there was talk of reaching 1 million. Such a figure would surely mean that there could be no war. The PPU, of course, was not the only organization in the field. In their different ways, both the Fellowship of Reconciliation and the National Peace Council sought to further the cause of peace. They experienced some modest reinvigoration in Sheppard's slipstream. Sheppard was insistent that he was a pacifist because he was a Christian, but the PPU had no kind of religious

[2] R. Ellis Roberts, *H.R.L. Sheppard: Life and Letters* (London, 1942), 226, 237.

[3] The text is reprinted in Sybil Morrison, *I Renounce War: The Story of the Peace Pledge Union* (London, 1962), 99–100.

[4] This summary of Sheppard, the Peace Pledge Union and 'pacifism' generally owes a great deal to various accounts by Martin Ceadel. His writing, too, has helped to distinguish 'pacificism' from 'pacifism'. The detailed categorization of opinions cannot be traced in detail here. Martin Ceadel, *Pacifism in Britain 1914–1945: The Defining of a Faith* (Oxford, 1980); 'Christian Pacifism in the Era of Two World Wars' in W.J. Sheils, ed., *The Church and War*, Studies in Church History 20 (Oxford, 1987), 391–408; *Semi-detached Idealists: The British Peace Movement and International Relations, 1854–1945* (Oxford, 2000). See also the discussion of 'Christian Pacifism' in A. Wilkinson, *Dissent or Conform? War, Peace and the English Churches 1900–1945* (London, 1986), 101–36.

test. He was unstinting in his condemnation of the leaders of the churches. If they had insisted unequivocally that war was wrong 'the effect would have been enormous'. He wanted to lead his 100,000 men to meet the leaders of the Christian church and say what he thought of them. Asked whether he would rather see the disintegration of the British Empire than a new war, he replied simply: 'I would'. If war should come, however, he accepted that a great number of PPU members would leave its ranks.[5] So, indeed, it proved, though Sheppard, who died in November 1937, did not live to see it.[6] The million members proved to be a delusion, but it is not an exaggeration to characterize the PPU as 'the strongest pacifist association in history'. Even so, his 'shock troops', as he referred to his 'highly trained and devoted pacifists', failed to prevent war in 1939.

Despite Sheppard's strictures for failing to become his kind of pacifists, 'church leaders' had spoken frequently on the subject of peace. It was the height of madness to be contemplating a new war. Both nationally and locally, resolutions had been repeatedly passed. The Bristol and District Association of Baptist Churches, for example, both in 1935 and 1937, declared its 'continued support for international peace'—a conclusion which could not have come as a surprise.[7] Almost all thinking Christians, it seemed, had believed in the League of Nations, though whether it should seek to apply sanctions, and what kind of sanctions, had been controversial.[8] 'Let the Churches . . . organize intelligent support for the League of Nations in every way that their zeal and ingenuity may devise' had been a typical clarion call from a Methodist author. The League of Nations Union had a 'Christian Organizations Committee' on which representatives from the main denominations sat. The 1930 Lambeth Conference repeated its support of a decade earlier. By 1934, the statistics of the LNU revealed that 2,656 congregations had enrolled as corporate members—by far the largest number coming from the Free Churches (Methodist, Congregational and Baptist). The Anglican total (511) was not what some had hoped for from the largest church in England. It did, however, contrast sharply with the Catholic participation, a mere fourteen.[9] The Vatican had not displayed conspicuous enthusiasm for the League of Nations—its location in Geneva might even be provocative. Nevertheless, Cardinal Bourne joined the archbishop of Canterbury as a LNU vice-president and gave lukewarm support.

[5] D. Sheppard, *100,000 say No! Aldous Huxley and 'Dick' Sheppard Talk about Pacifism* (London, 1936), 3–6.

[6] Maude Royden, one of the contributors to a tribute published on his death, believed that he had become 'the incarnate conscience of the nation'. *Dick Sheppard: An Apostle of Brotherhood* (London, 1938), 80.

[7] Ian Randall, *English Baptists of the Twentieth Century* (London, 2005), 197.

[8] A.W. Harrison, *Christianity and the League of Nations* (London, 1928), 190.

[9] Donald S. Birn, *The League of Nations Union 1918–1945* (Oxford, 1981), 136–7.

By the mid-1930s, however, international developments tested the significance of this generalized 'support'. There were some who believed that 'One hundred per cent world disarmament reflected the mind of Christ'. Arthur Henderson, as its chairman, had laboured at the World Disarmament Conference in Geneva but it petered out unsuccessfully after March 1935. Henderson, the first Methodist to be awarded the Nobel Peace Prize, died, despondent, a few months later.[10] There was also a pervasive view, sometimes strongly expressed, that Britain had a lot to answer for. Reflecting on the Abyssinian crisis in 1935, Leslie Weatherhead, best-selling author, then still a Methodist minister in Leeds but shortly to become minister of the City Temple in London, had contributed an article in the *Leeds Mercury* arguing that British participation in sanctions against Italy would be the sheerest hypocrisy. There had to be an understanding of Italy's problem.[11] Even more, others wrote, there had to be an understanding of Germany's problem. There were few who could see any virtue in the Versailles settlement and the straitjacket it had imposed. Britain's past history meant that it had no moral authority to judge nations. The *Christian Pacifist* wondered whether concern for human liberty and self-determination was the goal of British policy in India, Africa, Palestine and Jamaica.[12] In seeking 'an equitable adjustment of economic and territorial advantage as between different nations of the world', Bristol Baptists echoed a not uncommon sentiment. 'Appeasement' was something which should necessarily commend itself to Christian opinion.[13] Trying to solve the 'world crisis' by insisting on maintaining the status quo, both in Europe and the wider world, must surely be mistaken.

A skit at the office Christmas party of the LNU in December 1937 produced its own more limited but symbolic crisis. An 'International Peace Campaign' had been launched in France in 1935 and had been embraced by Lord Cecil and the LNU leadership. It was not too difficult, however, to identify it as a communist front. At the party, a staff member, Cecil's former secretary, lampooned him. Morale was generally low, the IPC was contentious, and the heavens fell in. The lampoonist was John Eppstein, a lonely Catholic on the staff as well as being a lonely Catholic enthusiast for the League.[14] In the end, he retained his job, but had to say that he supported complete co-operation between the LNU and the IPC. The episode,

---

[10] He was due to have given the (Methodist) Beckly Social Service Lecture in 1936. It was given instead by the Swiss Adolf Keller. Keller found in Henderson 'an increasing pain in his voice as he came to feel how difficult it was to combine the real or apparent interests of the State with the ideal message of the Church'. Adolf Keller, *Church and State on the European Continent* (London, 1936), 9.

[11] John Travell, *Doctor of Souls: A Biography of Dr. Leslie Dixon Weatherhead* (Cambridge, 1999), 106.

[12] Ceadel, *Pacifism in Britain*, 279–80.

[13] Keith Robbins, *Appeasement* (Oxford, 1988).

[14] John Eppstein, *Ten Years Life of the League of Nations* (London, 1929); *The Catholic Tradition of the Law of Nations* (London, 1935) and *A Catholic Looks at the League* (London, 1937).

however, signalled the withdrawal of the Catholic Church's co-operation. Archbishop Downey in Liverpool, detecting a 'sinister connection' between 'alleged peace movements' and communism, had resigned from his local LNU branch earlier in 1937. Archbishop Hinsley resigned in December 1938. It was a step, the Anglican Cecil told him tartly, which would be 'received with great pleasure by the Governments of Berlin and Rome'.[15]

What had led Hinsley to take this final step, however, had been the extent to which the LNU/IPC had committed itself to the republican cause in the Spanish Civil War. There was no doubt that, with few exceptions, English Catholic opinion was on the other side. Spain, shorn of wild republicanism, could enjoy a regime, like that of neighbouring Portugal, which would embody the best insights of that corporatist social thinking which the Vatican had espoused. The Spanish 'rebels', the Gibraltar-born Roman Catholic bishop of Southwark had declared in his cathedral in August 1936, were 'fighting for the church of God'. Amigo later expressed the view that any nation was entitled to rise against a government guilty of grave injustice and unable to maintain public order.[16] The grave injustice he was referring to was of course the treatment of the Catholic Church in Spain. A 'Bishops' Committee for the Relief of Spanish Distress' did not attempt to be impartial. There was no doubt where the Vatican itself stood and no likelihood that the hierarchy in England would see matters differently. Douglas Jerrold, a Quixotic Catholic, convinced that it was 'no use recalling men to Christ in London and burning those who have heard Him call in Spain' showed that his skills were not only literary. He helped to organize the aeroplane which took General Franco from the Canaries to Spanish Morocco at the beginning of the rebellion.[17] It was that same victorious general who was addressed by Hinsley in March 1939 as 'the great defender of true Spain, the country of Catholic principles where social justice and charity will be applied for the common good under a firm peace-loving Government'. Firmness, at any rate, seemed not in doubt. Anything would be better for Spain, it seemed, than the 'Red Terror' being exposed so relentlessly by Sir Arnold Lunn.

The Catholic Church in Spain, however, had not sprung to mind when British Protestants identified defenders of 'religious liberty' in Europe.[18]

[15] K. Aspden, *Fortress Church: The English Roman Catholic Bishops and Politics 1903–1963* (Leominster, 2002), 207–8.

[16] M. Clifton, *Amigo: Friend of the Poor* (Leominster, 1987), 142–3. Amigo was the most outspoken of the Catholic bishops, but his colleagues usually agreed. J. Flint, ' "Must God go Fascist?" English Catholic Opinion and the Spanish Civil War', *Church History* 56 (1987), 464–74.

[17] Douglas Jerrold, *Georgian Adventure* (London, 1937), 361.

[18] W.J. Callahan, *The Catholic Church in Spain, 1875–1998* (Washington, DC, 2000); Frances Lannon, *Privilege, Persecution, and Prophecy: The Catholic Church in Spain 1875–1975* (Oxford, 1987). T. Buchanan, *Britain and the Spanish Civil War* (Cambridge, 1997) places the Catholic stance in the national context.

Terror against Catholics and their churches was wrong, but the prospect of a Catholic *reconquista* drew no applause. Protestants in Spain were only a small minority but they had their British supporters. In these circumstances, 'Spain', in all its complexity, was not going to create a united 'Christian Front' in the British Isles.[19] Two expeditions of non-Roman British churchmen were invited to Spain by a Spanish government eager to dispel the notion that it was anti-religious. The deans of Chichester and Rochester were in the first and the dean of Canterbury in the second. In the Basque country they reported that they had never been anywhere in Europe where religion 'was more real and a greater social force'. Hewlett Johnson gave 'a true factual account of the situation' on his return. It was no surprise that the archbishop of Canterbury disapproved both of his dean's journey to Spain and of his returning sentiments.[20]

Applied to other aspects of the 'European crisis' after 1933—the remilitarization of the Rhineland (1935), the Austrian *Anschluss* (1938) and the Czechoslovak crisis (1938–9)—the mindset of the churches predisposed them to favour what were deemed prudent concessions—'peaceful change'. There were, of course, exceptions. It comes as no surprise, for example, to find Hensley Henson congenially swimming against the tide in his denunciation of the 1938 Munich agreement.[21] For its part, *Peace News*, organ of the Peace Pledge Union, had called for concessions to the Sudeten Germans, believing that 'Czecho-Germano-Slovako-Hungaro-Polono-Ruthenia' was not a nation-state at all and should not have been treated as one.[22] Weatherhead, while admitting that he was 'entirely incompetent to offer political advice' and further accepting that the pulpit was not the place to offer it, nevertheless argued that if there was any situation in which 'the law of Christ' was being broken, 'the pulpit must speak out'.[23] There were, indeed, examples of political incompetence to be had from preachers. It was apparent to the young Donald Soper in London, if to few others, that in November 1937 Europe was on the verge of a pacifist landslide.[24] Soper's belief that pacifism could solve most of the world's problems might have been an aspect of his youth. Unlike the older Christian pacifists, such as

[19] Frederick Hale, 'The Spanish Gospel Mission: Its Origins and Response to the Spanish Civil War', *Baptist Quarterly* 40 (2003), 152–72 and 'English Congregational Responses to the Spanish Civil War, 1936–1939', *Journal of the United Reformed Church History Society* 7/3 (2003), 166–79.

[20] Hewlett Johnson, *Searching for Light* (London, 1968), 142–8.

[21] Andrew Chandler, 'Munich and Morality: The Bishops of the Church of England and Appeasement', *Twentieth Century British History* 5 (1994), 77–99.

[22] Cited in Ceadel, *Pacifism in Britain*, 280–1.

[23] Travell, *Doctor of Souls*, 107.

[24] William Purcell, *Odd Man Out: A Biography of Lord Soper of Kingsway* (London, 1983), 134. Philip S. Bagwell, *Outcast London: A Christian Response: The West London Mission of the Methodist Church 1887–1987* (London, 1987). Soper moved from the South to the West London Mission.

Sheppard, whose beliefs stemmed from their retrospective meditation on the Great War (and their own involvement in it as chaplains) Soper was only 15 when the war ended. Retrospective meditation certainly played a part in the conversion to pacifism on the part of Charles Raven. Asking himself in a lecture series in 1934 whether war was obsolete, he could reach only one conclusion. In *War and the Christian*, published in May 1938 when he was Regius Professor of Divinity at Cambridge, he repeated his view that it would be wise to meet the advances of Mussolini or Hitler with 'generosity and "sweet reasonableness"'. It would be wrong to disbelieve their assertions of peace. It would not be foolhardy to treat them with friendship.[25] Two years earlier, Raven had been claiming that nine out of ten of the most virile young men at his university would go to prison rather than go into the army.[26] If 'non-virile' undergraduates, supposing that any such existed, had been counted, the army might not have had any Cambridge recruits.

It was, however, not only a clerical professor who was advocating 'sweet reasonableness'. In April 1937, George Lansbury, attempting an 'Embassy of Reconciliation', had an interview with Hitler. Lansbury, a Christian Socialist veteran, had been savaged by Ernest Bevin, leader of the Transport and General Workers' Union, at the Labour Party conference in October 1935 for hawking his conscience around from place to place. Leaving behind his Exmoor childhood, and living in Bristol as a young man, Bevin had been active in chapel life, being baptized as a Baptist, but trade union politics soon took over.[27] He did not hold back, for reasons of Christian charity, from destroying the aged Anglican politically. Lansbury had then resigned the leadership of the Labour Party. This left him free to go on his septuagenarian friendship visits. He returned impressed by Hitler's courtesy. The Führer spotted that George had a gouty foot and immediately ordered a stool on which it could be rested. 'A man as thoughtful as this', Lansbury commented on his return, 'cannot be as bad as some of you think he is.'[28] Unfortunately, this considerate man with the Charlie Chaplin moustache was indeed as bad as some did think.

Not all the Christian churches were swept along by 'pacifism', as defined by the Peace Pledge Union, but the tendency in this direction was strong. The Free Churches all had their own pacifist societies and in the mid-1930s

[25] Charles Raven, *War and the Christian* (London, 1938), 156.

[26] F.W. Dillistone, *Charles Raven: Naturalist, Historian, Theologian* (London, 1975), 222. His biographer finds 'no obvious answer' to why Raven committed himself irrevocably to pacifism in 1930, 211.

[27] Alan Bullock, *The Life and Times of Ernest Bevin*, vol. i (London, 1960), 8–10.

[28] Ursula M. Niebuhr, *Remembering Reinhold Niebuhr: Letters of Reinhold and Ursula M. Niebuhr* (San Francisco, 1991), 122.

these were gaining in numbers, though by no means all ministers joined.[29] What was striking, however, was that whilst dissent amongst Nonconformists might be expected, Anglican names were becoming as, if not more, prominent. The rather moribund Anglican Pacifist Fellowship came back, for a time, to energetic life. Bishops, however, remained pacifistically inclined rather than pacifist. Even the bishop of Birmingham gave the Peace Pledge Union a berth, though not a wide one. George MacLeod, holder of a Military Cross, announced his conversion to pacifism and spread the message in the Church of Scotland. Garth McGregor, a Glasgow University professor, expounded what he believed to be pacifism's New Testament basis. There were even mild stirrings amongst the Catholic laity. *Pax* was the inspiration of the well-known writer E.I. Watkin in 1936. The group took the view that wars between nations for national ends were 'morally unjustifiable'. Such a formulation no doubt made room for the hierarchy's view that wars for some other end might be justifiable. A speaker (actually an Anglican) at a *Pax* meeting in June 1937 saw the 'peace question' in generational terms. It was 'for the coming generation of Christians to give the lead which their elders have not given'.[30] *Pax* was not formally a Catholic organization, although its members were mostly Catholics—a position which enabled it to publish without ecclesiastical censorship. The hierarchy regarded it with suspicion. Eric Gill, the sculptor, was a lonely Catholic in his support for 'absolutism' and identification with the PPU, his unorthodoxy in this respect matching his private life.[31]

Sheppard had written that if huge numbers actively insisted that they would never take part in any war, the government would have to 'begin to take notice'. In the event, they were not forthcoming. When the 'Peace Ballot' had been held in 1934/35, some eleven and a half million people answered questions (about the role of the League of Nations and the imposition of sanctions, military or economic) and only around 15,000 people wished to be identified as 'Christian Pacifist' and therefore to decline to answer.[32] Ingli James, a Baptist minister in Coventry, tried to start a Christian Pacifist Party in October 1936 but, eighteen months later, it could only claim 140 supporters.[33] It was certainly the case that the government did in fact 'take notice' of the mood in the country—excessively, in the eyes

---

[29] Keith Robbins, 'Nonconformity and the Peace Question' in Alan P. Sell and Anthony R. Cross, eds., *Protestant Nonconformity in the Twentieth Century* (Carlisle, 2003), 216–39.

[30] Humphry Beevor, *Peace and Pacifism* (London, 1938), 212.

[31] Fiona McCarthy, *Eric Gill* (London, 1989).

[32] Adelaide Livingstone, *The Peace Ballot: The Official History* (London, 1935), 34.

[33] Ceadel, *Semi-detached Idealists*, 337; J.G.C. Binfield, *Pastors and People: The Biography of a Baptist Church, Queen's Road, Coventry* (Coventry, 1984), 249.

of some—but it did so from another perspective. And Mr Baldwin had more than 140 supporters in the Christian churches.

ii. Interpreting Europe's 'New Civilizations'

It might be a particularly British Christian vice to suppose that 'sweet reasonableness' was the way to deal with foreign dictators. The British did not seem to understand what these new civilizations were about. In March 1938, the month which saw the Austrian *Anschluss*, a foreign visitor observed what he called 'the sacred play' of debate in the House of Commons. Decisions about the future of the world were being taken there which, humanly speaking, could be regarded 'with some degree of confidence'. He became so fond of the people of England and Scotland that, if he were not Swiss, he would like best to be British. On another visit, a year earlier, he concluded that the British had an admirably sound view of the world situation. They had an unhysterical assurance about always finding a middle way. It reflected the most wholesome way of life which he encountered in the island kingdom. The day began there, at least in Scotland, with porridge (ugh) and ended with whisky. It was not the kind of atmosphere in which you could be cross with anyone. It almost seemed as if you had to commit atrocities to earn the wrath of your hosts. The trouble, though, was that such very nice people still lived in a world of moral optimism and activism. If they were Anglicans, they talked about the virtues of a 'comprehensive Church'.[34] The world he had been experiencing in Germany was very different.

The visitor was the 52-year-old Karl Barth, newly returned to Basel university after ending an academic career spent in German universities. His two British visits had been to deliver the Gifford Lectures at the University of Aberdeen. Not perhaps a natural choice as an expounder of natural theology, Barth had nevertheless contrived a topic which could be squeezed within the appointed rubric.[35] A running translation was provided for those of his audience not able to understand German. Arguably, however, 'translating' Barth was not, if translation ever can be, a matter of simple equivalents. The English translators of the plea for theological freedom which Barth had written in June 1933 confessed their difficulty with 'the

---

[34] Eberhard Busch, *Karl Barth* (London, 1976), 280–1, 287. Barth found St Andrews very beautiful but it was very remote from the continental kingdom of darkness. Bernd Jasper, ed., *Karl Barth–Rudolf Bultmann: Letters 1922–1966* (Edinburgh, 1982).

[35] The lectures were published as *The Knowledge of God and the Service of God according to the Teaching of the Reformation recalling the Scottish Confession of 1560* (London, 1938). W.R. Matthews took the view that Barth 'totally rejected natural theology and gave no reason for believing that Revelation was true', *Memories and Meanings* (London, 1969), 148.

thunder roll and tone' of his prose.[36] Could the sparks which a Swiss had struck in the disorientated and dislocated world of German Protestantism, both before and after 1933, be 'received' both by British academic theology and by the British churches? Did Barth's language not have its resonance in a political, social and cultural milieu in Germany far removed from easy-going porridge and whisky in wholesome Aberdeen? There was, however, a strong body of opinion in the Church of Scotland which wanted to keep lines open to all of the contending elements in Germany. An elder from Paisley apparently received applause from the floor in the General Assembly in 1934 when he thought the 'German Christians' were only following the Church of Scotland's example in identifying themselves with the aspirations of their nation.[37] Barth's, apparently, was a 'theology of crisis', but what was the crisis?

In Britain, 1931 had certainly been a year of political and economic crisis though not all churchmen prepared for it in the manner of J.H. Oldham and his wife. They spent three weeks that summer at a 'nature cure resort' existing entirely on a diet of oranges, an experience apparently not repeated. September had witnessed the disintegration of a Labour government con-fronted by demands for stringency which some of its members, less devoted to oranges, could not stomach. It had seen the emergence of a 'National' government, still under Ramsay MacDonald, which had obtained massive endorsement in the general election of that year. Labour suffered a severe setback. Despite the presence of some Liberals, the tone of the administra-tion was Conservative. This dominance was confirmed, though with a smaller majority, when Baldwin became prime minister in 1935, to be followed in turn by Neville Chamberlain in 1937. An administration which had been created in a crisis seemed to have become permanent even if—in the eyes of the weak Labour Opposition—the 'National' label was a fig-leaf. It did, however, signify some notion that the times demanded more than 'ordinary party politics'. What it did not signify was an accept-ance of the bankruptcy or obsolescence of parliamentary democracy. Its opponents were aghast at the apparent blindness or gullibility of the British electorate, but could not gainsay what it had done. The 'National' govern-ments, however, had not been formed by 'new men' such as were to be seen

[36] Karl Barth, *Theological Existence To-Day! A Plea for Theological Freedom* (London, 1933). The translators, R. Birch Hoyle and Carl Heath, were, respectively, a Baptist and a Quaker. Heath thought Barth a theological prophet but one who was in danger of producing a *reductio ad absurdum* (*The Challenge of Karl Barth* (London, n.d.), 46). Hoyle, who took a post in America, also published an introduction to Barth's teaching.

[37] Stewart J. Brown, 'The Campaign for the Christian Commonwealth in Scotland, 1919–1939' in W.M. Jacob and Nigel Yates, eds., *Crown and Mitre: Religion and Society in Northern Europe since the Reformation* (Woodbridge, 1993), 217–18.

contemporaneously at the helm of governments in Europe, men without 'pedigree' or 'past record' such as Adolf Hitler. British governments were full of established faces and, 'votes for women' notwithstanding, the faces remained overwhelmingly male. Moreover, the men still wore suits and hats—even, in the case of Mr Eden, being personally identified with the style of the latter—rather than the uniforms and funny headgear popular on the continent. In addition, there was no significant presence in British government of that 'popular' anti-clerical or indeed anti-Christian component also evident there.

The most powerful man in the government, Stanley Baldwin, walking in the hills above Aix-les-Bains, as was his summer habit, concluded in September 1933 that the world was 'stark mad'. It was not merely evidence of foreign rearmament or aggression (Japan in Manchuria)—to be followed, of course, in the years after he became prime minister in 1935, by further examples—which produced this conclusion. Things went deeper. Hitler's Germany, Mussolini's Italy and Stalin's Soviet Union, to name only three 'new orders' on display on the continent, were clearly not 'the same' but there were common elements. It was probable that Stalin's Communism, in the phase then emerging, was the most abhorrent. As a politician, he could see that Britain might, eventually, have to make unpalatable choices if Europe was again moving towards war. Such choices should be postponed as long as possible. For the moment, he stumbled towards a terminology which could embrace the character of these regimes—'dictatorship' or 'totalitarianism' did duty for the moment. They sprang, it seemed, from social changes evident in the wake of the war, if not caused by it. These changes, Baldwin supposed, included acceptance of the view that popular opinions, however uninformed and crude, were the best; that all problems could be solved by the state; that material advance was all that mattered; that 'science' could solve everything; that societies could be experimented with, and human beings justifiably regulated, in the name of some supposed common good. What Baldwin understood by freedom was in grave jeopardy. Millions of people, from the Rhine to the Pacific, were being trained to be 'either Bolshevik robots or Nazi robots' as he put it publicly in December 1934. The British people were 'the sanest but the disease is catching'.[38]

The attack on the churches, perceived as common aspect to both Nazism and Communism, was presented as central to this assault on freedom. It has been noted that in Baldwin's party addresses in 1935 and 1936 'the

---

[38] Philip Williamson, 'Christian Conservatives and the Totalitarian Challenge, 1933–40', *English Historical Review* 115 (2000), 615. Material in the following paragraph also derives from this article. See also Philip Williamson, *Stanley Baldwin, Conservative Leadership and National Values* (Cambridge, 2000).

maintenance of religion' was steadily elevated in importance. Addressing the National Free Church Council conference in April 1935, he affirmed that in a 'slave state' Christianity would have to go because Christianity and slavery could not live together. This was not merely the kind of rhetoric congenial to his audience. It reflected his deepest convictions. The great question had become whether the civilization of Europe was to be Christian or pagan. It was the spiritual rather than the political foundations of democracy which really counted. Although his speech was drafted for him by an agnostic, Baldwin reiterated, on retiring from government in May 1937, that the torch which he wished to hand on was a Christian truth which had to be rekindled anew in each generation; the brotherhood of man implied the fatherhood of God. The bishop of Durham noted in his journal that it was infinitely consoling that such a 'magnificent *prophecy*' should have been delivered in the face of the world by the prime minister of Great Britain. Baldwin and Lang were as close as it was possible for any two holders of their respective offices to be in the twentieth century.[39] The Book of Common Prayer, opined Rudolf Otto, the Marburg author of *The Idea of the Holy*, was the reason why 'England is still the most religious country in Europe'. Indeed, it was perhaps the only one in Europe in which large sections of the population were guided in public and private affairs by Christian principles.[40]

Nor did the torch flicker out with Baldwin's departure from power. Lord Halifax, Eden's successor as foreign secretary, picked it up and delivered substantially the same message in speech and writing over the next few years. Although not as prominent as a would-be agent of ecclesiastical reconciliation as his father, Halifax was perhaps the leading layman in the English Church Union. When young, in 1909, he had published a biography of John Keble. He spoke about the development of 'the Christian personality'. His own Christian personality was not perhaps 'typical'. It had been formed as a fellow of All Souls, Oxford, as an infantry officer, as a viceroy of India, as a master of hounds and as a working landowner. He had yet to learn to drive a motor-car. Such posts, and motoring innocence, did not suggest that he would be at home either in the cultural pessimism of Weimar Germany in which the new dialectical theology was fashioned, or in the world of Mr Morris's factory in Cowley where the automobile revolution was fashioned. It was puzzling to Halifax that Hitler should want to harass churches, but he felt certain that the Führer would harass

---

[39] Keith Robbins, 'Prime Ministers and their Primates', in *History, Religion and Identity in Modern Britain* (London, 1993), 223.

[40] Matthews, *Memories and Meanings*, 218. It would appear that he was specifically thinking of England (and excepting a Scotland which lacked the beneficent impact of the Book of Common Prayer). Otto was not familiar with the Irish Free State.

them more if he were criticized for doing so. When the two men met, in November 1937, the German account of the meeting records Halifax as stating that the Church of England was following the Church question in Germany 'with anxiety and disquiet' but he did not press the matter. 'In spite of these difficulties', Halifax recognized that the Chancellor had performed great services in Germany. Further, in preventing the entry of communism into his own country, he had barred its passage further west.[41]

Nor should these expressions of personal belief be thought eccentrically restricted to a prime minister and a foreign secretary. 'Christian Idealists' with more than nominal religious commitment, whether Conservative or National Liberal, were to be found in the higher reaches of the National governments under both Baldwin and Chamberlain. The Cecil clan was naturally to be found everywhere, though rarely contented, but there were other committed Anglicans in prominent positions. Amongst the inner circle in the Cabinet, Sir Samuel Hoare was a Quaker-descended Anglo-Catholic with a bishop as a brother-in-law.[42] Before the war, as an MP for Chelsea no doubt should, he had mounted a strong but unsuccessful opposition to disestablishment in Wales. On the opposite wing of the Church of England, Sir Thomas Inskip had not only successfully co-ordinated evangelical opinion in the Commons against the Revised Prayer Book but also now, as the government minister responsible, was co-ordinating national defence, perhaps less successfully.

Free Churchmen, were also to the fore in government. The Baptist Ernest Brown was a regular Sunday preacher and ran the Ministry of Labour during the week.[43] The Methodist Kingsley Wood, whose father had latterly ministered at Wesley's Chapel in the City Road in London, had come to political maturity in connection with health insurance. He had later shown ministerial skill in expanding the telephone service. In appointing him to the Air Ministry in 1938, the incoming prime minister hoped he would be as successful with aeroplanes as he had been with telephones. In 1940, his experience as treasurer of Wesley's Chapel no doubt assisted him when he became chancellor of the exchequer. His predecessor in the latter office, Sir John Simon, was the son of a Congregational minister. Simon could be persuaded to speak to the National Free Church Council. Walter

---

[41] Maurice Cowling, *The Impact of Hitler: British Politics and British Policy 1933–1940* (Cambridge, 1975), 275. *German Documents on Foreign Policy 1918–1945* D, vol.1, no. 31. It has been held by his friend and confessor that Halifax's religion was 'completely transcendental'. His biographer suggests that his religious convictions played little or no part in his day-to-day politics. Andrew Roberts, *'The Holy Fox': A Biography of Lord Halifax* (London, 1991), 50–1.

[42] J.A. Cross, *Sir Samuel Hoare: A Political Biography* (London, 1977).

[43] Brown, son of a Baptist fisherman, won an MC in the war. He had the most powerful voice, though not the greatest influence, in the government. He became president of the Baptist Union in 1948–9.

Runciman, another Methodist, served as president of the Board of Trade until 1937. Recalled to lead a special mission to Czechoslovakia in July 1938, he then returned to the Cabinet until the outbreak of war in 1939. Quite what the inherited Unitarianism of Neville Chamberlain amounted to was not clear, but it did not entail dissent from the language used by colleagues.

Highlighting the prominence of these leading laymen from different denominations, however, should not be taken to imply that this broad 'Christian front' produced detailed policy statements about what should be done. The great question might be whether Europe was to have a Christian or a pagan civilization, but neither Baldwin nor anybody else could explain how the former might be preserved or the latter contained, if not overthrown. Hoare's 'settlement' of the Ethiopian question in 1935 in an agreement with the French foreign minister greatly upset Christian enthusiasts for the League of Nations and cost him his job. What these backgrounds did provide, however, was a Christian ethos, admittedly understated, which transcended, or at least aspired to transcend, the ordinary cut and thrust of party politics. Indeed, one young historian at the time, viscerally hostile to Nonconformity, saw a country being led to its doom by the jaded exponents of an outworn 'conscience'. Their 'characteristic self-righteousness', as he put it, was 'all the more intolerable in the palpably wrong'.[44] Individual Christian commitment, however, did not translate into an identification with the manifestations of an ostentatious 'Christian polity' to be found in clerico-fascist regimes of various kinds, as for example those in Austria or Portugal. The Conservative Party was able to monopolize the ground on which any fascist movement might hope to base itself.[45]

There was little prospect, in these circumstances, that the British Union of Fascists would be able to drum up significant support from the churches, although Catholics were targeted—and some were attracted.[46] It was also the case, however, as in some Catholic quarters on Merseyside, that the zeal to take the offensive against 'the Communist menace' led to an approach to the Italian Information Bureau in London to 'secure the wider distribution of literature explaining the true nature of Fascism'. A few priests in Liverpool explicitly linked Communists and Jews (with Freemasons

---

[44] A.L. Rowse, *All Souls and Appeasement* (London, 1961), 19.

[45] As John Stevenson, 'Conservatism and the Failure of Interwar Fascism in Britain' in Martin Blinkhorn, ed., *Fascists and Conservatives* (London, 1990), 276 argues. Peter Catterall, 'The Party and Religion' in Anthony Seldon and Stuart Ball, eds., *Conservative Century: The Conservative Party since 1900* (Oxford, 1994), 648–50.

[46] K.L. Morris, 'Fascism and British Catholic Writers 1924–1939: Part One', *New Blackfriars* 80 (1999), 32–45 and '. . . Part Two', *New Blackfriars* 80 (1999), 82–95.

thrown in for good measure) because both they were supposedly engaged in a common conspiracy against the church.[47] There was a regular column in *The Fascist Week* by a clerical gentleman of undisclosed denomination who explained the fruitfulness of association between Christianity and fascism. The archbishop of Westminster had correspondence on fascism. Some Catholic ladies, as they wrote to him, liked the sight of patriotic young men marching (the Anglican archbishop of Armagh, visiting Italy, thought he understood the wonderful success of the Fascisti movement—it had grasped the enthusiasm of youth for work and service, not for selfish aims).[48] Asked by a young Catholic enquirer whether a Catholic could be a fascist, Westminster replied that it was possible, though the state was not the be-all and end-all. If some Catholics did belong to the BUF they should ensure that this pagan principle was not supreme. As a general rule, it was said, the church did not favour or condemn any 'legitimate' form of government, being above all particular regimes, whether democracy or dictatorship. Later, in January 1939, he stated publicly that he could not understand 'how a Catholic in this country can adopt wisely and safely this foreign label "Fascist" '.[49]

It was this sense of being in an exceptional country that Karl Barth experienced as he sat around 'well-banked-up British fires' smoking and talking. British churchmen he met did have 'special qualities'. Some of them, he found, even in Glasgow in 1930, adjourned weighty conversation to find out 'how the Test Match was getting on', whatever that was. They had their share of that confidence in deciding about the political future of the world which he had detected watching speakers in the House of Commons. It was, however, a puzzling country in which a chaplain to the king could be a pacifist. But perhaps this British confidence was misplaced? Barth suggested to George Bell that he was too much of an English gentleman to understand Hitler.[50] There *was* a 'crisis' in Europe even if its gravity seemingly could not be grasped on the island. When in Oxford in March 1938 to receive an honorary doctorate, Barth also lectured there, and then in Birmingham, on 'The German Church Struggle: Tribulation and Promise'. He concluded with 'a summons to the Church Universal'. There were no certainties to be had. The church in Germany might

[47] Aspden, *Fortress Church*, 211–15.

[48] C.F. D'Arcy, *Adventures of a Bishop*, (London, 1934), 268.

[49] Thomas Moloney, *Westminster, Whitehall and The Vatican: The Role of Cardinal Hinsley 1935–43* (Tunbridge Wells, 1935), 58–62.

[50] E.H. Robertson, *Unshakeable Friend: George Bell and the German Churches* (London, 1995); Gordon Rupp, *I Seek My Brethren: Bishop George Bell and the German Churches* (Norwich, 1975). See also Andrew Chandler's Introduction to his edition *Brethren in Adversity: Bishop George Bell, the Church of England and the Crisis of German Protestantism 1933–1939* (Woodbridge, 1997).

be coming to an end or might win through. What he stressed, however, was that it was not only the German church whose future was veiled. So was 'the path of the *whole Church of Christ*'. The tribulation and promise of the German church struggle were hovering over the churches of all countries and, sooner or later, would become visible in their midst.[51]

The trouble with Barth, sensible Englishmen thought, was that he exaggerated everything extravagantly. Evelyn Underhill thought he was rather like a bottle of champagne, too intoxicating to be taken neat, but excellent with a few dry biscuits.[52] It had fallen to a baronet, a holder of the Military Cross and the son of a bishop, namely Edwyn Hoskyns, of Corpus Christi, Cambridge to draw on the mastery of German which he had acquired in pre-war Berlin, to translate the second edition of Barth's *Römerbrief*. When it appeared in 1933, the translator conceded that its wealth of allusions would be largely unfamiliar to the English reader. Hoskyns told Barth that Englishmen experienced very real barriers to understanding him—different political and theological traditions, different qualities of piety.[53] Germans, for their part, were shocked by English ignorance of, and apparent indifference towards, the heroic work of Martin Luther and all that 'Lutheranism' had come to signify. Archbishop Lang, for example, had seen no reason in 1930 to have the Church of England officially represented at the 400th anniversary commemoration of the Augsburg Confession. German Lutherans, rather oddly Lang thought, seemed to regard it as having some importance outside their ranks. It could not be right to identify the Church of England with the Evangelical Church at home or on the continent.[54]

In Scotland, of course, theologians of the established church did not experience such Anglican anxieties, nor, naturally, were they greatly disturbed by Barth's evident lack of interest in bishops. Indeed, in a lecture series delivered in the University of Glasgow (which had honoured Barth as early as 1930), a lecturer proudly proclaimed that Scottish theology was thoroughly attuned to 'continental minds'. Scots apparently did not share peculiar English hang-ups regarding the miasma emanating from Basel. The return of John Baillie to Edinburgh from New York in 1934 meant too that there were strong American as well as European influences at play in Scotland.[55] There was indeed some justification for the view that Scottish reactions were different. J.K. Mozley seemed very English and very

[51] Karl Barth, *The German Church Struggle: Tribulation and Promise* (London, 1938), 16.
[52] Charles Williams, ed., *The Letters of Evelyn Underhill* (London, 1943), 214.
[53] Ian R. Boyd, *Dogmatics among the Ruins: German Expressionism and the Enlightenment as Contexts for Karl Barth's Theological Development* (Oxford and Bern, 2005).
[54] His letter to George Bell to this effect is cited in Chandler, *Brethren in Adversity*, 9.
[55] George Newlands, *John and Donald Baillie: Transatlantic Theology* (Oxford and Bern, 2002).

Anglican when, reviewing in the journal *Theology*, he found the absence of any trace of qualification in Barth disconcerting. The Swiss seemed to delight in words which shocked those, like Mozley himself, who had experienced 'the friendliness of God'. It was thought in England that God's friendliness had not been much emphasized in Scotland. 'Engagement' with Barth seemed a particularly Scottish phenomenon, initially in the persons of John McConnachie, J.H. Morrison and H.R. Mackintosh.[56] Barth, these writers believed, was asking the right questions even if, for some of them, he did not provide entirely the right answers. The assessment by H.R. Mackintosh, posthumuously published in 1939, was thought by many to strike a good balance. Mackintosh had been engaged with W.R. Matthews in producing a major translation of Schleiermacher's *Christliche Glaube*. By the time of its appearance, however, the Englishman had reluctantly to concede that 'even in Scotland' Schleiermacher had gone out of fashion and his place been taken by Karl Barth.

Talk of the friendliness of God, or at least exclusive dwelling upon it, also smacked to some of that tired and emollient liberalism which appeared to have established itself in 'Nonconformity' in Wales. So it appeared to the youthful J.E. Daniel, brilliant Oxford graduate and subsequent student of Bultmann in Marburg, who brought the message of Barth to the world of Welsh theology from Bangor where he had a post in the college of the Welsh Independents.[57] A younger generation bought into crisis. It was time to talk again of the transcendence of God and not shy away from 'the strange new world of the Bible'. Controversy raged in periodicals and in public addresses given in both Welsh and English. A corollary of Daniel's message was that the church was not the rather loose mutual support association of the spiritually minded, an interpretation which might have been drawn from an address recently given to the Union of Welsh Independents by Professor W.J. Gruffydd. On the contrary, Daniel proclaimed, the church of Christ was essential for the gospel of Christ. It was simply not true that there was as much religion on the golf-links as there was in chapel.[58] The

---

[56] Richard H. Roberts, 'The Reception of the Theology of Karl Barth in the Anglo-Saxon World: History, Typology and Prospect' in his *A Theology on its Way? Essays on Karl Barth* (Edinburgh, 1991), 107. Roberts errs, however, in 'presuming' that A.J. MacDonald moved in this Scottish intellectual world. H.R. Mackintosh concluded that Barth's message, explosive and often unduly emphatic though it was, was none the less of 'incalculable import' for the church. *Types of Modern Theology* (London, 1937), 319.

[57] *Torri'R Seiliau Sicr: Detholiad o Ysgrifiau J.E. Daniel* (Llandysul, 1993). D. Densil Morgan writes a substantial introduction to this collection of Daniel's writings. See also Morgan's article 'The Early Reception of Karl Barth's Theology in Britain: A Supplementary View', *Scottish Journal of Theology* 54/4 (2001), 504–27.

[58] D. Densil Morgan, *The Span of the Cross: Christian Religion and Society in Wales, 1914–2000* (Cardiff, 1999), 134–7.

words Daniel delivered echoed through Welsh-speaking 'Nonconformity' and were given a further contentious edge from being delivered alongside a nationalist message. The Welsh 'crisis' was evidently a multi-faceted one. A message forged in the cultural crisis of Weimar might therefore have more resonance in Wales than it did in England. Even so, at least in English-speaking 'Nonconformity' in Wales, the 'theology of crisis' shook but did not shatter the foundations of 'enlightened' Protestantism. The Church in Wales, for its part, having at length got its new structures into some kind of working order, had had enough of crisis talk. In any event, theologians of note were as rare as Welshmen themselves were on the staff of its theological college at Llandaff. The cause of scholarship had not been helped by the devotion of one warden, admittedly an Englishman, to the golf course, not on one day a week, but every day. It is not clear whether he was the particular target of J.E. Daniel's negative verdict on the spiritual value of golf.[59] Followers of Barth in England, reported Daniel Jenkins in 1939, had begun almost to despair of his ever being understood by the mass of English theological writers. A similar verdict could have been delivered on the situation in Jenkins's native Wales.

In January 1937 Evelyn Underhill wrote to Edwyn Hoskyns, Barth's translator, to thank him for his review of her book on *Worship*. One of her young friends had lately been asked by her rector what she had been reading and had replied 'Karl Barth' (*The Epistle to the Romans*). There had been a short silence and the reply came: 'Ah well! We all come back to Mr Baldwin in the end'.[60] The bishop of Birmingham had thought himself broadminded in allowing his clergy to be lectured to on Barth's thought 'if it can be so termed'. He himself considered it 'the outcome of an anti-intellectual reaction', adding that the Providence which had allowed Emil Brunner to pose as a theologian—another Swiss, often, though misleadingly, then lumped with Barth—had, fortunately, also enabled man to invent the wastepaper-basket.[61]

Mr Baldwin and Professor Barth never met.

The young lady's Advent reading preference was not widely shared at this time by the laity of the Church of England as a whole (or by that of any other church). Nevertheless, in one way or another, the questions posed by 'Germany' penetrated the life of all churches, to varying degrees, in both the United Kingdom and the Irish Free State. 'Interpreting' Nazism naturally occupied politicians, journalists and historians at this time. The issues thrown up by information from German church sources touched insular

[59] Owain W. Jones, *Saint Michael's College, Llandaff, 1892–1992* (Llandysul, 1992), 51.
[60] Gordon S. Wakefield, 'Hoskyns and Raven: The Theological Issue', *Theology* 58 (1975), 571 n.
[61] John Barnes, *Ahead of his Age: Bishop Barnes of Birmingham* (London, 1979), 296.

raw nerves on the subject of the relationship between 'church' and 'state'. They had, however, different implications and significance in different parts of the British Isles.

Information about the treatment of Jews and of 'non-Aryan' Christians in Germany brought to the fore both the deeply complicated relations between Christians and Jews, over the centuries, in Europe, and the current state of those relations in the British Isles themselves.[62] The reactions cannot be straightforwardly summarized.[63] On the one hand, there remained church societies specifically committed to the conversion of Jews to Christianity—and some under Anglican episcopal patronage.[64] Such a mission reflected a long-held and deeply entrenched understanding that Christianity had superseded Judaism. Its existence could be interpreted to imply that Christianity was inherently anti-Semitic (or perhaps the word should be anti-Judaic). It has been held that amongst Christians, Quakers apart, 'only very few other individuals, men like Bell, William Paton, Viscount Cecil' helped Jewish refugees from the Nazis.[65] It might also be pointed out, however, that some British Jews were wary of too much 'support' if it meant placing Jewish children in non-Jewish homes. There was a letter in the *Jewish Chronicle* protesting in strong terms about the appointment of a Jewish young man 'of German nationality' to the ministry of a London synagogue. The youth in question was subsequently to become the Chief Rabbi of the United Hebrew Congregation.[66] 'Anti-Semitic attitudes', it is claimed, 'were among the stock responses of many Christians, as among the

---

[62] C. Klein, *Anti-Judaism in Christian Theology* (London, 1978); Tony Kushner, 'James Parkes, the Jews, and Conversionism: A Model for Multi-Cultural Britain' in Diana Wood, ed., *Christianity and Judaism*, Studies in Church History 29 (Oxford, 1992), 451–61. In the late 1930s, arising out of extra-mural classes given by Manchester University, a series of volumes appeared, with Jewish and Christian contributors, under the general title *Judaism and Christianity*. In his 'Foreword' to the volume on 'Law and Religion', William Temple hoped that it would help 'modern English people' to appreciate 'their double debt to Judaism and Christianity, and so the more readily . . . to regard with sympathy and friendliness the Jewish people who now so urgently need both' (London, 1938), v. See also Richard Gutteridge, 'The Churches and the Jews in England, 1933–1945', in O. Kulka and P. Mendes-Flohr, eds., *Judaism and Christianity under the Impact of National Socialism, 1919–1945* (Jerusalem, 1987), 353–80. The Church of Scotland had a long-established mission to the Jews in Budapest. A missioner in the late 1930s was the Old Testament scholar George A.F. Knight, a Glasgow graduate in Semitic languages. George A.F. Knight, *The Queen of the Danube: An Account of the Church of Scotland's Jewish Mission in Budapest* (Edinburgh, 1937).

[63] Andrew Chandler, 'A Question of Fundamental Principles: The Church of England and the Jews of Germany 1933–1937', and 'Lambeth Palace, the Church of England and the Jews of Germany and Austria in 1938', in the *Leo Baeck Yearbook* 38 (1993), 221–61 and 40 (1995), 225–47 give detailed assessments.

[64] George Stevens, *Tell my Brethren: A Short Popular History of Church Missions to Jews (1809–1959)* (London, 1959). Edwyn Bevan offered 'Considerations on a Complaint regarding Christian Propaganda among Jews' in *International Review of Missions* 22/4 (1933), 481–99.

[65] Adrian Hastings, *A History of English Christianity 1920–1990* (London, 1991), 344.

[66] Geoffrey Alderman, *Modern British Jewry* (Oxford, 1998), 300.

general population of Britain'. Only after the Holocaust did 'people' realize to what horrifying actions such commonplace attitudes could lead.[67] Certainly, criticism of Nazi anti-Semitism could often be accompanied by a 'but' which criticized Jews as either Bolsheviks or bloated capitalists. For example, the Roman Catholic archbishop of Birmingham, Thomas Williams, in 1933 was publicly protesting against the discrimination against Jews in Germany, but also adding that, if it was true, as Nazis claimed, that Jews were Communists, his sympathy was with the Nazis 'though their methods may not be very wise'. In Liverpool, however, Downey appears to have had good relations with local Jewish figures.[68] The prominent Congregationalist A.E. Garvie, who had spent his childhood in Poland, stated that he hated anti-Semitism and deplored the record of Christendom but added that Jews in Poland had constituted an economic though not a political danger. In Germany, there were grounds for supposing that they had become both. Even so, the brutal attempt to solve the problem could not be excused.[69] He had earlier written that Jews always seemed to be *in* a country for what they could get *out* of it, rather than *of* a country to give what they could *to* it. It was, however, Christendom, by its persecutions of the past, which had made them what they were.[70] It was a perspective not dissimilar from that of Arthur Headlam, bishop of Gloucester, who thought himself to be hostile to anti-Semitism but was also forthright in his criticism of Jewish conduct in Germany.

Henson, on the other hand, in 1935 and subsequently, in speeches and writing, denounced what was going on. The general press praise for his stance perhaps calls into question the notion of a 'stock' British anti-Semitism. Henson contributed an introduction to *The Yellow Spot* published by the English Jewish publisher Victor Gollancz which included extracts from Streicher's virulent *Der Stürmer*.[71] Later, his diocesan conference asked Henson to communicate to the Chief Rabbi its deep sympathy with the Jewish people, a message which was much appreciated. *The Yellow Spot*, in its full title, referred to the *extermination* of the Jews in Germany, not to their persecution. Henson, however, did not suppose that Nazi policy was a legacy of Christendom. On the contrary, Germany seemed to have 're-pudiated the restraints of traditional Christianity more completely than any other community in Christendom'.[72] Obliquely alluding to reasons why he

[67] Wilkinson, *Dissent or Conform?*, 143.
[68] Aspden, *Fortress Church*, 215.
[69] A.E. Garvie, *Memories and Meanings of My Life* (London, 1938), 49–50.
[70] A.E. Garvie, *The Fatherly Rule of God* (London, 1935), 127–8.
[71] Ruth Dudley Edwards, *Victor Gollancz: A Biography* (London, 1987).
[72] *The Yellow Spot: The Extermination of the Jews in Germany* (London, 1936), 6.

held Germany in high regard, he hoped that this violation of the 'fundamental principles of civilised human intercourse' would not last much longer. Now in his early 70s, the bishop was inclined to believe that youth was to blame, though youth did often come to its senses quickly. No doubt accustomed in the Church of England to leadership being provided by men of Henson's ripeness, the Anglican evangelical weekly *The Record* in 1933 had expressed wonderment that Hitler had become Chancellor when not yet 42.[73] It would probably be unwise, however, to suppose that civilization could be saved merely by the return of elderly wisdom.

The German churches could not be directly held responsible for the measures being taken by the German government. However, taken in the round, their manifest acquiescence in, and indeed, in some quarters, enthusiastic support for, the 'cleansing' of German life from allegedly injurious Jewish presence could not be denied, even if some protection for 'non-Aryan' Christians was also sought. What was happening suggested to James Parkes nothing less than a complete recasting of the relationship between Judaism and Christianity.[74] Over decades, the views he advanced were to gain increasing acceptance in the churches, but he had no official position and little direct influence. If, in retrospect at least, it can appear that George Bell, to take one example, was more concerned about the fate of 'non-Aryan' Christians in Germany rather than with Jews as such this was at least in part initially because some British Jews gave the impression that they would look after their own 'nation'.[75] The notion, too, that Christian anti-Semitism was virtually the same as, or was the effective precursor of, the racial anti-Semitism evident in Germany, advanced by some British Jewish writers, was resented in some Christian circles.[76] The tensions arising out of the British mandate in Palestine and the ambitions of 'Zionism' brought an additional complication. Christian Arabs had their supporters. The question of whether Jews constituted a nation, or whether Judaism was a religion, or whether such a question was *mal posée* again surfaced. It is scarcely surprising, in these circumstances, that stances, statements and actions are to be

---

[73] Chandler, *Brethren in Adversity*, 12.

[74] Rupert Everett, *Christianity without Antisemitism: James Parkes and the Jewish–Christian Encounter* (Oxford, 1993). Parkes published his *The Conflict of the Church and the Synagogue: A Study in the Origins of Antisemitism* in 1934. His own autobiography is *Voyages of Discovery* (London, 1969).

[75] A proposition put forward in Tom Lawson, *The Church of England and the Holocaust: Christianity, Memory and Nazism* (Woodbridge, 2006). In a prayer 'For Jews and Non-Aryans', published in his diocesan gazette in 1936, Bell both asked for succour and sympathy for the Jews and asked who spoke a word of comfort for the Non-Aryan Christians who had rejected Judaism. Paul Foster, ed., *Bell of Chichester (1883–1958)* (Chichester, 2004), 83.

[76] Charles Singer, *The Christian Approach to the Jews* (London, 1937).

found which can be placed along a continuum which extends from anti- to philo-Semitism.[77]

For the British churches, the Hitler regime revived all those issues about 'Germany' which had smouldered on in church, no less than in political circles, concerning the 1914 war and the peacemaking in 1919.[78] Detailed knowledge of developments in Germany, unsurprisingly, was limited to the relatively few people, clerical or lay, who had 'first-hand' information derived from travel or from German correspondents.[79] What the controversy was 'all about', however, could not be explained simply. When visitors were told, and reported back, 'reasons' for the 'success' (and acceptability) of the regime it was difficult to tell whether this was merely reportage or represented personal acceptance of what they were told. Interpretations varied widely and some did indeed see different things depending on where they went in Germany or where their correspondents were coming from, both geographically and institutionally. Given the confusing nature of the German scene, it is not surprising that outside onlookers changed their minds—as, of course, did participants—as events unfolded.[80] It would also have been surprising if the level of interest and attention in Britain had remained constant—and it did not. The Church of England established a Council on Foreign Relations under the chairmanship of the bishop of

---

[77] Matters referred to in this paragraph continue to generate both historical and theological controversy worldwide as evinced, for example, in W. and H. Rubinstein, *Philosemitism: Admiration and Support in the English-Speaking World for Jews, 1840–1939* (London, 1999); Gisela Lebzelter, *Political Anti-Semitism in England, 1918–1939* (London, 1978); T. Kushner, ed., *The Jewish Heritage in British History: Englishness and Jewishness* (London, 1992); Sidney Dark of the *Church Times* was a keen supporter of the Jews in *The Jew Today* (London, 1933). See also his autobiography *I Sit and I Think and I Wonder* (London, 1943). Initially, like many others, Dark thought Nazism a confusion of ideas, some strange, some stupid and some sane. Who knew which ideas would triumph?

[78] Catherine Cline, 'Ecumenism and Appeasement: The Bishops and the Church of England and the Treaty of Versailles', *Journal of Modern History* 61/4 (1989), 683–703; Keith Robbins, 'Reconciliation? Democracy, Peacemaking and the Churches in Britain in 1918/19' in Katarzyna Stoklosa and Andrea Strübind, eds., *Glaube—Freiheit—Diktatur in Europa und dem USA: Festschrift für Gerhard Besier zum 60. Geburtstag* (Göttingen, 2007), 321–36; Gerhard Besier, *Krieg—Frieden—Abrüstung* (Göttingen, 1982).

[79] Keith Robbins, 'Church and Politics: Dorothy Buxton and the German Church Struggle', reprinted in Robbins, *History, Religion and Identity in Modern Britain* (London, 1993), 183–94. Amongst her many other activities, it was Mrs Buxton who arranged for the publication of Barth's Oxford lecture and persuaded him to write an introduction to it for the benefit of her 'ignorant fellow countrymen'. The German theologian Otto Piper, who lost his Chair in Münster in 1933, gave academic lectures in Manchester on 'Recent Developments in German Protestantism'. They were published in the following year under that title. The SCM Press also published a Swiss interpretation, Arthur Frey, *Cross and Swastika: The Ordeal of the Christian Church* (London, 1938). A common theme was that the British churches should understand that the struggle was not 'a German problem' but was vital 'to the whole of Protestantism'.

[80] Victoria Barnett, *For the Soul of the People: Protestant Protest against Hitler* (New York, 1992); Gerhard Besier, *Die Kirchen und das Dritte Reich: Spaltungen und Abwehrkämpfe 1934–1937* (Berlin and Munich, 2001).

Gloucester, Arthur Headlam, with a London rector, A.J. Macdonald, as its librarian. It was to have four sub-committees dealing, respectively, with the Roman Catholic Church, the Orthodox Church, other Eastern churches and with the continental churches. The Council had its first meeting in February 1933 and, over the years that followed, it was to be the 'German question' which aroused most internal controversy, and in the Church Assembly, to which it reported.[81] Headlam also received reports from various quarters. Bishop Bell had his own network of informants, amongst whom was the young Dietrich Bonhoeffer when he was a pastor to a German-speaking congregation in Forest Hill, London.[82] What one believed about what was going on tended to depend on who one knew.

Nor were differences of understanding and interpretation confined to the Church of England. Baptists and Methodists had particular difficulties stemming from the fact that leading figures amongst their German 'counterparts' dissented from the picture of persecution that was being presented in Britain.[83] Indeed, often in their relatively small numbers disparaged as 'sects' by Evangelical Lutherans, they now found themselves, or so they said, with more freedom and greater legal status in Germany than they had previously enjoyed. Their acknowledgement of this fact was, of course, a benefit to the regime which had seen the propaganda advantage in such treatment. Tensions were very manifest at the congress of the Baptist World Alliance held in Berlin in 1934. A session was suspended so that delegates might listen to the funeral service of President Hindenburg, relayed to the hall from Tannenburg, site of his former military triumph. This was a compromise. The proposition that it, together with Hitler's oration, should have formed part of a congress session had been rejected. Aspects of Nazi social policy were agreeable in German Baptist and Methodist circles (as in the wider German evangelical community)—for example, censorship of press, theatre and film in relation to sexual content, arrest of prostitutes, attacks on make-up and French fashions, and on homosexuality.[84] The 'purification' agenda, which such measures seemed to represent, did not strike British Free Church onlookers as notably objectionable. Even so, the strains within the 'Baptist family' were considerable. British Baptists of different generations with strong German connections, such as

---

[81] Andrew Chandler's 'Introduction' to *Brethren in Adversity* presents an account of the controversy.

[82] Keith Clements, *Bonhoeffer and Britain* (London, 2006).

[83] Keith Clements, 'A Question of Freedom? British Baptists and the German Church Struggle', in Clements, ed., *Baptists in the Twentieth Century* (London, 1982), 96–113.

[84] Nicholas M. Railton, 'German Free Churches and the Nazi Regime', *Journal of Ecclesiastical History* 49/1 (January, 1998), 104. Railton's article is illuminating on their general position.

J.H. Rushbrooke and E.A. Payne, tried to steer a path between criticism of and solidarity with German Baptists.[85]

Perhaps what was happening was more than the normal boundary disputes between 'state' and 'church'. Questions were being asked about the very nature of 'religion'. It seemed that Europe, and Germany in particular, was witnessing a 'politics' that was 'religious' (but not ecclesiastically religious). It seemed appropriate to some writers to speak of 'the Hitler cult'.[86] Otto Piper, leaving Germany, argued in Manchester that his country was experiencing a religious revival separate from and contrasting with Christianity. National Socialism was an enormous whirlpool. In the opinion of the 'masses' it was considered 'as the most perfect religion, because it comprised all the special religious tendencies'.[87] The appropriateness of the term 'political' or 'secular' religion has indeed been an abiding topic of debate. An American Methodist bishop in 1938 considered Hitlerism not only a religion but also an organized (and therefore rival) church.[88] Bishop Bell, visiting Berlin in 1937, was invited to believe that Hitler's religion combined mystical symbolism and the Enlightenment. That appealed to those many Germans who 'were seeking Christianity without the Church'.[89] F.A. Voigt, both of whose parents had been born in Germany, for long a *Manchester Guardian* journalist in France and Germany, published *Unto Caesar* in April 1938—a powerful and influential analysis of the European situation. He had become deeply disillusioned with the German left which had once engaged his sympathies. It seemed that only Christianity could resist this new 'totalitarianism' and, rather to his surprise, he gradually came to accept its value.

British diplomats at the time could not resist religious analogies. Sir Horace Rumbold had written privately from Berlin in 1932 describing Hitler as 'a Revivalist preacher' even if one with the appearance of a greengrocer who happened to be sporting an Air Force moustache. Likewise, to Frank Ashton-Gwatkin in 1934, Hitler's methods, 'were those of a

---

[85] Rushbrooke, with a German wife and fluent German, translated for Barth in London in 1937. Payne was a student in Marburg and listened to Bultmann's lectures in 1928. For the Berlin Congress see E.A. Payne, *John Henry Rushbrooke, 1870–1947: A Baptist Greatheart* (London, 1954), 56–8 and W.M.S. West, *To Be a Pilgrim: A Memoir of Ernest A. Payne* (Guildford, 1983), 48–9.

[86] Wyndham Lewis, who had earlier written a study of Hitler (1931), used this term in the title of his 1939 book.

[87] O.Piper, *Recent Developments in German Protestantism* (London, 1934), 157.

[88] Cited in Gerhard Besier, *Das Europa der Diktaturen: Eine neue Geschichte des 20. Jahrhunderts* (Munich, 2006), 673–4 in the context of his discussion of 'political religion'. The following selection of titles, from many, can also be mentioned: Michael Burleigh, 'National Socialism as a Political Religion', *Totalitarian Movements and Political Religions* 1 (2000), 1–26 and his book *Sacred Causes* (London, 2006); Michael Ley and Julius H. Schoeps, eds., *Der Nationalsozialismus als politische Religion* (Bodenheim, 1997).

[89] The opinion is that of Professor Seeberg. Chandler, *Brethren in Adversity*, 130.

revivalist preacher'. The very antithesis of an aristocrat, the Führer epitomized 'the little fellow' whose era had apparently dawned. The emotion
which greeted his speeches, however, was thought to well up from an
audience yearning to be born again. The ejaculated 'Heils' were unquestionably impressive—evidently 'like the Allelujahs which greet Mrs Aimée
Macpherson and her like'.[90] Hitler, it seemed, might almost be a certain
kind of Methodist local preacher. It did not appear inappropriate, to some,
to see a German national 'salvation'—the concept was not thought
far-fetched—emerging from the slough of despair. In their liturgical chore-
ography, the parades and rallies of National Socialism appealed to millions of
Germans for whom neither the arcane academic debates of university
theology nor the fusty formality of fossilized church structures had any
appeal. 'Little fellows' did not have much of a role in either of these
contexts. It was perhaps no surprise, therefore, that patriotic pastors, in
large numbers, saw no reason to challenge the regime fundamentally. Some,
like Martin Niemöller, later to be identified as a Christian hero, if one with
'limitations', had in fact earlier voted National Socialist.[91] His trial in 1938, it
was said, had made the British more aware of continental Christianity than
at any time since the early days of the Reformation.[92] However, Barth
wrote to Bell in 1939 pointing out Niemoller had never ceased to be 'a
fervent German nationalist'.[93]

Interpretations were indeed varied. Readers of *Theology* in England in
1933, for example, had been presented by a young Englishman, who had
been in Germany, with a picture of a revitalized and excited people. It
would be premature, the writer suggested, to criticize churches that were
simply going with the flow. A church which cut itself off from its community would atrophy.[94] Others considered that 'German Christians' were no
doubt going too far but, in the existing crisis, it was laudable, in conditions
of national revival, to want to be both 'German' and 'Christian'.[95] The

[90] The views of the diplomats are cited in M. Gilbert, ed., *Britain and Germany between the Wars*
(London, 1964), 97–8.

[91] Keith Robbins, 'Martin Niemöller, the German Church Struggle and English Opinion',
Journal of Ecclesiastical History 12 (1970), 149–70, republished in Robbins, *History, Religion and
Identity*, 161–82. Niemöller's autobiographical *From U-Boat to Pulpit* appeared in English in 1936.
James Bentley, *Martin Niemöller: 1892–1984* (New York, 1984).

[92] Nathaniel Micklem, *The Box and the Puppets* (London, 1957), 109.

[93] Chandler, *Brethren in Adversity*, 256. A yearning for a reconciliation of church and nation was
not, of course, confined to Protestants. Karl Adam, the Tübingen Catholic theologian, wanted
Catholics to be 'Catholic to the last fibre of our hearts' but also 'German to our very marrow'.
Robert A. Krieg, *Catholic Theologians in Nazi Germany* (London and New York, 2004), 102.

[94] Richard Gutteridge, 'German Protestantism and the Hitler Regime', *Theology* 36/12 (1933),
243–64.

[95] Doris Bergen, *The Twisted Cross: The German Christian Movement in the Third Reich* (Chapel
Hill, NC, 1996).

'German Christian camp' looked a capacious one. English modernists, some supposed, would not have found themselves too uncomfortable with some of the presuppositions held by leading German Christians, for example in relation to the continuing utility of the Old Testament. What seemed important to the bishop of Gloucester, after a further visit to Germany, was that Hitler should learn to respect Christianity. He would not do that 'if Christianity is used to oppose National Socialism, and if scatterbrained English divines flirt with Bolshevism'.[96]

In short, the issues posed by 'Germany' seemed so multi-layered that even that minority in the churches which did interest itself in 'foreign affairs' did not see clearly what could or should be done. English Christians, clerical and lay, it has been concluded, 'maintained prior to 1939 a most unjudgemental respect for their political neighbour, while they looked decently the other way from their true neighbour in his desperate need'.[97] Hensley Henson certainly took issue with those who thought that Germany should be left to take her own course without outside interference. States and nations could not live in isolation. Their membership of what he liked to call 'the comity of civilised peoples' imposed on them certain obligations which could not be repudiated. In his view, the solidarity of modern civilization was jeopardized by the persecuting policy of Germany. The nations, and by implication, the churches, were confronted by no small issue.[98] This was fine rhetoric but, as one looked at Europe, 'modern civilization' did not seem to evoke much sense of solidarity anywhere. Henson himself had shocked the House of Lords by the vehemence with which he had denounced the 'betrayal' of Abyssinia. Lord Halifax thought it was unbecoming in a bishop to distrust the word of dictators. But was not European civilization, with few exceptions, now in the hands of dictators of one kind or another?

British experts in the matter of religion, such as Bertrand Russell and Maynard Keynes, had already concluded in the 1920s that Bolshevism constituted a new 'political religion'. It could easily be concluded, from a church perspective, that Soviet Communism constituted a graver threat to Christianity than National Socialism. There appeared still to be some elements of Christianity, no doubt distorted and unacceptably intermingled, in the latter. Marxism–Leninism appeared, on the other hand, to offer no ideological space for religion. 'National Socialism', whatever it was, at least seemed to be an offering restricted to Germans. 'Fascism', of which it might be a particular manifestation, appeared to flourish by emphasizing the

---

[96] Chandler, *Brethren in Adversity*, 152.
[97] Hastings, *History of English Christianity*, 345.
[98] *Yellow Spot*, 8.

attributes of particular peoples. 'International Fascism' might therefore be something of a contradiction in terms. Communism, in principle, was as indifferent to nationality as Christianity was supposed to be. Its establishment in an entity called 'the Union of Soviet Socialist Republics', devoid of national name, was a harbinger. Communism (or 'socialism') might for the moment perforce display some Russian features, but they would only be temporary.

The 'defence' that National Socialism offered against communism was a powerful element in its appeal for Christian circles in Germany, both Protestant and Catholic. It was this aspect above all which blunted criticism and, in the future, in fighting in the East, was to ease Christian consciences. German visitors to England thought that churchmen would understand. Adolf Deissmann had taken a prominent part in orchestrating, with Bell, the exploratory gatherings of English and German theologians which had taken place in the Wartburg, Eisenach, and in Canterbury and Chichester between 1927 and 1931. These meetings—on the English side they included both Anglicans and Free Churchmen—had gone some way to overcoming wartime animosities. It was claimed that the differences which emerged were individual rather than national in discussing 'The Kingdom of God' and 'The Presence of Jesus Christ in the Word and the Sacraments'.[99] In May 1933, meeting W.R. Inge in London, Deissmann told him that Hitler had saved Germany from the imminent danger of a Bolshevik revolution. Inge did not believe it, but thought it very significant that such an intelligent man should have held this view. Since Inge's dislike of any kind of socialism was no secret, his dismissal of the suggestion is also very significant.

The Soviet Union was very far away but Bertrand Russell, George Bernard Shaw and, most recently, Sidney and Beatrice Webb, had been to see it for themselves. The latter pair, on their return in 1932, published *Soviet Communism: A New Civilisation?* a few years later. A subsequent edition removed the question mark. Losing the faith which he had hitherto placed in Social Credit as expounded by Major Douglas, and disappointed by what he had found in Alberta, the dean of Canterbury disappeared mysteriously to the Soviet Union for three months in 1937. He came back with the conviction that the Soviet Union was well on the way to becoming the perfect society. Since, 'in the main' the Communists were right, he would henceforth speak out on their behalf. It was a great advantage that a local Workers Educational Association lecturer, fully equipped with voluminous data on Soviet progress, was to hand in order

---

[99] R.C.D. Jasper, *George Bell, Bishop of Chichester* (London, 1967), 65–8. G.K.A. Bell and A. Deissmann, *Mysterium Christi: Christological Studies by British and German Theologians* (London, 1930) referred in their introduction to 'a strong and growing feeling of friendship'.

to draft the dean's writings for him. Enthusiasm for the Soviet Union was not only something which attracted publicity-seeking former engineers in their mid-sixties. It appealed to bright young men, whether or not this led to formal membership of the Communist Party of Great Britain. It had a particular attraction for those emerging, like A.J.P. Taylor and Michael Foot, from a Quaker schooling or, like Christopher Hill, from a Methodist home. It made a spy of Donald Maclean, diplomat son of the Liberal MP and prominent English Presbyterian, Sir John Maclean. In the beginning, these men supposed, Christianity probably had a simple message about equality, but it had been obscured by ecclesiastical encrustations. It would now be possible, however, to step directly into an egalitarian future and dispense, en route, with Christianity's meaningless and tiresome accompanying mumbo-jumbo. In March 1939 the dean published a tract urging Britain to make common cause with the Soviet Union in the struggle between Fascism and Socialism. It was frequently reprinted over subsequent months. In August 1939 the Nazi–Soviet Pact was signed. Johnson pressed on regardless with the composition of his *The Socialist Sixth of the World*.

It would, of course, be wrong to see Johnson as a 'representative' figure. Even if he had had the capacity, his penchant for extensive foreign travel precluded the organization of an effective Communist phalanx within the Church of England. There was, however, a current, if not a tide, which seemed to be propelling 'Christian Socialism' forward. Charles Raven introduced a volume on *Christianity and Social Revolution* by revealing that contemporaries were living in an epoch of revolution. They had discovered the necessity for the unifying power of an ideal. The two claimants for attention were Christ's way of life as 'interpreted by the forward-looking thought of His modern-followers' and the social revolution of Russia. The conflict for the dominance of the future would appear to lie between these two loyalties—but Raven did not want to see a clear-cut antithesis.[100] A variety of contributors, Christian and Communist, British and Russian, were enrolled to explore the theme. In trying to move towards a synthesis, the philosopher John Macmurray did not think it proven that there was any practical incongruity or any logical inconsistency between being at once a convinced Communist and a sincere Christian.[101] Cambridge Christian undergraduates, many of whom were strangers as yet to the 'working

---

[100] John Lewis, Karl Polanyi and Donald K. Kitchin, eds., *Christianity and the Social Revolution* (London, 1935), 17.

[101] Lewis, Polanyi and Kitchin, *Christianity and the Social Revolution*, 506. Macmurray, who held the Grote Chair at University College London at this time, was an influential philosopher in these circles. Only at the end of his tenure of the Chair of Philosophy at Edinburgh in 1958, however, when he became a Quaker, did he have any formal connection with institutional Christianity. D. Fergusson and N. Dower, eds., *John Macmurray: Critical Perspectives* (Edinburgh, 2002).

class', travelled out to listen to Conrad Noel at Thaxted and were thrilled. One of them, Mervyn Stockwood, nurtured in a 'minor public school', was propelled further along the path towards ordination.

At another level, Sir Stafford Cripps, KC and chemist, treading a perilous path within the politics of the Labour Party, combined Christian conviction with a desire to achieve a 'Socialist Commonwealth' in Britain 'within a world-wide system of Socialism'. He had a well-developed capacity for seeing fascism everywhere, but denied that he wished to be a socialist (and Christian) dictator. There were those, however, who thought his scorn for the muddle that was English democracy had much in common with the stance of his fellow Wykehamist, Sir Oswald Mosley, now a Fascist. The forced industrialization of Russia seemed to Cripps one of the greatest marvels of the world. Speculation about what Sir Stafford was 'up to' was endemic, but what was certain was that he had no fear of the 'godless civilization' of the East.[102] Cripps and Stockwood, a decade later, found themselves at one in bringing their message to the godless of East Bristol.

The Christian worlds of the bishop of Durham and Stafford Cripps did not intersect. Henson felt no call, in his retirement, to join the snappily named Council of Clergy and Ministers for Common Ownership when it was formed early in the forthcoming war. However, in delivering Gifford Lectures in St Andrews in 1935/6 on *Christian Morality*, he had not ignored the challenge which 'Soviet civilization' presented.[103] Reflecting on 'the Russian Mystery', and reading the Webbs's book, he found most unpleasant its 'almost complete absence of moral feeling'. The authors suggested that Soviet Russia had found a solution to all the old obstinate problems which had darkened western civilization for centuries. It was, he thought, an amazing picture but he had grave reservations about it. The cost of the great experiment had been excessive. It had implied a treatment of human nature so violent as to be ultimately intolerable. Further, it was premature to reach a 'progressive' verdict on a scheme of government which had not been adequately tested. The statistics were more impressive than convincing. All told, he doubted whether the system would survive and foresaw failure 'in the not very distant future'. He conceded that religion was apparently fading out of Russian life but did not think Christianity in Russia would be extirpated. He suspected that in fact, external appearances to the contrary, pre-revolutionary Christianity was 'the salt which had lost its savour'.[104]

---

[102] Keith Robbins, 'Stafford Cripps' in Kevin Jefferys, ed., *Labour Forces: From Ernest Bevin to Gordon Brown* (London, 2002), 63–79.

[103] Dr Norman errs, in his discussion of Henson's opinions in *Church and Society in England*, 326–8, in supposing that Gifford Lectures are given in Oxford.

[104] H. Hensley Henson, *Christian Morality: Natural, Developing, Final* (Oxford, 1936), 318–34.

iii. Protestants and Catholics: Being International

It was time, however, to ask whether civilized morality could survive the abolition of Christianity. It seemed to Henson that Christianity and civilization, which had grown together in Europe, must share a common ruin. Whether or not that was true, there was a growing sense, amongst office-holders in the non-Roman churches, that it was no longer possible, and certainly not desirable, to be thinking of insular church life as a self-contained and discrete entity. It was necessary to draw a clearer distinction, as J.H. Oldham put it, 'between the Church of Christ and what we have been accustomed to speak of as Christian civilization'.[105] But if such a distinction could and should be drawn, how was this 'Church of Christ' to be identified and manifest itself? The way forward had seemed to be to tackle both 'Life and Work' and 'Faith and Order' across national boundaries. British Christians, clerical and lay, committed themselves and, more dubiously, in so far as they were able, the churches to which they belonged, to this precarious enterprise and set about developing the necessary personal networks still further.

The bishop of Chichester pressed on with calling Christendom to realize, through Life and Work, the visible unity for which Christ had prayed. British speakers at the 1925 Stockholm conference—Anglican and Free Church—took a very prominent part in its proceedings.[106] Theodore Woods, now bishop of Winchester, a guest of the crown prince of Sweden, preached the opening sermon.[107] Until his death in 1932, Woods played a major part in the work of the continuation committee—which turned into the Universal Christian Council. The Anglican archbishop of Dublin felt that Christians were an integral part of the 'materialized and mechanized world'.[108] The more they were united the more they would work with growing authority from within it. Bell, president of the British section of the Universal Christian Council, chaired its administrative committee. He produced the English version of its proceedings. Speaking as chairman at the council meeting at Fanö in Denmark in August 1934, he stated that

---

[105] Keith Clements, *Faith on the Frontier: A Life of J.H. Oldham* (Edinburgh, 1999), 140.

[106] British speakers at what was billed as the biggest ecumenical Christian conference since the Council of Nicaea included Dr Alfred Garvie, the dean of Worcester, Sir William Ashley, Miss Constance Smith, Revd Will Reason, Mrs George Cadbury, Sir Henry Lunn, Lord Salvesen, Revd Henry Carter, the bishop of Lichfield, Lord Parmoor, Sir Willoughby Dickinson, Revd Harold Buxton, Dr Carnegie Simpson, Mr E.F. Wise, and the bishop of Plymouth. The Stockholm conference brought British, French and German leaders together for the first time, on any scale, since the end of the war. The details can be found in *The Universal Christian Council for Life and Work (Stockholm): Membership and Directory of Addresses*.

[107] Edward S. Woods and Frederick B. MacNett, *Theodore, Bishop of Winchester: Pastor, Prophet, Pilgrim* (London, 1933), 287–92.

[108] G.K.A. Bell, ed., *The Stockholm Conference on Life and Work 1925* (Oxford, 1926), 107.

what had been a dream in 1925 had become a vital necessity. The budget constraints were severe but progress in making contacts between churches and between nations was impressive. The British delegation, which included the unlikely figure of young Mr R.H.S. Crossman, was the largest present. Bell reported to the archbishop of Canterbury that there had been all sorts of scares and possibilities of explosion as the delegates skirted round the question of how to handle the German situation. Eirenic endeavours could not altogether disguise the rifts that were present. The Council did agree that the relation between church, state and community was becoming *the* issue in country after country. The debate between the Christian faith and 'the secular tendencies of our time' constituted a struggle in which 'the very existence of the Christian Church is at stake'.[109] The main lines of a major conference on this topic to be held in Oxford in July 1937 were agreed in 1935.

The preparation of the programme was put in the able administrative hands of the Scotsman-in-England, Dr J.H. Oldham, whose backstage influence grew steadily.[110] He set out the agenda in a preparatory publication. An opportunity presented itself 'to bear an effective Christian witness to the world as a whole at a critical moment in history when mankind stands at the parting of the ways'. The best minds available were to probe how the church should relate to the communal life with which its own life was 'inseparably intertwined'.[111] Oldham was firm that Christian faith could make an impact only through the multitudes of lay men and women conducting 'the ordinary affairs of life'. It was not proposed that any large part of the time of the conference should be devoted to theological discussion, but so far as possible the theological issues were to be elucidated by the publication of pertinent volumes in advance. Various draft reports to provide a basis for discussion had been circulated in advance.

It was not only this 'world conference' meeting in Oxford which signified the centrality of the British churches in the consideration of these weighty matters. The conference 'list of delegates' records their presence in strength. There was a substantial bloc of Church of England official delegates, together with one each from the Scottish Episcopal Church and the Church in Wales. The bishop of Down represented the Church of Ireland—there was no attendance at all from the Irish Free State. Presbyterians from England, Ireland, Scotland and Wales were there, together with

---

[109] *Minutes of the Meeting of the Council: Fanö August 24th–30th, 1934*; Jasper, *Bell*, 118.

[110] See the chapter 'Oxford 1937' in Clements, *Faith on the Frontier*, 307–31. Graeme Smith, *Oxford 1937: The Universal Christian Council for Life and Work Conference* (Frankfurt am Main and New York, 2006) is the most comprehensive analysis of the conference. Oldham's deafness was one reason why he was not much of a stage performer.

[111] J.H. Oldham, *Church, Community and State* (London, 1935), 20, 27, 45.

English and Welsh Baptists and English and Welsh Congregationalists. Quakers, Unitarians and the Salvation Army brought up the 'tail'.

Almost without exception, over the preceding years, the churches in Britain had all been giving much attention to cognate issues. It had proved necessary, for example, for the Church Congress, meeting in Bournemouth in October 1935 to discuss 'Church and State', to engage the Pavilion Ball Room for an overflow meeting.[112] Overflow meetings had not latterly been characteristic of the Church Congress. British prominence is further illustrated by the fact that there were more British contributors to the nine published volumes of the Oxford conference than were drawn from any other nationality. 'Nothing stood out more clearly' for those present than 'the recognition that the Church in its essential nature is a universal society'. That inevitably placed it 'in the front of the battle where there is an attempt to make the nation or race the ultimate authority over human life'.[113] The absence, however, of the German Evangelical Church delegation and the complicating presence of a German Methodist and a German Baptist pointed to the practical difficulties ahead. The concluding 'Message to the Christian Churches' was published as a pamphlet for wide distribution.

The following month, a decade after the Lausanne meeting, the second world conference on 'Faith and Order' met in Edinburgh. Its character was manifestly less 'political'. Its concluding report reiterated that 'the divisions of Christendom in every land are such as to hamper the manifestation of the unity of Christ's body'. It recommended educational and other steps to promote mutual understanding and co-operation but it had to recognize that 'behind all particular statements of the problem of corporate union lie deeply divergent conceptions of the Church'.[114] There was strong, though not unanimous support for the view that the time had come to set in motion processes which could bring together the work of 'Life and Work' and 'Faith and Order'. A 'World Council of Churches' was to be 'in process of formation'.

The two meetings in England and Scotland in 1937 therefore constituted, in their different ways, crucial stages towards the creation of some kind of universal body, perhaps a 'World Council of Churches'. How such a body might function and be financed and structured lay in the future. The role of English and Scottish Christians (there appears to be little Irish or Welsh input), both clerical and lay, was vital in this evolution, most of them being linked in some way with the Student Christian Movement whose publications furthered the cause. J.H. Oldham stressed that the conference was no

---

[112] The proceedings are to be found in Maxwell S. Leigh, ed., *Christianity in the Modern State* (London, 1936).

[113] *The Churches Survey their Task* (Oxford, 1937).

[114] *Report of the Second World Conference on Faith and Order, Edinburgh, August 3–18, 1937*, 35.

more than an incident in this continuing process. It had to be admitted too that it took place without the official participation of the Roman Catholic Church, though some individual Catholic thinkers had given 'unofficial help'. That absence, in itself, indicated that 'the fight against Modern Paganism' had not produced a Christian 'Common Front'. The only basis, it seemed, on which full global Christian unity could be achieved would be if Protestants and Orthodox submitted to Rome. British writers, observing what they thought was happening to the British Empire, sometimes thought that the future Christian church might be 'federal', but at best that looked a remote possibility. Lord Lothian, a man much obsessed by federalism, even wrote in the wake of the Oxford Conference to a German participant that when Christianity reached the point when it was able to bring the Kingdom of Heaven upon earth it would 'establish a world federation of some kind as the necessary institutional condition by which alone the Kingdom can be maintained in being'.[115] Such a thought had presumably not altogether disappeared from his mind by the time he reached Washington in August 1939 as the new British Ambassador to the United States. He was the first Christian Scientist to hold the post.

These developments were impressive so far as they went, though how a 'Protestant International' might be made a reality remained uncertain. The contrast with the existence of a 'Catholic International' visible in the independent state of the Vatican was strong. Pope Pius XI had been wholly negative towards 'Pan-Protestantism'. After the Lausanne Faith and Order Conference, he had issued an encyclical *Mortalium Animos* in January 1928 which stated that the Apostolic See could not take part in such assemblies, nor was it in any way lawful for Catholics to give such enterprises their encouragement or support. If they did so, they would be giving countenance to a false Christianity. That was clear enough. If there was ever again to be 'the church' it could only come about when false bodies which purported to be churches 'saw the light' and became reunited to the Visible Head of the church. Such guidance, indeed instruction, left the Roman Catholic Church in England and Wales, Scotland and Ireland with little room for manoeuvre in relation to these false bodies, not that such room was ardently sought. The Roman Catholic archbishop of Edinburgh sent a message of greeting to the 1937 Faith and Order conference in Edinburgh but there was no sign of any engagement of minds.

International political developments impacted significantly differently, in two respects. First, while German developments were no less of interest for British Catholics than for British Protestants, what was happening in 'Catholic' Italy and 'Catholic' Spain touched them much more intimately, for

---

[115] J.R.M. Butler, *Lord Lothian* (London, 1960), 100.

obvious reasons. Indeed, such 'Roman Catholic solidarity' as existed could, in these circumstances, seem to some to preclude rather than to create a 'Christian front'. Sidney Dark, editor of the *Church Times*, fervent philo-Semite and socialist, later wrote with pride on how, through the newspaper, he had 'successfully scotched' attempts to create a 'United Christian Front' in Britain in favour of General Franco. He spoke of having prevented the Church of England succumbing to Franco's allure.[116] Secondly, the two states of the British Isles could not forget their recent differences. It was very apparent that Dublin and London (and, subordinately, Belfast) were not likely to forge a 'United Front'. The reality remained, however, that notwithstanding three separate hierarchies and two (or two and a half) political jurisdictions, the Roman Catholic Church, in its membership, straddled these divisions and remained fully enmeshed in the awkward national ambivalences and antagonisms of the British Isles.

There had, however, been a change at the top of the Roman Catholic Church in England and Wales. Cardinal Bourne had died on New Year's Day, 1935. He was replaced by a 69-year-old Yorkshireman, Arthur Hinsley, a village carpenter's son, whose post-war career had been entirely outside England—in Rome and Africa. Although no deviation from the papal encyclical could be expected, there were some occasional gestures which appeared to indicate that Catholic/Protestant differences might be discussed in a more eirenic spirit. Hinsley was willing to provide a letter which Micklem, the principal of Mansfield College, Oxford, could take to Cardinal Faulhaber of Munich. Micklem was investigating the Roman Catholic Church in Germany on behalf of the Royal Institute of International Affairs. The letter opened many doors. It was an unusual mission for an English Congregationalist.[117] When the archbishop of Canterbury courteously sent Hinsley a message of welcome it was to a complete stranger. No one 'who mattered' knew Hinsley. That, however, was not only a comment which reflected Anglican–Roman Catholic mutual ignorance 'at the top'. It could also have been uttered by Catholics, particularly titled ones, who did not quite know what to expect, and did not want their proprietorial role in matters political unduly disturbed.

---

[116] Sidney Dark, *The Church Impotent and Triumphant* (London, 1941), 6, 22. In his autobiography, *Not Such A Bad Life* (London, 1941), Dark expressed the view that the Roman Catholic alliance with Franco had made a reunion of the churches both impossible and intolerable. Dark brought to his analysis past experience gained as a professional singer, gossip columnist on the *Daily Mail* and special correspondent at the Paris Peace Conference. He edited the *Church Times*, not altogether in agreement with its proprietor, from 1924 to 1941. Bernard Palmer, *Gadfly for God: A History of the* Church Times (London, 1991).

[117] Micklem, *Box and Puppets*, 110–13. His report, *National Socialism and the Roman Catholic Church*, was published in 1939.

The Foreign Office was advised by the British minister at the Holy See that the pope had wanted someone in London who was 'as English and as "Roman" as possible'. Other conceivable candidates, the minister speculated, were probably deemed to have had inadequate experience, to display insufficient culture or to be in indifferent health—or to be 'men of Irish origin'. Perhaps the Vatican, as the Irish Free State and Britain moved further apart, wanted an Englishman. The British minister, however, in making these observations, may not have known that Hinsley's mother had been a Bridget Riley. Kilkenny-born, but Liverpool-raised, Richard Downey, archbishop of Liverpool since 1928 and, at the time of his appointment, the youngest Catholic archbishop in the world, might have been thought likely to come to the capital. At 5′4″, but 18 stone, Downey made his presence felt in many places. It proved necessary, subsequently, for Westminster to assert its precedence over the three other provincial archbishops of England and Wales (Liverpool, Birmingham and Cardiff). The Catholics of Liverpool might have been mollified by the appointment, after much diplomatic exchange, of Liverpool-born William Godfrey as the first Apostolic Delegate to the United Kingdom when he arrived in London in February 1939. If so, they were almost alone. The hierarchy, and Hinsley particularly, had opposed the idea of a delegate, but to no avail. The archbishop thought that the coming of 'an extraordinary representative of the Pope to England' at this particular juncture would be dangerous to the cause of the church in this country. Even an Englishman delegate would be looked upon, in some quarters at least, as an agent of Mussolini. Hinsley was to prove determined to ensure that the Catholic centre of gravity in England and Wales should be Westminster rather than Wimbledon (where the Apostolic Delegation was established). There was also the fact that the Apostolic Delegate was to 'Great Britain' and thus, in ways yet to be discovered, overriding the England and Wales/Scotland hierarchies. The Vatican was not moved by these objections. The bishops had gingerly to come to terms with this new presence—as did the Foreign Office. If nothing else, the diplomatic susceptibilities all round which this episode provoked were a reminder that both the relationship of the hierarchies and the Vatican to the United Kingdom, at one level, and the 'domestic' relationship between the Roman Catholic Church and other churches, at another level, both nationally and locally, remained subject to particular constraints and suspicions.

In Liverpool, the unabashed triumphalism of Downey, unsurprisingly, did not commend itself to the Protestant Truth Society. And, while it has been claimed that Archbishop Downey 'contributed much to the easing of sectarian tension on Merseyside', his relations with the Anglican bishop,

David, were frigid over the sixteen years in which they overlapped in office.[118] Downey did succeed, by energetic dieting, in reducing his weight by approximately half, but even his reduced form made a social statement. Diminutive he might be, but he was determined to cut the Anglicans down to size (and, his will, in the early 1950s, when both men died, revealed an estate which was more than ten times that of the Anglican). With the aid of Sir Edwin Lutyens, and the financial assistance of a 'Catholic Emancipation Fund', he would build a bigger and better cathedral than they were con-structing. Indeed, it would be likely to put St Peter's in the shade. Despite the expressed view of a local councillor that he would prefer 'a poison germ factory' on the site, construction began—though in the event only the crypt of the original scheme was completed (in which Downey was in due time buried). No one supposed that the scheme was an expression of ecumenical goodwill.[119]

The Anglican bishop, by contrast, was not a local Irish boy made good. He had a First in Classical Moderations and Greats from Oxford and had been headmaster both of Clifton and Rugby and been translated from St Edmundsbury to Liverpool in 1923. His *Life and the Public School* (1932) showed that Liverpool had not entirely blotted out his previous career. He and the archbishop of York had been to the same Oxford college, though this did not prevent Temple's reprimand when David upheld the invitation which had been given to Dr L.P. Jacks, the Unitarian, to preach at a 'special service' in the Anglican cathedral in 1933. The 'worlds' of two bishops in one city could not be further apart and, while arguably it was only in Liverpool that their numbers put Catholics in a position to 'challenge' Anglicans, thus giving the city a distinctive flavour, the contest for 'pre-eminence' was never far away anywhere.[120] It was a reminder, if one were needed, that the 'Universal Christians' on display at Oxford in 1937, as they well knew, did not 'comprehend' the diversity of the world's Christianity, or even that part of it present in the British Isles.

The sophisticated Catholic interpretation of the European crisis did not come, however, from the insights developed by Hinsley and Godfrey from their respective rectorships of the English College in Rome. Indeed, it has been argued that college life manifested a very English sort of

---

[118] Moloney claims this in *Westminster, Whitehall and the Vatican*, 18. Much of the material in this paragraph derives from his book.

[119] For his own words see Richard Downey, *Public and Platform Addresses* (London, 1933) and *Rebuilding the Church in England* (London, 1933). J. Davies, ' "Rome on the Rates": Archbishop Richard Downey and the Catholic School Question, 1929–1939', *North West Catholic History* 18 (1991), 16–32.

[120] P.J. Waller, *Democracy and Sectarianism: A Political and Social History of Liverpool 1868–1939* (Liverpool, 1981).

existence—cricket against a British Embassy XI—contact with the City being strictly ecclesiastical and even this being restricted and supervised.[121] The most prolific interpreter of the 'Crisis in the West' was Christopher Dawson, son of a Yorkshire landowner rather than carpenter. He was, in Dean Inge's description, a 'brilliant philosophic historian', disposed to write in a manner which did not commend him to prevailing academic historical opinion.[122] A stream of books flowed from his pen, all, in one way or another, emphasizing that the church was no sect or human organization but a new creation. Christianity was in no way bound up with the 'individualist' culture that he thought to be 'passing away'.[123] He had agreed, alongside C.H. Dodd, Paul Tillich and others, to speak at the 1937 Oxford Conference on the subject of the Kingdom of God and history. As a former Anglican, he emphasized that the Catholic faith in the church was faith in a 'real historic society' not in an invisible communion of saints or spiritual union of Christians. He foresaw that the Kingdom of God would come 'not by the elimination of conflict but through an increasing opposition and tension between the Church and the world'.[124] By 1939, he had identified, even in England, a totalitarian trend which could not be reconciled with its traditions of liberty and individuality. It was only in the intelligentsia that a degree of cultural independence remained. He was pretty certain that liberal optimism, which he deemed so characteristic of 'Anglo-Saxon' religious thought over the previous half-century, was dead.

iv. Church, Community and State: British/Irish Belonging

Reinhold Niebuhr, lanky German-American, had played his part in dispelling such optimism amongst his growing number of British readers, though personally he seemed surprisingly genial.[125] Part of his success in Britain had

---

[121] Michael E. Williams, *The Venerable English College Rome* (London, 1979), 157.

[122] Michael Bentley, *Modernizing England's Past: English Historiography in the Age of Modernism 1870–1970* (Cambridge, 2005), 56.

[123] Educated at Winchester and Trinity College, Oxford, Dawson edited a series, *Essays in Order*, in the early 1930s with T.F. Burns designed to bring such European writers as Jacques Maritain, Carl Schmitt and Nicholas Berdyaev before an English readership. His own contribution was *Christianity and the New Order* (London, 1931). His writing included *Progress and Religion* (London, 1929), *The Making of Europe* (London, 1932), *Enquiries into Religion and Culture* (London, 1933), *Religion and the Modern State* (London, 1935). See also Christina Scott, *A Historian and his World: A Life of Christopher Dawson* (London, 1984) and G. Caldecot and J.S. Morrill, eds., *Eternity in Time: Christopher Dawson and the Catholic Idea of History* (Edinburgh, 1997); Tom Burns, *The Use of Memory: Publishing and Further Pursuits* (London, 1993).

[124] *Church, Community and State*, vol. iii: *The Kingdom of God and History* (London, 1938), 214–16.

[125] Niebuhr had visited Britain and Europe in 1923–4. The books alluded to are *Does Civilization Need Religion?* (1927), *Leaves from the Notebook of a Tamed Cynic* (1929), *Moral Man and Immoral Society* (1932), *Reflections on the End of an Era* (1934).

lain in the extent to which he saw himself as mediating between the 'Anglo-Saxon' and German worlds.[126] He was an 'insider-outsider'. Trying to translate Paul Tillich into comprehensible American prose, however, made it evident to him what a problem being a 'go-between' was.[127] 'Belonging' was a complicated business. How, in the 1930s, could the Christian reconcile loyalties to church, community and state in a Britain and Ireland (or, to put it differently, a United Kingdom and an *Eire)* with such confused yet intermingled understandings of each of these words?

The taming of Niebuhr's cynicism had been completed by contact with his new wife's country. Niebuhr was clearly an Anglophile, and not only because he had lately married an English wife in Winchester Cathedral. The English were quite wonderful, though that they knew it was a touch annoying. Their empire was beginning to crumble, he thought, but it would probably outlast his lifetime.[128] For her part, in 1936, coming back home after three years, Ursula Niebuhr had been struck by the 'salt of the earth' to be found in an English country church. There they were, old clerics, old squires, old barristers, avuncular colonial administrators and tanned young empire-builders home on leave.[129] Her brother was a district commissioner in Nyasaland (Malawi). It was all curiously reassuring. It was obvious that 'Reinie' was the man to come over and speak at Oxford on 'The Christian Church in a Secular Age', but talking to nice people in Oxford it was rather difficult to believe that England was very secular. Bishop Barnes arranged a delightful lunch at what he called 'our ridiculous House of Lords', an institution the bishop wanted to abolish. The Niebuhrs returned to the United States on the *Queen Mary*. Travelling tourist class, they noted other Oxford participants, bishops and bureaucrats, travelling second or even first class. They virtuously attended to the text of the next book, *Beyond Tragedy*. In September 1939 Reinhold was in Edinburgh

---

[126] In writing his 'autobiography', the exiled Hans Ehrenberg confessed how difficult it was to understand what the English took Christianity to be. His whole life—he had been born a Jew—had been a struggle for truth. Life did not seem to go on in the same way in England. He wondered whether the quality of the country's Christianity might perhaps be infected by a scepticism, matured over centuries, about the possibility of finding truth. While deeply admiring the society he encountered, he began 'to fear for the future of your Christian religion'. Hans P. Ehrenberg, *Autobiography of a German Pastor* (London, 1943), 9; Holger Roggelin, *Franz Hildebrandt. Ein lutherischer Dissenter im Kirchenkampf und Exil* (Gottingen, 1999) records the career of another 'go-between' who puzzled over the meaning of 'church' in England, Scotland and Germany.

[127] Paul Tillich, *My Travel Diary 1936: Between Two Worlds* (London, 1970). Newly arrived in England, Tillich was much impressed by Lord Lothian's Blickling Hall, where he was whisked away for a theological conference and, 'religious socialist' or not, seemed much impressed by butlers and by early morning tea brought to his bedroom. Niebuhr, *Remembering Reinhold Niebuhr*, 93. Lothian had a Roman Catholic upbringing. His Oxford tutor, H.A.L. Fisher, put in print his abomination of all that Christian Science stood for.

[128] Niebuhr, *Remembering Reinhold Niebuhr*, 112. Niebuhr died in 1971.

[129] Ibid., 100.

giving the Gifford Lectures. German bombers aiming at the Forth Bridge provided an apocalyptic background to his thoughts on 'The Nature and Destiny of Man'.

Amidst all the chatter at an Oxford conference tea party, one quiet former American sat by himself. He was T.S. Eliot. It was explained that he *was* rather quiet. Nearly two years later, in March 1939, Eliot was delivering his thoughts on 'The Idea of a Christian Society' in Corpus Christi, Cambridge. E.C. Hoskyns, who had preached so often in its chapel, was dead. It seems that he was worn-out prematurely by wrestling with intractable words. Eliot too wrestled with terms which he considered unsatisfactory—'freedom' and 'democracy' among them. We were living, he thought, in a kind of doldrums between opposing winds of doctrine. Britain was not a Christian society in contrast to that of Germany or Russia. Such a term simply meant that there was in Britain no penalty for the formal profession of Christianity. The Christian sociologists—and here he was referring to V.A. Demant, M.B. Reckitt and those associated in the 'Christendom' group—had pointed out the actual values of society and pointed the way to a real Christian society.[130] The complicated argument which Eliot then proceeded to develop was not supposed to be either an anti-communist or an anti-fascist manifesto. The Kingdom of God on earth would never be realized, but it was always being realized. He was adamant that unless the national church was a part of the universal church it could have no claim upon him. Nevertheless, he wanted a kind of 'establishment' to continue and, for him, only the Church of England could be 'the national church' he wanted.[131] Disestablishment would presuppose that the division between Christians and non-Christians in England was clear and could be reduced to statistics. Eliot believed that the great majority of people were 'neither one thing nor the other, but are living in a no man's land'.[132] 'Democracy', he felt, did not in itself have enough positive content. In the published version of the lectures Eliot stated that the possibility of war was always in his mind. The alignment of forces revealed in September 1939 'should bring more clearly to our consciousness the alternative of Christianity or paganism'.[133]

---

[130] Amongst Demant's writings at this time are, *God, Man and Society: An Introduction to Christian Sociology* (London, 1933), *Christian Polity* (London, 1935) and *The Religious Prospect* (London, 1939). Amongst Reckitt's are *Faith and Society* (London, 1932) and *Religion and Social Purpose* (London, 1935). See also his biography by J. Peart-Binns, *Maurice Reckitt: A Life* (Basingstoke, 1988), his autobiography *As It Happened* (London, 1941) and his Scott Holland Lectures *Maurice to Temple: A Century of the Social Movement in the Church of England* (London, 1947).

[131] T.S. Eliot, *The Idea of a Christian Society and Other Writings* (London, 1982). First published in 1939, this second edition has a helpful introduction by D.L. Edwards.

[132] Eliot, *Idea of a Christian Society*, 73.

[133] Ibid., 82.

Another poet, Wystan Auden, was found willing to tell readers what 'The Good Life' might be. His Oxford English degree, not a distinguished one, had been followed by ten months in Germany writing and reading widely in psychology. In *The Orators* (1932) he had castigated his country's spiritual and public torpor. He had little sympathy, however, with the notion that Jesus had promulgated a political theory. It would require the ingenuity of a Seventh-Day Adventist to believe that. His teaching was wholly concerned with the relation of the individual to God and his neighbour. Auden had no doubt that if communism triumphed in England the church would be persecuted. In such a circumstance, deprived as he saw it of all economic and social support, the Christian would have to see if what occurred in the first century could occur again in the twentieth. A truth was not tested until 'oppressed and illegal, it still shows irresistible signs of growth'.[134] The evidence did not seem to suggest, however, that the churches in the British Isles were anxious to put truth to the test in this manner. Nor was Auden, wheeling through Iceland, Spain and China in the years that followed, on hand to offer them further psychological counselling. Bishop Bell, something of a poet, showed the visiting Niebuhrs a copy of Auden and Isherwood's *Journey to a War*. It was not until 1940 that Auden became a practising Anglican.[135]

Prevailing church opinion, however, held that it was premature to prepare the path to the catacombs. The civilization that was present in the British Isles was still saturated with Christianity. The task, rather, was to nourish and sustain in the public sphere that pervasive if elusive and perhaps alarmingly evaporating presence. Percy Dearmer, indeed, believed in 1933 that a stronger religious spirit was now emerging 'from the confusions and disloyalties of the post-war decade'. There was no reason to despair. The crisis would be solved—'unless Christianity perishes'. What Christianity was, however, was 'a very large thing, larger perhaps than any of us can yet know'. It ultimately meant, for him at least, 'the religion of all good men'.[136] To this end he enrolled good men—Maude Royden was predictably the only 'good woman' available—who were drawn from the Church of England and the English Free Churches, leavened by a Welsh economist, whose task it was to outline 'the present chaos', to say what Christianity was and what solution it offered. Much illumination came from archbishops, bishops and universities. It was felt appropriate, however, to find space for 'the demands of the ordinary man'. The chosen spokesperson of the 'ordinary man' was a Companion of Honour and the recipient of an honorary

---

[134] Wystan Auden in Lewis, Polanyi and Kitchin, *Christianity and the Social Revolution*, 32, 50.
[135] Arthur Kirsch, *Auden and Christianity* (New Haven and London, 2005).
[136] Percy Dearmer, ed., *Christianity and the Crisis* (London, 1933), 10–12.

doctorate of laws. It was Albert Mansbridge, founder of the Workers' Education Association. Ghastly things had been done in the name of Christianity, Mansbridge thought, but there had been no higher or better force in the whole story of English life. The churches were still the most widespread institutions in the national life. The ordinary man did not think it the task of their clergy to solve economic and social problems. Their job, rather, was to strive, and induce their flocks to strive, 'for conformity with the spiritual in life, and to place diminishing reliance on material things'. He looked for sincerity and radiance.[137]

Hensley Henson was sincere but not altogether radiant in 1939 (stopping being a bishop had turned him into a 'nobody', he supposed). He had come to believe that the day of nationalism was over. Civilized mankind, he supposed, had outgrown the garments of its nationalist past. It followed that 'the epoch of national churches is closed'. Of all the national churches the Church of England had been the most magnificent and the most efficient, but it too was passing. Disestablishment would give but formal recognition to an accomplished fact. He could not tell what the future pattern of 'the Christian ideal of Catholicity' would be. 'Neither nationalism, nor totalitarian institutionalism [here he was thinking of the papal system], nor denominationalism can finally satisfy the human hunger for spiritual fellowship.'[138]

But was 'the past' really over? The dean of St Paul's went to Marburg in 1939, the university town where he had been a student in 1912, for the obsequies of Otto (discovering, on arrival, that Otto had apparently committed suicide). He found a church in which a meeting was being held as a protest against persecution. He supposed that it was against Nazi persecution, but then found that the target was the atheistic tyranny of Russian Communism and its victims. A substantial collection for the relief of Christian refugees was taken up. It was, he thought, all very puzzling. A German professor told him that if he really wanted to understand what was happening in Germany he should read about Elizabethan England and the only partially successful Elizabethan settlement.[139]

The archbishops of Canterbury and York had set up a commission to examine the relations between 'church and state' in 1930 under the chairmanship of Viscount Cecil of Chelwood, with York himself an inevitable

---

[137] Albert Mansbridge, 'The Demands of the Ordinary Man' in Dearmer, ed., *Christianity and the Crisis*, 40–9.

[138] H. Hensley Henson, *The Church of England* (Cambridge, 1939). T.S. Eliot gave Henson an alpha plus for his prose style but disagreed with his opinion. Garbett equally admired the prose but thought he would not want to be a member of the Church of England if it was only what Henson described, Charles Smyth, *Cyril Forster Garbett* (London, 1959), 412.

[139] Matthews, *Memories and Meanings*, 221.

member. It seems to have judiciously excluded opponents of the Revised Prayer Book or advocates of disestablishment. Its nine lay members, with two exceptions, all possessed titles. There was one woman, but, happily, she did have a title. One MP with a courtesy title was replaced in 1932 by another similarly blessed. Carlisle and Chichester represented the bishops.

It was inevitable that Temple should serve. Now in his early 50s, his energy and fecundity were formidable. No major Anglican or burgeoning ecumenical activity was without his presence, as speaker or chairman. Lectures, addresses, papers, talks and sermons streamed out—these very terms indicate the range and nature of his thinking and the type of audiences he addressed. He was always vulnerable, however, to the concern (or charge) that such a prodigal distribution could only mean that he was treading intellectual water.[140] All this, of course, was quite apart from the routine concerns of the northern province of the Church of England and of the diocese of York itself. He zoomed, in so far as it was then possible to zoom, from the Isle of Man to Chicago, from Paris to Cairo, to pluck only a few places in a peripatetic existence. He was always being asked to make statements on issues of the moment and rarely refrained. Many found his confident ebullience irresistible. Only in the Quantocks, on modest holidays, could he relax and do what a rounded Englishman in such circumstances ought to do, namely read aloud *Alice through the Looking-Glass* in a Somerset garden.

Ernest Barker, now Professor of Political Science at Cambridge, in presenting evidence to the commission, had a dim feeling 'at the back of his mind'. It was that it was very difficult for people to divorce utterly the different compartments in which they lived. Life flowed from one into the other. That was why no clear antinomy between church and state was ever possible.[141] Temple, with whom Barker had much dealing, illustrated the point perfectly. Temple was an established Englishman, although one engaged on damage limitation, but he also had a calling to prophecy.[142] Reconciling the two strained his substantial frame. August 1939 found him at Chatsworth, celebrating, on a magnificent scale, the coming-of-age of his

---

[140] Writing of this period included *Christian Faith and Life* (London, 1931), *Nature, Man and God* (London, 1934), *Christianity in Thought and Practice* (1936). Subsequent evaluations include J.F. Padgett's *The Christian Philosophy of William Temple* (The Hague, 1974); A.M. Suggate, *William Temple and Christian Social Ethics Today* (Edinburgh, 1987); S. Spencer, *William Temple: A Calling to Prophecy* (London, 2001).

[141] J. Stapleton, *Englishness and the Study of Politics: The Social and Political Thought of Ernest Barker* (Cambridge, 1994); E. Barker, *Age and Youth* (Oxford, 1953).

[142] J.H.S. Kent, 'William Temple, the Church of England and British National Identity' in A. Beach and R. Weight, eds., *The Right to Belong: Citizenship and National Identity in Britain 1930–1960* (London, 1998), 19–34; Miles Taylor, 'Patriotism, History and the Left in Twentieth-Century Britain', *Historical Journal* 33 (1990), 971–87.

cousin, William Hartington, whose father had joined the Cecil commission in 1932. It also found him with copies of his newly published *Readings in St. John's Gospel*. The following month, however, saw him announcing, from his throne in York Minster, that the country was at war.

Evidence for the commission was taken from church bodies of differing ilk—the Church Association, the Church Self-Government League, the English Church Union, the Modern Churchman's Union and the National Church League, together with both clerical and lay individuals. The latter were largely Anglican. Two bishops declined to give evidence. Birmingham said he thought the appointment of the commission a mistake. Henson, observing that his published opinions left no room for obscurity, thought 'revision' could not be obtained.[143] The 'wide and widening discord between Church and Nation' as he put it, made establishment on the English model 'unreal, arbitrary and spiritually paralysing'. The three Free Churchmen—Aubrey (Baptist), Manning (Congregationalist) and Simpson (Presbyterian) did not dissent from his view.[144] What is noteworthy, however, is that their opinions were expressed eirenically. Aubrey, speaking personally rather than officially as general secretary of the Baptist Union, thought that there had never been such goodwill as now existed towards the Church of England. Manning, however, thought that the commission should not suppose that Free Churchmen did not continue to feel the injustices caused by establishment in England, just because they were now better behaved and were less likely to brawl! However, he was in a quandary. He well knew, as a historian, that self-government, even in the Body of Christ, was a difficult business. Venerating some parts of the Church of England though he did, he had no wish to trust them to self-governing episcopalians. Things theoretically and rationally indefensible often did serve a useful purpose in England. The thought of 'unrestrained episcopal government' taking over was fearful indeed.[145]

The unremarkable outcome of the five-year commission was the recommendation to the archbishops that they should summon a Round Table Conference 'to secure agreement between the various schools of thought'. What was 'especially' to be considered were permissible deviations from the Order of Holy Communion as contained in the 1662 Prayer Book. It had

[143] Henson drew attention to his *Disestablishment* (London, 1929) and sundry subsequent articles. N.P. Williams, *The Bishop of Durham and Disestablishment* (London, 1929) was a rejoinder from Oxford.

[144] P.C. Simpson, *The Church and the State* (London, 1929). See also his *Recollections* (London, 1943). Anthony Tucker evaluates 'Nathaniel Micklem and the Ecumenical Movement' in *Journal of the United Reformed Church History Society* 6/9 (2001), 700–10.

[145] Church Assembly, *Church and State: Report of the Archbishops' Commission on the Relations between Church and State 1935*, vol. ii: *Evidence of Witnesses*. Aubrey's is at 248–9 and Manning's at 79–91.

indeed been the fate of the Revised Prayer Book which had prompted the commission. In the event, there was deadlock. The 'Prayer Book' question, by the time the commission reported, was being resolved, bit by bit, at a diocesan level. The mass of submitted material had produced a mouse of a conclusion. Some pamphleteering polemic on the wider constitutional issues continued, but formally they had been gently rolled into the short grass of the cathedral close. Most churchmen, it was clear, remained 'wedded to the national character of their Church'.[146] The case for disestablishment was 'strong' but it was not recommended 'in present circumstances'. The commission's composition precluded any other conclusion.

It was, however, the national character of the *English* church in the *United Kingdom* state that was being husbanded, though it would not have occurred to those concerned to have so titled their report. There was, however, some attention to the kind of 'establishment' which had just been reached in Scotland, but any suggestion that it might be an appropriate model did not find favour. Scotland had such a different history (no submission from the reunited Church of Scotland was solicited, or at least received). The same was true of the Roman Catholic Church. The secretary of the governing body of the Church in Wales gave evidence, in a personal capacity, which, broadly, gave a positive picture of a disestablished church. There was apparently general satisfaction, even enthusiasm, over the method of electing bishops in Wales. The archbishop of Dublin likewise gave the impression that the Church of Ireland was making the best of what he still regarded as a bad job. Such reports were interesting but did nothing to shake the centrality which the English church should have in the British state. When the new Christian king, Edward VIII of Great Britain and Northern Ireland, came to be crowned, assuming that he would be later in 1936, the archbishop of Canterbury and the Church of England would be 'in charge'. Hensley Henson, it appeared, had got it wrong. The commission had taken the view that disestablishment, at this juncture, might make England 'seem to become neutral in the fight between faith and unfaith in Christianity'. That would be a calamity 'for our own people and, indeed, for the whole world'.

Would the Irelands be neutral in the fight between such faith and unfaith? A visitor to Belfast in July 1935 would have witnessed a less abstract fight going on in parts of the city. Vicious rioting and house-burning had taken place arising out of an Orange procession. The casualties were largely

---

[146] Matthew Grimley, *Citizenship, Community, and the Church of England: Liberal Anglican Theories of the State between the Wars* (Oxford, 2004), 146–7; S.J.D. Green, 'Survival and Autonomy: On the Strange Fortunes and Peculiar Legacy of Ecclesiastical Establishments in the Modern British State *c.*1820 to the Present Day' in S.J.D. Green and R.C. Whiting, eds., *The Boundaries of the State in Modern Britain* (Cambridge, 1996), 299–324.

Catholic. A ban on further processions was imposed by the Northern Ireland prime minister. In suggesting that those attacked were 'disloyal', however, he appeared to condone what had happened. 'In retaliation' for events in the North, Anglican, Presbyterian and Methodist churches in the Free State were destroyed. De Valera expressed regret and offered funding to repair the damage. The communal damage, in both jurisdictions, could not be repaired so readily. It was a reminder, if one were needed, of unresolved conflicts of loyalty. Catholic opinion in the North still wanted to regard 'Northern Ireland' as a temporary aberration. The stance justified abstention from political participation in its institutions. Were 'church leaders' to be viewed as 'part of the problem' rather than 'part of the solution'? Certainly, initially, in July 1935, the Church of Ireland bishop of Down, MacNeice, and the dean of Belfast, Kerr, denounced the violence. Protestant ministers went to the shipyards with handbills urging peace.[147] The Catholic bishop of Down, Mageean, insisted that there should be no reprisals. This 'truce', however, did not last. There remained a disposition by clergy to exonerate clergy. Blame lay elsewhere. It appeared that while 'leaders', to some degree, might want to escape from the lenses through which they viewed their society, to do so risked forfeiting the support of the wider communities in which their churches were embedded. Craig, a Presbyterian, told the Stormont parliament in 1934 that he was more proud of being the Grand Master of the Loyal County Down Orange Lodge than of being prime minister. That was the real context. While, superficially, the leadership positions of the two bishops of Down might look the same, in practice, within their communities, they were not. Northern Catholic nationalism and Northern Protestant unionism were both complicated, in part reflecting regional 'senses of place and past' even within a small province. Presbyterians remained disinclined to defer to bishops, and Anglicans insisted on their necessity. The General Synod of the Church of Ireland in 1935 declined to accept a proposal that it should recognize 'the validity, efficacy and spiritual reality' of ordination and sacraments as administered by the Presbyterian Church. Presbyterians concluded that further negotiations—they had been going on spasmodically—were out of the question. As compared with their forefathers, who had known massacre, hunger and persecution, they were, in the words of a sermon in 1942 in Belfast, celebrating three hundred years of Presbyterianism in Ireland, '*at ease in Zion*'.[148] They were not likely to want to give that up.

---

[147] Christopher Fauske, *Side by Side in a Small Country: Bishop John Frederick MacNeice and Ireland* (Dublin, 2004). The bishop's son, Louis, made his career as a poet in England.

[148] Cited in Mitchel, *Evangelicals and National Identity in Ulster*, 236.

Éire was the term used in the new constitution promulgated in Dublin in 1937. Irish men and women should be at ease in their refashioned community. The island of Ireland was one. The government was easing itself out of as many links with the British Crown as possible (the rejection, symbolically, of the notion that 'the British Isles' constituted a 'community'). Éire could already be said to be *de facto* a republic. The ethos of the state left no doubt that it was not neutral in the fight between faith and unfaith. De Valera, broadcasting on St Patrick's Day in 1935, claimed Ireland as 'a Catholic nation' which set the eternal destiny of man above contemporary 'isms'. Various state services, including the *Garda Síochána* (the police force), had been placed under the protection of the Sacred Heart of Jesus or of the Blessed Virgin Mary. The nation, moreover, would find itself again in its use of its language—not that the language of the Mass was either English or Irish. Everything seemed to be being done to make language, religion and nationality a seamless robe. Professor Timothy Corcoran, a clerical figure of note in educational matters, explained in the *Catholic Bulletin*—in English, for he had no Irish—that the Irish nation was the Gaelic nation. It was not a racial synthesis, not a patchwork. Any other elements only had a place in as far as they were assimilated into 'the very substance of Gaelic speech, life and thought'.[149]

However, 'the Catholic nation', conceived as an integrated whole, only had plausibility as a description of the inhabitants of the Free State. The 1937 Constitution had recognized the 'special position' of the Catholic Church as 'the guardian of the Faith professed by the great majority of the citizens', though recognition was also extended to Anglicans, Presbyterians, Methodists, Quakers and Jews by name as well as the 'other' denominations which existed. What that 'special position' amounted to was not clear. It was only broadly true as a characterization, however, so long as the North was detached. It did indicate that Ireland was itself 'special' in the extent to which the teaching of the church should inform the legislation of the state. Almost without exception, political parties accepted the appropriateness of this relationship. It expressed itself in the maintenance of a censorship designed to shield society from influences, internal or external, which would undermine Christian values as Catholics understood them. Much emphasis was placed upon the 'natural rights' of the family. The 'recognition' extended to non-Catholic churches by the state did not mean that the church itself wished to recognize them. It was the rare Catholic in the archdiocese of Dublin who defied the ban placed upon attendance at Trinity College. Intermarriage between Catholics and Protestants, it could

---

[149] Cited in Terence Brown, *Ireland: A Social and Cultural History 1922–79* (Dublin, 1981), 63. E.B. Titley, *Church, State and the Control of Schooling in Ireland 1900–1944* (Dublin, 1983).

be hoped, would ensure the further, and in time, final, attrition of a small minority.[150] As always, in particular instances, marriage and the upbringing of children yielded opportunities for bitter controversy, occasionally erupting into the public arena.

v. 1939–1945: Crusading Together

The position of the British and Irish churches in relation to the Second World War therefore not surprisingly presented many paradoxes. The war came, as has been earlier noted, after more than a decade in which, in Britain, almost universally, it had been routinely denounced as contrary to the mind of Christ. Yet, when it came, the 'pacifist' tide diminished to a trickle. After all, it seemed, there were indeed worse things than war. Even Maude Royden, to the dismay of her friends, changed her mind. After decades of ardent pacifism, she declared, 'I believe now that Nazi-ism is worse than war.'[151] The 'development of events' had compelled Hugh Martin to reconsider his position and sever his connection with the Christian pacifist movement.[152] There were many others like him. Edwyn Bevan took a long view. He told his readers that there was 'no greater difficulty in reconciling the war of 1939 and 1940 with God's Providence than there is in reconciling the Diocletian Persecution in the years 303–13'.[153] Yet, precisely because the war appeared to transcend the mere pursuit of national interest, it was perceived to contain an inherent danger. Church leaders were acutely aware of the 'mistakes' which they or their predecessors thought they had made in the Great War. In retrospect, British claims about 'the issues' being made then and largely endorsed by the churches, had come to be thought excessive, even jingoistic. This time, however, it might look as though talk of a 'crusade' really was justified, though it might not be necessary to insist on 'unconditional surrender'.

While it was understandable and proper that church leaders, with some regularity, advised against the sin of self-righteousness and wrote at some length on future peace and harmony, there was a war to be won. The commander of British forces in North Africa, son of a bishop, struck different notes when he spoke to his troops. Bernard Montgomery code-named CRUSADER the operation which broke Rommel's siege of Tobruk in

---

[150] Richard O'Leary, 'Change in the Rate and Pattern of Religious Intermarriage in the Republic of Ireland', *The Economic and Social Review* 30/2.2 (1999), 119–52. Naturally, whatever the overall picture, which at this point was still largely one of endogamy, even a small change could rapidly destabilize Protestant congregations.

[151] Sheila Fletcher, *Maude Royden: A Life* (Oxford, 1989), 374.

[152] Hugh Martin, *The Christian as Soldier* (London, 1939), 5.

[153] Edwyn Bevan, *Christians in a World at War* (London, 1940), 35.

November 1941. Whilst some serving officers apparently wanted to retch at the mention of 'crusade', others felt earnestly that what they were engaged in was far more of a crusade than the crusades had ever been. Not that Britain was perfect...[154] Chaplains had a very definite role in raising morale. It was not absurd to talk of defending the faith. Montgomery had nothing but the 'highest praise' for the work of the YMCA.[155] Commanders, it is argued, had a well-founded conviction that religion was a crucial and sustaining force. The commander-in-chief of British troops in Cairo in 1940 found great support from the sermons of the bishop in the cathedral—when all seemed lost.[156] And, when victory eventually came, would it now be possible, Alec Vidler asked in 1940, sitting in Gladstone's library in North Wales, that the re-christianization of Europe would begin in England?[157]

The events of May 1940 jolted churchmen in all denominations whether in Winchester, Durham, Chichester, Lambeth, Edinburgh or Belfast (and in non-belligerent Dublin). Cyril Garbett, the 65-year-old bishop of Winchester had been suffering for months from persistent insomnia and was losing weight. Evenings at home were dreary. He went to bed miserable and even the combination of a devotional book and one of P.G. Wodehouse's stories failed to give him good nights. He had acute mental depression. He had a Lent book to write—*We Would See Jesus*—but could not, as it were, focus. Nevertheless, he went about his daily duties. May found him in Jersey conducting confirmations. Summoned back to Parliament, he hurried to England on what might be the last mail plane. In London, it was perhaps reassuring to be informed by the bishop of Birmingham that, even in defeat, the inner life of a nation could not be destroyed, provided it preserved the best stocks by careful breeding. On 26 May, the 'Day of National Prayer', Garbett preached in Winchester Cathedral to what he described as an enormous congregation. In Southampton, later in the day, he addressed a huge crowd in the Guildhall and gave a blessing at an open-air service at the Sports Centre—thousands being present on both occasions. He worried about the death or capture of one of his former chaplains who had not returned from Dunkirk. He thought it wrong of his suffragan bishop (of Southampton) to be calling for corporate repentance. People needed comfort and help rather than scolding. He worried about the Channel Islanders. He did his bit for the war effort by releasing his chauffeur

---

[154] These examples are drawn from the discussion in Michael Snape, *God and the British Soldier: Religion and the British Army in the First and Second World Wars* (London, 2005), 184–6.

[155] Ion Megarry, *The Y.M.C.A. and the Italian Prisoners of War* (London, 1945?) describes one activity.

[156] Snape, *God and the British Soldier*, 245, 230.

[157] A.R. Vidler, *God's Judgment on Europe* (London, 1940), 76.

of twenty years to be a fitter in an aircraft factory. He learnt to drive a car, but his manoeuvres, deemed hazardous by his staff, were not helped by the removal of those local signposts which, while assisting a bishop, would also assist an invader. He was himself, two years later, to be pointed, rather unwillingly, in the direction of York where, as archbishop, he was to find himself among 'rather rough and uncultured clergy' some of whom, however, were 'probably really good men'.[158]

The removal of signposts, as experienced by one motoring bishop, can serve as a metaphor for pervasive disorientation, though underlying convictions remained firm. In Durham, however, Cyril Alington struck a strong note, admittedly not delivered in an academic context. He published a pamphlet *The Last Crusade* in the belief that Britain had a clear claim to be engaged in a crusade—though it might be optimistic to think of it being the last. Apparently, however, the word 'crusade' did not have the resonance amongst the general population that, as a former headmaster of Eton, he had assumed would be the case.[159] There was also a little irony in the fact that, only two years earlier, his son-in-law, Lord Dunglass, had been the messenger, as his parliamentary private secretary, who had revealed to the prime minister that Herr Hitler was willing to meet him in Munich—a crusade for peace.[160] Church people, in particular, appeared to be uncomfortable with the language of 'crusade'.

From Chichester, Bishop Bell declared that the church could not speak of any earthly war as a 'crusade' because the one thing for which it was impossible to fight was the Cross: the supreme concern of the church was not 'the victory of the national cause'.[161] Enunciated in November 1939, this underlying contention informed everything Bell said and did throughout the war. Within 'the universal church', links should be strengthened between the churches in warring countries on both sides, probably with the help of churches in neutral countries. There should be an effort, through the ecumenical movement, to find out what a just and acceptable peace—for all parties—would be like.

---

[158] This paragraph draws on Charles Smyth, *Cyril Forster Garbett* (London, 1959), 238–85. Garbett, like Fisher, was the son and grandson of clergymen. His whole life, until York, had been spent in London and the south of England. He had been president of the Oxford Union as an undergraduate and, while he knew more about bad housing than any other bishop, his closest clergy, in Portsea, Southwark and Winchester, were cultured.

[159] C.A. Alington, *A Dean's Apology: A Semi-Religious Autobiography* (London, 1953).

[160] Lord Home, *The Way the Wind Blows* (London, 1976), 55–6, 76–83 for his impressions of his headmaster and father-in-law and his influence on his own Christian faith.

[161] Whether victory should be prayed for was contentious. Garbett disagreed with Temple's view that God should not be set up as being against the country's enemies, writing 'unless we thought it was God's Will that we should war against the Nazis, we ought to have opposed the war: if it is His Will, then we must pray for victory'. Smyth, *Garbett*, 291.

In January 1940 Bell wanted the Allies to be able to say that Germany would not be humiliated and dismembered. Wrong would have to be righted, but Germany's independence and integrity had to be preserved.[162] In such statements he had the Versailles settlement very much in mind and assumed that he was right to be doing so.[163] In the years that followed, without fear or favour, in the House of Lords and outside, in speeches and in writing, he made use of his considerable range of contacts, nationally and internationally, to try to give substance to his fundamental propositions. He attacked the bombing of cities in a famous speech in the House of Lords in February 1944.[164] A few months earlier, in his diocesan gazette, he had been explicit that to bomb cities as cities was wrong, whether carried out by the Nazis or the Allies. The stance he took on this matter evoked predictably different responses. Some of his correspondents said that they had been longing to hear some 'authoritative voice' raised in public against obliteration bombing. Others thought it strange that he should be concerned with the sufferings of the people of Berlin while allegedly ignoring the suffering in Britain. Bell recorded that supporters outnumbered critics by three to one. It is more difficult to judge whether the speech—which did not trigger sustained protests from other church leaders—did have an impact on British policy thereafter. It clearly had no immediate consequence. More generally, Bell attacked 'Vansittartism', the assumption that no distinction should or could be made between the generality of Germans and the followers of Hitler. At the close of the war he vigorously opposed the trial of those who could be accused of war crimes.

Dietrich Bonhoeffer, on the eve of his execution in 1945, sent a message to Bell reiterating that they both believed in a Universal Christian brotherhood, one which rose above all national interests. Their ultimate victory was 'certain'.[165] If so, however, it was not easy to identify what form victory could take. The translation of ideal into reality proved intractable. That there was a kind of 'Protestant International' amongst church leaders was undeniable but whether it constituted a 'community' was another matter.[166]

---

[162] Bell's *Christianity and World Order* appeared in 1940.

[163] Nathaniel Micklem went so far as to claim that 'the source of moral power necessary if we are to avoid "another Versailles" . . . can only come from the Christian Church'. *May God Defend the Right!* (London, 1939), 142–3.

[164] Andrew Chandler, 'The Church of England and the Obliteration Bombing of Germany in the Second World War', *English Historical Review* 108 (1993), 920–46.

[165] Jasper, *Bell*, 256–87. This informative chapter is headed 'The Statesman in Wartime' but, whatever the value of Bell's observations and the attractiveness of his vision, 'statesman' he was not nor could be.

[166] P.W. Ludlow, 'The International Protestant Community in the Second World War', *Journal of Ecclesiastical History* 29/3 (1978), 311–62. The conviction that the 'Christian oecumenical fellowship and unity minister to the need for an international *ethos* that shall underpin the structure of law' was offered by William Paton in *The Church and the New Order* (London, 1941), 170. In his *Christian Europe Today* (London, 1942), 232, a book derived from lectures in America in 1941, the Swiss Adolph Keller thought British Christianity 'a religious continent in itself'.

A broad picture of common 'resistance' was presented, though it was a rather partial evaluation.[167] Drawing attention to the newly formed trans-national fellowships in Britain, William Paton, secretary of the International Missionary Council, a major figure in these circles before his unexpected death in 1943, thought that they were 'beginning to create in this country a new sense of the universal Church'.[168] But was it really possible to rise above all national interests, particularly if those interests were more than national? Bell seems to have had little doubt that by his speeches during the war he had ruined his chances of succeeding Temple when the latter died in October 1944.

In York and then in Canterbury, Temple had continued to hold out hope of a new world.[169] Britain fell short at too many points to be called a Christian civilization. The country was rather, he believed, fighting for the opportunity to make a Christian civilization.[170] A Christian citizen, he further contended, would be a 'genuine patriot' but never a 'Jingo'. It was right for a British Christian to be glad of the British Empire—but in respect of its record of justice, freedom and trustworthiness not because of its capacity to impose the will of the British people on others.[171] He organized a conference at Malvern in January 1941 amidst hills on which, pertinently, many centuries earlier, the visionary 'Piers Plowman' had roamed. It was designed, from an Anglican point of view, to determine 'the fundamental facts' which would be relevant to the ordering of the new society. It was not the objective to construct a political programme. The speakers—W.G. Peck, M.B. Reckitt, Dorothy Sayers, Donald Mackinnon, V.A. Demant, Sir Richard Acland, Kenneth Ingram, Middleton Murry and

---

[167] Hugh Martin, Douglas Newton, H.M. Waddams and R.R. Williams, *Christian Counter-Attack: Europe's Churches against Nazism* (London, 1943). Readers of the book were alerted to the existence of an Anglo-Czechoslovak Christian Fellowship, a Scoto-Czechoslovak Christian Fellowship, a British and Dutch Christian Fellowship, the Scandinavian–British Christian Fellowship, the Christian Fellowship of French-Speaking and British Peoples and the German–British Christian Fellowship. For Waddams's later 'fact-finding' mission to Sweden and Finland see Hanna-Maija Ketola, 'Teaching "Correct" Attitudes: An Anglican Emissary to Sweden and Finland in 1944', *Journal of Ecclesiastical History* 55/1 (2004), 75–101. Waddams, an Anglican priest, was on the staff of the Ministry of Information, becoming general secretary of the Church of England Council on Foreign Relations in 1945.

[168] The fellowships concerned are those listed in the foregoing footnote. William Paton, *The Church and the New Order* (London, 1941), 182. Paton was also a contributor to the volume edited by William Temple *Is Christ Divided?* (Harmondsworth, 1943). Eleanor M. Jackson, *Red Tape and the Gospel: A Study in the Significance of the Ecumenical Missionary Struggle of William Paton (1886–1943)* (Birmingham, 1980).

[169] William Temple, *The Church Looks Forward* (London, 1944). Inge was no doubt in a minority in taking the view that 'All that interests the Archbishop is the flirtation of a certain group to which he himself belongs with Left-wing politics.' The conventional picture was that Temple was a 'world figure' as Bell described him.

[170] William Temple, *The Hope of a New World* (London, 1940), 64.

[171] William Temple, *Citizen and Churchman* (London, 1941), 92.

T.S. Eliot—were old hands at this kind of thing. They expected their audience to share their concepts and language. Young Mr Mackinnon claimed that the obscurity of his paper was due to the complexity of its theme ('Revelation and Social Justice').[172] Temple admitted that much of what was said had been said before but he nevertheless believed that the 'findings' of the conference had 'found a public ready to attend to them with a new eagerness'. The spirit of Malvern was carried on in a further volume of essays which pointed *Towards a Christian Order*. Here, too, the contributors were not unanimous: Temple ventured the comment that common ownership might be quite as bad as private ownership—and might even be worse—but the tide seemed to favour the former. It was even felt 'provocative' by the editorial committee for one essayist to assert that Marxism was radically anti-Christian.[173] Temple took to great meetings to demonstrate how the church was looking ahead. His new colleague of York was dutiful but did not really think it a good thing that both arch-bishops should tour round 'with what is rather like a political pro-gramme'.[174] Temple published *Christianity and Social Order* as a Penguin paperback in 1942, a volume which sold 132,000 copies.[175] Mervyn Stock-wood, newly installed as a vicar in East Bristol, was able to tell parishioners in air-raid shelters 'that the Archbishop was running a show to put the world right'.[176] They were reportedly eager to find out how he was getting on. Two years later, however, the archbishop was dead.

In Edinburgh, in May 1940, in an atmosphere of foreboding, the General Assembly of the Church of Scotland tried to come to terms with what was happening. It set up a commission, convened by John Baillie, to seek 'the

---

[172] Mackinnon's *God the Living and the True* (London, 1940) was a contribution to a series in which a new generation of men born between 1903 and 1913 argued that what was out of date was not traditional Christian theology but the attempts that were being made to 'bring it up to date'.

[173] Canon S.J. Marriott in *Towards a Christian Order* (London, 1942), 16.

[174] Smyth, *Garbett*, 293. The express purpose of these meetings in London, Birmingham, Leicester and Edinburgh was to affirm 'the right and duty of the Church to declare its judgment upon social facts and social movements and to lay down principles which should govern the ordering of society'. A.E. Baker, ed., *William Temple and His Message* (Harmondsworth, 1946), 36.

[175] It is argued that *Catholics and the New World Order*, a joint pastoral of the English hierarchy issued in July 1942, was influenced by Temple. Aspden, *Fortress Church*, 251.

[176] *Malvern 1941: The Life of the Church and the Order of Society*, 4–5. One show Temple was not running, however, was 'The Moot', a private gathering which met twenty times between April 1938 and December 1944. Orchestrated by Oldham, its inner core consisted of H.A. Hodges, Karl Mannheim, Alec Vidler, Walter Moberly and Eric Fenn, but also with notable participation by T.S. Eliot and John Baillie, amongst others. The philosophical, theological, sociological and educational issues involved in 'planning for freedom' formed the core of these 'elite' discussions. It was essentially an English gathering, Baillie being the exception—though Mannheim was a non-Christian 'incomer'. 'The Moot' is discussed in Clements, *Faith on the Frontier*, 363–88, 502–3. See further the articles by Clements, 'John Baillie and the Moot' in David Fergusson, ed., *Christ, Church and Society* (Edinburgh, 1993), 199–219; Marjorie Reeves, ed., *Christian Thinking and Social Order: Conviction Politics from the 1930s to the Present Day* (London, 1999).

Interpretation of God's will in the Present Crisis'. This gathering of theologians and elders also sought to engage in their own way with the destruction of the shrines of western Christendom. They reported annually to the General Assembly. The returning 'spirit of community' was welcomed after 'the long reign of individualism' but a true community needed the Christian church, whose existence was based on something that transcended community. Economic power, it was said in 1942, had to be made 'objectively responsible to the community as a whole'. The 'common interest', as perceived in 1944, apparently demanded a far greater measure of public control of capital resources and of the means of production. Given that the Baillie Commission was an official Church of Scotland body and that its reports were 'approved' by the General Assembly, the church appeared to be committed to the need for 'a new social and economic order'.[177] The language reflected the belief that there were 'middle axioms' which the church could set forth to prescribe a basis for modern society, even if it could not or should not endorse particular detailed policies. Baillie himself was moderator in 1943 and naturally reflected on what had happened in Scotland since 1843. What he observed was a 'diffused Christianity' in which the impulse of worship had failed and belief had grown shadowy and dim. Scotland might revert to 'paganism' but it was not pagan yet and it should not be addressed as though it were.[178] The challenge was to find a strategy to bring 'diffused Christianity' and 'living church' together again. It was wrong, he argued elsewhere, 'to think of earthly civilization and the Christian ideal of community as standing in simple anti-thesis to one another' since the true relationship was dialectical. He was certain, however, that as a society relaxed its hold upon the eternal it ensured the corruption of the temporal.[179]

In Armagh, Gregg, who had been installed as Church of Ireland Primate in 1938, had no hesitation in saying, a year later, '*our* [my italics] country is at war'. If he had still been in Dublin, he could not have said that. German bombs landed on Belfast, not on Dublin (except by mistake). A few fire engines, obligingly sent north by de Valera to deal with their aftermath, did not extinguish the animosity between North and South. It was scarcely

---

[177] Extracts from all the reports were published as *God's Will for Church and Nation* (London, 1946). A detailed assessment is A.R. Morton, ed., *God's Will in a Time of Crisis: A Colloquium Celebrating the 50th Anniversary of the Baillie Commission* (Edinburgh, 1994); Duncan B. Forrester, 'God's Will in a Time of Crisis: John Baillie as a Social Theologian' in Fergusson, ed., *Christ, Church and Society*, 221–3.

[178] James A. Whyte, 'Church and Society in the Thought of John Baillie' in Fergusson, ed., *Christ, Church and Society*, 235.

[179] John Baillie, *What is Christian Civilization?* (Oxford, 1945), 58–9. H.G. Wood, the Baptist-turned-Quaker Professor of Theology at Birmingham had given his thoughts on the same theme in lectures in Cambridge in 1942 on *Christianity and Civilisation* (Cambridge, 1942).

conceivable, in these circumstances, that there would be a common pan-Ireland Protestant and a pan-Ireland Catholic interpretation of the war's significance. Cardinal MacRory and other Catholic bishops in the North had warned (successfully) against conscription, saying that Catholics could not be expected to fight for their oppressor. Protestants, on the other hand, though not known for their admiration of Catholic Poland, thought they understood 'what the war was about'. No doubt, some Catholics did too, but it looked as though 'Catholic Ireland' had 'opted out' of a struggle to save 'Christian civilization' in Europe. The statement which came from the Catholic hierarchy in Maynooth in October 1939 gave the impression that, for Ireland at least, there were no great issues at stake in whatever it was that was happening on the continent.

Both Catholics and Protestants were organized within pan-Ireland structures but were citizens of states whose governments in Dublin and Belfast/London took radically different views on the war. The geographical position of Northern Ireland in the 'Atlantic world' gave it a strategic significance and left ample opportunity for its government to emphasize the loyalty of the province, or at least its majority Protestant population—who were deemed fully to understand how significant the war was for Christian civilization. In Dublin, however, while the government was not neutral in the fight between faith and unfaith, it saw no reason to involve itself in the war and studiously emphasized its neutrality and non-belligerence. Even so, there was a supply of Irish labour in Britain and of volunteers in the British Army, volunteers who included deserters from the Irish Army.[180] And the government itself, despite its public stance of detachment, could make some quiet gestures, particularly after the United States came into the war. It was not the high politics of the war which formed the content of the letters exchanged between the Catholic archbishops of Birmingham and Dublin but the welfare of Irish girls working in England. Some students at Trinity College, Dublin had ill-advisedly begun to sing 'God save the King' on VE Day in 1945 but, if there was Dublin gratification in the victory of 'Christian Civilization', Irish Catholic opinion did not relish the thought that it might also be a British and Protestant victory.

'Events' pushed the Roman Catholic Church in Britain down unusual paths. It made a change, when thinking and writing about 'downfalls', for it to be thinking about France rather than the Church of England. Catholic

---

[180] Brian Girvin and Geoffrey Roberts, 'The Forgotten Volunteers of World War II', *History Ireland* 6/1 (1998); Enda Delaney, 'The Churches and Irish Emigration to Britain, 1921–60', *Archivium Hibernicum* 52 (1998). Mervyn O'Driscoll, *Ireland, Germany and the Nazis: Politics and Diplomacy, 1919–1939* (Dublin, 2004); John P. Duggan, *Neutral Ireland and the Third Reich* (Dublin, 1985); Claire Wills, *That Neutral Island: A Cultural History of Ireland during the Second World War* (London, 2007) brings a new dimension.

Eire might be neutral but Catholics in Britain were in a delicate position. On the eve of the war there had been an attempt to improve contacts between the hierarchies of the two islands. In March 1939 a first joint meeting had been held in Dublin. Was there a common 'Catholic mind' on the issues ahead? The new Vichy regime established after the fall of France had its English Catholic sympathizers.[181] A further indication of the delicacy of the situation arose a little later when, on the advice of the Foreign Office, Father de Zulueta, the Catholic chaplain at Oxford, who had retained his Spanish nationality, was removed. He was replaced by a proper ex-Anglican Englishman.[182] Apprehensive about a propaganda campaign which could make Catholics appear anti-British, Hinsley wrote to the editor of *The Tablet* advising against publishing statements or comments which gave support to the government of France. He was blunt. Recent quotations from *Osservatore Romano* and the Vatican Radio had given 'a wrong impression' to many of our fellow countrymen—Catholic and Protestant.[183] The editor, predisposed to look favourably upon Pétain, might well have been surprised by the solicitude for Protestant opinion on the part of his correspondent. Hinsley, however, could see how vulnerable the church would be to accusations that it was a potential 'Fifth Column'. He had no enthusiasm for the 'Latin Bloc' of authoritarian regimes in 'Catholic countries'. If that bloc was 'against our country' he told Christopher Dawson, editor of *The Dublin Review*, then 'we' are against it. Hinsley was an Englishman whose speeches were comfortingly laced with cricketing metaphors. He was a good man, politicians thought, to be broadcasting to 'our kith and kin' in Australia. What a boon for mankind, 'down under' was told, 'if the cricket spirit inspired all our intercourse, social, economic, and political'.[184]

He was not well-briefed on the spirit of Anglo-Australian cricketing encounters, but he despatched to the boundary a suggestion that he might urge the British government to give serious consideration to recent German

[181] Gavin White, 'The Fall of France', in W.J. Sheils, ed., *The Church and War*, Studies in Church History 20 (Oxford, 1983), 431–41.

[182] Walter Druma, *The Old Palace: The Catholic Chaplaincy at Oxford* (Oscott, 1991).

[183] Hinsley to Woodruff, 13 July 1940, cited in Stuart Mews, 'The Sword of the Spirit' in Sheils, ed., *The Church and War*, 419. The section that follows is indebted to Mews and to M.J. Walsh, 'Ecumenism in War-Time Britain: The Sword of the Spirit and Religion and Life, 1940–1945', pt. 1, *Heythrop Journal* 23 (1982), 243–58 and 'Ecumenism in War-Time Britain: The Sword of the Spirit and Religion and Life, 1940–1945', pt. 2, *Heythrop Journal* 23 (1982), 377–94. Walsh relates subsequent developments in *From Sword to Ploughshare: Sword of the Spirit to Catholic Institute for International Relations, 1940–80* (London, 1980). Thomas Greene, 'Vichy France and the Catholic Press in England: Contrasting Attitudes to a Moral Problem', *Recusant History* 21/1 (1992), 111–33; Joan Keating, 'Discrediting the "Catholic State": Britain and the Fall of France' in F. Tallett and N. Atkin, eds., *Catholicism in Britain and France since 1789* (London, 1996), 27–42.

[184] Arthur, Cardinal Hinsley, *The Bond of Peace and Other War-Time Addresses* (London, 1941), 139–40.

peace proposals—even when consideration was apparently approved by the pope.[185] Also, on 1 August, he launched 'The Spirit of the Sword', which aimed to provide a more united Catholic effort in support of the struggle which the country had been forced to enter. It was an initiative which was backed by, if not inspired by, Dawson and A.C.F. Beales, both convert historians. Hinsley gave the movement necessary protection—Dawson was at predictable loggerheads with Jerrold, publisher of the *Dublin Review*. Most of his fellow bishops were suspicious, and some hostile, perhaps in part because lay enterprise was not welcome.[186] The prominent role of a woman, and a woman under thirty at that, Barbara Ward of *The Economist*, was disturbing (it may be noted, in passing, that the Church of Scotland, in setting up the Baillie Commission, had not looked to any woman as a possible interpreter of God's will). Over the following months, Hinsley tried to balance the political 'Left' and 'Right', and did so with difficulty.

From the outset, whether 'the Sword' should associate with Protestants in a 'common' concern for 'Christendom' was contentious. Just what was 'common'? There had been hints, from the beginning of the war, that relations between Canterbury and Westminster need not be quite so frosty. George Bell and the newly appointed and rather young auxiliary bishop of Westminster, David Mathew, took tea in the Athenaeum. The former suggested that there was an 'unprecedented opportunity' for contact to develop between 'the historic Churches' and the Church of Rome. The latter, a historian with an unusual grasp both of Catholicism and of the complexity of the British Isles, showed interest.[187] Initial soundings in Rome, however, led nowhere.

Even so, in all the circumstances, there was something of a new mood. Lang, Hinsley, Armstrong (moderator, Free Church Federal Council) and Temple—in that order—put their name to a letter to *The Times* on 21 December 1940 endorsing the 'Five Peace Points' which the pope had just made.[188] The signatories added their names to five standards by which economic situations and proposals were to be considered. Taken together,

---

[185] It did not seem to the Vatican that Britain was likely to survive. The French mother of Basil Hume, later archbishop of Westminster, was of the same mind. She supposed that her son might have to prepare for martyrdom. Owen Chadwick, *Britain and the Vatican during the Second World War* (Cambridge, 1986), 138–9.

[186] Further details of this hostility are provided in Aspden, *Fortress Church*, 234–61.

[187] Mathew, Oxford-educated, had published *The Celtic Peoples and Renaissance Europe: A Study of the Celtic and Spanish Influences on Elizabethan History* (London, 1933) and *Catholicism in England 1535–1935: Portrait of a Minority: Its Culture and Traditions* (London, 1935).

[188] The protocol to be observed in the matter of joint letters became—later—contentious. Griffin conceded that the established church should have precedence but held that this should only apply to Canterbury. The archbishop of Westminster should sign above the archbishop of York. Fisher did not agree. In consequence, the number of common letters purporting to speak with 'a common voice' diminished.

they constituted the objectives of 'The Sword'. It was an impressive statement, though not likely to be of much consequence. Some Free Churchmen still complained about the absence of any commitment to religious liberty. They were disquieted by the apparent Catholic position that 'Truth' required a special constitutional status. For their part, some Catholics thought that the cardinal was compromising Truth by putting his name alongside heretics. It is impossible to say what most Catholics and most Nonconformists thought of the letter. Most of them never read *The Times* anyway.

In May 1941 two successful public meetings under the auspices of the 'Sword', presided over respectively by the archbishops of Westminster and Canterbury, were held in the secular neutrality of the Stoll Theatre (and other meetings were held in other parts of the country). Hinsley talked about the need to have 'a regular system of consultation and collaboration'. Together, they could win the peace. Apparently at the prompting of Bell, who had been the speaker, the cardinal agreed to lead the assembly in saying the Lord's Prayer. Both gestures caused more than a stir. Agitated correspondence followed between the cardinal's episcopal colleagues. Could Hinsley not see how Catholic consciences would be offended by praying with heretics? Hinsley had to make it clear that non-Catholics could only be associate members of the 'Sword'—a clarification which led to the establishment of a parallel 'Religion and Life' movement among non-Catholics. Such co-operation as still occurred, however, caused anathemas to be pronounced in some evangelical circles. Theo Bamber, a prominent Baptist minister, addressed a Protestant Truth Society rally in opposition to the Sword of the Spirit at Caxton Hall in October 1941.[189] Some, perhaps most, Catholic bishops thought that any joint meetings were dangerous in so far as they could give rise to the clearly erroneous notion that the Catholic Church was just 'one of the churches'. From then on, the chief players stumbled in pursuit of some kind of collaboration—one example being the Council of Christians and Jews, founded in 1942. Its driving figure was W.W. Simpson, a Methodist minister.[190] Hinsley became one of its presidents. It may be, too, that near the end of his life the archbishop, after initial enthusiasm, was no longer capable of giving sustained encouragement to any enterprise. The 'Sword' lost its early glint and Griffin, his successor after an interval of nine months, had no intention of burnishing it. Twelve years after joining the Council of Christians and Jews, Catholics withdrew.[191] The

---

[189] Randall, *English Baptists*, 256.

[190] W.W. Simpson, *Jews and Christians Today* (London, 1940); Marcus Braybrooke, *Children of One God: A History of the Council of Christians and Jews* (London, 1991).

[191] Bernard, Cardinal Griffin, *The Catholic Church and Reunion* (London, 1950) made the position clear.

international body to which the council was affiliated appeared to be canvassing ideas of religious toleration which Pius XII judged to be encouraging 'religious indifferentism'.

At Hinsley's funeral, however, Temple was present, something which seemed 'so right and proper' to the *Church Times*. The paper noted that few realized how great a departure from precedent his attendance represented. 'Good personal relations' clearly now meant something, though equally clearly not everything. The exploratory fumbling, which 'the Sword' episode represented, again displayed how tangled up were social, cultural and dogmatic considerations. Hinsley's biographer, who had an acute eye for the latter, saw the 'demon' restlessly active all the time. Bishop Mathew thought 'northern Catholics' in these matters to be rather a different breed. Yet that may be a misapprehension. The enthusiasm of the very large audiences—'unsophisticated laity'—in Blackpool and Preston was such that it might have had to be curbed.

Certainly, however, the lay leadership of the 'Sword' came from different stables and moved in different circles. Beales, who wrote his *Penguin Special* on *The Catholic Church and International Order* independently of Bell's *Christianity and World Order*, nevertheless expressed 'profoundest admiration and deepest gratitude' for the book.[192] He dedicated his volume to the memory of Henry Richard, the nineteenth-century Welsh Congregationalist MP and peace activist about whom he had written in his non-Catholic days (he had converted only in 1935). As one Oxford man to another, Mathew explained to Bell that he was unusual among Catholic bishops—though this was beginning to change—in having gone to an English university. When paths did not cross, minds found it hard to meet. Just as a particular set of war circumstances and personalities seemed to open windows, so their passing closed them. There was also a reminder, in these encounters, that the churches of Britain could not simply come to a mutual understanding between themselves. Whereas all the Protestant churches were insularly autochthonous, ultimate authority in the Catholic Church naturally lay elsewhere. The letter to *The Times* in December 1940 also revealed another playing field that was not level. The church leaders concerned were English but they were clearly seeking to influence a United Kingdom government. It was not a letter which was signed by church leaders outside England, though no one in London seemed to think that mattered.

It was evident, therefore, that the walls which separated the churches exhibited modest crumbling under the impact of war. Ronald Selby Wright, the Church of Scotland minister who made a name for himself as

---

[192] A.C.F. Beales, *The Catholic Church and International Order* (Harmondsworth, 1941), v. He had previously written *A History of Peace* (London, 1931).

the 'Radio Padre', edited a volume entitled *Front Line Religion* (1941), which was broadminded enough to include a piece on 'St. George of England'.[193] For Hugh Martin, the Baptist who had made the SCM Press such a significant publishing enterprise and who was an honorary secretary of the 'Friends of Reunion', it was time to move on beyond the visible evidence of improved personal relations amongst Christians.[194] The business of Christian unity required haste, even though he admitted that it would be desperately hard to overcome inertia and break routine. He argued for such a step because it was the will of God but also because of the 'appalling waste' which the existing divisions perpetuated. The immense strength of the forces which opposed the Christian church 'should make us the more concerned to remove any possible element of weakness within its ranks'.[195] In 1940 the Free Church Federal Council came into being, its two predecessor bodies, the National Council of Evangelical Free Churches and the Federal Council of the Evangelical Free Churches having 'gone out of existence'. The word 'federal' however, continued to be problematic.

The new body's constitution insisted that each of the federating churches should preserve their own autonomy as regards faith and practice. There was talk of covering the whole country with Free Church Federal Councils. It was claimed that seven million Free Churchmen—many women must have been included to have achieved such an imaginative figure—could now speak with a united voice. The inaugurating moderator, a Methodist, asserted that the seed of unity might develop into the fruit of union, but offered no guidance on how the new Council might facilitate such a process.

In 1942 the British Council of Churches was formed, with William Temple as its first president. It brought together, for the first time, representatives of all of the main non-Roman Catholic churches in one organization. As such, it was the 'logical outcome' of that closer contact which had been a feature of the previous two decades. That contact had indeed not brought 'unity' but had at least brought 'a better spirit'. The council appeared to point to the future. It was an important, but nevertheless uncertain step. All 'umbrella' bodies possess an inherent instability and the British Council of Churches was no exception. When two such bodies, namely the FCFC and the BCC, overlapped to some extent, there was confusion, not to say irritation. 'Our greatest single hindrance', the FCFC 1948 Report stated, 'has been the attitude of those who say that the British Council of Churches has made the Free Church Federal Council

[193] For his autobiography see R.S. Wright, *Another Home* (Edinburgh, 1980).
[194] A.R. Cross, 'Dr Hugh Martin: Publisher and Writer, Part 1', *Baptist Quarterly* 37/1 (1997), 33–48; 'Dr Hugh Martin: Ecumenist, Part 2', *Baptist Quarterly* 37/2 (1997), 71–86; 'Revd Dr Hugh Martin: Ecumenical Controversialist and Writer', *Baptist Quarterly* 37/3, 131–46.
[195] Hugh Martin, *Christian Reunion: A Plea for Action* (London, 1941), 191.

unnecessary'. It observed that in many places there was no Council of Churches because the local clergy refused to co-operate and, further, the Free Church approach on drink, gambling and the Sunday question was different from the Anglican.[196] So, from the outset, the question of whether the British Council of Churches should be the 'mouthpiece' of the British churches was uncertain. Some might think so. Others, however, did not consider that it could arrogate to itself any such function. It should not have and could not have any intrinsic authority of its own. Its members, drawn from all the churches, had no 'mandate' to commit them. Such 'structural' questions, however, did not detract from the sense that a step forward had been taken. Writ large, this structural question was even more of a problem for the World Council of Churches 'in process of formation'.

These were organizational questions for the future. There were deeper questions to be pondered. In 1953 the Professor of Modern History at Cambridge reflected on *Christianity, Diplomacy and War* before his fellow Methodists.[197] Looking back over twenty years, Herbert Butterfield had come to the conclusion that it was a heresy to believe that one final war could eradicate human evil. He knew, of course, that there was now a weapon to hand which could be used utterly to destroy an enemy who was believed to be the embodiment of evil. In his diary, in August 1945, he had described the atomic bomb as the ultimate prostitution of human endeavour. It was 'the judgment of God on our civilisation'.[198] He advocated what he called the 'scientific' as opposed to the 'moralistic' approach to the study of international affairs. In lectures delivered in Cambridge in 1948, subsequently broadcast and published, Butterfield reflected—in too imprecise a way for some—on *Christianity and History*. His observations were warmly received, almost without exception, across the denominations. He had stopped being a Methodist local preacher in 1936 but that did not stop him wrestling with 'technical history', moral judgements, patriotism and statecraft—all within his understanding of Christian belief. In *Christianity in European History* he asked his audience to reflect on what could happen in a given country when Christianity was thoroughly uprooted. He suspected that people in England were living more than they knew on the 'old capital' of Christian assumptions. It was clearly possible for a generation to be brought up which was not 'squeamish' about cruelty.[199] He did not want

---

[196] Cited in Basil Amey, 'The Free Church Federal Council: A Retrospective View', *Journal of the United Reformed Church History Society* 7/3 (December 2003), 195.

[197] Ian Hall, 'History, Christianity and Diplomacy: Herbert Butterfield and International Relations', *Review of International Studies* (2002), 719–36.

[198] C.T. McIntire, *Herbert Butterfield: Historian as Dissenter* (New Haven and London, 2004), 167.

[199] F.R. Barry, and others, had argued during the war that if the Christian church failed in leadership at this juncture, what had happened in Germany 'was going to happen everywhere'. *Church and Leadership* (London, 1945), 31.

to see the imposition of 'Christian principles' by the state. That had led to too much abuse in the past. It was, rather, a matter of individuals 'by an autonomous act of judgement' going over to the Christian religion.[200]

The historian's pursuit of detachment was perilous. It had left some, in the 1930s and beyond, wondering about Butterfield's stance towards events in Nazi Germany.[201] On the other hand, in 1940, he told radio listeners that Hitler was more terrible than Napoleon, but privately noted that it would be quite wrong to treat Germans as sub-human. He wanted to ask what 'we' had done wrong. His *The Englishman and His History* was published just as the Normandy landings were taking place in June 1944. It seemed, to some, a Whiggish view of English liberty of a kind which he had in the past excoriated. He found in Churchill a hero. He had learnt how to deal with a German bomb should it ever land on his college, Peterhouse, but, beyond occasional broadcasting and his own writing, took no active part in winning the war.

Butterfield was elected to his Chair in Cambridge in the month when the Allies bombarded German forces ensconced in the ancient monastery of Monte Cassino. The 'general guidance' in the Italian campaign of 1943–5, much debated, had been that Italy's shrines should be regarded as sacrosanct unless military necessity dictated otherwise. If one of the most venerable shrines in Western Christendom could be destroyed, that was an odd reflection on the defence of Christian civilization. A Cambridge historian and a gunner at Monte Cassino were, in their different ways, drawing attention to the inherent ambiguity of noble wars. In different places, throughout the war, churches grappled with these uncomfortable paradoxes.

vi. Rebuilding Exercises

The journalist reporting *Malvern 1941* suspected that the bishops, deans, archdeacons and other clergy smiled at the response of the 'fish-and-chip public', as reported by Mervyn Stockwood when he had let that public know that the archbishop was running a show to put the world right.[202] If the conference did indeed smile, it was a commentary on the social character of the gathering. Certainly, the 'fish-and-chip' saloon, perhaps a location not entirely devoid of Christian patronage, would have been at a loss whether to agree, or not, with Mr MacKinnon that St Thomas Aquinas was right in his insistence on the ultimacy of ontology. Putting the world

---

[200] H. Butterfield, *Christianity in European History* (London, 1952), 61–3.
[201] Martina Steber, 'Herbert Butterfield, der Nationalsozialismus und die deutsche Geschichts-wissenschaft', *Vierteljahrshefte für Zeitgeschichte* (April 2007), 269–308.
[202] The writer was Bernard Causton.

right was an ambitious agenda. It was being set by men, and just a few women, whose operational milieu was rather different from that of 'ordinary' pew occupiers. As they began to build again did churches not need to ask questions, unpalatable questions, about their own buildings and ways of operating? It was likely, as appeared to have happened after the Great War, that soldiers returning from the war, might not slip back into old church routines (supposing they had them). There were formidable issues of leadership.

Bristol offers one example of 'starting again'. The heart of the old city had been practically destroyed by German bombs in 1940.[203] Of the two ancient churches of St Mary-le-Port and St Peter's little remained but the towers. The spire of St Nicholas stood out against the sky amidst shattered buildings, but the church was in ruins. The prime minister, chancellor of the city's university (itself damaged), sent a message of sympathy and came to see the devastation. So did the king. The bishop and the lord mayor were frequently out and about together visiting devastated sites and supporting homeless people throughout the war years. The dean, holder of a DSO and MC in the Great War, never expected to see the scene all around him. He set up a committee of clergy and members of all denominations to act as the agents of the Social Welfare Committee of the City Council in caring for people whose homes had been rendered unusable by the air raids. It received much local praise.[204] The bishop was himself rendered homeless in the air raids, though not enduringly so. Of course, German bombers had not single-mindedly concentrated upon the established church. All denominations in the city had seen some of their buildings smashed.[205] Bristol's experience was shared, to one extent or another, up and down the country. Nor, apparently, was damage only being caused by the enemy. The bishop of Lincoln expressed some consternation that the constant tramping up and down of the Home Guard in their military boots was damaging the lead on the roof of a church near Sleaford. It was not certain, also, that the church tower in which, on occasion, the men slept, would survive unscathed from their occupation. In Liverpool, London, Coventry and elsewhere, hallowed ecclesiastical landmarks had simply disappeared—even if the talismanic survival of St Paul's in London could be taken as some kind of encouraging miracle.

---

[203] Helen Reid, *Bristol under Siege* (Bristol, 2005).

[204] T.H. Underdown, *Bristol under Blitz* (Bristol, 1941), 15–16.

[205] Methodists suffered 2,607 cases of War Damage (these include cases of 'major' damage only). About £2.5 million was paid out in war damage compensation. During the war, the amalgamation of circuits and the sale of churches which had modestly followed Methodist Union came to a halt. Rupert Davies, 'Methodism' in Rupert Davies, ed., *The Testing of the Churches 1932–1982* (London, 1982), 58–9.

How should the churches be rebuilt? The struggle between heritage and 'the future' could be poignant. What happened in Bristol occurred in other cities too. The city's expansion had seen new churches erected in the 1920s. Reorganization schemes, involving the disappearance of ancient parishes, had started when war broke out. One central church in 1937, for example, could seat 800 but had an electoral roll of only 55. Before the planned demolition took place, however, it found itself being used as a mortuary during the air raids. Fifteen Anglican churches were totally destroyed and more badly damaged. A diocesan reorganization committee, with the new bishop, F.A. Cockin, grappled with the task of reconciling the frequent desire of congregations, sometimes much depleted, to restore what had been with the need to build for relocated populations in new housing 'estates'. The bombers, further, had not even-handedly destroyed Anglo-Catholic and Evangelical churches: a further complication. Individual clergy were determined not to be shifted. Fierce battles over the surviving city centre churches were the order of the day, in some cases lasting more than a decade, as petitions streamed in and enquiries were set in motion. There was general agreement that new churches for new estates were needed (and were provided, to some degree) but individual congregations always found good reasons why others should move and they should stay. The war had had tragic consequences but it also provided an opportunity for denominational bodies to think strategically about 'church planting'.[206]

The problems in this regard faced by Anglicans were faced, on a smaller scale, by all the denominations in Bristol. Baptists, Methodists, Congregationalists and Presbyterians all lost prominent places of worship. They wondered how, or whether, to 'relocate'. The Free Churches made some attempt to co-ordinate their building programmes. There was general agreement that the new estates should not be 'spiritual deserts' but 'transplanting' raised predictable issues. In architectural terms, what should new churches look like? Were they and their ancillary buildings to be squat, compact, multi-functional centres within 'communities' which had little sense of community? Or should they 'look like proper churches'?[207] Whatever specific answers were given, 'buildings' loomed ever larger in the practical life of all churches. Heating and running maintenance costs bulked

---

[206] The London North Presbytery of the Presbyterian Church of England's break from tending the growing suburbs around London to planting congregations in towns further afield would probably not have happened were it not for the war. Michael Hopkins, 'The Second World War and the Church Extension Policies of the Presbytery of London North', *Journal of the United Reformed Church History Society* 7/5 (2004), 327; E. Benson Perkins and Albert Hearn, *The Methodist Church Builds Again* (London, 1946).

[207] William Whyte, 'The Architecture of Belief' in Jane Garnett, Matthew Grimley, Alana Harris, William Whyte and Sarah Williams, *Redefining Christian Britain: Post-1945 Perspectives* (London, 2007), 190–5.

ever larger for congregations, many of whom now never regularly filled the space their buildings provided, and perhaps, in some cases at least, had never done. Buildings which had once met notions of 'sacred space' for some generations failed to move, and even repelled, their successors. If they once inspired, perhaps they now impeded. These issues, while they affected all denominations, hit the Church of England most severely. It, not the state, was the guardian of a central part of the nation's architectural heritage—and eager commentators were beginning to reassert the value of Victorian buildings which their users might wish to 'vandalize' or even destroy and replace. There were no simple answers.

A concern with buildings made people think of 'going to church' rather than 'being the church'. So what went on inside had urgently to express 'being in communion'. It had to link liturgy and life. In 1935, Gabriel Hebert published *Liturgy and Society*, which offered a vision of Christian worship as a focal point for society as a whole.[208] O.C. Quick, writing from Durham, hoped the book would have a wide and deep influence. Modern masters of the spiritual life were saying that it was necessary to cultivate private mystical powers, but he did not feel anxious to possess them. What was needed was a 'genuinely corporate and incorporating religion'.[209] Hebert, at one level, seemed by background as 'conventional' as his Oxford contemporary, the bishop of Chester. He too was the son and grandson of clergymen and had likewise taken a first in Theology. Thereafter, however, their paths had diverged significantly. Hebert had varied experiences in the parish of Horbury, West Yorkshire, in the Community of the Resurrection, in the Society of the Sacred Mission at Kelham, in South Africa and in Sweden. Worship sustained a sense of Christian identity. It was the sphere in which Christians, united with Christ, were enabled to become his co-workers in creating a more humane society, modelled on the Body of Christ. He wished to return to what he considered to be the practice of the early church and adopt the Parish Eucharist with Communion as the principal service of the Sunday. Other enthusiasts took forward the idea of 'the Parish Communion' but by no means all clergy were convinced.[210] It remained the case that a stray visitor seeking to worship in an Anglican

---

[208] A.G. Hebert, *Liturgy and Society* (London, 1935). Donald Gray, *Earth and Altar: The Evolution of the Parish Communion in the Church of England until 1945* (London, 1986), 196–208 stresses both that the idea of the Parish Communions did not spring new-born from the work of Hebert and that the activity of the Roman Catholic Church on the continent had no particular influence.

[209] Letter, March 1936, cited in Gray, *Earth and Altar*, 205.

[210] A.G. Hebert, ed., *The Parish Communion* (London, 1937). Christopher Irvine, *Worship, Church and Society* (Norwich, 1993) is an exposition of Hebert's work. See also P.J. Jagger, *Bishop Henry de Candole: His Life and Times 1895–1971* (Leighton Buzzard, 1975) and *A History of the Parish and People Movement* (Leighton Buzzard, 1977).

church on a Sunday could have no certainty about what it would entail. The pattern was liable to give rise to strong emotions if an incumbent made substantial alteration—whether in a 'Protestant' or 'Catholic' direction. The ornate interior of the parish church of St Hilary in Cornwall was wrecked in 1932 when militants of the Protestant Truth Society, armed with crowbars and hammers, set to work. A few years later, a broken man, the vicar resigned the living.[211]

Hebert, whose seventeenth-century ancestors had been French Huguenots, knew well how difficult it was to find a true catholicity.[212] It would not be sufficient for English Anglicans and Free Churchmen to come to a common mind. They should not blot out Lutherans, Roman Catholics and Orthodox, difficult though it was to envisage what a coming Great Church might be. He kept himself informed on the 'Liturgical Movement' as it manifested itself in French and German Roman Catholicism, a movement which, at the time, impinged little on the Roman Catholic Church in the British Isles. Hebert had much congenial contact with Free Churchmen who shared his concern for the form and nature of worship and its central significance.[213] Congregationalists mooted a new denominational hymnbook which would take account of hymn scholarship by eminent men in their ranks. Delayed by the war, it eventually appeared in 1951 as *Congregational Praise*. A young man, son of a Congregationalist father but educated at Fisher's Repton, had frequent interchange with Hebert. He was Michael Ramsey, whose first book spoke of there being 'no limit to what may be done through the sections of Christendom learning of one another's thought and ways and worship'.[214] Schemes of unity without such a recovery could have no meaning. 'Priests', 'Pastors' and 'People' did not find it easy, however, to assimilate different ways of worshipping. There was an undeniable element of eccentricity in Hebert. He could never be relied upon to be travelling with pyjamas and shaving equipment. His 'unworldliness' might indicate his proper sense of priorities, but whether

---

[211] Nicholas Orme, ed., *Unity and Variety: A History of the Church in Devon and Cornwall* (Ereter, 1991), 158.

[212] The Congregationalist Daniel Jenkins acknowledged Hebert's kindness in commenting on his *The Nature of Catholicity* (London, 1942) in manuscript.

[213] N. Micklem, ed., *Christian Worship* (Oxford, 1936). A common concern should not be taken to imply detailed agreement. Nor should one suppose that the Free Church service books being drawn up in this period by various figures were in fact 'typical' of the thinking of their congregations. Anglican interlocutors also failed to understand that hymns were not merely liturgical interludes but, rather, sung texts integral to the service. N. Wallwork, 'Developments in Liturgy and Worship...' in Sell and Cross, eds., *Protestant Nonconformity*, 103. Young Irish Methodists were apparently calling upon their leaders 'to worship God in the beauty of holiness', which would mean 'dignity without stodginess in conducting sacramental and other services'. A. McCrea, ed., *Irish Methodism in the Twentieth Century: A Symposium* (Belfast, 1931), 190.

[214] Michael Ramsey, *The Gospel and the Catholic Church* (London, 1936), 225.

'the world' would listen to his rather high-pitched voice was another matter.

There were other ways of rebuilding, broadening and deepening. Coventry Cathedral had been destroyed by fire bombs on the night of 14 November 1940. In consequence the outer walls and the tower and the spire remained intact. In 1951, after a competition open to architects of the British Commonwealth, it was announced that the design submitted by Basil Spence had been accepted. The ruins would still be there, as a reminder, but something new was being attempted. At a cost of one million three hundred and fifty thousand pounds (one million of which was war damage compensation) the new cathedral was consecrated in May 1962. Cuthbert Bardsley had come to Coventry as bishop six years earlier. He had made a name for himself in south London during and after the war. A product of Eton and New College, Oxford, he might not have been thought a man for the Midlands. His distinctive Oxford 4th in Politics, Philosophy and Economics did not suggest that motor industry moguls would be beating their path to his door for industrial advice, yet in his twenty years in the city he made a considerable impact. Not only was he credited with naming the University of Warwick, he also was president of Coventry City Football Club. He showed what a bishop could still do as a 'local figure'. With its Chapel Unity and Ministry of International Reconciliation, the cathedral's ministry, in the words of its provost, H.C.N. Williams, was so organized 'on the widest possible front' that it could establish 'points of entry' for the whole community.[215]

The point at which the personal, the local, the national and the universal intersected in the life of the churches was hard to define. 'Great utterances by "Church leaders"', F.R. Barry admitted, 'may change the whole trend of national policy. But the Church's primary responsibility and the normal exercise of its influence is through the local group or congregation . . .'.[216] The Church of England, he thought, was more than one church amongst other churches. It had to think in terms of the whole body of the king's subjects. Free Churches, on the other hand, might be thought to focus on the 'local'.[217] It was hard to disguise, however, that the 'local' had been in trouble in the 1930s and there was little sign of amelioration. Both Baptists and Congregationalists, classically with an emphasis on the local church,

[215] H.C.N. Williams, *Coventry Cathedral* (London, 1971), 18; Sir Basil Spence, *Phoenix at Coventry: The Building of a New Cathedral* (London, 1962).

[216] Barry, *Church and Leadership*, 146.

[217] Though 1944 witnessed, in publication terms, a tussle between Arthur Dakin of Bristol College and Ernest Payne, which revealed how Baptists were not of one mind. A. Dakin, *The Baptist View of the Church and Ministry* (London, 1944); E.A. Payne, *The Fellowship of Believers: Baptist Thought and Practice: Yesterday and Today* (London, 1944).

were experimenting with general superintendents, and moderators, respectively, whose role it was to provide 'oversight' within 'areas' or 'provinces'. Yet precisely what their status and function was, or might become, was to a degree contentious. A suggestion that their geographical areas might match Anglican dioceses, at least in some parts of the country, got nowhere. There were those, too, who felt that additional tiers, together with what was perceived to be bureaucratization at 'the centre' of their respective 'Unions', far from giving impetus to evangelism, was a sign that the Free Churches had lost their way. At 'the centre' a 'general secretary' provided essential continuity but also required, in the individual appointed, an ability to steer a path through contrary tendencies.[218] Since 'leadership' was so problematic, it is difficult to identify 'representative' figures. Presidents of the Methodist Conference, chairmen of the Congregational Union and presidents of the Baptist Union did their annual turn and were then replaced. They could make little or no impact beyond their own denominations, and only a limited and transient one within. In such circumstances, 'names' remained men who had a wider audience by virtue either of their preaching ability—on which a premium, though with diminishing success, continued to be placed, or who published 'middlebrow' books and articles. Dr W.E. Sangster at the Central Hall, Westminster and Dr Leslie Weatherhead at the City Temple came into this category.[219]

At a more 'humble' level, ministers laboured locally, recognizing, as one put it in 1937, that the days were past when they could be 'pulpit Hitlers'. Their context, too, was one where financial questions were never far away. An obituarist in 1932 remarked of a departed Methodist minister that not only had he been a leader in the religious revival of 1905/6 but 'To this record should be added the timely repair of a dangerous roof at Hebron and the renovation of the church premises on an extensive scale.'[220] A Baptist superintendent in 1952 noted that the 'old idea' of what a minister did—conducting Sunday services and a weeknight devotional service, together with pastoral visitation of his congregation, was 'outmoded' but it was not clear what the 'new idea' should be.[221] Denominations worried both about

---

[218] The historian Ernest A. Payne was appointed general secretary of the Baptist Union in 1951. His predecessor, M. E. Aubrey, had served for twenty-six years. West, *To Be a Pilgrim*, 76–82. R.N. Newall, *Methodist Preacher and Statesman: Eric W. Baker, 1899–1973* (London, 1984).

[219] Paul Sangster, *Dr Sangster* (London, 1962) and A. Kingsley Weatherhead, *Leslie Weatherhead: A Personal Portrait* (London, 1975) are studies by their respective sons. Weatherhead was a prolific author and in such books as *Psychology and Life* (1934) and *Psychology and Healing* (1951) addressed a Christian constituency anxious to learn what 'psychology' had to say. His influential *The Mastery of Sex through Psychology and Religion* (1931) might have been better titled.

[220] These examples come from K.D. Brown, *A Social History of the Nonconformist Ministry in England and Wales, 1800–1930* (Oxford, 1988), 228 and 234. Brown also provides more detail on numbers and finance.

[221] Cited in Randall, *English Baptists*, 290–1.

the diminishing number and quality of men who offered themselves for ministerial training and then about the level of the stipend churches could afford to pay those who were in service. Principals of colleges wondered whether students knew enough about the needs of 'the general mass of men and women'. Further, as 'professionalization' became ever more apparent across society, wherein lay the 'professional skills' of the clergy? Were they jacks of all trades and masters of none? There was a limit to the 'training' that could be provided. Even bishops had to come face to face with the conclusions of their diocesan boards of finance. Budgets and balance-sheets did not make comfortable or congenial reading, and did not come naturally to them, but it was an aspect of leadership. Rebuilding did need leaders.

The archbishop of Canterbury, following Temple's early death, was Geoffrey Fisher, bishop of London, a man of a very different stamp. No one could doubt his energy. The England with which he had been familiar from childhood to middle age was rural and intimate. He had himself been born 'over the shop' in a rectory (which was itself an old manor house) in a small Leicestershire village where his father, grandfather and great-grandfather had all held the benefice. He was teaching in the village Sunday school at the age of twelve. He knew in his bones what the parochial round entailed. A headmaster of Repton for eighteen years, he had devoted himself to his school (a rather special kind of parish). He had not even been stirred into public utterance on the subject of the Revised Prayer Book. It was his wife who had more local 'church prominence' as president of the Mothers' Union in the diocese of Derby. She was also prominent in giving birth to six boys, a record amongst the wives of bishops in her era (the Temples, the Hensons and others were, to their sadness, without children). The Fishers did therefore know the joys and strains of family life upon which bishops were frequently called to comment.

He had been appointed bishop of Chester in 1932. In his first six months in office he had driven (driven himself) more than six thousand miles, held over one hundred confirmations, instituted some twenty incumbents, conducted four ordinations and visited one hundred churches. He thereafter took some steps to 'rationalize' his use of time. What was it to 'lead' and 'shepherd' three hundred priests (though not all wanted to be called priests) who were firmly protected by freehold, together with 'church people' (however defined) in a diocese he hardly knew in a county of three million people? He was installed in York Minster. If any of the people from the Chester diocese who travelled to York by special train included Birkenhead shipyard workers, and there must be doubt on that score, they were likely to find the sermon, delivered by Fisher's former tutor at Oxford, a shade elusive. The new bishop's skill in controlling 'high-spirited adolescents' and their brilliant but strong-willed teachers, it seemed, made him ideal for the world of the Wirral. A Merseyside Crusade, planned before his appointment, took place in autumn 1933. The church, as Fisher put it, was going 'to plunge into the great industrial areas'. He knew that the gospel meant nothing to thousands and that the church, if it conveyed anything, was 'utterly misunderstood'. He himself, however, understood little about 'great industrial areas'. He knew little about 'crusades' either, and was a bit dubious about them, though conceding that they might connect the church with the people. He realized, in the outcome, that this might take a long time.

The bishop did, however, have the advantage of a dean whose vision and energy, over more than a decade, had made Chester Cathedral full of life from end to end. He had been spurred to action by the shocking knowledge that many local people had never darkened the cathedral's doors. Its 'coming to life' served as a model to be copied by deans in other English cathedrals—not that Fred Dwelly, appointed the first dean of Liverpool in 1931, needed any prompting.[222] Prior to that, as 'Ceremonarius' in the new cathedral, Dwelly had shown a genius for a new pattern of Anglican ceremonial. There was more than just a splash of colour in his arrangements. It was even claimed that he taught the Church of England how to process.[223] Cathedrals, whether old or new, gained in significance, both as centres of church life and as locations for civic occasions. Yet, as Evelyn Underhill noted, having a taste of 'music, beauty and liturgy' from time to time was a good thing but they were 'the chocolate creams of religion'.[224] It was a matter of trying to give spiritual quality to every detail of everyday lives, as she put it in broadcast talks in Advent 1936.[225] 'Big shows' could give a misleading impression of what it was to seek to lead a spiritual life.

Some in Chester had been surprised to find a headmaster become a bishop—though there was a regular controlled release of public school headmasters onto the episcopal bench. A.T.P. Williams, former headmaster of Winchester and dean of Christ Church, Oxford, succeeded Henson at Durham in 1939. No 'ideal type' of bishop existed. Some deftly delegated what could be regarded as administrative chores. In consequence, their archdeacons, whose number was increasing, felt themselves overburdened. The day of the suffragan bishop was dawning. Some bishops who might have been scholars came to wish that they had been. Others plumped for a

---

[222] Peter Kennedy, *Frederick William Dwelly, First Dean of Liverpool, 1881–1967* (Lancaster, 2004).

[223] F.S.M. Bennett, *The Nature of a Cathedral* (Chester, 1925).

[224] Charles Williams, ed., *The Letters of Evelyn Underhill* (London, 1943), 168. Underhill (1875–1941) having herself undergone an experience of religious conversion in 1907, wrote widely on 'the inner life'. In her role as a retreat conductor and spiritual writer one of her concerns was with the reconciliation of the personal and the institutional in the life and experience of a Christian. Dana Greene, *Evelyn Underhill: Artist of the Infinite Life* (London, 1991).

[225] Evelyn Underhill, *The Spiritual Life* (London, 1937), 133.

mode of heroic industry, relishing the rich array of civic as well as ecclesiastical roles open to them. There were also, however, in their ranks men who had no administrative zeal or capacity. Tommy Strong of Oxford, receiving one of his clergy for some leisured, and as it turned out, protracted, conversation remarked that he was delighted to see his visitor since he 'found it hard to occupy my time here' (here being his palace at Cuddesdon).[226] Garbett of Winchester groaned at the thought of going to London to discuss with fellow bishops whether grants could be made from Queen Anne's Bounty to provide an incumbent with a new lavatory. Differences of character, temperament and theology were only to be expected. A 'balanced bench', which reflected the comprehensive character of the Church of England itself, was always at the heart of those who guided the mysterious process which led the prime minister to make his recommendations to the Crown. It could not always be achieved. Fisher disappointed those who wanted radical change. His enthusiasm for an overhaul of canon law could be ridiculed by those with priorities for reform which they deemed more immediately relevant. It was disconcerting, however, that he had such a firm grasp of what could and could not be done.

The archbishop gave inter-church discussions a further impetus, preaching in Cambridge in November 1946. The archbishop asked that the Free Churches should take episcopacy into their own systems. As in the previous war, the Church of England's national stance appeared enhanced, at least temporarily. 'Free Churchism' lacked potency as a concept in the circumstances of war. Even so, the Free Churches would not move rapidly. Not for the first, nor the last time, the essence of 'episcopacy' within and outside the Church of England (not to mention the Roman Catholic Church, though it did not feature in these discussions) proved difficult to define. Controversy surrounding the creation of the Church of South India in 1947—a coming together of Anglicans, Methodists, Presbyterians and Congregationalists—provided ample evidence of that. The non-Anglican ministers had not been re-ordained but all future clergy would be episcopally ordained. There was much agonizing, however, on what CSI clergy should be permitted to do in the Church of England were they to venture to England and encounter it. A steady stream of publications and conferences followed, both at home and abroad, but scholarship could not emerge with a consensus on the nature of ministry or, indeed, of the church itself.[227] The inauguration of the World Council of Churches, in Amsterdam in

---

[226] F.R. Barry, *Period of My Life* (London, 1970), 27.

[227] The Methodist R. Newton Flew published *Jesus and His Church* in 1938 and played a notable role in these matters both within Methodism and in national and international discussion. G.S. Wakefield, *Robert Newton Flew 1886–1962* (London, 1971). R. Kissack, *Church or No Church? A Study of the Development of the Concept of Church in British Methodism* (London, 1964). K. Kirk, ed., *The Apostolic Ministry* (London, 1946); K.M. Carey, ed., *The Historic Episcopate* (London, 1954).

1948, placed all such insular debate in a wider framework. Bishop Bell was elected chairman of its Central Committee and as a consequence its first meeting was held in Chichester. There was no lack of material for the student of comparative ecclesiology to consider, but the way forward proved elusive. There was a conference in Lund in Sweden in 1951 at which a notable contribution was made from Britain—Tomkins (Church of England), Payne (Baptist), Flew (Methodist), Torrance (Church of Scotland). C.H. Dodd was also one of the speakers. One of the consequences was that it became fashionable to talk about the 'non-theological factors'—class and nationality in particular—as underlying stumbling-blocks on the path to unity.[228]

Recognition of such realities was arguably overdue, though it was a revelation which seemed to suppose that theology itself could somehow escape cultural contextualization. The quest for unity, an official Methodist statement declared in 1952, had assumed an urgency which could not be exaggerated when seen against the background of a generation which had either repudiated Christian values or separated them from the Christian faith.[229] People were indeed talking and writing reports about unity, but could not decide in what it essentially consisted. Some thought that it could and should mean the creation of 'one church'. Fisher dismayed enthusiasts, however, by saying that one 'centrally organized church' would merely guarantee that either heresy, or at least folly, would dominate the whole situation.[230] What he wanted was for separate churches to be in close harmony and in full inter-communion with each other. Each could then preserve its special ethos, direction and freedom. What inter-communion would mean, he wrote in 1950 in contributing a foreword to a report submitted to him by a group of Free Churchmen, was that each believed that the other held the essentials of the Christian faith.[231] To his critics, this approach sounded too much like that of a practical mind.

vii. Welfare: Minds and Bodies

Material in the previous section has illustrated how the churches, particularly in England, pondered reconstruction. They were inevitably concerned

---

[228] C.H. Dodd, G.R. Cragg and J. Ellul, *Social and Cultural Factors in Church Divisions* (London, 1952).

[229] Cited in J.M. Turner, *Conflict and Reconciliation: Studies in Methodism and Ecumenism 1740–1982* (London, 1985), 194.

[230] Edward Carpenter, *Archbishop Fisher: His Life and Times* (Norwich, 1991), 317.

[231] R. Newton Flew and Rupert E. Davies, *The Catholicity of Protestantism* (London, 1950), 8–9. In the same year Cardinal Griffin put the position, as he saw it, very plainly in *The Catholic Church and Reunion* (London, 1950). During the war, Vincent McNabb, with unusual sympathy, had considered the position of Nonconformists in *Catholics and Nonconformists* (London, 1942)—but McNabb was unusual. F. Valentine, *Father Vincent McNabb OP* (London, 1955).

with 'internal matters'. Leading figures, however, looking at what had happened in Europe over the previous quarter-century, argued that education had to be more than instilling knowledge. It had to convey, by ethos or explicit instruction, values which held society together. Government seemed prepared to concede that such values should be Christian, at least in a broad sense.

The Education Act of 1944 in England and Wales had many aspects, but a central one in this regard was the requirement that all schools had to begin the day with a collective act of worship and that all children should receive regular religious 'instruction'.[232] The Anglican report *Towards the Conversion of England* (1945) paid tribute to the apparent recognition by the state that 'true Christian education is far more than to teach a certain kind of subject at a certain time'.[233] In 'Aided Schools', largely Anglican or Roman Catholic, the churches concerned retained control over the content of religious instruction. In other schools, what 'religious instruction' meant was determined by four panels who would have to settle, at local authority level, on an 'agreed syllabus': the Church of England (except in Wales), 'other denominations' as the LEA saw fit, the LEA itself and, finally, teachers' associations. Political accommodations had apparently been made which had substantially succeeded in overcoming previous entrenched denominational confrontations. Some denominations, even so, continued to feel that others had been the 'winners' in the settlement.

The Roman Catholic Church continued to stand out most vigorously in its determination to retain (and extend) its school network and to call upon the faithful for the financial support which was still vital. Griffin lobbied hard. Butler, the education minister, was rewarded for the outcome with a copy of Butler's *Lives of the Saints*. Perhaps this would contribute to the minister's spiritual development. Heenan, however, thought that Butler's behaviour had been awful, and took to wondering whether he slept with a copy of *Mein Kampf* under his pillow. By 1950, however, even though there were now some 400,000 children in Catholic schools, Griffin, conscious of the financial burden which the Act still placed, was coming to consider it, rather exaggeratedly, as the 'death sentence of Catholic schools'.[234] The network continued to expand, though there were Catholic voices who

---

[232] S.J.D. Green, 'The 1944 Education Act: A Church–State Perspective', *Parliamentary History* 19 (2000), 148–64; W. Earl, 'The 1944 Education Act—Forty Years On', *British Journal of Religious Education* 6 (1984), 88–92. Gerald Parsons, 'There and Back Again? Religion and the 1944 and 1988 Education Acts' in Gerald Parsons, ed., *The Growth of Religious Diversity: Britain from 1945*, vol. ii (London, 1994), 165–8; J. Hull, *Studies in Religion and Education* (Lewes, 1984). The relevant section of the Act is published in R.P. Flindall, ed. *The Church of England, 1815–1948: A Documentary History* (London, 1972), 431–3.

[233] Cited in Flindall, *Church of England* 469.

[234] Michael de la Bedoyère, *Cardinal Bernard Griffin* (London, 1955).

wondered whether too much emphasis was placed upon 'the Catholic school'.[235] The church itself, however, did not seem to be under a death sentence. The year 1950 was not only a Holy Year for the Universal Church but the centenary of the restoration of the Catholic hierarchy. Wembley Stadium was filled for an episcopal Mass. Separate education, a natural right, would secure the crowds for the future, or so it was hoped.

The all-pervasive assumption of the agreed syllabi, as they evolved locally, was that in large measure 'religion' meant 'Christianity'. D.C. Somervell, author of the best-selling *History of Our Religion* (1934), could reasonably assume that everybody knew that 'our religion' was Christianity. Little had changed a decade later. Some syllabuses, further, were explicit that 'Christianity' meant 'the church'. Sunderland's enjoined schools to do their 'positive best' to guide children into church membership. Derbyshire's hoped to bring pupils, by studying the Bible, to fashion their own lives on the pattern of the life of Christ. Surrey's hoped that children would gain knowledge of 'the common Christian faith' which their fathers (and perhaps mothers?) had held for nearly two thousand years.

There was, however, the deeper question of whether this 'common Christian faith' was in fact held in common. What might be held in common was a 'Christian ethic' loosely linked to churches. Different views could be expressed as to whether, detached from the churches, the 'Christian ethic' might express the country's 'values'. Perhaps the 'ordinary man in the street' wanted neither a creed of 'secularism' nor 'churchiness' but a diluted form of Christianity.[236] For some, there was an ever broadening chasm between what the churches taught and what legislators should permit or perhaps even encourage. 'It would be well', Dean Inge declared, 'if Christians quite openly professed and acted upon a higher standard than that of the world around them.' That was unquestionably the Christian method of leavening society.[237] But was it desirable to seek to impose these standards legislatively? Even if desirable, however, it was becoming steadily less and less feasible in the realm of personal behaviour to do so.

The Matrimonial Causes Act (1937), which provided more possibilities of divorce, is a clear example. Lang decided that it was no longer feasible to impose 'the full Christian standard by law on a largely non-Christian

---

[235] A detailed account is J. Davies, ' "L'Art du Possible": The Board of Education, the Catholic Church and Negotiations over the White Paper and the Education Bill, 1943–1944', *Recusant History* 22 (1994), 231–50. A very influential figure in shaping the Catholic response was George Beck, a headmaster, in 1951 bishop of Brentwood and subsequently and successively bishop of Salford and archbishop of Liverpool. F.R. Phillips, *Bishop Beck and English Education 1949–1959* (Lampeter, 1990).

[236] An assertion of a holistic *Christian Education* (London, 1947) came from Spencer Leeson, headmaster and later bishop of Peterborough.

[237] W.R. Inge, *Christian Ethics and Modern Problems* (London, 1930), 392.

population' and he had abstained in the vote in the Lords, as did all the other bishops, with one exception. All that the Church of England could do was to 'commend' its view of marriage to the state. What the church could still attempt—though it could not be completely carried out—was to prohibit the remarriage in church of divorced persons. On these matters, however, there was not a common mind across the churches. The Methodist Conference had approved the 1937 measure by a large majority, but the opposition of the Roman Catholic hierarchy to divorce remained implacable. Even so, while a Roman Catholic peer reminded their lordships that divorce was 'contrary to the teachings of Christ', most of the twenty-three Roman Catholic MPs did not vote and certainly did not attempt to mobilize a 'Roman Catholic opposition'. The Independent MP (for Oxford University) behind the measure, A.P. Herbert thought of himself as an Anglican, but wanted an honest recognition of the misery which could occur in some marriages. Church people might be able to offer 'Marriage Guidance' (the Council was formed in 1938) but they could not control what the state would regard as legal. The trend of divorce began to move upwards. 'Christian Marriage', as an issue, was symbolic of other areas where what the churches, with differing degrees of denominational emphasis, saw as 'ideal behaviour', whether in regard to Sunday observance, the drink licensing laws or gambling, was at loggerheads with what growing numbers of the population ignored or deliberately challenged, or so it appeared.[238] But whether 'the state' should be indifferent as between all forms of human behaviour, whether some behaviour might be regarded as 'normative' (and, if so, on what grounds), and whether 'individual rights' and 'a sense of community' (conceived as 'national') could be reconciled— all these matters were becoming increasingly problematic even as a kind of 'educational restoration' was being attempted.

There was, however, apparently no need to consider these issues other than in terms of a dialogue (or even a confrontation) within a traditional 'church and state' framework. A limited place for studying 'world religions' did exist in 'RE', but there was no serious expectation that there would ever be substantial adherents of 'foreign' religions in the British Isles. The first new arrivals from outside Europe, unexpectedly, might indeed be bringing Christianity 'back' to Britain. Some at least of the arrivals from the Caribbean on the *Windrush* in 1948, and subsequently, had spiritual homes in churches which may have been, through past missionary activity, 'made in Britain', but which had now come to have their own style and

---

[238] Matter in this paragraph is derived from G.I.T. Machin, *Churches and Social Issues in Twentieth-Century Britain* (Oxford, 1988), 99–106.

characteristics. For the moment, however, the assumptions of 1944 largely held. They would not do so for very much longer.

The National Health Service which Labour had created in 1948 endured under its successor. Its central concern was with medical provision, at every level, for 'health'. Churches, although not using the language, also saw themselves as providing a national health service. There was a possible threat if the NHS embodied the assumption that 'health' was solely a matter of the body. There was a spiritual dimension. The NHS, however, did permit, and fund, hospital chaplains and some space and provision for religious services. The non-Catholic churches in the United Kingdom, in general, found little to quarrel with these arrangements. Even so, as with education, there lurked questions about medical ethics which could lead to conflict about what a National Health Service, under the direction of law, should provide in hospitals.

Roman Catholics, however, had anxieties about an enveloping and all-embracing welfare state—whether expressed in education or health. There was no need to search for examples of what states had been doing in the recent past of Europe. Cardinal Griffin was very wary. He wondered what would happen if people thought that Whitehall could provide every-thing.[239] Downey of Liverpool urged resistance against 'Stateolatry' and John Heenan, who became bishop of Leeds in 1951, feared the country was in danger of becoming 'National Socialist'. In Cardiff, Archbishop McGrath, an Irishman who thought that most projects for social reform were not worth the paper on which they were written, did battle with Aneurin Bevan, the South Walian apostate Nonconformist, who was cre-ating the National Health Service. For the state to take over the voluntary hospitals, McGrath wrote to Bernard Griffin, who had succeeded Hinsley as archbishop of Westminster in 1943, was 'expropriation and pure robbery quite in line with J. Stalin's methods'. Catholic voluntary hospitals with-drew from the NHS and, constituting only a tiny proportion of hospital provision, struggled to survive.[240] In Britain, however, the Catholic Church was powerless to prevent the apparently relentless expansion of state as opposed to voluntary provision.

Evelyn Waugh, as an English Catholic, dyspeptically observing this development, had momentarily sought a house in Ireland. Having failed to find one, or at least one which measured up to his requirements, he concluded that his failure had been a blessing. Irish peasants were malevo-lent, with smiles as false as Hell. Their priests were suitable for them, but not for foreigners.[241] Leaving such an assessment aside, it was true that the

---

[239] Peter Coman, *Catholics and the Welfare State* (London, 1977).
[240] Cited in Aspden, *Fortress Church*, 266–7.
[241] Mark Amory, ed., *The Letters of Evelyn Waugh* (London, 1980), 373.

boundaries of the state were being drawn differently in Ireland. In 1950–1, the 'Mother-and-Child' controversy, at least in the eyes of the *Irish Times*, demonstrated that the hierarchy provided the effective government of the country. That newspaper, by its tradition, could reach that conclusion easily but it was not alone in doing so. The minister of health, Dr Noel Browne, had introduced a bill which would have provided free medical care for mothers and children without a means-test. It is generally agreed, in retrospect, that there were many ingredients in the controversy that then erupted—among them Browne's less than emollient personality and the medical profession's concern for its own welfare—besides the hierarchy's identification of the proposal as 'a ready-made instrument for future totalitarian aggression'. McQuaid's opposition should not be taken to indicate an indifference to social welfare. He had been vigorous within the diocese in this regard. His own contribution to the debate, however, gained added depth from his being the son of a doctor. The scheme, with Browne deserted by his colleagues, was abandoned. It was easy to conclude, though an overstatement, that the hierarchy could do what it liked.[242]

There was nothing accidental in the reference by the Irish bishops to 'future totalitarian aggression'. They stated their fear that state officials would not respect Catholic principles, principles which they were determined to see maintained in hospitals (as in schools). The statement did not concede that an Irish state could operate in this matter on any other basis than one which it approved, The hierarchy in Northern Ireland, however, accepted, or at least acquiesced in, Catholics using a comparable scheme as the Stormont government, with some satisfaction, implemented it in the North (as its variant of the 'welfare state' in Britain). The church claimed to fear 'totalitarian aggression' but its stance seemed itself to some contemporary critics to exhibit a totalitarian frame of mind. *The Tablet* in London, however, expressed its profound gratitude to the Irish hierarchy for the stand it had taken. What the Irish minister of health had advocated as 'social justice', it said, 'was the very reverse of justice'.

The Anglican Lambeth Conference in 1948, however, thought that national 'mobilization' in the United Kingdom was inevitable and not likely to be reversed. It did, however, present voluntary and free associations with new problems, in particular in 'altering the boundaries of the respective spheres of Church and State'. A subsequent commentator, arguing that it was 'the welfare role of religion which made it relevant to society' suggested that in relegating its historic charitable role to the sidelines many traditional

---

[242] Browne's autobiography is *Against the Tide* (Dublin, 1986). Browne's advocacy owed something to his own time in medical practice in England. A Protestant wife, who shared his 'left-wing' stance, did not increase his popularity in circles where popularity mattered.

parishioners were 'estranged'.[243] In providing 'welfare', who decides what 'welfare' is?[244] Bishop Lucey of Cork thought bishops should be the final arbiter of 'right and wrong' even in political matters. But should 'authority' and 'power' be the same? The belief in a cohesive national moral community with 'common values' was powerfully present both in 'new Ireland' emerging from its struggle and in a Britain emerging from its wartime 'common struggle'. The outcome for the churches, Catholic and Protestant, for the moment at least, seemed significantly different in the two countries. It seemed also that they were content with this difference. The Church of England appeared to have reached the conclusion, as Garbett put it, that the welfare state was the contemporary embodiment of the principle 'Bear ye one another's burdens and so fulfil the law of Christ'. Donald Soper, who had campaigned for it from his soapbox in Hyde Park, was able, as president of the Methodist Conference in 1953, to declare that he thanked God for its creation.[245]

Further, the degree to which 'Christian values' should be, or could be made to be, 'common' remained to be tested. The peoples and churches of the British Isles sought to 'learn the lesson' from the European 'civil war' of the previous twenty years. The churches might find themselves functioning in plural societies with little sense *au fond* of common values or on what basis (if required as a precondition of 'integration' and social harmony) 'common values' might be constructed. It might, indeed, already be too late for such an enterprise.

viii. Crowning Moment

In June 1953 in a fairy-tale golden coach drawn by eight greys, a 27-year-old queen arrived at Westminster Abbey to be crowned by a 66-year-old archbishop.[246] The 'New Elizabethan Age' was beginning. Sir William Walton composed a splendid coronation march, though it was a little less splendid than the one he had composed in 1937. Here, it seemed, was

[243] Frank Prochaska, *Christianity and Social Service in Modern Britain: The Disinherited Spirit* (Oxford, 2006), 96.

[244] Geoffrey Finlayson, 'A Moving Frontier: Voluntarism and the State in British Social Welfare, 1911–1949', *Twentieth Century British History* 1 (1990), 183–206 and *Citizen, State and Social Welfare in Britain 1830–1990* (Oxford, 1994).

[245] Prochaska, *Christianity and Social Service*, 151 sees in the obeisance to the 'omnicompetent' state by the British churches (though he makes no distinctions between them in this regard) 'an abdication of a historic responsibility'. Christian leaders 'failed to appreciate the consequences of endorsing a collectivist secular world without redemptive purpose' since 'Collective provision eroded community religious life, partly because charities linked so many families to churches and congregations'. With their disappearance, religious observance was bound to suffer.

[246] Roy Strong, *Coronation* (London, 2006).

continuity. Church and state had together 'come through' after two turbulent decades. Yet, despite the solemnity, the splendour and the excitement, there was an underlying uncertainty, perhaps a sadness. Coronation was a time to take stock. The 'Age of Austerity' was perhaps giving way to an 'Age of Affluence'. That seemed positive progress. Few guessed how difficult it would be for the churches to endure prosperity.[247]

The aged prime minister again in Downing Street thought his last great contribution might be to make Washington and Moscow deal with each other. He found how limited was Britain's capacity. One war had ended in 1945 but another 'cold war' was ongoing. The *de facto* division of Europe was not what church leaders had looked for when they had endorsed plans for a new United Nations Organization and a 'new world order'. In the 1930s 'atheistic communism', which had alarmed, had been restricted to the Soviet Union. Now there was a 'Soviet Empire' which could be perceived as a 'threat', and perhaps was one. But what did it threaten? Was the 'Christian West' confronting the 'Communist East'? If so, were the churches in the front line?

Back in the war, Garbett's translation to York had turned him, rather to his surprise, into a wartime globetrotter, taking him notably to Britain's partners, Russia and the United States, amongst other places.[248] Some 'religious rehabilitation' of the Soviet Union, in existing conditions, seemed expedient. In the post-war world, it was apparently necessary to take sides in the unfolding conflict. Canterbury and York saw no reason to dissent from British foreign policy as it was fashioned in these years and indeed to play their part rallying the West.[249] A prominent Catholic, Barbara Ward, wrote busily on the fate of 'the West'.[250] Oliver Franks, six months later to be appointed British ambassador to the United States, wrote on 'The Tradition of Western Civilization'.[251] Churchill had famously, if somewhat

[247] Avner Offner, *The Challenge of Affluence: Self-Control and Well-Being in the United States and Britain since 1950* (Oxford, 2006).

[248] Dianne Kirby, 'Anglican–Orthodox Relations and the Religious Rehabilitation of the Soviet Regime during the Second World War', *Revue d'Histoire Ecclésiastique* 96/1–2 (2001), 101–23.

[249] Detailed aspects of this involvement are considered by Dianne Kirby in a book and in articles *Church, State and Propaganda: The Archbishop of York and International Relations. A Political Study of Cyril Foster Garbett 1942–1955* (Hull, 1999); 'Truman's Holy Alliance: The President, the Pope and the Origins of the Cold War', *Borderlines: Studies in American Culture* 4/1 (1997), 1–17; 'The Archbishop of York and Anglo-American Relations during the Second World War and Early Cold War, 1942–55', *Journal of Religious History* 23/3 (1999), 327–45; 'Harry S. Truman's International Religious Anti-Communist Front, the Archbishop of Canterbury and the 1948 Inaugural Assembly of the World Council of Churches', *Contemporary British History* 15/4 (2001), 35–70.

[250] Barbara Ward, *The West at Bay* (London, 1948), *Policy for the West* (Harmondsworth, 1951) and *Faith and Freedom: A Study of Western Society* (London, 1954).

[251] In the *Congregational Quarterly* 27/4 (1949), 296–303. The author's father, R.S. Franks, was a distinguished Congregationalist theologian, principal of the Western College, Bristol.

ambiguously, spoken in Zurich in 1946 about 'some kind of United States of Europe'. The churches throughout Europe would be vital to this end. Archbishop Fisher eventually agreed in May 1947 to preside over the inaugural meeting at the Royal Albert Hall of the United Europe Movement at which Churchill spoke. Other bishops indicated their support. There was talk of the restoration of the spiritual unity that was once western civilization and Christendom.[252] There appeared to be, at the 'leadership' level, an endorsement across the churches of a 'Europe' seen in this light. At pew level, however, the picture was far less clear. Keen supporters of the Labour government saw in 'Europe' a Churchillian ploy. Much capital could be gained by painting the Christian Democracy to be found in Western Europe as 'right-wing'. At a deeper level, however, just as declarations of 'spiritual unity' found it difficult to achieve ecclesiastical form so the 'political unity' could not disguise the continuing reality of national aspirations. What did 'unity' actually mean? Neither churches nor political parties knew, but they seemed, in general terms, to suppose it desirable, even necessary.

The Catholic bishops expressed deep concern about the fate of their counterparts in Soviet-dominated Eastern Europe. A modest, but not perhaps crucial, financial contribution was made to assist the Christian Democrats in the Italian general election of 1948. Cardinal Griffin in 1949 had no difficulty in releasing a Lenten pastoral letter which stated that Catholics could vote for any political party except for the Communist Party of Great Britain. Catholic enthusiasm for 'Europe', though it was not universal, in turn aroused some Protestant suspicions, which could even extend to the Labour Cabinet, that a Catholic plot was being hatched. A Catholic-dominated Europe was not an attractive prospect.[253] There was, of course, in these matters continuity with positions in relation to communism which had been taken in the 1930s—except that now the threat seemed much graver. And if war should come, church leaders were obviously aware of the possibility that it might resume where Hiroshima and Nagasaki had left off.[254]

[252] Philip M. Coupland, *Britannia, Europa and Christendom* (London, 2006), 92–6. J. Zeilstra, *European Unity in Ecumenical Thinking, 1937–1948* (Zoetermeer, 1995).

[253] For 'Christian Democracy' in general see Joan Keating, 'The British Experience: Christian Democrats Without a Party' in David Hanley, ed., *Christian Democracy in Europe: A Comparative Perspective* (London, 1994) and 'Looking to Europe: Roman Catholics and Christian Democracy in 1930s Britain', *European History Quarterly* 26/1 (1996), 57–79.

[254] One of the first enquiries set in train by the British Council of Churches produced *The Era of Atomic Power* (London, 1946). The Church of England produced *The Church and the Atom* (London, 1948) which criticized the use of the bombs on the Japanese cities but defended their retention. Dianne Kirby, 'Responses within the Anglican Church to Nuclear Weapons, 1945–1961', *Journal of Church and State* 37 (1995), 599–622.

Critics, though in a minority in all churches, criticized what they regarded as the 'compromise' which church leaders had apparently made with the 'Capitalist West'. The dean of Canterbury, to the constant chagrin of the archbishop, was able to add China to the list of communist countries which he eagerly visited and on which he gave encouraging reports. The fact that the Soviet Union had emerged at the end of the war with more millions incarcerated in concentration camps than had been similarly detained in Nazi Germany had not greatly troubled its Christian admirers. Whether communism was or was not a secularized version of Christianity continued to provoke discussion. The relationship between 'Christian Faith' and 'Communist Faith' was again explored by scholars.[255] Theoretical debate, however, only got one so far. What were things really like behind the 'Iron Curtain'? The Revd Mervyn Stockwood, with his wide experience as a city councillor, set out from Bristol in 1953 to see for himself.[256] Perhaps a new era was dawning, perhaps not. There was, therefore, much anxiety behind the flag-waving exuberance of the coronation procession. Everything might not be as solid and safe as it seemed inside Westminster Abbey.

It was the customary right of the primate of All England to preside over the supreme act of crowning and anointing the sovereign. Fisher was not disposed to modernize the rite, though *The Times* suggested he should. Canon Raven also helpfully reported that Canadian opinion, even in 1937, had wanted something more 'modern'. Canadian bishops had been peeved not to have been invited. However, episcopal griping from the 'dominions' was not the real problem (it might have been consoling that Westminster Abbey's organist was Australian). Difficulty arose because the British Empire was no more. It was a British Commonwealth, perhaps now only a Commonwealth. As such, it could not be a Christian Commonwealth. The *raj* had ended six years earlier. India in 1950 became a republic. The new queen was not an empress, she was 'Head of the Commonwealth', a title

---

[255] The contributors to D. Mackinnon, ed., *Christian Faith and Communist Faith: A Series of Studies by Members of the Anglican Communion* (London, 1953) tried to be 'balanced' in their identification of the points of compatibility and incompatibility. Of course, the British consideration of these matters was part of—or perhaps peripheral to—the debate which was going on elsewhere and in the context of a more active communist presence in the political sphere than was the case in Britain. Charles West, *Communism and the Theologians: Study of an Encounter* (London, 1958). Dianne Kirby, 'Christian Faith, Communist Faith: Some Aspects of the Relationship between the Foreign Office Information Research Department and the Church of England Council on Foreign Relations, 1950–1953', *Kirchliche Zeitgeschichte* 13/1 (2000), 217–41. Herbert Waddams, 'Communism and the Churches', *International Affairs* 25/3 (1949), 295–306.

[256] In his autobiography, *Chanctonbury Rings*, Stockwood recalled that he found Russia 'a servile state ruled by terror and corruption' but the reader of the book he published on his return, *I went to Moscow* (London, 1954) would not have formed this impression. Stockwood had been very vocal in his criticism of 'Christian Democracy' in western Europe.

whose exact significance was obscure. In these circumstances, options for Commonwealth involvement in the coronation were explored but not pursued.

The 'crowning moment' also sharply served to bring out the contrasts within the British Isles. It was not only the contrast between a monarchy and a republic but also between a small state and a 'world power'. The contrast, however, went deeper. There was an intensity about the Catholicism of the Irish state which was now largely lacking, in public comment at least, about the Protestantisms of the United Kingdom. The Dublin government in 1953, unlike its predecessor in 1937, had not expressed views on the coronation. *Eire* under the inter-party coalition of John Costello became the Irish Republic in 1948–9 and left the Commonwealth. The Church of Ireland Prayer Book omitted prayers for the monarch after 1949—an act of 'liturgical regicide' as some of its members considered it. The republic was an established fact, Archbishop Gregg told his synod, and reality had to be accepted. The death of George VI in February 1952 seems to have passed virtually unnoticed in the Republic. The three-hour newsreel film of the coronation, however, was very widely shown in Church of Ireland parish halls.[257] Even so, despite that interest, there could be no sense, even for Protestant people, that Elizabeth was still 'our queen'. In this sense, the coronation drew a line under lingering 'Protestant Britishness' as it had existed in the decades since 1922 in the Irish Free State/Irish Republic.

There still remained, however, prominent English Anglicans who felt themselves to some extent 'stranded' by all that had happened over the previous couple of decades. F.R. Barry, made bishop of Southwell in 1941, considered himself to be 'half Irish and half-English' and 'at home' in both islands.[258] Some opinion in Whitehall in 1949 thought that the population of the British Isles, for historical and geographical reasons, was essentially one. Whether they liked it or not, the Irish 'were not a different race from the ordinary inhabitants of Great Britain'.[259] That contention might be true or not, but there were now indubitably two countries who were 'foreign' to each other, though foreign in a rather idiosyncratic way. Ireland retained some special citizenship and trade preferences with Britain.[260] Notwithstanding the country's departure from the Commonwealth, its relationship

[257] Martin Maguire, 'The Church of Ireland in Dublin since Disestablishment' in Raymond Gillespie and W.G. Neely, eds., *The Laity and the Church of Ireland, 1000–2000: All Sorts and Conditions* (Dublin, 2000), 298.

[258] Barry, *Period of My Life*, 19.

[259] Cited in Kathleen Paul, *Whitewashing Britain: Race and Citizenship in the Postwar Era* (London, 1947), 108.

[260] Charles Raven, in Liverpool as a residentiary canon at the Anglican cathedral, with immigration to Merseyside from the Free State increasing, expressed disquiet about 'the entry of labour of an inferior quality' and referred to 'Irish invaders'. Dillistone, *Raven*, 152.

with the United Kingdom was through the Commonwealth Office (then separate) rather than the Foreign Office. The relationship between Protestants, Catholics and the state in the republic was now three-sided, not four-sided.[261]

Yet, for all the constitutional clarity which had perhaps been achieved, there were aspects of British–Irish relations which remained obstinately ambiguous, both negatively and positively. When members of the Irish hierarchy visited Pope Pius XII in late 1947 the pontiff raised the question of Irish emigration. He was told that the bishops were perturbed by the mass emigration from Ireland, much of it to Britain.[262] 'Foreign agents' [British] were recruiting female labour for work in Britain. The associated dangers to the faith of the emigrants needed no elaboration. A ban on emigration to Britain was even contemplated but not proceeded with. An attempt to persuade men to return to participate in 'the grand adventure of building up a new state' met with little success, and, in any case, it was only skilled workers who were needed for this adventure. The issue, also involving as it did the question of Irish living conditions in Britain, pointed to the continued intermeshing of politics, economics, culture and religion in the British–Irish relationship.

The final move towards a republic, however, had not been taken in a mood of exuberant optimism in Dublin. Politically, economically and culturally, the country seemed to be stagnant, maybe even moribund. In these circumstances, the church, at least in the person of the archbishop of Dublin, John Charles McQuaid, had not been reluctant, since his appointment in 1940, to give moral leadership to a rather demoralized nation.[263] There was, therefore, the paradox, if paradox it was, of a poor country in which population was declining but the church was still growing (if the actual number of priests, nuns and brothers—the 'religious personnel'—defines vigour). No other western European country could match Ireland in the number of priests per head of population. In addition, the country's capacity to produce priests, sisters and brothers for Britain and other 'missionary' countries beyond Europe (chiefly in what was still, ironically, largely 'British' colonial territory) gave Ireland a special status in the eyes

[261] There were, however, still many-sided aspects of the Northern Ireland situation. Should the archbishop of Westminster take up with the United Kingdom government the treatment of Catholics in Northern Ireland to which his attention had been drawn by the Catholic bishop of Down and Connor? United Kingdom ministers tended to suggest in reply that enquiries should be directed to Belfast. See the chapter on 'Ireland' in Moloney, *Westminster, Whitehall and The Vatican*, 103–18.

[262] Enda Delaney, *Demography, State and Society: Irish Migration to Britain, 1921–1971* (Liverpool, 2000), 189–93.

[263] John Cooney, *John Charles McQuaid, Ruler of Catholic Ireland* (Dublin, 1999). McQuaid had not risked modifying his low opinion of 'the English' by visiting them in their homeland.

of the Vatican. Significant investment went into seminaries, monasteries and convents. Substantial church building took place in Dublin in the post-war decade. Some new churches ensured that grandeur was not confined to cathedrals in Protestant hands. President O'Kelly, visiting Rome in the 1950 Holy Year, placed not only his personal homage but also that of 'my people' at the feet of the pope. Two years earlier, the incoming external affairs minister, Sean MacBride, had indicated his willingness to be 'summoned' by McQuaid. It would be a favour, apparently, to be placed at His Grace's disposal. Obsequiousness, however, was not a general characteristic of the minister. The relationship had about it the appearance of a 'Celtic Mystery' of a kind favoured by his mother, Maud Gonne. No minister in London would be willing to be 'summoned' by an archbishop.

Northern Ireland, however, was not going to be left out of the coronation. Its wartime record loomed large.[264] 'Ulster people' had played their part and everybody knew who they were. It was not surprising, therefore, that in 1953, Viscount Brookeborough, who had been prime minister of Northern Ireland for a decade, was rubbing shoulders with the other Commonwealth prime ministers at the Buckingham Palace coronation party—in an implausible appearance of parity with them. Protestant Ulster had played its part and could not be 'cast off'. He had been educated at Winchester and Sandhurst. He had seen no reason to visit the foreign country which lay to the south of Co. Fermanagh. His family had owned an estate in that county since the seventeenth century. Northern Ireland, the Act had declared, would not cease to be a part of His Majesty's dominions and the United Kingdom without the consent of its parliament. 'Partition' was constantly denounced by Dublin, but its campaign gained little international support. Its existence was given as the reason why, in 1949, the republic declined to join the new North Atlantic Treaty Organization. A subsequent appearance of Dutch naval vessels in the province, for NATO purposes, triggered protests to London, to no avail, protests evoked by long memories of an earlier visiting Dutchman.

Queen Elizabeth came to Belfast in 1953—a visit which revealed, unsurprisingly, that the status of Northern Ireland remained contentious.[265] For Catholics in the North, the declaration of a republic in the South came as a

---

[264] Brian Barton, 'The Impact of World War II on Northern Ireland and on Belfast–London Relations' in Peter Catterall and Sean McDougall, eds., *The Northern Ireland Question in British Politics* (London, 1996), 47.

[265] It was significant that it was on 'Empire Day', just after her wedding, that Princess Elizabeth had been given the freedom of Belfast when she and her new husband visited the province in 1949. She had then declared that she felt as much at home in Ulster as in any other part of the United Kingdom. The Crown was the focus of 'our unity, comradeship and moral standards'. David H. Hume, 'Empire Day in Ireland 1896–1962' in Keith Jeffery, ed., *An Irish Empire? Aspects of Ireland and the British Empire* (1996), 162–3.

shock. It might, after all, be necessary to recognize that the northern state might last. The reception of Her Majesty reflected the ambivalences, evolving all the time, inherent in this situation: Catholic councillors, or at least some, would not have come—if they had been invited—to the City Hall lunch to welcome her, but they were angry at not being invited. The queen, it had been claimed, might have been insulted or injured, but one Nationalist councillor complained that that was a most damnable and insidious thing to say. Nationalists wished this young woman well, though she was not their queen.[266]

One of the archbishop's correspondents, at least aware of some of these 'larger issues' which swirled around, concluded that their resolution was being postponed until the next coronation, which he wisely supposed would probably be at least fifty years off. Some tinkering satisfied liturgical scholars but impinged on nobody else. The archbishop, in any case, was clear that it was the spiritual significance of the religious act in Westminster Abbey which mattered. It was 'all or nothing'. At the heart of the rite was Holy Communion. Fisher knew that the queen understood that, but he produced a short article for the *Radio Times* for the benefit of the people. The 'Commonwealth' issue was effectively shelved, but there might be problems arising from the fact that Her Majesty was indubitably Queen of Great Britain and Northern Ireland. The Eucharist would be celebrated according to the manner of the Church of England. Fisher, unlike his two predecessors, was an Englishman. At his elbow, however, in relation to the sensitivities which this matter posed, stood a Scotsman, the dean of Westminster, who had been Lang's chaplain in 1937. There were signs of a changing mood in Anglo-Scottish relations. There had been strong support in the Church of Scotland for the 'National Covenant' launched in Scotland in 1949 calling for a Scottish parliament. The General Assembly a year later called for a royal commission on the subject. A daring raid in 1951 had returned the Stone of Scone on which Scottish kings had been crowned to Scotland from the Abbey (in the event, only temporarily, though much later it was to be formally and permanently restored). The Moderator of the General Assembly of the Church of Scotland was clearly not a bishop, but in a United Kingdom should he not have a part in the rite? It was decided that he should participate in presenting the Scriptures to the queen. He could not receive the sacrament.

What about Roman Catholics? In October 1952 Fisher wrote to the archbishop of Westminster, Griffin, concerning the coronation. In their exchange of letters, the latter made it clear that if he and other Roman Catholic bishops were to receive personal invitations they would not be

---

[266] Marianne Elliott, *The Catholics of Ulster* (London, 2000), 396–400.

accepted. No Roman Catholic bishop attended. It was, however, a bishop of the Church in Wales who caused a flurry six months later by preaching a sermon in which he attacked the oath which asked the Sovereign to maintain in the United Kingdom the 'Protestant Reformed Religion established by Law', to maintain inviolably 'the Settlement of the Church of England, and to preserve the rights and privileges of the Bishops and Clergy of England'. It had been contentious in 1937. Morris, the bishop of Monmouth—who happened to be an Englishman in Wales—was determined to make it more so. He did not like the word Protestant. It was only because it was Catholic (albeit reformed) that the Church of England had the moral right of its position. In Wales, too, both the Roman clergy and Nonconformist ministers were, 'strictly speaking', intruders. A public controversy followed in which the Dixie Professor of Ecclesiastical History at Cambridge learnedly joined. There was much discussion of what the word 'Protestant' meant. Fisher soon had enough of Morris's intervention. He was not a bishop of the Church of England, Fisher wrote to him, and was therefore not directly concerned. He should stop trailing his coat. Fisher admitted that the word 'Protestant' had misleading associations, but so did 'Catholic'. There were many people, 'himself included', who would apparently 'resist to the death' the removal of 'Protestant' from the coronation oath. It was all the more necessary to retain it since the Roman Catholic Church was 'becoming ever more heretical in doctrine and intolerant in spirit and aggressive in action' (his reference being to the proclamation, in 1950, of the dogma of the Bodily Assumption of the Virgin Mary).[267] It is not surprising that the word 'Protestant' was retained.

It is against this background that the United Kingdom still appeared a kind of Protestant state, although it was only England's particular, and perhaps peculiar, form of 'Protestant Reformed Religion' which was under the protection of the Crown. The general secretary of the Presbyterian Church of England, addressing the annual congress of the Free Church Federal Council in 1954, repeated both that the Roman Catholic Church was an institution alien to his understanding of the gospel, and that, as a political power, it was 'alien to the main stream of our British social and political insights'.[268] It was noticeable, too, that the new queen did not seem to regard her faith frivolously, although the Lord's Day Observance Society had not allowed her attendance at races in Paris on a Whit Sunday to go unnoticed. This same attendance had even been used in 1949 by opponents of admitting women to the diocesan and general synods of the Church of Ireland. Her attendance indicated what their presence might lead to. This

[267] John S. Peart-Binns, *Edwin Morris: Archbishop of Wales* (Llandysul, 1990), 87–94.
[268] *The Free Church Chronicle* (May 1954), 11.

time, however, they lost the vote. Her husband, Prince Philip, who was born in Greece, had remained Orthodox but had been received into the Church of England shortly before their wedding in 1947. Unprompted, to mark that occasion, the princess had given an oak screen to the restored Iona Abbey and, a few years after her coronation, had made a point of attending Sunday morning worship there on the occasion when it was dedicated. The 'Iona Community' had been the inspiration of the fiery but also somewhat ethereal George MacLeod who had waded through controversy over a decade in an effort to bring harmony between pink stone in ancient sunlight and the tenements of Govan, Glasgow, which he knew so well.[269] Started in 1938 as MacLeod's personal vision (but eventually in 1949 brought under the jurisdiction of the General Assembly), the community had seen crafts-men and ministerial licentiates working and living together on the island in restoring the monastic buildings and forging a sense of fellowship. The fusion of work and worship, not to mention politics, which had then evolved had often been controversial. The Crown, however, was evidently able to be at the service of all Protestant churches.

The director-general of the BBC, a former general, wrote after the coronation to Fisher to congratulate him on his 'splendid performance'. 'The full effect', he continued, 'spiritual as much as ceremonial, was per-fectly conveyed and must have had a profound impression on everyone.'[270] The 'everyone' no doubt included the millions who watched on television, giving it its largest audience to date.[271] There had been much agitation in predictable quarters beforehand about whether cameras would be both too obtrusive and intrusive, but in the end the televising had gone ahead. The capacity of television to trivialize everything had been apparent to the BBC hierarchy, particularly, no doubt, if its own monopoly was taken away. The archbishop of Canterbury agreed and supported a newly formed National Television Council whose manifesto declared that *Britain Unites against Commercial Television*. On the day itself, however, sections of the press took pleasure in the fact that 'the people' got a better peep than some ermined peers, imprisoned as the latter were behind obtrusive pillars.

---

[269] George MacLeod, *Govan Calling* (London, 1934). R. Morton, *The Iona Community* (Edin-burgh, 1977).

[270] Carpenter, *Fisher*, 263. Much of the material on the coronation in this section derives from Carpenter. In 1938, when it had been necessary to find a successor for Sir John Reith as director-general, the governors of the BBC had ruled out one candidate because, in the words of one of them, the historian H.A.L. Fisher, it would be quite impossible 'that the supreme executive control of one of the most important organs of public education in this country should be placed in Roman Catholic hands'. Leonard Miall, *Inside the BBC: British Broadcasting Characters* (London, 1994), 80.

[271] The experience, it so happens, as for so many others, was this author's first encounter with the medium.

How 'profound' the impression had really been was impossible to tell. British viewers, however, had been spared the advertisement for Blake's shampoo, a product which 'made every girl look queenly'. American viewers on NBC had watched it shortly before the crown was placed on the queen's head.[272] The mood surrounding the coronation, however, did suggest that a kind of Christian self-understanding was an integral element in the self-understanding of the United Kingdom. Nevertheless, as the golden coach rolled through the streets, symbolizing continuity, few in the churches (or for that matter in the state) grasped that the reign that was beginning would witness changes challenging the assumptions which surrounded the very 'splendid performance'.

[272] For discussion of certain aspects of the coronation see Richard Weight, *Patriots: National Identity in Britain, 1940–2000* (London, 2002), 240–2.

6

THE PERILS OF PROSPERITY, 1953–1975

The enchantment of the 'new Elizabethan age' had a brief existence. Twenty years on, historical parallels had lost their attraction. Certainties about the story of the islands began to dissolve both within and between Britain and Ireland. Empire faded, leaving contested legacies. African freedom ambiguously dawned. The shape of a 'New Europe' began to be discernible. 'Cold War' continued in fluctuating intensity. The United States guarded the 'Free World'. The 'British story' contracted so that the coming generation found it difficult to grasp the 'world' which had framed the lives of their parents.[1] Yet, paradoxically, as it also contracted, it became ever more open to the 'outside' world. On the one hand, eventually, the United Kingdom (and Ireland) 'joined' Europe. On the other, the languages, cultures and religions of the non-European world arrived in increasing numbers. These developments may be labelled as 'political' but they were more than the 'background' to the life of the churches. Their life, perhaps to a greater degree than they were aware of, was part of that story. That interaction is sampled in what follows. Yet, if they were part of that story, they also offered a parallel 'master narrative', though whether it could or should be delivered by the evangelical means shortly to be considered, looked unlikely. Trying, as ever, to relate the two stories became both more urgent and more complex. It necessarily required churches to look again at themselves, and their relations with each other. There were times, as is also implied in what follows, when that introspection became self-absorption and 'irrelevant'. It prompted some to jettison 'piety' in favour of 'politics'. Moreover, it took place at a time of accelerating prosperity—but could it last?—in a burgeoning 'consumer society'. Churches, with greater or lesser success, had seen themselves as alleviating poverty. It began to look as though their 'offering', at least within its customary structures, might be defeated by 'prosperity'. The sweeping social and economic changes, characteristic of the time, have been most frequently identified as 'secularizing forces', but whether such forces would really create a secular state or a secular society, assuming the one to be different from the other, was not

---

[1] Keith Robbins, ed., *The British Isles* (Oxford, 2002), 1–10.

clear. Such uncertainty could not do otherwise than force the churches to engage, as always, in the constant unsettling dialogue between 'text' and 'context'.

i. Evangelism: Call to the Nation(s)

In 1946, a young American Southern Baptist, Billy Graham, had a dream. He would save Britain from 'the abyss'. He toured the country speaking at over three hundred meetings. In subsequent winters, he held short mission events in the Albert Hall. In 1952, he spelt out what was needed to a gathering of Anglican Evangelicals in Church House, Westminster. Meticulous planning began. What was to happen for three months (March–May) in 1954, however, exceeded any campaign which had been attempted before. His fame as a preacher back home, which really began in 1949, had been consolidated in the interval. He had a bestseller in *Peace with God* (1953). He had knelt on the White House lawn. He had come close to converting the gangland figure Mickey Cohen. His popularity was far greater than that of racially exclusive white fundamentalists. In this same year, 1954, he was consistently to desegregate his crowds. Martin Luther King, another dreamer, co-operated with him. Graham understood celebrity culture and had mastered electronic communications. He might look a bit of a hick and a huckster to the liberal luminaries in the great theological seminaries of New York—but perhaps their day was passing.[2] Of course, he was not the first American with a mission to appear in London. The memory of Moody and Sankey lingered on, at least in evangelical circles. There was now, however, a different context. The United States was indubitably 'top dog'. Global power had shifted. Millions of Americans had been 'over here'. They had won the war. They had stockings. They had the money. There was an exhilaration and excitement about the States. There were full churches there.[3]

Receiving Billy Graham meant receiving America, loud and clear, including the bonus of cowboy Roy Rogers and his horse *Trigger*. For some, that might be an ambivalent prospect, but it had been understood elsewhere that the big bucks from North America were vital. Canterbury Cathedral had received £124,000 in 1947—nearly half of its target—from Thomas

---

[2] John Pollock, *Billy Graham: The Authorised Biography* (London, 1966); W. Martin, *The Billy Graham Story: A Prophet with Honour* (London, 1991); Dianne Kirby, 'The Cold War' in Hugh McLeod, ed., *The Cambridge History of Christianity: World Christianities c.1914–c.2000* (Cambridge, 2006), 285–8 comments on 'counter-faith' construction.

[3] Young bishops, visiting the United States for the first time, thought that if they had been younger they would have liked to stay and work there. Bartha de Blank, *Joost de Blank* (Ipswich, 1977), 81.

W. Lamont of the J.P. Morgan Co.[4] In coronation year, Westminster Abbey had received an anonymous gift of 100,000 Canadian dollars. To rebuild the City Temple required more money than the congregation could raise. Its minister, Leslie Weatherhead, set off for a speaking and preaching tour in America designed to boost the Rebuilding Fund. He returned with promises of over half a million dollars, a major part of which sum came from Mr and Mrs John D. Rockefeller. Just before he had set off, Weatherhead had attended one of Graham's meetings and told the American press that what Graham was doing was magnificent. He only wished, he said, that he *could* do that sort of thing himself.[5] So, there could be no sense, apparently, in thinking that the Atlantic constituted a divide. The English-speaking peoples were on a roll together. Geoffrey Fisher, indeed, on his first visit to New York in 1946, had been driven through the streets, sirens shrieking, in a car placed at his disposal by Governor Dewey. Canterbury apparently counted.

There was home-grown evangelism to match. English Methodists, post-war, had launched 'Christian Commando Campaigns' to take the Christian message to people who seemingly had no idea what it was. If a Christian order of society was ever to be achieved, millions more Christians were needed. In January 1953, preaching in the Central Hall, Westminster, Dr Sangster indicated ten ways in which a revival of religion would benefit Britain. All the national newspapers, the *Daily Worker* excepted, carried this good news. It would pay old debts, reduce sexual immorality, disinfect the theatre, cut the divorce rate, reduce juvenile crime, lessen the prison population, improve the quality and increase the output of industry, restore to the nation a sense of high destiny, make Britain invincible in the war of ideas and, finally, give happiness and peace to the people.[6] Sangster later initiated 'The Call to the Nation' and, at least to judge by the large congregations in the Central Hall, it was one that was being heard. In Scotland, from late 1953, a Church of Scotland minister, Tom Allan, spearheaded and consolidated various initiatives under the banner 'Tell Scotland'.[7] The year 1955 was to be the year of outreach, though in fact it turned into one of crisis over the involvement of Billy Graham. Allan returned to the parish ministry. The bishop of London, William Wand, somewhat unbuttoned after his years in Australia,

[4] Robbins, in Patrick Collinson, Nigel Ramsay and Margaret Sparks, ed., *A History of Canterbury Cathedral* (Oxford, 1995), 326–7.

[5] John Travell, *Doctor of Souls: A Biography of Dr. Leslie Dixon Weatherhead* (Cambridge, 1999), 205.

[6] George Thompson Brake, *Policy and Politics in British Methodism 1932–1982* (London, 1984), 406.

[7] T. Allan, ed., *Crusade in Scotland* (London, 1955).

had promoted a mission to London in 1949 with the slogan 'Recovery Starts Within', but the result was disappointing.

There was, therefore, in many church quarters, a propitious climate in which Graham would be received—but not in all. Use of advertising and the media had a razzamatazz about it which some church leaders found hard to stomach. Was this 'circus' ancient or modern? Whatever it was, it was American. Probably without exception, bishops had never been skating or attending boxing matches at Harringay Arena and were not sure that it was the place to be, even for different purposes. They were a bit surprised to see two US Senators, one from each party, giving the evangelist 'support' on the opening night. They were equally not used to listening to mass choirs running into thousands, though it was nice to see them in black and white. Graham's audiences totalled some one and a half million (precise figures vary and, of course, some undoubtedly attended on more than one occasion). Additionally, there were relay services.[8] On the final day, some 65,000 people packed the White City greyhound stadium in the afternoon and 120,000 were present in the evening at Wembley football stadium. On this latter occasion, Graham was flanked by the lord mayor of London and the archbishop of Canterbury. It was the latter, however, who gave the blessing. Fisher had initially been circumspect, but in June he was able to confirm that there was a massive spiritual revival under way. It was an encouraging note on which to leave the country for two months.[9] Graham had a second coming in 1955, on this occasion attracting more than a million attendances in Scotland in a Glasgow-centred campaign. There was a massive rally in Hampden Park football stadium. He then moved on to Wembley Stadium. After one evening service, Fisher apparently felt moved to comment, 'We'll never see such a sight again until we get to Heaven.'[10]

The sight was certainly not seen again in the years that followed. Graham's campaigning continued, but in different parts of the world, although he paid visits from time to time, as in a Greater London Crusade in May 1966 and later.[11] The evangelist himself, in 1956 and on other occasions, stressed that if 'ordinary' churches sought to reach out then he and his kind

[8] Frank Colquhoun, *Harringay Story: A Detailed Account of the Greater London Crusade 1954* (London, 1955). Callum Brown, *Religion and Society in Twentieth-Century Britain* (Harlow, 2006), has a comprehensive discussion which claims that Graham 'plugged into and helped breed the sense of guilt in fifties Britain', 188–96.

[9] Amongst other assignments, Fisher attended the assembly of the World Council of Churches in Evanston. It is extraordinary that his biographer, Carpenter, devotes a chapter to this North American tour but makes no allusion to the Billy Graham crusade.

[10] Randle Manwaring, *From Controversy to Co-Existence: Evangelicals in the Church of England 1914–1980* (Cambridge, 1985), 95.

[11] John Pollock, *Crusade 66: Britain Hears Billy Graham* (London, 1966).

would be unnecessary. There was the rub. What was the relation between this extraordinary activity and the 'real world' of churches as their members experienced it and outsiders observed it? Graham had 'star' quality (and, it had to be admitted, was not the simple rabble-rouser suspicious people thought he must be). He knew how to disarm criticism when he came to Cambridge university—he humbly asked a professor for a theological reading list.[12] Such success as he had, both in Scotland and England, may have benefited very considerably from being an outsider. He seemed to be able to speak with and to Clydeside shipyard workers and university students, meet the Queen Mother at Clarence House, or take tea with the Queen at Windsor Castle—all with equal facility. He did not have all the social and cultural baggage which would have handicapped a native evangelist operating in such different milieux. But, unless those who had decided for Christ became 'plugged in' to local churches, their new commitment would rapidly fade. Counsellors were trained and efforts were made to ensure that such contact happened, but it was difficult. To which particular church should enquirers be directed? Over 36,000 people in England and over 26,000 in Scotland 'came forward' in 1954/5, of whom the clear majority were women and under thirty, but it was known that grown men, from fish-paste manufacturers to admirals of the fleet, confessed that their lives had been transformed as they accepted Christ as their Saviour. There was no news of such a transformation, however, from 10 Downing Street, though its ancient inhabitant, rather grumpily, did receive Dr Graham.

For the moment, longer-term impact could only be guessed at. The whole affair, however, was something of an affront to the left-leaning intelligentsia. It was disturbing that a man could still speak so blatantly about 'sin' in public. It did not like the fact that the chairman of the Crusade executive committee was a major-general. It was alarming to find a man advocating 'militant Christianity' as the only real defence against the communism which was claimed to be infiltrating British life. It was annoying to see how widely that message was accepted and perpetrated locally.[13] Members of the Federation of British Industries, however, were not sufficiently convinced either about the former, or about the latter, to make financial contributions of any substance. It might reluctantly be admitted on the left that communism was a God that had failed, but 'old-time religion' was supposed to have failed more comprehensively. The whole idea of 'conversion' was rather irritating.

---

[12] The professor was John Burnaby and allegedly it was the newly arrived Mervyn Stockwood who had fed this suggestion to Graham.

[13] I. Jones, 'The Clergy, the Cold War and the Mission of the Local Church: England ca. 1945–60', in Dianne Kirby, ed., *Religion and the Cold War* (Basingstoke, 2003), 188–99.

The enterprise, however, did give a boost to evangelicals whatever their particular denomination. It happened, too, that 1955 was the 400th anniversary of the martyrdom of Latimer and Ridley. Christopher Chavasse, bishop of Rochester, came to Oxford to commemorate the fact that from the martyrs had come the Protestant Reformed Religion which had now expanded into the worldwide Anglican Communion.[14] Baptists reported new evangelistic initiatives. Two British evangelists, Eric Hutchings and Tom Rees, modelled themselves on Graham and held meetings up and down the country.[15] The bishop of Barking, Hugh Gough, had been a strong supporter and other prominent Anglican names in the London area included Frank Colquhoun, Tom Livermore and Maurice Wood. New magazines, in particular a 'glossy', *Crusade*, holiday camps and minor missions kept some impetus going. Allegations that the converts were 'flash in the pan' Christians were rebutted.[16] Even so, as early as 1959, Gough was concluding that 'we missed what God intended for us'. Part of the explanation, he thought, lay in the fact that many church people themselves had been sceptical or even hostile. There were indeed ministers and clergy who felt, as one Baptist minister put it, that the key to advance lay 'not in stunts and spasmodic spurts, but in solid patient pastoral work'.[17]

The opposition to which Gough alluded, however, was more than a concern about 'stunts'. Rather unexpectedly, it came to be most clearly expressed by the new bishop of Durham, Michael Ramsey—shortly to be translated to York. Perhaps he had in his memory his listening, appalled, as a Cambridge undergraduate to an Irish Presbyterian missioner. Ramsey did not like crusades. Graham's meetings, he thought, might involve the stifling of the mind. In an article in the diocesan *Bishoprick* in February 1956 entitled 'The Menace of Fundamentalism', he strongly expressed his disquiet.[18] Ramsey emphasized that a crude view of conversion abstracted a man from his place and duty in society; 'The moral will is separated from its context, because the appeal is made to less than the whole man as a reasoning being, and a social being.' 'Fundamentalism' was indeed back on the agenda.

In criticizing what was deemed unreasoning moralizing, there was a certain continuity in the voice coming from Durham. It was Ramsey's predecessor but one, Hensley Henson, who had published a blistering attack

[14] Chavasse had chaired the group which had produced *Towards the Conversion of England*. Selwyn Gummer, *The Chavasse Twins* (London, 1963).

[15] Jean Rees, *His Name was Tom: The Biography of Tom Rees* (London, 1971).

[16] D.W. Bebbington, *Evangelicalism in Modern Britain: A History from the 1730s to the 1980s* (London, 1989), 258–9.

[17] Cited in Ian Randall, *English Baptists of the Twentieth Century* (London, 2005), 273.

[18] Owen Chadwick, *Michael Ramsey: A Life* (Oxford, 1990), 92.

on 'the Oxford Group' which, inspired by another American evangelist, Frank Buchman, was then moving out of the universities and spreading across the country, from Worthing to Edinburgh.[19] 'Life-changers' had spoken then of their own surrender. They had been as 'modern' in their day as Graham was in his. There had been much use of first names—then still unusual—and an ostentatious lack of 'stuffiness'.[20] Advertising slickness had been demonstrated by placing the Group slogan on four million milk bottle tops. Traditional theological language had been eschewed. Buchman himself was controversial. He had returned from attending the 1936 Olympic Games in Berlin declaring 'I thank heaven for a man like Adolf Hitler'—as a barrier to communism. In 1938 the Oxford Group became Moral Re-Armament. As such, it was enjoying a fresh lease of life in the early 1950s, parading a number of public figures who committed themselves to the absolute honesty, purity, unselfishness and love which it espoused.[21] It had a centre at Caux in Switzerland and was reputed to be influential 'behind the scenes' at the highest levels of German and French politics. For a couple of decades, as journalist and Labour MP, Tom Driberg had devoted himself to exposing the mystery of Moral Re-Armament.[22] There was, of course, no mean mystery about Driberg himself. It would perhaps be unwise to see in him the model High Churchman.

Billy Graham and Frank Buchman, the Greater London Crusade and Moral Re-Armament, should not be equated, although there was a similar concern for the 'moral health' of the nation. They looked, though with different emphases, to 'conversion'. The 1945 Anglican report had been directed *Towards the Conversion of England*. Yet was not England (and the UK) a Christian country? The BBC apparently thought so. The director-general had stated only a few years earlier that it should base its policy 'upon a positive attitude towards Christian values'. It sought to safeguard them and foster their acceptance. A parliamentary committee on broadcasting rejected the notion that religious broadcasting should seek converts to one particular church but it did have a duty to maintain 'the common element in all religious bodies' against those who denied spiritual values. What belief was actually 'out there', how it was characterized, how it related to 'culture', how differently it was embedded in particular classes and

---

[19] David Bebbington, 'The Oxford Group Movement between the Wars' in W.J. Sheils and D.Wood, eds., *Voluntary Religion*, Studies in Church History 23 (Oxford, 1986), 495–507.

[20] A number of prominent Church leaders in the 1950s and 1960s, when younger, had been involved in the Oxford group—for example, de Blank. De Blank, *De Blank*, 25–7.

[21] Anne Wolrige Gordon, *Peter Howard: Life and Letters* (London, 1969).

[22] T. Driberg, *The Mystery of Moral Re-Armament: A Study of Frank Buchman and his Movement* (London, 1964); F. Wheen, *The Soul of Indiscretion: Tom Driberg: Poet, Philanderer, Legislator and Outlaw* (London, 1990).

communities, remained unclear, though subject to increasing investigation. Whether puzzled but not disbelieving people, who appeared to be a clear majority, should be regarded, in some sense at least, as being 'inside' one or other church or were regarded as 'outside', requiring explicit 'conversion' and 'incorporation', remained something over which the churches themselves puzzled. The relationship between 'believing' and 'belonging', and what both of these terms entailed, remained problematic. 'Change', however, was 'in the air', more than usual, many thought. The question, scarcely a new one, was bound up with what was happening to the United Kingdom in the world and what 'national values', if any, it might be said to possess.[23]

The 65-year-old Donald Coggan faced this challenge when he became archbishop of Canterbury in 1974. The 'permissive' age was very different from that twenty years earlier when Billy Graham had been in town. Coggan had been translated from York, having been bishop of Bradford before that. Earlier, he had spent seven years in Canada, before returning in 1944 to head the London College of Divinity. He was no mean Semitic scholar—his subject at Cambridge, but the cast of his mind was not philosophical. He was a firm evangelical—though not a 'fundamentalist'—and had thus 'balanced' Ramsey at Canterbury. Unlike Ramsey, there was little eccentric about him and he could conduct meetings effectively. He was sometimes called the 'layman's archbishop' largely on the ground that he had famously discussed God, sex and 'the teenager' on television in January 1962 with a 'popstar' of the time, Adam Faith. His background led him to speak of 'evangelism' and 'mission' with little inhibition. When at York, he had given enthusiastic support to an inter-church 'Call to the North' in 1973. The campaign had tried, though not very successfully, to avoid being an 'old-style' short, sharp burst of mission activity. It aimed rather to trigger

---

[23] The director-general was Sir William Haley, subsequently editor of *The Times*. These matters are discussed in Brown, *Religion and Society in Twentieth-Century Britain*, 181–3. Contemporary investigations alluded to in this paragraph include Mass-Observation, *Puzzled People: A Study in Popular Attitudes to Religion, Ethics Progress and Politics in a London Borough prepared for the Ethical Union* (London, 1947); Geoffrey Gorer, *Exploring English Character* (London, 1955); B. Seebohm Rowntree and G.R. Lavers, *English Life and Leisure: A Social Study* (London, 1951); Mark Freeman, 'Britain's Spiritual Life: How Can It be Deepened? Seebohm Rowntree, Russell Lavers and the "Crisis of Belief"', ca 1946–54', *Journal of Religious History* 29/1 (2005), 43–66. The extent to which 'the full picture' can be captured by means of questionnaires, how questions should be posed, how responses should be correlated with 'attendance' figures and how far a consequential 'Christian behaviour' can be measured of course raises acute questions in social science. Rather contrary reflections on substantially the same data relating to this period are to be found in Brown, *Religion and Society in Twentieth-Century Britain*, Grace Davie, *Religion in Britain since 1945: Believing without Belonging* (Oxford, 1994) and S.J.D. Green, 'Was there an English Religious Revival in the 1950s?', *Journal of the United Reformed Church Historical Society* 7/9 (2006), 517–38.

a sustained programme of local 'outreach'. In 1975, together with his successor at York, Stuart Blanch, who had moved from Liverpool, a 'Call to the Nation' had been launched from Lambeth Palace with full press and television coverage, accompanied by a pastoral letter to be read in all Anglican churches. The message was that the nation was in trouble. There could be no answer to its problems unless there was a 'concentrated effort' to lift 'our whole national debate' into the moral sphere.

It is difficult to judge quite what response was expected. There was certainly a substantial postbag to Lambeth Palace indicating a belief that 'leadership' from the church was indeed necessary. On the other hand, archiepiscopal statements to the effect that good work mattered, or that strong family life meant a strong nation, did not in themselves resolve current problems. That the archbishops had sent out their call, apparently, with little consultation irked some. It smacked of a 'leadership' style inappropriate in the new synodical age. Mervyn Stockwood, bishop of Southwark, chose to write in the Communist *Morning Star* suggesting that the evils which Coggan deplored were the product of 'the system'. Undeterred, Coggan pressed on, though critics were divided between those who spoke of his initiative as a damp squib and those who called it a fiasco. 'Calls to the Nation', it seemed, were not being answered. All of the 'mainline' churches in all parts of Britain, with the exception of the Roman Catholic, experienced falls in their 'memberships' when compared with twenty years earlier. The 'national' churches of England and Scotland could still, on some measures, be deemed to remain 'national' but Roman Catholic growth increasingly placed this status in jeopardy. The Free Church decline was steepest. Since population was growing, the proportion of the population with a firm allegiance inevitably diminished. Collecting statistics, even though they always had problems of definition, became depressing. The world, as a whole, could also seem depressing. Some wondered whether there was not at some profound but indistinct level a connection between losing members and losing national power. If there was 'decline' perhaps it was collective.

ii. *Relocations: Empire and Europe*

The Suez expedition in 1956, and its failure, dramatically demonstrated the limitation on British power. In the Lords, Fisher attacked the expedition in strong terms. Like other speakers, of course, he was not aware of the 'full story'. Selwyn Lloyd, the foreign secretary, had been at Cambridge a college friend and Union contemporary of Ramsey (who, as an undergraduate, was himself thinking of possibly following a political career—as a Liberal). It does not appear, however, that the archbishop of York reopened contact on this occasion.[24] Some less prominent figures found themselves, in the words of J.A.T. Robinson—then dean of Clare College, Cambridge—shattered by political events to a degree that they could seldom, if ever, remember before. He had to admit, however, that most people did not appear to be shaken to any significant degree, and that was probably true of 'church people' too. Members of the Baptist Union council, for example, could not agree on a motion deploring the Anglo-French invasion. It was agreed simply to support the United Nations.[25] If the motion had been passed, the president of the Union, a knighted builder from Luton, threatened to resign. Sir Cyril Black, MP for Wimbledon and a prominent support of the Graham Crusade, backed the government. Robinson felt that the expedition had destroyed the only basis on which Britain could 'hope to exercise leadership in our post-war situation'. Britain was finally finished as a great power.[26] 'Suez' meant the end of an era, though not in the sense used by the Peckham Baptist pastor, Theo Bamber, who was arguing that there was little point in passing resolutions at this juncture since a battle of blood without parallel in the history of the human race was about to begin.

Empire, once supposed to have been acquired absent-mindedly, may also have been disposed of with equal insouciance. How 'consciousness of empire' is measured, and what it entailed for the population of the United Kingdom raises complex issues of interpretation. It is arguable that the churches thought 'globally' more than any other domestic institution. 'We British', wrote the general secretary of the British Council of Churches in 1964, 'feel we only belong in a very partial way to Europe'. British 'lines' had gone out to Canada and Nyasaland, to New Zealand and India every bit as much as across the narrow straits of Dover.[27] The Canadian prime minister of the day, John Diefenbaker, himself a Baptist, addressed the Baptist Assembly in 1960.

Nyasaland [Malawi] was not Canada, but it was not idly mentioned. The fate of Central Africa in particular had been of special concern to Scottish church people in the 1950s and 1960s. Dr Hastings Banda, erstwhile elder of Guthrie Memorial Church, Easter Road, Edinburgh, returned to Nyasaland in July 1958. George Macleod, then moderator of the General Assembly of the Church of Scotland, saw him off and wished him well. It was arguably Banda's experience of church government as an elder which equipped him to run the numerous committees of the nationalist movement in his home

---

[24] Silence on the part of his biographer leads to this conclusion—and indeed he makes no mention of the Suez expedition in the book. Lloyd had Methodist roots.

[25] Randall, *English Baptists*, 310–11. There were three MPs at this time who were Baptists, two Labour and one Conservative.

[26] Eric James, *A Life of Bishop John A. T. Robinson: Scholar, Pastor, Prophet* (London, 1987), 57.

[27] Cited in Philip M. Coupland, *Britannia, Europa and Christendom* (Basingstoke, 2006), 138.

country. At the General Assembly in 1959, after Banda had been arrested, Macleod declared that 'for the time being someone must speak for the African—and that someone will be the General Assembly of the Church of Scotland'. The Kirk was opposed to bringing Nyasaland under the hegemony of white-ruled Southern Rhodesia (Zimbabwe).[28] Historical connections still had substantial resonance and had a distinctive Scottish significance. A different part of Africa was on the mind of the English Free Churches. Events in Angola led Baptists to lobby ministers and express their 'grave concern'.[29] In this and other instances, missionary connections with particular 'trouble spots' meant that a lively political interest continued.

It was South Africa, however, in which there was most active involvement. It was necessarily controversial. The presence of a succession of English churchmen as bishops in South Africa—Joost de Blank and Ambrose Reeves—and their networks back home, ensured that the Church of England had a prominent place in the debates about South African internal affairs. The plight of Africans received more space than would otherwise have been the case. Yet, for all their outspokenness, these men were 'imperial implants' sent out from a 'mother country' only recognized as such by a white English-speaking minority. Joost de Blank may have been a 'spokesman for Black people' but he insisted on travelling in a big American car, flying a pennant—'foreign ostentation'. Despite, or perhaps because of, his Dutch ancestry, he seemed to loathe all Afrikaners.[30]

It is difficult to judge how significant the publicity these men engendered was in the general evolution of successive phases of British government policy, and indeed in the course of events in South Africa, but it certainly cannot be discounted. Trevor Huddleston, speaking and writing, was a charismatic figure who reached out far beyond a 'church constituency'.[31] Their prophetic utterances, unsurprisingly, were balanced by other voices calling for caution and 'prudence' but no other body in British public life could match the 'knowledge on the ground' which the Church of England possessed.

---

[28] J. McCracken, *Politics and Christianity in Malawi, 1876–1940* (Cambridge, 1977) provides background. See Andrew Ross, 'The Scottish Church and Central Africa, 1859–1964' in Stewart J. Brown and George Newlands, eds., *Scottish Christianity in the Modern World* (Edinburgh, 2000), 285–310 and Michael Fry, *The Scottish Empire* (Edinburgh, 2001), 421–4. The British Council of Churches issued a pamphlet on Central Africa which it hoped would provide a basis for inter-party agreement. L.B. Greaves, *Everyman's Concern: The Rhodesias and Nyasaland* (London, 1959), 13.

[29] Brian Stanley, *The History of the Baptist Missionary Society, 1792–1992* (Edinburgh, 1992), 454.

[30] John Stuart Peart-Binns, *Archbishop Joost de Blank: Scourge of Apartheid* (London, 1987) conveying the impressions of an English-speaking white South African Anglican bishop.

[31] De Blank, *De Blank*; Deborah Honoré, ed., *Trevor Huddleston: Essays on his Life and Work* (London, 1988); John Stuart Peart-Binns, *Ambrose Reeves* (London, 1973); Trevor Huddleston, *Naught for Your Comfort* (London, 1956).

The Church of England, the bishop of Southwell had written at the close of the war, having grown into the Anglican Communion, 'the indigenous Church of the English-speaking world', could 'exert a planetary influence'.[32] It was for the Anglican churches that 'Empire to Commonwealth' had the greatest significance. D.W. Brogan, not a member, wrote that it had 'more first-hand knowledge of all parts of the British Empire than any secular body'.[33] Over the next couple of decades, and beyond, there were senior bishops of the Church of England who had spent significant periods of their lives working overseas. Leslie Brown became bishop of St Edmundsbury and Ipswich in 1966, having served in India and Africa since 1939. Robert Stopford, who became bishop of London in 1961, had been a college principal in Sri Lanka and Ghana in the decade 1935–45.[34] Such men certainly did not only England know. The ties seemed to remain tight. The summer of 1954 found the archbishop of Canterbury in North America, covering seven thousand miles in thirty days. Amongst many other activities, he dedicated a window at Christ Church Cathedral, Victoria, Vancouver Island, in memory of his predecessor as bishop of London, Winnington-Ingram. It was an action which appeared to confirm some common sense of belonging, but would it endure? What was the ecclesiastical 'English-speaking world'?

When Fisher presided over the 1958 Lambeth Conference, 30 per cent of the bishops attending were non-white. Ten years later, when Ramsey presided, breaking tradition by not wearing gaiters, the non-whites had just slipped into being a majority.[35] Such a transformation in composition, not to mention the increase in overall numbers which went with it—from 300 or so in 1958 to 462 in 1968—particularly reflected the rapid Africanization which had begun in 1951 with the establishment of the province of West Africa. This 'granting of independence' took place before the achievement of political independence by the countries concerned. Fisher was present in Freetown, Sierra Leone, in person, as he was to be in many other parts of the world in a decade of intensive journeying made possible, as it had never been for his predecessors, by air travel. Fisher, who liked legal and constitutional issues, was just the man to wrestle with them in province after province across the globe. 'Indigenization' had wide ramifications as,

[32] F.R. Barry, *Church and Leadership* (London, 1945), 53.

[33] D.W. Brogan, *The English People: Impressions and Observations* (London, 1943), 113.

[34] Brown worked in Kerala from 1939 and was a creator of the Church of South India before becoming the first (and last) English archbishop of Uganda in 1953. Stopford went out to Sri Lanka in 1935 and transferred to Ghana in 1941. His strong educational background made him an ideal person to become general secretary of the National Society (1952). He was bishop of Peterborough, 1956–61.

[35] John Howe, *Highways and Hedges: Anglicans and the Universal Church* (London, 1985), 14.

all over the world, churches emerged out of their missionary pasts and constructed, to take but one example, *A Liturgy for Africa*. Nor was this question merely one for Africa or Asia. It was time, in an 'Old Dominion', for Anglicans to start thinking of belonging to something more appropriate than 'The Church of England in Australia'. At differing speeds and to different degrees, it was being made ever more clear that the 'Anglican Communion' was not the Church of England writ large. The provinces had to fashion their own relationships with the states in which they were situated and uniformity was not to be expected.[36]

It was perhaps fortunate that the substantial steps which changed the character of the Anglican Communion were taken while Fisher was archbishop. The organizational issues did not necessarily require an acute theological mind. Ramsey, who had not been a great traveller and did not much enjoy jamborees, was also persuaded to travel. He was not averse to the notion that the European and North American churches were receivers not merely givers. He found much variety in the Anglican provinces he encountered. Between them, Anglican leaders knew at first hand those not only in the dissolved British Empire but also in South America or Japan. This sense of mutual responsibility and interdependence—given more vital content by Ramsey's expression that the church which lived to itself would die to itself—was growing. The Anglican churches of the British Isles were enmeshed in something greater—tangible relationships increasingly given expression by the 'twinning' of dioceses in different parts of the world. The pace of change, however, was such that it was difficult to pin down precisely what the Anglican Communion was. One statement by a committee on liturgy, endorsed by the 1958 conference, stated that 'Our unity exists because we are a federation of Provinces and Dioceses of the One Holy, Catholic and Apostolic Church, each being served and governed by a Catholic and Apostolic Ministry, and each believing the Catholic faith.' The word federation, however, might not be quite the right one. The archbishop of Canterbury had a 'primacy of respect' though it was quite clear that the Lambeth Conference which he chaired had quite outgrown the 'house-party' which it had begun as. He neither exercised, nor sought to exercise, the kind of authority which the pope exercised in the Roman Catholic world. The newly created Anglican Council, which 'steered' the Communion between conferences, had an executive officer—the first appointee, significantly, being an American. It would also be money from the United States which oiled the wheels and made possible the meetings and formal business of the Communion.

---

[36] W.M. Jacob, *The Making of the Anglican Church Worldwide* (London, 1997), 278–85.

The Church of England, in short, may have 'founded' the Anglican Communion but it no longer 'controlled' it. The fact that Anglican 'summits' were held in England was 'an accident of history' and in the future they might be held elsewhere. Parallels were not infrequently drawn with the Commonwealth of Nations whose members were all self-governing states. Only a few of its expanding membership acknowledged the queen as their head of state, although she was recognized as 'Head of the Commonwealth'. The Commonwealth was ceasing to be serviced by the British government, having a separate secretariat with a secretary-general who was unlikely to be British. Its 'summits' met around the globe. But was Britain not its vital core? Could it survive if, for whatever reason, Britain wished to withdraw? Could the Commonwealth require Britain itself to pursue a particular policy? Such questions, particularly in relation to successive phases of decolonization in Africa and in relation to South Africa, were not academic.

The relationship between the Church of England and the Anglican Communion raised parallel questions. While attention naturally concentrated on the path which would be followed as the new provinces 'indigenized', the more fundamental question might be where such processes left 'the mother church' itself. Could one man both 'represent' the Church of England and also embody 'the Anglican Communion'. Would he have to be English? The Anglican provinces of the British Isles and their self-definition arose out of the particular circumstances of insular history. In England at least, the Church of England saw its own difficult but essential 'checks and balances', its own reconciliation of freedom and order, and of Protestantism and Catholicism, as something which both expressed and sustained 'understandings' which, in aspiration at least, underpinned the state itself. Its 'myths' might become, if they were not so already, incomprehensible in other parts of the Communion. Just as the word 'British' had dropped from the 'Commonwealth of Nations' might not 'Anglican' seem an unhelpful term—as indeed, from time to time, Irish, Scottish and Welsh bishops in the British Isles thought when they met together and wished to avoid being thought English. Would it be possible to sustain the 'unity' of the Anglican Communion if the Church of England were to enter into 'union' with other churches in England or Britain on a basis which might not commend itself to other provinces, and vice versa?

There were other complicating considerations. Fisher made history in 1960 when he visited the pope in the Vatican, as did Ramsey in 1966. The Church of England was an interesting church, no doubt, and the occasion had its significance in English history, but it was the archbishop of Canterbury's status as, in some sense, representing a Communion which was, though patchily, world-wide, which gave the visit another dimension.

There was the further complication that the 'English-speakingness' of the Anglican Communion could seem to run counter to the increasing, if reluctant, engagement of successive British governments with 'Europe'. Only Anglicans in the British Isles, and of course English Anglicans in particular, had problems of identity and self-understanding which were so implicitly related to the disappearance of empire. No other saw itself as the 'hub' of a 'Communion' whose current world presence largely derived from that empire. In short, signposts pointed in many directions. It might not be possible to follow all of them without collision or crash. The period up to 1975 demonstrated that this was indeed the case.

In 1973 Michael Ramsey, as the head of a British churches delegation, attended a special service for the European Economic Community in Brussels Cathedral. In his address, he suggested that a Christian Europe would be one which looked to the needs of other continents with poverty and hunger. He wanted a Europe in which God was honoured and worshipped, in which men and women asked God's forgiveness and held the family sacred. He wanted to see a Europe in which the divine image in every man and woman was reverenced and in which the love of money and material things was not supreme. Perhaps above all he wanted a Europe which knew that beyond the sovereignty of states there was the sovereignty of the righteous God.[37] The UK government had taken the country into the Community in January. In June 1975 electors were asked in a referendum whether they wished the country to remain a member. Nearly two-thirds of the electorate voted, with 67.2 per cent in favour and 32.8 per cent against. This result appeared to settle a matter which had reverberated through British politics for two decades. Britain had not signed the 1957 Treaty of Rome which had brought the EEC into existence. The Macmillan government announced in 1961 that, on suitable terms, Britain did wish to join. Edward Heath, the chief negotiator, declared that Europe had to unite or perish. Gaitskell, the Leader of the Opposition, raised the spectre of a European federation in which Britain would be reduced to being like a state of the United States or Australia. Britain, he said, was 'the centre and founder member' of a much larger and still more important group, the Commonwealth. President de Gaulle brought the negotiations to an end in January 1963. A further attempt had failed by the end of 1967.

Fisher was not a 'natural European'. He had visited Germany in 1948 and saw something of the 'queer life' going on around him. It was reported that the British community in Germany thought his visit a 'big thing'. He preached to a joint British–German congregation in Hamburg. Thereafter, however, he gave no sustained attention to the processes which led to the

---

[37] Chadwick, *Ramsey*, 402.

creation and consolidation of the EEC. His preoccupation, during his last decade, was with the 'Anglican world' in Africa, Asia and America. *Ecclesia Anglicana*, of course, was not conspicuously present in Europe. Ramsey, too, although a very different man, was also not a 'natural European'. His 'formation' had been very English, with only a glimpse of Germany being refracted through the Cambridge lectures of E.C. Hoskyns. The theology he wrote about was the theology of Englishmen and it was in the United States that he delivered his thoughts on the fifty years of Anglican theology which ended in 1939. His travels as an archbishop took him primarily beyond Europe, although he did give an address in Germany on Martin Luther's birthday, visit both Bec and Taizé in France and develop a friendship with Cardinal Suenens of Belgium. The nature of the 'Anglican world', however, dictated his priorities.

Mental dispositions and travel itineraries naturally only constitute a limited basis on which to make pronouncements about 'realignment'. They do suggest, however, that even if there had been a 'committed European' as archbishop, the reality of the global demands placed upon him would have squeezed 'Europe' to the margin of his attention. To have attempted a more vigorous promotion of 'European unity' would in any event not have been likely to be well-received by the churches. An ecclesiastical 'champion' for Europe of stature was as rare as a political. Edward Heath's long distant days working on the *Church Times* by no means secured him the support of that readership in his committed and exceptional endorsement of a 'united Europe'. That did not mean, certain exceptions apart, that the notion of 'Europe' was greeted with pervasive hostility. Since so much had been said in church gatherings, for so long, about the evil consequences of nationalism, at least in its 'excessive' form, it was difficult to take issue with a project which, it was claimed, would give Europe a fresh start. The general church tone was captured by what Ramsey had to say in Brussels Cathedral. He was not explicit about what direction the EEC should take with the UK as a member—whether it might become some kind of European Union. Sovereign states should be mindful of the sovereignty of the righteous God, but he did not suggest that they should accept some attrition of that sovereignty. God should be honoured and worshipped but he did not advocate 'Christian Europe'. What the 'ever closer union' of the Treaty of Rome entailed remained obscure.

The Christian Democrat parties in the countries concerned had played a significant part in that consolidation of 'western Europe' which the United Kingdom at length was joining. To that extent, a Christian label might loosely be applied. These parties all sought to establish a broad platform which rejected both free-market liberalism and socialism. It could be claimed that they were neither 'Right' nor 'Left'. They asserted a Christian foundation but sought to avoid clerical control or the imputation that they existed to impose in detail the specific doctrines of the Catholic Church. Their hostility to communism was clear. Their particular fortunes had varied, as did their specific policies, but they had succeeded in creating a certain ethos. The corollary, however, was that attaching the label 'Christian' to any political party carried with it the imputation that other political parties were 'not Christian' and might possibly be 'anti-Christian'. It was this underlying divide which continued to complicate the relationships between UK political parties and churches and their 'counterparts' on the continent.

Throughout the ups and downs of the UK's relationship with 'Europe', however, there had been dedicated Christian enthusiasts who talked in federal terms: the nation state was at once too small and too big. The international department of the British Council of Churches was particularly active in taking this view. One document which emanated from a working party under its auspices was *Christians and the Common Market*. The secretary/rapporteur of this and other working parties was Noel Salter, a Congregationalist with a theology degree who had been working as a civil servant at Western European Union.[38] He saw the failure of British applications to join as merely a setback. It was not a question of *whether* Britain should join the EEC but *what kind* of Community Christians might hope to develop. The composition of the working party excluded opponents of membership. Such packing was apparently compatible with the claim that 'the Body of Christ must never be demeaned into becoming a political pressure group'. Later, though after Salter had left, the international department was actively engaged in the political lobbying and manoeuvring of the early 1970s with the objective of mobilizing opinion in favour of accession. In 1971, the conclusions of the earlier report were summarized and circulated to Anglican and Roman Catholic priests and to the secretaries of around 700 local Councils of Churches. Ramsey's support for a 'yes' vote in his diocesan newsletter was released to the press. In the House of Lords in October 1971 the two archbishops and the other bishops voted in favour of membership. In the referendum campaign in 1975, there was no doubt that 'leaderships' wanted 'the voice of the churches' to favour 'staying in'. Opponents of entry naturally criticized this stance. The assistant secretary of the British Council of Churches, Hugh Wilcox, retorted that he was quite sure that Christian people in Europe would regard a negative decision by Britain as 'a betrayal of our commitment to internationalism'. It is likely, though cannot be established, that 'church voters' probably voted 'yes',

---

[38] For the context see Philip M. Coupland, 'Western Union, "Spiritual Union" and European Integration, 1948–1951', *Journal of British Studies* 43 (July 2004).

possibly in a higher proportion than that of the electorate as a whole. It must be doubted, however, whether they shared the 'federal' aspirations to be found amongst those who offered advice. In this respect, a somewhat paradoxical situation was disclosed. Individual member churches could rarely draw, from their own members, upon the expertise which the British Council of Churches could 'pool', but only the constituent churches could 'deliver' whatever conclusions the Council's advisory bodies reached.[39]

Yet there was also a qualification. Ramsey thought that Christian influence from Britain would help to make Europe more outward-looking. The view from the British Council of Churches was that a negative decision would let down the less developed countries. Advocates of a 'no', however, and they included some Christian voices, argued that by its very nature the 'European project' was inward-looking. 'Christian influence' would do little to alter that fact. It also followed, they thought, that it would be a betrayal of the needs of the less developed countries to *join*. Such propositions, however, did not carry the day. Refusal to join might indeed be a 'betrayal of internationalism', but the reality was that the EEC was but one bloc among many in the power politics of the world. Its members—with the exception of Ireland, if it joined—were all members of NATO. They were part of 'the West' against 'the East'. There was danger, it was argued in some quarters, in yielding to a view of 'Christian Europe' which happened to suit the requirements of American foreign policy. 'Christendom' neither could nor should be revived. There were Christians behind the 'Iron Curtain' who should be supported, not only in respect of 'religious freedom' but also for the positive spin which some applied to the 'new order' of communism. Some were sympathetic to the views of some Christian leaders in the German Democratic Republic, Czechoslovakia and Hungary, for example, who thought that it was possible to find a creative way of engaging with communist regimes. The 'international Christian community' should transcend barriers, not strengthen barricades. The appeal of Eastern Orthodoxy had remained strong for some Anglicans. Ramsey felt it too. His first overseas visit as archbishop of York, in July 1956, was to Russia. It was to prove his happiest. His dealings thereafter with the Russian church were inescapably complicated. Who could he trust? Some compromise was no doubt inevitable but was the core of the Russian church safe or had it been penetrated? Whatever conclusions he (and others who also had contacts) came to in this regard were always likely to be affected by political events which—as in Hungary in 1956 or Czechoslovakia in 1968—showed how

---

[39] These matters are discussed more fully in Philip M. Coupland, *Britannia, Europa and Christendom* (London, 2006), 170–99. It was, of course, not only in relation to Europe that this was the case.

little individuals could achieve on the basis of personal contacts. Michael Bourdeaux, a Russian-speaking Anglican priest, embarked on what was to prove his life's work—providing information on what was happening to Christians in the Soviet sphere. Some believed that this work was 'unhelpful'.

For the churches, therefore, the United Kingdom, Europe and the 'Cold War' were all interconnected in a world living under the shadow of nuclear weapons.[40] It was again the British Council of Churches which had set the pace in examining their implications. Early post-war reports were followed by *Christians and Atomic War* (1959). Christian pacifism, it argued, could be defended as an act of individual obedience but could not form the basis of a policy to be responsibly adopted by a government. This report, and subsequent documents covering the same ground, showed that there was no single Christian perspective. The dilemmas were obvious, but the solutions were unclear whenever these matters were considered within denominational contexts. There were some, but not a majority, who were attracted by the Campaign for Nuclear Disarmament which was founded in 1958. One of its most prominent figures was Canon John Collins, now of St Paul's, who had been widely identified previously with 'Christian Action'. It had aimed to put pressure 'by active democratic means' on governments to 'maintain the application of Christian principles in national and international affairs'.[41] CND's marches and rallies attracted a great deal of publicity but the UK governments retained its nuclear weapons. Harold Macmillan and his successor, Alec Douglas-Home, both Etonian Anglicans, stood firm. So did the vestigially Congregationalist Harold from Huddersfield who succeeded them, though with more difficulty from his party.[42]

'Peace' and its related issues tested the structures and functioning of the evolving World Council of Churches. Was it really possible to be 'non-aligned' and to speak, in some sense, on behalf of an 'international Christian community' in a clearly divided world? The context in which its second assembly was to be held was a case in point. Ernest Payne, the Baptist, travelled to the United States, where it was to be held, three weeks after returning from a pioneering visit to Russian Baptists. The passport official let him in with the observation that he was clearly attending the

---

[40] Owen Chadwick, *The Christian Church in the Cold War* (Harmondsworth, 1992).

[41] Collins had been an RAF chaplain and dean of Oriel College, Oxford. Diana Collins, *Christian Action* (London, 1949); L. John Collins, *A Theology of Christian Action* (London, 1949); L. John Collins, *Faith under Fire* (London, 1966) ; Diana Collins, *Partners in Protest: Life with Canon Collins* (London, 1992); Haddon Willmer, 'John Collins, Gadfly of the Resurrection' in Stuart Mews, ed., *Modern Religious Rebels* (London, 1993), 245–67.

[42] Wilson's parents were Congregationalists and his wife was the daughter of a Congregational minister.

'economical conference'. Payne knew that, whatever he had come for, it was not that. The World Council was not immune from McCarthyite accusations. At one point, it had looked as though only the relocation of the Assembly to Canada would ensure the presence of Eastern European delegates. President Eisenhower, addressing the Assembly, asked that every person in every country who believed in the power of prayer should engage in a mighty simultaneous act of faith. Fisher, in his speech, could not avoid some reference to the time when, on the battlefields of Europe, Britain and the United States stood together in a grand alliance, but he nevertheless insisted that the roles of the United States government and the World Council were different. Payne preached a sermon which did not disguise the degree of tension at the Assembly. Not for the first, nor the last, time he advised patience in dealing with 'the long and devious story of the Christian church'. It would be a mistake to suppose that 'the mind of Christ' at any one moment in its pilgrimage would be fully expressed by either the majority or the minority. He went on to become vice-chairman (subsequently chairman) of the Central Committee which would endeavour to 'steer' the World Council between its assemblies. The chairman was an American. Payne returned home to help organize the conference of the Baptist World Alliance to be held in London in 1955. Its financial success was made possible by the American participation—some half of the 8,500 delegates. It had been at Oxford in 1951 that the Ecumenical Methodist Conference had decided to call itself the World Methodist Council and to meet henceforth at five-yearly intervals across the globe.

These and comparable developments in other Protestant denominations emphasized the extent to which the 'history of the Christian Church in the British Isles' could no longer be considered in insular isolation. Church leaders found themselves increasingly enmeshed in a web of international relationships—the sustaining of which required time, energy and money. Globalization brought with it the seemingly never-ending necessity to assess priorities. The gap between aspiration, pretension and reality could be wide. The World Council professed not to be a super-church, but it needed some kind of superstructure and a general secretary. There could be no certainty that pronouncements made at exalted level on the issues of the day resonated with the 'base communities' which were the local congregations throughout the British Isles. The Russian Orthodox and other Soviet bloc Orthodox churches joined the Council in 1961. Such a step could scarcely have been taken without it being perceived by the Soviet government as a way of advancing its own 'peace' policy objectives. It was a membership welcomed by some delegates from the 'non-aligned' world as a means of lessening the influence of American churches, though nothing could lessen the significance of financial support from that quarter. Assemblies at such

conspicuously 'neutral' locations as New Delhi (1961) and Uppsala (1968)
did not bring any attenuation of political controversy. In the latter case, the
young added their own sloganizing ingredients. A Programme to Combat
Racism emerged. A stormy period began and had not abated by the time the
next Assembly was held, eventually, in Nairobi in 1975.[43]

Consideration of these controversies belongs properly to the history of
the World Council and cannot be considered further here. Brief consideration, however, of the career of Ernest Payne, elected after Uppsala as (at
that time) the sole British figure among the presidents of the World
Council—in recognition of the contribution he had made to its affairs
over a decade and a half—brings out just how multi-layered were the
alignments which now presented themselves to leading churchmen in the
British Isles. His 'day job', on successive reappointments, had been as
general secretary of the Baptist Union. His commitment to the British
Council of Churches had been firm—and in his retirement he wrote a
short history of its work to date.[44] He served a term as moderator of the Free
Church Federal Council. The Baptist World Alliance could not be
neglected. He 'spoke for' Baptists, though he well knew the limits of his
'authority' and, if he had not known it, criticism of the World Council in
particular would not have left him in doubt on this score.[45] He had been
present at world assemblies which had talked of world mission but knew, to
his sadness, that 'back home', at national level, it had proved impossible,
organizationally, to get the Baptist Union and the Baptist Missionary
Society to come together. And finally, at local level, the only local church,
at the beginning of his career, of which he had been the minister, Bug-
brooke in Northamptonshire, was by 1974 dropping the label 'Baptist' and
had purchased a local manor house to develop a form of 'community living'
which attracted television cameras. One man's story showed that 'being the
church', globally, nationally and locally, was now a complicated business.

iii. *Churches, Nations and States: Insular Turbulence*

The United Kingdom and the Republic of Ireland (and Denmark) entered
the European Economic Community together in 1973. Such a step, however, did not constitute a conscious British–Irish act of togetherness and

---

[43] Gerhard Besier, Armin Boyens and Gerhard Lindemann, *Nationaler Protestantismus und
Ökumenische Bewegung: Kirchliches Handeln im Kalten Krieg (1945–1990)* (Berlin, 1999); Nicholas
Hope, 'The Iron Curtain and its Repercussions for the Churches in Europe', *Kirchliche Zeit-
geschichte* 9/2 (1999), 426–40.

[44] E.A. Payne, *Thirty Years of the British Council of Churches, 1942–1972* (London, 1972).

[45] E.A. Payne, 'Baptists and the Ecumenical Movement', *Baptist Quarterly* 18 (1960), 258–67;
D.M. Thompson, 'Baptists and the World Fellowship of the Church' in J.H.Y. Briggs, ed., *Bible,
Church and World* (London, 1989), 54–63.

neither government, at the time, could guess the extent to which common membership would affect their relationships. The previous twenty years had seen the steady emergence of Ireland on the international stage. The Soviet veto over its membership of the United Nations had been lifted in 1955. In 1960 it had opened its first embassy in Africa—in Nigeria at the moment of that country's independence. The civil war that broke out there in 1967 provided an ironic comment on the UK/Ireland/Commonwealth triangle. Irish Catholic missions had been very active during British rule, particularly among the Ibo people. There was, therefore, much emotional support in Ireland for the secessionist 'Biafran' cause. The Irish government, however, mindful of the secessionist parallel with Northern Ireland, supported Nigerian unity. A decade earlier, spasmodically, the possibility of Ireland rejoining the Commonwealth had been floated in various quarters. Cardinal d'Alton of Armagh did so publicly—'on the same basis as India'—in 1957 but the official reaction in the three capitals was cool.[46] Frank Pakenham (later Lord Longford) the Catholic Anglo-Irish Labour former minister and historian of the 1921 treaty was told by de Valera that ending partition was a prerequisite for any such step. Neither Home, the Commonwealth secretary, nor Macmillan, the prime minister, were enthusiastic. Further gestures on similar lines were sometimes made, but to no effect.[47] They did, however, indicate that, independence notwithstanding, there still remained something special about the relationship between the two islands.

The 1971 UK census disclosed that the Irish were the largest 'ethnic minority' in Britain. Over seven hundred thousand Irish-born people were concentrated in urban Britain, particularly as skilled and unskilled manual workers in the Greater London area. It did look, at one point, as though the right of Irish citizens to enter Britain freely (under the British Nationality Act of 1948) might be affected by British legislation, culminating in the 1971 Act designed to control entry from the 'New Commonwealth', but, substantially, that did not turn out to be the case.[48] Generalization about how such a large community—supposing it to be a community—perceived itself in different parts of Britain is perilous. As in the past, pressures to assimilate and to differentiate were both present.[49] Commentators reached different conclusions in particular localities. One way of not 'becoming English' was

---

[46] The 'D'Alton plan' is discussed more fully in D. Ó Corráin, *Rendering to God and Caesar: The Irish Churches and the Two States in Ireland, 1949–73* (Manchester, 2006), 51–7. The *Derry Journal*, which he cites, thought that if Ireland were again to become part of the Commonwealth 'family' it would not make Unionists any more willing to accept the removal of the border.

[47] Deirdre McMahon, 'Ireland, the Empire and the Commonwealth' in Kevin Kenny, ed., *Ireland and the British Empire* (Oxford, 2004), 216–18.

[48] Enda Delaney, *Demography, State and Society: Irish Migration to Britain, 1921–1971* (Liverpool, 2000), 264–71.

[49] Steven Fielding, *Class and Ethnicity: Irish Catholics in England, 1880–1939* (Buckingham, 1993).

to stick firmly to Catholicism and to heed the exhortation of church authorities to send children to Catholic schools. Investigators in Sparkbrook, Birmingham, concluded that the Roman Catholic Church was the biggest Irish migrant organization of all. Mass attendance rates were high. Priests from Ireland were in attendance.[50] As also in the past, however, this 'Irish Catholic' equation was not without its complexities for the Catholic Church in England, Scotland and Wales. In every decade, it almost seemed, its efforts to remove the notion that it was an 'alien' presence were 'jeopardized' by fresh tranches of Irish settlement (which might, or might not, be permanent).[51] It remained the case, however, that many dioceses relied on large numbers of Irish priests, though the proportion began to drop.[52]

If the island of Ireland had been harmonious, the perpetuation of 'Irish Catholicism' in Britain as a conscious cultural enterprise within the world of British Catholicism would have been no more problematic than the survival, to some degree at any rate, of other European cultural heritages within it. But the island of Ireland was not harmonious. The Northern Ireland 'Troubles' are conventionally taken to have their starting point in 1968 when police baton-charged the civil rights march from Belfast to Londonderry. In August 1969, the United Kingdom government agreed to deploy troops in the province as it slid ever deeper into violence. The Downing Street Declaration reiterated that it would not cease to be part of the United Kingdom without the consent of the people but also declared that every citizen was entitled to equality of treatment and freedom from discrimination, irrespective of political views or religion. Internment, introduced in August 1971, deeply divided the churches, and not simply on a Catholic/Protestant basis. Cardinal Conway and the Northern Catholic bishops were, on occasion, openly criticized by both wings of the IRA. It was the Church of Ireland clerical leadership, however, which was perhaps most on the wrack. Any statement congenial to its Northern members was liable to be criticized by its Southern.[53]

---

[50] John Rex and Robert Moore, *Race, Community and Conflict: A Study of Sparkbrook* (London, 1967).

[51] J.V. Hickey, *The Irish Rural Immigrant and British Urban Society* (London, 1960) and *Urban Catholics: Urban Catholicism in England and Wales from 1829 to the Present Day* (London, 1967); Michael Hornsby-Smith, 'Irish Catholics in England: Some Sociological Perspectives', *Social Studies* 6 (1979), 179–208 and *Roman Catholics in England: Studies in Social Structure since the Second World War* (Cambridge, 1987).

[52] Robert E. Finnegan and George T. Bradley, eds., *Catholicism in Leeds: A Community of Faith 1794–1994* (Leeds, 1994) shows that in 1950 64 per cent of priests in the diocese were Irish and 54 per cent a decade later. The first Catholic Lord Mayor of Leeds—in 1950—was a man of Irish descent.

[53] These matters are discussed more fully in Ó Corráin, *Rendering to God and Caesar*, 156–69.

In the same month, January 1972, in which the Irish republic signed the treaty of accession to the EEC, thirteen apparently unarmed civilians were killed by British soldiers in Londonderry/Derry in the context of a banned civil rights march.[54] Three weeks later, an IRA bomb killed seven people at Aldershot army barracks. The British Embassy in Dublin was burned down in the following month. By the end of the year, 474 people had been killed in spiralling sectarian warfare. In March, Heath, the UK prime minister, suspended the Northern Ireland parliament and brought in 'direct rule' through a secretary of state. It did not stop the violence. About the only thing that was clear, in a chaotic situation, was that 'Northern Ireland', as it had functioned for half a century, was at an end. Not much more could be said about how it would function in the future. History, it seemed, had not gone away. Certainly, there were two camps. Frightened population shifts produced a situation in Londonderry/Derry in which the River Foyle could be regarded as a 'religious frontier'. The very duality of the city's name pointed to competing claims to 'ownership'. Segmentation and segregation accelerated in Belfast and in other parts of the province.

It might look as though nothing had changed—but some things had. The political/religious dynamics of 1973 were not quite what they had been in 1953. Both within Britain and Ireland, meanings which had been firmly attached to the commonplace terminology of secular and ecclesiastical politics, most notably on the subject of 'unity' and 'community', wobbled uncertainly. Factors, both secular and ecclesiastical, in the world beyond Britain and Ireland destabilized, though not at the same rate and to the same degree, the working perceptions and assumptions, political and ecclesiastical, which had held sway both within and between the two islands and the 'territories' they contained. They destabilized, but did not destroy. 'Loyalties' in churches and states were stretched in unexpected directions, as a certain amount of awkward trespassing across boundaries took place, but perhaps, at bottom, they remained intact. The instability might even lead, as seemed to be the case in Northern Ireland, to a potent reaffirmation of 'old truths'. Clerical leaders were inclined to suggest that they might 'go further' but could not carry their 'flocks' with them. Some latitudinarian laity thought that what prevented change was clerical vested interest and theological nit-picking of an egregious kind. Political leaders, likewise, appeared to welcome 'change' but knew they had to face the ballot box—and, in Northern Ireland, it might also be a bullet. Some, at least, of their constituents complained that leaders were failing to lead. Where was

---

[54] What precisely happened, and why, was the subject of one inquiry and, at the time of writing, of a further one under Lord Savile, one of no mean duration and expense but, as yet, no conclusion.

the vision? The difficulty, of course, was that there was no uniformity of vision. Politicians, secular and ecclesiastical, bobbed about precariously in the boat called democracy, not sure whether they were being pulled in the same or contrary directions.

The grim reality of violence in Northern Ireland in the early 1970s naturally occupied most of the headlines, bringing, in turn, substantial addition to the already dense literature which sought to explain the cause of 'The Troubles', and possibly identify a cure. This volume cannot hope to trace in detail the tortuous course of politics in both parts of the island in the 1950s and 1960s. It seeks, rather, to illustrate both 'change' and the constraints upon further 'change' and where the churches found themselves. The 1961 census disclosed that the population of Northern Ireland, nearly one and a half million, was nearly half that of the republic. The aggregate Protestant population of the latter had diminished to a mere 4.6 per cent of the population and a further 0.5 per cent decline was recorded in 1971. Familiar discussion took place on emigration, intermarriage and late marriage as explanations for this decline. Extrapolation of what was going to happen from one census to the next had become a topic of intense interest in Northern Ireland, for obvious reasons. The Catholic population crept up but still stopped significantly short of a majority. It quivered somewhere between a third and a half. When, and indeed whether, it would achieve a majority was the subject of much punditry. Some supposed that such a majority would overnight 'solve' the 'Northern Ireland' question. That remained to be seen. Fears and hopes attended the topic, but such speculation was of no immediate assistance.

Given the exiguous Protestant minority in the Republic and the still existing non-Catholic majority in Northern Ireland, the contemporary characterization of the two entities as 'Catholic' and 'Protestant' still seemed obviously pertinent. The different balances, however, had obvious political significance. If Protestants in the Republic had grievances, which they normally said they did not have, their numbers did not make them a significant political force. That was not true in Northern Ireland. Whatever the overall position in the province, Catholic majorities existed locally. That said, it still seemed that one point emerged 'all too clearly' in the view of scholars. Grace Davie, writing from England, thought that there could be 'no doubt that the Northern Ireland conflict is a religious one'.[55] Other factors were crucial to a full understanding of the tragedy but she cited with approval the view of another sociologist, who had been resident in Northern Ireland, that it was 'the fact that the competing populations in Ireland adhered to and still adhere to competing religious traditions' which gave the

---

[55] Davie, *Religion in Britain*, 98.

conflict 'its enduring and intractable quality'.[56] She noted the irony, as she saw it, in the way in which the 'actively religious' Protestants of Northern Ireland clung to a union with a Britain which had 'long since' lost the religious disciplines that continued, 'sometimes very positively', to motivate Ulster. What underpinned Northern Irish 'aspirations' was simply not present, therefore, in the goal of their political undertakings. Another Northern Ireland-based scholar advised against the view, often expressed, that because religion was judged not to be important in western European societies 'it cannot and *should not* be important in Northern Ireland and cannot *really* be contributing to the violent conflict here'.[57]

What also has an enduring and intractable quality, however, is the presumption that without elaboration of other 'crucial' factors, 'religion' must leap to the head of the queue and so make the entire conflict 'a religious one'. There is, too, some sly footwork with words, as between 'competing' and 'conflicting', and between 'contributing to' and 'causing'. What is all too clear in most situations of conflict is that nothing is clear. 'Competition', in a broad sense, has been characteristic of churches across the British Isles as they have sought to draw in adherents either from 'outside' or by movement between themselves. 'Competition' between religious institutions can take such a form as to become 'conflict' but it is most often only when a cultural/linguistic 'national' ingredient is present that the genie is released. It might be that 'Protestant murder gangs' and 'Catholic bombers', engaging in conflict, exemplified in their conduct the noblest insights of Protestant and Catholic tradition, but that was by no means certain. What was true was that in its half-century of semi-independence, and perhaps particularly in the twenty years up to the dissolution of Stormont, Northern Ireland's inhabitants, in their tight corner, were so inwardly focused that both 'communities' failed to grasp the extent to which Ireland and Britain were changing. Neither country, in 1973, was quite what it had seemed in 1953. With some common, but some different drivers, and at different speeds, the churches, states, nations and societies of the British Isles were all engaged in a renegotiation (formal or informal) of relationships both within and between each of those four categories. Turbulence, though deep and more violent than anywhere else, was not confined to Northern Ireland.

In 1966, in a manner of speaking, 'Wales' emerged. The 44-year-old Gwynfor Evans became the first Plaid Cymru MP when he was elected for Carmarthen in a by-election. Four years earlier, Saunders Lewis had delivered a BBC lecture on 'The Fate of the Language'. Without the language, it

---

[56] S. Bruce, *God Save Ulster: The Religion and Politics of Paisleyism* (Oxford, 1986), 249.

[57] J. Hickey, *Religion and the Northern Ireland Problem* (Dublin, 1984), 110–11; Bill McSweeney, 'The Religious Dimension of the "Troubles" in Northern Ireland' in Paul Badham, ed., *Religion, State and Society in Modern Britain* (Lampeter, 1989), 67–84.

was argued, there was no nation. *Cymdeithas yr Iaith Gymraeg* (the Welsh
Language Society) began its campaigns—including civil disobedience—for
equal language rights. The result was the 1967 Welsh Language Act which
gave English and Welsh equal legal status. Yet in a rapidly changing economic and social scene it was far from clear what the future of the Welsh
language would be. Plaid Cymru did make some further electoral progress
but did not make the all-Wales breakthrough which it desired. The future of
the heavy industries and their supporting communities, so often thought to
be 'typical' of Wales, looked increasingly precarious. Where was Wales
going? Did it exist? 'Chapel' did not speak with one voice. Gwynfor
Evans, the victor of Carmarthen, an Oxford-educated Welsh-speaking
Independent (Congregationalist) and Christian pacifist, pointed to a new
national future. George Thomas, a Cardiff MP and secretary of state for
Wales (1968–70), an English-speaking Methodist, saw himself as a proud
Welshman but he would have no truck with separatism.[58] 'Church' too did
not speak with one voice. Until 1968 its archbishop, Morris was an Englishman, though one whose adult career had been spent in Wales. His lack of
Welsh had occasioned much adverse comment from Welsh-speakers on his
appointment in 1957. Was the post only to be occupied by a priest drawn
from the minority of Welsh clergy who spoke Welsh? His successor, Glyn
Simon, was equally controversial in his brief years in office—though for
quite contrasting reasons. Morris pronounced against unilateral nuclear
disarmament, Simon pronounced in favour. The extent to which the
Church in Wales should 'shake off the shackles of the past' and identify itself
with the 'new nationalism' remained contentious. The editor of *Crockford's
Clerical Directory* had noted in 1954 that not a few Welsh parsons seemed to
prefer the shackles of an established church (in England) to the delights of
serving at home. In 1962 700 priests ordained in Wales were serving in
England, but only ten priests ordained in England were ministering in Wales.
Simon held that there was nothing unscriptural or unChristian in nationalism
as such. Wales was a nation, not a region. The church had to be 'truly
bilingual'. Simon's successor, Gwilym Owen Williams, had Welsh as his first
language and, as bishop of Bangor, was determined, if he could, to make
comprehensive bilingualism more than a pious expression.[59]

---

[58] Thomas, a local preacher, explicitly linked his Christianity and his socialism. He was to become
Speaker of the House of Commons and Viscount Tonypandy. See his *George Thomas, Mr Speaker*
(London, 1986) and *My Wales* (London, 1986). Contributors to Lionel Madden, ed., *Methodism in
Wales: A Short History of the Wesleyan Tradition* (Llandudno, 2003) perforce discuss separately the
English-speaking and Welsh-speaking aspects of that tradition and also highlight those Welshmen
whose Methodist ministerial careers were passed largely in England such as Maldwyn Edwards,
Harold Roberts and, most recently, Leslie Griffiths, Lord Griffiths of Burry Port.

[59] David Walker, ed., *A History of the Church in Wales* (Penarth, 1976), 176–81; D.T.W. Price,
A History of the Church in Wales in the Twentieth Century (Penarth, 1990), 30–7; O.W. Jones,

In October 1973 Lord Kilbrandon reported the findings of the commission which had been set up to examine the UK constitution. It had not been set up merely as an interesting academic exercise. It reflected what had been happening in Wales but more importantly it was a reaction to the rapid advance which the Scottish National Party was making electorally. It won the normally safe Labour seat of Hamilton at a by-election in November 1967. A new political situation was clearly developing.[60] While it was not clear exactly what Scottish voters were after, the existing structure no longer satisfied. Edward Heath, in Opposition, told Scottish Conservatives in 1968 that he favoured a Scottish Assembly, but when he came into government in 1970 nothing happened.[61] Scottish Unionists had been forced to call themselves Conservatives in 1965 and were by no means enamoured of what Heath put forward in 1968. Most of the members of the Kilbrandon commission favoured legislative assemblies for both Scotland and Wales but there was disagreement as to whether there should also be 'devolution' in England. Whatever the precise remit of these assemblies, it was proposed that Scotland and Wales should retain their secretaries of state in the Cabinet. Nothing happened. In the 1974 general elections, the SNP made further advances. Labour would have to do something.

Many factors fed into the shifting pattern of Anglo-Scottish relations. The 'church question' was one of them. The ambiguities of 'union' were again apparent. The drawing together of the Church of England and the Church of Scotland in some way was one obvious area to be explored in the wake of the sermon Fisher had given in Cambridge in 1946, but the attempt to do so proved prickly and problematic. The General Assembly of the Church of Scotland agreed in 1947 that discussion should take place but should it only involve the two 'national' churches? Should the Scottish Episcopal Church also participate and, if it did, should the equally small Presbyterian Church of England do so too?[62] A formula was eventually found. After some stop-go, discussions eventually proceeded and a *Report on the Relations*

Glyn Simon: His Life and Opinions (Llandysul, 1981); Glyn Simon, *A Time of Change* (Penarth, 1967); G.O. Williams, *The Church's Work* (Caernarfon, 1959). Williams, strong Welshman though he was, had nevertheless graduated from Oxford with a first class degree in English.

[60] Richard J. Finlay, *A Partnership for Good? Scottish Politics and the Union since 1800* (Edinburgh, 1997), 146–60.

[61] James Kellas, 'After the Declaration of Perth: All Change!' in William L. Miller, ed., *Anglo-Scottish Relations from 1900 to Devolution and Beyond* (Oxford, 2005), 51–62.

[62] Some elements in the Episcopal Church, in the decades after the adoption of the Scottish Book of Common Prayer in 1929, had been keen to fortify it against the wicked accusation that it was simply the Church of England north of the Border. I.B. Cowan, in 1966, thought this adoption 'did something to rectify the balance, but probably not enough'. See I.B. Cowan and Spencer Ervin, *The Scottish Episcopal Church* (Ambler, PA, 1966), 65.

of the Anglican and Presbyterian Churches was published in Edinburgh in 1957. Inter-communion had naturally been a central focus. Its proposal was not that there should be a single church of Great Britain but Anglicans and Presbyterians in England and in Scotland would each unite, thus creating two churches which would be in full communion with each other. A year later, its inter-church relations committee was willing to recommend to the General Assembly that the Church of Scotland should accept a form of episcopacy. Each presbytery would choose its own 'Bishop in Presbytery'. Episcopacy in England was supposed to be going to develop a more corporate and conciliar character.

What no one anticipated, however, was that Lord Beaverbrook would rediscover his Presbyterian roots and that his *Scottish Daily Express* would be instructed to fight the proposal at whatever cost.[63] Those in Scotland who were willing to 'sell the pass' must be defeated. A vigorous campaign followed and had an impact on the presbyteries (to whom the issue had been remitted) so that by early 1959 it was clear that they were not minded to take episcopacy into their system. Nevertheless, continuing dialogue with the Church of England was authorized but the *Scottish Daily Express* remained ever watchful, over the years ahead, for any sign of a 'sell-out'. In the wake of a further conference in 1966 in Edinburgh, the bishop of Bristol publicly criticized the 'tyrannous pretensions' of the Fourth Estate which had scuppered progress. Hugh Montefiore, later bishop of Birmingham, referred to 'less pleasing aspects of national sentiment' which were being played on under cover of religious conviction. Neither man, of course, could easily see how their own reactions had an arrogance that was not only Anglican but English to boot. Few on the Anglican side had any grasp of the mood in Scotland at this juncture and what combination of factors made the Anglican–Presbyterian relationship so sensitive. Able journalists had indeed shown themselves steadfast in the faith of their forebears, even though it was no longer their own. The customary tensions between 'popular' Glasgow— expressed by Ian Henderson, a Glasgow university divinity professor in his explosive *Power without Glory*—and 'snooty' Edinburgh were triggered.[64] His exposure of the power politics, as he perceived it, at the heart of ecumenical activity, brought a new note. It contributed to a weakening, in the future, of that Scottish contribution which until this juncture may be judged 'disproportionate'. On every front, it was claimed, Scotland was

[63] Tom Gallagher, 'The Press and Protestant Popular Culture: A Case-Study of the *Scottish Daily Express*' in Graham Walker and Tom Gallagher, *Sermons and Battle Hymns: Protestant Popular Culture in Modern Scotland* (Edinburgh, 1990), 193–212.

[64] Ian Henderson, *Power Without Glory* (London, 1967). See also Andrew Herron, *Kirk by Divine Right: A Peaceful Coexistence* (Edinburgh, 1985); Mabel Small, *Growing Together: Some Aspects of the Ecumenical Movement in Scotland, 1924–1964* (Edinburgh, 1975).

being trampled on. Why had the Post Office not issued a stamp in 1960 to commemorate the 400th anniversary of the Scottish Reformation? That year had seen a special sitting of the General Assembly. Sir Thomas Taylor, principal of Aberdeen university, and perhaps the leading layman in the Church of Scotland, spoke vigorously in defence of the Scottish Reformation.[65] The wife of the minister of St Giles, biographer of John Knox, was scarcely surprised—though angry—that in 1971 the 400th anniversary of his death was similarly ignored. The previous year, in the general election, she had stood unsuccessfully against Sir Alec Douglas-Home as an SNP candidate (studies by political scientists made it clear that Protestants rather than Catholics were likely to vote for the SNP). The professor of ecclesiastical history at Edinburgh had written in 1960 that 'in time both Anglicans and Presbyterians may come to realize that the ineffectiveness of their witness is due in no small part to mechanical defects in the organization of their ministries'. Their inherited order, he thought, had been imperfectly adapted to 'the vastly changed conditions' in which they found themselves.[66] One constant source of irritation was the apparent failure of English Anglicans to understand what the office of moderator of the General Assembly really entailed.[67] Few of those who took part in the controversy, however, could be unaware of those vastly changed conditions to which the historian alluded. It was at this very point that the Church of Scotland's membership and the vitality of its ancillary organizations began to go steeply downhill.[68] The struggle against the bishops, therefore, had its paradoxical aspects. The cord between 'Scottishness' and Presbyterianism was not umbilical, despite the joined-up sentiments that could still be evoked. Dispassionate consideration of Presbyterian and Episcopalian systems might indeed be possible in time, but that time was not yet. To Geoffrey Fisher, in his retirement in a Dorset village, Scotland's identity struggles

---

[65] T.M. Taylor, *Where One Man Stands* (Edinburgh, 1960). He also called, however, for closer understanding of and co-operation with Roman Catholics.

[66] J.H.S Burleigh, *A Church History of Scotland* (Oxford, 1960), 420.

[67] The robust entry on 'Moderator' in Nigel de S. Cameron et al., eds., *Dictionary of Scottish Church History and Theology* (Edinburgh, 1993), 596–7 makes it clear that 'he' 'is not a minister plenipotentiary, a "Church Leader", or an authorized spokesman of the church'. The first 'she' moderator was to be elected in 2004—Alison Elliott, an elder, not an ordained minister, who was an academic psychologist. Andrew Herron, author of the entry, knew more about constitutional matters than any other minister in his generation and was not reluctant to deploy that knowledge in the handling of business. See his *Kirk Lore: Answers to some Interesting Questions on the Constitution and History of the Kirk in Scotland* (Edinburgh, 1999).

[68] The Glasgow sociologist John Highet's investigations, published in *The Churches in Scotland Today: A Survey of their Principles, Strength, Work and Statements* (Glasgow, 1950) and *The Scottish Churches: A Review of their State 400 Years after the Reformation* (London, 1960) did not disguise problems but did not forecast doom. Callum Brown, *Religion and Society in Scotland since 1707* (Edinburgh, 1997), 158–61.

seemed very far away. He no longer needed to try to keep the primus of the Scottish Episcopal Church in line. It might be, however, that, in the abortive attempt to come closer together, the experience of four churches revealed how far England and Scotland were, to some degree, drifting apart. The paradox of the divisions which surfaced the more ardently unity was desired was no more evident than in the parallel turbulence of the churches themselves.

iv. Inside Story: Church Unity?

In 1963, aged 58, John Heenan was driven to Lime Street station in Liverpool in an open car. He had been told, apparently without irony, that the faithful 'wanted to see the last of you, Your Grace' as he left to become archbishop of Westminster. They sang 'Faith of our Fathers'. Heenan had been enthroned in Liverpool in 1957, after spending six years as bishop of Leeds. He had found Liverpool, as he described it, a city which was alive with ebullient friendliness and religious fervour. On the Sunday after his enthronement, more than 40,000 people attended an open-air service on the site of the future metropolitan cathedral. It was from his cathedral in Leeds that Mass had been shown on British television for the first time—a Pontifical High Mass. It had been good to have known that at least a million pagans, 'many of them good but dense', had been watching, one correspondent had written to him afterwards, though others expressed the view that they wanted 'Rome dope' to be kept in the Vatican rather than be exposed to it on British television. Heenan left behind him a half-completed cathedral but he had successfully scuppered Downey's original plans. He returned in 1967 for its solemn opening.[69]

He had interpreted the 'demonstrative faith' which he had encountered as evidence of the love of the laity for their clergy and 'the esteem for their archbishop' held by the Catholics of Liverpool, practising or lapsed, educated or unlettered. Heenan in turn, as a communicator in the new television age, had qualities which his predecessor, both in Liverpool and at Westminster, William Godfrey, had not possessed. Heenan was able to fit into that 'public Catholicism' which Downey had so successfully encouraged. It all seemed further evidence of the consolidation of Catholicism and the maintenance of its self-contained ethos, at least within Liverpool. 'More of the same' would keep the steady flow of converts coming (nationally around 12,000 per annum until 1962). The provision of Catholic education still brought financial strain, though government in 1959 made further

---

[69] John C. Heenan, *A Crown of Thorns: An Autobiography, 1951–1963* (London, 1974).

concessions in England and Wales, but it seemed to ensure the consolidation of the Catholic population. Heenan, in Liverpool, had wrestled with secondary education issues but, on the whole, it seemed not unsuccessfully. At another level, Catholics were prominent in public life. William Rees-Mogg was editor of *The Times*, when it was still a paper for 'top people'. Charles Curran became director-general of the BBC and George Woodcock the general secretary of the TUC. As has been noted, whatever statistic one considered, the position of the church 'seemed almost wholly rosy'.[70]

A combination of external and internal developments made this picture less settled. In 1959, John XXIII, the elderly new pope, announced his intention to call a general council of the church.[71] Observers from other churches could attend its deliberations.[72] He may have been under the impression that there was a general yearning amongst Protestants to return to unity with the see of Peter. The agenda was prepared by some 800 theologians and other experts. The church's 2,500 bishops and the faculties of many Catholic universities were all asked what they thought were the major problems facing the church. *Aggiornamento* seemed to open a new era and no one could tell how it would all end. 'We need not expect anything dramatic' declared the Hexham and Newcastle diocesan paper in February 1962.[73] The *Northern Cross* was wrong. Prompted by the proceedings of the various sessions of the council, the church was being cast out into the deep waters of the world.

The papal initiative—did he know what he was doing?—would not have suggested itself as the obvious way ahead to the hierarchies in any part of the British Isles in 1959. With the possible exception of the abbot of Downside, B.C. Butler, who had converted from the Church of England, no British or Irish Catholic in significant office seemed to swim in the intellectual world inhabited by those Dutch, Swiss or German Catholics whose ideas were bandied about. At this level, the judgement that the English contribution to the council—and by extension that of the British Isles—was not outstanding, holds. Yet, in relation to two of the most distinctive documents of the council—the 'Pastoral Constitution on the Church and the Modern World' and the 'Declaration on Religious Liberty', it is not implausible to suggest that the experience of British Catholics of living within a religiously plural and democratic society did have a bearing, by way of example, on the

[70] Adrian Hastings, *A History of English Christianity 1920–1990* (London, 1991), 563.

[71] Adrian Hastings, ed. *Modern Catholicism: Vatican II and After* (London, 1991).

[72] J.R.H. Moorman, *Vatican Observed: An Anglican Impression of Vatican II* (London, 1967). More generally see two articles by Alberic Stacpoole, 'Ecumenism on the Eve of the Council: Anglican/Roman Catholic Relations', *Clergy Review* (1984), 300–6, 333–8 and 'Anglican/Roman Catholic Relations after the Council 1965–1970', *Clergy Review* (1985), 55–62, 91–8.

[73] Antony Archer, *The Two Catholic Churches: A Study in Oppression* (London, 1986), 126.

outcome.[74] Even so, it was obvious that the 'fundamental new definition of the relation of the Church to the world' embodied in *Gaudium et Spes* (Joy and Hope) and the conception of the church as 'the people of God' descended upon, rather than sprang from, the Catholics of the British Isles.

Suddenly, the assumptions which had underpinned the church politics of the British Isles for centuries, seemed to be thrust into a quite different context. Boundaries which had seemed certain and secure now seemed porous. A church in which, in theory at least, there was a place for everybody, but everybody knew their place, was rocking from side to side. Conservatives and liberals, in so far as such terminology can capture the range of opinion, all recognized that a great change was occurring. The argument was whether it had gone far enough—or too far. It was one thing to make inspiring pronouncements and another to devise appropriate mechanisms to put them into effect.[75] It was all either exhilarating or depressing. It was taken in some quarters to presage the 'liberation' of the church from structures and modes of thought and procedure which no longer made sense in 'the modern world' or, alternatively seen as the abandonment of all that had made Catholicism 'different'. Veterans of the Catholic cause were dismayed. Frank Sheed, who attended every session of the council, claimed never to have encountered optimism. Both excitement and dismay required subtle management if the boat was not to capsize. A Secretariat for Unity certainly opened up prospects, but the debates of Vatican II tested to the full how 'unity' was to be interpreted in a global church existing in very different cultures and drawing support from very different ethnic and social communities. The Catholic Church in the British Isles would still be moulded from outside but 'national styles' would be inescapable—to some degree. What did 'unity in diversity' actually mean?

Heenan had dipped his toe tentatively in the water. Godfrey's manifest lack of enthusiasm for ecumenism had enabled him to set up a secretariat in Liverpool. It would show those outside the church that the hierarchy was determined to reflect the pope's fatherly zeal for Christian unity. Heenan organized a conference, which had a good deal of media coverage, whose proceedings were designed to demonstrate that the bench of bishops was not, as was sometimes suggested, restraining an eager laity, and some priests, from engaging in ecumenical endeavour. He chose a visit to Northern Ireland in 1962 to remark that being a Christian was more important than being a Catholic or a Protestant. Some of his English correspondents

---

[74] Jeffrey Paul von Arx, 'Catholics and Politics' in V. Alan McClelland and Michael Hodgetts, eds., *From Without the Flaminian Gate: 150 Years of Roman Catholicism in England and Wales 1850–2000* (London, 1999), 267.

[75] Nicholas Atkin and Frank Tallett, *Priests, Prelates and People: A History of European Catholicism, 1750 to the Present* (London, 2003), 294–6.

thought the remark appalling. It gave the impression that the Christian church had *branches*. Heenan endeavoured to issue 'rules for ecumenical conduct' which would try to make sure both that the Catholic Church was the one true church and at the same time concede that there were real Christians who were not Catholics. It would not be right to take part in public worship with non-Catholics. Something was clearly afoot, but in the apprehension and excitement of the moment, no one quite knew what. Some doors were open, some cautiously ajar, others still apparently tight shut.

Returning from 'exile' in the North of England in 1963, the new arch-bishop of Westminster had little inkling of the scale of turbulence ahead of him. Only in 1973, after a stormy decade, did he see, as he put it, light beginning to break through. He encountered, as he saw it, a bitter attack on the Catholic Church being mounted by her own children. The faithful, he recorded, had revolted by then against the prophets of doom and had looked to their bishops and priests for protection and guidance. The struggle had been fierce and there had been many casualties. Eventually, however, he thought, 'the true spirit of Pope John prevailed'. 'True spirit', however, could never be reduced to propositions, and 'ownership' could not be other than contentious. The paradoxes in the process which was being set on foot could not be avoided. 'Never before', it has been noted, 'had so many and such sudden changes been legislated' and never before had the laity been expected to adjust so radically across so many aspects of what had hitherto been presented as a compact and indivisible whole.[76] The question of power was inescapably present in such circum-stances, though rarely addressed as such. Men who exercised power, and had been formed to exercise it, were now in the business of saying that it all had to be exercised differently, but did not quite know how to do it. Heenan, looking back on his time in Leeds, recognized that he had been an autocrat, but had not supposed so at the time. It was not easy for a man in his sixties to start behaving differently. What was true of archbishops was also true of bishops and priests, all of whom had been formed within a conception of 'church' which was 'theirs' to administer and direct at all levels. Now, things were to be different, but how different? When the Conference of English Bishops gathered to consider how best to implement the council, their first (probably jocular) thought was: 'How are we to persuade the laity not to kiss our episcopal rings any more?'[77] It was one thing to be mouthing the new terminology of 'co-responsibility' and to be admitting the necessity of

[76] John O'Malley, *Tradition and Transition: Historical Perspectives on Vatican II* (Wilmington, 1989), 17.
[77] Alberic Stacpoole, ed., *Vatican II by Those who were There* (London, 1986) citing Augustine Harris, incoming bishop of Middlesbrough, 2.

consultation (of some kind) but difficult to know what this meant in practice. The laity were thrust into prominence but did not know how to behave in a 'representative' manner, at least not initially. It was also apparent, when it came to deeds (and even more to words) that there was no such thing as a homogenous 'Catholic laity'. Those who 'came forward' were people who were used to doing so in their working lives. There were evidently different kinds of laity.[78] When so much had been said about 'participation' and 'dialogue', what were 'church leaders' to make of Cardinal Heenan's scathing attack in 1972 on 'discussion'—words before and instead of deeds. He revealed that he was never over-confident of hearing God's voice at conferences—but presumably felt more confident when on his own.[79]

The 'faithful', of course, did not react uniformly to the directive that they should be participatory neophytes. It was odd, some thought, not to be consulted about the fact that they should be consulted. For others, it was a relief not to have to be infantile any longer. It was, however, puzzling that what many had supposed to be essential features of the practice of Catholicism simply disappeared. It was not long before social anthropologists and sociologists were busy.[80] A fully vernacular Mass was permitted in 1967 and the priest was now to celebrate facing the people. The reality, it was frequently conceded, was that there was no widespread demand for liturgical change. The English, an American observed, still saw the liturgy as having as its principal function the differentiation of Catholics from the Protestant majority. The changes, Archbishop Dwyer of Birmingham thought, had 'launched a movement which will uproot all kinds of age-old habits, cut psychological and emotional ties, shake to the foundations the ways of thought of three to four million Catholics'.[81] All of that, he wondered, just to place an emphasis on communal responsibility? It was undoubtedly true that much uprooting did take place and there was much uncertainty about the new arrangements. The structure, it was observed,

---

[78] Hence the thesis advanced in Archer, *Two Catholic Churches* that a new middle-class form of Roman Catholicism was coming into existence which was effectively excluding the working class. There was no enquiry concerning what 'the working class' needed or wanted. I. Hamnett and J.O. Mills, eds., 'Class and Church: After Ghetto Catholicism: Facing the Issues raised by Antony Archer's *The Two Catholic Churches*', *New Blackfriars* 68 (1987). M.P. Hornsby-Smith, *The Changing Parish: A Study of Parishes, Priests and Parishioners after Vatican II* (London, 1989).

[79] Michael P. Hornsby-Smith, 'A Transformed Church' in Hornsby-Smith, ed., *Catholics in England 1950–2000: Historical and Sociological Perspectives* (London, 1999), 7.

[80] Mary Douglas, *Natural Symbols: Explorations in Cosmology* (Harmondsworth, 1973), 59–76 considers the symbolic significance of Friday and Lenten fasting.

[81] M.A. Fitzsimons, 'England' in M.A. Fitzsimons, ed., *The Catholic Church Today: Western Europe* (London and Notre Dame, IN, 1969), 335–7. He cites Dwyer's remarks. Desmond Ryan, *The Catholic Parish: Institutional Discipline, Tribal Identity and Religious Development in the English Church* (London, 1996) is a study of the archdiocese of Birmingham undertaken nearly thirty years after Dwyer and has much material, obtained in interviews, on the local impact of Vatican II.

still gave the priest total control over everything and everybody in his parish. He could be as democratic or as autocratic as he wanted to be. A change of priest could result in a total change in the whole attitude and style of a parish. It was very confusing.[82] Men who had been taken to be, in their different ways, talismanic Catholics—such as Christopher Dawson or Evelyn Waugh—hated what was going on. Dawson supposed that a liturgy in English constituted a regression into nationalism. That the English language that was used was 'basic' (and the music, as it evolved, was so 'banal') did not escape the attention of men of high culture.[83] Indeed, some of them came to think that use of an unintelligible *lingua sacra* enabled the worshipper to escape from the tyranny of the present: emphasis upon 'plain English' gave the false impression that the mystery of God could be easily made plain.

This unsettlement reverberated across the British Isles. Naturally, the hierarchies could not 'pick and mix' amongst the decrees that emanated from the council, but that did not mean that enthusiasm abounded. The majority of the Irish hierarchy had spent the council cocooned in the Irish College, where they were fortunately fortified by running water in each room, specially installed. The Irish Ambassador to the Holy See had no difficulty in concluding that their attitude had been 'the reverse of exuberant'. He further observed that they and the archbishop of Westminster were at one in requiring the unqualified adherence to every iota of Catholic doctrine as it then existed. They were wary of 'Europeans' who seemed to be soft-pedalling. Heenan, however, knew how not to wave the Roman sceptre, and the ambassador thought that reflected the difference between Ireland and England.[84]

In the Irish case, so much seemed to show a 'successful' church. Why meddle with it? In parish after parish, the priest seemed to be the man who held the community together. It was not unusual, as one found himself in the diocese of Achonry in 1959, to be patron of eight different local committees which included the boxing club and the agricultural show. Generously, he ceded the presidency of the local golf club to the bishop.[85] The laity appeared to be willing to pay and obey. Archbishop McQuaid, on his return from the council, an experience which had not enthused him, felt able to reassure the faithful that no change would disturb 'the tranquillity of

---

[82] Hornsby-Smith, *Changing Parish*, 194–5.

[83] A later historian, himself a convert, seems to have found more 'loss' than 'gain' in a period which left 'a whole generation of Roman Catholics caught between ecclesiastical nostalgia and a half-digested modernism'. Sheridan Gilley, 'A Tradition and Culture Lost, To be Regained?' in Michael P. Hornsby-Smith, ed., *Catholics in England 1950–2000: Historical and Sociological Perspectives* (London, 1999), 30–45.

[84] The observations of the ambassador are cited in Ó Corráin, *Rendering to God and Caesar*, 203–4.

[85] Liam Swords, *A Dominant Church: The Diocese of Achonry 1818–1960* (Blackrock, 2004), 527.

your Christian lives'. Certainly, no significant change in the manner in which he exercised his own office was discernible. However, the Irish hierarchy published the vernacular text in January 1965 and in the following year gave permission for Catholics to attend non-Catholic baptism, marriages and funerals. Ecumenism, in McQuaid's view, was a gravely delicate process. Non-Catholics stood for 'the English remnant' who had tried to destroy the one true Faith. In 1966—the 50th anniversary of the Easter Rising—he did not renew the ban on Catholics attending Trinity College, reversed the decision the following year, but finally lifted it in 1970. The pattern of its admissions changed dramatically thereafter. In 1972 the clause in the constitution which gave a special position to the Catholic Church was abolished by referendum. McQuaid himself resigned in that year from the see to which he had been appointed in 1940.

By that juncture, at least in the eyes of those who wrote in critical periodicals, Irish Christian lives had been successfully kept too tranquil. Articulate members of the laity complained that they were kept inarticulate, but the inarticulate members did not seem greatly seized by the opportunities before them. Some Knights of St Columbanus were rather depressed that their job-distributing skills were being restrained. Bishops still moved in mysterious ways and it was not certain, in their conclaves in Maynooth, that they were performing wonders. There had been formal changes, it was true, but it seemed to be asking too much of men to change their underlying habits and assumptions. What critics claimed was a 'claustrophobic atmosphere in the parishes' could alternatively be portrayed as evidence of a deep loyalty to the Faith, undisturbed by passing fashion. Why talk of change when a 1971 survey was claiming a 96 per cent Mass-going rate among Catholics? A historian in that year, admittedly one who was to become Provost of Trinity, wrote that 'the forces that favour the maintenance of the status quo are by no means routed'.[86] Ireland, it seemed, was still very firmly 'a Catholic country'.

'Vatican II' across the British Isles therefore evoked a broadly similar response—a grudging and somewhat bewildered acceptance at all levels of the Roman Catholic Church was accompanied, on the wings, by ardent enthusiasts and malcontents in roughly equal measure. It was in Ireland that its implications could have the most far-reaching consequences. In rendering inappropriate language in which ecclesiastical and theological controversy had been conducted, it could, in time at least, render obsolete (politically) both the partition of Ireland and the gulf between Britain and Ireland. The conditional tense, however, is used deliberately. Whether

---

[86] F.S.L. Lyons, *Ireland since the Famine* (Glasgow, 1973 edn.), 690.

approached politically, culturally or religiously, the scene across the British Isles, against the background which has been sketched, was set for a complicated dance as 'leaders' circled the floor, warily looking over new 'partners'. Outside the hall, the men with the gun were operating. The Lord of the Dance, meanwhile, looked on.

The Protestantisms of the British Isles had been confirmed in their own self-justification by contrasting themselves, to greater or lesser degree, with the Roman Catholic Church. They had done so with varying degrees of self-confidence and stridency. Protestants clearly disagreed among themselves, in denominational terms, but what united them, at a certain level, was that they were not inclined to be Roman Catholics. For some, disinclination inadequately expressed their feelings. As the Vatican Council got under way an editorial in the Anglican evangelical journal *Churchman* perceived it to be 'still a monstrous authoritarian machine, relentless in its purpose, intolerant of change, insensitive to the claims of individuals and minorities'. The Scottish Reformation Society thought that non-Catholics should not accept the papal invitation to be present as observers. Three years later the tone of the *Churchman* was a little more positive, but still highly critical. When, in 1968, Michael Ramsey came to preach in Westminster Cathedral he was greeted outside with banners which declared 'Bible Truth or Roman Error: Britain Must Choose'. Such a proclamation at least added variety to the banners being displayed in some profusion elsewhere in 1968. The consensus of English commentators, however, was that the 'primitive' anti-Romanism which this display epitomized was something which should only be seen on the periphery of the United Kingdom, say in Skye or Co. Antrim.[87]

That did not mean to say, however, that everything had changed. Ecumenically-minded Baptists were still being reminded by other Baptists in 1962 that the teaching of Rome was utterly divorced from Scripture. The Baptist World Alliance did not send observers to Vatican II. Yet others, while not unmindful of the iniquity evident in the extent to which Catholic parish life apparently depended financially on funds raised by football pools—or, subsequently, by Bingo—did see quite extraordinary and unexpected promise in what was unfolding in Rome. It was not so much 'the Reformation in danger' as that the Roman Church, in so many respects, appeared at long last to be accepting 'Reformation insights'. Of course, it was accepted that the Catholic Church did not want to admit that it was doing so, but it would have been churlish not to recognize and welcome change. And, once started, who knew where change would really end?

---

[87] John Wolffe, 'Change and Continuity in British Anti-Catholicism, 1829–1982' in Frank Tallett and Nicholas Atkin, eds., *Catholicism in Britain and France since 1789* (London, 1996), 67–83.

Nor would it be prudent to derive a simple satisfaction from the fact that, in some at least of their assertions, Protestants could be held to have been right 'all along'. 'Bible Truth' as contrasted with 'Roman Error' might still have some powerful resonance, but perhaps all the churches were moving beyond such simple antitheses as they tried to accommodate both tradition and change. Was there to be a return to the past or a voyage to the future?

The entry of Rome into the ecumenical arena, whatever it precisely betokened, had one major consequence. It either rendered obsolete or brought fresh urgency to the kind of discussion of 'church unity' which had been followed, erratically and spasmodically, and without tangible outcome, since Fisher's 1946 Cambridge sermon. It was rendered obsolete, particularly for those Anglicans who had hitherto looked in vain for a 'sign' from Rome of a formal kind. The great rift in western Christianity represented by 'the Reformation' could now be addressed, formidable though such an undertaking would be. It was rendered urgent in another way if one took the view that, notwithstanding the welcome tone from Rome, 'unity' in any constitutional sense was only a remote prospect. It would be better, rather, to seek the consolidation of the separated strands of Protestantism ahead of any eventual and distant 'solution' with Rome. The ecclesiastical landscape of the British Isles might then be simplified so that it consisted, as it had not done since the Reformation, of a single Protestant Church and a single Roman Catholic Church. The reality, however, was that both processes were entangled. Each step, at whatever level, had consequences which the participants in both processes could not anticipate.

Public gestures were necessary and occupied headlines. Behind the headlines, much anxious diplomatic and theological protocol had accompanied the meeting between Archbishop Fisher and Pope John XXIII in December 1960, on the initiative of the former. The visit was not 'official'. Lady Scarlett, wife of the British Minister to the Holy See, seemed rather fiercely anti-Roman and wanted the archbishop to show the flag (it is not clear which flag). Not everybody in the Vatican was prepared to think that Fisher was really an archbishop. Having stressed to the pope that Anglicans were not really Protestants, Fisher deplored the lack of contact between Roman Catholics and Anglicans. He reiterated his liking for a 'Commonwealth of Churches'. It was agreed, though not reported immediately, that an Anglican priest should live in Rome, no doubt unobtrusively, to serve as a link between Lambeth and the Secretariat for Christian Unity. Fisher's present was a copy of the Coronation Service—which he stressed had followed the ancient Catholic Consecration Rite. He made no allusion to his vigorous support for the royal Coronation Oath and the Protestant Reformed Religion. Two old men, with such different backgrounds, exchanging courtesies, would not move mountains but did make possible the beginning of more substantial dialogue. The Vatican allowed no photograph of 'Dr Fisher' with the pope. When the next archbishop came to meet the next pope in 1966 the atmosphere was different, and not only because the two men were different. Paul revealed that as a younger man he had visited both Durham and Canterbury. Ramsey was surprised to find the pope slipping on his finger—a layman whose Orders were null and void— the episcopal ring which he had been given as archbishop of Milan. It was a moving gesture (though it did not nullify the nullifying of Anglican Orders). They were friends. They signed a common declaration.[88]

A mutual interest, 'at the top', in the life and thought of St. Anselm was gratifying but in the ordinary course of events 'normal' Anglican and Roman Catholic congregations in England did not find Anselm so ready a common bond. Newman could be a link, of an awkward kind, between Catholics and Anglicans—though who 'owned' the 'real' Newman? Translating elevated and elevating gestures into specific action was much more problematic, and there were toes waiting to be trodden on. How to go about meeting, reading and even, just conceivably, praying together? What annoyed him in Roman Catholics, Ramsey told the students at the English College in Rome, where he was staying during his visit, was the fact that they exhibited the natural inferiority complex of any minority group but spiced it with a certain bumptiousness. Everybody laughed. It would not indeed have been difficult to compose a comprehensive picture of what annoyed everybody about everybody else. Heenan, reputedly, sponsored a bring-your-own-picnic-lunch meeting of Roman Catholics and Methodists at Westminster because he supposed that his flock would be able to get along together more easily with Methodists than with Anglicans (supposing, rather fondly, Methodists to be 'working-class'). A Roman Catholic–Methodist Committee got under way. The Ecumenical Commission of England and Wales began its work in 1970 under the presidency of Bishop Alan Clark.

At a wider level, what was to be formalized as the Anglican–Roman Catholic International Commission (ARCIC) began its main work in 1970. There were indeed difficult issues to be addressed but in quick order there was supposed to be 'substantial agreement' on Eucharistic Doctrine (1971) and on Ministry (1973). Yet, despite this remarkable set of developments, it was not a world without boundaries. Heenan told the Birmingham Church Leaders Conference in 1972 that only in the most unfavourable circumstance—he instanced maybe in a concentration camp—might

[88] For a general background see Bernard and Margaret Pawley, *Rome and Canterbury through Four Centuries* (London, 1974). The accounts of the archiepiscopal visits are drawn from Edward Carpenter, *Archbishop Fisher: His Life and Times* (Norwich, 1991), 730–44 and Chadwick, *Ramsey*, 316–29.

non-Catholics be permitted to receive communion. The Anglican chairman suggested, as an appropriate response, that the thing to do might be
to pray for a multiplication of concentration camps. The suggestion was
apparently not followed up. Its absurdity, however, did raise the question:
how far can you go? And it was in that same city that a professor of English
was working on a novel with that title which encapsulated the dilemmas
which were increasingly being experienced. *Real Life is Meeting*, J.H. Oldham had written in his book of 1942. By the time of his death in 1969,
'meeting' was taking place between Christian persons at levels, 'high' and
'low', which could not have been anticipated when the British Council of
Churches had been formed in the year the book was published. Moreover,
the 'meeting' of long separated 'brethren', and perhaps 'sister' churches,
involved more than meetings, though there was no lack of them.

It was, of course, in the island of Ireland that the potential scope for
change was perhaps greatest. If 'religion' was *the* issue, or *perceived to be the
issue* in Northern Ireland then the change brought by Vatican II would
surely contribute to 'religious peace' which in turn would help to halt the
spiralling violence. Again, it was time for public statements and gestures
which unfroze a long past. In 1968, the president of the Irish Republic and
the Taoiseach, for the first time, attended a funeral in a Protestant church.
Presbyterian, Anglican and Methodist figures all made statements which
saw the prospect of a new beginning. The *Presbyterian Herald* in 1965
forecast that over the next twenty years Ireland would be an exciting
place in which to live. In a way, though perhaps not the way it hoped,
that was to be the case. That these statements were at a predictable level of
generality should not detract from the difficulty, in the political circumstances, of making them at all. There was base-up as well as top-down. Ray
Davey, a Presbyterian minister, founded the Corrymeela Community at
Ballycastle, Co. Antrim, in 1965 as a place for individuals to explore the
process of reconciliation. In Dublin, Michael Hurley, a Jesuit, became the
first director of the Irish School of Ecumenics, with encouragement from
both sides. At another level, 'high-ranking experts' began to meet from
1973 to discuss issues which divided the churches, both theological and
practical. Mixed marriage was never long off the agenda (it was no accident
that Archbishop Simms, then still in Dublin, had been the Anglican chairman of the ARCIC consideration of the theology of marriage which met
between 1967 and 1975). The Irish Catholic–Protestant conferences took
place at Ballymascanlon, Co. Louth, in the republic, but not too far from
Northern Ireland. More than one kind of border was obviously involved.[89]

---

[89] Cahal B. Daly and A.S. Worrall, *Ballymascanlon: A Venture in Inter-Church Dialogue* (Belfast
and Dublin, 1978).

The political background, however, gave them a dimension which was lacking when analogous questions were being discussed in Britain. An inter-church group, set up in 1970, jointly chaired by Bishop Cahal Daly and the Methodist minister Eric Gallagher produced a notable report on *Violence in Ireland* which was both a mutually agreed analysis and an outline of possible courses of action in which all churches could be involved. There was always an underlying anxiety, however, whether 'the centre' could hold. Group members were well aware that 'delivering' their churches might be another matter, and there were times when they found themselves further apart from each other than they had originally supposed.[90]

The picture in the province at this juncture also brought out the interplay of cultural/political/religious connections across the British Isles as it looked north and south, east and west. G.O. Simms arrived in Armagh as Church of Ireland archbishop from Cork and Dublin in 1969.[91] Born in Donegal, he had been educated (and taught) in England and in Trinity College, Dublin. His spoken English was 'Anglo-Irish' but he spoke Irish fluently. Northern Ireland he did not know at all intimately. Some of his Southern flock reacted to 'The Troubles' by criticizing their Northern brethren. Then again there was the question whether 'The Troubles' would give fresh vigour to the Ulster/Scottish/Presbyterian axis. In 1971 the Scottish grand secretary of the Orange Order toured Orange halls in Scotland seeking to enrol men with National Service or Territorial Army experience who would be willing to join in the defence of their 'own people'. There were rumours of arms and explosives going across.[92] Presbyterian and Methodist leaders, in particular, were worried that moving into ecumenical ground, however tentatively, always carried with it the possibility of disaffected elements drifting out of what they regarded as the Protestant mainstream. Splitting up came naturally to the powerful figure of Ian Paisley, as it had done to his father before him. Armagh-born Paisley had become pastor of the Ravenhill Evangelical Mission, but in 1951, aged 25, he led followers out of it to set up a new Free Presbyterian Church. Unlike other moder-ators, he was permanent. In 1969 the Ravenhill Road Martyrs' Memorial Free Presbyterian Church in East Belfast was opened and became the religious headquarters of the denomination. Other churches were opened in due course, though in number they did not seriously challenge the

---

[90] E. Gallagher and S. Worrall, *Christians in Ulster 1968–1980* (Oxford, 1982).
[91] Lesley Whiteside, *George Otto Simms: A Biography* (Gerrards Cross, 1990).
[92] Steve Bruce, 'The Ulster Connection' in Graham Walker and Tom Gallagher, eds., *Sermons and Battle Hymns: Protestant Popular Culture in Modern Scotland* (Edinburgh, 1990), 240–52 con-cludes, however, that the bulk of Scottish Protestants distanced themselves from the mindset which saw Presbyterians in Northern Ireland as 'our own people'.

existing denominations. 'God's man in Ulster', through the new Demo-cratic Unionist Party, was determined that 'Rome' would not win.[93]

The ingredients of Ulster Christianity, thus manifested, were difficult for English Christians to engage with. Ian Paisley might see himself as a latter-day John Knox, but John Knox had little resonance in England. It was easy to think that Paisley belonged to a different world.[94] There was a realization, too, that any attempt at intervention or mediation by any particular church or by churches collectively from across the water would be likely to be misconstrued. As things were, for the English Catholic hierarchy, the substantial Irish immigration continued to pose the custom-ary conundrum of identity and allegiance.[95] Part of a 'successful' integration seemed to entail 'the Irish' adopting, amongst other things, the English habit of infrequent churchgoing (as it was perceived) but to keep the Irish 'good Catholics' by encouraging Irish cultural activities and group solidarity unfortunately reinforced the English notion that Catholicism was 'Irish religion'. Whether the hierarchy could really determine matters, one way or the other, was at least questionable.

The archbishop of Canterbury thought he ought to go to Ireland. Perhaps this apparently very English Englishman (normally, but not always) remembered that his own Irish grandfather had been a preacher on the steps of Belfast Customs House whose services had reputedly gone on all day and all night. He might also have recalled, though with a shudder, his memory of the sensational preaching at Cambridge of the Belfast Presbyterian Wil-liam Nicholson.[96] Cultured ears were not used to Nicholson's rugged directness, but this mission in the university had produced many converts, although Ramsey had not been among them. It seemed better to go to Northern Ireland first (in 1964) and Ramsey could think of no better way to be with all of the Church of Ireland than to join in a pilgrimage on St Patrick's Day. He lectured in Dublin in 1967 on 'Rome and Canterbury' and had lunch with President de Valera. A momentary solidarity was discovered in the revelation that the president, a mathematician, had used mathematical textbooks written by Ramsey's father. As the situation

[93] Patrick Mitchel, *Evangelicalism and National Identity in Ulster, 1921–1988* (Oxford, 2003), 171–212 is the most probing discussion of the blend of ideas in 'Paisleyism'.

[94] Paisley himself, at this juncture, had had very little contact with England. His training to be a pastor had been at a school of evangelism in Barry near Cardiff and in Belfast.

[95] Mary J. Hickman, 'The Religio-Ethnic Identities of Teenagers of Irish Descent' in Hornsby-Smith, *Catholics in England 1950–2000*, and her book *Religion, Class and Identity: The State, the Catholic Church and the Education of the Irish in Britain* (Aldershot, 1995). Hickman argues strongly against the view expressed by Hornsby-Smith, *Roman Catholics in England*, 116–32 that Irish Catholics had been very largely assimilated into British Catholicism.

[96] S.W. Murray, *W.P. Nicholson* (Belfast, 1977). Nicholson's career, apart from occasional forays into England, classically spanned Ulster, Glasgow, the United States and the 'Old Dominions'.

deteriorated over the subsequent years, the archbishop found it difficult to decide whether his presence would or would not be beneficial. In 1973 he saw Cardinal Conway in Armagh and flew into Londonderry by helicopter, a scene he found both depressing and bewildering.

This, and subsequent visits, always attracted the personal attention of Ian Paisley, The two men had already met. Paisley was on the aircraft which took Ramsey to the pope so that he could point out the error of the archbishop's ways. When they formally, though reluctantly, met in Northern Ireland, Ramsey offered to shake hands but Paisley would not do so with a man who had shaken hands with the pope. In New York in 1970, Ramsey had indicated that he would not call Ian Paisley a man of God and no doubt that sentiment was reciprocated.[97] It could be understood why a future generation might wish to move beyond this apparent impasse. Michael Hurley, in his own contribution to a volume on Irish Anglicanism which he edited in 1970, chided the disestablished Church of Ireland for insufficiently freeing itself from the Church of England. Amongst other unhappy consequences, he criticized its failure, as he saw it, to see its destiny as that of a minority church. It had therefore failed to show 'the rest of us' how to be 'the minority Church which all Christians must now be, in fact if not in theory'.[98] 'Churches', as manifested in the public arena, however, did not yet seem ready to welcome minority status.

The engagement of Roman Catholics with other Christians was necessarily problematic by virtue of its novelty, but the discussions between non-Catholic Christians were scarcely less difficult despite their pedigree. It was in 1953 that the Methodist Conference, alone of the Free Churches, approved a suggestion that exploratory conversations should be held with the Church of England. The Convocations of the Church of England agreed, two years later, that such discussion should be deemed to be taking place 'within the Body of Christ'. A committee was set up with nothing less than visible union as its goal. It was evident from the outset, however, that the 'unification of ministries' would be the major hurdle, involving as it did debate on the necessity and nature of episcopacy. There was also the obvious fact that both churches were ecclesiastical coalitions.[99] After only twenty years of union, the 'backgrounds' from which Methodists came

---

[97] Chadwick, *Ramsey*, 198–206; Michael de-la-Noy, *Michael Ramsey: A Portrait* (London, 1990), 16–17.

[98] M. Hurley, ed., *Irish Anglicanism* (Dublin, 1970), 222. It was a sign of the times that these essays on the role of Anglicanism in Irish life were presented to the Church of Ireland on the occasion of the centenary of its disestablishment by a group of Methodist, Quaker and Roman Catholic scholars. After a little prodding, modest financial support for the volume was produced by the Irish Department of Education. An approach to the Northern Ireland Education Department for similar support did not yield fruit.

[99] W.S.F. Pickering, ed., *Anglican–Methodist Relations: Some Institutional Factors* (London, 1961).

could still be evident. The 'parties' of the Church of England had not disappeared. Some Methodists had been accustomed to thinking of themselves as Free Churchmen, some felt closer to Anglicans. Some Anglicans did not want to jeopardize their position in the wider ecclesiastical scene by reaching a 'Protestant' accommodation with Methodists.

After a series of interim reports, the joint committee produced *Conversations between the Church of England and the Methodist Church* in 1963. It envisaged proceeding in two stages. In the first, the two churches would enter into full communion but retain their separate identities. However, in accepting Stage One, they would commit themselves to a Stage Two which would be a union, perhaps after twenty years. Such a church, it was hinted, might then have a different relationship with the state. The means of effecting 'reconciliation' was to be a mutual re-commissioning of the ministry of both churches. It was not difficult, however, for opponents in both churches to fasten on the ambiguity which surrounded 're-commissioning'—was it really 're-ordination'? In 1965, however, the two churches each nominated twelve representatives to prepare a detailed scheme of union. Two years later, the group produced an Interim Statement. It worked, however, in the context of evident public division, particularly initially among Methodists—a minority report had been submitted to the 1963 *Conversations* document. Two organizations sprang to life urging opposing courses. The Church Union, for its part, recommended that no bishop or priest should take part in the proposed Service of Reconciliation without some more positive statement on the role of the ministerial priesthood as it was traditionally understood in Catholic Christendom. As books, articles and pamphlets proliferated, the scheme appeared to be running into ever-increasing difficulty.[100]

The final report was published in April 1968. It was a long document which had observations on all the pertinent issues, not least a lengthy consideration of the 'Service of Reconciliation'. In its aftermath, a 'continuing' Church of England and a 'continuing' Methodist Church had their advocates amongst the opponents of the proposed union. Those involved did not all come from clearly identifiable 'wings' in their respective churches. The temperature rose as some people equated use of ambiguous language, particularly in relation to the Service of Reconciliation, with deliberate dishonesty. The archbishop of Canterbury and his vocal retired predecessor were at loggerheads in public.[101] Fisher, in a letter to *The Times*

---

[100] J.I. Packer, ed., *The Church of England and the Methodist Church* (Marcham, 1963); R.E. Davies, *Methodists and Unity* (London, 1962); S.L. Greenslade et al., *Conversations between the Church of England and the Methodist Church: Comments and Criticisms* (London, 1963).

[101] G.F. Fisher, *The Anglican–Methodist Conversations and the Problem of Church Unity* (Oxford, 1964).

in January 1969, referred to 'open double dealing'. Ramsey rebutted the charge in his presidential address to the Convocation of Canterbury in the same month. After much discussion it was agreed that a 75 per cent approval was required in both churches for the scheme to go ahead. The vote in both churches took place in July 1969 and the Methodist Conference recorded a majority in favour of 77.4 per cent. The two Church of England Convocations, meeting together in London, only recorded a majority of 69 per cent.

There was, however, one other development which, some believed, might yet save the scheme—besides the knowledge that Methodists had endorsed it again by an increased majority. In November 1970 the queen opened the first session of the new General Synod of the Church of England in Westminster Abbey in the presence of the political establishment. It came into being by fusing the Convocations and the Church Assembly. The Church of England was not disestablished but *de facto* it was ruling itself. It had set up yet another commission on *Church and State* under the historian Owen Chadwick. Reporting in 1970, it had recommended that the Crown should still appoint bishops but that a permanent electoral board (which might or might not include the prime minister) should oversee the selection process. It still remained to be seen precisely how that would work out. The supposition that General Synod might yet come round to supporting the union scheme was ill-founded. In the final vote, in May 1972, the majority was only 65.81 per cent in favour, less than it had been in 1969. Bishops had shown themselves more in favour than either clergy or the laity, though six of their number had voted against. After its long agony, the scheme was dead.[102] The most substantial attempt in English history to bring together two churches had collapsed ignominiously and it had been the Church of England which had been responsible. Anglicans had positioned themselves as leaders in England in the matter of Christian unity. They had failed. Ramsey identified in his church a fear of change which had deepened and become obsessive. He asked himself, as others did, whether he should have spoken and acted differently, at particular junctures. There was no doubt that he felt deeply the failure of a project to which—unexpectedly in the eyes of some—he had become committed. Of course, there could be some things which could be rescued from the wreck—the existence, for example, of the joint Anglican–Methodist Queen's College in Birmingham—which testified that it was still possible to work together. Basically, however, there was no alternative but to think denominationally. Rebuffed, Methodists, in the words of one participant, found themselves afflicted 'with a certain

---

[102] J.M. Turner, *Conflict and Reconciliation: Studies in Methodism and Ecumenism, 1740–1982* (London, 1985), 194–232; Brake, *Policy and Politics in British Methodism*, 99–150.

numbness, followed by a slightly feverish preoccupation with denominational affairs'.[103] They settled down to the rather grim task of restructuring
their church as a single entity. They did so with a membership of some
600,000 in the year the scheme failed. When serious discussion had begun, it
had been near 750,000. They were not alone in the apparently accelerating
erosion of their base.[104]

There was some realignment to celebrate in 1972 but it did not constitute a development on the scale which an Anglican–Methodist coming
together would have represented. In England and Wales, the Congregational Church—the Union had become a church five years earlier—and
the Presbyterian Church of England came together to form the United
Reformed Church.[105] It had not been a swift process—the project having
been mooted, with fluctuating seriousness, for four decades. A minority of
Congregationalist churches dissented and were linked in a Congregational
Federation which hallowed the emphasis on independency which the new
structure appeared to abandon, at least in certain central aspects. On the
day of the union the archbishop of Canterbury came to Westminster
Central Hall to join the celebration and apparently received a tumultuous
reception. It may have been remembered by those present that his father
had been a Congregationalist. Now that his father was dead, and Methodist union buried, Ramsey may have been more ready than in his
ecclesiastically rebellious youth to see the positive aspects of Free Church
tradition.

It might be, however, despite the optimism which a union might en-
gender, that that tradition was anaemic. 'Old Dissent' in 1962 looked back
three hundred years to 1662 when there had been another failure of
comprehension which had produced the split in English religious life over
the ensuing centuries. A Welshman produced a celebratory history which
was not very celebratory. The battle against infidelity, he thought, had been
at its hottest around the local church. The rapid numerical decline which
they had been experiencing at this point was bewildering Congregationalists. There were some who were quite certain of the way ahead, but he left it
to the generation which would observe the quatercentenary of the 1662

---

[103] Rupert Davies in Rupert Davies, A. Raymond George and Gordon Rupp, eds., *A History of the Methodist Church in Great Britain*, vol. iii (London, 1983), 379.

[104] J. Munsey Turner, *Modern Methodism in England* (Peterborough, 1998).

[105] Arthur MacArthur, 'The Background to the Formation of the United Reformed Church (Presbyterian and Congregational) in England and Wales in 1972', *Journal of the United Reformed Church History Society* 4/1 (1987), 3–21; David M. Thompson, ed., *Stating the Gospel: Formulations and Declarations of Faith from the Heritage of the United Reformed Church* (Edinburgh, 1990) includes 'The Basis of the United Reformed Church, 1981', 249–65; C. Binfield, ed., 'Reformed and Renewed 1972–1997: Eight Essays', *Supplements to the Journal of the United Reformed Church History Society* 5 [Supp. 2] (1997).

ejection to decide whether they were right.[106] In the same year, 1962, a young layman, asking himself whether the Free Churches had a future, thought not. Unless 'fairly radical' changes of direction were soon made, the situation would become irretrievable. The rising generation would need to feel that change would happen within its lifetime or a new stampede out of the chapels would begin. There was ultimately no future short of church reunion, but he had no wish to be stampeded into that either. He hoped, however, that within twenty years the Church of England would be visibly united with the Methodists, in full communion with the Church of Scotland and moving, by this means, towards visible organic union with what by then would be the other mainstream English confession, namely a union of Congregationalists, Presbyterians and Baptists.[107] A decade later, only the Congregationalist–Presbyterian union had taken place. (Baptists, despite the ecumenical engagement of many of their leading figures, tended generally to see their distinctive understanding of baptism as precluding union with any other body.)[108]

In 1964, at its meeting in Nottingham university, 500 delegates attending a British Faith and Order conference had been overcome with impatience. It called upon the member churches of the British Council of Churches to covenant together to inaugurate a union by an agreed date. It dared to suggest that it should not be later than Easter 1980.[109] There were still a few years to go before that date was reached but in 1972 prospects looked remote. A certain weariness, or perhaps disillusion, began to set in. Colin Morris, a pungent Methodist preacher, thought that the churches were demonstrating once again how implausible was their offer of a gospel of reconciliation. Their pitch rang as shallow as that of a bald man selling hair restorer.[110] Yet, despite the apparent failure of the central project, one deeply involved figure could still see behind him a decade of ecumenical progress.[111] It was time to start talking again, this time through a Churches'

---

[106] R.T. Jones, *Congregationalism in England 1662–1962* (London, 1962), 460–2.

[107] Christopher Driver, *A Future for the Free Churches?* (London, 1962). Percipient journalist though he was, it is notable that the author was envisaging there being two 'mainstream' English confessions. Roman Catholics, apparently, were not thought to be 'mainstream'.

[108] *Baptists and Unity* (London, 1967). There was a certain irony in the fact that it was in the end a kind of 'Free Church' union which had happened when the Baptist writer Alec Gilmore had been declaring that 'The time for Free Church union has long passed. The curious inheritance of division and intercommunion, of co-existence without cost, has sanctified the scandal and dried up the springs of healing.' A. Gilmore, ed., *The Pattern of the Church: A Baptist View* (London, 1963), 163–4.

[109] *Unity Begins at Home: A Report from the First British Conference on Faith and Order* (Nottingham, 1964).

[110] Colin Morris, *Include Me Out!* (London, 1968).

[111] Norman Goodall, *Ecumenical Progress: A Decade of Change in the Ecumenical Movement, 1961–1971* (London, 1972). See also his memoirs, *Second Fiddle: Recollections and Reflections* (London, 1979).

Unity Commission in 1974 which, this time, included Roman Catholics alongside representatives of most of the mainline churches.

The Nottingham conference, in urging the churches to covenant together for 'One Church Renewed for Mission', spoke of them doing so 'in appropriate groupings such as nations'. Though this aspect was not much remarked upon, the Church of *England* had been in discussion with the Methodist Church in *Great Britain*. In the May District Synods of 1969 Methodists in Wales and Scotland—except Shetland—had all voted against—in what was a matter of a possible union to take place in England (this was not a multilateral pan-British Anglican discussion with Methodists). As has already been mentioned, the pertinent decade was one in which 'nations' were indeed being thought appropriate 'groupings'. The abortive Church of Scotland–Church of England discussions, already referred to, had been complicated by national considerations. Now, Scotland proceeded on its own in matters ecclesiastical. In 1963 the moderator of the Church of Scotland paid his first visit to the Vatican. Inevitably, it was a controversial step, but it pointed to the different character which ecumenism would possess in Scotland. The theological and ecclesial issues which divided the Church of Scotland and the Roman Catholic Church in Scotland had certainly not disappeared. However, there was no 'complication' caused by the pervasive existence of a church which saw itself as a 'bridge' (a very wobbly bridge it now appeared) between the two. In 1975, Archbishop Winning of Glasgow became the first Catholic to address the General Assembly of the Church of Scotland. He spoke of the need to replace the climate of 'sterile polemics' with an atmosphere of 'genuine brotherly love'. Only a little knowledge of history was needed to realize how difficult this would be, but, however matters developed, a dialogue between the Reformed and Catholic traditions could take place without major 'third parties' causing substantial complication by claiming to be both Catholic and Reformed.

The denominational configuration in Wales inevitably meant that unity here would involve a different set of players. A Council of Churches for Wales came into existence in 1956 but its impact was slight. The idea of a unity plan for a 'Free Church of Wales' was firmed up in 1965, arising out of the largely Welsh-speaking milieux of the Presbyterians, Independents, Baptists—those in membership of the Baptist Union of Wales—and Methodists (the Committee of the Four Denominations). While it could still be plausibly claimed in that year that about half the Welsh-speaking population attended a place of worship, who knew whether or to what degree this was a way of 'being Welsh'? This attendance was believed to be roughly four times the proportion among English-only speakers in Wales. Church/chapel/language/social convention remained all mixed up as aspects of 'being Welsh'. In a rural diocese like St Davids, it was not uncommon for men and women to sit on different sides of a church. There had also been a recent public controversy concerning the Sunday opening of public houses. In the event, in the vote of 1961, only the counties of Carmarthenshire, Cardiganshire and Pembrokeshire voted against. It is difficult to judge whether the voice of the Bishop of St Davids had swayed the voters.[112] Reservations about the unity plan were particularly expressed by Baptists and Independents and the idea petered out by the end of the decade. The Council of Churches, which included the Church in Wales, put up its own plan, in the wake of Nottingham, also in 1965. Further discussions, with fluctuating participants, led to a report *Covenanting for Union in Wales*. Churches were asked to state their intentions by 1974. It looked as though those who wished to do so would have to accept a church order which was essentially Anglican. All the denominations, apart from Welsh-speaking Independents and Baptists, publicly covenanted in 1975 to work and pray together so that they might be brought into one visible church. It remained to be seen whether this had any significance. In that same year, the popular Welsh singer Max Boyce had a song the last verse of which ran:

> When He sees that empty chapel with its locked and shuttered doors,
> And sees that dusty Bible, cobweb-covered floors,
> The numbers slowly dwindling, much fewer now each day
> Calfaria now a bingo hall, I wonder what He'll say.[113]

In England, Lord Fisher was apparently canvassing the idea that the pursuit of a united church, hammered out around somebody's table, would not yield fruit. Roman Catholics and Anglicans, at least, building on their recognition of baptism, could surely exist side by side in full fellowship and communion. That didn't make sense said the archbishop of Wales in 1972, at least not in rural Wales where so many different denominations coexisted in small communities and could scarcely keep going, let alone cope with the change that frequently surrounded them. For his part, however, the Welshman who could still attract some large congregations in Wales, thought that all of these 'unity' schemes only served to reveal the theological and spiritual bankruptcy of those who sought to

---

[112] The bishop crossed swords with the retired archbishop, Edwin Morris, now living in his diocese, who expressed a lively opposition to teetotalism in a pamphlet *The Christian Use of Alcoholic Beverages* (1961).

[113] Roy Jenkins, 'Extinct Volcanoes', *Baptist Quarterly* 40 (2004), 307. Between 1962 and 1972 Presbyterians lost 17,000 members, Independents 25,000, Baptists 22,000 and Methodists 5,000—the total 'Free Church' constituency came down from 363,000 to 284,000. The denominational institutions were in crisis and closures were inevitable. D. Densil Morgan, *The Span of the Cross: Christian Religion and Society in Wales, 1914–2000* (Cardiff, 1999), 252.

perpetrate them. The Evangelical Movement of Wales, hitherto one of individuals of evangelical persuasion, now opened its rank to 'new' and existing congregations whose members dissociated themselves from the historic churches and their ecumenical entanglements. The Welshman was Dr Martyn Lloyd-Jones, who occupied the pulpit of Westminster Chapel in London from 1939 to 1968. The preference for a *via media*, he thought, was a very English thing. He disliked Anglicanism's apparently amiable but really imperial ambitions. It was either Calvinism or Catholicism for Wales. Adherents of one or other were the only people who really knew where they stood. He told his English congregation in England that the 'peculiar quality' of the Welsh language meant that it had the capacity to convey aspects of the glory of the gospel 'in a way which . . . a Welshman alone can do'. It is not clear that his congregation, in this respect, understood what he was talking about.[114] In his old age, however, Saunders Lewis was not sure that the Catholicism which he had embraced was now quite in trim to confront Lloyd-Jones's Calvinism. The abolition of the Latin Mass had left Lewis very bitter. While the archbishop of Cardiff had no enthusiasm for the outcome of the Vatican Council, its changes had to be implemented. It also meant that the vernacular was most often English, a language which perhaps also had its peculiar qualities. In stages, but very slow stages, the Catholic Church indicated a wish to 'observe' the proceedings of the Council of Churches for Wales. But was 'speaking the same language' an impossibility?

v. Texts and Contexts

All churches read the Bible. They all understood themselves to live under the Word of God. What that meant in practice, however, penetrated to the heart of division. The Word of God was expressed in words. It was normally received and read not in the language in which it had been written. Words had meaning in their context. The Bible 'meant' different things to different people. Its truth was acknowledged but differently understood. So were Prayer Books and other devotional works used in all churches, to greater or lesser degree. How to translate 'another world' into the second half of the twentieth century?

   Pope Paul VI told a visiting English layman, Sir Gilbert Inglefield, that he had a great affection for the Book of Common Prayer. It contained very beautiful poetry and must not be abandoned. Yet, was it really the text for

---

[114] J.F. Brencher, '"A Welshman Through and Through" David Martyn Lloyd-Jones (1899–1981)', *Journal of the United Reformed Church History Society* 6/3 (1998), 204–25; C. Catherwood, *A Family Portrait* (Eastbourne, 1995); *D. Martyn Lloyd-Jones. Letters 1919–1981* (Edinburgh, 1994); Iain H. Murray, *David Martyn Lloyd-Jones: The Fight of Faith, 1939–1981* (Edinburgh, 1990).

the mid-twentieth century? In 1954, following a request from the Convocations, the Anglican archbishops appointed a liturgical commission which began work the following year. A decade later it produced a series of experimental eucharistic services—Series I (1965), II (1967) and III (1973). Series III even addressed God as 'You'. It is not surprising that they were variously received for, in many Anglican quarters, the thought of losing even a part of '1662' was to betray a heritage. Although these new services were 'alternatives' not 'replacements', there were suspicions that this is what they, or their successors, would turn out to be. Moreover, there was the additional problem that the Book of Common Prayer was sometimes seen as a 'national cultural inheritance'. It was appalling that the church should be severing the nation from its past. All churches, during this period, were, to greater or lesser degree, grappling with their inherited texts and trying to find appropriate new language. Only the Church of England, in doing so, had the burden of also being the carrier of a 'national responsibility'. And, of course, 'modernizing' any text, and the structure of a service in which texts were to be located, could not be done without raising questions of meaning, perhaps particularly in relation to the Eucharist. As always, the problem was to speak to the present without obliterating the past. In turn, no reconciliation was likely to be other than temporary before being subject to further revision as time passed. Given that there was fresh attention to and emphasis upon lection, this applied even more to Holy Scripture itself.

The Bible had been offered to the queen at her coronation as the book that offered the best wisdom that this world afforded. It was a book on which the majority of citizens in a court of law chose to swear that they were telling the truth, the whole truth and nothing but the truth. Read or unread, in its black covers, it was to be found in the majority of those homes in the British Isles where books were to be found. Some of the stories it contained remained implanted in the cultural heritage of the people. It was regularly read in churches, whether according to a fixed lectionary or according to the whim of a preacher. Its authority had been acknowledged by all churches. An 'appeal to Scripture' was customarily made in order to explain or defend particular doctrines or practices. To what extent its meaning was 'patent', however, was not self-evident. Whether the Bible 'controlled' the church, or the church 'controlled' the Bible, had long been debated in terms much more sophisticated than this simple formulation might suggest. Oxford philosophers at this time were particularly pondering on how to do things with words. The language of the Bible, in places at least, was not very ordinary. Unless it could be 'accessible', there could be no communication. There might be a mysterious core. Meaning might only be disclosed gradually, fitfully and incompletely. But the 'plain man', whose existence in the mid-century British Isles was thought to be almost universal, needed help. The text in general use outside the Roman Catholic Church was written in the language of seventeenth-century England. That language had deep resonances for those whose ears and eyes were accustomed to it, but it was not 'everyday use'. It was time to try once more to let the reader follow what the Bible had to say.

In 1946 it had been the Church of Scotland which had suggested that a new translation of the Bible in the language of the present day be prepared.[115] The proposal was well-received across the denominations. A joint committee was set up in 1947 with the bishop of Truro, J.W. Hunkin, as chairman and Dr G.S. Hendry of the Church of Scotland as secretary. The vice-chairman was C.H. Dodd and, on his retirement from his Cambridge chair in 1949, he accepted the general directorship of the whole enterprise. The work of translation fell to four panels dealing respectively with the Old Testament, the New Testament, the Apocrypha and the literary revision of the whole. Dodd had ex-officio membership of all four panels. From the beginning of 1950, until the completion of the project in March 1970, three years before his death, Dodd directed this massive enterprise, which drew upon the accumulated wisdom of contemporary scholarship. It was published as being 'planned and directed' by representatives of the Baptist Union of Great Britain and Ireland, Church of England, Church of Scotland, Congregational Church of England and Wales, Council of Churches for Wales, Irish Council of Churches, London Yearly Meeting of the Religious Society of Friends, Methodist Church of Great Britain, Presbyterian Church of England, together with the British and Foreign Bible Society and the National Bible Society. The alphabetical listing of participating bodies deliberately avoided hierarchy. It was an enterprise in which the non-Roman Catholic churches of the British Isles were 'together'. The director was a Congregationalist—one who was to be uniquely honoured after his death by a memorial service in Westminster Abbey. His friends did not recognize in him the Jesuit-poisoned character discerned from Northern Ireland by the Revd Ian Paisley. Moreover, he was a Welshman, familiar from childhood with the coexistence of languages and their inexact correspondence. The chairman of the committee (1950–68) was A.T.P. Williams, bishop of Durham. He was succeeded, in the final phase, by Donald Coggan, by then archbishop of York.[116] It should be noted too that work had begun in 1961, based at the university in Bangor to provide a new translation into Welsh—and here the problem of deciding what kind of Welsh was appropriate was even more complicated than that which

---

[115] The Revised Version of 1881 could no longer be considered 'present day'. Dr James Moffat, a Scot, had produced his own translations which had been widely used between the wars.

[116] Dodd and Coggan—a Semitic scholar—had been academic colleagues for a time at the University of Manchester.

confronted the translators into English. The New Testament became available in 1975.

Dodd always opened panel sessions by reciting in Latin a prayer of St Thomas Aquinas. There were the inevitable disagreements amongst scholars to be ironed out, sometimes with difficulty, by patient discussion, but that is what they were. They were not disputes between the churches from which they came. There was, however, a more fundamental problem. Scholars, by definition, are not plain men. Their meetings were held in Oxford and Cambridge colleges, with occasional forays to Fife and elsewhere, where masters of language were to be found. Where was the boundary to be drawn between literary English, standard English and colloquial English? Did plain prose have to be prosaic? How to steer a path between archaism and a modernism which might well be transient? The New Testament had appeared in 1961 and its reception had been mixed. Altogether *The New English Bible* was recognized as a considerable achievement. It came into widespread but not universal use. It was not *the* replacement of the King James Bible. That could scarcely be the case since others too had been trying to meet the need of the 'modern reader'. Even so, the Authorized Version was still apparently 'the Bible of choice' at a Keswick Convention youth meeting in 1970.[117]

The *New English Bible* had been a translation by committee. One man had had a major impact on his own since translating *Letters to Young Churches* in 1947. He went on to publish *The Gospels in Modern English* (1952) and *The New Testament in Modern English* (1958 and, in a revised edition, again in 1972). J.B. Phillips, then a mere vicar on the southern edge of London, thought that the scholar was all too often isolated from the workaday world. He had a Third in Classics at Cambridge and could not hold a candle to Dodd's scholarship. He was convinced, however, that he had found 'a perfectly sound English vocabulary which was very widely used, quite outside intellectual circles'. The sales figures which he achieved suggested that he had succeeded. The price of success, however—in his personal case, being transported into a whirl of broadcasting and correspondence—contributed to a period of depressive illness. Successful translators, Phillips was certain, could not be 'detached'. They had to enter into and communicate the passionate urgency disclosed in an extraordinary short period of human history. Merely to concentrate upon the accurate reproduction of patterns of thought and ways of human living two thousand years ago might make the gospel seem more than ever far away and long ago.[118] The perfectly

---

[117] The American *Revised Standard Version* (1952) and the *Good News Bible* (1976), the latter being a joint production of the American and British Bible Societies. Bebbington, *Evangelicalism in Modern Britain*, 268.

[118] J.B. Phillips, *The Price of Success* (London, 1984), 150–2.

sound English vocabulary of Phillips, however, was not altogether that of E.V. Rieu, who also tried his hand at *The Four Gospels*.[119] Nor was it that of Ronald Knox, who was, of course, not trying his hand at 'the Protestant Bible'. Having left the Oxford Catholic chaplaincy to seek rural shelter in English country houses, where he was supported by well-connected ladies, he had settled down to learning Hebrew and tackling the Vulgate. He had a committee above him but he did not take that to mean 'edit, revise, or collaborate'. His efforts were not fully appreciated within the hierarchy and he was somewhat mortified. However, duly authorized by the Catholic archbishops and bishops of England and Wales, the New Testament had duly appeared in 1945. A decade later, the Knox Bible was complete. It was, he thought, the unique child of one man's literary life. Who could tell how long it would last? He entered a plea, however, that when it came to be seen as dated—and that was perhaps rather earlier than he had hoped—it should be scrapped. Somebody else should sit down and start again. A pale rehash of the Knox Bible, thought Knox, would be terrible.[120] 'Bibles' were indeed to come from various quarters, all judged by users in different contexts and for different purposes to be meeting different needs. 'The Bible' would never be the same again.

It was impossible not to realize, when looking at the 'competing' versions, that conveying *the* meaning of the Bible for *today* was not so easily done. All the translators spoke of the complexity of their task.[121] 'Ordinary' Christians may not have absorbed the insights of Form Criticism, Tradition Criticism, Redaction Criticism, to mention only some modes of approach—now academically fashionable, now not—but the Bible was clearly a complicated compilation. The translators, too, normally spoke, as Moffat had earlier done, of being 'released' from the theory of verbal inspiration.[122]

What were the implications? Where were 'fundamentals'? Old controversies were revived in the wake of the Graham crusade.[123] A.G. Hebert launched an attack in 1957 on the 'grave menace to the Church of God' which he believed 'fundamentalism' to constitute. He had in mind the 'conservative evangelicalism' to be found in the Church of England and other churches and expounded in the Inter-Varsity Fellowship of Christian Unions. Conservative evangelicals were not in fact precisely of one mind on

[119] E.V. Rieu, *The Four Gospels* (Harmondsworth, 1952).

[120] Evelyn Waugh, *Monsignor Ronald Knox* (London, 1959), 312.

[121] Ronald Knox, *On Englishing the Bible* (London, 1949). The sermon preached by Dodd in Westminster Abbey to commemorate the 350th anniversary of the Authorized Version and the inauguration of the New English Bible is reproduced in F.W. Dillistone, *C.H. Dodd: Interpreter of the New Testament* (London, 1977), 244–8.

[122] James Moffat, *The New Testament: A New Translation* (London, 1934 revised edition), vii.

[123] John Stott, *Fundamentalism and Evangelism* (London, 1956).

the meanings to be attached to 'the authority of scripture' but did not recognize themselves as a menace. The real menace, they thought, came from a subjectivism which set up the human mind as the measure and test of truth.[124]

In 1954 a novelist made the head of a university department answer the phone by saying 'History speaking'.[125] The reality, however, was that 'History' was not speaking, though historians certainly were, at least to themselves.[126] The nature of the authority of the Bible had preoccupied Dodd over many decades.[127] While others had concluded that the search for what had actually happened was not a worthwhile pursuit, might even be seen as seeking to minimize the risk that was faith, he pressed on.[128] At the end of his life, he produced a distillation of his endeavours in an accessible form which was rapidly reprinted.[129] It was adopted as a textbook by the Gregorian University in Rome. It avowedly had a 'story' to tell and historians were then not enamoured of narrative. Professor Hugh Trevor-Roper did not like the book. A foreword was provided by John A.T. Robinson. That his recommendation was thought by the publisher to be advantageous was a measure of what had happened over the previous decade. A New Testament scholar himself, it had appeared to Robinson that 'coming to terms' was a more than technical task of translating texts. The kind of exegesis provided in his almost inexhaustible supplies of 'notes' by the Glasgow New Testament professor, William Barclay, met the particular needs of church members. His series of daily Bible studies sold over three million copies and brought him a world-wide correspondence.[130]

Robinson and others wanted to go further. They sensed a connection, intangible though it might be, between Britain being 'finished' as a great power and the Church of England being 'finished'—in the form in which it had existed. Cradled in the precincts of Canterbury Cathedral, where his father was a canon, he had 'C of E' in his blood. In an article in *Theology* in June 1952, however, he argued that the only hope for the church, economically as well as evangelistically, was to recognize that the coming

[124] A.G. Hebert, *Fundamentalism and the Church of God* (London, 1957); J.I. Packer, *Fundamentalism and the Word of God: Some Evangelical Principles* (London, 1958) supposed that the Bible asked to be regarded as a God-given, error-free and self-interpreting unity. Kenneth Hylson-Smith, *Evangelicals in the Church of England, 1734–1984* (Edinburgh, 1989), 297–302.

[125] Kingsley Amis, *Lucky Jim* (London, 1954).

[126] Michael Bentley, *Modernizing England's Past: English Historiography in the Age of Modernism 1870–1970* (Cambridge, 2005), 194–218.

[127] Starting with *The Authority of the Bible* (London, 1928).

[128] C.H. Dodd, *Historical Tradition in the Fourth Gospel* (Cambridge, 1963).

[129] C.H. Dodd, *The Founder of Christianity* (London, 1971).

[130] R.D. Kernohan, ed., *William Barclay* (London, 1980); C.L. Rawlins, *William Barclay* (Exeter, 1984).

pattern of its ministry was 'bound to be largely non-professional'. Its priesthood, in great proportion, would consist of men working in secular jobs.[131] Mervyn Stockwood, whose curate he had been at St Matthew's, Moorfields, East Bristol, had come to Cambridge as vicar of Great St Mary's. In 1959 Robinson became bishop of Woolwich under Stockwood when the latter moved to become bishop of Southwark. Being the church in the world would mean something different. The word 'revival' was problematic. A radical, which is what Robinson felt he was, did not want to revive what could not be revived. He did not yet use the term, but the notion was already present: 'New Reformation'.

In March 1963 Robinson issued *Honest to God* with the SCM Press, whose publisher was David Edwards. It was a short book, designed to overcome the 'growing gulf' between 'the traditional orthodox supernaturalism' and the categories which the 'lay' world found meaningful. He found it extremely depressing that Christianity should be equated in the public mind with 'organized religion'. That showed how far the church had departed from the New Testament. The last thing the church should be was an organization for the religious. The author reflected on his own deep dissatisfaction with the traditional framework of metaphysics and morals. The fact that old landmarks were apparently disappearing, however, was something to be welcomed rather than deplored. Perhaps the lay world might understand, with the Cambridge philosopher R.B. Braithwaite, that to assert that God was love was to declare one's intention to follow an agapeistic way of life. A basic commitment to Christ might in the past have been buttressed by a particular projection of God, a particular 'myth' of the Incarnation, code of morals, or pattern of religion, but it was no longer necessary to insist upon them. The bishop was not an unknown figure. He had appeared at the Old Bailey in a celebrated case in which he had claimed that D.H. Lawrence's *Lady Chatterley's Lover* had neither the intention nor the effect of depraving and corrupting. A storm had followed but he appeared to have weathered it. The book's publication was preceded by an article in *The Observer*, 'Our Image of God Must Go', which Robinson had not suggested, but in which he had acquiesced. The book, which had an initial print run of only 6,000, turned rapidly into a world-wide best-seller—over 300,000 by the end of the year. The critical reception ranged from the adulatory to the dismissive. The publishing success certainly testified to more than clever marketing. It fitted alongside other publications, such as the Cambridge essays in *Soundings* (1962) which also challenged traditional formulations. It was rare to find any scholar who resisted

---

[131] James, *Robinson*, 43. In the same year he published *The Body: A Study in Pauline Theology* (London, 1952).

the temptation to say what he thought, one way or another, about *Honest to God*. The archbishop of Canterbury had little option, but came to think his initial attempt less than adequate.[132] Honesty was much prized. Some, but not many, agreed with what Robinson wrote, but thought that a bishop should not have written. Others, appalled, spoke of 'damage' and sought its limitation. Thousands were apparently shocked to learn that God was not a daddy in the sky. Admirers thought windows had to be thrown open wide. The press, for its part, had a field day with headlines, but was less astute in determining whether 'The End of Theism' had indeed been reached. Robinson believed that he was articulating the mind of the 'lay world' and he certainly received a substantial postbag.[133]

In Wales, though emerging from a different social and cultural milieu from that of Robinson, the Swansea philosopher J.R. Jones, writing in Welsh, wrote on the crisis of meaninglessness which he thought character-ized the age in which he was living. For a time, partly because he gave support to the civil disobedience campaign of the Welsh Language Society, Jones became the 'equivalent' in the Welsh press and media of Robinson in England. Believed to be a Calvinistic Methodist, Jones's scathing denunci-ation of 'salvation mongers' and supposition that what had been said about Jesus in the New Testament had only been a dream, was not what was customarily associated with Calvinistic Methodism.[134]

The difficulty was that the 'modern' thoughts and categories which Robinson and other writers employed stemmed substantially from German sources forged, in exile or martyrdom, in the particular circumstances of Germany between 1933 and 1945.[135] Not unusually, it was a Scot, Ronald Gregor Smith, professor in Glasgow from 1956 until his death in 1968, who had the most intimate familiarity with 'the continental mind'.[136] Not that

[132] A.M. Ramsey, *Image Old and New* (London, 1963). *Sacred and Secular: A Study in the Other-Worldly and This-Worldly Aspects of Christianity* (London, 1965) and *God, Christ and the World: A Study in Contemporary Theology* (London, 1969) were more substantial reflections.

[133] J.A.T. Robinson, *Honest to God* (London, 1963). James, *Robinson*, 72–188 deals with 'the Woolwich Years'.

[134] Morgan, *Span of the Cross*, 224–30. H.D. Lewis, formerly Professor of Philosophy at Bangor, the Welsh Calvinist Methodist who held the Chair of the Philosophy of Religion at King's College, London, joined in the controversy 'back home' from a different perspective. H.D. Lewis, *Our Experience of God* (London, 1959).

[135] Robinson embraced Tillich, who might, or might not, be 'an unintelligible Hegelian' as characterized by Owen Chadwick. He also built much upon the tantalizing and enigmatic last thoughts of Bonhoeffer. Ramsey, as a professor of divinity, had never felt any temptation to read Tillich. Bonhoeffer, he began to see, almost his exact contemporary, might be another matter. Tillich's *The Shaking of the Foundations* had been published by the SCM Press in 1949 and Bonhoeffer's *Letters and Papers from Prison* in 1953.

[136] Ronald Gregor Smith, *Secular Christianity* (London, 1966). Before moving to Glasgow he had been editor of the SCM Press and as such was a conduit for the publication of German theology. K.W. Clements, *The Theology of Ronald Gregor Smith* (Leiden, 1986).

such familiarity led to the same conclusions. Thomas Torrance, who had studied as a postgraduate under Karl Barth, was setting out a rather different conception of theological science.[137] 'Modern man', in his British garb, however, might already be in a different world. The generation below Robinson, initially at least, found itself 'liberated' by his iconoclasm. Theological tension mounted, to greater or lesser degree, in all denominations. Amongst Baptists, for example, the answer in 1971 given by Michael Taylor, then newly appointed as principal of the Northern College, to the question 'How much of a man was Jesus Christ?' triggered a deep crisis. Was there a limit to that tolerance of different theological opinions and emphases for which it was claimed Baptists had stood?[138] It was a question asked across the board.

Robinson's publisher wanted to know where Christian radicalism would now go. It could not stand still without degenerating. What had been achieved, he thought, amounted so far to little more than gestures to show that some Christians were anxious 'to enter into a real conversation with more typical citizens of our secular society'.[139] Radicals might be tempted to part company with their church—paradoxically 'to be the church'—but that point had not been reached. There should be a period of experimentation for no one claimed to know the whole truth. And, indeed, there were experiments, though they were neither as ubiquitous nor as 'successful' as radicals had hoped. Edwards was happy to note that they were a disunited crew and the appearance of a skipper would mean a quick mutiny. Certainly, handicapped by back pain and a rather awkward personality, Robinson, for all the publicity that he attracted, was not the man to lead a sustained 'New Reformation'.[140] He did not have the music in him to be a new Luther. By the end of the decade he had returned, rather uncomfortably, to Trinity College, Cambridge. Twenty years after the publication of *Honest to God* he was dead. 'The church' never came to terms with him nor he with 'the church'—as it existed. What was never

[137] Torrance (b. 1913) was Professor of Christian Dogmatics at New College. He was the founder of the *Scottish Journal of Theology* in 1948, which became one of the world's leading journals for systematic theology. A. McGrath, *Thomas Torrance: An Intellectual Biography* (Edinburgh, 1999, new edn. 2006).

[138] Randall, *English Baptists*, 365–75.

[139] John A.T. Robinson and David L. Edwards, *The Honest to God Debate* (London, 1963), 24. This volume contains some of the contrasting reviews evoked by the book. Reflections on 'Honest to God' are to be found in Brown, *Religion and Society in Twentieth-Century Britain*, 230–6. and A.D. Gilbert, *The Making of Post-Christian Britain: A History of the Secularization of Modern Society* (London, 1980), 122–3. Edwards, elected a fellow of All Souls as a historian, had raised some Oxford eyebrows by his ordination. He had not been cradled in the Canterbury Precincts, as Robinson had, but had been educated at the King's School in Canterbury. A prolific writer, he addressed himself more generally on the subject of *Religion and Change* (London, 1965).

[140] J.A.T. Robinson, *The New Reformation?* (London, 1965).

clear, however, was who the 'typical citizen' was, with whom 'to have conversation'. 'Our secular society' was a puzzle.

vi. Choice and Diversity

'Not for me', George Bell declared in his farewell address to his diocese in October 1957, 'a fugitive and cloistered Church, which slinks out of the race and refuses to meet the problems and crises of the modern world.'[141] 'Meeting the modern world', as previous sections have indicated, was what all churches, to one degree or another, thought they were doing. In his generation, there could be no more admirable example of that engagement than the life Bell had led.[142] When he died, in 1958, obituarists could not resist speculating about what might have happened to the Church of England if he, and not Fisher, had succeeded Temple. Bell's valedictory message was one which had come to have wide acceptance. In 'engaged' circles, it had been easy to speak disparagingly of those gathered together in holy huddles, and bourgeois ones at that. Now things were changing. Evangelicals in the Church of England also began to consider how they should meet the modern world. After considerable preparation, the first National Evangelical Conference was held at Keele university in 1967. It was promised that in their addresses eight evangelical clergymen would eschew platitudes. It was left to a layman, (Sir) Norman Anderson, to speak on 'Christian Worldliness, the Needs and Limits of Christian Involvement'. In a book published in the following year Anderson was emphatic that there was a Christian duty to get unjust laws changed and autocratic action restrained. In a democracy the Christian could and should 'play his full part in formulating policy and framing the laws under which he has to live'. 'Opting out' constituted a misunderstanding or misapplication of New Testament principles and was condemned.[143] The only novelty in such utterance stemmed from its milieu. It did not arise, however, from any sense that 'traditional' evangelicalism was moribund. On the contrary, it seemed that evangelical Anglicanism, diverse and fractious though it in turn was, had more vitality than any other part of the church. One of its most prominent figures was John Stott, for thirty years rector of All Souls,

---

[141] R.C.D. Jasper, *George Bell: Bishop of Chichester* (London, 1967), 378.

[142] Peter Raina, *Bishop Bell: The Greatest Churchman: A Portrait in Letters* (London, 2006).

[143] J.N.D. Anderson, *Into the World* (London, 1968). Anderson, director of the Institute of Advanced Legal Studies in the University of London and a specialist in Islamic law also played a prominent part in the work of the General Synod of the Church of England. For context see David Bebbington, 'The Decline and Resurgence of Evangelical Social Concern 1918–1980' in J. Wolffe, ed., *Evangelical Faith and Public Zeal: Evangelicals and Society in Britain 1780–1980* (London, 1995), 175–210.

Langham Place, situated beside Broadcasting House (or was it the other way round?). From this base, until his retirement in 1975, he became a major evangelical voice in the British Isles and beyond, through preaching, 'statesmanship' and prolific publication.[144]

It seemed, therefore, that few church leaders wanted to 'slink out of the race'. Yet, as a lawyer must have known, the 'Christian duty' of changing 'unjust laws' was no easy matter in a context where the criteria for determining what might or might not be 'just' seemed to be becoming ever more problematic. Christians, where they were busy in the public domain, seemed not so much seeking to change unjust laws as seeking to hang on to laws which reflected views which they had thought in the past, and perhaps still did in the present, to reflect a Christian perspective. It was understandable that church leaders should believe that Christian moral teaching was good for the country. They should be free to say so. What was becoming ever clearer, however, was that laws appeared on, or were removed from, the statute book in so far as they seemed to reflect, after parliamentary discussion, the public social consensus of the moment. It was not easy to say how that opinion was formed nor was there any certainty that lawmakers had invariably correctly interpreted it. It was increasingly assumed, nevertheless, that potential legislation could not be found acceptable or unacceptable by reference to the degree to which it did or did not conform to Christian teaching, or indeed to any coherently articulated general moral code. Lord Devlin and Professor H.L.A. Hart could argue whether morals could be enforced, and indeed more generally on the relationship between law and morality. In the upshot, United Kingdom governments could not be expected to uphold what the churches held to be Christian principles. The implications of democracy seemed to be making themselves apparent in field after field. Whatever the fulminations of the Lord's Day Observance Society, the British electorate would not allow a citizen's choice of how to pass Sunday to be restricted by a 'special interest' group. If Christians chose to 'keep Sunday special' they could do so. They could not compel others. That example, however, was a simple one. It was more problematic as one moved through the other topics which occupied the headlines—homosexuality, abortion, marriage and divorce,

---

[144] Timothy Dudley-Smith, *John Stott: The Making of a Leader* (London, 1999) and *John Stott: A Global Ministry* (Leicester, 2001). Alister Chapman, 'Secularisation and the Ministry of John R.W. Stott', *Journal of Ecclesiastical History* 56/3 (2005), 496–513. Stott had handed over day-to-day running of the church in 1970. He was only 50 at the time and still had many years of vigorous activity ahead of him. Graduating with Firsts in both Modern Languages and Theology from Cambridge, the milieu in which he originally moved can be seen in David Goodhew, 'The rise of the Cambridge Inter-Collegiate Christian Union, 1910–71', *Journal of Ecclesiastical History* 54/1 (2003), 62–88. Goodhew characterizes Stott as doctrinally sound but also well-read, urbane and upper-middle-class.

contraception, gambling, drink and pornography, punishment, prisons and the death penalty, sex and violence on screen—all of which were 'reported on', in one way or another, and which led to a greater or lesser degree of 'liberalization'.[145] The test to be applied, almost invariably, seemed to be the 'freedom of the individual'. Did it have any limit?

It proved impossible for the churches to undermine this fundamental principle. Part of the reason was that they did not speak with one voice on most of the particulars. Opinions varied within and between them: there were reservations, welcomes and hostility. The ecumenical picture was complicated by the fact that on some, though not all, of these issues 'extremes' met. 'Hard' Catholics and Protestants were united in criticizing 'compromisers', though few 'liberals' wanted to find a *via media* on every issue. The churches could make statements and pass resolutions which were not without significant insight into the social consequences of what was taking place. Such arguments, however, could have some impact only in so far as their conclusions were couched in utilitarian rather than dogmatic terms. All the while, leading churchmen were inclined to denounce the 'moral anarchy' which they saw before them, but knew that moral consensus, on their terms, was not achievable. Late twentieth-century democracy in the United Kingdom functioned, at least to some degree, as a market place of competing but also negotiating moralities. Just as Christian leaders said that Christianity could only be freely accepted, so, whatever morality, or moralities, stemmed from it had to be as an example not an imposition. The church, in this respect, had been improperly coercive in the past. And it had to be faced that Christianity had its own internal market. It could not be assumed, in any denomination, that individual members adhered to the teaching of their church in all matters of personal conduct. There was selection. Whatever Pope Paul had had to say in the encyclical *Humanae Vitae* in 1968, with its reiterated prohibition of all artificial methods of birth control, it appeared that increasing numbers of Catholics were using the pill.[146] The Lambeth Conference of the same year repeated that Anglicans found themselves unable to agree with the pope's conclusion. It was also turning out to be the case that Catholics did not seem to be any less prone to divorce than members of the population at large.[147]

---

[145] These matters are considered in more detail by G.I.T. Machin, 'British Churches and Moral Change in the 1960s' in W.M. Jacob and Nigel Yates, eds., *Crown and Mitre: Religion and Society in Northern Europe since the Reformation* (Woodbridge, 1993), 223–42 and in his *Churches and Social Issues in Twentieth-Century Britain* (Oxford, 1988), 175–210.

[146] Hastings, *History of English Christianity*, 575–8 presents a picture of the controversy occasioned by the encyclical.

[147] Timothy J. Buckley, 'English Catholics and Divorce' in Hornsby-Smith, ed. *Catholics in England, 1950–2000*, 199–218. Hornsby-Smith reached this conclusion in his *Roman Catholic Beliefs in England: Customary Catholicism and Transformation of Religious Authority* (Cambridge, 1991).

Besides, though not yet dramatically, the influx of adherents of other world religions into the United Kingdom set new parameters to debate and discussion.[148] It was 'race' not 'religion' that was debated. The extensive literature on 'race relations' produced in this period contains little reference to the religions of new arrivals.[149] The issue became particularly contentious from the mid-1960s onwards. Archbishop Ramsey vigorously opposed legislation in 1968 which restricted the immigration of Kenyan Asians. Two years earlier, he had accepted the chairmanship of the National Committee for Commonwealth Immigrants. However, the anxieties publicly articulated by Enoch Powell over this period, which led to his dismissal from the Opposition Shadow Cabinet for a speech in which he forecast future 'rivers of blood', were also those of a committed Anglican. On occasion, he preached from pulpits. Were Christian leaders not endorsing a change the consequence of which would be the end of that British/ Christian symbiosis, established over centuries, to which Powell was so deeply attached? It is difficult to judge what was the balance of opinion in the churches at the time. Abhorrence of 'racism' was strong but it mingled uneasily with the suspicion that over time, and perhaps not over a very long time, there would be areas of urban Britain in which Christians were a 'beleaguered minority'. The prospect might be opening up of a Britain which was made up of a patchwork of spatially concentrated ethnic/religious 'communities'. In respect of Jewry, on a limited scale, this had long been true, though in this period the pattern of concentration in London particularly, but also elsewhere, was shifting from the centre to the periphery of cities. This dispersal, and the fact that 'Jewry' was no more united than 'Christendom' had made it difficult to speak of any profound Jewish–Christian dialogue at local level.[150] And, although there was some intellectual engagement, on both sides, it had not penetrated deeply. Richard Harries, listening to James Parkes as a visiting speaker on 'Church and Synagogue' as an ordinand at Cuddesdon in the early '60s noted he was

---

[148] John Wolffe, 'How Many Ways to God? Christians and Religious Pluralism' in Gerald Parsons, ed., *The Growth of Religious Diversity: Britain from 1945*, vol. ii: *Issues* (London, 1994), 25–53; Myrtle S. Langley, 'The Challenge of the Religions' in Rupert Davies, ed., *The Testing of the Churches, 1932–1982* (London, 1982), 132–44. The issue is addressed, from different perspectives, in the following examples of contemporary writing: J.N.D. Anderson, *Christianity and Comparative Religion* (London, 1970); Charles Davis, *Christ and the World Religions* (London, 1970); Stephen Neill, *Christian Faith and Other Faiths* (Oxford, 1961); John Hick, *God and the Universe of Faiths* (London, 1973).

[149] John Wolffe, ' "And There's Another Country . . . ": Religion, the State and British Identities' in Parsons, ed. *Growth of Religious Diversity*, ii. 98.

[150] David Englander, 'Integrated but Insecure: A Portrait of Anglo-Jewry at the Close of the Twentieth Century', in Parsons, ed., *Growth of Religious Diversity*, vol. i: *Traditions* (London, 1993), 95–132.

being fitted in as an 'optional extra'. Christianity's approach to Judaism was not reflected in the main curriculum.[151]

In this context, the growth of Islam presented a challenge, the dimensions of which were only dimly appreciated in the churches as in the population at large. Simply in terms of numbers, observers in 1969 were quoting the number of adherents from a quarter of a million to a million and a half.[152] 'Old imperial hands' knew very well that Islam's understanding of 'religion, state and society' posited very different relationships than those which had emerged in 'the Christian world', though the general population as a whole had little notion. In everyday life, the compatibility and incompatibility of the great religions of the world had been something which could be left to missionaries to worry about. Now, the question was coming home. In 1970 the newly created Redundant Churches Committee found itself considering a difficult matter. Could a redundant church building be adopted for worship by a non-Christian faith? One paper accepted as axiomatic that in a democratic and plural society non-Christians should be able to worship in some building. Church people had varying perceptions of Islam but suggested that 'we shall communicate more of the God in whom we believe by an open-eyed offer than by a principled refusal'. There was also the risk that a refusal might be interpreted as discrimination on racial grounds. On the other hand, another paper pointed out that however high and noble a non-Christian faith might be, it was nevertheless sure to be 'in positive opposition to Christianity'.[153]

Confronted by the complexity which lay behind this symbolic example, there were those who would rebuild the fugitive fortresses which had perhaps been too rapidly dismantled in pursuit of openness.[154] Let there be no doubt, it was asserted, that collectively, the churches constituted a clear-cut (and clean-cut) 'Christian community' which did and should exist as a self-contained culture. Such recourse had many parallels in Christian history. There were times when a *kraal* might be the only way to ensure survival, and perhaps that time was coming. In the British Isles in the early 1970s, however, the possibility of a pervasive radical separation of cultures, one of which was 'Christian', in countries which had no 'common values',

---

[151] Richard Harries, *After the Evil: Christianity and Judaism in the Shadow of the Holocaust* (Oxford, 2003), 2. Writing as bishop of Oxford, after a long involvement in Christian–Jewish relations, Harries noted that this curriculum situation had changed little at the time of writing.

[152] John Wolffe, 'Fragmented Universality: Islam and Muslims' in Parsons, ed., *Growth of Religious Diversity*, ii. 145.

[153] Andrew Chandler, *The Church of England in the Twentieth Century: The Church Commissioners and the Politics of Reform, 1948–1998* (Woodbridge, 2006), 231–2. A particular case in Wakefield then proved very difficult to settle. Eventually, the church was demolished.

[154] Ronald H. Preston, *Church and Society in the Late Twentieth Century: The Economic and Political Task* (London, 1983), 133–9.

was still difficult to conceive. At the end of 1974, the general secretary of the British Council of Churches described British society as 'permanently characterized by a multiplicity of religious creeds' but Clifford Longley, then religious affairs correspondent of *The Times*, took the view that the Muslim, Sikh and Hindu presence had had scarcely any impact on the life of the Christian churches.[155] At another level, however, particularly in some of the new universities that were being founded in the 1960s—notably Lancaster—'Religious Studies' rather than 'Theology' was to be offered. How comfortably, in older universities, the two approaches could fruitfully coexist was only one facet of a much wider unsettlement.

vii. Fit for Purpose? Institutional Unsettlement

When Bell died in 1958, the 'modern world' already had a different feel about it. Austerity had had its day.[156] The consumer became queen. In the 'thirteen wasted years' after 1951, the lineaments of the 'consumer society' were already clear. The washing machine arrived. Car-ownership tripled— to reach roughly one-third of the population. Ten million TV licences were being issued in 1960. Refrigerators proliferated. Most of our people, the new prime minister, Harold Macmillan, had told a Bedford crowd in July 1957, 'have never had it so good'.[157] It was a state of prosperity 'such as we have never had in my lifetime'. 'Never had it so good' has lingered, though the thrust of the speech was to indicate anxiety about whether that state could last and whether, in particular, inflation could be contained. In that same year he had invented Premium Bonds. It was a wheeze which the archbishop of Canterbury described as 'squalid'. It was a 'rather second-rate expedient' which added nothing to 'the spiritual capital of the nation'.[158]

In 1960, in a sermon, Fisher chose to go back to Macmillan's Bedford speech. The church, he thought, was living in a time of England's greatest peril. The country had kept its freedom, and paid a price for it, but it was in danger of forgetting what freedom was for. In 'becoming tolerant', he suggested, 'we may become traitors to truth'. He contrasted the 'dreadful' phrase 'We've never had it so good' with 'How hardly shall they that have riches enter into the Kingdom of Heaven'. Macmillan, now prime minister,

---

[155] John Wolffe, 'How Many Ways to God? Christians and Religious Pluralism' in Parsons, ed., *Growth of Religious Diversity*, ii. 38–9.

[156] Ina Zweiniger-Bargielowska, *Austerity in Britain: Rationing, Controls and Consumption 1939–1955* (Oxford, 2000), 264.

[157] Dominic Sandbrook, *Never Had It So Good: 1956–1963: A History of Britain from Suez to the Beatles* (London, 2005).

[158] John Turner, *Macmillan* (London, 1994), 228; Paul A. Welsby, *A History of the Church of England 1945–1980* (Oxford, 1984), 73.

responded to him 'as a churchman', accepting that without 'spiritual values' a country would fail. But it was the function of government to try to improve material conditions. He had always thought that the church supported this effort.[159] The exchange was emblematic. It caught Macmillan going back in conversation to Eton and Oxford and the person of Ronald Knox. All that was a long time ago. Macmillan had not 'poped' but his belief in 'spiritual values' was real. Fisher, for his part, struggled with a world which declined to see in the possession of a washing machine evidence of riches which might make entry into the Kingdom of Heaven difficult. Neither man, one may presume, had much personal experience of what it was to do domestic washing in a world without washing machines. In a wider sense, 'materialism' was 'dreadful' but it was its 'vulgarity' which also offended Lambeth Palace. For both prime minister and archbishop, 'prosperity' was a two-edged sword. Different though they were, they both belonged to what was now being characterized as an 'establishment'—one which went beyond the traditional ecclesiastical use of this term.

It was an 'establishment' which was to find itself battered by satire and subverted by 'scandal' as the 'swinging sixties' swept in. 'Everything' changed as 'youth' paraded itself and 'style' became substance. Skirts were Quantified. Technological innovations tumbled out in rapid succession. Where's my transistor? The contraceptive pill penetrated Britain in 1962. Beautiful women were discovered, though perhaps not for the first time. The Beatles played on. It was time to visit India. Gurus had more to offer than clergy. Social hierarchies wobbled. Social conventions crumbled. The 'Permissive Society' appeared to have arrived. Deference was dead, or dying, and perhaps respect with it. The establishment of 'positive standards of value', the queen told the Boys' Brigade in 1966, was increasingly difficult for young people. They found it hard to know what or whom to respect. The propensity to indulge in what a senior generation judged to be unhygienic hairstyles was conclusive evidence that any form of authority had been jettisoned. Discipline and religion, her father had written to the same organization in 1943, were its twin pillars.[160] They might be crumbling together. This is obviously not the place to examine 'push' and 'pull' in tracing the cultural (though not the political) revolution which it embodied. It is sufficient to realize that, at last, 'liberation' was believed to have arrived. There had been nothing quite like it, wrote an historian who had lived through it. His concluding cliché was that nothing would ever be quite the

[159] Carpenter, *Fisher*, 407–8.

[160] Such was the view of a Boys' Brigade officer who disliked the worship of youth. The organization wrestled with the fact that the challenge it presented might be 'unwelcome or unacceptable'. John Springhall, Brian Fraser and Michael Hoare, *Sure and Stedfast: A History of the Boys' Brigade, 1883–1983* (London and Glasgow, 1983), 232.

same.[161] Another has supposed that those who were in charge of 'the organised Christian apparatus of the country' were at a loss what to do about the decline of discipline and Christianity. They were, he supposed, merely ranting uncontrollably.[162]

An angry Cardinal Heenan hoped that things might still be the same. He railed against those in his own fold (or who were departing from it) who seemed not to love 'Mother Church' but to think of it just as an institution, and a not very attractive one at that. Charles Davis, one such, came to think that the Vatican was saturated with the elements of the Constantinian order. It embodied a notion of power very remote from whatever authority had been entrusted to Peter the fisherman disciple.[163] It also embodied a notion of power uncongenial to the finely honed democratic instincts now evident in seminarians. It was time to get out of the church, find a wife and leave the country.

It also appeared, however, that women might be able to go 'into the church' (to use the quaint expression applied frequently to men who sought ordination within it). In July 1975 the General Synod of the Church of England considered a motion 'that there are no fundamental theological objections to the ordination of women to the priesthood'. Its predecessor body, the Church Assembly, had received two reports on *Gender and Ministry* (1962) and *Women and Holy Orders* (1966). These set out the considerations, for and against, which might apply, but did not make recommendations. Neither did the Church Assembly, in considering these documents, come to any conclusion, other than that a long period of education on the matter was required. A further report, *Women in Ministry: A Study*, followed two years later. This did make recommendations, the effect of which was to put all accredited lay workers, regardless of gender, on an equal footing, though precisely what that meant in terms of salaries, pensions and conditions of service required some elaboration. In 1969 women were allowed to join men in becoming Readers. The 1968 Lambeth Conference had concluded that the theological arguments for and against the ordination of women to the priesthood were 'inconclusive'. Churches in the Anglican Communion were requested to study and to report to the Anglican Consultative Council. Miss Christian Howard prepared a report, published in October 1972, on *The Ordination of Women to the Priesthood* for the Advisory Council for the Church's Ministry. She acknowledged that some believed that traditional male and female

---

[161] Arthur Marwick examined *The Sixties: Cultural Revolution in Britain, France, Italy, and the United States, c.1958–c.1974* (Oxford, 1998) at no mean length. He identified sixteen 'characteristics'. He admits to his cliché.

[162] Brown, *Religion and Society in Twentieth-Century Britain*, 249.

[163] Charles Davis, *A Question of Conscience* (London, 1967).

archetypes should not be disrupted but argued that it was very difficult – given what was happening in society generally and in the light of current scientific conclusions—to be precise about what they were. English dioceses were asked for their opinions in 1973 and thirty-three concluded that there was no fundamental objection to the ordination of women. However, only half that number concluded that the Church of England should take the necessary legal and other steps to make this possible. All three Houses of General Synod (bishops 28:10; clergy 110:96 and 2 abstentions; laity 117:74 and 3 abstentions) did then conclude that there was no fundamental theological objection. However, it was left to the bishops to bring forward proposals to ordain women priests when they judged 'the time for action to be right'. The arguments deployed on both sides had become familiar by this juncture. Some speakers spoke with apparent but conflicting authority on the psychological and biological characteristics of men and women. Some did not trouble themselves with the conclusions which 'the modern world' was coming to on such matters and supposed that St Paul had simply said the last word. Some thought that to move precipitately would split the Church of England. Some thought that to procrastinate would have the same effect. Some thought this was not a matter on which the Church of England should reach a conclusion. It should be a matter for the 'whole church'.

The other Anglican churches of the British Isles naturally watched the Church of England closely but were determined to move at their own pace in this matter. The Church in Wales set apart a very small number of women as deaconesses in the 1960s but ordination to the priesthood was as contentious as in England. The governing body also decided in July 1975 that there was no fundamental theological objection (bishops all in favour; clergy 87:18; laity 120:14) but also resolved that it would be inexpedient to take unilateral action at that juncture. Of course, a decision not to take unilateral action might be interpreted as a desire not to take any action. The Church of Ireland and the Scottish Episcopal Church moved with comparable circumspection, reservations being expressed, respectively, from the 'low' and 'high' standpoints which generally characterized these churches. Their decisions were made slightly 'behind' the Church of England.

The difficulty, of course, was that the 'whole church' did not exist. Those who emphasized this point naturally had in mind that ordination of woman would not be acceptable to the Roman Catholic, Eastern Orthodox and Old Catholic churches. It might constitute a block on further improved ecumenical relations. On the other hand, those Protestant churches which had not already ordained women, appeared on the brink of doing so. Women were first ordained in the Church of Scotland in 1969. Elizabeth Barr became the first moderator of a General Assembly of a Scottish

Presbyterian Church—the small United Free Church—in 1960 (her father had also been its moderator). Amongst Congregationalists, the Revd Elsie Chamberlain had become the first and, as it turned out, the only woman Chair of the Congregational Union when she took office in 1955. There was indeed scarcely any aspect of her life in which Elsie had not been a 'first' as a woman—in serving as an RAF chaplain during the war, in marrying an Anglican vicar—in the teeth of opposition from the bishop of London who warned her husband-to-be a post would not be found for him if, in their married life, she continued in her 'Free Church pastorate' and in leading *The Daily Service* on the BBC. She became a household name and frequently led *Lift Up Your Hearts*—an early morning broadcast story, hymn and prayer—until, to her dismay, the programme was axed in 1967. Her independence of mind and spirit was further displayed in her opposition to the United Reformed Church.[164] With her friend Viscountess Stansgate, wife, mother and grandmother of Labour politicians, she played a leading role in forming the Congregational Federation.[165] From the outset, the United Reformed Church was willing to ordain women. Methodists, though Conference had nearly unanimously voted in favour in 1971, had held back from ordaining women in the context of possible Anglican–Methodist union, but, when that failed, they went ahead. The numbers of ordained women involved, however, at this juncture remained small, and their ministry could be found unacceptable, or at least be regarded suspiciously, in some congregations. So, as the bishops of the Church of England waited to decide when the time was ripe, there was a general recognition that to place women in the ordained ranks of the church might be something momentous in its cultural history. Those who were hostile saw the possible outcome as a pandering to a 'secular' feminist fashion of the twentieth century. Those who were joyful suggested that the church was liberating itself from an entrenched masculinity, itself, they thought, a cultural phenomenon which had had its day. It was still difficult to say precisely what would happen, with what consequence and over what period of time. The institution of the church, for good or ill, would be unlikely to be the same once women 'emerged'. Back in 1918, J.H. Shakespeare, the Baptist leader, had written that the liberation of

---

[164] See the articles on Elsie Chamberlain by Alan Angell in the *Congregational History Circle Magazine* 4/1–3 (1999–2001); Elaine Kaye, 'From "Woman Minister" to "Minister"? One Hundred Congregational Ministers Ordained between 1917 and 1972 in England and Wales', *Journal of the United Reformed Church History Society* 6/10 (2002), 761–71.

[165] Margaret Stansgate, wife of William Wedgwood Benn, mother of Anthony Wedgwood Benn, 'Tony Benn', grandmother of Hilary Benn, left the Church of England in 1948 because she saw little hope that it would make progress towards ordaining women. She became a Congregationalist and, later, the first president of the Congregational Federation. Margaret Stansgate, *My Exit Visa* (London, 1992).

women was one of the most helpful features of his time. Only at its peril could the church make itself the last ditch of prejudice. In the new world which was opening up he thought 'the Church will be compelled to accept the principle that sex in itself can be no bar to position and service'.[166] It had taken time, but perhaps that point was being reached.

These issues in the church were being addressed in a period of general institutional fragility. People wanted to 'do their own thing' and did not feel 'bound' by any organization which entailed regular and sustained commitment. A body which had seemed so settled a feature of Christian activity in universities, and which had nourished so much ecumenical activity, the Student Christian Movement, imploded.[167] There was less and less need or, as employment patterns changed for women, less time, to 'join' or to be 'part of it'. Membership figures both for the Mothers' Union and the National Federation of Women's Institutes showed sharp decline. All collective self-definitions, whether of race, class or even gender, lost their comforting if constricting solidity. Sociologists, perhaps themselves an aspect of the social transformation they investigated, brought the 'secular society' under excited scrutiny. A journalist, writing from the outside, found it hard to avoid the conclusion that 'something' had the Church of England by the throat. For the moment, the attack was being contained, but for how much longer?[168]

Churches were institutions. 'Institutionalism', however, was something which individuals believed to be inhibiting the life of the Spirit. The 'charismatic movement'—not, of course, unique to the British Isles—erupted across denominational boundaries in the 1960s.[169] It was this incursion into 'mainline' churches—Roman Catholics, Baptists and Anglicans—which brought it attention. Pentecostalism had of course continued to be an aspect of Christianity in the British Isles throughout the century but had been perceived as 'marginal'. Pentecostals worked outside the central narrative of British Isles Christianity—as conceived from England by the 'mainline' churches. Their marginality was partly a matter of social distance but also of 'peripheral' geography. The 'Apostolic' networks, themselves rather fragile and prone to schism, linked, as nothing else did, Bournemouth, Glasgow and Penygroes (in the then mining part of Carmarthenshire). The Apostolic Church in Wales began in a Welsh-speaking milieu.

[166] J.H. Shakespeare, *The Churches at the Cross-Roads: A Study in Church Unity* (London, 1918), 9–11.

[167] Robin Boyd, *The Witness of the Student Christian Movement: Church Ahead of the Church* (London, 2007). The author has not been able to penetrate the 'conspiracy of silence' encountered when trying to establish quite how what amounts to a political coup occurred.

[168] Paul Ferris, *The Church of England* (Harmondsworth, 1964), 9.

[169] Allan Anderson 'The Pentecostal and Charismatic Movements' in McLeod, ed., *Cambridge History of Christianity*, 89–106 and his book *An Introduction to Pentecostalism: Global Charismatic Christianity* (Cambridge, 2004).

A temple in the small town was opened in 1933 capable of holding one thousand people. There D.P. Williams spoke his word of prophecy to the thousands who, year on year, attended the Penygroes International Convention. 'Prophecy', Williams declared, 'is a gift in the bowels of a prophet and is perfect. It cannot be touched by a subconsciousness or a conscious mind . . . '.[170] In 1967, his widow opened a new large convention hall with seating for 3,000 people. The work had become worldwide, notably in Nigeria. George Jeffreys, who originally worked as a salesman in the Maesteg Co-operative store, was another who took on the spirit of the Welsh revival and led another Pentecostal movement. In 1915, he founded the 'Elim Evangelistic Band' in Belfast and his team carried out gigantic missions. The hope was that the 'Elim Four Square Gospel Alliance of the British Isles' would bring together all Pentecostals, but the plan failed. Later Jefferys parted from the Elim Pentecostal Church, which went on to be the largest Pentecostal denomination in Britain. The Assemblies of God of Great Britain and Ireland had been formed in 1925. Its prominent figures could be said to have moved in an international circuit which had strong American connections, among both blacks and whites.[171] In all such bodies, a tension invariably existed between 'leader' and 'institution'. Some quite extraordinary careers, in and out of nations and denominations, can be detected.[172] Charismatics stood out in their experience of 'baptism in the Spirit'—a second blessing subsequent to conversion—and in the authentication of that experience by 'speaking with tongues'.

   'Speaking with tongues' received a good deal of attention and comment in the early sixties, often from 'mainline' church leaders who had little awareness of these pedigrees.[173] In 1964, an Anglican evangelical, the Revd Michael

---

[170] James E. Worsfold, *The Origins of the Apostolic Church in Great Britain* (Wellington, NZ, 1991), 187. Its historian describes the convention as 'still the Mecca of the movement's international ministry and fellowship'.

[171] William K. Kay, *Pentecostals in Britain* (Carlisle, 2000).

[172] Bryan R. Wilson, *Sects and Society* (London, 1961). Robert Jardine was brought up in the Church of Scotland in Liverpool, converted to Wesleyan Methodism, ministered on its behalf in the Shetland Islands, where he became a Baptist. After an unsuccessful period, (an English speaker) as pastor of a small Gaelic-speaking congregation, and short Baptist pastorates elsewhere in Scotland, he associated himself with the Apostolic Church in Wales in 1916. In 1923, however, he was ordained into the ministry of the Church of England, becoming vicar of Doncaster in 1937. He then moved swiftly to offer his services to the duke of Windsor and Mrs Wallis Simpson, performing a marriage for them in a French chateau. On his return, his parishioners were hostile, correctly regarding him as having flouted episcopal authority. He departed for the United States, accepting the pastorate of a small Los Angeles church which he renamed Windsor Cathedral with himself as bishop. His visitor's visa was not renewed and he returned to Britain. He died in 1950 while preparing to sail to South Africa, where he had accepted an episcopal offer from the breakaway South African Episcopal Church. Robert S. Jardine, *The Supernatural in a Commonplace Life* (Los Angeles, 1944).

[173] Walter J. Hollenweger, *The Pentecostals* (London, 1982) was the first author to put these British movements into a global context.

Harper, resigned as curate of All Souls, Langham Place and founded the Fountain Trust.[174] Certain parishes were seen to overflow with the distinctive marks of Pentecostalism. There were always elements who wanted to move outside established structures but Harper, David Watson and other figures restrained such tendencies. At Guildford in 1971 the Fountain Trust held a conference at which Roman Catholics, 'traditional' Protestants and members of designated Pentecostal churches appeared on the same platform.[175] Even so, while recognizing that it had brought 'renewal', the emphasis on the normality of 'speaking in tongues' and the 'second blessing' was controversial and, sometimes, acutely divisive.[176] It was not to be expected that an emphasis on the Spirit could easily be translated into precise formulae. Yet while doctrine might be disputed, the music and drama which was also a hallmark of the charismatic movement appealed to those who found the atmosphere of 'mainline' Christian worship too constipated.[177]

The expansion of white 'Pentecostalism'—to give it a generic description—more or less coincided with the emergence of black-led churches as a significant element in the Christianity of England in particular. The designation 'black-led', however, pointed to the central issue: integration or separate development? It seems clear that churchgoing immigrants from the Caribbean could find themselves stared at, ignored, treated with hostility or warmly welcomed—it was impossible to predict. Returning home in 1961, after spending six months in England, a former president of the Jamaican Baptist Union concluded that the new immigrants were not wanted by the churches. In addition, they found themselves being ridiculed at work by their English workmates for their interest in churchgoing. These are, of course, generalizations. Individual congregations did make specific and sometimes successful attempts to 'integrate' newcomers. In 1965, however, while it was estimated that there were 40,000 West Indians in Birmingham only a hundred were members of Baptist churches. 'Back home', the proportion would have been significantly larger. 'Christian migrants', it has been claimed, were 'confronted with the same prejudice and discrimination inside the churches as they were outside'.[178] This is a large claim and

---

[174] Michael Harper, *At the Beginning: The Twentieth Century Pentecostal Revival* (London, 1965).

[175] James Dunn, author of *Baptism in the Spirit* (London, 1970) was one of the theologians who participated.

[176] Randall, *English Baptists*, 397–402.

[177] C.O. Buchanan, *Encountering Charismatic Worship* (Nottingham, 1970).

[178] Iain MacRobert, 'The New Black-Led Pentecostal Churches in Britain' in Paul Badham, ed., *Religion, State and Society in Modern Britain* (Lampeter, 1989), 127. David Killingray, 'Black Baptists in Britain 1640–1950', *Baptist Quarterly* 40 (2003), 84 likewise speaks of black Christians from the Caribbean being 'often cold-shouldered out of churches' and being 'forced' to form their own. The author speaks of the presence of separate black churches as being 'a severe indictment on our recent Christian past'. Clifford Hill, *West Indian Migrants and the London Churches* (Oxford,

difficult, in this form, to verify one way or another. In so far as it is true, it combined with other factors to make black Christians form their own churches. Although not formally ethnic, in practice they became bodies, largely Pentecostal, which sustained a strong sense of black community. These churches went under a variety of names but by the early 1970s their presence in urban England was a marked feature of the ecclesiastical land-scape.[179] Black faces were not altogether absent from 'mainline' denomin-ations but it seemed, in practice, appropriate to speak of 'white-led' and 'black-led' churches. This phenomenon made it even more difficult than was already the case to think of the Christian presence in England as being evenly distributed or constituting a uniform whole. Lord Fisher, in his retirement Dorset village, would not have encountered much evidence of local activity by the New Testament Church of God. Another realignment of Christianity and culture was under way. The incidence of Caribbean—and later African—settlement meant that this adjustment was most marked in England, but it also had some impact elsewhere in the British Isles.

Contrasting what he saw as the 'reckless simplicity and freedom' of the early Church with the elaborate institutional frames of 'traditional' contem-porary Churches. one sociologist was struck by the sheer institutional weight which the latter carried. The early Christians, it seemed, had been makeshift in their organization. Their lack of a tightly hammered structure had of course made it possible for all subsequent churches, over the cen-turies, to see their own arrangements as proper inferences from the hints which the New Testament disclosed. The irritating failure of the early church to be precise beyond question could be explained by the fact that it did not suppose there would be future generations of churchmen who would worry about such matters.[180]

It could also be observed that the early church had not had to cope with cathedrals.[181] More and more people seemed to want to visit them. Cath-edral chapters were besieged by requests from artists—choirs, orchestras and organists—to perform. They were very expensive to maintain. They were 'tourist attractions'. The millions needed guides and guide books pitched at

1963); R. Gerloff, *A Plea for British Black Theologies: The Black Church Movement in Britain in its Transatlantic Cultural and Theological Interaction* ... (Frankfurt, 1992).

[179] Hastings, *History of English Christianity*, 559 notes that by the early 1970s there were eighteen different West Indian churches worshipping in Handsworth, Birmingham. The expansion of these churches was, of course, an example of 'bottom-up' enterprise rather than the result of some 'top-down' planning of church growth. It is difficult to speak of membership numbers in any precise way.

[180] Leslie Paul, *A Church by Daylight: A Reappraisal of the Church of England and its Future* (London, 1973), 301.

[181] Robbins, 'The Twentieth Century' in Collinson, Ramsay and Sparks, eds., *History of Canterbury Cathedral*, 335–8. Canterbury was to an extent a 'special case' but both its 'problems' and 'opportunities' were experienced by all other cathedrals.

various levels and in various languages. Visitors injected money into the local economy. Should they pay to go in? But what was a cathedral for? Had they become 'secular sites', glorified concert halls? There were those both inside and outside the church who supposed that was all they were. The picture was perhaps more complicated. Who could tell what meaning building and music—an ordered, ongoing worship—could convey to a twentieth-century tourist battered by words? 'Reckless simplicity and freedom' might now need to be recovered, but not everything had to go.

The sociologist reviewing these questions of 'fitness for purpose' was no 'ordinary' one. Leslie Paul had also revealed the 'Angry Young Man'. He produced a report on *The Deployment and Payment of the Clergy* in January 1964 in response to a commission from the Church of England's Central Advisory Council for the Ministry. Within a fortnight, 11,000 copies had been sold. His conclusion, not in itself surprising, was that the institution of the church was not fit for purpose. Viewing clergy as its manpower, it found them to be inefficiently and haphazardly deployed. Where clergy did splendid work, they did so in spite of rather than because of the system. Statistical data spelt out the details of uneven distribution and unequal pay for equal (notional) work. The report made sixty-two recommendations. They included the abolition of the parson's freehold and the ending of the distinction between beneficed and unbeneficed clergy. There was to be a central Clergy Staff Board, together with regional bodies. It was time to think beyond the traditional parish—which was losing and perhaps had lost its significance in both urban and rural areas. Paul was very obsessed by the bleak urban picture. Although the report generated much discussion, there was evidently need for more discussion. *Partners in Ministry* appeared in 1967. The outcome was the Pastoral Measure of 1968 which set out, in complex, not to say baffling, detail, new procedures for the reorganization of parish and ministries. It looked as though an appropriate way of dealing with redundant churches had been found. At the heart of the debate was a clash of cultures. Clerical critics disliked the 'management speak' which they detected. Priests, the editor of the *Church Times* opined, were not pawns 'on a vast impersonal, bureaucratic chessboard'.[182] Clergy had not been trained to think in terms of 'partnership'. The church was an institution but a peculiar one. Its men, apparently, could not be mobilized, measured and monitored as other men. That might be so, but the trouble was that the institution was expensive to run. It needed more money.

In the same year in which Fisher had been reminding the prime minister on the subject of riches, he received a letter from Sir Malcolm Trustram Eve (later Lord Silsoe) in which Eve reported that the work of the Church

---

[182] Cited in Welsby, *History of the Church of England*, 135.

Commissioners meant that the sums available for distribution were 'vastly larger than ever before'. 'The embarrassment of riches', he remarked, 'makes for difficulties...'. He wanted to know what suggestions for disbursement the archbishop might have. Fisher was staggered. It was very difficult to take in 'these vast sums', the benefit of which to the church could not be told. He did not think, however, that the Church Assembly needed to be turned to for any new proposals.[183] The Church Commission, after a protracted process, had finally been created in 1948 bringing together the Ecclesiastical Commission and Queen Anne's Bounty. Fisher, as perhaps did none of his successors, had both a serious personal involvement in the Commission's work and an understanding of its fundamental financial importance. It was a new body but the weight of English history hung heavily over all its work as it grappled with clergy stipends and pensions, parsonages, houses for bishops, and cathedrals. 'Reforming the parish' might seem a straightforward matter to reformers, but in practice it could entail the most arcane of legal and quasi-legal procedures. More suffragan bishops might be useful, but the bill for them had to be totted up. There were twenty-seven assistant bishops who were reported to be active 'or fairly active', in twenty-one dioceses. Who paid for them? No man, through lack of private resources, should be prevented from accepting a bishopric. The archbishop of Canterbury remembered the furniture which he had to buy when he became bishop of Durham. However, Lord Silsoe finally exploded in 1968. The church had to do something 'to reduce ostentation and expensive maintenance in clergy houses and, in particular in See houses'. Parts of Auckland Castle had been let out but that still left 30,000 square feet at the disposal of the bishop. Ian Ramsey, Durham's diocesan at the time, had come from meditating philosophically on religious language at Oxford. He was not very prelatical, but he reported, with respect, that only those who had lived in the castle could know just how suited to a bishop's ministry it was. The weight of history was there too. It was 'a symbol of tradition' and, difficult though it was to evaluate an influence of this kind, no one who had 'a concern for the spirit of man' would deny its existence.[184] Other bishops, where they still lived in 'palaces', did not relish the companionship of deathwatch beetles. They wanted a speedy escape from the symbols of tradition which they inhabited.

It is reasonable to suppose that 'average churchgoers' had little notion of who the Church Commissioners were, how they were appointed or how they operated. Viewed from this level, they were a particularly arcane

---

[183] Chandler, *Church of England in the Twentieth Century*, 63. Subsequent comments derive from this detailed study.

[184] Chandler, *Church of England in the Twentieth Century*, 190–1. David L. Edwards, *Ian Ramsey, Bishop of Durham* (London, 1973).

aspect of how the Church of England worked (not as a whole a system whose functioning could be swiftly understood).[185] The First and Third Commissioners were appointed respectively by the Crown and the archbishop of Canterbury. The Second, an unpaid post, was an MP who answered for the Commissioners in the House of Commons. It was acknowledged that the Church of England also needed voluntary contributions, but it seemed safe to assume that the investment strategy pursued by the Commissioners would give the Church of England that financial cushion which could keep its institutional structure afloat. It was this apparent security which made the Church of England different from all other churches. Free Churches knew that their ability to carry on rested very much more directly on the contributions of their members. Belt-tightening, both at local and national level, was their only recourse if contributions fell off. At regular intervals, when they considered 'wastage', that is to say men who left the ordained ministry, it was alleged that low salaries constituted the chief reason.[186] How the Roman Catholic Church was funded, both in the parish and nationally, was one of those mysteries on which there was no eagerness to enlighten and on which historians have thus far not shed much light.[187]

For a decade, Leslie Paul had been immersing himself in facts and figures and asked himself, finally, particularly in relation to the Church of England, what this tough, legal, historical, organizational muddle was all about. It was not worth keeping alive, at great cost, just because it was picturesque. It was only worth saving because of the tremendous and humbling assertion that it was the vehicle of God's mercy and redemption in the world. Writing disconsolately after the publication of his report, Paul accepted that the Church of England might just quietly fade away—decently. Its decline was statistically predictable, but it might never happen. The church did

---

[185] Paul A. Welsby, *How the Church of England Works* (London, 1960), subsequently updated, was an attempt by an insider to offer a succinct insight into its structure and procedure.

[186] Gordon A. Catherall, *Lord, Why Pick On Me?* (Liverpool, 1986) is a rare example of a ministerial memoir by a man who deliberately remained 'rooted close to the people'; A. Kenny, *A Path from Rome: An Autobiography* (Oxford, 1986), 153–8 relates how a Catholic curate, also on Merseyside, spent the most depressing years of his life. Catherall spoke with warm affection for his congregation, Kenny wrote that it would not have been easy to make friends in the parish, even if that had been encouraged. In time, the latter became rooted close to academic people.

[187] Finance, for example, does not feature specifically in the perspectives addressed by the contributors to Hornsby-Smith, *Catholics in England 1950–2000*. Hastings, *History of English Christianity*, 663 thought that the Church of England might be particularly vulnerable to 'intellectual bankruptcy', but his stimulating volume reflects the perspective of a professor of theology. He had no concern with how English Christianity, in any of the branches he considers, was institutionally financed. The only prospect of 'bankruptcy' which crossed his mind was that of the intellect.

change all the time, despite itself. In an anti-institutional mood, parishes were throwing up their own new forms.[188] 'Swings and roundabouts' might mean that, shrunken and shriven, the show somehow remained on the road.

---

[188] Paul, *Church by Daylight*, 332–3.

PLURALISM'S PUZZLES, 1976–2000

i. Millennial Moments

The year 2000 saw an English Anglican, George Carey, archbishop of Canterbury, standing beside a Polish Pope John Paul II, together with the Metropolitan Athanasios, pushing open the Jubilee Door of St Paul's basilica in Rome. A new millennium for Christianity was beginning. To have gathered such men together a century before would have been inconceivable. The ecclesiastical world was changing, perhaps had changed. The churches in the British Isles were determined not to let the millennial moment pass without celebration. Plaques were placed on church buildings as a reminder to any curious passers-by, and they remained in place. In the United Kingdom, the churches contrived to gain exposure on television and radio for the celebration of the millennium. A millennium 'Resolution' was broadcast at ten minutes to midnight as the New Year, 2000, appeared. London Weekend Television had just produced Melvyn Bragg's series *Two Thousand Years*—two volumes by Peter Partner being published to accompany it. Readers of the *News of the World* were treated to the archbishop of Canterbury's millennial message, courtesy of an indulgent editor. *The Times* on 1 January 2000 contained a 'Millennium Section'. Its contents, however, included nothing which reflected on the religious significance (or insignificance) of what was apparently being 'celebrated'. The newspaper's religious affairs correspondent did file a piece on 'events' which were taking place up and down the country. Its headline ran 'Blairs join Royal Family in prayers for a new era'. She noted that the heir to the throne was to be found marking the occasion in the High Kirk of St Giles in Edinburgh. Noting the participation of a Liberal Jewish Rabbi in a hospital service alongside an Anglican clergyman and a Roman Catholic priest, she supposed that 'even some non-Christian religious communities marked the date change'. The 'national' observance of the 'date change' reached its bathos in the erection of a secular 'Dome' in Greenwich, though one with a 'Spirit Zone' which Christianity shared with other religions.

The regius professor of ecclesiastical history in the University of Oxford, the dean of Christ Church and the bishop of Oxford wanted to offer the public more substantial fare. In public lectures given in the University of Oxford 'top experts' celebrated the highlights of two millennia of religious thought and practice. They took stock of how the church had emerged, how it had evolved over centuries, how it currently stood and what its future prospects might be. Contributors paid attention to Christianity's 'most fascinating contributions to the history of western civilization'. Yet the forms and structures of that civilization, with its attendant political, economic and military needs, might equally be said to have moulded the churches. Contemplating the complex processes of interaction, it might rarely be possible to be certain whether 'the church', in any century, was 'capturing' the world in which it lived or had been captured by it. The 'world' under scrutiny was 'Europe'. The church in the British Isles was part of that story. Lecturers in Oxford in 1899–1900 would have been comfortably familiar with 'the history of Christianity' within the framework of 'western civilization'. Their successors, a hundred years later, however, were well aware that they were 'taking stock' in a radically different world. The lecturers had to grapple with the fact, or so it appeared, that uniquely among world cultures, the descendants of Latin Christianity had begun to emancipate themselves from the bonds of traditional belief-systems.[1] In other public commentary it was held that the biggest single explanation for the retreat from organized religion lay in the fact that people could live without that constant encounter with death which had been the lot of previous generations. When that 'emancipation' had 'begun' was problematic, as indeed was whether 'emancipation' was the appropriate term to describe what was happening.[2]

So, jolted by the millennium, the whole 'Christian past' came under scrutiny in sermons, lectures and the occasional book.[3] In itself, a mere date could not signify a substantial 'turning point', and nothing extraordinary happened, as the year opened, to make it seem a specially 'new era'. If there was media focus on Palestine, it was not because of what had occurred in Nazareth and Bethlehem two thousand years earlier, but because of the three-cornered struggle in which Jews, Christians and Muslims were currently engaged. Nothing, it might seem, could more graphically illustrate the contrary imperatives of place, people and religious persuasion, or demonstrate the relationship between 'peace' and 'power', than the fate of the 'Holy Land'. When the British government gave up the 'mandate' to administer 'Palestine', which it had held since 1919, and British troops

---

[1] As Diarmaid MacCulloch puts it in Richard Harries and Henry Mayr-Harting, eds., *Christianity: Two Thousand Years* (Oxford, 2001), 161.

[2] Lecturing in 1953, the incoming Spalding Professor of Eastern Religion and Ethics at Oxford spoke of 'the de-christianization of the United Kingdom' as a nation-wide fact. Christians in England, he supposed, being Laodicean in tendency, had brought this condition upon themselves. R.C. Zaehner, *Foolishness to the Greeks* (Oxford, 1953), 8.

[3] Examples include Keith Ward, *God, Faith and the New Millennium* (Oxford, 1998); Martyn Percy, ed., *Calling Time: Religion and Change at the Turn of the Millennium* (Sheffield, 2000).

returned home in 1948, it was little suspected that, half a century later, the relationship between 'People of the Book' would become of critical importance in the 'Jerusalem' of 'England's green and pleasant land'.

It was in that England, from May to July in 2001, that serious civil disturbance erupted in Oldham, Burnley and Bradford. The Muslim population, over the last third of the century, had risen very substantially to reach some million and a half. It was substantially drawn, with the exception of a small number of 'native' conversions, from the populations which had come from Pakistan, Bangladesh and India (including Kashmir). Although it is no more easy to be precise about 'practising' Muslims than it is about 'practising' Christians, in major cities across England—Leeds, Birmingham, Leicester and of course London, being among them—the Muslim presence was significant. Nor was this only an English matter. Belfast had 10 mosques and a 4,000-strong 'community', Cardiff 11 mosques and a 5,000 community while Glasgow and Edinburgh together had 30 mosques and a 48,000 community.[4] Historically, and contemporaneously in different parts of the world, it was the relationship between the 'Three Faiths' which had exhibited, in varying degrees, both mutual hostility and respect. However, additionally, the presence of substantial Sikhs (600,000?) and adherents of Hinduism (400,000) further extended the complex religious mosaic of the United Kingdom. Such communities, necessarily, had a special connection with the tensions of the Indian sub-continent. The plurality thus disclosed was made even more diverse by the variety of the ethnic, linguistic and cultural traditions from which followers of these world religions had come, making problematic the identification of their 'communities' and 'leaders'.[5]

The encounter between Christianity and Islam, formerly largely 'external', which was taking place in what had still, in the first half of the century, been regarded as 'the mission field', now became ever more significant and problematic.[6] A mosque was 'next door'.[7] In 1994, as a further sign of interlocking worlds Michael Nazir-Ali, who had been a bishop in Pakistan and whose father had converted from Islam, was made bishop of Rochester and spoke prominently thereafter on Muslim–Christian relations. In practice, of course, that translated into an encounter (or, more often, the lack of

---

[4] Peter Leese, *Britain since 1945: Aspects of Identity* (Basingstoke, 2006), 185–6.

[5] H. Ansari, *'The Infidel Within': Muslims in Britain since 1800* (London, 2004). A local study is R. Singh, *Sikhs and Sikhism in Britain Fifty Years On: The Bradford Perspective* (Bradford, 2000).

[6] Some of the best accounts of Islam written by Christian scholars, for example Montgomery Watt and Kenneth Cragg, came out of a period when the geographical 'territory' of Islam was much clearer than it later became.

[7] One Anglican professor of theology in Wales marvelled at the way in which Karl Barth, he believed, had constructed a theology without ever having met a person of another faith, a person to whom God was profoundly real. Paul Badham, *The Contemporary Challenge of Modernist Theology* (Cardiff, 1998).

an encounter) between different kinds of Christians and different kinds of Muslims. Who constituted 'spokesmen', in relation to particular issues, could not be easily identified. Both faiths were in principle open to all human beings, and shared much in common, but what that meant for the social existence of their believers has diverged sharply. Christianity, to put it boldly, had been of its nature a shaper of nations and even of nationalism, whereas Islam has been profoundly anti-national. The one did not start with a clear political model of its own, the other did.[8] As will shortly be noted, the pope's visits, in their 'national' character, had illustrated this Christian synthesis again, with all its tensions. Islam in the British Isles had to operate in two nation states of the kind that had evolved in Western Europe, states which required 'loyalty'. What, over time, might 'British Islam' come to be?[9] In short, therefore, year after year, immigration was bringing the ethnic, linguistic, cultural and religious complexity of 'the world' into Britain on a scale and with an impact that was without precedent. Issues of identity and loyalty, of belonging and believing, took on a new dimension, raising, as they did, taxing but fundamental questions about the nature of 'communities' and 'sovereignties'. It was supposed in 1994 that the heir to the throne wanted to make sure that he might be regarded as 'defender of faith' rather than 'defender of the faith'.[10]

The complexity of this process, and its wide-ranging ramifications, cannot be considered in detail here. It brought with it, however, lengthy and unresolved debate on the meanings and consequences of a 'multi-faith' and 'multi-cultural' society.[11] The states of the British Isles, some supposed, should amount to little more than 'communities of communities', each community having its own value-system, conventions and practices recognized and safeguarded within a legal framework whose primary purpose was

---

[8] Such is the basic position which is then argued through in Adrian Hastings, *The Construction of Nationhood: Ethnicity, Religion and Nationalism* (Cambridge, 1997), 187 ff.

[9] J. Klausen, *The Islamic Challenge: Politics and Religion in Western Europe* (Oxford, 2005); Tariq Ramadan, *Western Muslims and the Future of Islam* (Oxford, 2005).

[10] Dr. E.R. Norman wrote a vigorous article which made it clear that the future monarch could only head one faith. To suppose otherwise, he thought, suggested that he had been listening to too many Anglican sermons. *The Times,* 28 June 1994.

[11] Publications written at different levels, designed for different audiences and with differing emphases, poured from presses. They include *In Good Faith: The Four Principles of Interfaith Dialogue: A Brief Guide for the Churches* (London, 1991), a reissue by the Council of Churches for Britain and Ireland of guidelines produced a decade earlier by the British Council of Churches. The Evangelical Alliance, *Christianity and Other Faiths* (Exeter, 1983); A.G. Hunter, *Christianity and Other Faiths in Britain* (London, 1985); M. Forward, ed., *God of All Faith: Discerning God's Presence in a Multi-Faith Society* (London, 1989) was published by the Methodist Church Home Division; C. Lamb, *Belief in a Mixed Society* (Tring, 1985). It is difficult to map the distribution and measure the impact of publications such as these which were primarily for in-church use. The fact remained that the 'multi-faith' character of the country was much more evident in some areas than in others.

just that, not to purport to express an 'agreed' social morality. The 'law of the land' would not attempt to embody a state 'norm' or reflect a common understanding of social morality—for there was not, and in the circumstances now pertaining, could not be, any such understanding. For others, however, such a notion was absurd, impractical and objectionable. A state could not survive on such a basis. The nation, or nations, could function only if the state embodied certain pervasive values, and it might be necessary to formulate either 'codes of conduct' or formal legislation to encapsulate those values. It was not clear how a 'plural society' should operate and how the constituent parts of that plurality understood their status and roles.[12] Philosophers and theologians conducted an enduring debate on justice and freedom, on the individual and the community, tradition and authenticity.[13] Books with 'pluralism' in their title, in one connection or another, mushroomed. The climate had changed. Much of this discourse was transatlantic, engaged in by academics who moved with some regularity between universities in the United Kingdom and North America and who read each other's books.[14] This learned discussion often had an abstract quality which took it beyond the range of 'ordinary' insular churchgoers, but the condition of society which it sought to explicate was felt more generally—and to a degree understood.

Outside academic debate, it was in the context of education that the issues became most lively. On the one hand, there was the question of the

---

The academic debate ranged far and wide and impacted, at different speeds and to different degrees, on the teaching, research and curricula of departments of theology in British universities and their relationships with 'Religious Studies'. The personal path followed by John Hick, who became Professor of Theology at Birmingham, proved attractive to many, but his position was by no means universally accepted. John Hick, *God and the Universe of Faiths* (London, 1973); *God Has Many Names: Britain's New Religious Pluralism* (London, 1980) and *Problems of Religious Pluralism* (London, 1985). Paul Badham edited *A John Hick Reader* (London, 1990). See, amongst many articles and reactions, the contributions in J. Hick and B. Hebblethwaite, eds., *Christianity and Other Religions* (Glasgow, 1981) and in D. Cohn-Sherbok, ed., *Many Mansions* (London, 1992).

[12] Adrian Hastings, 'Pluralism: Theology and Religious Studies' in *The Theology of a Protestant Catholic* (London, 1990), 27–42. This conference paper was written in 1987 and appeared in the conference proceedings, Ian Hamnett, ed., *Religious Pluralism and Unbelief: Studies Critical and Comparative* (London, 1987), in which volume there is other pertinent discussion. See also 'Church and State in a Pluralist Society' in Adrian Hastings, *The Shaping of Prophecy: Passion, Perception and Practicality* (London, 1995), 113–25.

[13] A pivotal figure in these exchanges was Alasdair MacIntyre, whose multi-phased intellectual and academic career took him from Britain to the United States. A. MacIntyre, *After Virtue* (London, 1981) and *Whose Justice? Which Rationality?* (London, 1990). Charles Taylor, *The Ethics of Authenticity* (Cambridge, MA, 1991); *Sources of the Self: The Making of the Modern Identity* (Cambridge, 1989) and, in giving the Gifford Lectures, *Varieties of Religion Today: William James* (Cambridge, MA, 2002) and on other occasions, has come in the opposite direction. James Mackey, *Power and Christian Ethics* (Cambridge, 1994) has been another 'go-between'.

[14] Paul J. Griffiths, *Problems of Religious Diversity* (Oxford, 2001); Gavin d'Costa, *The Meeting of Religions and the Trinity* (New York, 2000)—American author publishing in Britain and British author publishing in America.

specific content of 'Religious Education' and the extent to which its syllabus should have some kind of assumption of Christianity as normative, however 'open' its presentation should be. Did not religious 'pluralism' demand a 'neutral' or non-dogmatic presentation? There were lively exchanges over decades between exponents of different solutions. What the 1944 Education Act meant by a daily act of worship also became contentious and seemed to leave open rather different practice (or lack of practice). Few Christians dissented from the view that knowledge of all the major world religions was desirable (and atheists could not find 'knowledge' objectionable). The deeper issue was whether education 'about' religion was sufficient—for adherents of any faith. If religion was important it could not be reduced to 'knowledge'. It was not a 'subject' but sought to encapsulate an entire attitude to life and death, and to personal and collective conduct. Discussion was not helped by the apparent inability (or unwillingness) of official inquiries, as in the case of the Swann Report in 1985, to be sufficiently clear, conceptually, whether what was being considered was ethnicity or religion. The 1988 Education Act attempted to clarify what the state now required, and its passage through Parliament had been contentious. Every word had a potentially loaded significance. The 1988 Act spoke of 'religious education', that of 1944 had spoken of 'religious instruction'. The Agreed Syllabus was to reflect the fact that the religious traditions in Great Britain were 'in the main Christian'. The daily collective act of worship was to be 'wholly or mainly of a broadly Christian character'. In short, there was, and has remained, much debate on what precisely could or should be provided. It sometimes appeared that there had been a 'Christian reaffirmation' but ambiguity abounded. The churches themselves did not quite know how much of an opening they had. Battle lines were not quite what they had been. 'Church schools' (Roman Catholic or Anglican—and, in a small number of cases, joint) regained confidence after a period when, for financial and other reasons, the churches had been unusually hesitant about their justification and value. That Muslims and other traditions should have their own schools, in such a context, could not be thought unreasonable. However, an educational universe in which there were vibrant 'faith schools'—as they came to be known—was perceived as 'divisive' and threatened social and national cohesion (only apparently capable of being sustained on a 'secular' basis). The growth of Islam might alarm some Christians but there was also a Christian benefit. Christians grew more confident that 'secularity' was not some kind of inevitable future. It was encouraging, too, that 'faith schools' seemed, relatively speaking, so popular and 'successful'. Sceptics thought that parents wanted 'respectability' not 'religion' when they sent their children to such schools. They were reluctant to concede that there might be a deep connection between an ethos pervaded, however imperfectly, by religious conviction, and social behaviour.[15]

Yet this was no simple return to uncomplicated confessionalization. While Christians, and perhaps British Christians living at the heart of an imperial state in particular, had thought in the first half of the century in terms of the church one day embracing all humanity in a common fellowship, that vision faded. By the 1980s and 1990s, the 'missionary movement' as it had existed in British church life for two centuries was dwindling. Missionary societies not infrequently changed their names in an effort to see themselves as 'partners in world mission' rather than be thought 'purveyors of the Christian West'. Individual missionaries who had once 'on furlough' thrilled congregations with conversion stories from 'remote' regions of the world now seemed, in their retirement, 'remote' figures themselves, beached by the global tide of changed assumptions and relationships. It now seemed, at the end of the century, to an Anglican, the Regius Professor of Divinity at Oxford, to be 'an unrealistic possibility' to think that the world might become Christian. The inclusion of all human beings in one church would be possible only by the effective suppression of dissent, an unattractive prospect. It followed, he thought, that the church had to accept itself as one religious community amongst others, though that did not mean that it should cease to claim for itself truths which were important for the salvation of humanity. Further, the church itself should aim at a 'union of fellowship' rather than an institutional uniformity within a hierarchical and authoritarian structure.[16] That might leave open whether there could be 'group rights' for religious communities. These, and other cognate questions poured in on the churches by the end of the century. They were not in themselves new but, as the subsequent sections illustrate, the churches struggled to find answers, or at least common answers. Such 'displacements' from outside, the full extent of which cannot be elaborated here in more detail, required the churches of the British Isles in late century to find their own 'place' in a society and culture which, historically, they had axiomatically assumed to be 'theirs'. It was not easy to do so.

---

[15] Gerald Parsons, 'There and Back Again? Religion and the 1944 and 1988 Education Acts' in Gerald Parsons, ed., *The Growth of Religious Diversity: Britain from 1945*, vol. ii: *Issues* (London, 1994), 161–98; Leslie Frances and Adrian Thatcher, eds., *Christian Perspectives for Education* (Leominster, 1990) is a 'Reader' with contributions from various perspectives.

[16] Keith Ward, *Religion and Community* (Oxford, 2000), 358. His Cambridge opposite number was also grappling with contextual and cultural plurality. David F. Ford, 'Christian Wisdom for the New Millennium' in Philip L. Wickeri, Janice L. Wickeri and Damayanthi M.A. Niles, *Plurality, Power and Mission: Intercontextual Theological Explorations on the Role of Religion in the New Millennium* (London, 2000), 111–34; Jan van Lin, *Shaking the Fundamentals: Religious Plurality and Ecumenical Movement* (Amsterdam and New York, 2002).

On the one hand, it was ever more apparent that facets, at least, of the future before the churches were linked to developments far beyond the British Isles. If any demonstration of this was required, it was provided by the devastating terrorist attacks in New York and Washington on '9/11' in 2001, and all that stemmed from them thereafter. If there was an enveloping global 'clash of civilizations' gathering pace, Britain, and to a lesser extent, Ireland, could not escape its consequences. How such 'civilizations' might be defined was of course problematic. In so far as 'the West', under the leadership, if not the hegemony, of a United States with which the United Kingdom was so closely linked, constituted a 'civilization-player', it had a 'Christian' ingredient in its complex ideological stances, or at least was capable of being given one by enemies. Yet 'the West', if it had, or had had, Christianity at its core, was certainly no longer coextensive with the 'territory' of Christianity. 'World history' might indeed be disclosing, too, that the 'centre of gravity' of Christianity (supposing one could speak of Christianity in the singular) was shifting away from Euro-America.[17] Though that nexus might still possess the 'home' of Christianity's 'global' institutional locations—Rome or Geneva—and need to draw on its financial resources, dynamism was to be seen in Africa or, conceivably but more distantly, in China. The priorities that dynamism upheld might conflict with the 'native' cultural context in which the churches of the British Isles were 'at home'. The reversal of roles implied by the notion of an African mission to Europe was difficult to accommodate. The foundation of African Christian congregations in Britain, the Netherlands and elsewhere, specifically with such a purpose, stood history on its head.[18] Elements of all of these global shifts were already strongly evident. They were apparent at least to those 'at the top' in the British/Irish churches who urged 'global thinking' even before the issue of 'climate change' became, by definition, global. Some felt stifled by the burden of nationhood. There was not much sign that the United Kingdom was a 'failed state' but was it not time for it to 'fade' in Christian consciousness, which should be transnational.[19] Would it not be good to feel that the twentieth century might be the last in which a history of 'The Christian Church in the British Isles' could be conceived as a meaningful enterprise to attempt?

These, and surrounding and opposing views, formed the currency of somewhat bewildered millennial contemplation. The sections that follow

[17] The exploration of these shifts forms part of the substance of Hugh McLeod, ed., *The Cambridge History of Christianity: World Christianities c.1914–c.2000* (Cambridge, 2006); Keith Robbins, *The World since 1945: A Concise History* (Oxford, 1998).

[18] Gerrie ter Haar, *Halfway to Paradise: African Christians in Europe* (Cardiff, 1998).

[19] Bernard Thorogood, *The Flag and the Cross: National Limits and Church Universal* (London, 1988); contributors to Susanne Hoeber Rudolph and James Piscatori, eds., *Transnational Religion and Fading States* (Oxford/Boulder, 1997).

examine this condition by reference to specific developments within the churches over the previous quarter of a century in their interaction with their societies. The purpose is to show churches navigating both with and against the tide, both coming to terms with, and failing to come to terms with, the pluralism which they themselves constituted—all within the wider wobbly 'pluralism' of Britain and Ireland in this period, islands themselves exposed as sites of continental, even global, economic and political cross-currents.[20] The position of the churches remained a not insignificant element within the interlocking but problematic constitutional relationships of the time: between the Republic and Northern Ireland, between the Republic and the United Kingdom, between the 'communities' within Northern Ireland, between Northern Ireland and Great Britain within the United Kingdom. Further, the structure of Great Britain itself came under increasing strain, with the result, by the millennium, that there was a newly minted Scottish Parliament in Edinburgh and a Welsh Assembly in Cardiff. It remained to be seen how these institutions, with their different powers, would evolve. It also remained to be seen whether the United Kingdom, as the twentieth century had known it, would survive. How the United Kingdom and the Republic of Ireland positioned themselves within the precarious identity of Europe, possibly 'secular' or possibly not, offered much scope for speculation.

ii. Papal Encounter: Ireland, 1979

That a pope should visit the British Isles was a novelty. That he was Polish made his visits extraordinary. In October 1978 the Conclave gathered in Rome to choose a successor to John Paul I. They settled, though only on the eighth vote, on the 58-year-old Karol Wojtyla. The first non-Italian pope since 1522, he had for fifteen years been archbishop of Krakow. One year later, at the end of September, his plane touched down at Dublin airport and he was kissing Irish ground.[21] That he should come, and come so soon, was confirmation that Ireland was exceptional. Later, looking down from his helicopter, it might appear to John Paul II that 'all Ireland' had assembled for Mass in Phoenix Park. Two hundred cardinals were on hand to concelebrate and ten times that number of priests distributed the host to a reported figure of more than a million communicants. It was an event which dwarfed even the 1932 Eucharistic Congress, though the mood of the people was more sunny. From Dublin, he moved to Drogheda in the diocese of Armagh, and then across to Galway where a quarter of a million

---

[20] Andrew F. Walls, *The Cross-Cultural Process in Christian History* (Edinburgh, 2002); Robert Song, *Christianity and Liberal Society* (Oxford, 1997).

[21] *John Paul II in Ireland: A Historical Record* (Dublin, 1979).

young people greeted him on the Ballybrit racecourse. Eamon Casey, the popular and substantial bishop of Galway, newspaper columnist and frequent broadcaster, warmed up the crowd in advance. Father Michael Cleary, a popular priest in Dublin, was also on the platform. On the same day, John Paul II also visited the shrine of Knock in its centenary year.[22] His attendance there had been lobbied for intensively by its local guardians.[23] It seemed that both in the capital, and in the west, 'Catholic Ireland' was intact. Returning to Maynooth on 1 October, he told seminarians and religious that after two days in the country he was confident that the next generation of Irish men and women would be as faithful as their fathers (and mothers?) had been. An address at Limerick strongly condemned abortion, contraception and divorce.

Ireland and Poland were distant from each other. They neither shared the recent past of the Second World War nor what was then the present of communism, realities which had shaped the experience and thinking of the pope. Yet there was much in their pasts—occupation by or subordination to a powerful neighbour, and partition—capable of generating emotional sympathy. The Irish bishops had issued a pastoral letter in early September which compared Ireland's devotion to Mary with that of Poland. A pope who immersed himself, in various languages, in European literature and philosophy was determined also to show, in visiting Knock, his abiding involvement in 'popular ritual'. Indeed, as in his first overseas visit, to Mexico, the impression was almost given that he had been inspired to travel from a desire to pay homage, in due course, at each country's chief Marian shrine.[24] 'Backward' and 'peripheral' though they might seem from the perspective of sophisticated urban European opinion-formers, the 'ordinary people' of Ireland and of Poland were being fused in Catholic unity by a man whose style, for a pope, was far from ordinary. On arrival in Dublin, the pope had been greeted by the archbishop of Armagh, Tomás Ó Fiaich, newly made a cardinal. Ó Fiaich, formerly president of Maynooth, had succeeded William Conway in 1977. No mean historian, in his way, he would not have been the man to disabuse the pope of the notion that Ireland too, like Poland, was a martyr nation. He had his feet, rather large feet, firmly planted in Irish soil. His preferred language was Irish. The soil he most liked tramping over was in South Armagh, where he had been

---

[22] He took off from Knock by helicopter. The parish priest, Monsignor Horan, argued that Knock needed an airport to cope with the thousands of pilgrims who, following the pope's visit, could be expected in future. No other rationale for such an airport existed but, in controversial circumstances, it went ahead. Bruce Arnold, *What Kind of Country: Modern Irish Politics 1968–1983* (London, 1984), 167.

[23] Ethna Kennedy, ed., *Dame Judy Coyne: The Heroine Face of the Knock Shrine Story* (Cork, 2004), 221–7. Fr. M. MacGréil, SJ, *Monsignor James Horan: Memoirs 1911–1986* (Dingle, 1992), 133–54.

[24] Michael Walsh, *John Paul II* (London, 1994), 64.

born—though he had largely lived in the Republic. It was what the British Army called 'bandit country'. The pope would have known that the cardinal's 'solution' to the violence which continued in Northern Ireland was simple. He had articulated it in public already and was to continue to do so over the decade of his time in office. He received an unflattering press in England but Lord Longford, who became a connoisseur of bishops, Anglican and Roman Catholic, found him probably the friendliest, almost certainly the jolliest, and undoubtedly the most expansive and candid of them all.[25] The archbishop simply thought the British should withdraw from Ireland. They were ending their colonialism across the globe. It was time to do the same in Northern Ireland. The Northern Ireland problem could only be solved in an all-Ireland context.

The pope did not visit Northern Ireland. In both parts of the island there had been Catholic hopes, even expectations that he would do so.[26] The previous month, however, the last viceroy of India, earl Mountbatten of Burma, had been murdered in Co. Sligo. He had been in the habit of holidaying in the West of Ireland, with scant regard for his own security. His assassination added another element to an already tense situation, not least in respect of the internal politics of the Republic. The Drogheda allocution, therefore, provided a 'proxy'—though naturally pleasing or displeasing various elements. In the town where, 330 years earlier, Oliver Cromwell's troops had massacred all men found in arms after its capture, John Paul II stated that Christianity was 'decisively opposed to fomenting hatred or to promoting or provoking violence or struggle for the sake of struggle'. Do not believe in violence, he told his audience, and do not support violence. It was not the Christian way. The violence, however, did not stop.

Not surprisingly, Protestants both in the Republic and in Northern Ireland were in at least two minds about the significance of the papal visit. In a tight schedule in Dublin he had nonetheless briefly met Protestant church leaders and spoke of friendship. Such a gesture, even if it was responded to with some caution, showed that 1979 was not 1932. That the pope had come so early to Ireland was a source of some satisfaction. Yet, even though the atmosphere might even be described as joyful, the spectacle of 'national' mobilization for Mass in Phoenix Park was also disturbing. Did the ensemble of the papal visit not represent a more genial but nonetheless triumphal Catholicism? The Presbyterian moderator of the day, upset by the apparent intensity of the pope's Marian devotion, had been the only one of

[25] Frank Longford, *The Bishops* (London, 1986), 179.
[26] There remains some uncertainty, and conflict of testimony, as to whether or not a visit to Northern Ireland had been intended (and then abandoned) or whether it had been ruled out in an initial communication to the British Minister to the Holy See.

the main church leaders to decline to meet him. A subsequent Anglican bishop of Cork, an Irishman, watching and listening to the events at Knock, felt he was a stranger in a strange land in a way he had never felt before. To hear the phrase 'Mary, Queen of Ireland' compounded his sense of being 'in' but not 'of' the community in which he lived.

The pope moved on to the United States and the United Nations in New York (in reality Ireland was a 'stopover' on his way to greater things). He had, however, seen nothing which disturbed the notion of 'Catholic Ireland' as it had been formed in his mind and which could so easily be equated with Poland—a country also with only a very small Protestant minority. The most high-profile and, in presentational terms, the most 'modern' event in modern Irish history was over. At Knock, a plaque placed at the base of the re-erected altar used by the pope, described his visit as 'the most important event in Irish history since the coming of St. Patrick'. Only 'we Irish', one writer declared in *The Tablet*, could understand the chord which had been awoken by the presence of the pastor of pastors. Each man, woman and child, amidst the present excitement, voiced the soul stirrings of a people past.[27] Whether they pointed to the future, however, might be another matter.

iii. *Replacing the Past: Ireland, 2000*

In 2000, in the Republic, there were two mosques in Dublin and four others elsewhere. The basis of the new Muslim population was formed by Bosnians who were refugees from the Yugoslav conflict at the beginning of the 1990s and had remained. They were augmented by immigrants from the Horn of Africa and the Middle East. The booming Irish economy needed the kind of labour they supplied. The total size of the community was fluid as the state wrestled with asylum-seekers and the problem of distinguishing between legal and illegal immigration as did the state across the water. In aggregate it did not approach the levels in the United Kingdom, but the Republic's population was of course much smaller. Despite the continuing troubled condition of Northern Ireland, the same pattern of new arrivals also occurred in Belfast and elsewhere in the province. At the turn of the century, Catholics and Protestants in London/Derry found a Sikh *gurdwara* established in what had been a primary school.[28] A society culturally accustomed to emigration and exile, and to being 'a place of [occasional] return' for its global diaspora, now found itself accepting a

---

[27] Louis McRedmond on 6 October 1979 cited in Norman St John Stevas, *Pope John Paul II: His Travels and Mission* (London, 1982), 49.

[28] M. Nic Craith, *Plural Identities—Singular Narratives: The Case of Northern Ireland* (New York and Oxford, 2002), 20–5.

population which did not intend to be transient. The Jewish population, small and urban, had not been augmented by any significant disposition to take Jewish refugees in the 1930s.[29] A new religious pluralism was emerging, even though the numbers were relatively small and precedents were not readily to hand.

It seemed at least plausible, in 2003, for a round table discussion held outside Dublin by *Encounter*—a body established twenty years earlier by the British and Irish Governments 'to contribute to the improvement of relations between their peoples in the interests of peace, reconciliation and stability'—to have as its theme 'Post-Christian Society'. Its Irish/UK joint chairs took the view, in organizing such an occasion, that Ireland had 'begun to experience a similar diminution of religious belief and practice within the Christian tradition' though 'not necessarily to the same degree as had been experienced in Britain over a somewhat longer period'. It was suggested that 'pointers' might be communicated to governments and to agencies of civil society which 'might be helpful in understanding the tasks that have to be undertaken when the Churches are not nearly such influential institutions as they have been hitherto'. The heterogeneous gathering assembled for this purpose came from all parts of the islands, representing different traditions, varieties of Christian, humanist and atheist. It had, however, been decided by the organizers 'not to embrace for consideration the religious traditions not indigenous to the two islands'.[30] Not surprisingly the participants were not all of one mind, even in relation to the central premiss, but the very fact that it was held at all indicated that 'something had changed'. Ireland was not 'just like' Britain, nor was it necessarily 'programmed' to 'catch up' with the neighbouring island, but there was a dissolution of old assumptions. The papal visit, with surprising speed, came to be seen as something of a last hurrah.

The political, social and economic elements in this change intermeshed. The years immediately before the pope's arrival had seen political transitions that might be significant. Conor Cruise O'Brien might not make much direct impact on Post and Telegraphs as the department's minister, but he embarked on an unremitting personal campaign to cut off the 'Ancestral Voices' which, he believed, plagued the present.[31] Garret Fitzgerald, with a Protestant mother, abandoned his many careers and became, at the age of

---

[29] D. Keogh, *Jews in Twentieth-Century Ireland: Refugees, Anti-Semitism and the Holocaust* (Cork, 1999).

[30] Encounter, *Post-Christian Society*. A report of the round table discussion held 28–30 November 2003. This author was present. Robert Tobin, 'The Evolution of National and Religious Identity in Contemporary Ireland' in Jane Garnett, Matthew Grimley, Alana Harris, William Whyte and Sarah Williams, eds., *Redefining Christian Britain: Post 1945 Perspectives* (London, 2006), 284–66 is a useful sketch.

[31] Conor Cruise O'Brien, *Ancestral Voices: Religion and Nationalism in Ireland* (Dublin, 1994).

46, foreign minister in the Cosgrave Fine Gael government, a post his father had held in the new Free State.[32] Ireland's new membership of the EEC gave the post enhanced importance. It was also time, given what was happening in the North, to unpack pieties in relation to possible unification. The Republic's constitution came back into the frame. This new questioning attitude, it has been argued, marked 'the biggest single change in the nationalist response to the Ulster question in the 1970s'.[33] It would be a mistake, however, to suppose, for example, that O'Brien's ruthless dissection was universally commended. He lost his seat in the 1977 election. Jack Lynch and Fianna Fail emerged with the biggest majority in the Dáil which had ever been recorded. Fitzgerald had stated publicly in April 1976 that the state would take steps to eliminate 'legal anomalies' and remove such basis as might exist for the charge that the constitution and the laws of the Republic were 'unduly influenced by the teachings of one Church'.[34] He had let it be known, informally, when in Europe, that some 'new thinking' was afoot. The message he received from Paul VI was firm. Ireland was a Catholic country, perhaps the only one left. It should stay that way and should not be changed to make it less so.[35] John Paul II's message was the same, but the political class seemed less enamoured of the 'special relationship' which had been enunciated so fervently by Joseph Walshe, minister to the Holy See, thirty years earlier when he had declared that Ireland and the Holy See were 'one'.[36]

The Irish republic of 2000 had not ceased to be a 'Catholic country' but in its millennial condition it had ceased to be 'the only one left' in the way that Paul VI had thought of it. Northern Ireland was not a Protestant state for Protestant people, but the sequence of events over the previous years left it unclear quite what it was. That was not for lack of academic industry. The problems of the province had been examined on an epic scale in publication after publication. In 1998 the 'Good Friday' agreement was reached. Determination, snacks and adrenalin kept the show on the road, as *The Times* put it on 11 April. For *The Independent* on the same day, there had never been negotiations involving so many points of the political compass, and rarely has such a sense of historic new beginning been generated. It provided for a Northern Ireland Assembly, a North–South Council and a British–Irish Council—the 'Council of the Isles' which would link the devolved polities and also include the Isle of Man and the

---

[32] Garret Fitzgerald, *All in a Life: An Autobiography* (Dublin, 1991).
[33] J.J. Lee, *Ireland 1912–1985: Politics and Society* (Cambridge, 1989), 479.
[34] Cited in Marcus Tanner, *Ireland's Holy Wars: The Struggle for a Nation's Soul 1500–2000* (London, 2001), 385.
[35] Dermot Keogh, *Ireland and the Vatican* (Dublin, 1995), 363.
[36] Keogh, *Ireland and the Vatican*, 358.

Channel Islands. Alongside these institutional structures were measures protecting civil and political rights, policing justice and arms de-commissioning. The agreement was put to the electorate in a referendum and received a 70 per cent endorsement. The Presbyterian Church described the outcome as neither defeat nor assimilation but 'a political accommodation which could be the way out of the darkness of the last 30 years into a better future'.[37] David Trimble took office as the leader of the Ulster Unionist Party. Observers and commentators, who had developed a certain cynicism about agreements concluded in relation to Northern Ireland, watched and waited.

In 1985, Garret Fitzgerald, by then taoiseach, had concluded, with Margaret Thatcher, in the face of strong opposition from Ulster unionists, what came, rather puzzlingly, to be referred to as the Anglo-Irish Agreement.[38] Two years later, on Remembrance Day, a bomb set off in Enniskillen left eleven dead. The quality of the response made by the local Methodist, Gordon Wilson, whose daughter had been killed, was much admired, but violence continued.[39] In 1991 the Anglo-Irish Agreement was suspended to allow fresh constitutional talks. The following year the number of dead in 'The Troubles' passed 3,000. Ceasefires, from both sides of the divide, came and went, in the years that followed, as did talks, and talks about talks. London and Manchester were hit by bomb attacks in 1996. Confrontation and violence attended the Drumcree Orange Parade near Portadown, in Co. Armagh. 'Drumcree' in this year, and subsequently, brought fierce criticism in both the British and Irish press.[40] Ritual, memorialism and the cultivation of a cultural religious identity were worth bothering about 'only if they reinforce a central core of blazing charity'. Churchmen had to have the bottle to tell their congregations that 'love thy

---

[37] Cited in Patrick Mitchel, *Evangelicalism and National Identity in Ulster 1921–1998* (Oxford, 2003), 249.

[38] For general assessments at this date see B. Girvin and R. Sturm, eds., *Politics and Society in Contemporary Ireland* (Aldershot, 1986); A. Aughey, *Under Siege: Ulster Unionism and the Anglo-Irish Agreement* (Belfast, 1989). Fitzgerald gave his own account in 'The Origins and Rationale of the Anglo-Irish Agreement of 1985' in Dermot Keogh and Michael H. Haltzel, eds., *Northern Ireland and the Politics of Reconciliation* (Cambridge, 1993), 189–202.

[39] Wilson had been born in the Free State and educated at Wesley College in Dublin before moving to Enniskillen to open a drapery business. In 1987 Wilson was named 'man of the year' by BBC Radio 4's *Today* programme, well ahead of his nearest rival, Mikhail Gorbachev. The queen's Christmas message referred to him as a man 'who had impressed the whole world by the depth of his forgiveness'. He accepted a seat in the Senate of the Irish Republic in 1993.

[40] Dominic Bryan, 'Drumcree and the "Right to March": Orangeism, Ritual and Politics in Northern Ireland' in T. G. Fraser, ed., *The Irish Parading Tradition: Following the Drum* (Basingstoke, 2000), 191–207; Neil Jarman, 'Another Form of Troubles: Parades, Protests, and the Northern Ireland Peace Process' in Matthias Reiss, ed., *The Street as Stage: Protest Marches and Public Rallies since the Nineteenth Century* (Oxford, 2007), 255–72.

neighbour as thyself' was never negotiable. Being mealy-mouthed made 'Christianity in these islands a scandal and a laughing stock'.[41]

It was easy, in these circumstances, to feel sceptical about the 1998 agreement.[42] A bomb in Omagh in August left 28 dead and over 200 injured. The Good Friday agreement, wrote an Irish columnist in the *Irish Times* and the British *Daily Mail*, has now been followed by 'the Calvary of Omagh'.[43] All parties claimed that they were implementing the provisions in full, it was just that 'the other side' was not doing so. The electorate of the Irish republic, in a referendum in 1999, abandoned its claim to Northern Ireland. Earlier, in December 1993 in the 'Downing Street Declaration' made after talks between John Major and Albert Reynolds, the UK government had made it clear that if 'the greater number' of the inhabitants of the province wished to join the Republic it would not seek to prevent such an outcome. A protracted implementation process of a kind, however, was still in place, but at the millennium it could still not be said, with any certainty, that a lasting settlement would be reached.[44] 'Good Friday', nevertheless, remained the only basis on which it could be constructed. That it did happen to have this reference to one of the most significant days in the Christian calendar, with its ambivalently dark 'goodness' was pointedly pertinent. The churches, too, were struggling, North and South, though in different circumstances, with diversity and unity. The 'reconciliation agenda' pressed on them.[45] They were uncomfortably aware, too, of

---

[41] Libby Purves, 'Christ Dies in Drumcree: Real Protestants or Catholics would be Praying for Peace, not Burning Churches', *The Times*, 7 July 1998. Anglican and Presbyterian leaders struggled to put distance between their churches and the Orange Order in this matter. Not unnaturally there was some tension within the Church of Ireland between South and North. One Southern bishop, John Neill, later archbishop of Dublin, was critical of Eames for not closing Drumcree parish church. Eames thought that to have done so would have led to bloodshed.

[42] Some immediate interpretations are to be found in J. Ruane and J. Todd, eds., *After the Good Friday Agreement: Analysing Political Change in Northern Ireland* (Dublin, 1999).

[43] For reflections on how men, women and children from all walks of life and both sides of the identity divide began the process of healing see John Paul Lederach, *The Moral Imagination: The Art and Soul of Building Peace* (Oxford, 2005), 157–8.

[44] It was not to be until May 2007, that 'the Northern Ireland peace process reached its journey's end', as a British newspaper felt able to say, when, in the presence of the taoiseach, Bertie Aherne, and the prime minister, Tony Blair, the new first minister, Ian Paisley, leader of the Democratic Unionist Party, and his deputy, Martin McGuinness of Sinn Féin all pledged themselves 'to promote the interests of the whole community represented in the Northern Ireland Assembly towards the goal of a shared future . . .'. 'If anyone had told me that I would be standing here to take this office, I would have been totally unbelieving.' *The Times*, 9 May 2007. Doubtless his two previous biographers would be sharing such disbelief: D. Cooke, *Persecuting Zeal: A Portrait of Ian Paisley* (Dingle, 1996) and C. Smyth, *Ian Paisley: The Voice of Protestant Ulster* (Edinburgh, 1987), written as their books were at different stages in his career and published in significantly different locations.

[45] M. Haley, ed., *Reconciliation in Religion and Society* (Belfast, 1994). See, particularly, various writing by Duncan Morrow, *The Churches and Inter-Community Relationships* (Coleraine, 1991), 'Church and Religion in the Ulster Crisis', in S. Dunn, ed., *Facets of the Conflict in Northern Ireland* (Basingtoke, 1995), 151–67 and 'Churches, Society and Conflict in Northern Ireland', in A. Aughey

the view, expressed in articulate quarters, that it was time to get the whole 'religious business' out of the way.[46] A proper resurrection would require the churches in Ireland to forfeit their cultural hegemonies and, if necessary, be paraded, protesting, into the broad sunlit uplands of secularity.

Some twenty years after he had written the best-seller *The Council and Reunion* on the eve of Vatican II, the Swiss theologian Hans Küng came to speak in Dublin. The Congregation for the Doctrine of the Faith had withdrawn his right to be called a 'Catholic theologian' (within the German university system). He had come to believe that there could be no world peace without religious peace and sought an ecumenical way between what he called 'fanaticism for truth and forgetfulness of truth'.[47] He was not in the habit of mincing words. The pope, on his visit to Ireland, had been given 'an ecumenical opportunity of historical dimensions' but he had not taken it. But if nothing was done, it would not only be the departure from the church of such great Irish personalities as James Joyce 'but also, in the long run, the masses'. Seán Freyne, in introducing the published version of the lecture—in which Küng went on to spell out what steps the pope might have taken—was concluding that Vatican II had not been able to make an impact on Irish life 'because the questions the Council sought to grapple with had never been seriously posed in this country'. The inter-church discussions which had taken place had in truth been 'mere token events as far as the grass-roots in all churches are concerned'. He thought this especially true of the Roman Catholic Church.[48] Vision was one thing, reality another, notwithstanding the efforts of individuals.[49] It had to be

and D. Morrow, eds., *Northern Ireland Politics* (London, 1996), 190–8. Morrow's father, incoming moderator of the General Assembly of the Presbyterian Church in Ireland in 2000, had a deep personal involvement in these issues. See John Dunlop 'The Self-Understanding of Protestants in Northern Ireland' in Enda McDonagh, ed., *Irish Challenges to Theology: Papers of the Irish Theological Association Conference 1984* (Dublin, 1986) and his *A Precarious Belonging: Presbyterians and the Conflict in Ireland* (Belfast, 1995). After his return to Belfast in 1978, after ten years in Jamaica, Dunlop was a key figure in Presbyterian–Roman Catholic relationships. He became moderator in 1992. Protestants had had a traditional fear of Roman Catholics but he thought that the threat which they both now faced came from 'the increasingly pervasive secularisation of people's thinking'. John Dunlop 'A Response: The Disengaged' in S. MacRéanmonn, ed., *The Church in a New Ireland* (Dublin, 1996), 85.

[46] M. O'Doherty, *I was a Teenage Catholic* (Cork, 2003) presents a vivid personal picture of 'getting away'.

[47] Hans Küng, *My Struggle for Freedom: Memoirs* (Grand Rapids, MI, and Cambridge, 2003).

[48] Hans Küng, *Church and Change: The Irish Experience* (Dublin, 1986), 85–90. English translations of Küng, *Infallible?* and *On Being a Christian* had appeared in 1971 and 1977 in London. Freyne's remarks are on page 10. Contributors to A. Falconer, E. MacDonagh and S. MacRéamonn, eds., *Freedom to Hope? The Catholic Church in Ireland Twenty Years after Vatican II* (Dublin, 1985) had some hope. Küng had also been paying occasional visits to Britain and his case had received considerable attention in the British press, viz. Patricia Clough, *The Times*, 28 January 1980, where Küng also explained why he remained a Catholic.

[49] I.M. Ellis, *Vision and Reality: A Survey of Twentieth-Century Irish Inter-church Relations* (Belfast, 1992).

admitted in the mid-1990s that, for the new generation, 'Vatican II' was merely part of church history, of only the vaguest significance.[50] Küng could be, and was, dismissed in the mid-1980s as an outsider who did not understand. In fact, the 'defection' he forecast proved to come rather more quickly than in 'the long run'. A statement published in 1989 remained in the conditional tense. 'If religion were to no longer fulfil its historic civilizing mission', as Professor Lee saw it, 'as a substitute for internalised values of civic responsibility, the consequences for the country no less than for the church could be lethal.'[51]

By the end of the century, however, commentators already had in print accounts of the 'fall' of the Catholic Church.[52] The indices of withdrawal were already there in terms of falling attendances at Mass. The young were losing interest. Women seemed increasingly unwilling to accept their 'natural' place. Of course, these were generalizations, but they had substance. The ready supply of men for ordination began to dry up. The Maynooth which Ó Fiaich had apparently left in good health began to spiral downhill as numbers declined and threatened its very existence.[53] Its president resigned in 1994. The civil and church sides of the institution were separated. Two centuries after its foundation, what would be left? Various publications from 'ground level', by priests and others, chronicled this process of decline, or perhaps collapse.[54] The reduction in numbers brought into question whether the Church had the capacity to maintain its customary role in health and education. There were acute problems in what now seemed the over-provision of buildings. It was not too difficult to identify 'the whole patriarchal, male-dominated presence of the Catholic Church' (and 'middle-aged' might have been added for good measure) as in crisis. One who did so was Mary Robinson, from a Catholic family in Co. Mayo, the successful candidate in the 1990 presidential election, the first woman to reach this office.[55] She attributed her victory to the women of Ireland. She had entered politics twenty years earlier as the youngest senator and had subsequently, in her support for 'progressive' causes, become an icon of 'new Ireland'. With a Protestant husband, she was more 'Protestant' in sentiment—having

---

[50] Seán MacRéamonn, ed., *The Church in a New Ireland* (Dublin, 1996), 21. A veteran of ecumenism asked himself what had happened and whether there might be a fresh start. Michael Hurley, *Christian Unity: An Ecumenical Second Spring?* (Dublin, 1998). Dermot Lane, 'Vatican II: The Irish Experience' in Liam Bergin, ed., *Faith, Word and Culture* (Dublin, 2004), 54–70.

[51] Lee, *Ireland 1912–1985*, 657.

[52] T. Inglis, *Moral Monopoly: The Rise and Fall of the Catholic Church in Modern Ireland*, 2nd edn. (Dublin, 1998); Mary Kenny, *Goodbye to Catholic Ireland* (Dublin, 2000 edn.).

[53] P. Corish, *Maynooth College, 1795–1995* (Dublin, 1995).

[54] T. Flannery, *From the Inside, a Priest's View of the Catholic Church* (Cork and Dublin, 1999).

[55] L. Siggins, *Mary Robinson: The Woman who Took Power in the Park* (London and Edinburgh, 1997).

thought the 1985 Anglo-Irish Agreement too harsh on Unionists—than some Protestants who had previously decorously occupied her office.

The English Catholic columnist William Rees-Mogg was very happy. Although not invariably an enthusiast for the Enlightenment, he thought her victory opened the gates to 'an enlightened Ireland'. Middle-class Protestants in Belfast, he thought, might not feel particularly English but they were at least given, by the British connection, a link with a government based, however imperfectly, on liberal values. Now, however, 'enlightened Protestants' of Belfast could deal with an 'enlightened President of Ireland'. Further, he added that 'we do not ourselves belong to either tribe, nor they to us. English Protestants, he considered, had 'few cultural links' to the Protestants of Northern Ireland, and English Catholics, like himself, while owing a great debt to Irish spirituality and Irish priests, were not Irish. The two Irish tribes, he concluded, belonged culturally to each other rather than 'to us' and Britain did not want to retain the role of the neighbour who intervenes in a family dispute.[56]

Those interested in the statistical detail of decline had plenty of information to dwell on. What interested the media, however, was scandal, and there was a good deal of that to dwell on too. The beaming bishop who had greeted the pope in Galway, together with his friend from Dublin, hit the headlines in 1992. Eamon Casey had fathered a child who was in America and, further, had supplied the mother with money which was not his. The curious, and there were many such, found much to savour in the picture of deceit and hypocrisy that emerged.[57] His rattled episcopal colleagues, in their response, seemed in disarray, but this was only the beginning. In June 1995, Cardinal Daly, who had succeeded Ó Fiaich in Armagh in 1990, delivered a strong defence of celibacy in an address at Knock, only to find a fresh storm breaking. Michael Cleary, who had been with Casey in Galway in 1979, and was equally a 'media figure', had died at the end of 1993. The press now revealed that his 'housekeeper' was the mother of his two sons. The woman's subsequent book filled out the picture.[58] The media were now in full cry, and were not starved of further material. Even more damaging, however, was the information which came out about child sex abuse on the part of priests.[59] Throughout the 1990s, the cases multiplied,

[56] William Rees-Mogg, 'The Gates Open to an Enlightened Ireland', *The Independent*, 12 November 1990. It would seem that the author was either not aware of the 'cultural links' between Scotland and Ulster or may have supposed that 'we' in England constituted Britain. G. Ecclestone and E. Elliott, *The Irish Problem and Ourselves* (London, 1977) offered an earlier perspective published by the Church Information Office.

[57] Joe Broderick, *Fall from Grace: The Life of Eamon Casey* (Dingle, 1992).

[58] P. Hamilton, *Secret Love: My Life with Father Michael Cleary* (London and Edinburgh, 1995).

[59] C. Moore, *Betrayal of Trust: The Father Brendan Smyth Affair and the Catholic Church* (Dublin, 1995) was one such (Belfast) case.

and digging back into the past did not stop thereafter.[60] Bishops were subjected to relentless questioning about their knowledge of these matters and how they had 'covered up'. It seemed as if every Catholic schoolboy in Ireland had been beaten by a Christian Brother. Apologies were issued, but they seemed inadequate. When, in the new century, Cardinal Connell, archbishop of Dublin, resigned, after much criticism, his replacement came from outside the circle of existing Irish bishops. The church, it seemed, was on the run. Its apparatus had been shown to be incompetent and corrupt, and possibly worse. It was unacceptable to plead in mitigation that harshness and severity was what 'society', until very recently, had expected in the upbringing and education of children. Some said—if this was a helpful perspective—that what was being disclosed was not some latter-day infection in the church but a condition which had been 'normal'. All that was different was that the media were in charge and that the church could not now prevent exposure. The tables were turned, old scores were being settled and the house of cards might fall in. Priests returning to Ireland in the 1990s, having served overseas for several decades, contrasted the universal respect which had attended them when they left with the widespread suspicion, even hostility, which they now encountered. The Church of Ireland took no pleasure from the turmoil in the Catholic Church but felt a fresh confidence in publicly stating its position in areas of personal and public ethics where its views differed from the Roman Catholic. Its normally uxurious bishops were not burdened with the celibacy which was clearly 'a problem' for their Catholic colleagues, some of whom, though not themselves falling from grace, were thought by the Vatican to be 'wobbling' on the subject of its necessity.

Viewed from Britain, one English Catholic commentator thought it no bad thing that the unchecked power and unchallenged influence of the Irish Catholic Church had come to an end. Such power as the church exerted in the future would have to be earned. Rather than a matter for regret, that was an exciting opportunity. Ireland's religious glaciers were thawing fast and any church, Catholic or Protestant, which tried to resist would accelerate the dechristianization of the whole island.[61] It was indeed Mary Robinson's successor as president of the Republic, Mary McAleese, a practising Catholic, who in December 1997 received communion at a service in the

---

[60] For example, Seamus Hegarty, bishop of Derry, held an unprecedented press conference in October 2005, two days after the publication of an Irish government report into the diocese of Ferns, Co. Wicklow, which revealed it as having the world's highest rate of clerical abuse allegations. Bishop Hegarty, albeit over a slightly long period of review, was able to top the Ferns figures by detailing, though not naming, 26 priests. He expressed his heartfelt and unreserved apology. *The Times*, 28 October 2005.

[61] Clifford Longley, 'Priestly Scandal that can Help Bring Peace to Ireland', *Daily Telegraph*, 15 March 1996.

Church of Ireland cathedral, Dublin.[62] The rebuke she received from the archbishop of Dublin, and the 'spat' between the two churches over the incident, demonstrated that in this particular matter the glacier did not seem to be thawing.

In short, it was unclear, even more than was the case across the water, how the society of the Republic should be characterized and where 'ultimately' it was going. It was difficult to avoid newspaper articles and television programmes in Ireland which revealed, in title after title, that an Irish 'identity crisis' was in full spate and the 'church crisis' was both separate from and yet integral to it. The same period, in fits and starts, had seen notable constitutional battles, even if the outcome lacked the clarity which was supposedly being sought. Such a comment applies to the 1983 referendum on an amendment to the constitution which stated that the state acknowledged 'the right to life of the unborn' though with due regard for 'the equal right of the mother' and to give appropriate legal guarantees. It was passed by a two-to-one majority, though only half the population voted. Broadly speaking, there was a division in the voting between urban and rural and between east and west. Catholic bishops had made it clear that they looked to the faithful to support the amendment. Predictably, opponents thought their intervention untimely and inappropriate. But, in a country which allowed 'the people' not politicians in legislatures to decide such a matter, why should they not speak? There was a conservative voice which had a right to speak (if not perhaps in the terms sometimes deployed) and liberals had to stomach it.

At the end of the century various attempts were made to discern beliefs and values. One such inquiry concluded that despite the well-publicized 'decline' of the 1990s the church showed what to some was an unexpected resilience in adversity. The devout had become less conspicuous, but there was not an army of atheists. Mary Robinson had described herself as a non-practising Catholic—what did that mean? Although the findings of specific polls varied, it was virtually certain that a majority of Catholics neither agreed with, nor adhered to, the church's teaching on contraception. There were other indications, too, of *à la carte* Catholicism. 'The people' did not want to 'say goodbye' but appeared to want a Catholic menu which had

---

[62] McAleese, born and educated in Belfast, was the first 'Northerner' to become president. She was known to hold 'liberal' views on homosexuality and women priests. Before her election as president, she had addressed a large gathering, at the Jesuit Conference Centre, Milltown Park in Dublin in March 1995, of an Irish network formed two years earlier to petition for all ministries and offices in the church to be equally open to both women and men. She spoke fiercely against what she called the 'demonization' within the church of those, like herself, who supported this cause. Mary McAleese, 'Coping with a Christ Who Does Not Want Women Priests Almost as Much as He Wants Ulster to Remain British' in *Women—Sharing Fully in the Ministry of Christ?* (Dublin, 1995), 11–21.

options. The pope who had come in 1979 was not likely to offer it. A significant element in Ireland still did not want him to. They thought that the wheel would surely turn as the hollow hedonism, which economic success of an unparalleled kind was spawning, lost its charm. Ireland should forge its own kind of pluralism. It was much to be regretted that public decision-makers were taking their ideas from 'the bankrupt stock of our large neighbours in Europe and America'.[63]

Both Catholics and Protestants in Northern Ireland had kept a watchful eye on what had been happening in the Republic. The continuing all-Ireland church structures ensured a good deal of exchange of information and opinion. Even so, the stance of the churches took place within a 'province' (whether conceived as of Ireland or of the United Kingdom) which remained *sui generis*, the site for the interplay of pan-insular linkages and where, in a sense, both culturally and politically 'America' and 'Europe' were actively engaged.[64] 'Leaders' and 'flocks' continued their testing relationships within and between their respective 'communities' and in interaction with the UK government. Both continued to find themselves in circumstances where every word or gesture was capable of being used in the propaganda war. Some, walking a tightrope, fell off.[65] No one could doubt the strength of Cardinal Ó Fiaich's commitment to the nationalist cause. Fear that the church was losing ground in the Northern nationalist community may have been a strong factor in his appointment. He was not a favourite figure in government circles in London. However, despite his obvious sympathies and outspoken comments, particularly in relation to the treatment of hunger-strikers, he deplored violence (but if the pope could not stop it, nor could he). If he deplored a particular episode, as for example the Enniskillen bomb, however, he could upset other members of the 'Catholic community' because a statement from him could be taken to imply that it was indeed responsible. It was, of course, individual priests who

---

[63] So the historian and commentator Liam de Paor had written in 1985, cited in Lee, *Ireland 1912–1985*, 658. More generally see Eoin G. Cassidy, *Faith and Culture in the Irish Context* (Dublin, 1996). The author is executive secretary of the Irish Centre for Faith and Culture based at Maynooth.

[64] This operated at different levels. American Catholics and Presbyterians set up various programmes and activities hoping thereby to preserve Christianity 'from the discredit that arises from the frequent description of the troubles in Protestant–Catholic terms'. There was a religious dimension but it was a misleading metaphor to characterize the conflict as a whole. Josiah Horton Beeman and Robert Mahoney, 'The institutional Churches and the Process of Reconciliation in Northern Ireland: Recent Progress in Presbyterian–Roman Catholic Relations' in Dermot Keogh and Michael H. Haltzel, eds., *Northern Ireland and the Politics of Reconciliation* (Cambridge, 1993), 150–1. At another level, the involvement of the American Senator George Mitchell in facilitating the peace process was of great importance, as were the programmes supported by the European Commission.

[65] G. McElroy, *The Catholic Church and the Northern Ireland Crisis, 1968–86* (Dublin, 1991).

were 'at the front line' and found themselves torn. It remained difficult for some bishops to breathe the words 'Northern Ireland'.[66] Cahal Daly, Ó Fiaich's successor in 1990, was of a different stamp. Antrim-born and Belfast and Maynooth educated, he had lectured at Queen's university in scholastic philosophy. One of those who listened to his lectures was a young man, twenty years his junior, Robin Eames. Daly, at the age of 65, had been made bishop of Down and Connor in 1982. His disposition was more ecumenical (he had been a *peritus* at Vatican II). His nationalism was firmly rooted in the notion that a united Ireland could only come about by common consent. His tone and his willingness to engage with the UK government and the Royal Ulster Constabulary presented a marked difference from his predecessor, but by the same token lost him some influence in the 'nationalist community'. There was no wavering, however, in his opposition to 'integrated' schooling, whatever might be said about the barrier to mutual understanding which separate systems were alleged to preserve.[67]

Robin Eames, enthroned as Church of Ireland archbishop of Armagh in February 1986, was to become a key figure in that office in Northern Ireland for the next twenty years. His father, a Methodist minister, had uprooted his family and 'come north' in the 1920s. Increasingly, Eames became a major figure in the world-wide affairs of the Anglican Communion, helping, in the process, to dispel the notion that the Church of Ireland was a backwater.[68] He accepted a life peerage from John Major in 1995. He had been appointed bishop of Derry and Raphoe in 1975 at the age of 38, followed by Down and Dromore in 1980. It is revealing that, born and bred in the east of the province, he had only visited Derry once before taking up his post. The contrast with his Catholic counterpart, Edward Daly, whom he invited to his consecration, could not be more marked. He found himself taking office just at the juncture when, in the wake of the Anglo-Irish Agreement, it was the 'Protestant community' which felt itself most aggrieved by the way in which, so it perceived, it had been by-passed by the two sovereign governments. It now felt alienated and 'sold out'.[69]

Since it now appeared that both 'communities' had an experience of 'alienation' from the structures of government, might it now be possible for

---

[66] Edward Daly, *Mister, Are You a Priest?* (Dublin, 2000), 11. Apart from studying in Rome and a brief period in Dublin, the whole life of the bishop of Derry was spent 'on the border', in more senses than one.

[67] Cahal Daly, *The Price of Peace* (Belfast, 1991).

[68] Alf McCreary, *Nobody's Fool: The Life of Robin Eames* (Belfast, 2004); interview with Eames in Simon Lee and Peter Stanford, *Believing Bishops* (London, 1990), 166–9.

[69] Thousands of loyalists, in their protests outside the City Hall in Belfast, sang hymns and read from the Bible. Eames thought that to dismiss this as idolatry or an insult to religion was to fail to appreciate how deep within Ulster Protestantism was the 'siege mentality'. Robin Eames, *Chains to be Broken* (Belfast, 1993), 142.

Catholics and Protestants to develop greater respect for their 'traditions'? Such a notion blended with a contemporary initiative, in the shape of the Cultural Traditions Group, an ad hoc committee, with government funding, to promote understanding of and constructive debate about the different cultural traditions in Northern Ireland. It was impossible to disguise the extent to which 'religion' was integral to such discussion.[70] Identification of the constituent elements of this 'pluralism', however, was no straightforward matter. There was also the possibility that delineating and constructing the integrity of a community's 'traditions' had the effect of solidifying them. It needed little wisdom to appreciate, perhaps particularly at this juncture, that the 'Protestant community' in fact consisted of different and often competing strands. One writer 'within the evangelical camp' analysing its ideas in these decades wrote that Paisleyism represented 'a retreat into an inviolable Pharisaical self-righteousness that idolizes the myth of the Protestants of Ulster as God's people in God's chosen land'. It was fundamentally opposed to 'the radical, boundary-breaking Good News of the Gospel'.[71] Paradoxically, perhaps, it was only a dose of 'secularism' which might compel both Catholics and Protestants to accept the Good News. Indeed, Archbishop Eames, in his address to the General Synod of the Church of Ireland in 1991, went so far as to see it as 'an opportunity, not a defeat, for the Christian ethos'.[72] The reality for the present, however, was that Ian Paisley was a waxing figure in the religious-political landscape, as was Gerry Adams. Cardinal Daly might not relish the IRA, and Archbishop Eames might not relish Protestant paramilitaries, but those sitting in ecumenical and ecclesiastical armchairs could not control 'their people'.

Flitting between Somerset and London, as he did, Lord Rees-Mogg might indeed suppose that Englishmen did not 'belong' to either of the 'two tribes' of Ireland, though, at the end of the century, the new archbishop of Westminster had names which did not seem very English. The reality was that boundary-breaking (and boundary-strengthening) remained significantly bundled up across the British Isles. The archbishop of Canterbury preached in Dublin in November 1994, in the presence of President Robinson, asking forgiveness for 'our often brutal domination and crass

---

[70] See the comments by Terence Brown, 'The Cultural Issue in Northern Ireland, 1965–1991' in Dermot Keogh and Michael H. Haltzel, eds., *Northern Ireland and the Politics of Reconciliation* (Cambridge, 1993), 168–9. Two significant conferences were held in 1988 and 1990. At the second, held in Enniskillen, this author gave the keynote address on 'Varieties of Britishness', following the earlier lecture on 'Varieties of Irishness' by Roy Foster. Maurna Crozier, ed., *Cultural Traditions in Northern Ireland: Varieties of Irishness* (Belfast, 1989) and Maurna Crozier, ed., *Cultural Traditions in Northern Ireland: Varieties of Britishness* (Belfast, 1990).

[71] Mitchel, *Evangelicalism and National Identity in Ulster 1921–1998*, 212.

[72] Cited in Alan Megahey, *The Irish Protestant Churches in the Twentieth Century* (Basingstoke, 2000), 182.

insensitivity in the 800 years of history of our relationships'. In the following January, Cardinal Daly, in Canterbury Cathedral, asked 'the English' to forgive the wrongs inflicted by Irish people.[73] Such gestures played their part in the complex series of acts which constituted a process of reconciliation.[74]

It was, of course, Northern Ireland which had featured on British television screens in the years since 1975. The pope's visit to Ireland made rather a change from the images of violence and destruction. A peregrinating pope in 1979 was still an extraordinary novelty. A Catholic member of the British Cabinet, moved by what had been said in Drogheda in particular, wrote to the prime minister, Margaret Thatcher, suggesting that, while the IRA would be unlikely to desist, there was 'at least a good chance of separating the Catholic population of Northern Ireland from the terrorist'. An earlier visit to the detention camp at Long Kesh, followed by one to the Stormont parliament building, had convinced him that he was encountering 'two races fighting for one territory'. The letter writer, Norman St John Stevas, did not see himself as 'belonging' to either. The 'problem', he thought, was social rather than religious. It was time for the secretary of state for Northern Ireland to launch a new 'initiative'. Mrs Thatcher did permit one, but it soon ran into the sand. Indeed, over the next couple of years, the fate of the 'hunger strikers' in the Maze prison entrenched opinion in both parts of the island and in Britain.[75] It was almost inevitable, in such circumstances, that the papal visit had been looked at, politically, in the triangular context of Ireland, Northern Ireland and Britain. In so far as he had not been to Northern Ireland, the ecclesiastical significance of the visit had been limited. He had not engaged with its Protestant worlds. They remained, to him, a mystery, as indeed did Protestants in general. He had never lived amongst them. Indeed, viewing Ireland as in practice substantially an English-speaking country, it was only his second to one such. He might have made himself 'at home' with the English language but he was not as fluent in it as he was in German. The expression of his philosophical thought reflected its linguistic-cultural sources. It was to prove not easy to translate into English. While there were exponents, in both islands, of 'phenomenology' and 'personalism'—terms and concepts dear to the pope's way of approaching

[73] *Irish Times*, 19 November 1994 and *The Times*, 23 January 1995.

[74] See the observations by Trevor Williams, the first Anglican priest to become leader of the Corrymeela Community, in Andrew Wingate, Kevin Ward, Carrie Pemberton and Wilson Sitshebo, eds., *Anglicanism: A Global Communion* (London, 1998), 286–93. For a general assessment see J. Liechty and C. Clegg, *Moving Beyond Sectarianism: Religion, Conflict and Reconciliation in Northern Ireland* (Dublin, 2001). Other, not very substantial, evidence has been used to suggest, on the contrary, that at the end of the century there has been 'an intensifying culture of bigotry and sectarianism' in Northern Ireland, with 'militant religion' still a really significant force. Callum Brown, *Religion and Society in Twentieth-Century Britain* (Harlow, 2006), 111.

[75] See Padraig O'Malley, *Biting the Grave: The Irish Hunger Strikes and the Politics of Despair* (Boston, 1990) for an examination of their cultural significance.

issues—they were neither 'mainstream' within philosophical circles nor with significant general impact. A papal visit to Great Britain clearly would not be a simple affair. It would obviously have 'history' to negotiate and would provide a window from which to perceive how the churches really stood in relation to each other and in relation to the society in which they operated. Precedent, protocol, power and personality were all mixed up.

iv. British Domestic Politics: Confronting Convictions

The years 1979–80 brought change in state and church. In the United Kingdom it saw the end of Labour government and the return of the first ever woman prime minister. In England it saw the appointment of Robert Runcie as archbishop of Canterbury. Margaret Thatcher remained in office until her involuntary departure in November 1990. Runcie stepped down in the same year. Their conjuncture proved to be of unusual interest. After a shaky start, the prime minister stamped her mark on a decade of social and economic turbulence. At the end of 1985 the Board of Social Responsibility of the Church of England published *Faith in the City*. The archbishop had set up a Commission on Urban Priority Areas in 1983 and this report was its work. It drew attention to very high levels of unemployment, poverty, homelessness or unsatisfactory housing conditions. It recommended a major redistribution of resources and priorities to tackle these problems. In the furore that followed it was often thought to confirm the view that the English established church was engaging in open battle with the United Kingdom government. There were times, during this decade, when the Labour Party's own internal problems made a coherent Opposition impossible. Viewed as institutions, the churches all had their own serious internal problems but the Church of England could suddenly be seen, across a variety of social and economic issues, to be 'speaking for England' and even 'speaking for Britain'.[76]

It was possible, in the press, to polarize the situation in personal terms: Thatcher vs Runcie.[77] The position, however, was more complex than might appear. The two had first met each other in the context of Conservative undergraduate politics at Oxford in 1946—though only their later

[76] Henry Clark, *The Church under Thatcher* (London, 1993); Peter Catterall entitled a section of his 'The Party and Religion' in Anthony Seldon and Stuart Ball, eds., *Conservative Century: The Conservative Party since 1900* (Oxford, 1994), 'Church against State', 657–67.

[77] In terms of press attention, however, it was rather David Jenkins, newly appointed bishop of Durham in 1984, who was chief critic of the government. Kenneth Medhurst and George Moyser, eds., *Church and Politics in a Secular Age* (Oxford, 1988), 294–6 identify 'a certain division of episcopal labour', with Jenkins at Durham (1984–94) making attacks of a kind which the archbishop, with national-level responsibilities, eschewed. His previous post had been as professor of theology at Leeds University. His theological views excited media attention. David Jenkins, *God, Miracle and the Church of England* (London, 1987) and *God, Politics and the Future* (London, 1988). See his autobiography, *The Calling of a Cuckoo* (London, 2003).

prominence gave this mild early link any interest. This might at first sight suggest that they came, in state and church, from well-groomed 'established' stables. The reality was that both were 'unconventional' in their origins. Their 'unexpected' elevations as 'outsiders' in the Conservative Party and the Church of England, respectively, however, resulted not in their sharing a common perspective but rather in an uncomfortable and sometimes confrontational relationship. The turbulence of the 1980s posed questions for each about identity and 'spheres of influence', about Christianity and politics, in a world very different from that in which the two had been born in the early 1920s. The clashes can be seen in terms of 'principles'. It is instructive, however, to see something of the social complexity of 'religion and politics' through the prism of the two outstanding persons. There was 'religion and politics' in both.

Margaret Thatcher was the daughter of a grocer, a Methodist, in a small Lincolnshire town. It was in Wesley's Chapel in City Road that she married in 1951, though she gravitated loosely into the Church of England. In so far as that happened, however, it was not a drift into cosy conservative Conservatism. Her 'puritan streak' has been identified as making her see those on the right or the left who toyed with ideas for their own sake as frivolous. She seemed to despise people who pontificated about solving the unemployment problem but did not look as though they could run even a grocer's shop. Of course, there had to be analysis but only with a view to finding solutions. She liked making decisions. Making decisions inevitably meant being divisive. She was intelligent but not intellectual. She was the first woman prime minister and had an immaculate hairstyle. That apart, she did not seem excessively endowed with that sensitivity for the feelings of others often believed to be characteristic of her sex. A dissenter began a long march through the institutional consensus which she believed to be paralysing the country. Some intellectuals announced their 'conversion' but the majority found themselves amongst the cultured despisers of the prime minister and her government.[78] She was English. Her language, as she enunciated it, was not as enunciated in Glasgow, Cardiff or Belfast. On coming into the premiership, she had quoted before the cameras the alleged prayer of St Francis, but church leaders soon decided that searching for harmony did not completely encapsulate her political stance.

Robert Runcie had an electrical engineer as father, and a freelance hairdresser as mother (who was apt, with little notice, to ply her trade across the globe). He was brought up in the Crosby suburb of Liverpool. He was a Liverpool kind of Englishman, though his speech did not betray this fact. It was

---

[78] Brian Harrison, 'Mrs Thatcher and the Intellectuals', *Twentieth Century British History* 5/2 (1994), 206–45.

not a 'cultured' household. Nor would his father, who reputedly never trusted parsons or policemen, have wanted an archbishop in the family. The faith Robert found and formulated, therefore, was not that moulded in habitual Anglican surroundings. Like Margaret, he proceeded to Oxford as a 'first-generation' student, but he went to war with the Scots Guards and gained a Military Cross. He achieved a First in Greats in a philosophical climate saturated by A.J. Ayer's *Language, Truth and Logic*. It was an influence which produced in him a lasting distrust of metaphysical systematizing. His decision to be ordained surprised many of his friends. Two years as a curate in Gosforth (1950–2) proved his only experience of working in a parish before he was whisked back to Cambridge, first to Westcott House (where he had himself been trained) and then as Dean of Trinity Hall. It did not seem likely, however, that he would write a big book, indeed any book. He married the daughter of an atheist don, and although his wife was a Christian believer that did not extend to a particular partiality for the goings-on of the Church of England. He spent ten years as principal of Cuddesdon, the Anglican theological college outside Oxford, before becoming bishop of St Albans in 1970. Ten years later—having declined, in the interval, to succeed Coggan at York—he reached Canterbury. The prime minister, for the first time, had had to choose between the two names placed before her by the Crown Appointments Commission. A 'conviction' prime minister had chosen a man who was not without conviction but one whose style, some thought, was 'laid-back'.

Runcie was a clever man who could readily see both sides of a question (he had also, as an undergraduate, joined the Labour Club). In politics, he professed himself not to be a party man but to be stirred by particular matters. In 'church' terms he could be categorized as 'Liberal Catholic' with some placing more emphasis on the one and some on the other. He himself thought that an archbishop should resist a label. What an archbishop should be, however, was not clear. An immediate 'Call to the Nation' was unlikely but Runcie had a sense of national history. An archbishop should still speak to the nation, preferably not in platitudes. It happened that the home secretary, William Whitelaw, had been with him in the war. There were members of the Cabinet who were personally 'accessible'. A churchman should not confine his acquaintance to churchmen, but the 'management' of the Church of England had to be his first charge. Then there was still the diocese of Canterbury itself, though it was to be decided in due course that the bishop of Dover would really look after it.[79]

---

[79] This sketch contains material derived from the biographies written by Margaret Duggan, *Runcie: The Making of an Archbishop* (London, 1983) and Adrian Hastings, *Robert Runcie* (London, 1990) together with the 'biography' by Humphrey Carpenter, *Robert Runcie: The Reluctant Archbishop* (London, 1996) which prints interview material with Runcie and others. There are also glimpses in David L. Edwards, ed., *Robert Runcie: A Portrait by His Friends* (London, 1990).

Subsequently, Lady Thatcher thought that *Faith in the City* 'could have been written very differently'.[80] There seems little reason to dispute such a statement. Its authors, however, couched the document within a well-honed tradition of Anglican social comment, one which certainly did not merit a Marxist label. The question was whether such a tradition, as it had unfolded and been elaborated since the days of William Temple, really now fitted the social and economic circumstances in which the country found itself. It was easy to set the arguments in terms of categories which placed the prime minister and her supporters on the 'wrong side': private/public, individual profit/community benefit, state intervention/free market. She made no bones about her belief that what she was doing was to create wealth which would help many people out of poverty. Industrial and economic change was a painful business, but it had to be gone through. There was no need to apologize for capitalism. What was needed was to liberate enterprise. The general consensus of church comment, however, was that her emphasis was dangerously wrong. It was not something which escaped her notice. She took the very unusual step of addressing the General Assembly of the Church of Scotland in May 1988, elaborating the general contentions which have been sketched above. Her remarks—often referred to as 'The Sermon on the Mound'—did not receive entire approbation.[81] Yet she was not without support. Graham Leonard, appointed bishop of London in 1981, regretted that some Christians seemed to believe that only one viewpoint on social and political matters was possible. He contrasted this with a theological climate in which, so he suggested, they were prepared to accept almost any opinion. From his academic and clerical vantage point, Dr Edward Norman found further confirmation that there was nothing very Christian about the social consensus of the churches. Brian Griffiths, an economist and evangelical Christian, with close experience of government, issued a strong defence of the market economy. The arguments were joined across all the Christian churches, and continued through until the millennium, by which juncture, the economic climate had changed very markedly from that of the mid-1980s.[82] 'New Labour'

---

[80] Interviewed in Carpenter, *Runcie*, 277. Elaine Graham, 'Theology in the City: Ten Years after "Faith in the City"', *Bulletin of the John Rylands University Library of Manchester* 78/1 (Spring 1996), 173–91.

[81] The Assembly Hall of the Church of Scotland is on Edinburgh's Mound.

[82] See the essays in Digby Anderson, ed., *The Kindness that Kills: The Churches' Simplistic Response to Complex Social Issues* (London, 1984); Brian Griffiths, *Morality and the Market Place: Christian Alternatives to Capitalism and Socialism* (London, 1982) and *Monetarism and Morality: A Response to the Bishops* (London, 1985); G. Moyser, ed., *The Church and Politics Today: The Role of the Church of England in Contemporary Politics* (Edinburgh, 1985); R. Tingle, *Another Gospel? An Account of the Growing Involvement of the Anglican Church in Secular Politics* (London, 1988); R. Plant, 'Conservative Capitalism: Theological and Moral Challenges' in A. Harvey, ed., *Theology in the City* (London, 1989); J. Davies, ed., *God and the Market Place: Essays on the Morality*

in 1997 under a prime minister who did not disguise, although neither did he elaborate, his Anglican convictions, seemed willing to accept many 'Thatcherite' axioms.[83] So did his chancellor of the exchequer, and successor, son of a Church of Scotland minister, who apparently carried his father's moral compass with him wherever he went. That would not be the whole story. It was a sufficient reality, however, to suggest that the churches needed a completely fresh look at 'markets', though no doubt tension between liberals and communitarians, of one stripe or other, would remain.[84]

Whatever work was done in this respect, however, there remained some continuing discordant elements. Much of the discussion of 'wealth creation' was conducted by clerical or lay spokesmen who had never themselves created wealth. The 'Christian businessman', so prominent a figure in the life of many churches, had not completely disappeared but he was rare (and she was even rarer). In part, that reflected the changes in the nature and control of British industry. It was a situation in which 'wealth creators' and their critics talked past each other not to each other. Then there was the fact, or probable fact, that in England, notwithstanding the supposed polarization of 'church' and 'state', a majority of church people voted Conservative and supported Margaret Thatcher. Even if that had not been the case, in England at least, she had a 'mandate' from the people. When 'the church' was at loggerheads with government, whether it be in relation to unemployment, housing, or welfare benefits, there was no 'Christian party' behind it.[85] There never had been. It did not appear that there ever would be. Critics of government had therefore to adopt the mantle of prophet, a role for which there was some competition. It was not always certain, however, that difference of opinion arose from prophetic discernment, or that prophets had reconciled themselves to the legitimacy of the electoral process. Be that as it may, the churches collectively had for a time a place in the public arena in which, arguably, they 'punched above their weight'. Certain symbolic interventions were made by individuals at particular moments of tension. Habgood, together with the Roman Catholic archbishop of Liverpool and other church leaders, held a meeting with Arthur

---

of Wealth Creation (London, 1993); Catholic Bishops' Conference, *The Common Good and the Catholic Church's Social Teaching* (London, 1996); L. Boeve, 'Market and Religion in Postmodern Culture', *Theology* 80/5 (1999), 28–36.

[83] It is not easy to see Blair as the embodiment of the 'Christian Socialist' tradition. A. Wilkinson, *Christian Socialism: Scott Holland to Tony Blair* (London, 1998).

[84] Malcolm Brown, *After the Market: Economics, Moral Agreement and the Churches' Mission* (Oxford and Bern, 2004), 22. The entire book is relevant to this theme.

[85] The 1987 general election, for example, had seen statements from Christian politicians in the three main political parties. John Selwyn Gummer, Eric Heffer and Alan Beith, *Faith in Politics* (London, 1987).

Scargill at Bishopthorpe palace, but to little consequence. In Wales, also during the coal strike, with feelings running high and where a taxi-driver had been killed, clergy and ministers had held secret talks with South Wales area leaders of the miners. They advocated an independent body which would plan the coalfield responsibly but protect social values and cohesion.[86] The search was on, joined by the Anglican and Roman Catholic archbishops, for what was described as an equitable peace. It was not achieved. Such endeavours were no more successful than had been other initiatives in 1926, and for the same reasons.

v. Christian Business: John Paul II in Britain

It had come to be assumed that an archbishop of Canterbury would pay a visit to a pope. The 'success' or otherwise of such visits was a matter both of personality and of the ambient ecclesiastical climate worldwide. Donald Coggan visited Paul VI for a few days in April 1977. At the age of 65, he had become archbishop three years earlier, having been translated from York and having previously been bishop of Bradford.[87] Coggan had a supportive wife, herself one of the first women 'readers'.[88] It was the case, however, that the Church of England's 1975 decision that it saw no objection in principle to the ordination of women, amongst other factors, inevitably made his visit to Rome more difficult than that of his predecessor. By 1977 both churches had had some time to mull over the 'Agreed Statements' which had emerged from the work of ARCIC. In a 'Common Declaration' the two leaders agreed that theological dialogue should continue but also, since it was reaffirmed that organic unity should be the objective, practical steps to that end should be encouraged. Preaching in Rome on the evening before he met the pope, the archbishop stated his belief that joint participation in the sacrament of Christ's body and blood would make evangelism more effective. Some thought it impolitic of Coggan to state publicly what he believed. He had what *The Times* called a 'headlong approach'.

In March 1976 George Hume, in religion Basil, the 53-year-old abbot of Ampleforth, near York, was installed as archbishop of Westminster, a post he held for twenty-three years. He left the altar to embrace non-Roman church leaders. Afterwards, he and his brother Benedictine monks sang the old Latin Vespers in Westminster Abbey—the first time this had happened since the

---

[86] D. Densil Morgan, *The Span of the Cross: Christian Religion and Society in Wales, 1914–2000* (Cardiff, 1999), 269–71.

[87] M. Pawley, *Donald Coggan* (London, 1987).

[88] She was the first archbishop's wife to receive a biography. A. Arnott, *Wife to the Archbishop* (London, 1976). Her successor, if an author had contemplated her biography, would not have wished it to have such a title.

Reformation. He had known Coggan well as a 'neighbour' in Yorkshire and had attended his enthronement in Canterbury. Two months later, he was appointed cardinal. He did not seem very like his predecessors. He had a quiet authority stemming both from his spiritual discipline and social ease. He was not Irish, though he was not as 'typically English' as he appeared. His mother was French. He had taught A-level French, and European History at Ampleforth where he had himself been at school. His 'continent' lacked the customary firm Roman impress. He had not studied at the College of the Venerable Bede in Rome but at the University of Fribourg in Switzerland. No previous archbishop of Westminster had coached a school 1st XV (in which side he had himself starred as a boy). His father, a medical knight, was mildly Anglican. Priests might wonder what a monk knew about running parishes but, with a brother-in-law who was Cabinet Secretary, he might have picked up something about running the country. From the Vatican, it seemed he was worth the risk, though it would have to get used to being told that the English did things differently. There were even those, following the inconvenient death of John Paul I, who supposed he might be history's second English pope. The fact that he said that he would not have been very good at being pope was often deemed a substantial commendation. Early on, he reiterated what had often been said before, namely that Christians who were divided from each other were in a poor position to preach peace and reconciliation to an unimpressed world.[89]

The British Isles were troubled. Notwithstanding the Silver Jubilee of Queen Elizabeth II, celebrated in June 1977, which suggested confident continuity, Britain seemed to be sliding to occupy the position of 'the sick man of Europe'. In December 1976, inflation had reached 17 per cent. Two years later, the country endured what came to be known as 'The Winter of Discontent' as government wrestled with pay policy and industrial unrest. Membership of 'Europe' remained contentious. So did the constitutional structure of Britain. In March 1979, votes were held in Wales and Scotland on proposals for devolution. They failed, very clearly in Wales, but in Scotland only because the size of the majority did not pass the stipulated hurdle. Amongst Presbyterian social activists, in the years leading up to the vote, it was often thought likely that Geoffrey Shaw might have become Scotland's First Minister in a new Parliament. An Edinburgh divinity graduate, he had thrown himself into social work in Glasgow before becoming convener of the then new Strathclyde Regional Council.[90] The

---

[89] Tony Castle, ed., *Basil Hume: A Portrait* (London, 1986); Clifford Longley, 'George Haliburton Hume' in *Oxford Dictionary of National Biography*; Anthony Howard, *Basil Hume: The Monk Cardinal* (London, 2005).

[90] R. Ferguson, *Geoff: The Life of Geoffrey M. Shaw* (Gartocharn, 1979); John Harvey, *Bridging the Gap* (Edinburgh, 1987). Shaw died prematurely in 1978.

issue of 'devolution' would be unlikely to make an early political return, but some observers supposed it unwise to presume that the structure of Britain, and the relationships between its peoples, had been settled for all time. The condition of Northern Ireland, at this particular juncture, as has already been indicated, appeared 'insoluble'. It poisoned relations between the United Kingdom and the Republic. Four months after Hume's installation, the British ambassador in Dublin was assassinated.

The prime minister to be grappling since April 1976 with these apparently interlocking crises was James Callaghan. In his own person, he knew some of their constituent elements in his bones. Portsmouth-born, of a Birmingham-born father who had served in the Royal Navy—in which he had also served during the war. His father, however, was of Irish descent. It had been Callaghan, as home secretary in 1969, who had sent in British troops to Northern Ireland, an action, whatever the subsequent course of events, initially designed to protect the non-Unionist population. He had become a Cardiff MP in 1945 and, over thirty years representing his constituency, he knew how much Wales had changed in this time. His mother had been a keen and committed Baptist and he had been raised in a chapel ethos. By this juncture, however, his early faith had soured. *A House Divided*, his account of Northern Ireland, revealed that he was among those unimpressed by the healing capacity of religion.[91]

The pope and Robert Runcie had met for the first time in Accra, Ghana, in May 1980. It illustrated how both leaders were projecting their respective Communions 'away from home'. Their assignations in Africa were for separate purposes, but an encounter was rather hastily cobbled together. The pope's retinue was significantly larger than the archbishop's. This was not, however, the occasion for a deep exchange. John Paul II simply said that he did not understand much that went on in western theology and attitudes. He had spent his ministry in an atheistic country and saw communism as the enemy in the East. However, he also conveyed his criticism of self-indulgent consumer hedonism, which he equated with the West. This yearning for some kind of 'Third Way', of course, had already been publicly articulated on many occasions, though pinning down what it entailed was proving difficult. Both men were sizing each other up. A visit to Britain might be full of significance. Who should invite him? Who would he be visiting? The foreign secretary did not seem notably enthusiastic. There was tricky diplomacy. The 'official' invitation was presented in person by Cardinal Hume and Derek Worlock, since 1976 archbishop of Liverpool, a man deeply knowledgeable about Vatican ways. The queen

---

[91] James Callaghan, *A House Divided: The Dilemma of Northern Ireland* (London, 1973). His autobiography is *Time and Chance* (London, 1987). Kenneth O. Morgan, *Callaghan: A Life* (Oxford, 1997).

and the duke of Edinburgh paid a state visit to the Vatican in the following October and referred approvingly to 'the growing movement of unity between the Christian Churches'. The pope, however, Hume told a press conference, would not be making a state visit but a pastoral one to the Roman Catholic community of England and Wales. It was also announced that Cardinal Gray's invitation to Scotland had been accepted. Gray, now seventy, had been archbishop of St Andrews and Edinburgh since 1951. The first resident cardinal in Scotland since the Reformation— appointed in 1969—Gray had neither the linguistic skill nor quiet charisma of his English colleague. He had not been a speaker of consequence at Vatican II, partly because, unusually amongst those assembled, he could not cope with Latin. He was not going to let Scotland be left out. He had endured six years in Surrey in the 1930s but showed no signs of anglicization. It would be important to get the pope to understand that the church in Scotland was not run, ecclesiastically, from Westminster. One of Gray's surprising qualities was to possess an understanding of the importance of the media.

The visit, lasting five days, took place between 28 May and 2 June 1982, after the FA Cup Final at Wembley, but before the onset of Wimbledon. It was expensive and even the entrepreneurial ingenuity in disposing of souvenirs of Mr Mark McCormack, at a generous commission, did not generate sufficient funds to cover the costs. Hume settled down to the task of trying to anticipate such banana skins as could turn the event into a disaster. Runcie also settled to the same task, having assured the cardinal that the Pope would be received with affection in England by Anglicans and other Christians.[92] Neither man, in contemplating contingencies, could have been expected to anticipate the Falklands War. Runcie, of course, had no authority to speak on what 'other Christians' might or might not feel. There was a determination that the visit should be a sign that Roman Catholics and Anglicans were really 'getting down to business'. That was the cusp. The pope should experience Anglican worship but could/should it be a Eucharist? Would Canterbury be the place? These were matters for reflection and negotiation. The Anglican Professor Henry Chadwick, then Regius Professor of Divinity at Cambridge, was despatched in January 1982 for direct conversation with the pope. There was awareness, on all sides, of the delicacy of the situation. If the pope had been present during the Eucharist it would have been interpreted as giving it authenticity—something which would doubtless have pleased some Catholics but upset others. So it would not be possible. Some degree

---

[92] That affection was not universal. David Samuel, a fervent Anglican evangelical, produced *Pope or Gospel?* (London, 1982) for the occasion of the visit.

of recognition of their Orders, for which there were quite high Anglican expectations in the context of the visit, looked unlikely, but the hope was not abandoned.

Perhaps because he had been miserable at the Methodist Sunday school to which his mother had sent him, Runcie had not personally been crestfallen by the failure of Anglican–Methodist unity. In St Albans, he had been president of the local Council of Churches and worked well with its chairman, the Baptist minister Morris West, president of the Baptist Union in 1979–80 and moderator of the Free Church Federal Council in 1981–2.[93] Yet, courtesies apart, it was a fresh accommodation with Rome that was at the top of Runcie's agenda. Indeed, it was Hume who did not want the Free Churches to feel left out. He addressed the Federal Council, meeting in his native city of Newcastle in March 1982, urging that Christians should not only pray for reunion but come together to pray into reunion. The process of working to achieve full organic union should not obscure the profound unity which baptism already brought.[94] He received a cordial reception and had 'prepared the way' for the imminent presence of the pope. David Sheppard, bishop of Liverpool since 1976, wanted Runcie and the pope together to hold two or three great public meetings. He thought it appropriate that 'a Free Churchman of appropriate stature' should appear on the platform with them.

Such combined meetings did not in the event happen, but Sheppard's suggestion is revealing. How was this 'stature' to be determined—and by whom? It was a difficulty which had become ever more pronounced in a media age accustomed to dealing with 'leaders'. Rotating presidents or moderators, normally annually, were here today and gone tomorrow. They left no mark on the public mind. It was a situation of which the Free Churches were conscious, indeed arguably it was accelerating, both ecclesiastically and socially, a sense of their marginality. Donald, Lord Soper, increasingly crippled with arthritis, could no longer be centre stage. He had stepped down from being superintendent of the West London Mission at the age of 75 in 1978, by which date its congregations had dramatically dwindled. Amongst the next generation of Methodists, perhaps the most 'public' figure, through his broadcasting, lecturing and preaching, was Donald English. In 1978, at the age of 47, one of the three youngest men ever to have held the post, he was elected president of the Conference. He

---

[93] W.M.S. West, *Baptists Together* (London, 2000), 10.

[94] A few months earlier, at Lima in Peru, the Faith and Order Commission of the World Council of Churches agreed, after very long gestation, a document on *Baptism, Eucharist and Ministry* in which two English representatives had played a prominent part, the Anglican Mary Tanner and the Baptist Morris West. Writing in the Catholic review *One in Christ* West regarded himself as having taken part, over a long time, in producing an 'ecumenical miracle'. West, *Baptists Together* (London, 2000), 24–5.

became leader of the Methodist Home Mission Division in 1982. In a step without precedent, he become president again in 1990, perhaps in part an indication that a 'public face' was increasingly necessary. What was significant, both about English and about Leslie Griffiths, appointed minister of Wesley's Chapel in 1996, was that they had spent substantial periods outside the British Isles, in Africa and Haiti respectively. Another Methodist with a 'profile' beyond his own denomination, where he was a long-serving secretary of Conference, was Kenneth Greet. However, the Free Churches could not solve this problem without in the process abandoning their 'democratic' sense of the 'mind of the church' evolving, however muddily and muddledly, in the hands of men and women some of whom might perhaps not be of 'appropriate stature'.

Jeering Protestants still existed, as Runcie found when he was interrupted on a visit to his native city in March 1982, but most 'other Christians' recognized in John Paul II a man of exceptional personal stature. He had survived an attempt on his life in the previous year. Even so, charisma could perhaps be carried too far. Leadership was one thing, a cult another. The pope, some noted with suspicion, had begun acting at the age of eight.[95] Runcie's successor at St Albans, however, thought it unlikely that a few days of papal over-exposure, as he put it, would sweep Anglicans unthinkingly into the arms of Rome. The Englishman, he supposed, was too canny to let that happen (he did not speculate on whether the Englishwoman shared this canniness). It was a reassuring acknowledgement, for those who needed it, that *au fond* Anglicanism and Englishness really had a shared base of sense and sentiment.

It was possible, however, that English Catholics also had a share in this canniness. They lived in a democracy, indeed one thought by some observers to be so eager to express and obstruct that it was one becoming, in the phrase of the moment, 'ungovernable'. They knew that their church was not a democracy nor likely to become one and, in this sense, were used to inhabiting different homes, but even so 'consulting the faithful' had to be made to mean something. The National Pastoral Congress of England and Wales meeting in Liverpool in May 1980 chaired by Archbishop Worlock was to be an expression of the notion that the church existed in dialogue.[96]

---

[95] That he had also turned his hand to writing plays (originally under a pseudonym) had also become known. Arrangements were in hand for one of them, *The Jeweller's Shop*, to be staged in London to coincide with his visit.

[96] *Liverpool 1980: Official Report of the National Pastoral Congress* (1981); George Moyser, 'Patterns of Social Representation in the National Pastoral Congress', *Month* (March 1980), 95–101; Michael Hornsby-Smith and Elizabeth Cordingley, *Catholic Elites: A Study of the Delegates to the National Pastoral Congress* (Guildford, 1983); P. Jennings, 'An Assessment of the National Pastoral Congress', *Clergy Review* (July 1980), 233–9; M. Hornsby-Smith 'Two Years After: Reflections on Liverpool 1980', *New Blackfriars* (June 1982), 252–60.

Such an assembly had been a long time coming, but it had now arrived. It was a gathering of some two thousand lay people, full of articulate middle-class enthusiasm, with an almost equal balance of men and women. Loyalty to the church could be shown to be perfectly compatible with particular criticisms. The suggestions, not in themselves surprising, had been frequently advanced in 'Catholic Renewal' circles. Some 'development' was looked for on the question of birth control and 'easement' of admission to Mass of Catholics who had remarried after divorce (a steadily rising number).[97] Limited inter-communion, the establishment of communion of both kinds as the norm, the ordination of married men (and even the ordination of women) were additionally included as worthy of consideration. It was time to join the British Council of Churches. This was a 'liberal' agenda which could be portrayed by an 'old guard' as being bent on turning Catholics into Anglicans. 'Traditionalist' voices had been raised for some time against 'the enemy within'.[98] If, however, the Congress was indeed 'the mind of the Catholic laity' on such matters it would nevertheless fall to Hume and Worlock to present the propositions to the pope. It was in the context of doing so that they gave him the invitation to visit England and Wales. Here was a 'national' voice—that of 'England and Wales', the 'national' entity which the church continued to embody in its structure—which the pope, serenely sitting above nationality, had to consider. The presenters could hardly have supposed that the document would be eagerly received. And so it proved. It fell to Hume and Worlock to try to keep the spirit, if not the substance, of Liverpool alive.[99] In retrospect, particularly for those involved, the National Pastoral Congress represented not the firm establishment of enduring internal dialogue but rather the highpoint from which, twenty years later, much of the excitement and inspiration had 'ebbed away'.[100] It was against this background that what the pope said on these matters, and how he said it, was as much a matter of delicacy within the Catholic Church as it was in its inter-church implications.

[97] Timothy J. Buckley, 'English Catholics and Divorce' in M. Hornsby-Smith, ed., *Catholics in England 1950–2000: Historical and Sociological Perspectives* (London, 1999), 199–218.

[98] Adrian Hastings, *A History of English Christianity 1920–1990* (London, 1991), 638–9 characterizes 'traditionalists' as equally 'loyal'. Hastings, as a 'liberal', was of course retrospectively assessing controversies in which he himself was active at the time.

[99] In assessing Hume, his obituarist in *The Times* (18 June 1999) judiciously commented that 'his anti-dogmatic manner persuaded Catholic liberals that he was at heart one of them; and many conservatives assumed that he was a theological liberal too. But he was seen in Rome as a safe pair of hands: and whatever his personal sympathy for individuals, he always defended the authority of Rome in the end...'.

[100] Philip L. Daniel, 'Have We Seen the Death of Dialogue?' in Hornsby-Smith ed., *Catholics in England, 1950–2000*, 97. The author, a civil servant, was prominent in many Catholic lay organizations.

Also in the background was the 'Final Report' of the Anglican–Roman Catholic International Commission (ARCIC) which concluded its meetings at Windsor in September 1981.[101] The Commission, though 'international', had a majority of English members. It concluded by saying that in its view the two churches had grown together in faith and charity as, over the years, they had together explored the Eucharist, ministry and authority (on the last they had reflected further and this had led to a formulation which tried to reach a 'balanced' presentation). The need for a primacy in a united church could be acknowledged but its *modus operandi* should fully embrace 'collegiality'. The two co-chairmen, introducing the report on 29 March 1982, spoke with academic caution and commended their findings to their churches (being themselves without authority on the 'authority' of which they spoke) over the coming years. However, it took only one day for the Congregation for the Doctrine of the Faith, under the presidency of Cardinal Ratzinger, to conclude, by means of a press release, that there was no substantive agreement. Some of the formulations, it was said, not only could not easily be reconciled with Catholic doctrine but, apparently, left themselves open to divergent interpretations. Such a swift release, two months before the pope was due in England, blunted expectations. All that could be done, pope and archbishop agreed when they met in Canterbury, was to set up another international commission to further consider the outstanding doctrinal differences.

Ratzinger's press release was not the only disturbance in early April. A day later, Argentine forces invaded the Falkland Islands. Argentina was a 'Catholic country'. William Wolfe, then president of the Scottish National Party, referred to the need to protect the Falkland islanders from 'the cruel and ruthless fascist dictatorship of a Roman Catholic state'.[102] Could the pope come to a country sending a task force, supported by the archbishop of Canterbury in the Lords, to undo this 'armed aggression'? If, however, he cancelled, it could suggest that 'when the chips were down' there was, after all, a 'Catholic International'. There could be no better way of reviving the deep suspicions which the visit was apparently relegating to the past. It may have been the archbishops of Liverpool and Glasgow, who flew to Rome, who persuaded the pope in a private meeting, that the visit should go ahead. A way out was found by re-emphasizing the pastoral purpose of the visit. The pope would meet the queen, but the government would be discreetly

---

[101] William Purdy, *The Search for Unity: Relations between the Anglican and Roman Catholic Churches from the 1950s to the 1970s* (London, 1996). The author was one of the two joint secretaries of ARCIC almost from its origins to the Final Report of 1981. Frederick Bliss, *Anglicans in Rome* (London, 2007) gives an account of the vicissitudes of the Anglican Centre in Rome.

[102] T. Gallagher, *Glasgow: The Uneasy Peace: Religious Tension in Modern Scotland* (Manchester, 1987), 323.

in the background. Even so, this crisis in the South Atlantic produced diplomatic complications all round. Runcie repeated his admiration for British forces. The pope, when he came to Coventry—with its history and its ministry of international reconciliation—denounced all warmongering. Words the pope used, that war should have no place on humanity's agenda for the future, were picked up in the sermon the archbishop delivered in St Paul's Cathedral in July. It was an address which, in the eyes of some correspondents and a section of the press, indicated that Runcie had become a trendy cleric who dabbled in politics. His forthright support for the government in April, however, had upset some 'trendy clerics'. After the war, the British Council of Churches made the first group visit to the Falklands and to Buenos Aires to meet church leaders and politicians—a further demonstration of a determination not to be 'triumphalist'.

The Falklands War complicated the papal visit but did not disrupt the programme. The pope preached in Canterbury Cathedral on 29 May. He talked of the hope of full restoration of unity in faith and love. The form of the service, which had gone through many drafts, was well-received. Intercessions were led by the archbishop of York, archbishop Methodios of Thyateira, Cardinal Hume and Dr Greet (for the Free Churches). There was judicious clerical hugging. The relationship between two churches and, using Canterbury symbolically, between England and the Vatican, had been moved to a different plane. The heir to the throne was in the congregation. The sun shone.[103]

The pope proceeded on his rounds. He came to Liverpool on Pentecost Sunday, deliberately driving through the Toxteth which had witnessed serious rioting. The pope-mobile arrived first at the Anglican cathedral, where he was greeted by a cheering, clapping and singing congregation drawn from the non-Roman Catholic churches of Merseyside. He gave a blessing and then progressed to the Roman Catholic cathedral, where he celebrated Mass. Bishop Sheppard and Archbishop Worlock took him to be endorsing all they had done since, only slightly acquainted, they had come to the city in 1976. They gave high priority, from the outset, to creating a positive partnership in Christian mission out of the residual sectarianism in a 'hurt city' whose social and political problems occupied press headlines. They not only worked at this on the ground but wrote books about doing

---

[103] There had, of course, been ample opportunity for 'misapprehensions'. A proposal had come to the chapter that a medallion should be struck with the image of the pope on one face and the cathedral on the reverse. It was made clear that it could be approved only if the pope and the archbishop were shown together on one side. Robbins, 'The Twentieth Century, 1898–1994' in Patrick Collinson, Nigel Ramsay and Margaret Sparks, eds., *A History of Canterbury Cathedral* (Oxford, 1995), 338–40.

it. And not only Roman Catholics and Anglicans were 'better together'. A moderator from the Free Churches was specifically assigned to work alongside them. In due course the Merseyside and Region Ecumenical Assembly was constituted.[104] Sheppard had done what no bishop had ever done. Twenty years earlier he had become the first priest to represent England at cricket (before ordination he had captained the side). He had come to Liverpool after six years as bishop of Woolwich, succeeding John Robinson. Previously, he had been for many years warden of the Mayflower Settlement in Canning Town in the East End of London. Worlock had been secretary to no fewer than three archbishops of Westminster before becoming bishop of Portsmouth. He had seemed the obvious candidate to succeed Heenan, but it did not happen. His parents had converted from the Church of England. He had always wanted to be a priest and had never wanted to play cricket for England. Sheppard's background was evangelical but was deemed to be 'broadening'. 'Partnership', therefore, had to be worked at. It did not just 'happen', but if it worked on Merseyside, observers said, it could happen anywhere. There was hope in Hope Street.[105]

In coming to Glasgow, the pope might have experienced a form of the 'Northern Ireland' which he had never visited. The death of Bobby Sands in Northern Ireland in 1981, and other disturbing events there, saw the emergence of a few republican flute-bands in the West of Scotland expressing support for the IRA. On the other side, 'Scottish Loyalists' emerged in 1980 from within the Orange Order in Scotland. Their vice-chairman announced plans 'to smash the Mass' and wreck the papal visit. In the event, however, the promised violence did not materialize. The leadership of the Orange Order had been distancing itself from its more militant members. While devoted to the Reformed Church, its grand secretary, a few years earlier, had claimed that the order was more than an anti-Catholic organization.[106] It was against all terrorist groups, whatever their motivation. So, the pope was able to arrive to a huge gathering, perhaps 300,000 strong, of happy Catholics in Bellahouston Park in Glasgow. The mood seemed to confirm that over the previous thirty years the Catholic condition in the west of Scotland had been transformed. So, in many respects, it had, but in the 1970s there was

[104] The second such moderator was the Methodist, John Newton. See his 'Protestant Non-conformists and Ecumenism' in Alan P.F. Sell and Anthony R. Cross, eds., *Protestant Nonconformity in the Twentieth Century* (Carlisle, 2003), 376–8.

[105] Derek Worlock and David Sheppard, *Better Together: Christian Partnership in a Hurt City* (London, 1988); David Sheppard, *Steps along Hope Street* (London, 2002). Hope Street linked the two cathedrals. The pope passed along it. J. Furnival and A. Knowles, *Archbishop Derek Worlock: His Personal Journey* (London, 1998).

[106] Steve Bruce, 'The Ulster Connection' in Graham Walker and Tom Gallagher, eds., *Sermons and Battle-Hymns: Protestant Popular Culture in Modern Scotland* (Edinburgh, 1990), 245–6.

3. The moderator and the pope: Professor John McIntyre and John Paul II, Edinburgh, 1982

clear evidence of declining numbers, falling birth rates and diminishing vocations.[107] Communities were experiencing economic, cultural and social upheaval. Thomas Winning, archbishop of Glasgow, was a robust man and he needed to be to cope, amongst other matters, with the grave financial problems of the diocese. Ecumenical gestures, however, had to be made. In 1975 he had been the first Catholic priest to address the General Assembly of the Church of Scotland: a tentative first step.[108] Speaking for a moment to the 'larger community of believers in Christ' the pope in Glasgow had asked for a joint pilgrimage 'hand-in-hand'. Both Catholics and Presbyterians knew

[107] Bernard Aspinwall, 'Perennial Problems of Scottish Catholicism: Morale, Resources and Divisions 1820–2000' in Tony Schmitz, ed., *A Garland of Silver: A Jubilee Anthology in Honour of Archbishop Mario Conti* (Aberdeen, 2002), 192–216 gives a personal sketch of these problems. His *The Catholic Experience in North Ayrshire* (2002) provides a detailed account of the Catholic parishes in this area.

[108] Vivienne Bett, *Cardinal Thomas Winning: An Authorised Biography* (Dublin, 2000), 92–3, 138–9.

that Northern Ireland might 'spill over' to Scotland. Leaderships were determined to prevent that happening. They both knew, too, that they were experiencing not dissimilar miseries.[109] Outside New College in Edinburgh, beneath the statue of John Knox, John Paul II was greeted by the moderator and other church leaders.[110] He had blessed angry protestors, perhaps 800 strong, on his way to the meeting. The moderator of the year was John McIntyre, Professor of Divinity in the University of Edinburgh. A quarter of a century earlier, he had accepted that historical events were in part at least the outcome of the free decisions of persons, decisions which could not be reduced to 'forces' whether economic, social or political. It was impossible, he thought, to know fully what the motives were which motivated the behaviour of persons.[111] At this moment, perhaps those words came back to his subtle mind.

The pope could not do other than round off his tour by coming to Cardiff. There was a comparable welcome, though not on the Scottish scale, and there were no significant anti-Catholic protests. Roman Catholic and Anglican bishops had begun to meet reasonably regularly in Wales over the previous decade. A new archbishop, John Aloysius Ward, was to come to the metropolitan see of Cardiff in 1983 from the diocese of Menevia. It could be expected that within a few years he would be addressing the governing body of the Church in Wales, as indeed happened. Plans were afoot to reorganize the diocesan structure of the Roman Catholic Church in Wales. The pope said farewell in Welsh. The visit was over. It had been historic. It had occupied the headlines. It encouraged the faithful. But, two decades later, did it 'make a difference'?

vi. Affectionate Friction: Struggling for Unity

John Paul II was still on his global peregrinations in 2000 but he did not come to the British Isles again. The atmosphere, on his departure, was excited. His visit had served to dispel some stereotypes and disperse some historical legacies. The diplomatic relations between the United Kingdom and the Vatican were upgraded.[112] It was possible to believe that the

---

[109] T.M. Devine, *The Scottish Nation 1700–2000* (London, 1999), 582–4 sees the change in denominational allegiances in the context of economic restructuring and political realignment.

[110] This meeting, apparently, was a late rearrangement. The Church of Scotland had indicated that it would not have been appropriate for a representative, as had been suggested, to join *English* non-Catholic leaders in Canterbury. The pope had to understand that what happened there was an *English* occasion.

[111] John McIntyre, *The Christian Doctrine of History* (Edinburgh, 1957), 114.

[112] This matter had great delicacy in relation to Ireland. The Irish government expressed great concern that Irish Catholics would feel much bitterness if those of the Six Counties were placed under the jurisdiction of a Nuncio or Internuncio in London. Emphasis on the unity of the Irish

churches would collectively escape the weight of their pasts. Ecumenism, the departing pope had told the bishops in Liverpool, was not only of the intellect, it was a matter of the affections. Affections had indeed been displayed, but it was soon clear that intellects would not be curbed. What at the time had seemed like a new beginning before long appeared to be an evanescent moment. Undertakings and statements made in all quarters at the time were not disingenuous but it looked as though the future would again be a matter of working parties and protracted discussion. There would be ARCIC documents to consider further, and then more from other quarters. There was no lack of skilled academic expertise able to demark denominational doctrinal divisions with precision—but did it all matter? 'Already', one experienced Baptist noted in 1982, 'numbers of church members move easily from one denomination to another when they change their place of living'.[113] An analysis in the same year found it difficult to offer *one* explanation, with regard to ecumenism, for the elements of support, indifference and opposition—all of which could be clearly seen.[114] The intricate steps involved in the gradualist 'Covenant for Unity' which had been drawn up in the wake of the failure of the Anglican–Methodist proposals proved too complicated and had failed by 1982. There were, of course, the mechanisms of contact to be looked at again, most notably the British Council of Churches—certainly if Roman Catholics were to join either it or some refashioned body. What was difficult, perhaps impossible, was to bring the various levels of contact and understanding into purposeful articulation. 'Not Strangers but Pilgrims' was an exercise, backed by the British Council of Churches and the Catholic Bishops' Conference, set on foot during Lent 1986 in which some 70,000 local inter-church house groups composed of 'ordinary churchgoers' were to consider 'what on earth the church was for'. There was a notable participation in this exercise from the black-led churches—a further illustration of 'mainstreaming'. Local 'Pilgrims', in the process, found love and friendship but felt the institutional weight above and beyond them. Speaking in Scotland, where earlier he had been an Episcopalian rector for five years, John Habgood, who had moved from being bishop of Durham to being archbishop of York in 1983, acknowledged, in the aftermath, that the clear message that had come through was that people wanted to be closer together but they valued

church was a way of advancing the cause of political unity. In fact the *sui generis* diplomatic relations with the Vatican remained unaltered even when a Pro-Nunciature was established in Britain in 1982. D. Ó Corráin, *Rendering to God and Caesar: The Irish Churches and the Two States in Ireland 1949–73* (Manchester, 2006), 59–63.

[113] L.G. Champion in Keith Clements, ed., *Baptists in the Twentieth Century* (London, 1982), 14.

[114] Christopher Lewis, 'Unity: A Sociological Perspective' in Rupert Davies, ed., *The Testing of the Churches 1932–1952: A Symposium* (London, 1982), 157. The contributors to this volume were all conscious that they were writing half a century after the conclusion of Methodist union in 1932.

their differences.[115] They wanted 'you at the top' to get on with it, but those so positioned did not quite know what to do.

The papal visit, however, made explicit that a 'settlement' of the 'British church question' could not be 'made in Britain'. Galling though it might be, a pope, certainly this pope, did not think the British Isles constituted the centre of the Christian universe. There could be no special deals. In the eyes of 'the historian', only five years later, it was already being concluded that the ecumenical movement was 'the great ecclesiastical failure of our time'.[116] Clearly, the absence of substantive 'organic unions' would support this conclusion. So much effort by devoted 'ecumaniacs', so many conferences, so many publications, but all had apparently had so little tangible outcome. For those who felt the existing church divisions most keenly, and continued to regard them as a major hindrance to the promotion of the gospel, it was difficult to know how to proceed. One illustration of this lies in the discussion about the future of the British Council of Churches. In 1990, now with Roman Catholic participation, it became the Council of Churches for Britain and Ireland, a significantly pan-insular title. However, quite what the structure of this new body should be and what 'remit' it had, not to mention financial issues, was problematic from the outset. Individual member churches in the old council had been apprehensive about the way in which, on occasion, it had appeared to be claiming to 'speak for' the churches. Roman Catholic involvement necessarily meant that the new body had to be careful in this regard. That involvement, not unexpectedly, had triggered unease and some outright opposition to 'Churches Together' amongst evangelical constituencies, particularly amongst Baptists, although eventually most churches in the Baptist Union had decided that Roman Catholics were fellow-pilgrims. Cardinal Hume, in 1998, addressed the annual Baptist Assembly and he received a prolonged ovation.[117]

It was evident that the new body could facilitate the collection and dissemination of information, particularly on social and international issues, which it would be silly for individual member churches to try to do on their own. It had to try to establish its role, however, at a time of weariness with 'top-down' initiatives. That expressed itself in the strong desire of the nations of the British Isles to have their own 'ecumenical instruments'—and this saw the formation of ACTS (Action of Churches Together in Scotland), CTE (Churches Together England), CYTUN (Churches Together in Wales)

---

[115] John Habgood, *Confessions of a Conservative Liberal* (London, 1988). Habgood had the unique experience of having been principal of Queen's College, Birmingham when it turned into an ecumenical college.

[116] Or at least of one such, John Kent, *The Unacceptable Face: The Modern Church in the Eye of the Historian* (London, 1987), 203. H. J. Hanham puts 'Kent in Context: Some Personal Reflections' in Stuart Mews, ed., *Modern Religious Rebels: Presented to John Kent* (London, 1993).

[117] Ian Randall, *English Baptists of the Twentieth Century* (London, 2005), 495.

alongside the existing Irish Council of Churches. Further thinking led in 1999 to a rebranding as Churches Together in Britain and Ireland, but financial and structural issues would not go away. These difficulties were compounded by the fact that, to an extent, the 'mainline' churches had taken 'the ecumenical dimension' on board, at national level, in the way in which they functioned. And, at local level, instances of co-operation which had been fostered under the heading Local Ecumenical Projects were redesignated as Local Ecumenical Partnerships in the mid-1990s. Some of these arrangements, which required careful but cordial planning, seemed to work well, especially in new towns where there were no 'heritages' to be wrestled with in terms of buildings and sentiments. In new Milton Keynes, for example, the Development Corporation made available a prime site for the building of a central church to be used jointly by all the mainstream churches. It was opened in 1992 and used for worship by Roman Catholics, Anglicans, Baptists, Methodists and United Reformed Church Christians. The clergy and ministers worked as an integrated team under the leadership of a moderator, the first of whom happened to be a Baptist. In old Swindon, different arrangements applied. Merseyside was different again. By definition, 'local partnerships' were local—some 600 were in existence over England and Wales. Their vitality often depended on the ethos of a diocese as established by particular bishops and their equivalents in other churches. All of this, however, represented 'inter-church co-operation' of a meaningful kind. Christians were friends in the way they had not invariably shown themselves to be. It did not, however, constitute 'church unity' in a single structure.[118] It did not seem likely, at the millennium, that one would emerge. Further areas of disagreement, as will now be noted, within and between churches, had sharply arisen in the two decades since the papal visit. These issues made it seem unlikely, from the perspective of the millennium, that 'organic unity' was at all imminent.[119]

vii. *Women: Accepting and Rejecting*

The question of the ordination of women to the priesthood in the Church of England had rumbled on since the General Synod had decided in 1975 that there could be no objection to this step, but there had been no

---

[118] Hugh Montefiore thought that John 17.20–23a, so often simplistically translated as 'that they may all be one' clearly was not a prayer for a particular form of outward or even simple organic unity but a spiritual unity of believers which could be expressed in a way best adapted to the circumstances in which the church found itself. Hugh Montefiore, *So Near and Yet so Far: Rome, Canterbury and ARCIC* (London, 1986), 130. J.S. Peart-Binns, *Bishop Hugh Montefiore* (London, 1990).

[119] Such a conclusion, however, should not be taken to imply that ecumenical discussion had come to an end.

immediate enabling legislation brought forward. The capacity of the issue to divide, and perhaps destroy, the Church of England needed little rehearsal. It was also one, however, where decisions being made elsewhere in the Anglican Communion reduced the scope for indefinite procrastination, though the fact that they were being made in this autonomous fashion was itself a commentary on its own character. Some thought that no decision should have been taken anywhere before the whole Communion had come to a common mind, however long that might take. There was also the even more fundamental question of whether the Church of England was 'entitled' to take an action which would, in all likelihood, put itself at variance with the 'universal church'. A Vatican Declaration in 1976 had reiterated that, in fidelity to the example of the Lord, the church did not consider herself authorized to admit women to priestly ordination. The Old Catholics, almost unanimously, took the same view and in 1978 declined to share in consecrations of bishops in those provinces of the Anglican Communion which had decided to ordain women. The Anglican–Orthodox Joint Doctrinal Commission in July 1978 recorded that by ordaining women Anglicans would sever themselves from continuity in Apostolic faith and spiritual life. Dialogue with the Orthodox, on which Anglicans had set much store over decades, was being brought to a point of 'acute crisis'. The 1978 Lambeth Conference declared its acceptance of provinces where women were and were not ordained and urged mutual respect. There was, however, the tricky question of what was to happen to women lawfully ordained abroad who came to England. In the same year the General Synod debated a motion which requested legislation to remove the barriers to the ordination of women to the priesthood and their consecration to the episcopate. Voting in the House of Bishops and the House of Laity was in favour but the House of Clergy was against. The same division occurred the following year in relation to a temporary measure which, on certain conditions, would have allowed women priests ordained abroad to exercise their priesthood in England.

The battle lines were fairly clearly drawn. The pleas for charity were not universally respected. Lobbying began in earnest. In July 1979 the Movement for the Ordination of Women was founded with the bishop of Manchester, Stanley Booth-Clibborn, as moderator and Margaret Webster as secretary. It produced literature, and subsequently a journal, in support of the cause. Members could also be seen in public places with banners. Contrary bodies, the Association for the Apostolic Ministry, and Women against the Ordination of Women, followed a few years later. The latter's arguments were particularly directed against the 'secular feminism' which seemed to be creeping in everywhere in the church. 'Christian feminism' should not be seduced by it. So, just as one side wanted to show that some men wanted ordination for women as ardently as some women, the other wanted to show that some women opposed it as ardently as some men.

What St Paul really thought about the place of women, and whether, if one could be certain, it still mattered, filled many columns. Not much new was being said, on one side or the other. Fundamentally, the nature of 'tradition' and 'the authority of the Bible' were at stake. Those of a Catholic disposition, alarmed by what 'unilateral' action would do for relations with Rome, did not think tradition was malleable.[120] The prospect of women at the altar was deeply alarming. Those of an evangelical disposition, who were not so troubled by Rome's reaction, thought the sight of women in the pulpit deeply alarming. But not all Catholics or Evangelicals were alarmed by either of these things. The fall-out did not divide into straight-forward categories. Was this all a matter of the generations? Not so, apparently. Some ardent young female opponents were produced, but they were matched by some elderly male supporters. Some thought that to proceed would lead to a debilitating split. Opponents wished to assert the headship of men over women and their proper subordination. A male priesthood would testify to the purposes of God in creation and redemp-tion. Supporters thought it obscured the gospel in twentieth-century Eng-land. Some argued that not to proceed would lead to a debilitating haemorrhage, particularly because of the 'signal' it gave to women. Some considered that it was not in the least important that the church seemed to be going quite against 'gender equality'. Some were certain that to do so would confirm the impression that the church was 'stuck in the past'. Some feared that the whole nature of the priesthood would be upset. Some hoped it would. Some thought that the whole affair was really a technical question of 'personpower' planning and were not greatly excited. Some thought that 'feminism', in its imperial march across the globe, wanted to go far beyond the achievement of the ordination of women. The more powerful 'Chris-tian feminism' became, 'the more abundant will be the Church's bitter harvest of division, anger, suspicion and all uncharitableness'.[121] In some quarters, nothing less than the wholesale reconstruction of Christian belief was thought to lurk beneath the apparently plausible, but surely 'secular', aspiration to 'equal rights'. Beneath opposition of that kind some detected a

---

[120] In *Women Priests: Obstacles to Unity?* (London, 1986) the Catholic Truth Society published, amongst other items, a 1984–6 exchange of letters from John Paul II, Robert Runcie and Jan Willibrands (President of the Vatican Secretariat for the Promotion of Christian Unity).

[121] William Oddie, *What Will Happen to God? Feminism and the Reconstruction of Christian Belief* (London, 1984), 155. The author, at the time an Anglican priest, subsequently became a Roman Catholic and, for a time, editor of *The Catholic Herald*. In her *Theology and Feminism* (Oxford, 1990), Daphne Hampson thought patriarchy could not be eliminated from the Christian tradition. Subsequent writing made it clear that, largely for this reason, she could no longer find Christianity acceptable. Lisa Isherwood and Dorothea McEwan, *An A to Z of Feminist Theology* (Sheffield, 1996).

not very thinly disguised misogyny.[122] Some thought that it was a mistake to be bullied into delay by the known disapproval of Rome. There were believed to be millions of Catholics world-wide who were sympathetic to women priests. Sooner or later, though probably later, the Vatican would have to find a way out of the intransigence on this issue which John Paul II displayed. The Church of England should not be afraid to 'lead the way'.

Given these and other pertinent opinions, it is not surprising that tension grew in the mid-1980s and thereafter as the bishops and the General Synod wrestled with the matter in various further documents, discussions and proceedings. Factions proliferated. The lobbying and arm-twisting that went on was not very edifying, but passions had become engaged.[123] Clergy and laity let it be known that they were 'considering their positions' if the church were to be so foolish as to proceed to ordain. It was manifest that no agreement which pleased all parties was possible. Runcie seemed disinclined to give a clear-cut 'lead'. He was not enthusiastic for women's ordination but neither was he fundamentally opposed. It was possible to ordain women, but it was not worth it if in the process the Church of England was destroyed. He was not anxious to hurry along. His propensity to occupy the fence upset both sides. Graham Leonard, now bishop of London, led the opposition with unbridled determination.

Another of pluralism's puzzles had presented itself. Just how much difference could one church accommodate? In 1987, 'Cost of Conscience' had been formed by clergy opposed to the ordination of women. What would the future be for clergy who remained opposed and what provision would be made for those who left? The secular press became greatly interested as the prospect of years of litigation and dissent lay ahead.[124] A system of 'alternative episcopal oversight' was proposed. In the same year, following the presentation of a further report to Synod, all three Houses approved a motion by the archbishop that a draft measure should be brought forward to ordain women.[125] The following year it was approved by all three Houses (Bishops 28:21; Clergy 137:102; Laity 134:93). Together with draft canons, this was then remitted to diocesan synods for consideration (which was

---

[122] Richard Holloway, ed., *Who Needs Feminism? Men Respond to Sexism in the Church* (London, 1991) contains various reflections on the roles of men and women and their relationships.

[123] Charles Moore, A.N. Wilson and Gavin Stamp, *The Church in Crisis* (London, 1986) is one contemporary assessment. The authors could do no better than copy the title used thirteen years earlier by a clerical commentator Trevor Beeson, *The Church of England in Crisis* (London, 1973). Monica Furlong, *A Dangerous Delight: Women and Power in the Church* (London, 1991).

[124] For example *The Independent*, 29 December 1990.

[125] Supporters of the 1993 Act of Synod, in this respect, regarded it as a lifeline enabling many to stay within the Church of England, but it has been a source of outrage in so far as it seems to discriminate against women priests. Paul Avis, ed., *Seeking the Truth of Change in the Church: Reception, Communion and the Ordination of Women* (London, 2004).

overwhelmingly approved, 38 out of 45). One 1992 survey claimed that 90 per cent of English people wished to see women ordained. Further consideration was given in Synod in the summer of 1992, but it had been agreed that the final vote would be held on 11 November 1992. The outcome was uncertain since a two-thirds majority was required. Despite the date, no sudden armistice overtook the speakers on that day. Media interest was intense, leading to the partial broadcasting of the debate, but little new could be said. In the end, the motion was carried in all three Houses (Bishops 39:13; Clergy 176:74; Laity 169:82). The result was indeed tight. It had only needed two lay members to vote the other way and all would have been lost.[126]

The measure then had to go before the ecclesiastical committee of the Commons. In the House itself, it was approved on 29 October in a free vote by 215 to 21 (slightly less than two-thirds of MPs did not deem it appropriate to vote). MPs also backed—195 to 19—plans to compensate those priests who felt that they had to leave the church in consequence of the decision. Opponents explained that their objections were doctrinal. They were not against women. John Gummer, then environment minister, son of a clergyman and a former member of the General Synod, said that he was 'agnostic' on the ordination of women but believed that the Church of England had no right to take what he called a unilateral decision. Many people would be 'forced out' by this decision (and that was to be true in his case). Another minister, Ann Widdecombe, had already joined the Roman Catholic Church in protest at Synod's decision. If women were allowed to give the sacrament, she thought, and be a representative of Christ, 'then you might as well have males representing the Virgin Mary in nativity plays'. She was joined in the lobby by three Democratic Unionist MPs, at least one of whom, the Revd Ian Paisley, seemed disinclined to follow her into the Roman Catholic Church. From the Labour benches, Tony Benn, a true son of his mother, thought that however much the debate was dressed up in ecclesiastical terms it was all about a prejudice against women. The Liberal Democrat Simon Hughes, another former member of the Synod, thought it was a great day for the church, for the nation and 'for the cause which all Christians are here to serve'.[127] A special session of the Synod rubber-stamped the necessary change of law. Its members, on arrival at Church House, Westminster, had been greeted with the spectre of a coffin with the words Church of England daubed on the side and a wreath saying RIP. Five and a half years of legal argument and decades of debate finally came to an end on 22 February.[128]

---

[126] Sean Gill, *Women and the Church of England: From the Eighteenth Century to the Present* (London, 1994), 252–9.

[127] *The Times*, 30 October 1993.

[128] *The Times*, 21 and 23 February 1994.

On 12 March 1994 the first thirty-two women priests were ordained by Bishop Rogerson in Bristol Cathedral.[129] Over the months that followed, ordinations took place in other dioceses. It was reported at the time that about 1,300 women were queuing up to be ordained. Two years later, nearly 1,500 had been. The percentage of clergy who were women began steadily to increase. Women claimed that men and women were returning to church because of the ministry of women priests. Some men claimed that this was just what women would say. Anecdotal evidence was tossed around. Laity, it was said, welcomed the different styles and the emphasis on collaboration which they detected among women.[130] It was also supposed that women were less interested in hierarchy, though the fact that, as yet, there were very few women indeed who were even in its lower echelons was not to be taken to indicate a lack of interest.[131] Ahead still lay the question of their admission to the episcopate. In hospital in York, Dame Christian Howard, founder-member of the Movement for the Ordination of Women, veteran Church Assembly and General Synod member and eager ecumenist, had a purple tea-towel on the wall in her ward proclaiming 'A woman's place is in the House of Bishops'. The first woman bishop was to be consecrated in the United States in 1989. At the Lambeth Conference of 1998 eleven women bishops were present. The bishop of Birmingham said they had been hardly noticed, hastening to add that this was because they had been accepted 'naturally'. Like men, he said, they were a mixed bunch. There had been no rush to consecrate a bishop in the British Isles. There was much talk of watersheds. In the eyes of some clergy interviewed at the time, what had been done was not so much an opportunity for the church to flourish as the only way to prevent it from perishing.[132] The Church of England debate had naturally been followed closely by the other Anglican churches of the British Isles. It was highly likely that they would follow the same course, but they would do so within their own procedures and structures. So it proved.

[129] This diocese, through a succession of bishops, had been very active ecumenically. In 1984 and 1985 there had been parallel Anglican and United Reformed ordinations in Bristol Cathedral. Ronald Bocking, 'Parallel Ordinations (Church of England and the United Reformed Church)', *Journal of the United Reformed Church History Society* 7/5 (October 2004), 329–33.

[130] Hilary Wakeman, ed., *Women Priests: The First Years* (London, 1996) is a collection of experiences.

[131] Carrie Pemberton and Christina Rees, 'Five Years In: Where are Women in the Church of England?' in Andrew Wingate, Kevin Ward, Carrie Pemberton and Wilson Sitshebo, eds., *Anglicanism: A Global Communion* (London, 1998), 22–6; Elaine Graham, *Making the Difference: Gender, Priesthood and Theology* (London, 1995). Natalie K. Watson, *Introducing Feminist Ecclesiology* (Sheffield, 2002).

[132] Mary Loudon, *Revelations: The Clergy Questioned* (London, 1994).

viii. Anglican/English Anxieties

The archbishops of the moment, George Carey at Canterbury and John Habgood at York, pointedly emphasized that the Church of England belonged to the people of England 'not only to those who regularly worship in our churches' and wished there to be harmony and tolerance all round. It had not fallen to Runcie to be in office when the final decision had been made. He was merely visited by one of the leaders of the opposition who wept for an hour in his presence. Bishop-watchers in 1990 had identified Carey as the man to succeed if the clergy and the laity had been allowed to vote. It was estimated, rather ambitiously, that the 'low-church Protestant tradition' made up 80 per cent of the church and that Carey was one of the few 'of that ilk' to have become a bishop in recent times.[133] That was not the only respect in which Carey was unusual. The son of a hospital porter in the East End, he was the first archbishop to have left his 'secondary modern' school at fifteen, not to have gone to Oxford or Cambridge, and to have served in the RAF in Iraq. He had earned himself a Ph.D. Prior to his brief experience as a bishop—of Bath and Wells—he had been principal of the evangelical Trinity Theological College in Bristol. Habgood, at York, was also unusual, though not in the same way. He was the first Etonian archbishop of the century, the first with First Classes in the Natural Science Tripos at Cambridge and the first former atheist. He had turned away from an academic career in pharmacology. Until his appointment as bishop of Durham in 1973, when he was 45, his career had largely been spent in theological colleges—latterly as principal of the ecumenical Queen's College, in Birmingham. He might subsequently have moved to London (the post went to Graham Leonard) and to Canterbury either to succeed Ramsey or, later, Coggan—but no offers were made. Instead, from 1983 until 1995, he served in York. Carey remained in office at the millennium and delivered the millennial message. It fell to these two men, therefore, who plugged into very different networks in English life, to play their different parts in shaping the Anglican future in England.[134] There continued to be vigorous discussion, in which academically distinguished bishops joined, concerning the 'distinctive identity of Anglicanism'.[135] One thing which the protracted debate over the ordination of women brought home was the

[133] Lee and Stanford, *Believing Bishops*, 184.

[134] Carey was characterized as 'Academic who seeks to reach "ordinary folk" ', *The Independent*, 26 July 1990 or, a decade later, as 'People's Primate', *The Times* (2), 19 April 2001.

[135] For example, S.W. Sykes, *The Integrity of Anglicanism* (London, 1978) and *Unashamed Anglicanism* (London, 1995); P.D.L. Avis, *Anglicanism and the Christian Church: Theological Resources in Historical Perspective* (Edinburgh, 1989); R. Hannaford, ed., *The Future of Anglicanism* (Leominster, 1996); A. Warren, ed., *A Church for the Nation? Essays on the Future of Anglicanism* (Leominster, 1992). Succinct statements of Anglican positions appeared in Stephen Sykes, John Booty and Jonathan Knight, eds., *The Study of Anglicanism* (London, 1988, 1998).

extent to which the Church of England, while the *fons et origo* of 'Anglicanism' was no longer the 'pacemaker' in its global evolution.[136] Yet again, as had been the case in each recent appointment, questions were asked about how the archbishop of Canterbury could carry both his national and his international commitments. Both pressed urgently upon him.

The archbishops might be right in supposing that the Church of England belonged to the people of England but what did this mean? Periodically, those who wished to see the 'church and state' question once more subjected to formal constitutional examination pressed their case for disestablishment, but this remained a minority enthusiasm.[137] Who were the 'people of England'? Was the Church of England still an untrumpeted aspect of what it was to be English? Glorious English cathedrals were part of the heritage of England, but they were expensive to maintain. The state, however, did not pay for them. Even if they were part of 'Englishness', their priority had to be as places of worship. The Archbishops' Commission noted that they were 'a spiritual asset available to enormous numbers of people . . . some of whom do not otherwise encounter the ministry of the Church'.[138] Commentators, reflecting on Carey's appointment, noted, as though it were a discovery, that the Church of England was a complex and ancient institution. It embodied a set of Christian values that were historically distinctive. At its best, it limited sectarian exclusiveness, reactionary authoritarianism and vacuous liberalism. It was, *mirabile dictu*, the mirror image of what 'England' was, at its best. *The Independent* published a celebratory photograph of Canterbury Cathedral with the caption, 'a set of values well suited to express the religious genius of the English people'.[139] Other authors, reacting to the General Synod's decision to introduce a book of Alternative Services in 1980, expressed their love and reverence for the work of Cranmer and his contemporaries. The impulse towards new translation and liturgical revision was wholesome, but the matchless masterpieces of the Authorized Version of the Bible and the Book of Common Prayer should not be banished.[140] They were part of the birthright of every English person, not an Anglican preserve. But all those who could be

[136] Kevin Ward, *A History of Global Anglicanism* (Cambridge, 2006) is the most recent assessment.

[137] Two expositions, from different wings of the church, can be found in Peter Cornwell, *Church and Nation: The Case for Disestablishment* (Oxford, 1983) and Colin Buchanan, *Cut the Connexion: Disestablishment and the Church of England* (London, 1994). Cornwell subsequently became a Roman Catholic. Paul Avis, *Church, State and Establishment* (London, 2001) is a recent overview.

[138] *Heritage and Renewal: The Report of the Archbishops' Commission on Cathedrals* (London, 1994), 8.

[139] Keith Ward, 'An Established Morality', *The Independent*, 1 August 1990.

[140] Brian Morris, ed., *Ritual Murder* (Manchester, 1980), 7–9; C.H. Sisson, *Is there a Church of England?* (Manchester, 1993). R.C.D. Jasper and Paul F. Bradshaw, *A Companion to the Alternative Service Book* (London, 1986).

enrolled to this end, the heir to the throne and A.L. Rowse included, might only be manning the last ditch. If so, they had, as company, organists and choirmasters who saw their 'birthright' tunes and hymns being ditched for guitars and 'songs'. The variety of what was on offer, and the increasing impossibility of determining, in any denomination, what form a service of worship might take, was depressing to 'cultured' Christians.[141] Everything was changing. Compilers of hymnbooks staggered to keep up. New every Sunday morning were printed sheets. Alternatively, worshippers gazed, not always in rapture, at trite words projected onto a screen.

Even so, expressing himself proud to be English, Rees-Mogg weighed in with a powerful tribute in 1993 to an Anglican church which embodied one of the greatest cultures in man's history. Peace, justice, tolerance, good nature, democracy—these were the traditional virtues of the English polity. They were built into the Church of England and were valued by many people outside that church—as he was himself.[142] Yet neither church nor nation were perhaps at this juncture 'at their best', sharing a collective grumpiness which reflected a deep uncertainty about the future of inherited structures. In its 'settlement' of the ordination of women to the priesthood the Church of England had endeavoured, through the provision of extended episcopal oversight—'flying bishops'—for those clergy and parishes where women priests were unacceptable, to maintain its capacity for comprehensiveness. Critics of the arrangements, as they began to work in practice, identified a competing rather than a complementary system of authority. It was argued by some that the valued comprehensiveness of the past had actually been made possible within a single hierarchy. Alternative hierarchies were not sustaining comprehensiveness so much as creating parallel churches. There remained cries that both women priests and their opponents were not being 'fully valued'. The question would return.

There had been press speculation for more than a decade, not least by commentators who were themselves Catholics, that the decision to ordain women would result in a mass exodus of priests and laity. In all parts of England there were press reports of clergy who proposed to boycott, or worse, their apostate bishops. In April 1994 Graham Leonard, the former

---

[141] Ian Jones and Peter Webster, 'Anglican "Establishment" Reactions to "Pop" Church Music in England, 1956–c.1990' in Kate Cooper and Jeremy Gregory, eds., *Elite and Popular Religion*, Studies in Church History 42 (Woodbridge, 2006), 429–41. Noting that the majority of Baptist churches in England had opted for 'praise songs', one Baptist author thought this a great mistake. 'Too often, the only criterion for what is sung by God's people, particularly in those fellowships dependent solely on OHPs or video projectors, is popularity, often primarily with the musicians. When any one style of music excludes all others, the church loses some of its universality.' Michael Ball, 'Baptist Praise and Worship', *Baptist Quarterly* 40 (October 2003), 214.

[142] William Rees-Mogg, 'Proud to be English: The Anglican Church Embodies One of the Great Cultures in Man's History', *The Times*, 14 October 1993.

bishop of London, a married man, announced that he had become a Roman Catholic priest as the result of a conditional ordination. Special instructions had arrived from the pope. Leonard departed, he said, in sorrow rather than in bitterness. The heading of the report in *The Times* spoke of his move as being expected to 'inspire a wave of converts', and various numbers were suggested.[143] The ecclesiastical atmosphere was difficult. The duchess of Kent had recently converted to Roman Catholicism. One columnist identified in other sections of the press a powerful corps of journalists who were engaged, he thought, in a 'consistent onslaught on the Church of England'.[144] It was not argued that Cardinal Hume had sanctioned 'corrosive articles' but it seemed that there were those who thought that the 'second spring', so long hoped for, had at last arrived. At one moment, the cardinal himself seemed excited by the prospect. Precise figures for Anglican conversions to Rome are difficult to provide since the position over the following years was not static, and some returned. It was more than a year before the pope approved rules which opened up a 'fast track' for married former Anglican clergy to become Roman Catholic priests and work full-time in parishes. The figure for those departing, by the millennium, may be around 400. Both departure and reception raised difficulties, financial and legal, for Carey and Hume, who were naturally drawn into contact on the matter. It would appear that their dealings were not acrimonious. Even so, there were wounded ecumenical feelings. As departing Anglican priests, for example in 1998, urged 'faithful Anglicans' not to go on attempting 'to revive the corpse of the Church of England', and told parishes to have no part in 'the apostasy of priestesses', the 'Canterbury moment' of 1982 seemed far away.[145]

The corpse of the Church of England was still twitching, indeed, rather to its surprise, ten years after his appointment, *The Times* declared that Carey had 'overcome the forecasters of doom'.[146] The avoidance of doom, however, could not disguise the reality of manifold tensions. The effect of departures to Rome was necessarily to weaken 'Anglo-Catholicism' seen, in so far as it ever had been, as a single 'wing'. There were rival answers as to how, within its remaining ranks, one should go 'forward in faith' or 'affirm'. Evangelicalism, broad church though that itself was, gained in stature and

---

[143] *The Times*, 27 April 1994.

[144] Tim Bradshaw, 'Anglicans Fear the Catholics who Conspire', *The Times*, 29 January 1994. Lord Rees-Mogg, in another column, noted, with dismay, that there was a different inter-church climate.

[145] 'Dissident Vicar Urges "Faithful" Anglicans to Defect', *The Times*, 22 September 1998. Christina Rees, of Women and the Church, the successor organization to the Movement for the Ordination of Women, suspected, though without firm evidence, that the departing priest might not be as safe as he thought. Women priests might come to the Roman Catholic Church as well.

[146] 'Archbishop of Change', *The Times*, 19 April 2001.

significance, though an archbishop from that background judiciously affirmed his appreciation of Catholic values. It was difficult to tell where 'the centre' now lay. The notion, much canvassed by critics in the Runcie years, and which had led to the bizarre and tragic death of an Oxford don arising out of the preface he had written in *Crockford's*—that a liberal clique was in control—no longer seemed to have substance, if it ever had. The church's plurality remained both its glory and its burden.

Carey was anxious, after so much time and attention had been given to the 'woman question', that the church should cease to give the impression that it was preoccupied with itself. It was true that the secular press had been attracted by the issue as by no other—but that was now over. It would take time to gauge the impact of women priests. Some members of what had been an all-male club, even if they had no 'principled' objection to women joining, nevertheless would find it difficult to work alongside women as equals, even in some cases as their superiors. Already, complaints were emerging that some women were being harassed or bullied by their colleagues. Men tended to think such suggestions exaggerated. Whatever the truth, the church was having to accommodate itself to the legal norms and assumptions governing 'human resources' in secular society.

Clergy, of whatever gender, required stipends and expected pensions. In July 1992 a piece in the *Financial Times* reported that £500 million had been wiped off the value of the church's property investments, suggesting that this had arisen from borrowings to fund speculative developments in Britain and the United States just as the market plunged. The Church Commissioners found themselves recipients of hostile mutterings, and more. People, naturally 'eminent' people, 'the Lambeth Group', were appointed by the archbishop in the autumn of 1992 to find out more. The secretary-general of the Synod, Philip Mawer, thought the group would soon realize that 'our institutional arrangements do not facilitate the co-ordinated management of the Church's financial resources. Nor is there any central system of policy direction for the whole Church'.[147] There were immediate issues of balancing income and expenditure to be addressed. Assets had been eroded. What should go? Who should decide? A decision to reduce the superior stipends of the bishops of Durham and Winchester, much mooted in the past, was to be implemented, but scarcely made a dent in the problem. Archbishop Carey admitted at a meeting in April 1994 that he had known in a general way that 'we were overspending at a remarkable rate'. Something had to be done, and done quickly, but any step, as the past had shown, inevitably trod

---

[147] Cited in Andrew Chandler, *The Church of England in the Twentieth Century: The Church Commissioners and the Politics of Reform, 1948–1998* (Woodbridge, 2006), 408. This summary paragraph scarcely does justice to the author's lengthy and subtle analysis of the forces and factors involved.

on the relationship between church and state and between 'the centre' and the dioceses. *Working as One Body*, the report of the Archbishops' Commission on the Organisation of the Church of England, which had been chaired by Michael Turnbull, bishop of Rochester, came through in 1995. Its title was optimistic. Out of the arguments and manoeuvres that followed came a new Archbishops' Council, which began its life in January 1998, to which the Commissioners had to relate. Whether, in consequence, the Church of England would operate as one body was another matter. Discussion of these matters in Synod and elsewhere, not to mention statements by bishops, had brought home what an enormous undertaking maintaining a national parochial structure was. The laity were to be repeatedly told that they had to pay more. *The Times* talked of 'The Church' needing to 'renew the historical alliance with the laity which has always been its best hope'. The financial losses should be a stimulus to reform not an excuse for Anglicans to resign themselves to inevitable institutional decline.[148] But if they were to provide more resources might they not want to 'monitor' the effectiveness of their clergy? Whose church was it?[149]

Against this background of financial uncertainty, any notion that things would 'settle down' after the ordination of women was short-lived. Issues in relation to sexuality would not go away, either in the Church of England or in other churches: marriage, divorce, cohabitation, the family, abortion, homosexuality. In relation to all of them, there were two aspects.[150] How should the churches respond to what the state, at any particular juncture, decreed on these matters and how did the churches enjoin their members to conduct themselves? On the former, as had been evident in earlier discussion, the state had moved in an apparently inexorable 'liberal' direction. It did not purport to base what was legal upon its conformity with 'Christian tradition'. The consequences for social behaviour of such decisions might, or might not, be judged to be deplorable. If they were, they might have to be altered but only on pragmatic grounds. The churches, in a democratic society, appeared to have accepted that 'Christian standards' could not be enforced. They might be amongst voices urging the modification of existing legislation but without a sense that it could be made to

---

[148] *The Times*, 21 April 1995.

[149] Its continuing national status, and the scale of the finance involved, necessarily put the Church of England in a special position, but the balancing of income and expenditure was a matter for grave concern in all churches. From time to time this led to explosions of discontent with the still pervasive reality of what was called 'the Christendom church'. It was time to liberate the laity from clericalism and conformism to play their full part in the 'diaconal church' (though it was recognized that not all lay people seemed eager for liberation). David Clark, *Breaking the Mould of Christendom: Kingdom Community, Diaconal Church and the Liberation of the Laity* (London, 2005).

[150] Fuller discussion of these matters is in G.I.T. Machin, *Churches and Social Issues in Twentieth-Century Britain* (Oxford, 1988), 221–6.

conform in its essence to those standards. There were, however, ironies in abundance. In 1988 the three Houses of the Church of England Synod approved a measure which would permit remarried divorcees to be ordained (or existing such clergy to remarry). It was the Ecclesiastical Committee of Parliament that threw it out on the grounds that the indissolubility of marriage was being abandoned in face of current trends. Subsequent resubmission, however, meant that the measure was passed in 1990. The exception might be the question of abortion. All churches had reservations and worries on what the law had allowed since the passage of the Abortion Act in 1967, but the Roman Catholic Church not only expressed its opposition but sought its amendment. It was a Roman Catholic Liberal Democrat MP, David Alton, who was able, in 1990, after a long parliamentary battle, to carry a bill which reduced the period within which abortion was permitted to twenty-four weeks. It was an issue on which the church was very willing to use such 'political muscle' as it possessed and on which it was determined to ensure that doctors who had conscientious objections could not be required to carry out operations.

How the members of the churches should interpret 'Christian standards' for themselves was the other side of the coin. All churches, at all levels, sought an elusive common mind, vacillating between a continuing commitment to 'ideals' with a desire to be pastorally accommodating. In approaching these matters, the Roman Catholic stance was invariably characterized as 'hardline', though its position was not unique, many conservative evangelicals taking a similar view. Debates and discussions on these matters were a constant feature. Such was the range of expressed opinion that it was impossible to speak unequivocally of the Methodist or the Anglican view. On the issue of homosexuality, however, equivocation was proving difficult to sustain. The Lesbian and Gay Christian Movement had been founded in 1976 with an Anglican clergyman, Richard Kirker, as its general secretary. The 1967 Sexual Offences Act had decriminalized homosexual acts between consenting adults in private. Decriminalization might be one thing, social approval another. It was twenty years later that the General Synod debated and rejected a motion that homosexual clergy should be removed from their posts. However, it did pass a motion that homosexual genital acts fell short of the ideal, as found in marriage, and required repentance. Four years later, considering *Issues in Sexuality* the House of Bishops considered that in certain circumstances the laity might have homosexual relationships but priests could not. Not everybody could see the force of this distinction. More reflection was needed. Was 'orientation' one thing, but practice another? Was it 'faithfulness' and 'mutual support' in a homosexual relationship, as in a heterosexual marriage, which was key to acceptability? Particularly where Anglicans were concerned, but not only for them, the global ramifications of decisions for the integrity of their structures could not be ignored. The Church of England, in these matters, left to itself might have been able to come to a relatively tolerable accommodation but it could not do so on its own.

In March 1995 a group of Anglican prelates from across the world assembled in Windsor Great Park to reflect. At its conclusion, Dr Carey told the press that the group rejected homophobia in any form. Homosexuals had to be treated as people made in the image of God. On what that meant in practice, he did not elaborate. The question, he concluded, would have to be analysed in a way which took account of human experience as well as Bible teaching. Such analysis, however, was not going to be possible in academic seclusion. Very shortly before the Windsor meeting Peter Tatchell, a Gay Rights activist, had attempted to 'out' Dr David Hope, the bishop of London. A letter which he had written to him in December 1994 appeared in the press.[151] Dr Hope felt obliged to say that he was celibate. His sexuality might be a 'grey area' but he had not put his to the test. The air was thick, however, with rumours as to which bishops and priests might have put theirs to the test. A service in Southwark Cathedral in November 1996 held in connection with the twentieth anniversary of the Lesbian and Gay Christian Movement caused another storm and another headline 'The Church Divided'.[152] The proceedings of the 1998 Lambeth Conference on this issue left no doubt that the storm had not abated. It would roll on disruptively into the twenty-first century.

The combination of 'human experience' and 'Bible teaching' which the archbishop recommended in this matter (as he had done in relation to the ordination of women and other cognate issues of sexuality) obviously constituted a recipe for reconciliation at a time of tension. In bold terms, it amounted to little more than a truism. How it might be fleshed out remained problematic, as it always had been, in the search for tenable truth. The millennial moment was no turning point at which all tensions had been removed, all issues clarified and all sentiments harmoniously integrated. There was still a long way to go.

ix. Insular Pluriformity

In the early 1990s a Roman Catholic lecturer in Westminster Abbey had argued that the pluriformity of Christian reality to be seen so positively in England—and even more in the British Isles—was something to be

---

[151] *The Times*, 15 March and 17 March 1995.

[152] *The Independent*, 15 November 1996. The House of Bishops made their statement *Issues in Human Sexuality* in 1991. See the essays in Duncan Dormor and Jeremy Morris, eds., *An Acceptable Sacrifice? Homosexuality and the Church* (London, 2007).

celebrated. Christian tradition had been flexible from its very start. Only when people started from a recognition of pluriformity could they move a bit nearer unity.[153] It was a remark which, at the millennium, applied to the future of Britain, the British Isles and the European Union.

The electorates in Wales and Scotland voted in 1997 on a specific 'package' of proposals for future government but perhaps devolution was a 'process' rather than an 'event'. Once started, it could not be reversed and would accelerate. As has been earlier noted, the Good Friday agreement at least both set in motion a solution for Northern Ireland itself and confirmed a strong working relationship between Ireland and the United Kingdom. A new situation had arisen in the British Isles. In Wales and Scotland, in the absence of discrete political institutions, the churches, implicitly or explicitly, had been throughout the century 'carriers' of their nations within a United Kingdom whose government (and monarch) was sometimes described, plausibly or implausibly, as English.[154] Now, as the new century lay ahead, in 'domestic' matters, the churches found themselves in a new position, relating significantly to administrations in Edinburgh and Cardiff. Those administrations, in turn, had their own cultural objectives and notions of what a nation was or should be. Not that the churches were unhappy, for the most part, at this turn of events. Individual churchmen had campaigned vigorously, in bad times and good, to bring this about. Yet the existence of these new institutions might mean that this role, conscious, or unconscious, was redundant.[155] Indeed, new administrations with a 'new nationalism' might see the churches as citadels of obsolete sectarianism which had 'no future' in a 'New Scotland' or 'New Wales'. These developments posed further questions about the way in which the churches in Britain, and in the British Isles, now perceived themselves in relation to an apparently sprouting multiplicity of complicatedly interlocking political institutions and relationships, north and south, east and west. Nor was this merely a matter of certain 'peripheral' adjustments. The process of change in Scotland and Wales, on which the English electorate had not had an opportunity to express its opinion in its own referendum, left England without any specific political institution of its own. There was a sense,

---

[153] Adrian Hastings, delivering the Gore Lecture in November 1991, printed in *Theology* (May/ June 1992), 171.

[154] The Irish Catholic hierarchy, for example, in 1958 in a letter to the papal nuncio, spoke of Ireland being partitioned against the will of the Irish people, one part being subject to the jurisdiction of the Republic and the other owing allegiance to 'the Queen of England'. Ó Corráin, *Rendering to God and Caesar*, 57.

[155] People in the 1980s, at a time when the 1979 vote appeared to have stopped the emergence of a 'political' Wales, had asked themselves whether the Church of England and the Church in Wales were really 'two radically different churches'. See the essay by Jeremy Winston in *Living Authority: Essays in Memory of Archbishop Derrick Childs* (Penarth, n.d.).

therefore, in which the Church of England functioned as an embodiment of Englishness at a time of uncertainty about 'England'. It was a role both relished and rejected—though in different quarters.[156]

The millennium in Wales saw a National Assembly for Wales and a Welsh Assembly government newly in existence. By a narrow margin, the Welsh electorate in September 1997 had voted in favour of a devolved administration within the United Kingdom and a significant political identity, though with limited powers. The 'British' political parties, Labour, Conservative and Liberal Democrat, rebranded themselves by adding the word Welsh, and *Plaid Cymru*, whose goal seemed, sometimes, to be independence, pushed itself, for English-speakers, as 'The Party of Wales'. Should there be an additional rebranding of a 'Welsh Christianity'?

There was a sermon preached in May 1999 in Llandaff Cathedral at the inauguration of the Assembly in the presence of the queen, politicians, church people and many others. The preacher was the newly appointed liaison officer of Cytun with the National Assembly. Those attending could not fail to be aware of the hopeful ambiguities surrounding the occasion. Beneath Jacob Epstein's *Christ in Majesty*, an image of a crucified God for a broken humanity, the preacher invited the congregation to think of transformation, of an opportunity, amidst the squabbles of politics, to build anew. That such a service could be held was an indication that there was a place for 'religion', but the emphasis, here and elsewhere, was upon an inclusive, just and reconciled society in which Christians and non-Christians could live together harmoniously. Much of the 'old Wales' had yet to die; its insecurities, false consciousness, fears and hegemonies of power.[157] There was not to be much room for simple triumphant assertion of old caricatures of what 'Wales' *really* was.

The last decades of the century had seen the shattering of old 'industrial Wales'. By 1985, some concluded that Wales was no longer a Christian country.[158] Yet there was a congregation in Llandaff. By the mid-1990s sociologists were concluding that the Church in Wales was still 'behind' England on some measures of 'secularization' (baptisms, confirmations and weddings) but 'catching up' fast. Observers thought that the population of active members was not replacing itself. Even to moderate its decline the church seemed to be implicitly relying on the idea that people drifted back to religion as they aged. Yet the Church in Wales, in terms of its public commentary, made a significant contribution during these decades when

---

[156] It was a church, however, which was to find itself in the new century with two archbishops, born and reared respectively in Wales and Uganda, who guided this 'English church'.

[157] Aled Edwards, *Transforming Power: A Christian Reflection on Welsh Devolution* (Bangor, 2001).

[158] Chris Williams, 'On a Border in History? Wales 1945–85' in Gareth Elwyn Jones and Dai Smith, eds., *The People of Wales* (Llandysul, 1999), 228.

administratively and politically Wales became an ever more significant unit.[159] Its reports *Faith in Wales* (1989–91) and *The Church in the Welsh Countryside* (1992) matched those produced in England.[160] For all the similarity in the problems identified in these and other documents of the eighties and nineties, they demonstrated that Wales was 'different'. That remained most evident in the cultural/linguistic sphere, but not exclusively there. Approximately a third of incumbents were able to preach in Welsh, and Welsh was used in some 37 per cent of services. What that meant in practice in local situations, however, was much more complicated. Keeping English-speakers and Welsh-speakers content could result in endless juggling. Could churches cater simultaneously for Welsh Welsh-speakers (the diocese of St Davids elected an English Welsh-speaker as bishop in 2002), Welsh English-speakers and the not inconsiderable number of English residents?[161] Should they embrace or reject absolutist notions of culture as expressed in the view that there was 'in the Welsh psyche a self-replicating pattern' which fuelled its tendency repetitively to produce 'despite cultures'?[162] Alongside it lay the unresolved ambiguities of multiculturalism in society at large, issues which necessarily had a different dimension from England.[163]

The issues behind whatever local arrangements were made could generate strong sentiment, drawing upon particular interpretations of history and national sentiment. Welsh culture was seen by some clergy as 'unchurched' rather than 'secular'. Church was the problem not the answer and would remain so until a new way of 'being church' was found.[164] Some thought that an old but fashionably rediscovered 'Celtic spirituality' offered a way forward, though historians had doubts about 'Celtic

[159] Keith Robbins, 'Wales and the "British Question" ', *Transactions of the Honourable Society of Cymmrodorion 2002*, new series, 9 (2003), 152–61 and 'Cultural Independence and Political Devolution in Wales' in H.T. Dickinson and M. Lynch, eds., *The Challenge to Westminster: Sovereignty, Devolution and Independence* (East Linton, 2000), 81–90.

[160] Christopher Harris and Richard Startup, *The Church in Wales: The Sociology of a Traditional Institution* (Cardiff, 1999), 22. P. Brierley, *Prospects for Wales from a Census of the Churches in 1982* (London, 1983).

[161] To what extent 'the English' in Wales constitute an 'ethnic minority' alongside other immigrants and minorities raises issues in a church which to a significant extent had been removing from itself the 'stain' of being 'the English church'. C. Williams, N. Evans and P. O'Leary, *Exploring Ethnic Diversity in Wales* (Cardiff, 2003).

[162] A thesis employing the problematic term 'meme' advanced by Jane Aaron in *The Welsh Survival Gene* (Cardiff, 2003), 1–2.

[163] Charlotte Williams, 'Can We Live Together? Wales and the Multicultural Question', *Transactions of the Honourable Society of Cymmrodorion 2004*, new series, 11 (2005), 216–30.

[164] A view stated in a book by an Anglican priest who still 'shared the myths of identity of non-conformist Wales' in which she had been brought up: Enid R. Morgan, 'Called to One Hope: The Gospel in Diverse Cultures' in Wingate, Ward, Pemberton and Sitshebo, *Anglicanism: A Global Communion*, 311–16.

Christianity'. 'Nonconformity', however, was in a more parlous state than in England. Was it reduced to being a long *Cymanfa Ganu* (Hymn-singing festival)? Yet, even though the churches appeared to be existing 'on the edge' their combined worshipping community in every part of the country remained substantially the most significant element in the 'voluntary sector'. In a Wales which was busy reinventing itself, the church could not and should not be merely a refuge. A Welsh-speaking Welshman, Rowan Williams, returning to Wales after years in academic life in England to be bishop of Monmouth, and then archbishop of Wales, detected in 2001 'less overt hostility to the Church than might have been the case even fifteen years ago'. Whether the churches could find a 'language' which gave them a continuing significant place had yet to be seen. It would not be easy or conflict-free but it could not be either a betrayal or retreat into the past.[165]

The national movement in Scotland appeared to have accepted the result of the 1979 referendum meekly. From a Westminster perspective, it appeared to indicate that what Scots told pollsters about their desire for a parliament and what they did in a ballot box were two different things. In 1997, however, 74 per cent of those who voted supported a Scottish Parliament and 63 per cent believed that it should have tax-varying powers. In the 1997 UK general election the Conservatives lost all their parliamentary seats in Scotland, having held 22 in 1979. Despite last minute gestures, such as the return of the Stone of Destiny to Scotland and the appearance of then secretary of state for Scotland in a kilt at the Scottish premiere of the film *Braveheart*, the Conservatives could not shake off their image as 'anti-Scottish'. The policies pursued by Mrs Thatcher had not shown sensitivity to the only basis on which the union could flourish, namely the recognition in London that Scotland was different. Unionism had not been, and could not be based on uniformity and assimilation. It was not just that particular decisions hit hard but worse was 'the imposition of an alien ideology that rejected community and expressed itself as an attack on our distinctive systems of education and local government'. The real enemy, the writer added, was the constitutional system itself. If Scotland was to be governed justly and democratically, it was not just a change of government but a change in the rules which was needed.[166] After the UK Conservative victory in 1987, what had been a comparatively feeble campaign for a Scottish Assembly took off. The SNP in 1988 proclaimed its aim as 'Independence in Europe'. Scotland could no longer live with what 'prominent Scots'

---

[165] Rowan Williams, 'The Churches of Wales and the Future of Wales', *Transactions of the Honourable Society of Cymmrodorion 2001*, new series, 8 (2002), 160. Rowan Williams subsequently became archbishop of Canterbury.

[166] Kenyon Wright, *The People say Yes* (Glendaruel, 1997), 55.

described as 'the English constitution'.[167] A Scottish Constitutional Convention was set up in 1989 in which neither the Conservatives nor the SNP took part, leaving the field open to Labour, the Liberals Democrats, the Greens and the Communists, together with local government representatives and others representing 'civil society'. The Scottish churches took part under the latter head. It produced its proposals on St Andrew's Day 1990 for a legislature elected under proportional representation. What all that meant in detail was uncertain but the involvement of Labour seemed likely to mean that if and when Labour formed a UK government again the Scottish people would be offered some kind of 'Home Rule'.

When the prime minister had addressed the General Assembly of the Church of Scotland in May 1988, it reflected the prevailing assumption that, in the absence of any political institution, it was still in some sense the place where 'Scotland' could be addressed.[168] The moderator of the day had made it plain, in turn, that the government was failing to tackle poverty in Scotland.[169] The General Assembly, however, left it to the fans at the Scottish Cup Final to show the prime minister not one, but a forest, of red cards. The Constitutional Convention had three chairs, Sir David Steel, erstwhile UK Liberal leader (and a son of the manse), Harry Ewing for Labour and Canon Kenyon Wright, the last named being chairman of the executive committee. It was Wright's attack on the 'alien ideology' which was quoted above. In the wake of the publication of the report, anticipating that a lady in Downing Street would say 'no' and also say 'and we are the state', Wright retorted 'we say yes and we are the people'. In fact the lady left office that very month, though her successor, was also inclined to say no, though more emolliently. Who really did represent 'the people' could only be tested when the matter did eventually come to a referendum.[170]

This unfolding, but still somewhat erratic, political pattern placed the Church of Scotland in something of a quandary, though one only

---

[167] The *Claim of Right for Scotland* was edited by a Scottish-resident Irish historian, Owen Dudley Edwards (Edinburgh, 1989). Its concluding statement is reproduced in Devine, *Scottish Nation*, 610–11.

[168] 'Insider' views of the Church of Scotland at this juncture include: Andrew Herron, *Kirk by Divine Right: Church and State, A Peaceful Coexistence* (Edinburgh, 1985) and his *Confessions of an Unrepentant Non-Conformist* (Edinburgh, 1990); R.D. Kernohan, *Our Church: A Guide to the Kirk of Scotland* (Edinburgh, 1985) (the author edited the Church of Scotland magazine *Life and Work*); Ronald Falconer, *The Kirk beneath my Cassock* (Edinburgh, 1978). (The author was Head of Religious Broadcasting at BBC Scotland); Peter Brierley, ed., *Prospects for Scotland: Report of the 1984 Census of the Churches* (1985).

[169] The church produced its own reports on housing and poverty, but *Faith in the City* also had a Scottish version: R. O'Brien, ed., *Faith in the Scottish City: The Scottish Relevance of the Report of the Archbishop's Commission on Urban Priority Areas* (Edinburgh, 1986).

[170] Further discussion of these developments can be found in Andrew Marr, *The Battle for Scotland* (London, 1992); James Mitchell, *Strategies for Self-Government* (Edinburgh, 1996).

reluctantly acknowledged. Few of its leaders had demurred from the notion that it constituted the voice of a stateless nation. Its influence on the campaign for a Scottish Assembly/Parliament has been described as 'out of proportion to its strength in Scottish society'.[171] Certainly, Wright achieved a notable prominence in the 1980s and 1990s. Yet, for all his eloquent espousal of the Scottish cause he was only just renewing an acquaintance with Scotland. Paisley-bred, he left for India as a Methodist missionary in 1955 and did not return—to England—until 1970. He transmogrified himself into an Anglican canon working out of Coventry Cathedral before coming to Scotland as general secretary of the Scottish Churches Council. All of this no doubt made him a thoroughly representative figure of the 'New Scotland'. Learning about the Scottish Episcopal Church was an early task for an English-formed Anglican.[172] Richard Holloway came back to Edinburgh as Episcopalian bishop in 1986 and made a mark beyond his own communion. Indeed beyond any church. There was a transparent existential authenticity about all he did and said. He was not a 'typical bishop'.[173] Individual figures within the Church of Scotland might have their reservations about the way in which 'their' cause had been hijacked by non-Presbyterian 'returnees', but there was a broad Home Rule consensus, even though it might break down when it came to detailed consideration of the future place, if any, of Scotland within the United Kingdom. From 1999 to 2004, while the new Scottish Parliament was being erected, the new parliament was sited in a Church of Scotland Assembly Hall on the Mound. That was a temporary arrangement pending the building of the parliament, but for those who wished to see it in this light it was an acknowledgement of the intimacy of 'church and nation'.[174] The then leader of the SNP wanted St Andrew to be given an upgrade as Scotland's patron saint. The articulation of 'Scottish identity' from a Christian perspective had been given particular attention in this evolving picture. William Storrar wrote influentially on this topic and campaigned prominently for a Scottish Parliament.[175]

---

[171] Graham Walker, 'Varieties of Scottish Protestant Identity' in T.M. Devine and R.J. Finlay, eds., *Scotland in the Twentieth Century* (Edinburgh, 1996), 257.

[172] Kenyon Wright, *Politics, Philosophy and Religion* (Edinburgh, 2003). Wright was educated at Glasgow and Cambridge universities.

[173] Holloway had been a priest in Glasgow and Edinburgh in the 1960s and 1970s before serving in the United States, where he had been a student, and in Oxford. He danced on the edge, to take the title of one of his many books.

[174] Harry Reid, *Outside Verdict: An Old Kirk in a New Scotland* (Edinburgh, 2002). The author, a former editor of the *Herald* in Glasgow, paints one picture of what such intimacy really amounted to.

[175] W. Storrar, *Scottish Identity: A Christian Vision* (Edinburgh, 1990). After the millennium, the author, a Presbyterian minister, moved to Princeton Theological Seminary whose new President, Iain Torrance, was also a Scottish Presbyterian—the Scottish Presbyterian 'New World' orientation was thus being maintained into the twenty-first century.

Such projections had appeal. Yet it was not altogether clear whether the resistance being offered to the 'alien ideology' coming up from the south did indeed reflect a fused national/Christian consensus.[176] If it came to the point, a nationalist appeal did not require much Christian buttressing in order now to be successful. However, the Church of Scotland, for all its numerical decline, remained a significant aspect of a Scottish 'democratic' identity, even as that identity was being reformulated.[177] The greater the solidarity of the old church with the new Scotland, however, the more complicated became its position in relation to minorities, whether identified as ethnic, cultural or religious.[178] For, as in Wales, there was also a powerful strand of thinking which sought to give 'New Scotland' an inclusive tone. What about the Muslims of Pakistani descent? The Church of Scotland, the Scottish Episcopal Church and some smaller bodies continued to be engaged in ecumenical discussion and, for a moment, it looked as though, on the eve of the millennium, a way might have been found, though in an exclusively Scottish rather than an Anglo-Scottish context, to find a way of 'dealing with bishops'. That would be the contribution which the non-Roman Catholic churches would make to the 'new order'. In the event, however, these proposals, like their predecessors, came to nothing.

What occupied the headlines, rather, was a lecture made at the Edinburgh International Festival in August 1999 by the young Scottish composer, James Macmillan.[179] A Catholic, he described Scotland as a land of 'sleep-walking bigotry' in which 'visceral anti-Catholicism' was present in the professions, academic and educational life, politics and the media. The problem, he supposed, was far more pervasive than being a matter of totemic abuse sung within the sanctity of Glasgow football stadiums. His remarks provoked controversy within and beyond the Catholic population. Opinions on the accuracy, or otherwise, of his opinions by no means corresponded with denominational allegiance. Some thought he was

[176] There was, however, very little sign in Scotland of that more positive evaluation of 'the market' to be found, as has been noted, in some Christian quarters in England. It was indeed the conservativeness of the self-defined radicalism which irked those English Conservatives who thought of themselves as really radical.

[177] Scottish social historians and sociologists can find themselves in sharp disagreement about the continuing presence or absence of the 'democratic intellect' as an aspect of the Presbyterian inheritance. Callum Brown, *Religion and Society in Scotland since 1707* (Edinburgh, 1997), 183 takes issue with David McCrone, *Understanding Scotland: The Sociology of a Stateless Nation* (London, 1992), 36, 99.

[178] According to the 2001 census, over 8 per cent were born in England and thus, if those who were so born considered themselves to be 'English', they constituted by far the largest minority. In some parts of Scotland the figure was considerably higher than 8 per cent.

[179] Macmillan considered himself a socialist with a radical criticism of conservative elements in society (and in his own church) and of 'the excesses of free-market capitalism'. His lecture, afterthoughts, and the responses from various quarters are reproduced in T.M. Devine, ed., *Scotland's Shame: Bigotry and Sectarianism in Modern Scotland* (Edinburgh and London, 2000).

right, others thought that what might have been true of the 1950s and 1960s was true no longer. Macmillan's salvo can be seen as a determination to break the link between Scotland and Presbyterianism. Some observers thought that the heat was probably going out of religious discrimination but it was a slower process than, twenty years earlier, they had supposed likely.[180] It also seemed to be the case, at least viewed from England, that Scottish ecclesiastical disputes had their own particular brand of intensity. When the London press got over its surprise at the knowledge that the lord chancellor of England, a Scot, was a member of the small Free Presbyterian Church of Scotland, it expressed its sympathy with him in the suspension meted out for attending the Requiem Mass of a friend. Lord Mackay of Clashfern subsequently left the Free Presbyterian Church.[181]

The 'ethnic' element in such discrimination as existed, given that a majority of Scottish Catholics could be deemed, according to varying definitions, to be of 'Irish descent', had not altogether gone away, although the 'Irish-born' constituted only 1 per cent of the population in 2001. Cardinal Gray's successor as archbishop of St Andrews and Edinburgh, Keith Patrick O'Brien, had been born in Northern Ireland, but the fact was not unduly held against him.[182] It was possible, however, at community level, for discrimination to work against Protestants, as the conduct of Monklands District Council appeared to show. The reality was that both the Catholic and Protestant communities were diverse and generalizations which pretend otherwise carry little conviction. Scotland itself, also, remained a diverse country. In these circumstances, there could be considerable variation in how the two main churches behaved in their relation to each other and the extent to which they 'owned' a common vision of the future. They wished to distance themselves, at leadership level, from that virulent sectarianism which provided easy ammunition for those who wished to discredit Christianity. On the other hand, the attractions of the 'numbers game' in trying to assess the respective 'real strength' of the Church of Scotland and the Roman Catholic Church in Scotland proved irresistible to some. Particular issues, as for example the case of the appointment of a Roman Catholic to the Chair of Divinity at Edinburgh, three years before the papal visit, could still see a closing of the ranks.[183] On the other hand, the Church of Scotland Church and Nation Committee was now being joined by observers from the Scottish Episcopal Church, the

---

[180] Tom Gallagher in Devine, ed., *Scotland's Shame*, 50.

[181] In 2005/6 he served as lord high commissioner to the General Assembly of the Church of Scotland.

[182] O'Brien had been rector of the national junior seminary at Blairs which was closed in 1986.

[183] The affair is discussed by S.J. Brown in his article 'Presbyterians and Catholics in Twentieth-Century Scotland' in S.J. Brown and G. Newlands, eds., *Scottish Christianity in the Modern World* (Edinburgh, 2000), 255–81.

Salvation Army and the Roman Catholic Justice and Peace Commission. One sociologist came to the conclusion that at the end of the century the mainstream churches had all come to share a broadly similar identity. In key respects, he thought Scottish Catholics were much more similar to other Scots than they were to their co-religionists elsewhere in Britain.[184] Yet, notwithstanding the steady swell of ecumenical contact, the terms on which 'unity' might be obtained remained elusive. In January 1999, at a ceremony in Glasgow at which the now Cardinal Winning's 50th anniversary of his entry into the priesthood was celebrated, he reportedly left no doubt in his hearers that there could be no movement on doctrine or on the seven sacraments in the interests of unity. When Catholics spoke to other churches, they had the right to say to them, 'Look right back to the beginning and ask yourselves, why did you abandon us.'[185] Non-Catholics did not quite see matters in those terms. Winning's vocal public opposition to homosexuality and to abortion could attract some support, including financial support, across the confessional divide, but other Protestants were repelled by the supposition that he had become Scotland's Christian voice.[186] Whether he was, or not, as in the case of the Westminster parliament so in the incoming Scottish parliament there was fierce debate on how the church should present its case and seek to groom support. Some appeared to think that the best contribution the Roman Catholic Church could make to 'plural' Scotland was to shut up.[187] In short, at a politically auspicious millennium, the relationship between church, nation, people and culture in Scotland had not lost its contentious character. Further, how it played in the territories of the British Isles was in turn now caught up in 'the question of Europe'. 'As a Catholic', Bishop Devine of Motherwell had

[184] Remarks by David McCrone, author of *Catholics in Scotland: A Sociological Review* (Edinburgh, 1997) cited by David Sinclair in Devine, ed., *Scotland's Shame*, 180.

[185] Remarks reported in *The Scotsman* and cited by Gallagher in Devine, ed., *Scotland's Shame*, 49. It was sometimes supposed that this 'harder tone' to some degree reflected Winning's concern to steady the Catholic ship. In 1996, it was found that the bishop of Argyll and the Isles, Roddy Wright, had joined the bishop of Galway in succumbing to feminine charm and fathering a child. Winning felt himself to have been betrayed. He remarked that this was the worst personal problem he had to deal with.

[186] The Church of Scotland embraced both 'conservative' and 'liberal' exponents of opinion on these matters. The incoming moderator in 2003/4 was to cause a storm when he declared that he was utterly untroubled by the appointment of gay ministers, provided they were disciplined and effective. His successor in the following year repudiated this view. George Newlands, Professor of Divinity in Glasgow University, and the moderator's cousin-in-law wrote liberally in a liberal vein. He also had the distinction, as rarely sought as it was welcomed, of being both a Church of Scotland minister and a Church of England priest. He had been Dean of Trinity Hall, Cambridge, a post once occupied by Robert Runcie. George Newlands, *Generosity and the Christian Future* (London, 1997) arose out of the Henson Lectures delivered in Oxford in 1995.

[187] If a 'Catholic vote' was there to be delivered, the SNP was particularly anxious to prise it away from Labour—a fact of which Cardinal Winning was well aware.

stated in 1979, campaigning for a 'Yes' vote, 'I belong to an international church, but internationalism flourishes best when rooted in a keen sense of one's nation, culture and identity.' You cannot have internationalism without nations, he concluded, and Scotland was a nation.[188] Was Europe, but what kind of Europe, something to be 'rooted in' too?

x. *Europe: Secular and Christian?*

The end of the century saw the churches not only themselves struggling to cope with pluriformity and unity but finding themselves operating within shifting political structures which had the same problem. Each successive phase in the expansion in the membership of the European Union brought with it questions about its structure, functions, purposes and 'essence'. The collapse of communism at the end of the 1980s and the disintegration of the Soviet Union gave such questions an even greater complexity. So did the related crisis in the Balkans which brought back memories of a century or so earlier. Some Christians, amongst whom might be found the prime minister, supported military action to halt 'ethnic cleansing' and mass murders; others of pacifist conviction thought it unjustifiable. Yet others, relatively few but vocal, feared for Serb or Croat Christians, perceived to be threatened by Bosnian or Kosovar Muslims. The United Kingdom found itself with new structures of government whose efficacy had yet to be demonstrated. Contrary opinions were expressed as to whether the devolved parliament in Scotland, with its law-making powers, and the assembly in Wales, which lacked them, would constitute an enduring 'solution' or would merely be a transitional stage on the way to the 'break-up' of Britain. A problematic and ambiguous integration into a contentious new structure seemed to go hand in hand with the problematic and ambiguous disintegration of an old structure. Whether this was a fortuitous or causal relationship could be argued over. Neither process, at the millennium, was complete and both 'integration' and 'disintegration' could be variously interpreted. This was, however, the context in which the churches of the British Isles now functioned.

Both the United Kingdom and the Republic of Ireland were part of a European *Community* which had changed itself into a European *Union*. They had joined together but their strategies within it, over a quarter of a century, had been markedly different. Whereas successive British governments gave the impression of being reluctant participants, Irish governments appeared eager. The 'Europeanization' of Ireland was a 'project' which, in general, had public support and brought both direct economic benefit and a

---

[188] Cited in Gallagher, *Glasgow: The Uneasy Peace*, 328. It was Gallagher's 'Is One Community Emerging' in that book to which he was alluding in 2000.

higher national profile (not to mention an alternative focus from London). The British, or at least the English, seemed manifestly less eager. Like the churches in their relationships with each other, the European Union talked of 'unity in diversity'. Indeed, it recognized and, some said, encouraged, greater cultural and even political diversity than the nation states had allowed in their fully sovereign heyday. It also required a degree of 'harmonization' if it were to function properly, but what degree? Freedom of movement and employment within its member states began to blur, but not eliminate, perceptions of 'insiders' and 'outsiders'.

The election of Cardinal Hume as president of the Council of European Bishops' Conferences in 1979 and his re-election in 1984 brought an English Roman Catholic, perhaps unexpectedly, to the heart of European affairs as communism collapsed.[189] His influence could not be compared with that of John Paul II but he brought to the deliberations of his fellow cardinals the subtleties of a life lived in a multi-confessional democracy. He spoke powerfully about 'remaking Europe' after 1989 but, even though the multi-European composition of the Roman Catholic faithful in Britain was higher than that of any other church, eagerness to do so was not substantially higher amongst their number than amongst Christians as a whole or the population at large.[190] There was an obvious sense, however, in which Catholics from the British Isles, living or holidaying in Europe, could participate in 'Catholic Europe'.

'European Anglicanism' was a more complicated affair. The diocese of Gibraltar in Europe was reconstructed in 1980 and embraced the former Fulham jurisdiction of the bishop of London in Northern and Central Europe. It embraced some 200 congregations in more than 30 countries and was 'deemed to belong' to the Church of England, with the archbishop of Canterbury as metropolitan. In partnership with American Episcopalians it ministered to the ever-increasing numbers of English-speakers on the continent. By the millennium, its 'constituency' had become ever more complicated. Its congregations included short- and long-term expatriates and local nationals; first- or second-language English-speakers or Anglicans from a different linguistic background; or people from different confessions. In such circumstances it has not been easy to define 'Anglicanism' and indeed it has been that very difficulty which has made it attractive to adherents coming from more specific confessional profiles.[191] Depending

---

[189] Keith Robbins, 'The British Churches and the Process of Transformation and Consolidation of Democracy in Central Eastern Europe since 1985', *Kirchliche Zeitgeschichte* 1 (2007), 81–96.

[190] Basil Hume, *Remaking Europe: The Gospel in a Divided Continent* (London, 1994); David L. Edwards, *Christians in a New Europe* (London, 1990).

[191] John Hind, 'Why Have an Anglican Church on Mainland Europe?' in Wingate, Ward, Pemberton and Sitshebo, eds., *Anglicanism: A Global Communion*, 114–19.

on the local circumstances, it has also been able to act as an ecumenical stimulus for surrounding Roman Catholics, Protestants and Orthodox. The church did not encourage proselytism but did not turn away 'foreigners' who were drawn to it.

Apart from this Anglican presence in Europe, however, the mid-1990s saw what was being described as the most significant ecumenical step taken by the Church of England in the entire century. Following the Meissen agreement with the German Evangelical Church in 1992 it entered into the Porvoo Agreement with the Lutheran national churches of Sweden, Finland, Estonia, Latvia and Lithuania (which had retained the historic succession of its bishops as the Church of England believed itself to have done) and with those of Denmark, Iceland and Norway, where this was not the case. Analogies were drawn with the Maastricht Agreement being reached within the European community. There was to be inter-communion and mutual recognition of ministries. There was further debate about what a bishop was. The opposition from within the Anglican churches of the British Isles came from those who were unhappy that all of these churches were now to be seen as equally valid, but it did not prevail. The 'rank and file' of the churches may not immediately have taken on board the implications of these agreements, though, over time, new diocese-to-diocese relationships across northern Europe began to appear. One disgruntled historian thought both that 'the Englishness of the English experience' was being fundamentally redefined and that Anglicans were 'turning away from the challenges of reconciliation with the majority in favour of politically easy accommodations with minorities'.[192]

The formation of an Anglican–Lutheran axis was a significant development. It again made the Anglican churches of the British Isles 'European'. The contacts made by British Baptists, particularly in central Europe, where an International Baptist Seminary was established in Prague, also represented a significant 'Europeanization'. While it was an effort which engaged particular individuals, a growing sense of being part of a 'European Baptist family' can be detected.[193] In an ecumenical context, British Baptists had frequently been perceived as 'difficult' but they supplied general secretaries for the 1959-founded Conference of European Churches. The contribution to this organization might be judged to be 'disproportionately' large. Its president, from 1986 to 2001, was John Arnold, dean of Durham.[194]

It happened that the millennium coincided with a further stage in the debate about 'Europe'. Another expansion in the membership of the

---

[192] Jonathan Clark, 'A "Maastricht" for the Church', *The Times*, 28 November 1994.

[193] Bernard Green, *Crossing the Boundaries: A History of the European Baptist Foundation* (Didcot, 2003).

[194] John Arnold, 'Europe, the Churches and the Conference of European Churches', *Kirchliche Zeitgeschichte* 12/2 (1999), 473–87 and 'New Pilgrimage', *Theology* (May/June 1992), 182–9.

European Union was in prospect. There was also the possibility, at a later stage still, that Turkey, a 'secular' state but with an overwhelmingly Muslim population, might be admitted. To talk about Europe as 'Christian' might be one way, for those who so desired, of excluding it. It would be time to begin the process of drafting a European constitutional treaty—popularly referred to as the 'constitution'—and it was already apparent that what could be held to be the 'heritage' at the basis of such a document would be contentious. The former French president, Valéry Giscard d'Estaing, presiding over the drafting convention, wanted to claim that 'Europeans live in a purely secular political system, where religion does not play an important role.' The interweaving of 'Europe' and Christianity might be grudgingly admitted but, in so far as it was, it was only a part of 'the past'. The battle lines in relation to a reference, of some kind, to 'Christian roots' were being drawn up both within and between the states.[195] The government of the United Kingdom resisted any explicit acknowledgement of the link. The Irish government's advocacy was guarded. In the event, the 'constitution' never left the drawing board. The adverse referendums in France and the Netherlands were to kill it off, though, reformulated, it was likely to return. There can be little doubt if a vote had ever been held in the United Kingdom the 'constitution' would have been defeated. However, it would be wrong to suppose that the 'religious question' had been uppermost in the minds of those who had voted. It was a reminder that 'Europeans' were not all of one mind—about anything. The episode made it apparent that in 'leading circles' not only was the 'Christian heritage' to be downplayed, its survival was presented as an obstacle to the peaceful evolution of Europe. 'Religion', for some, was to be associated with intolerance, obscurantism and even fratricide. It was something which belonged to a past from which escape had to be made. In March 2000, however, Pope John Paul II led a Day of Pardon at St Peter's. A cardinal (later his successor) asked God's pardon for times when Christians used methods which, in the course of their sacred duty of defending the truth, had not been in keeping with the gospel. The pope reaffirmed his conviction that a Europe conceived in merely geographic or economic terms would lack substance. He talked in terms of a new model of unity in diversity. The Catholic bishops of Europe met in Rome for a month in October 1999 reflecting on how they might best be witnesses to Christ who had 'set us free'.[196] That task would never end.

---

[195] For a discussion of 'adaptation' or 'preservation' see the essays in Christine Lienemann-Perrin, Hendrik M. Vroom and Michael Weinrich, *Contextuality in Reformed Europe: The Mission of the Church in the Transformation of European Culture* (Amsterdam and New York, 2004).

[196] George Weigel, *The Cube and the Cathedral: Europe, America, and Politics without God* (Leominster, 2005), 59–61. Lucia Faltin and Melanie Jo Wright, eds., *The Religious Roots of Contemporary European Identity* (London, 2007).

xi. Ambivalent Messages

Whatever tides of global change had been taking place, and however much the religious landscape of the British Isles was changing, the churches were rooted in their cultural inheritances. They could not readily be detached (supposing such detachment to be even theoretically possible) from the network of associations and assumptions which the history of their societies bequeathed and which democracy, as it functioned within the islands, now required them to share in. Once again there was tension between the local and the universal.[197] Even though it was the arrival of 'outsiders' that was most conspicuous, 'displacement' of 'indigenous' populations across the British Isles accelerated as their inhabitants increasingly 'moved around', both socially and geographically, leaving uncertainty about the existence of rooted communities anywhere. Should/could churches constitute 'islands of community' for atomized, mobile people swimming or sinking in cyberspace?

It was becoming increasingly clear that generalizations could not readily be made about the islands as a whole. Long-established patterns of denominational allegiance, despite mobility, in some respects remained surprisingly resilient.[198] The attempts to prise open how the churches stood 'nationally' could only be meaningfully done region by region, locality by locality. Anthropological and ethnographical reflection on embedded structures of belief and sentiment could disclose elastic 'Christian communities'.[199] Their very historical embeddedness, however, made comparison with other religious 'communities' difficult, if not impossible. While it might be necessary, for certain purposes, to speak of the churches collectively as constituting a 'Christian community' which happened to find itself in the British Isles, the artificiality of doing so in a sharply delineated fashion hindered any such effort (supposing it to have been desirable).[200] The moderator of the General

[197] It was time to stop thinking of the church as an institution. It was a 'form of existence' or 'way of being'. So wrote a Greek theologian, who taught for a time in Glasgow university and whose thinking had an influence beyond the 'Orthodox world'. John D. Zizioulas, *Being as Communion* (London, 1984, 2004).

[198] K.D.M. Snell, *Parish and Belonging: Community, Identity and Welfare in England and Wales 1700–1950* (Cambridge, 2006). Different patterns between town and country were still being thrown up. Douglas Davies, Charles Watkins and Michael Winter, *Church and Religion in Rural England* (Edinburgh, 1991); Leslie J. Francis, *Rural Anglicanism: A Future for Young Christians?* (London, 1985).

[199] Timothy Jenkins, *Religion in English Everyday Life: An Ethnographical Approach* (Oxford and New York, 1999). Jenkins here reflects, as observer-participant, on life in Kingswood, Bristol. Robin Greenwood, *Practising Community: The Task of the Local Church* (London, 1996) is one of a number of cognate books by the then ministry officer for the Church in Wales.

[200] Daniel W. Hardy brought a transatlantic perspective in his English exploration, in the University of Cambridge, of 'Christian community' and practising Christian faith. D.W. Hardy, *God's Ways with the World: Thinking and Practising Christian Faith* (Edinburgh, 1996) and *Finding the Church: The Dynamic Truth of Anglicanism* (London, 2001); David F. Ford and Dennis L. Stamps, eds., *Essentials of Christian Community: Essays for Daniel W. Hardy* (Edinburgh, 1996); Peter Selby, *Belonging* (London, 1991).

Assembly of the Church of Scotland, reflecting on gloomy figures in 1991, lamented the loss of a vision of the parish church forging links with 'the total life of a community'. He criticized congregations which saw themselves as a gathering of the theologically like-minded extracted from the community.[201] Here was the crux of the problem of definition.

The conduct of an 'English Church census' in 1989, undertaken not for its own sake but with a view to enabling the churches to conduct effective evangelism, published its findings inside inverted commas: 'Christian' England.[202] The data, in the view of the new archbishop of Canterbury, George Carey, constituted 'serious and uncomfortable realities for us all'. It showed that on a particular Sunday in October, 10 per cent of adults went to church. In the year 2000, the English church attendance survey appeared with the title *The Tide is Running Out*. The population of England had increased from 46 million in 1979 to 50 million in 1998 but the number who went to church on a 'typical' Sunday in September declined from 5.4 million to 3.7 million. Church of England attendances fell from 1,671,000 to 980,600 and Roman Catholic from 1,991,000 to 1,230,100. Methodist decline was sharp. Only Baptist, black-led and independent evangelical churches seemed to be holding their own.[203] In inner London, it was thought that more black people than white people went to church. However, what was also true was that significant figures in both the 'mainline' white churches and the black-led churches were taking active steps to come closer together. There was increased awareness of the cultural complexities such engagement entailed. The shape of this pluralism, as it evolved, was slowly altering the public face of Christianity in England.[204]

It seemed appropriate to Callum Brown, as a social historian of religion, to speak at the end of the century of the 'death of Christian Britain' and, taking a timeframe of two hundred years, to see 'secularization' as something which had occurred with great speed since the 1960s.[205] He posited a

[201] The Very Revd Robert Davidson, *The Independent*, 23 May 1991.

[202] Peter Brierley, *'Christian' England: What the English Church Census Reveals* (London, 1991), to be read alongside his *Prospects for the Nineties: Trends and Tables from the 1989 English Church Census* (London, 1991). The survey was undertaken by MARC Europe. *Prospects for the Eighties* had appeared in 1980, being a census of the churches in 1979 which had been undertaken by the Nationwide Initiative in Evangelism. There were companion *Prospects for Wales* and *Prospects for Scotland*. The same organization was responsible for an annual publication of data.

[203] P. Brierley, *The Tide is Running Out: What the English Church Attendance Survey Tells Us* (London, 2000). It was concluded in Scotland, for example, that while Baptists were not very numerous they had 'remained relatively strong because of their wholehearted identification with Evangelical Christianity'. D.W. Bebbington, ed., *The Baptists in Scotland: A History* (Glasgow, 1988), 86.

[204] Gerald Parsons, 'Filling a Void? Afro-Caribbean Identity and Religion' in Gerald Parsons, ed., *Growth of Religious Diversity: Britain from 1945*, vol. i: *Traditions* (London, 1993), 258–65.

[205] Callum Brown, *The Death of Christian Britain* (London, 2002) and *Religion and Society in Twentieth Century Britain* (Harlow, 2006). The essayists in Jane Garnett, Matthew Grimley, Alana Harris, William Whyte and Sarah Williams, eds., *Redefining Christian Britain: Post 1945 Perspectives*

'discourse revolution' and a move from female piety to women's liberation. In a further book, he elaborated this picture. It seemed appropriate to speak of the period from 1974 to 2000 as 'The shaping of secular society'. It was one which witnessed 'the increasing marginalisation of religion from British public life, intellectualism and popular culture' and in which the Christian faithful 'dwindled'. Society was pushing its Christian heritage further and further 'from the rules of social behaviour and personal identity', religious culture in the broadcast media was waning, religious marriages were collapsing, the young were deserting in droves, *Christian names* were disappearing, church buildings were finding better use as night clubs, car showrooms and carpet warehouses, and so on. Religion was now 'lost', to be recalled either with affection, as part of a happier and homelier society, or, with horror, as the agency of a social oppression in which not everything had been permitted. In short, Britain was 'turning secular', and indeed other comments seemed to suggest that Britain had in fact reached 'the secular age'.

Church leaders themselves had indeed already, for some decades, fallen into the habit of talking about 'the secular age'.[206] They were also busily writing, from various angles, on the nature of contemporary culture, its perceived deficiencies and challenges.[207] Hugh Montefiore, now bishop of Birmingham, did so with the galling knowledge that *The Sun*, in 1987, had not printed an article on Christmas which he had been commissioned to write. He was told that a story about violence on the London Underground had broken and he would understand that it had to have priority.[208] The British Council of Churches had asked Bishop Lesslie Newbigin to draft a programme statement defining how the churches should seek to address the 'culture' question. It was published in 1983 as *The Other Side of 1984: Questions for the Churches*. Newbigin, recently retired, was an English Free Churchman, but had spent decades in South India and had served as bishop in the Church of South India in Madras. He was, therefore, something of an insider/outsider. Some controversy followed and led to the establishment of 'The Gospel and Our Culture' programme with a 'national consultation'

(London, 2007) offer alternative ways of looking at generational change. The Introduction argues that Christian Britain has not ceased to exist but rather has to be conceived in relation to 'other Britains', such as 'Muslim Britain' and to 'global identities'. The 'navigational tools' suggested by the contributors for negotiating a 'constantly changing religious seascape' and their desire to escape the constant parameters imposed by 'secularization' or 'life' and 'death' language in relation to 'Christianity' is, broadly, in line with the cultural/political framework of this book. Although the contributors have 'Britain' in their title, their book is about England.

[206] As, for example, John Habgood, *Church and Nation in a Secular Age* (London, 1983).

[207] J.R.W. Stott and R. Coote, eds., *Down to Earth: Studies in Christianity and Culture* (London, 1980).

[208] Hugh Montefiore, *Reclaiming the High Ground: A Christian Response to Secularism* (Basingstoke, 1990), 2.

planned for July 1992 as its climax. Meanwhile, Newbigin published a series of books which criticized prevailing cultural modes and assumptions.[209] The 1992 consultation brought together some four hundred people under the heading 'The Gospel as Public Truth'. It had been prepared for by a series of study groups, and their position papers were subsequently edited and published.[210] A further ongoing series of consultations and publications were set in train. The churches themselves would have to change and demonstrate a depth of community in what was held to be an age of increasing fragmentation and alienation. A cultural crossroads had been reached at the end of the twentieth century. 'We' in the West were no longer comfortable with the assumptions of our culture.[211] For Cormac Murphy-O'Connor, cardinal archbishop of Westminster, Christianity 'as a background to people's lives and moral decisions and to the Government and social life of Britain has almost been vanquished'.[212]

By 2000, Professor Brown had concluded, the people had overwhelmingly rejected faith-based morality and displayed large-scale indifference to the faith itself. What was happening/had happened constituted one of the greatest cultural changes of all time. 'Never', he concluded, 'had something as close to a secular society existed before the late twentieth century'. Yet, while the 'markers' adduced could scarcely be gainsaid, the language in which he conveyed their significance seemed at variance with the outcome of the millennial UK census of 2001. This disclosed that 77 per cent of the population reported themselves as having a religious affiliation and indicated what it was. Given the supposed large-scale indifference and overwhelming rejection identified as being characteristic of society as a whole, the free decision of such a massive percentage, 71.6 per cent of which registered as 'Christian', is astonishing. In the UK as a whole, only 15.4 per cent stated that they had no religion (27.5 per cent in Scotland, 19 per cent in Wales and 3 per cent in Northern Ireland). Professor Brown concedes that this picture discloses 'an apparent contradiction'. The figures, notwithstanding

---

[209] *The Other Side of 1984* was published by the World Council of Churches (1983). Newbigin's books were *Foolishness to the Greeks* (London, 1986), *The Gospel in a Pluralist Society* (London, 1989) and *Truth to Tell* (London, 1991). He had written *A Faith for This One World?* (London, 1961) when general secretary of the International Missionary Council (as it was then still called).

[210] Hugh Montefiore, ed., *The Gospel and Contemporary Culture* (London, 1992).

[211] So argued a former co-ordinator of the programme, Lawrence Osborn, in *Restoring the Vision: The Gospel and Modern Culture* (London, 1995), viii; Robert Miller, *Arguments against Secular Culture* (London, 1995); John W. O'Malley, *Four Cultures of the West* (Cambridge, MA, and London, 2005) presents a more complex picture of what 'we' in the West might be. Further reflections on modernism/postmodernism were being offered by John Drane, *Cultural Change and Biblical Faith* (Carlisle, 2000) and Andrew Walker, *Telling the Story: Gospel Mission and Culture* (London, 1996).

[212] The cardinal was speaking at the National Conference of Priests as reported in *The Daily Telegraph*, 6 September 2001.

all he has said, do tell us 'that religious belonging was still important to British people at the end of the twentieth century'. It is indeed difficult to probe behind these figures and determine their significance. Those who recorded themselves as having no religion might have done so for varied reasons—that 'religion' (if that meant belief in God as understood within one or other of the traditions available) made no sense and therefore could not be 'had', or that it was impossible to decide whether or not it did have meaning, or that religion did make sense, but that sense was too disturbing to want to 'have' it. For Professor Brown, 'belonging to a religion' and 'practising one' were different matters, and the test of whether a religion was being practised was something to be measured in terms of actually going to church. Whether the 'apparent contradiction' can be so simply resolved is questionable.[213]

The quandary in which historians find themselves in this matter is of course fully shared by the churches themselves. The census could appear to indicate that 'Christianity' was accepted and acknowledged by the overwhelming majority—granted that such an acknowledgement would disclose, if further analysis were possible, a most diffuse range of understandings of what Christianity meant and entailed. If this was indeed the case, it might be that such 'Christianity', tangentially connected with 'church', would wither and fade, if one accepted that the two were indeed 'the same'. It was a situation which could be, and was, interpreted in at least two ways. It indicated that 'the death of Christian Britain' had been overstated: the position was much more subtle and complex. It could also be claimed that the existence of this 'secular Britain', asserted as fact and promulgated as such routinely in the media, was an aspect of vociferous militant 'nonreligious' or 'secularist' propaganda. The more frequently it was said, the more likely it was to come to be believed. It was, therefore, necessary to assert that 'Christianity' could not be pushed aside and left to the tender care of the heritage industry. It was, and had every right to be, a continuing significant element in 'national life'.

Yet, to draw attention to the continuing presence of 'Christianity' also had the consequence of highlighting how ineffective, unappealing and 'irrelevant' the life of 'church', conceived as an institution with its organizational paraphernalia, actually was: 'churchiness', not for me, 'the people' seemed to say. Statistics of 'membership' continued to decline. The Church of Scotland counted just over a million members in 1975, a figure which had

---

[213] Brown, *Religion and Society in Twentieth-Century Britain* is the welcome addition to a series of which this author is the general editor. The discussion alluded to above takes place in chapter 7. That in relation to the 2001 census appears on 6–8. Paul Avis, ed., *Public Faith? The State of Religious Belief and Practice in Britain* (London, 2003) contains contributions, largely from sociologists, on the general problem of interpretation. Leslie Francis, 45–64 discusses the 2001 census.

dropped to around 650,000 by the end of the century. There had been a Methodist community in the British Isles of nearly 600,000 in 1975, a figure which had dropped to around 400,000 by 2000. Baptists had more or less held their own, but the creation of the United Reformed Church had done nothing to stem the outflow from Congregationalism. Anglican UK membership had fallen to around one and a half million. Roman Catholic weekly Mass attendance fell away from two and a half million to 1,750,000. These round figures and much other statistical information was available for the churches to pore over. Of course, they could still be open to an interpretation which suggested that the 'church community' was wider and more obscure than was disclosed either by 'membership' or 'irregular attendance' but no one could say how it should be measured. The United Kingdom was not uniform. It was calculated that per 1,000 adult population in 1995 there were 111 church members in England, 175 in Wales, 301 in Scotland and 769 in Northern Ireland—and these figures had all been dropping over the previous two decades.[214]

'Spirituality' looked to have escaped from the realm of 'church' and be available as a personal DIY. Church leaders could ritually repeat that it was a fundamental misunderstanding to suppose that Christianity could viably and meaningfully exist as a vital element in individual and social existence *extra ecclesiam*. They still declared that believing, belonging and 'practising' all hung inextricably together, but millions appeared to disagree.[215] Yet perhaps nothing was as simple as it seemed. The Church of England buried Diana, Princess of Wales. After a civil ceremony it blessed the second marriage of the heir to the throne. How was one to interpret both of these events?[216] How was one to interpret the outpouring that followed the death of the princess? Was this 'secular' Britain? Was it 'Christian' Britain? All churches again asked themselves what 'being the church' now meant.[217] It was asserted that only a transformation, of a kind which neither

---

[214] These and other figures have been taken from the many to be found in the *UK Christian Handbook* 1994/5 edition.

[215] R. Gill, *Churchgoing and Christian Ethics* (Cambridge, 1999) reflects on aspects of these points.

[216] Grace Davie 'A Papal Funeral and a Royal Wedding: Reconfiguring Religion in the Twenty-First Century' in Garnett, Grimley, Harris, Whyte and Williams, eds., *Redefining Christian Britain*, 106–9 uses these events to argue that while the historic churches could no longer discipline beliefs and behaviour they still remained significant players. Willem Marie Speelman, 'The "Feast" of Diana's Death' in P. Post, G. Rouwhorst, L. van Tongeren and A. Scheer, eds., *Christian Feast and Festival: The Dynamics of Western Liturgy and Culture* (Leuven, 2001), 775–801 is a meticulous examination of the liturgical dynamics of the event and its Christian and 'wider' significance.

[217] Two 'millennial' examples are Paul Avis, *The Anglican Understanding of the Church: An Introduction* (London, 2000) operating at one level, and Nicholas M. Healy, *Church, World and the Christian Life: Practical-Prophetic Ecclesiology* (Cambridge, 2000) at another.

'professionals' nor 'supporters' appeared eager to contemplate, had any chance of turning 'unattached Christians' into 'church Christians'.[218] Such perspectives, however, appeared to others to be either incomprehensible, in terms of the abstruse language sometimes deployed by advocates, or mere flatulent gestures of iconoclastic radicalism. No matter what changes were made—and accepting that much that had declined ought to have declined—it was an illusion, some said, to suppose that a vague if pervasive Christianity could be 'firmed up' into full participation in 'church', with all its joys, irritations, challenges, rebukes and consolations. The 'Way of the Cross' did not make a good television advertisement—not that religion could easily be allowed to advertise. Here, again, on the cusp of the millennium, were being played out, within new contexts, tensions which had arguably been invariably present in the history of Christianity. Martha and Mary seemed to be looking for different things. What for some was a lamentable 'decline' was, for others, a timely release from 'Constantinian captivity': not so much a doleful end as a liberating beginning. Confronted by the puzzle before them, pastors and priests, mystics and managers, prophets and politicians emphasized now one, now the other, of the facets of this situation.[219]

A historian cannot predict the future, except to caution against any self-evident linear teleological trajectory.[220] Much of late twentieth-century writing and public comment hinged on meanings to be attached to the word 'secular', both as a characterization of society and as a definition of a stance it should take. There had been, and were still, secular states determined to root out religion and enforce 'secularism', as there had been, and were still, secular states which functioned acceptably to all parties within mono-faith or multi-faith societies and which had no such determination. It was evident, both globally and within the late twentieth-century British Isles, that the word secular was being used in different ways for different purposes. Pluralism entailed an acceptance of diversity and division and, with it, a recognition that there was always the possibility of disturbance to the civil order. The scale of diversity and the gravity of division might need to be monitored and, to a contentious degree, limited and contained. The

---

[218] Robin Greenwood, *Transforming Church: Liberating Structures for Ministry* (London, 2002).

[219] Bernice Martin, *A Sociology of Contemporary Cultural Change* (Oxford, 1981). Paul Avis, *A Church Drawing Near: Spirituality and Mission in a Post-Christian Culture* (Edinburgh, 2003). H. Richard Niebuhr's *Christ and Culture* (New York, 1951) remains a classic text. See the essays in G.H. Stassen, D.M. Yeager and J.H. Yoder, eds., *Authentic Transformation: A New Vision of Christ and Culture* (Neuhalten, 1996); Mary C. Grey, *Prophecy and Mysticism: The Heart of the Post-Modern Church* (Edinburgh, 1997); Keith Robbins, 'Religion and Culture: A Contemporary British/Irish Perspective', *Schweizerische Zeitschrift für Religions- und Kulturgeschichte* 100 (2006), 331–44.

[220] The contributors to G. Davie, L. Woodhead and P. Heelas, eds., *Predicting Religion: Christian, Secular and Alternative Futures* (Aldershot, 2003) do make some such attempt.

public space was an awkward and unstable market-place in which 'the church' and 'non-church' should be free to set out their stalls, without fear of the coercive capacity of the one over the other. It was a specious piece of secularist fundamentalism to suppose that only those without religious belief were capable of being objective, fair and balanced.

SELECT BIBLIOGRAPHY

The books and articles used in the preparation of this book have been fully documented in the notes. The following titles, listed by broad subject, give guidance, selected from the source notes, for further reading.

General

BADHAM, PAUL, *Religion, State and Society in Modern Britain* (Lampeter, 1989).

BROWN, CALLUM, *The Death of Christian Britain* (London, 2001).

—— *Religion and Society in Twentieth-Century Britain* (Harlow, 2006).

BROWN, STEWART J., *Providence and Empire* (London, 2007).

COWLING, MAURICE, *Religion and Public Doctrine in Modern England* (1980–2001).

GARNETT, JANE, GRIMLEY, MATTHEW, HARRIS, ALANA, WHYTE, WILLIAM and WILLIAMS, SARAH, *Redefining Christian Britain: Post-1945 Perspectives* (London, 2006).

GILLEY, S. and SHEILS, W.J., eds., *A History of Britain: Practice and Belief from Pre-Roman Times to the Present* (Oxford, 1994).

HEMPTON, DAVID, *Religion and Public Culture in Britain and Ireland: From the Glorious Revolution to the Decline of Empire* (Cambridge, 1996).

MCLEOD, H., ed., *The Cambridge History of Christianity: World Christianities c.1914–c.2000* (Cambridge, 2006).

MCLEOD, H., and USTORF, WERNER, eds., *The Decline of Christendom in Western Europe* (Cambridge, 2003).

ROBBINS, KEITH, *History, Religion and Identity in Modern Britain* (London, 1993).

WARD, KEVIN, *A History of Global Anglicanism* (Cambridge, 2006).

WOLFFE, JOHN, *God and Greater Britain: Religion and National Life in Britain and Ireland 1843–1945* (London, 1994).

England

ASPDEN, K., *Fortress Church: The English Roman Catholic Bishops and Politics 1903–1963* (Leominster, 2002).

HASTINGS, A., *A History of English Christianity 1920–1990* (London, 1991).

HORNSBY-SMITH, M., *Catholics in England 1950–2000: Historical and Sociological Perspectives* (London, 1999).

MCCLELLAND, V. ALAN and DODGETTS, MICHAEL, eds., *From Without the Flaminian Gate: 150 Years of Roman Catholicism in England and Wales, 1850–2000* (London, 1999).

TALLETT, FRANK and ATKIN, NICHOLAS, eds., *Catholicism in Britain and France since 1789* (London, 1996).

WARD, KEVIN, *A History of Global Anglicanism* (Cambridge, 2006).

WELSBY, P., *A History of the Church of England 1945–1980* (London, 1984).

Ireland

ACHESON, A., *A History of the Church of Ireland 1691–1969* (Dublin, 1997).

CASSIDY, E.G., *Faith and Culture in the Irish Context* (Dublin, 1996).

ELLIOTT, MARIANNE, *The Catholics of Ulster* (London, 2000).

FULTON, JOHN, *The Tragedy of Belief: Division, Politics and Religion in Ireland* (Oxford, 1991).

HAMILTON, T., *A History of Presbyterianism in Ireland* (Belfast, 1992).

HARRIS, MARY, *The Catholic Church and the Foundation of the Northern Irish State* (Cork, 1993).

KEOGH, DERMOT, *Ireland and the Vatican* (Dublin, 1995).

MEGAHEY, ALAN, *The Irish Protestant Churches in the Twentieth Century* (Basingstoke, 2000).

MILLER, D.W., *Church, State and Nation in Ireland 1891–1921* (Dublin, 1973).

MURRAY, PATRICK, *The Oracles of God: The Roman Catholic Church and Irish Politics 1922–1937* (Dublin, 2000).

Ó CORRÁIN, D., *Rendering to God and Caesar: The Irish Churches and the Two States in Ireland 1949–73* (Manchester, 2006).

Scotland

BROWN, CALLUM, *Religion and Society in Scotland since 1707* (Edinburgh, 1997).

BROWN, S.J. and NEWLANDS, G., eds., *Scottish Christianity in the Modern World* (Edinburgh, 2000).

BURLEIGH, J.H.S., *A Church History of Scotland* (Oxford, 1960).

GALLAGHER, T., *Glasgow: The Uneasy Peace: Religious Tension in Modern Scotland* (Manchester, 1987).

—— *Edinburgh Divided: John Cormack and No Popery in the 1930s* (Edinburgh, 1987).

McCRONE, DAVID, *Catholics in Scotland: A Sociological Review* (Edinburgh, 1997).

SMITH, D.S., *Passive Obedience and Prophetic Protest: Social Criticism in the Scottish Church 1830–1945* (New York, 1987).

Wales

BALLARD, P. and JONES, D.H., eds., *The Land and People: A Symposium on Christian and Welsh National Identity* (Cardiff, 1979).

HARRIS, C., and STARTUP, R., *The Church in Wales: The Sociology of a Traditional Institution* (Cardiff, 1999).

HUGHES, TRISTAN OWAIN, *Winds of Change: The Roman Catholic Church and Society in Wales, 1916–1962* (Cardiff, 1999).

MORGAN, D. DENSIL, *The Span of the Cross: Christian Religion and Society in Wales, 1914–2000* (Cardiff, 1999).
POPE, R., ed., *Religion and National Identity: Wales and Scotland c.1700–2000* (Cardiff, 2001).

Church/State/Government Relations

AVIS, PAUL, *Church, State and Establishment* (London, 2001).
BEESON, TREVOR, *The Church of England in Crisis* (London, 1973).
BELL, P.M.H., *Disestablishment in Ireland and Wales* (London, 1969).
CHADWICK, OWEN, *Hensley Henson: A Study in the Friction between Church and State* (Norwich, 1994).
CHANDLER, ANDREW, *The Church of England in the Twentieth Century: The Church Commissioners and the Politics of Reform, 1948–1998* (Woodbridge, 2006).
CLARK, HENRY, *The Church under Thatcher* (London, 1993).
FERGUSSON, DAVID, *Church, State and Civil Society* (Cambridge, 2004).
GRIMLEY, MATTHEW, *Citizenship, Community and the Church of England: Liberal Anglican Theories of the State between the Wars* (Oxford, 2004).
SMITH, GRAEME, *Oxford 1937: The Universal Christian Council for Life and Work Conference* (Frankfurt am Main and New York, 2006).

Free Churches

BINFIELD, J.C.G., *So Down to Prayers: Studies in English Nonconformity 1780–1920* (London, 1977).
CLEMENTS, K.W., ed., *Baptists in the Twentieth Century* (London, 1982).
DAVIES, RUPERT, GEORGE, A. RAYMOND and RUPP, GORDON, eds., *A History of the Methodist Church in Great Britain*, vol. iii (London, 1983).
JONES, R.T., *Congregationalism in England, 1662–1962* (London, 1962).
MUNSON, JAMES, *The Nonconformists: In Search of a Lost Culture* (London, 1991).
RANDALL, IAN, *English Baptists of the 20th Century* (London, 2005).
SELL, A.P.F., and CROSS, A.R., eds., *Protestant Nonconformity in the Twentieth Century* (Carlisle, 2003).
TURNER, J.M., *Modern Methodism in England* (Peterborough, 1998).

War, Peace, Conflict

CEADEL, M., *Pacifism in Britain 1914–1945: The Defining of a Faith* (Oxford, 1980).
LAWSON, TOM, *The Church of England and the Holocaust: Christianity, Memory and Nazism* (Woodbridge, 2006).
LIECHTY, L., and CLEGG, C., *Moving Beyond Sectarianism: Religion, Conflict and Reconciliation in Northern Ireland* (Dublin, 2001).
SNAPE, MICHAEL, *God and the Soldier* (London, 2005).
WILKINSON, ALAN, *The Church of England and the First World War* (London, 1978).
—— *Dissent or Conform? War, Peace and the English Churches 1900–1945* (London, 1986).

Women

AVIS, P., ed., *Seeking the Truth of Change in the Church: Reception, Communion and the Ordination of Women* (London, 2004).

GILL, SEAN, *Women and the Church of England from the Eighteenth Century to the Present* (London, 1994).

MACDONALD, L. ORR, *A Unique and Glorious Mission: Women and Presbyterianism in Scotland 1830–1930* (Edinburgh, 2000).

MALMGREEN, G., *Religion in the Lives of English Women, 1760–1930* (London, 1986).

Worship

DAVIES, HORTON, *Worship and Theology in England: The Ecumenical Century 1900 to the Present* (Princeton, 1995).

WATSON, J.R., *The English Hymn: A Critical and Historical Study* (Oxford, 1999).

Secularization

BRUCE, S., ed., *Religion and Modernization: Sociologists and Historians Debate the Secularization Thesis* (Oxford, 1992).

DAVIE, G., *Religion in Britain since 1945: Believing without Belonging* (Oxford, 1994).

GILBERT, A.D., *The Making of Post-Christian Britain: A History of the Secularization of Modern Society* (London, 1980).

GREEN, S.J.D., *Religion in the Age of Decline: Organization and Experience in Industrial Yorkshire 1870–1920* (Cambridge, 1996).

MARTIN, DAVID, *On Secularization: Towards a Revised General Theory* (Aldershot, 2005).

Social and Political Issues

MACHIN, G.I.T., *Churches and Social Issues in Twentieth-Century Britain* (Oxford, 1988).

MEDHURST, KENNETH and MOYSER, GEORGE, eds., *Church and Politics in a Secular Age* (Oxford, 1988).

MOYSER, GEORGE, ed., *The Church and Politics Today: The Role of the Church of England in Contemporary Politics* (Edinburgh, 1985).

NORMAN, E.R., *Church and Society in England, 1770–1970: A Historical Study* (Oxford, 1976).

OLIVER, J.K., *The Church and Social Order: Social Thought in the Church of England 1918–1939* (London, 1968).

PRESTON, RONALD H., *Church and Society in the Late Twentieth Century: The Economic and Political Task* (London, 1983).

PROCHASKA, FRANK, *Christianity and Social Service in Modern Britain: The Disinherited Spirit* (Oxford, 2006).

REEVES, MARJORIE, ed., *Christian Thinking and Social Order: Conviction Politics from the 1930s to the Present Day* (London, 1999).

SONG, ROBERT, *Christianity and Liberal Society* (Oxford, 1997).

THOMPSON, KENNETH, *Bureaucracy and Church Reform: The Organizational Response of the Church of England to Social Change* (Oxford, 1970).

WILKINSON, ALAN, *Christian Socialism: Scott Holland to Tony Blair* (London, 1998).

WILLIAMSON, PHILIP, *Stanley Baldwin, Conservative Leadership and National Values* (Cambridge, 2000).

INDEX